Data Structures, Algorithms and Applications in C++

C++

Second Edition

SARTAJ SAHNI

Universities Press

Universities Press (India) Private Limited

Registered Office
3-5-747/1/A & 3-6-754/1 Himayatnagar
Hyderabad 500 029 (A.P.), India
e-mail: info@universitiespress.com

Distributed by
Orient Longman Private Limited

Registered Office
3-6-752 Himayatnagar, Hyderabad 500 029 (A.P.), India

Other Offices
Bangalore / Bhopal / Bhubaneshwar / Chennai
Ernakulam / Guwahati / Hyderabad / Jaipur / Kolkata
Lucknow / Mumbai / New Delhi / Patna

First Published in India by
Universities Press (India) Private Limited 2005
Reprinted 2006, 2007 (Twice)

ISBN-13: 978 81 7371 522 8
ISBN-10: 81 7371 522 X

Printed in India at
Graphica Printers, Hyderabad 500 013

Published by
Universities Press (India) Private Limited
3-5-747/1/A & 3-6-754/1 Himayatnagar
Hyderabad 500 029 (A.P.), India

To my mother,
      Santosh

My wife,
      Neeta

and my children,
      Agam, Neha, and Param

PREFACE

The study of data structures and algorithms is fundamental to computer science and engineering. A mastery of these areas is essential for us to develop computer programs that utilize computer resources in an effective manner. Consequently, all computer science and engineering curriculums include one or more courses devoted to these subjects. Typically, the first programming course introduces students to basic data structures (such as stacks and queues) and basic algorithms (such as those for sorting and matrix algebra). The second programming course covers more data structures and algorithms. The next one or two courses are usually dedicated to the study of data structures and algorithms.

The explosion of courses in the undergraduate computer science and engineering curriculums has forced many universities and colleges to consolidate material into fewer courses. At the University of Florida, for example, we offer a single one-semester undergraduate data structures and algorithms course. Students coming into this course have had a one-semester course in Java programming and another in discrete mathematics/structures.

Data Structures, Algorithms, and Applications in C++ has been developed for use in programs that cover this material in a unified course as well as in programs that spread out the study of data structures and algorithms over two or more courses. The book is divided into three parts. Part I, which consists of Chapters 1 through 4, is intended as a review of C++ programming concepts and of methods to analyze and measure the performance of programs. Students who are familiar with programming in C should be able to read Chapter 1 and bridge the gap between C and C++. Although Chapter 1 is not a primer on C++, it covers most of the C++ constructs with which students might have become rusty. These concepts include parameter passing, template functions, dynamic memory allocation, recursion, classes, inheritance, and throwing and catching exceptions. Chapters 2 and 3 are a review of methods to analyze the performance of a program—operation counts, step counts, and asymptotic notation (big oh, omega, theta, and little oh). Chapter 4 reviews methods to measure performance experimentally. This chapter also has a brief discussion of how cache affects measured run times. The applications considered in Chapter 2 explore fundamental problems typically studied in a beginning programming course—simple sort methods such as bubble, selection,

v

insertion, and rank (or count) sort; sequential search; polynomial evaluation using Horner's rule; and matrix operations such as matrix addition, transpose, and multiply. Chapter 3 examines binary search. Even though the primary purpose of Chapters 2 through 4 is to study performance analysis and measurement methods, these chapters also ensure that all students are familiar with a set of fundamental algorithms.

Chapters 5 through 16 form the second part of the book. These chapters provide an in-depth study of data structures. Chapters 5 and 6 form the backbone of this study by examining the array and pointer (or linked) methods of representing data. These two chapters develop C++ classes to represent the linear list data structure, using each representation method. We compare the different representation schemes with respect to their effectiveness in representing linear lists by presenting experimental data. The remaining chapters on data structures use the representation methods of Chapters 5 and 6 to arrive at representations for other data structures such as arrays and matrices (Chapter 7), stacks (Chapter 8), queues (Chapter 9), dictionaries (Chapters 10, 14, and 15), binary trees (Chapter 11), priority queues (Chapter 12), tournament trees (Chapter 15), and graphs (Chapter 16).

In our treatment of data structures, we have attempted to maintain compatibility with similar or identical structures that are available in the C++ Standard Templates Library (STL). For example, the linear list data structure that is the subject of Chapter 5 is modeled after the STL class vector. Throughout the book we make use of STL functions such as copy, min, and max so students becomes familiar with these functions.

The third part of this book, which comprises Chapters 17 through 21 (Chapters 20 and 21 are available from the Web site for this book), is a study of common algorithm-design methods. The methods we study are greedy (Chapter 17), divide and conquer (Chapter 18), dynamic programming (Chapter 19), backtracking (Chapter 20), and branch and bound (Chapter 21). Two lower-bound proofs (one for the minmax problem and the other for sorting) are provided in Section 18.4; approximation algorithms for machine scheduling (Section 12.6.2), bin packing (Section 13.5), and the 0/1 knapsack problem (Section 17.3.2) are also covered. NP-hard problems are introduced, informally, in Section 12.6.2.

A unique feature of this book is the emphasis on applications. Several real-world applications illustrate the use of each data structure and algorithm-design method developed in this book. Typically, the last section of each chapter is dedicated to applications of the data structure or design method studied earlier in the chapter. In many cases additional applications are also introduced early in the chapter. We have drawn applications from various areas—sorting (bubble, selection, insertion, rank, heap, merge, quick, bin, radix, and topological sort); matrix algebra (matrix addition, transpose, and multiplication); electronic design automation (finding the nets in a circuit, wire routing, component stack folding, switch-box routing, placement of signal boosters, crossing distribution, and backplane board ordering); compression and coding (LZW compression and Huffman coding); computational geometry (convex hull and closest pair of points); simulation (machine shop simulation); image processing (component labeling); recreational mathematics (Towers of Hanoi, tiling a defective chessboard, and rat in a maze); scheduling (LPT schedules); optimization (bin packing, container loading, 0/1 knapsack, and matrix multiplication chains); statistics (histogramming, finding the minimum and maximum, and finding the kth smallest); and graph algorithms (spanning trees, components, shortest paths, max clique, bipartite graph covers, and traveling salesperson). Our treatment of these applications does not require prior knowledge of the application areas. The material covered in this book is self-contained and gives students a flavor for what these application areas entail.

By closely tying the applications to the more basic treatment of data structures and algorithm-design methods, we hope to give the student a greater appreciation of the subject. Further enrichment can be obtained by working through the more than 800 exercises in the book and from the associated Web site.

WEB SITE

The URL for the Web site for this book is

```
http://www.cise.ufl.edu/~sahni/dsaac
```

From this Web site you can obtain all the programs in the book together with sample data and generated output. The sample data are not intended to serve as a good test set for a given program; rather they are just something you can use to run the program and compare the output produced with the given output. Solutions to many of the exercises that appear in each chapter, codes for these solutions, sample tests and solutions to these tests, additional applications, and enhanced discussions of some of the material covered in the text also appear in the Web site.

HOW TO USE THIS BOOK

There are several ways in which this book may be used to teach the subject of data structures and/or algorithms. Instructors should make a decision based on the background of their students, the amount of emphasis instructors want to put on applications, and the number of semesters or quarters devoted to the subject. We give a few of the possible course outlines below. We recommend that the assignments require students to write and debug several programs, beginning with a collection of short programs and working up to larger programs as the course progresses. Students should read the text at a pace commensurate with classroom coverage of topics.

TWO-QUARTER SCHEDULE—QUARTER 1
One week of review. Data structures and algorithms sequence.

Week	Topic	Reading
1	Review of C++ and program performance.	Chapters 1–4. Assignment 1 given out.
2	Array-based representation.	Chapter 5. Assignment 1 due.
3	Linked representation.	Sections 6.1–6.4. Assignment 2 given out.
4	Bin sort and equivalence classes.	Sections 6.5.1 and 6.5.4. Assignment 2 due.
5	Arrays and matrices.	Chapter 7. Examination.
6	Stacks and queues.	Chapters 8 and 9. Assignment 3 given out.
7	Skip lists and hashing.	Chapter 10. Assignment 3 due.
8	Binary and other trees.	Sections 11.1–11.8. Assignment 4 given out.
9	Union-find application. Heaps and heap sort.	Sections 11.9.2, 12.1–12.4, and 12.6.1. Assignment 4 due.
10	Leftist trees, Huffman codes, and tournament trees.	Sections 12.5 and 12.6.3 and Chapter 13.

TWO-QUARTER SCHEDULE—QUARTER 2
Data structures and algorithms sequence.

Week	Topic	Reading
1	Binary search trees. Either AVL or red-black trees. Histogramming.	Chapters 14 and 15. Assignment 1 given out.
2	Graphs.	Sections 16.1–16.7. Assignment 1 due.
3	Graphs.	Sections 16.8 and 16.9. Assignment 2 given out.
4	The greedy method.	Sections 17.1–17.3.5. Assignment 2 due.
5	The greedy method and the divide-and-conquer method.	Sections 17.3.6 and 18.1. Assignment 3 given out.
6	Divide-and-conquer applications.	Section 18.2. Examination.
7	Solving recurrences, lower bounds, and dynamic programming.	Sections 18.3, 18.4, and 19.1. Assignment 3 due.
8	Dynamic-programming applications.	Sections 19.2.1 and 19.2.2. Assignment 4 given out.
9	Dynamic-programming applications.	Sections 19.2.3–19.2.5. Assignment 4 due.
10	Backtracking and branch-and-bound methods.	Chapters 20 and 21.

SEMESTER SCHEDULE
Two weeks of review. Data structures course.

Week	Topic	Reading
1	Review of C++.	Chapter 1. Assignment 1 given out.
2	Review of program performance.	Chapters 2–4.
3	Array-based representation.	Chapter 5. Assignment 1 due.
4	Linked representation.	Sections 6.1–6.4. Assignment 2 given out.
5	Bin sort and equivalence classes.	Sections 6.5.1 and 6.5.4.
6	Arrays and matrices.	Chapter 7. Assignment 2 due. First examination.
7	Stacks and queues. One or two applications.	Chapters 8 and 9. Assignment 3 given out.
8	Skip lists and hashing.	Chapter 10.
9	Binary and other trees.	Sections 11.1–11.8. Assignment 3 due.
10	Union-find application.	Section 11.9.2. Assignment 4 given out. Second examination.
11	Priority queues, heap sort, and Huffman codes.	Chapter 12.
12	Tournament trees and bin packing.	Chapter 13. Assignment 4 due.
13	Binary search trees. Either AVL or red-black trees. Histogramming.	Chapters 14 and 15. Assignment 5 given out.
14	Graphs.	Sections 16.1–16.7.
15	Graphs. Shortest paths.	Sections 16.8, 16.9, 17.3.5, and 19.2.3. Assignment 5 due.
16	Minimum-cost spanning trees. Merge sort and quick sort.	Sections 17.3.6, 18.2.2, and 18.2.3.

SEMESTER SCHEDULE
One week of review. Data structures and algorithms course.

Week	Topic	Reading
1	Review of program performance.	Chapters 1–4.
2	Array-based representation.	Chapter 5. Assignment 1 given out.
3	Linked representation.	Chapter 6.
4	Arrays and matrices.	Chapter 7. Assignment 1 due.
5	Stacks and queues. One or two applications.	Chapters 8 and 9. Assignment 2 given out.
6	Skip lists and hashing.	Chapter 10. Assignment 2 due. First examination.
7	Binary and other trees.	Sections 11.1–11.8. Assignment 3 given out.
8	Union-find application. Heaps and heap sort.	Sections 11.9.2, 12.1–12.4, and 12.6.1.
9	Leftist trees, Huffman codes, and tournament trees.	Sections 12.5 and 12.6.3 and Chapter 13. Assignment 3 due.
10	Binary search trees. Either AVL or red-black trees. Histogramming.	Chapters 14 and 15. Assignment 4 given out. Second examination.
11	Graphs.	Sections 16.1–16.7.
12	Graphs and the greedy method.	Sections 16.8, 16.9, 17.1, and 17.2. Assignment 4 due.
13	Container loading, 0/1 knapsack, shortest paths, and spanning trees.	Section 17.3. Assignment 5 given out.
14	Divide-and-conquer method.	Chapter 18.
15	Dynamic programming.	Chapter 19. Assignment 5 due.
16	Backtracking and branch-and-bound methods.	Chapters 20 and 21.

ACKNOWLEDGMENTS

This book would not have been possible without the assistance, comments, and suggestions of many individuals. I am deeply indebted to the following reviewers of the first edition of this book. Their valuable comments have resulted in a better manuscript.

Jacabo Carrasquel	Carnegie Mellon University
Yu Lo Cyrus Chang	University of New Hampshire
Teofilo F. Gonzalez	University of California at Santa Barbara
Laxmikant V. Kale	University of Illinois
Donald H. Kraft	Louisiana State University
Sang W. Lee	University of Michigan
Jorge Lobo	University of Illinois at Chicago
Brian Malloy	Clemson University
Thomas Miller	University of Idaho
Richard Rasala	Northeastern University
Craig E. Wills	Worchester Polytechnic Institute
Neal E. Young	Dartmouth College

Special thanks go to the students in my data structures and algorithms class who provided valuable feedback and helped debug the manuscript. Additionally, I am grateful to the following individuals at the University of Florida for their contributions: Justin Bullard, Edward Y. C. Cheng, Rajesh Dasari, Thomas Davies, Pinkesh Desai, Vinayak Goel, Haejae Jung, Kun-Suk Kim, Haibin Lu, Jawalant Patel, Sanguthevar Rajasekeran, Gauri Sukhatankar, Gayatri Venkataraman, and Joe Wilson.

Sartaj Sahni
Gainesville
June 2004

CONTENTS IN BRIEF

CONTENTS

PART II   DATA STRUCTURES

PART III   ALGORITHM-DESIGN METHODS

WEB CONTENTS

CHAPTER 1

C++ REVIEW

BIRD'S-EYE VIEW

Well, folks, we are about to begin a journey through the world of data structures, algorithms, and computer programs that solve many real-life problems. The program development process will require us to (1) represent data in an effective way and (2) develop a suitable step-by-step procedure (or algorithm) that can be implemented as a computer program. Effective data representation requires expertise in the field of data structures, and the development of a suitable step-by-step procedure requires expertise in the field of algorithm design methods.

Before you embark on the study of data structures and algorithm design methods, you need to be a proficient C++ programmer and an adept analyst of computer programs. These essential skills are typically gained from introductory C++ and discrete structures courses. The first four chapters of this book are intended as a review of these skills, and much of the material covered in these chapters should already be familiar to you.

In this first chapter we discuss some features of the C++ language. However, this chapter is not intended as a C++ primer, and we do not cover basic constructs such as assignment statements, if statements, and looping statements (e.g., for and while). This chapter covers the following C++ language features:

- The different modes of parameter passing in C++ (by value, by reference, and by const reference).

1

- The different modes in which a function or method may return a value (by value, by reference, and by const reference).

- Template functions.

- Recursive functions.

- Constant functions.

- The C++ memory allocation and deallocation functions **new** and **delete**.

- The C++ exception handling constructs **try**, **catch**, and **throw**.

- Classes and template classes.

- Public, protected, and private class members.

- Friends of a class.

- Operator overloading.

- The standard templates library.

Additional C++ features that may not have been covered in a first C++ course are introduced in later chapters as needed. Chapter 1 also includes codes for the following applications:

- Dynamic allocation and deallocation of one- and two-dimensional arrays.

- Finding the roots of a quadratic function.

- Generating all permutations of n items.

- Finding the maximum of n elements.

Chapter 1 concludes with tips on how to test and debug a program.

1.1   INTRODUCTION

Some of the questions we should ask when examining a computer program are

- Is it correct?

- How easy is it to read the program and understand the code?

- Is the program well documented?

- How easy is it to make changes to the program?

- How much memory is needed to run the program?

- For how long will the program run?

- How general is the code? Will it solve problems over a large range of inputs without modification?

- Can the code be compiled and run on a variety of computers or are modifications needed to run it on different computers?

The relative importance of some of these questions depends on the application environment. For example, if we are writing a program that is to be run once and discarded, then correctness, memory and time requirements, and the ability to compile and run the code on a single computer are the dominating considerations. Regardless of the application, the most important attribute of a program is correctness. An incorrect program, no matter how fast, how general, or how well documented, is of little use (until it is corrected). Although we do not explicitly dwell on techniques to establish program correctness, we provide informal proofs of correctness and implicitly develop programming habits conducive to the production of correct codes. The goal is to teach techniques that will enable you to develop correct, elegant, and efficient solutions.

Before we can begin the study of these techniques, we must review some essential aspects of the C++ language, techniques to test and debug programs, and techniques to analyze and measure the performance of a program. This chapter focuses on the first two items. Chapters 2 through 4 review performance analysis and measurement techniques.

1.2   FUNCTIONS AND PARAMETERS

1.2.1   Value Parameters

Consider the C++ function abc (Program 1.1). This function computes the expression a + b * c for the case when a, b, and c are integers. The result is also an integer.

In Program 1.1 a, b, and c are the **formal parameters** of the function abc. Each is of type integer. If the function is invoked by the statement

```
int abc(int a, int b, int c)
{
    return a + b * c;
}
```

Program 1.1 Compute an integer expression

```
z = abc(2,x,y)
```

then 2, x, and y are the **actual parameters** that correspond to a, b, and c, respectively.

In Program 1.1 the formal parameters a, b, and c are actually **value** formal parameters. At run time the value of the actual parameter that corresponds to a value formal parameter is copied into the formal parameter before the function is executed. This copying is done using the **copy constructor** for the data type of the formal parameter. If the actual and value formal parameters are of different data types, a type conversion is performed from the type of the actual parameter to that of the value formal parameter provided such a type conversion is defined.

When the invocation abc(2,x,y) is executed, a is assigned the value 2, b is assigned the value of x, and c is assigned the value of y. In case x and/or y are not of type int, then a type conversion between their type and int is performed prior to the assignment of values to b and c (provided such a type conversion is defined). For example, if x is of type double and has the value 3.8, then b is assigned the value 3.

When a function terminates, **destructors** for the data types of the formal parameters destroy the value formal parameters. *When a function terminates, formal parameter values are not copied back into the actual parameters.* Consequently, function invocation does not change the actual parameters that correspond to value formal parameters.

1.2.2   Template Functions

Suppose we wish to write another function to compute the same expression as computed by Program 1.1. However, this time a, b, and c are of type float, and the result is also of this type. Program 1.2 gives the code. Programs 1.1 and 1.2 differ only in the data type of the formal parameters and of the value returned.

Rather than write a new version of the code for every possible data type of the formal parameters, we can write a generic code in which the data type is a variable whose value is to be determined by the compiler. This generic code is written using the template statement as shown in Program 1.3.

From this generic code the compiler can construct Program 1.1 by substituting int for T and Program 1.2 by substituting float for T. In fact, the compiler can

```
float abc(float a, float b, float c)
{
    return a + b * c;
}
```

Program 1.2 Compute a floating-point expression

```
template<class T>
T abc(T a, T b, T c)
{
    return a + b * c;
}
```

Program 1.3 Compute an expression using a template function

construct a double-precision version or a long-integer version (or both) of the code by substituting double or long for T. Writing abc as a template function eliminates the need to know the data type of the formal parameters when we write the code.

1.2.3 Reference Parameters

The use of value parameters in Program 1.3 increases the run-time cost. For example, consider the operations involved when a function is invoked and when it terminates. When a, b, and c are value parameters, the copy constructor for type T copies the values of the corresponding actual parameters into the formal parameters a, b, and c upon entry into the function. At the time of exiting the function, the destructor for type T is invoked, and the formal parameters a, b, and c are destroyed.

Suppose that T is the user-defined data type matrix whose copy constructor copies all entries of the matrix and whose destructor destroys the matrix entries one by one (assume that the operators +, *, and / have been defined for the data type matrix). If abc is invoked with each actual parameter being a matrix with 1000 elements, then copying the three actual parameters into a, b, and c would require 3000 operations. When abc terminates, the matrix destructor is invoked to destroy a, b, and c at a cost of an additional 3000 operations.

In the code of Program 1.4, a, b, and c are **reference parameters**. If abc is invoked by the statement abc(x,y,z) where x, y, and z are of the same data type, then these actual parameters are bound to the names a, b, and c, respectively. Therefore, during execution of the function abc, the names x, y, and z, respectively, are used in place of the names a, b, and c. Unlike the case of value parameters, this program does not copy actual parameter values at the time of invocation and does not invoke the type T destructor upon exit.

```
template<class T>
T abc(T& a, T& b, T& c)
{
    return a + b * c;
}
```

Program 1.4 Compute an expression using reference parameters

Consider the case when the actual parameters that correspond to a, b, and c are matrices x, y, and z with 1000 elements each. Since the values of x, y, and z are now not copied into the formal parameters, we save the 3000 operations needed to do the copying when value parameters are used.

1.2.4   Const Reference Parameters

C++ provides yet another mode of parameter passing, **const reference**. This mode designates reference parameters that are not changed by the function. For example, in Program 1.4 the values of a, b, and c do not change, so we may rewrite the code as shown in Program 1.5.

```
template<class T>
T abc(const T& a, const T& b, const T& c)
{
    return a + b * c;
}
```

Program 1.5 Compute an expression using const reference parameters

Using the const qualifier to designate reference parameters that the function does not change has an important software-engineering value. The function header tells the user that the function will not change the actual parameters.

Using the syntax of Program 1.6, we can obtain a more general version of Program 1.5. In the new version each formal parameter may be of a different type, and the result is of the same type as the first parameter (for example).

1.2.5   Return Values

A function may make a value return, a reference return, or a const reference return. The preceding examples make value returns. In such a return, the object that is

```
template<class Ta, class Tb, class Tc>
Ta abc(const Ta& a, const Tb& b, const Tc& c)
{
    return a + b * c;
}
```

Program 1.6 A more general version of Program 1.5

being returned is copied into the invoking (or return) environment. This copying is necessary in all versions of the function abc, as the result of the expression computed by this function is saved in a local temporary variable. When the function terminates, the space allocated to this temporary variable (as well as to all other temporary variables, local variables and value formal parameters) is freed and its value is no longer available. To avoid losing this value, we copy it from the temporary variable into the return environment before releasing the space allocated to temporary variables, local variables and value formal parameters.

We specify a reference return by adding the symbol **&** as a suffix to the return type. The function header

```
T& mystery(int i, T& z)
```

defines a function mystery that makes a reference return of type T. It could, for example, return z using the following statement:

```
return z;
```

Such a return would not involve copying the value of z into the return environment. When function mystery terminates, the space allocated to the value formal parameter i and all local variables is released. Because z is simply a reference to an actual parameter, it is not affected.

A const reference return is specified by adding the keyword **const** to the function header as in

```
const T& mystery(int i, T& z)
```

A const reference return is similar to a reference return except that the item returned is designated a constant object.

1.2.6 Overloaded Functions

The **signature** of a function is defined by the data types of the method's formal parameters and the number of formal parameters. The signature of the method abc of Program 1.1 is (int, int, int). C++ allows you to define two or more functions with the same name provided no two functions with the same name have the same signature. The ability to define several functions with the same name is called **function overloading**. Because of the availability of function overloading, we can write a program that includes both the function abc of Program 1.1 and the function abc of Program 1.2. By matching the signature used by a function invocation statement to the signature in a function definition, the C++ compiler can determine which of the overloaded functions is meant.

EXERCISES

1. Explain why the swap method of Program 1.7 fails to swap (i.e., interchange) the values of the integer actual parameters that correspond to the formal parameters x and y. How would you change this code so that it correctly swaps the values of the actual parameters.

```
void swap(int x, int y)
{// swap the integers x and y
   int temp = x;
   x = y;
   y = temp;
}
```

Program 1.7 Incorrect code to swap two integers

2. Write a template function count that returns the number of occurrences of value in the array a[0:n-1]. Test your code.

3. Write a template function fill that sets a[start:end-1] to value. Test your code.

4. Write a template function inner_product that returns $\sum_{i=0}^{n-1} a[i] * b[i]$. Test your code.

5. Write a template function iota that sets a[i] = value + i, $0 \le i < n$. Test your code.

6. Write a template function is_sorted that returns true iff a[0:n-1] is sorted. Test your code.

7. Write a template function mismatch that returns the smallest i, $0 \le i < n$ such that a[i] $\ne$ b[i]. Test your code.

8. Do the following headers define functions with different signatures? Why?

(a) `int abc(int a, int b, int c)`

(b) `float abc(int a, int b, int c)`

9. Suppose we have a program that contains both of the `abc` functions given in Programs 1.1 and 1.2. Which `abc` function is invoked by each of the following statements. Which will result in a compile-time error? Why?

(a) `cout << abc(1, 2, 3);) << endln;`

(b) `cout << abc(1.0F, 2.0F, 3.0F);) < endln;`

(c) `cout << abc(1, 2, 3.0F);) < endln;`

(d) `cout << abc(1.0, 2.0, 3.0);) << endln;`

1.3   EXCEPTIONS

1.3.1   Throwing an Exception

Exceptions are used to signal the occurrence of errors. For example, the evaluation of the expression a+b*c+b/c with a = 2, b = 1, and c = 0 requires us to divide by zero, which is an error. Although this error is not detected by C++, your hardware will detect the error and throw an exception.

We can write C++ programs that check for exceptional conditions and throw an exception when such a condition is detected. For example, the task performed by function `abc` (Program 1.1) may be defined only when each of its three parameters is greater than 0. In this case we would modify the code of Program 1.1 to first check that the values of a, b, and c are actually > 0. If one or more of these parameters is ≤ 0, we can signal an exceptional condition by throwing an exception as is done in Program 1.8. The exception thrown by this program is of type `char*`.

```
int abc(int a, int b, int c)
{
    if (a <= 0 || b <= 0 || c <= 0)
         throw "All parameters should be > 0";
    return a + b * c;
}
```

Program 1.8 Throwing an exception of type `char*`

We get more flexibility in processing exceptions when we define an exception class for each of the different kinds of exceptions (e.g., divide by zero, illegal parameter value, illegal input value, array index out of range) that our program may throw. For example, C++ has a hierarchy of exception classes with the class `exception` as root. Standard C++ functions signal exceptional conditions by throwing exceptions of a type that is derived from the root or base class **exception**. For example, the C++ operator **new** that does dynamic memory allocation throws an exception of type **bad_alloc** when it is unable to make the requested memory allocation; **bad_alloc** is derived from the base class **exception**. Similarly, the C++ function **typeid**, which determines the type of an object, throws an exception of type **bad_typeid** when you attempt to determine the type of the NULL object; **bad_typeid** also is derived from the base class **exception**. In Section 1.6 we shall see how to define an exception class.

1.3.2   Handling Exceptions

Exceptions that might be thrown by a piece of code can be handled by enclosing this code within a **try** block. The **try** block is then followed by zero or more **catch** blocks. Each **catch** block has a parameter or argument whose type determines the type of exception that may be caught by that **catch** block. For example, the block

```
catch (char* e) {}
```

catches exceptions of type **char*** while the block

```
catch (bad_alloc e) {}
```

catches exceptions of type **bad_alloc**. The block

```
catch (exception& e) {}
```

catches exceptions of type **exception** as well as of all types derived from **exception** (e.g., **bad_alloc** and **bad_typeid**). The block

```
catch (...) {}
```

catches all exceptions regardless of their type.

A **catch** block typically contains code to recover from the exception that has occurred, or if recovery is not possible, the code in the **catch** block prints out an error message. Program 1.9 shows an example of the **try-catch** construct. The method **abc** that is invoked within the **try** block is the one given in Program 1.8.

Although Program 1.9 has a single **catch** block following the **try** block, it is possible to follow a **try** block with several **catch** blocks. When the code within a **try** block terminates with no exception, we bypass the **catch** blocks. When an exception is thrown, normal execution of the **try** block terminates and we enter the first **catch** block that can catch an exception of the type thrown. Following the execution of the code within this matching **catch** block, we bypass the remaining **catch** blocks. If no **catch** block matches the thrown exception type, then the exception propagates through the hierarchy of nested enclosing **try** blocks to the

```
int main()
{
  try {cout << abc(2,0,4) << endl;}
  catch (char* e)
     {
         cout << "The parameters to abc were 2, 0, and 4" << endl;
         cout << "An exception has been thrown" << endl;
         cout << e << endl;
         return 1;
     }
   return 0;
}
```

Program 1.9 Catching an exception of type char*

first catch block in this hierarchy that can handle the exception. If the exception is not caught by any catch block, the program terminates abnormally.

When Program 1.9 executes, abc throws an exception of type char*. This exception causes abc to terminate without the evaluation of the expression. Also, the try block terminates immediately (the cout in the try block doesn't complete). Since the type of the exception thrown by abc is the same as that of the catch block's parameter e, the exception is caught by this catch block; e is assigned the thrown exception; and the catch block is entered. Figure 1.1 gives the output generated by Program 1.9.

```
The parameters to abc were 2, 0, and 4
An exception has been thrown
All parameters should be > 0
```

Figure 1.1 Output from Program 1.9

EXERCISES

10. Modify Program 1.8 so that it throws an exception of type int. The value of the thrown exception should be 1 if a, b, and c are all less than 0; the value should be 2 if all three equal 0. When neither of these conditions is satisfied, no exception is thrown. Write a main function that uses your modified code; catches the exception if thrown; and outputs a message that depends on the value of the thrown exception. Test your code.

11. Do Exercise 2. Your code for the function should throw an exception of type char* in case $n < 1$. Test your code.

1.4   DYNAMIC MEMORY ALLOCATION

1.4.1   The Operator new

Run-time or dynamic allocation of memory may be done using the C++ operator new. This operator returns a pointer to the allocated memory. For example, to dynamically allocate memory for an integer, we must declare a variable (e.g., y) to be a pointer to an integer using this statement:

```
int *y;
```

When the program needs to actually use the integer, memory may be allocated to it using this syntax:

```
y = new int;
```

The operator new allocates enough memory to hold an integer, and a pointer to this memory is returned and saved in y. The variable y references the pointer to the integer, and *y references the integer. To store an integer value, for example 10, in the newly allocated memory, we can use the following syntax:

```
*y = 10;
```

We can combine the three steps–declare y, allocate memory, and assign a value to *y–into a smaller number of steps as shown in the following examples:

```
int *y = new int;
*y = 10;
```

or

```
int *y = new int (10);
```

or

```
int *y;
y = new int (10);
```

1.4.2   One-Dimensional Arrays

This text includes many examples of functions that work with one- and two-dimensional arrays. The size of these arrays may not be known at compile time and may, in fact, change from one invocation of the function to the next. Consequently, memory for these arrays needs to be allocated dynamically.

To create a one-dimensional floating-point array x at run time, we must declare x as a pointer to a `float` and then allocate enough memory for the array. For example, a floating-point array of size n may be created as follows:

```
float *x = new float [n];
```

The operator `new` allocates memory for n floating-point numbers and returns a pointer to the first of these. The array elements may be addressed using the syntax x[0], x[1], ..., x[n-1].

1.4.3   Exception Handling

What happens when the statement

```
float *x = new float [n];
```

is executed and the computer doesn't have enough memory for n floating-point numbers? In this case `new` cannot possibly allocate the desired amount of memory, and an exception of type `bad_alloc` is thrown. We may detect the failure of `new` by catching the exception with the `try` - `catch` construct:

```
float *x;
try {x = new float [n];}
catch (bad_alloc e)
{// enter only when new fails
   cerr << "Out of Memory" << endl;
   exit(1);
}
```

1.4.4   The Operator delete

Dynamically allocated memory should be freed when it is no longer needed. The freed memory can then be reused to create new dynamically allocated structures. We can use the C++ operator `delete` to free space allocated using the operator `new`. The statements

```
delete y;
delete [] x;
```

free the memory allocated to *y and the one-dimensional array x.

1.4.5   Two-Dimensional Arrays

Although C++ provides several mechanisms for declaring two-dimensional arrays, most of these mechanisms require that both dimensions be known at compile time. Further, when these mechanisms are used, it is difficult to write functions that allow a formal parameter which is a two-dimensional array whose second dimension is unknown. This is so because when a formal parameter is a two-dimensional array, we must specify the value of the second dimension. For example, a[] [10] is a valid formal parameter for a function; a[] [] is not.

An effective way to overcome these limitations is to use dynamic memory allocation for all two-dimensional arrays. Throughout this text we use dynamically allocated two-dimensional arrays.

When both dimensions of the array are known at compile time, the array may be created using a syntax similar to that used for one-dimensional arrays. For example, a seven by five array of type char may be declared using the syntax:

```
char c[7][5];
```

When at least one of the dimensions is unknown at compile time, the array must be created at run time using the new operator. A two-dimensional character array for which the number of columns–for example, 5–is known at compile time may be allocated using the following syntax:

```
char (*c)[5];
try {c = new char [n][5];}
catch (bad_alloc)
{// enter only when new fails
   cerr << "Out of Memory" << endl;
   exit(1);
}
```

The number of rows n may be determined at run time either via computation or user input. When the number of columns is not known at compile time, the array cannot be allocated by a simple invocation of new (even if the number of rows is known). To construct the two-dimensional array, we view it as composed of several rows. Each row is a one-dimensional array and may be created using new as discussed earlier. Pointers to each row may be saved in another one-dimensional array. Figure 1.2 shows the structure that needs to be established for the case of a three by five array x.

x[0], x[1], and x[2] point to the first element of rows 0, 1, and 2, respectively. So if x is to be a character array, then x[0:2] are pointers to characters and x is itself a pointer to a pointer to a character. x may be declared using the following syntax:

```
char **x;
```

Figure 1.2 Memory structure for a three by five array

To create the memory structure of Figure 1.2, we can use the code of Program 1.10, which creates a two-dimensional array of type T. The array has numberOfRows rows and numberOfCols columns. The code first gets memory for the pointers x[0] through x[numberOfRows-1]. Next it gets memory for each row of the array. This code invokes new numberOfRows + 1 times. If one of these invocations of new throws an exception, program control is transferred to the catch block and the value false is returned. If none of the invocations of new throws an exception, the array construction is successful and make2dArray returns the value true. The elements of the created array x may be indexed using the standard x[i][j] notation, $0 \leq i <$ numberOfRows, $0 \leq j <$ numberOfColumns.

```
template <class T>
bool make2dArray(T ** &x, int numberOfRows, int numberOfColumns)
{// Create a two dimensional array.

    try {
          // create pointers for the rows
          x = new T * [numberOfRows];

          // get memory for each row
          for (int i = 0; i < numberOfRows; i++)
              x[i] = new int [numberOfColumns];
          return true;
        }
    catch (bad_alloc) {return false;}
}
```

Program 1.10 Allocate memory for a two-dimensional array

In Program 1.10 the exception (if any) thrown by new is reported to the invoking function as the Boolean value **false**. The failure of **make2dArray** may also be reported to the invoking function by simply doing nothing. If we use the code of Program 1.11, the invoking function can catch any exception thrown by **new**.

```
template <class T>
void make2dArray(T ** &x, int numberOfRows, int numberOfColumns)
{// Create a two-dimensional array.

   // create pointers for the rows
   x = new T * [numberOfRows];

   // get memory for each row
   for (int i = 0; i < numberOfRows; i++)
      x[i] = new T [numberOfColumns];
}
```

Program 1.11 Make a two-dimensional array but do not catch exceptions

When **make2dArray** is defined as in Program 1.11, we can use the code

```
try {make2dArray(x,r,c);}
catch (bad_alloc)
{
   cerr << "Could not create x" << endl;
   exit(1);
}
```

to determine a shortage of memory. Not catching the exception within **make2dArray** not only simplifies the code for this function but also allows the exception to be caught at a point where the user is better able to report a meaningful error or attempt error recovery.

We can free the memory allocated to a two-dimensional array by Program 1.10 by first freeing the memory allocated in the **for** loop to each row and then freeing the memory allocated for the row pointers, as shown in Program 1.12. Notice that this code sets **x** to zero, which prevents the user from accessing the memory that was freed.

EXERCISES

12. Write a general version of **make2dArray** (Program 1.11) whose third parameter is a one-dimensional array **rowSize** rather than the integer **numberOfColumns**. Your function should create a two-dimensional array in which row i has **rowSize[i]** positions.

```
template <class T>
void delete2dArray(T ** &x, int numberOfRows)
{// Delete the two-dimensional array x.

   // delete the memory for each row
   for (int i = 0; i < numberOfRows; i++)
      delete [] x[i];

   // delete the row pointers
   delete [] x;
   x = NULL;
}
```

Program 1.12 Free the memory allocated by make2dArray

13. Write a template function changeLength1D to change the length (i.e., number of positions) of a one-dimensional array from oldLength to newLength. Your function should allocate space for a new one-dimensional array of length newLength; copy the first min{oldLength, newLength} elements of the old array into the new one; and free the space allocated to the old array. Test your code.

14. Write a function changeLength2D that changes the dimensions of a two-dimensional array (see Exercise 13). Test your code.

1.5 YOUR VERY OWN DATA TYPE

1.5.1 The Class currency

The C++ language supports data types such as int, float, and char. Many of the applications we develop in this text require additional data types that are not supported by the language. The most flexible way to define your own data types in C++ is to use the class construct. Suppose you wish to deal with objects (also referred to as instances) of type currency. Objects of type currency have a sign component (plus or minus), a dollar component, and a cents component. Two examples are $2.35 (sign is plus, 2 dollars, and 35 cents) and −$6.05 (sign is minus, 6 dollars, and 5 cents). Some of the functions or operations we wish to perform on objects of this type follow:

- Set their value.

- Determine the components (i.e., sign, dollar amount, and number of cents).

- Add two objects of type currency.

- Increment the value.

- Output.

Suppose we choose to represent objects of type currency using an unsigned long variable dollars, an unsigned integer cents, and a variable sign of type signType where the data type signType is defined as

```
enum signType {plus, minus};
```

We may declare a C++ class currency using the syntax of Program 1.13. The first line simply says that we are declaring a class whose name is currency. The class declaration is then enclosed in braces ({}). The class declaration has been divided into two sections public and private. The public section declares functions (or methods) that operate on objects (or instances) of type currency. These functions are *visible* to the users of the class and are the only means by which users can interact with objects of type currency. The private section declares functions and data members (simple variables, arrays, and so on that may hold data values) that are not visible to users of the class. By having a public section and a private section, we can let the user see only what he or she needs to see while we hide the remaining information (generally having to do with implementation details). *Although C++ syntax permits you to declare data members in the* public *section, good software-engineering practice discourages this procedure.*

The first function in the public section has the same name as the class name. Member functions that have the same name as that of the class are called **constructor** functions. Constructor functions specify how to create an object of a given type and are not permitted to return a value. In our case the constructor has three parameters whose default values are plus, 0, and 0. The implementation of the constructor function is provided later in this section. Constructor functions are invoked automatically when an object of type currency is being created. Two ways to create objects of type currency are

```
currency f, g(plus, 3, 45), h(minus, 10);
currency *m = new currency (plus, 8, 12);
```

The first line declares three variables (f, g, and h) of type currency. f is to be initialized using the default values plus, 0, and 0, whereas g is to be initialized to $3.45 and h to −$10.00. Notice that the initialization values correspond to the constructor parameters from left to right. If the number of initialization values is less than the number of constructor parameters, the remaining parameters are assigned their default values. Line 2 declares m as a pointer to an object of type currency. We invoke the new operator to create an object of type currency and store a pointer to this object in m. The created object is to be initialized to $8.12.

```
class currency
{
   public:
      // constructor
      currency(signType theSign = plus,
               unsigned long theDollars = 0,
               unsigned int theCents = 0);
      // destructor
      ~currency() {}
      void setValue(signType, unsigned long, unsigned int);
      void setValue(double);
      signType getSign() const {return sign;}
      unsigned long getDollars() const {return dollars;}
      unsigned int getCents() const {return cents;}
      currency add(const currency&) const;
      currency& increment(const currency&);
      void output() const;
   private:
      signType sign;           // sign of object
      unsigned long dollars;   // number of dollars
      unsigned int cents;      // number of cents
};
```

Program 1.13 Declaration of the class currency

The next function, ~currency, has a name that is the class name preceded by a tilde (~). This function is called the **destructor**. It is automatically invoked whenever an object of type currency goes out of scope. The object is destroyed using this function. In our case the destructor is defined as the null function ({}). For other classes, the class constructor might create dynamic arrays (for example) and the destructor will need to free the space allocated to these arrays when the object goes out of scope. Destructor functions are not permitted to return a value.

The next two functions allow the user to set the value of a currency object. The first requires the user to provide three parameters, while the second permits setting the value by providing a single number. The implementations are provided later in this section. Notice first that both functions have the same name. The compiler and user are able to tell the functions apart because they have different signatures. C++ allows the reuse of function names as long as their signatures are different! Notice also that we have not specified the name of the object whose sign, dollars, and cents values are to be set. This is because the syntax to invoke a class member function is

```
g.setValue(minus,33,0);
h.setValue(20.52);
```

where g and h are variables of type currency. In the first case g is the object that invokes setValue, while in the second the object h invokes setValue. When we write the code for the setValue functions, we will have a away to access the object that invoked them. Therefore we do not need to include the name of the invoking object in the parameter list.

The functions getSign, getDollars, and getCents return the appropriate data member of the invoking object. The key word const states that these functions do not change the invoking object. We refer to functions of this type as **constant functions**.

The function add sums the currency amounts of the invoking object and the parameter currency object and then returns the resultant amount. Since this function does not change the invoking object, add is a constant function. The function increment adds the parameter currency object to the invoking object. This function changes the invoking object and so is not a constant function. The last public member function is output, which displays the invoking object by inserting it into the output stream cout. The function output, which does not change the invoking object, is a constant function.

Although both add and increment return objects of type currency, add does a value return, while increment does a reference return. As mentioned in Section 1.2.5, value and reference returns work like value and reference parameters. In the case of a value return, the object being returned is copied into the return environment. A reference return avoids this copying, and the return environment makes direct use of the return object. Reference returns are faster than value returns, as no copying is done. The code for add shows that it returns a local object, which is destroyed when the function terminates. Therefore the return statement must copy this object. In the case of increment, a global object is returned and there is no need to copy it.

A **copy constructor** performs the copying for value returns as well as for value parameters. Program 1.13 does not specify a copy constructor, so C++ uses the default copy constructor, which copies the data members only. The use of the default copy constructor is adequate for the class currency. We will also see classes where the use of the default copy constructor is not sufficient.

In the private section, we declared the three data members needed to represent an object of type currency. Each object of type currency has its own copy of these three data members.

The functions whose implementation is not given inside the class declaration must be defined outside of it by using the scope resolution operator :: to specify that the function we are defining is a member of the class currency. So the syntax currency::currency denotes the constructor of the class currency, while currency::output denotes the output function of this class. Program 1.14 gives the currency constructor, which simply invokes the three-parameter setValue function to initialize the object's data members.

```
currency::currency(signType theSign, unsigned long theDollars,
                                      unsigned int theCents)
{// Create a currency object.
   setValue(theSign, theDollars, theCents);
}
```

Program 1.14 Constructor for `currency`

Program 1.15 gives the codes for the two `setValue` functions. The first function validates the input and sets the **private** data members of the invoking object only if the parameter values pass the validation test. In case the parameters do not pass the validation test, an exception of type `illegalParametervalue` is thrown (defined later in Section 1.6). The second function does not perform validation and uses only the first two digits after the decimal point. Numbers of the form $d_1.d_2d_3$ may not have an exact computer representation. For example, the computer representation of the number 5.29 is slightly smaller than 5.29. This representation creates an error when extracting the cents component using the following statement:

```
cents = (unsigned int) ((theAmount - dollars) * 100);
```

`(theAmount - dollars) * 100` is slightly smaller than 29, and when the program does the conversion to an unsigned integer, it assigns `cents` the value 28 rather than 29. Adding 0.001 to `theAmount` solves our problem so long as the computer representation of $d_1.d_2d_3$ is not less by more than 0.001 or more by ≥ 0.009. For example, if the computer representation of 5.29 is equivalent to 5.28999, then adding 0.001 yields 5.29099 and the computed cents amount is 29.

Program 1.16 gives the code for the **add** function. This function begins by converting into integers the two currency values to be added. The amount \$2.32 becomes the integer 232, and −\$4.75 becomes the integer −475. Notice the difference in syntax used to reference the data members of the invoking object and those of the parameter x. `x.dollars` specifies the `dollars` data member of x, while the use of `dollars` with no object name before it refers to the `dollars` member of the invoking object. When function **add** terminates, the local variables a1, a2, a3, and **ans** are destroyed by the destructor for **long** and the space allocated to these variables freed. Since the currency object **ans** is to be returned as the value of the invocation, it must be copied into the invoking environment. So **add** must do a value return.

Program 1.17 gives the **increment** and **output** codes. In C++, the reserved word **this** points to the invoking object; *this is the invoking object itself. Consider the invocation g.increment(h). The first line of function **increment** invokes the **public** member function **add**, which adds x (i.e., h) to the invoking object g.

```
void currency::setValue(signType theSign, unsigned long theDollars,
                                         unsigned int theCents)
{// Set currency value.
   if (theCents > 99)
       // too many cents
       throw illegalParameterValue("Cents should be < 100");

   sign = theSign;
   dollars = theDollars;
   cents = theCents;
}

void currency::setValue(double theAmount)
{// Set currency value.
   if (theAmount < 0) {sign = minus;
                       theAmount = -theAmount;}
   else sign = plus;

   dollars = (unsigned long) theAmount;
           // extract integer part
   cents = (unsigned int) ((theAmount + 0.001 - dollars) * 100);
           // get two decimal digits
}
```

Program 1.15 Setting the private data members

The result is returned and assigned to the object *this, which is g. So the value of g is incremented by h. The function returns *this, which is the invoking object. Since this object is not local to function increment, it will not be automatically destroyed upon termination of the function. Hence we may do a reference return and save the copying that would take place during a value return.

By making the data members of the class currency private, we deny access to these members to the user. So the user cannot change their values using statements such as

```
h.cents = 20;
h.dollars = 100;
h.sign = plus;
```

We can assure the integrity of the data members by writing the member functions to leave behind valid values if they begin with valid data member values. Our codes for the constructor and setValue functions validate the data before using it. The

```
currency currency::add(const currency& x) const
{// Add x and *this.
   long a1, a2, a3;
   currency result;
   // convert invoking object to signed integers
   a1 = dollars * 100 + cents;
   if (sign == minus) a1 = -a1;

   // convert x to signed integer
   a2 = x.dollars * 100 + x.cents;
   if (x.sign == minus) a2 = -a2;

   a3 = a1 + a2;

   // convert to currency representation
   if (a3 < 0) {result.sign = minus; a3 = -a3;}
   else result.sign = plus;
   result.dollars = a3 / 100;
   result.cents = a3 - result.dollars * 100;

   return result;
}
```

Program 1.16 Adding two currency values

```
currency& currency::increment(const currency& x)
{// Increment by x.
   *this = add(x);
   return *this;
}

void currency::output() const
{// Output currency value.
   if (sign == minus) cout << '-';
   cout << '$' << dollars << '.';
   if (cents < 10) cout << '0';
   cout << cents;
}
```

Program 1.17 increment and output

remaining functions have the property they leave behind valid data if they start with valid data. As a result, the codes for functions such as add and output do not need to verify that the number of cents is, in fact, between 0 and 99. If the data members are declared as public members, their integrity cannot be assured. The user might (erroneously) set cents equal to 305, which would cause functions such as output to malfunction. As a result, all functions would need to validate the data before proceeding with their tasks. This validation would slow down the codes and also make them less elegant.

Program 1.18 gives a sample application of the class currency. This code assumes that the class declaration and all implementation codes are in the file currency.h. We would normally keep the class declaration and the function implementations in separate files. However, such a separation causes difficulties with template functions and template classes that we use heavily in subsequent sections and chapters.

Line 1 of the function main declares four variables, g, h, i, and j of type currency. The class constructor initializes all but h to $0.00. h has the initial value $3.50. In the two calls to setValue, g and i are, respectively, set to −$2.25 and −$6.45. The call to function add adds h and g and returns the resulting object whose value is $1.25. The returned object is assigned to j, using the default assignment procedure that copies the data members of the object on the right side into the corresponding data members of the object on the left side. This copying results in j having the value $1.25. This values of h, g and j are output by the next few lines of code. The remaining lines of code are self explanatory.

1.5.2   Using a Different Representation

Suppose that many application codes have been developed using the class currency of Program 1.13. Now we desire to change the representation of a currency object to one that results in faster codes for the more frequently performed operations of add and increment and hence speed the application codes. Since the user interacts with the class currency only through the interface provided in the public section, changes made to the private section do not affect the correctness of the application codes. Hence we can change the private section without making any changes in the applications!

The new representation of a currency object has just one private data member, which is of type long. The number 132 represents $1.32, while −20 represents −$0.20. Programs 1.19, 1.20, and 1.21 give the new declaration of currency and the implementation of the various member functions.

Notice that if the new code is placed in the file currency.h, we can run the application code of Program 1.18 with no change at all! *An important benefit of hiding the implementation details from the user is that we can replace old representations with new more efficient ones without changing the application codes.*

```
#include <iostream>
#include "currency.h"

using namespace std;

int main()
{
   currency g, h(plus, 3, 50), i, j;

   // try out both forms of setValue
   g.setValue(minus, 2, 25);
   i.setValue(-6.45);

   // do an add and output
   j = h.add(g);
   h.output();
   cout << " + ";
   g.output();
   cout << " = ";
   j.output(); cout << endl;

   // do two adds in a sequence
   j = i.add(g).add(h);
      // output statements omitted

   // do an increment and add
   j = i.increment(g).add(h);
      // output statements omitted

   // test the exception
   cout << "Attempting to initialize with cents = 152" << endl;
   try {i.setValue(plus, 3, 152);}
   catch (illegalParameterValue e)
   {
      cout << "Caught thrown exception" << endl;
      e.outputMessage();
   }
   return 0;
}
```

Program 1.18 Application of the class currency

```
class currency
{
    public:
        // constructor
        currency(signType theSign = plus,
                 unsigned long theDollars = 0,
                 unsigned int theCents = 0);
        // destructor
        ~currency() {}
        void setValue(signType, unsigned long, unsigned int);
        void setValue(double);
        signType getSign() const
            {if (amount < 0) return minus;
             else return plus;}
        unsigned long getDollars() const
            {if (amount < 0) return (-amount) / 100;
             else return amount / 100;}
        unsigned int getCents() const
            {if (amount < 0) return -amount - getDollars() * 100;
             else return amount - getDollars() * 100;}
        currency add(const currency&) const;
        currency& increment(const currency& x)
            {amount += x.amount; return *this;}
        void output() const;
    private:
        long amount;
};
```

Program 1.19 New declaration of the class currency

1.5.3   Operator Overloading

The class currency includes several member functions that resemble some of the standard operators of C++. For example, add does what + does, and increment does what += does. Using these standard C++ operators is more natural than defining new ones such as add and increment. We can use + and += by a process called **operator overloading** that permits us to extend the applicability of existing C++ operators so that they work with new data types or classes.

Program 1.22 gives the class declaration that substitutes the standard operators + and += for add and increment. The output function now takes the name of an output stream as a parameter. Program 1.23 gives the new codes for add and output. This program also includes code to overload the C++ stream insertion

```
currency::currency(signType theSign, unsigned long theDollars,
                                     unsigned int theCents)
{// Create a currency object.
   setValue(theSign, theDollars, theCents);
}


void currency::setValue(signType theSign, unsigned long theDollars,
                                          unsigned int theCents)
{// Set currency value.
   if (theCents > 99)
       // too many cents
       throw illegalParameterValue("Cents should be < 100");

   amount = theDollars * 100 + theCents;
   if (theSign == minus) amount = -amount;
}


void currency::setValue(double theAmount)
{// Set currency value.
   if (theAmount < 0)
      amount = (long) ((theAmount - 0.001) * 100);
   else
      amount = (long) ((theAmount + 0.001) * 100);
            // 2 decimal digits only
}
```

Program 1.20 New constructor and set value codes

operator <<.

Notice that we overload the stream insertion operator without declaring a corresponding member function in the class currency, and overload + and += by defining these operators as members of the class. We can also overload the stream extraction operator >> without defining this operator as a class member. Further, notice the use of the function output to assist in the overloading of <<. Since the **private** members of currency objects are not accessible from functions that are not class members (the overloaded << is not a class member, while the overloaded + is), the code that overloads << may not reference the **private** members of the object x that it is to insert into the output stream. In particular, the code

```
// overload <<
ostream& operator<<(ostream& out, const currency& x)
   {out << x.amount; return out;}
```

```
currency currency::add(const currency& x) const
{// Add x and *this.
  currency y;
  y.amount = amount + x.amount;
  return y;
}

void currency::output() const
{// Output currency value.
  long theAmount = amount;
  if (theAmount < 0) {cout << '-';
                          theAmount = -theAmount;}
  long dollars = theAmount / 100; // dollars
  cout << '$' << dollars << '.';
  int cents = theAmount - dollars * 100; // cents
  if (cents < 10) cout << '0';
  cout << cents;
}
```

Program 1.21 New code for add and output

is erroneous, as the member amount is not accessible.

Program 1.24 is a version of Program 1.18 that assumes that operators have been overloaded and that the codes of Programs 1.22 and 1.23 are in the file currencyOverload.h.

1.5.4   Friends and Protected Class Members

As pointed out earlier, private members of a class are visible only to class member functions. In some applications, we must grant access to these private members to other classes and functions. This access may be granted by declaring these other classes or functions as friends.

In our currency class example (Program 1.22), we defined a member function output to facilitate the overloading of the operator <<. Defining this member function was necessary, as the function

```
ostream& operator<<(ostream&, const currency&)
```

cannot access the private member amount. We may avoid defining the additional function output by declaring ostream& operator<< a friend of the class currency. Thus we grant this function access to all members (private and public) of currency. To make friends, we introduce friend statements into the declaration

```
class currency
{
   public:
      // constructor
      currency(signType theSign = plus,
               unsigned long theDollars = 0,
               unsigned int theCents = 0);
      // destructor
      ~currency() {}
      void setValue(signType, unsigned long, unsigned int);
      void setValue(double);
      signType getSign() const
        {if (amount < 0) return minus;
         else return plus;}
      unsigned long getDollars() const
        {if (amount < 0) return (-amount) / 100;
         else return amount / 100;}
      unsigned int getCents() const
        {if (amount < 0) return -amount - getDollars() * 100;
         else return amount - getDollars() * 100;}
      currency operator+(const currency&) const;
      currency& operator+=(const currency& x)
        {amount += x.amount; return *this;}
      void output(ostream&) const;
   private:
      long amount;
};
```

Program 1.22 Class declaration using operator overloading

of the class **currency**. For consistency, we shall always place **friend** statements just after the **class** header statement as in

```
class currency {
   friend ostream& operator<<(ostream&, const currency&);
   public:
```

With this friend declaration in place, we may overload the << operator using the code of Program 1.25. When the **private** members of **currency** are changed, we will need to examine its friends and make appropriate changes.

Later we shall see how a class A may be derived from another class B. Class A is called the **derived class**, and B is the **base class**. The derived class will

```
currency currency::operator+(const currency& x) const
{// Add x and *this.
   currency result;
   result.amount = amount + x.amount;
   return result;
}


void currency::output(ostream& out) const
{// Insert currency value into stream out.
   long theAmount = amount;
   if (theAmount < 0) {out << '-';
                       theAmount = -theAmount;}
   long dollars = theAmount / 100; // dollars
   out << '$' << dollars << '.';
   int cents = theAmount - dollars * 100; // cents
   if (cents < 10) out << '0';
   out << cents;
}


// overload <<
ostream& operator<<(ostream& out, const currency& x)
   {x.output(out); return out;}
```

Program 1.23 Codes for +, output, and <<

need access to some or all of the data members of the base class. To facilitate granting this access, C++ allows for a third category of members called **protected**. Protected members behave like **private** members except that derived classes can access **protected** members.

Class members that are to be accessible by user applications should be declared **public** members. Data members should never be in this category. The remaining members should be divided between the categories **protected** and **private**. Good software-engineering principles dictate that data members remain private. By adding member functions to access and change the value of data members, derived classes obtain indirect access to the data members of the base class. At the same time, we can change the implementation of the base class without having to change its derived classes.

1.5.5   Addition of #ifndef, #define, and #endif Statements

The entire contents of the file currency.h (or currencyOverload.h) that contains the declaration and implementation of the class currency should be preceded by

```
#include <iostream>
#include "currencyOverload.h"

using namespace std;

int main()
{
   currency g, h(plus, 3, 50), i, j;

   // try out both forms of setValue
   g.setValue(minus, 2, 25);
   i.setValue(-6.45);

   // do an add and output
   j = h + g;
   cout << h << " + " << g << " = " << j << endl;

   // do two adds in a sequence
   j = i + g + h;
   cout << i << " + " << g << " + "
        << h << " = " << j << endl;

   // do an increment and add
   cout << "Increment " << i << " by " << g
        << " and then add " << h << endl;
   j = (i += g) + h;
   cout << "Result is " << j << endl;
   cout << "Incremented object is " << i << endl;

   // test the exception
   cout << "Attempting to initialize with cents = 152" << endl;
   try {i.setValue(plus, 3, 152);}
   catch (illegalParameterValue e)
   {
       cout << "Caught thrown exception" << endl;
       e.outputMessage();
   }
   return 0;
}
```

Program 1.24 Using overloaded operators

```
// overload <<
ostream& operator<<(ostream& out, const currency& x)
{// Insert currency value into stream out.
   long theAmount = x.amount;
   if (theAmount < 0) {out << '-';
                        theAmount = -theAmount;}
   long dollars = theAmount / 100; // dollars
   out << '$' << dollars << '.';
   int cents = theAmount - dollars * 100; // cents
   if (cents < 10) out << '0';
   out << cents;
   return out;
}
```

Program 1.25 Overloading the friend <<

the statements

```
#ifndef currency_
#define currency_
```

and followed by the statement

```
#endif
```

These statements ensure that the code for **currency** gets included and compiled only once per program. *You should add corresponding statements to the program listings provided for the remaining class definitions in this book.*

EXERCISES

15. (a) What are the maximum and minimum currency values permissible when the representation of Program 1.13 is used? Assume that objects of type unsigned long and unsigned int are represented using 4 bytes. So objects of these types have the range 0 through $2^{32} - 1$.

    (b) What are the maximum and minimum currency values permissible when the representation of Program 1.13 is used and the data types of dollars and cents are changed to int?

    (c) If function add (Program 1.16) is used to add two currency amounts, what are their largest possible values so that no error occurs when converting from type currency to type long as is done to set a1 and a2?

16. Extend the class `currency` of Program 1.13 by adding the following `public` member functions:

    (a) `input()` inputs a currency value from the standard input stream and assign it to the invoking object.

    (b) `subtract(x)` subtracts the value of the currency object `x` from that of the invoking object and returns the result.

    (c) `percent(x)` returns a currency object whose value is `x` percent of the value of the invoking object. The data type of `x` is `double`.

    (d) `multiply(x)` returns the currency object that results from multiplying the invoking object and the number `x`, which is of type `double`.

    (e) `divide(x)` returns the currency object that results from dividing the invoking object by the number `x`, which is of type `double`.

    Implement all member functions and test their correctness using suitable test data.

17. Do Exercise 16 using the implementation of Program 1.19.

18. (a) Do Exercise 16 using the implementation of Program 1.22. Overload the operators `>>`, `-`, `%`, `*`, and `/`. When overloading `>>`, declare it as a friend function and do not define a `public` input function to facilitate the input.

    (b) Replace the two `setValue` functions by overloading the assignment operator `=`. An overload of the type `operator=(int x)` that assigns an integer to an object of type `currency` should replace the three-parameter `setValue` function. `x` represents the sign, dollar amount, and cents rolled into a single integer. An overload of the type `operator=(double x)` should replace the single-parameter `setValue` function.

1.6   THE EXCEPTION CLASS illegalParameterValue

Program 1.26 shows a user-defined class `illegalParameterValue` that may be used when signaling errors in which the value of an actual parameter to a function is improper. Program 1.27 is a version of Program 1.8 in which an exception of type `illegalParameterValue` is thrown instead of an exception of type `char*`. Program 1.28 shows how to catch an exception of type `illegalParameterValue`.

1.7   RECURSION

A **recursive function** or method invokes itself. In **direct recursion** the code for function `f` contains a statement that invokes `f`, whereas in **indirect recursion**

```
class illegalParameterValue
{
    public:
        illegalParameterValue() :
                message("Illegal parameter value") {}
        illegalParameterValue(char * theMessage)
                {message = theMessage;}
        void outputMessage() {cout << message << endl;}
    private:
        char * message;
};
```

Program 1.26 Defining an exception class

```
int abc(int a, int b, int c)
{
    if (a <= 0 || b <= 0 || c <= 0)
        throw illegalParameterValue ("All parameters should be > 0");
    return a + b * c;
}
```

Program 1.27 Throwing an exception of type `illegalParameterValue`

```
int main()
{
    try {cout << abc(2,0,4) << endl;}
    catch (illegalParameterValue e)
    {
        cout << "The parameters to abc were 2, 0, and 4" << endl;
        cout << "illegalParameterValue exception thrown" << endl;
        e.outputMessage();
        return 1;
    }
    return 0;
}
```

Program 1.28 Catching an exception of type `illegalParameterValue` the function **f** invokes some other function **g**, which invokes yet another function **h**, and so on until function **f** is again invoked. Before delving into recursive C++ functions, we examine two related concepts from mathematics—recursive definitions of mathematical functions and proofs by induction.

1.7.1   Recursive Mathematical Functions

In mathematics we often define a function in terms of itself. For example, the factorial function $f(n) = n!$, for n an integer, is defined as follows:

$$f(n) = \begin{cases} 1 & n \le 1 \\ nf(n-1) & n > 1 \end{cases} \qquad (1.1)$$

This definition states that $f(n)$ equals 1 whenever n is less than or equal to 1; for example, $f(-3) = f(0) = f(1) = 1$. However, when n is more than 1, $f(n)$ is defined recursively, as the definition of f now contains an occurrence of f on the right side. This use of f on the right side does not result in a circular definition, as the parameter of f on the right side is smaller than that on the left side. For example, from Equation 1.1 we obtain $f(2) = 2f(1)$. From Equation 1.1 we also obtain $f(1) = 1$, and substituting for $f(1)$ in $f(2) = 2f(1)$, we obtain $f(2) = 2$. Similarly, from Equation 1.1 we obtain $f(3) = 3f(2)$. We have already seen that Equation 1.1 yields $f(2) = 2$. So $f(3) = 3 * 2 = 6$.

For a recursive definition of $f(n)$ (we assume direct recursion) to be a complete specification of f, it must meet the following requirements:

- The definition must include a **base** component in which $f(n)$ is defined directly (i.e., nonrecursively) for one or more values of n. For simplicity, we assume that the domain of f is the nonnegative integers and that the base covers the case $0 \le n \le k$ for some constant k. (It is possible to have recursive definitions in which the base covers the case $n \ge k$ instead, but we encounter these definitions less frequently.)

- In the **recursive component** all occurrences of f on the right side should have a parameter smaller than n so that repeated application of the recursive component transforms all occurrences of f on the right side to occurrences of f in the base.

In Equation 1.1 the base is $f(n) = 1$ for $n \le 1$; in the recursive component $f(n) = nf(n-1)$, the parameter of f on the right side is $n-1$, which is smaller than n. Repeated application of the recursive component transforms $f(n-1)$ to $f(n-2)$, $f(n-3)$, $\cdots$, and finally to $f(1)$ which is included in the base. For example, repeated application of the recursive component gives the following:

$$f(5) = 5f(4) = 20f(3) = 60f(2) = 120f(1)$$

Notice that each application of the recursive component gets us closer to the base. Finally, an application of the base gives $f(5) = 120$. From the example, we see that $f(n) = n(n-1)(n-2)\cdots 1$ for $n \geq 1$.

As another example of a recursive definition, consider the Fibonacci numbers that are defined recursively as below:

$$F_0 = 0, \quad F_1 = 1, \quad F_n = F_{n-1} + F_{n-2} \text{ for } n > 1 \tag{1.2}$$

In this definition, $F_0 = 0$ and $F_1 = 1$ make up the base component, and $F_n = F_{n-1} + F_{n-2}$ is the recursive component. The function parameters on the right side are smaller than n. For Equation 1.2 to be a complete recursive specification of F, repeated application of the recursive component beginning with any value of $n > 1$ should transform all occurrences of F on the right side to occurrences in the base. Since repeated subtraction of 1 or 2 from an integer $n > 1$ reduces it to either 0 or 1, right-side occurrences of F are always transformed to base occurrences. For example, $F_4 = F_3 + F_2 = F_2 + F_1 + F_1 + F_0 = 3F_1 + 2F_0 = 3$.

1.7.2   Induction

Now, we turn our attention to the second concept related to recursive computer functions—proofs by induction. In a proof by induction, we establish the validity of a claim such as

$$\sum_{i=0}^{n} i = n(n+1)/2, n \geq 0 \tag{1.3}$$

by showing that the claim is true for one or more base values of n (generally, $n = 0$ suffices); we assume the claim is true for values of n from 0 through m where m is an arbitrary integer greater than or equal to the largest n covered in the base; and finally using this assumption, we show the claim is true for the next value of n (i.e., $m + 1$). This methodology leads to a proof that has three components—**induction base**, **induction hypothesis**, and **induction step**.

Suppose we are to prove Equation 1.3 by induction on n. In the induction base we establish correctness for $n = 0$. At this time the left side is $\sum_{i=0}^{0} i = 0$, and the right side is also 0. So Equation 1.3 is valid when $n = 0$. In the induction hypothesis we assume the equation is valid for $n \leq m$ where m is an arbitrary integer ≥ 0. (For the ensuing induction step proof, it is sufficient to assume that Equation 1.3 is valid only for $n = m$.) In the induction step we show that the equation is valid for $n = m + 1$. For this value of n, the left side is $\sum_{i=0}^{m+1} i$, which equals $m + 1 + \sum_{i=0}^{m} i$. From the induction hypothesis we get $\sum_{i=0}^{m} i = m(m+1)/2$. So when $n = m + 1$, the left side becomes $m + 1 + m(m+1)/2 = (m+1)(m+2)/2$, which equals the right side.

At first glance, a proof by induction appears to be a circular proof—we establish a result assuming it is correct. However, a proof by induction is not a circular proof for the same reasons that a recursive definition is not circular. A correct proof by induction has an induction base similar to the base component of a recursive definition, and the induction step proves correctness using correctness for smaller values of n. Repeated application of the induction step reduces the proof to one that is solely in terms of the base.

1.7.3   Recursive C++ Functions

C++ allows us to write recursive functions. A proper recursive function must include a base component. The recursive component of the function should use smaller values of the function parameters so that repeated invocation of the function results in parameters equal to those included in the base component.

Example 1.1 [Factorial] Program 1.29 gives a C++ recursive function that uses Equation 1.1 to compute n!. The base component covers the cases when $n \leq$ 1. Consider the invocation factorial(2). To compute 2*factorial(1) in the else statement, the computation of factorial(2) is suspended and factorial invoked with n = 1. When the computation of factorial(2) is suspended, the program state (i.e., values of local variables and value formal parameters, bindings of reference formal parameters, location in code, etc.) is saved in a recursion stack. This state is restored when the computation of factorial(1) completes. The invocation factorial(1) returns the value 1. The computation of factorial(2) resumes, and the expression $2 * 1$ is computed.

```
int factorial(int n)
{// Compute n!
   if (n <= 1) return 1;
   else return n * factorial(n - 1);
}
```

Program 1.29 Recursive method to compute n!

When computing factorial(3), the computation is suspended when the else statement is reached so that factorial(2) may be computed. We have already seen how the invocation factorial(2) works to produce the result 2. When the computation of factorial(2) completes, the computation of factorial(3) resumes and the expression $3 * 2$ is computed.

Because of the similarity between the code of Program 1.29 and Equation 1.1, the correctness of the code follows from the correctness of the equation.   ∎

Example 1.2 The template function sum (Program 1.30) computes the sum of elements a[0] through a[n-1] (abbreviated a[0:n-1]). When n is 0, the method returns the value 0.

```
template<class T>
T sum(T a[], int n)
{// Return sum of the numbers a[0:n-1].
    T theSum = 0;
    for (int i = 0; i < n; i++)
        theSum += a[i];
    return theSum;
}
```

Program 1.30 Add a[0:n-i]

Program 1.31 is a recursive method to compute the sum of the elements a[0:n-1]. The code for rSum results from a recursive formulation of the problem—when n is 0, the sum is 0; when n is greater than 0, the sum of n elements is the sum of the first $n - 1$ elements plus the last element.   ∎

```
template<class T>
T rSum(T a[], int n)
{// Return sum of numbers a[0:n - 1].
    if (n > 0)
        return rSum(a, n-1) + a[n-1];
    return 0;
}
```

Program 1.31 Recursive code to add a[0:n-1]

Example 1.3 [Permutations] Often we wish to examine all permutations of n distinct elements to determine the best one. For example, the permutations of the elements a, b, and c are abc, acb, bac, bca, cba, and cab. The number of permutations of n elements is $n!$.

Although developing a nonrecursive C++ function to output all permutations of n elements is quite difficult, we can develop a recursive one with modest effort. Let $E = \{e_1, \cdots, e_n\}$ denote the set of n elements whose permutations are to be generated; let E_i be the set obtained by removing element i from E; let $perm(X)$ denote the permutations of the elements in set X; and let $e_i.perm(X)$ denote the permutation list obtained by prefixing each permutation in $perm(X)$ with element e_i. For example, if $E = \{a, b, c\}$, then $E_1 = \{b, c\}$, $perm(E_1) = (bc, cb)$, and $e_1.perm(E_1) = (abc, acb)$.

For the recursion base, we use $n = 1$. Since only one permutation is possible when we have only one element, $perm(E) = (e)$ where e is the lone element in E.

When $n > 1$, $perm(E)$ is the list $e_1.perm(E_1)$ followed by $e_2.perm(E_2)$ followed by $e_3.perm(E_3) \cdots$ followed by $e_n.perm(E_n)$. This recursive definition of $perm(E)$ defines $perm(E)$ in terms of n $perm(X)$s, each of which involves an X with $n-1$ elements. Both the base component and recursive component requirements of a complete recursive definition are satisfied.

When $n = 3$ and $E = (a, b, c)$, the preceding definition of $perm(E)$ yields $perm(E) = a.perm(\{b, c\})$, $b.perm(\{a, c\})$, $c.perm(\{b, a\})$. From the recursive definition $perm(\{b, c\})$ is $b.perm(\{c\})$, $c.perm(\{b\})$. So $a.perm(\{b, c\})$ is $ab.perm(\{c\})$, $ac.perm(\{b\}) = ab.c, ac.b = (abc, acb)$. Proceeding in a similar way, we obtain $b.perm(\{a, c\})$ is $ba.perm(\{c\})$, $bc.perm(\{a\}) = ba.c, bc.a = (bac, bca)$ and $c.perm(\{b, a\})$ is $cb.perm(\{a\})$, $ca.perm(\{b\}) = cb.a, ca.b = (cba, cab)$. So $perm(E) = (abc, acb, bac, bca, cba, cab)$.

Notice that $a.perm(\{b, c\})$ is actually the two permutations abc and acb. a is the prefix of these permutations, and $perm(\{b, c\})$ gives their suffixes. Similarly, $ac.perm(\{b\})$ denotes permutations whose prefix is ac and whose suffixes are the permutations $perm(\{b\})$.

Program 1.32 transforms the preceding recursive definition of $perm(E)$ into a C++ function. This code outputs all permutations whose prefix is list[0:k-1] and whose suffixes are the permutations of list[k:m]. The invocation permutations-(list,0,n-1) outputs all n! permutations of list[0:n-1]. With this invocation, k is 0 and m is n-1. So the prefix of the generated permutations is null, and their suffixes are the permutations of list[0:n-1]. When k equals m, there is only one suffix list[m], and now list[0:m] defines a permutation that is to be output. When k < m, the else clause is executed. Let E denote the elements in list[k:m] and let E_i be the set obtained by removing $e_i = $ list[i] from E. The first swap in the for loop has the effect of setting list[k] $= e_i$ and list[k+1:m] $= E_i$. Therefore, the following call to permutations computes $e_i.perm(E_i)$. The second swap restores list[k:m] to its state prior to the first swap.

Figure 1.3 shows the progress of Program 1.32 when invoked with k = 0, m = 2, and list[0:2] = [a, b, c]. The figure shows the contents of list[0:2] immediately after each call to permutations, as well as immediately after the second swap is done following a return from permutations. The unshaded entries denote list[0:k-1], and the shaded entries denote list[k:m]. Configuration numbers are shown outside the array. Each edge of Figure 1.3 is traversed twice during the execution of permutations(list, 0, 2): once when a call to permutations is made in the for loop and once when a return from permutations is made.

We begin with configuration 1. The first swap done in the for loop has no effect on the array; configuration 2 shows the state just after permutations is invoked from within the for loop. From configuration 2 we move to configuration 3. Configuration 3 is output because, in this configuration, k = m. Following this output, we make a return and execute the second swap statement in the for loop. As a result, we restore configuration 2. From configuration 2 we move forward to configuration 4. and the permutation acb is output. Then we back up through earlier configura-

```
template<class T>
void permutations(T list[], int k, int m)
{// Generate all permutations of list[k:m].
   int i;
   if (k == m) {// list[k:m] has one permutation, output it
                copy(list, list+m+1,
                     ostream_iterator<T>(cout, ""));
                cout << endl;
                }
   else  // list[k:m] has more than one permutation
         // generate these recursively
         for (i = k; i <= m; i++)
         {
            swap(list[k], list[i]);
            permutations(list, k+1, m);
            swap(list[k], list[i]);
         }
}
```

Program 1.32 Recursive method for permutations

Figure 1.3 Generating the permutations of abc

tions until we can move forward again. We back up through configurations 2 and
1. From configuration 1 we move forward to configurations 5 and 6. The sequence
of configurations encountered in the complete execution is 1, 2, 3, 2, 4, 2, 1, 5, 6, 5,
7, 5, 1, 8, 9, 8, 10, 8, 1.   ∎

EXERCISES

19. Write a nonrecursive function to compute $n!$. Test your code.

20. (a) Write a recursive function to compute the Fibonacci number F_n. Test your code.

    (b) Show that your code for part (a) computes the same F_i more than once when it is invoked to compute F_n for any $n > 2$.

    (c) Write a nonrecursive function to compute the Fibonacci number F_n. Your code should compute each Fibonacci number just once. Test your code.

21. Consider the function f, which is defined in Equation 1.4. n is a nonnegative integer.

$$f(n) = \begin{cases} n/2 & n \text{ is even} \\ f(3n+1) & n \text{ is odd} \end{cases} \qquad (1.4)$$

    (a) Use Equation 1.4 to manually compute $f(5)$ and $f(7)$.

    (b) Identify the base and recursive components of the function definition. Show that repeated application of the recursive component transforms the occurrence of f on the right side to the occurrence of f in the base component.

    (c) Write a recursive C++ function to compute $f(n)$. Test your code.

    (d) Use your proof for part (b) to arrive at a nonrecursive C++ function to compute f. Your code should have no loops. Test your code.

22. [Ackermann's Function] Equation 1.5 defines Ackermann's function. In this definition, i and j are integers that are ≥ 1.

$$A(i,j) = \begin{cases} 2^j & i = 1 \text{ and } j \geq 1 \\ A(i-1,2) & i \geq 2 \text{ and } j = 1 \\ A(i-1, A(i, j-1)) & i, j \geq 2 \end{cases} \qquad (1.5)$$

    (a) Use Equation 1.5 to manually compute $A(1, 2)$, $A(2, 1)$, and $A(2, 2)$.

    (b) Identify the base and recursive components of the function definition.

    (c) Write a recursive C++ function to compute $A(i, j)$. Test your code.

23. [GCD] The **greatest common divisor (GCD)** of two nonnegative integers x and y is 0 when exactly one of them is 0. When at least one of x and y is nonzero, their GCD, $gcd(x, y)$, is the greatest integer that evenly divides both. So $gcd(0, 0) = 0$, $gcd(10, 0) = gcd(0, 10) = 10$, and $gcd(20, 30) = 10$. Euclid's GCD algorithm is a recursive algorithm that is believed to date back to 375 B.C.; it is perhaps the earliest example of a recursive algorithm. Euclid's algorithm implements the recursive definition given in Equation 1.6.

$$gcd(x, y) = \begin{cases} x & y = 0 \\ gcd(y, x \textbf{ mod } y) & y > 0 \end{cases} \tag{1.6}$$

In Equation 1.6 **mod** is the modulo operator that is implemented in C++ as the operator %. x **mod** y is the remainder of x/y.

(a) Use Equation 1.6 to manually compute $gcd(20, 30)$ and $gcd(112, 42)$.

(b) Identify the base and recursive components of the function definition. Show that repeated application of the recursive component transforms the occurrence of gcd on the right side to the occurrence of gcd in the base component.

(c) Write a recursive C++ function to compute $gcd(x, y)$. Test your code.

24. Write a recursive template function to determine whether element x is one of the elements in the array a[0:n-1].

25. [Subset Generation] Write a recursive C++ function to output all subsets of n elements. For example, the subsets of the three-element set $\{a, b, c\}$ are $\{\}$ (empty set), $\{a\}$, $\{b\}$, $\{c\}$, $\{a, b\}$, $\{a, c\}$, $\{b, c\}$, and $\{a, b, c\}$. These subsets may be denoted by the 0/1 vector sequence 000, 100, 010, 001, 110, 101, 011, and 111, respectively (a 0 means that the corresponding element is not in the subset, and a 1 means that it is). So it is sufficient that your C++ code output all 0/1 sequences of length n.

26. [Gray Code] The **Hamming distance** between two vectors is the number of positions in which the vectors differ. For example, the Hamming distance between 100 and 010 is 2. A (binary) Gray code is a subset sequence in which the Hamming distance between every pair of consecutive vectors (also called codes) is 1. The three-element subset sequence given in Exercise 25 is not a Gray code. However, the three-element subset sequence 000, 100, 110, 010, 011, 111, 101, 001 is a Gray code. This sequence also has the property that the first and last vectors differ in exactly one place. In some applications of subset sequences, the cost of going from one subset to the next depends on the Hamming distance between these two subsets. In these applications, we desire a subset sequence that is a Gray code. A Gray code may be compactly

represented by giving the sequence of positions in which the vectors of the code change. For the three-element Gray code given above, the position change sequence is 1, 2, 1, 3, 1, 2, 1. Let $g(n)$ be the position change sequence for a Gray code for n elements. Equation 1.7 gives a recursive definition for $g(n)$.

$$g(n) = \begin{cases} 1 & n = 1 \\ g(n-1), n, g(n-1) & n > 1 \end{cases} \qquad (1.7)$$

(a) Use Equation 1.6 to manually compute $g(4)$.

(b) Identify the base and recursive components of the function definition. Show that repeated application of the recursive component transforms both occurrences of g on the right side to the occurrence of g in the base component.

(c) Write a recursive C++ function to compute $g(n)$. Test your code.

1.8   THE STANDARD TEMPLATES LIBRARY

The C++ standard templates library (STL) is a collection of containers, adaptors, iterators, function objects (also known as functors) and algorithms. Through the judicious use of elements of the STL, the task of writing application codes is greatly simplified. In this book, we shall often solve a problem first using basic C++ language constructs to illustrate the mechanics of solving the problem. Later, we will show how the same problem can be solved more simply by using an element of the STL.

Example 1.4 [The STL algorithm accumulate] The STL has an algorithm accumulate that may be used to sum the elements in a sequence. The syntax is

```
accumulate(start, end, initialValue)
```

where start points to the first element to be accumulated and end points to one position after the last element to be accumulated. So, elements in the range [start, end) are accumulated. The invocation

```
accumulate(a, a+n, initialValue)
```

where a is a one-dimensional array, for example, returns the value

$$initialValue + \sum_{i=0}^{n-1} a[i]$$

```
template<class T>
T sum(T a[], int n)
{// Return sum of the numbers a[0:n-1].
   T theSum = 0;
   return accumulate(a, a+n, theSum);
}
```

Program 1.33 Summing a[0:n-1] using the STL algorithm accumulate

Program 1.33 uses the STL algorithm **accumulate** to provide the same functionality as is provided by Programs 1.30 and 1.31.

The STL algorithm **accumulate** accesses successive elements of the sequence to be summed by performing the ++ operator on **start** and terminating when the pointer value becomes **end**. So, this algorithm may be used to sum the values of any sequence whose elements may be obtained by repeated application of the ++ operator. One-dimensional arrays and the STL container **vector** are two examples of sequences whose elements may be accessed in this way. We shall see other examples later in this book.

The STL has a more general form of the **accumulate** algorithm, which has the following syntax

```
accumulate(start, end, initialValue, operator)
```

where **operator** is a function that defines the operation to be used during the accumulation process. Using the STL functor **multiplies**, for example, we can find the product of an array of elements using the code of Program 1.34.   ∎

```
template<class T>
T product(T a[], int n)
{// Return sum of the numbers a[0:n-1].
   T theProduct = 1;
   return accumulate(a, a+n, theProduct, multiplies<T>());
}
```

Program 1.34 Compute the product of the elements a[0:n-1]

Example 1.5 [The STL algorithms copy and next_permutation] The copy algorithm copies a sequence of elements from one location to another. The syntax is

```
copy(start, end, to)
```

where to gives the location to which the first element is to be copied. So, elements are copied from locations start, start + 1, $\cdots$, end - 1 to the locations to, to + 1, $\cdots$, to + end - start.

The algorithm next_permutation, which has the syntax

next_permutation(start, end)

creates the next lexicographically larger permutation of the elements in the range [start, end); it returns the value true iff such a next permutation exists. By starting with the smallest lexicographic permutation of a sequence of distinct elements and making successive calls to next_permutation, we can obtain all permutations. Program 1.35 does just this. The invocation of copy in this program copies the elements list[0:m] to the output stream cout; each copied element is followed by the null string (""). Program 1.35 is equivalent to Program 1.32 provided the initial sequence is the smallest lexicographic sequence. Notice that Program 1.35 outputs no permutation that is lexically smaller than the initial sequence whereas Program 1.32 outputs all permutations regardless of the initial ordering. The exercises examine ways to modify Program 1.35 so as to obtain all permutations.

```
template<class T>
void permutations(T list[], int k, int m)
{// Generate all permutations of list[k:m].
 // Assume k <= m.
   // output the permutations one by one
   do {
      copy(list, list+m+1,
           ostream_iterator<T>(cout, ""));
      cout << endl;
   } while (next_permutation(list, list+m+1));
}
```

Program 1.35 Permutations using the STL algorithm next_permutation

A more general form of the next_permutation algorithm takes a third parameter compare as in

next_permutation(start, end, compare)

When this form is used, the binary function compare is used to determine whether one element is smaller than another. In the two-parameter version, this comparison is done using the operator <.   ∎

The STL contains many algorithms in addition to the ones used in the preceding examples. Exercises 2 through 7 are solved quite easily using the appropriate STL algorithms. The exercises for this section explore STL algorithms further.

EXERCISES

27. Write C++ code for the three-parameter template function `accumulate`. Test your code.

28. Write C++ code for the four-parameter template function `accumulate`. Test your code.

29. Write C++ code for the template function `copy`. Test your code.

30. Modify Program 1.35 so that it outputs all permutations of distinct elements. Do this by sorting the list elements into ascending order prior to generating the permutations. To sort, use the STL algorithm

    ```
    sort(start, end)
    ```

    which sorts elements in the range [`start`, `end`) into ascending order. Test your code.

31. Modify Program 1.35 so that it outputs all permutations of distinct elements. Do this by first using `next_permutation` to generate permutations that are lexically larger than the initial permutation and then using the STL algorithm `prev_permutation` to generate permutations that are lexically smaller than the initial permutation. Test your code.

32. Modify Program 1.35 so that it outputs all permutations of distinct elements. Do this by using the fact that when `next_permutation` returns the value `false`, the sequence [`start`, `end`) is the lexically smallest sequence. Hence, subsequent invocations of `next_permutation` will get you the remaining (if any) permutations you need. Test your code.

33. Do Exercise 2 using the STL algorithm `count`, which has the syntax

    ```
    count(start, end, value)
    ```

34. Do Exercise 3 using the STL algorithm `fill`, which has the syntax

    ```
    fill(start, end, value)
    ```

35. Do Exercise 4 using the STL algorithm `inner_product`, which has the syntax

    ```
    inner_product(start1, end1, start2, initialValue)
    ```

36. Do Exercise 5 using the STL algorithm `iota`, which has the syntax

```
iota(start, end, value)
```

37. Do Exercise 6 using the STL algorithm `is_sorted`, which has the syntax

    ```
    is_sorted(start, end)
    ```

38. Do Exercise 7 using the STL algorithm `mismatch`, which has the syntax

    ```
    mismatch(start1, end1, start2)
    ```

39. Write C++ code for the STL template function `count` of Exercise 33. Test your code.

40. Write C++ code for the STL template function `fill` of Exercise 34. Test your code.

41. Write C++ code for the STL template function `inner_product` of Exercise 35. Test your code.

42. Write C++ code for the STL template function `iota` of Exercise 36. Test your code.

43. Write C++ code for the STL template function `is_sorted` of Exercise 37. Test your code.

44. Write C++ code for the STL template function `mismatch` of Exercise 38. Test your code.

1.9   TESTING AND DEBUGGING

1.9.1   What Is Testing?

As indicated in Section 1.1, correctness is the most important attribute of a program. Because providing a mathematically rigorous proof of correctness for even a small program is quite difficult, we resort to a process called **program testing** in which we execute the program on the target computer using input data, called **test data**, and compare the program's behavior with the expected behavior. If these two behaviors are different, we have a problem with the program. Unfortunately, however, even if the two behaviors are the same, we cannot conclude that the program is correct, as the two behaviors may not be the same on other input data. By using many sets of input data and verifying that the observed and expected behaviors are the same, we can increase our confidence in the correctness of the program. By using all possible input data we can verify that the program is correct. However, for most practical programs, the number of possible input data is too large to perform such exhaustive testing. The subset of the input data space that is actually used for testing is called the **test set**.

Example 1.6 [Quadratic Roots] A **quadratic function** (or simply a **quadratic**) in x is a function that has the form

$$ax^2 + bx + c$$

where the values of a, b, and c are real numbers and $a \neq 0$. $3x^2 - 2x + 4$, $-9x^2 - 7x$, $3.5x^2 + 4$, and $5.8x^2 + 3.2x + 5$ are examples of quadratic functions. $5x + 3$ is not a quadratic function.

The **roots** of a quadratic function are the values of x at which the function value is 0. For example, the roots of $f(x) = x^2 - 5x + 6$ are 2 and 3, as $f(2) = f(3) = 0$. Every quadratic has exactly two roots, and these roots are given by the formula:

$$\frac{-b \pm \sqrt{b^2 - 4ac}}{2a}$$

For the function $f(x) = x^2 - 5x + 6$, $a = 1$, $b = -5$, and $c = 6$. Substituting these into the above formula, we get

$$\frac{5 \pm \sqrt{25 - 4*1*6}}{2} = \frac{5 \pm 1}{2}$$

So the roots of $f(x)$ are $x = 3$ and $x = 2$.

When $d = b^2 - 4ac = 0$, the two roots are the same; when $d > 0$, the two roots are different and real numbers; and when $d < 0$, the two roots are different and complex numbers. In this last case each root has a *real* part and an *imaginary* part. The real part is $real = -b/(2a)$, and the imaginary part is $imag = \sqrt{-d}/(2a)$. The complex roots are $real + imag * i$ and $real - imag * i$ where $i = \sqrt{-1}$.

The function `outputRoots` (Program 1.36) computes and outputs the roots of a quadratic. We shall not attempt a formal correctness proof for this function. Rather, we wish to establish correctness by testing. The number of possible inputs is the number of different triples (a, b, c) with $a \neq 0$. Even if we restrict a, b, and c to 16-bit nonnegative integers, the number of possible input triples is too large for us to test the program on all inputs. With 16 bits per integer, there are 2^{16} different values for b and c and $2^{16} - 1$ for a (recall that a cannot be 0). The number of different triples is $2^{32}(2^{16} - 1)$. If our target computer can test at the rate of 1,000,000 triples per second, it would take almost 9 years to complete! A faster computer executing at the rate of 1,000,000,000 triples per second would take almost 3 days. So a practical test set can contain only a small subset of the entire space of input data.

If we run the program using the data set $(a, b, c) = (1, -5, 6)$, the roots 2 and 3 are output. The program behavior agrees with the expected behavior, and we conclude that the program is correct for this input. However, verifying agreement between observed and expected behavior on a proper subset of the possible inputs does not prove that the program works correctly on all inputs. ∎

```
void outputRoots(const double& a, const double& b, const double& c)
{// Compute and output the roots of the quadratic.

   double d = b * b - 4 * a * c;
   if (d > 0) {// two real roots
               double sqrtd = sqrt(d);
               cout << "There are two real roots "
                    << (-b + sqrtd) / (2 * a) << " and "
                    << (-b - sqrtd) / (2 * a)
                    << endl;
            }
   else if (d == 0)
          // both roots are the same
          cout << "There is only one distinct root "
               << -b / (2 * a)
               << endl;
       else //  complex conjugate roots
           cout << "The roots are complex"
                << endl
                << "The real part is "
                << -b / (2 * a) << endl
                << "The imaginary part is "
                << sqrt(-d) / (2 * a) << endl;
}
```

Program 1.36 Compute and output the roots of the quadratic $ax^2 + bx + c$

Since the number of different inputs that can be provided to a program is generally very large, testing is often limited to a very small subset of the possible inputs. Testing with this subset cannot conclusively establish the correctness of the program. As a result, *the objective of testing is not to establish correctness, but to expose the presence of errors*. The test set must be chosen so as to expose any errors that may be present in the program. Different test sets can expose different errors in a program.

Example 1.7 The test data $(a, b, c) = (1, -5, 6)$ causes outputRoots to execute the code for the case when there are two real roots. If the roots 2 and 3 are output, we can have some confidence that the statements executed during this test are correct. Notice that an erroneous code could still give the correct results. For example, if we omitted the a from the expression for d and mistakenly typed

```
double d = b * b - 4 * c;
```

the value of d is the same for our test data because a = 1. Since the test data (1,−5,6) did not execute all statements of the code, we have less confidence in the correctness of the statements that are not executed.

The test set {(1,−5,6), (1,3,2), (2,5,2)} can expose errors only in the first seven lines of outputRoots, as each triple in this test set executes only these seven lines of code. However, the test set {(1,−5,6), (1,−8,16), (1,2,5)} causes all statements of outputRoots to execute and so has a better chance of exposing the errors in the code.   ∎

1.9.2   Designing Test Data

When developing test data, we should keep in mind that the objective of testing is to expose the presence of errors. If data designed to expose errors fails to expose any errors, then we may have confidence in the correctness of the program. To tell whether or not a program malfunctions on given test data, we must be able to verify the correctness of the program behavior on the test data.

Example 1.8 For our quadratic roots example, the behavior on any test data may be verified in one of two ways. First, we might know the roots of the test quadratic. For example, the roots of the quadratic with $(a, b, c) = (1,−5,6)$ are 2 and 3. We can verify the correctness of Program 1.36 on the test data (1,−5,6) by comparing the output roots with the correct roots 2 and 3. Another possibility is to substitute the roots produced by the program into the quadratic function and verify that the function value is 0. So if our program outputs 2 and 3 as the roots, we compute $f(2) = 2^2 - 5*2 + 6 = 0$ and $f(3) = 3^2 - 5*3 + 6 = 0$. We can implement these verification methods as computer programs. In the first case, the test program inputs the triple (a, b, c) as well as the expected roots and then checks the computed roots against the expected ones. For the second method we write code to evaluate the quadratic at the computed roots and verify that the result is 0.   ∎

We can evaluate any candidate test data using the following criteria:

- What is these data's potential to expose errors?

- Can we verify the correctness of the program behavior on this data?

Techniques for test data development fall into two categories: black box methods and white box methods. In a **black box method**, we consider the program's function, not the actual code, when we develop test data. In a **white box method**, we examine the code in an attempt to develop test data whose execution results in a good coverage of the program's statements and execution paths.

Black Box Methods

The most popular black box methods are I/O partitioning and cause-effect graphing. This section elaborates on the I/O partitioning method only. In this method we partition the input and/or output data space into classes. The data in different classes cause the program to exhibit qualitatively different behaviors, while data in the same class cause qualitatively similar behaviors. The quadratic roots example has three different qualitative behaviors: the roots are complex, the roots are real and distinct, and the roots are real and the same. We can use these three behaviors to partition the input space into three classes. Data in the first class cause the first kind of behavior; data in the second cause the second kind of behavior; and data in the third cause the third kind of behavior. A test set should include at least one input from each class.

White Box Methods

White box methods create test data based on an examination of the code to be generated. The weakest condition we can place on a test set is that it results in each program statement being executed at least once. This condition is called **statement coverage**. For our quadratic roots example, the test set $\{(0,1,2), (1,-5,6), (1,-8,16), (1,2,5)\}$ causes all statements in Program 1.36 to execute. So this test set provides statement coverage. The test set $\{(0, 1, 2), (1,-5,6), (1,3,2), (2,5,2)\}$ does not provide statement coverage.

In **decision coverage** we require the test set to cause each conditional in the program to take on both true and false values. The code of Program 1.36 has three conditionals: a == 0, d > 0, and d == 0. In decision coverage we require at least one set of test data for which a == 0.0 is true and at least one for which it is false. We also require at least one test data for which d > 0 is true and at least one for which it is false; there should also be at least one set of test data for which d == 0 is true and at least one for which it is false.

Example 1.9 [Maximum Element] Program 1.37 returns the position of the largest element in the array a[0:n]. The program finds this position by scanning the array from positions 0 to n, using the variable indexOfMax to keep track of the position of the largest element seen so far. The data set $\{(a,-1), (a,4)\}$ with a[0:4] = [2, 4, 6, 8, 9] provides statement coverage, but not decision coverage, as the condition a[indexOfMax] < a[i] never becomes false. When a[0:4] = [4, 2, 6, 8, 9]}, we get both decision and statement coverage. ∎

We can strengthen the decision coverage criterion to require each clause of each conditional to take on both true and false values. This strengthened criterion is called **clause coverage**. A **clause** is formally defined to be a Boolean expression that contains no Boolean operator (i.e., &&, ||, !). The expressions $x > y$, $x + y < y * z$, and c (where c is of type Boolean) are examples of clauses. Consider the statement

```
if ((C1 && C2) || (C3 && C4)) S1;
else S2;
```

```
template<class T>
int indexOfMax(T a[], int n)
{// Locate the largest element in a[0:n-1].
   if (n <= 0)
      throw illegalParameterValue("n must be > 0");

   int indexOfMax = 0;
   for (int i = 1; i < n; i++)
     if (a[indexOfMax] < a[i])
         indexOfMax = i;
   return indexOfMax;
}
```

Program 1.37 Finding the position of the largest element in a[0:n-1]

where C1, C2, C3, and C4 are clauses and S1 and S2 are statements. Under the decision coverage criterion, we need to use one test set that causes ((C1 && C2) || (C3 && C4)) to be true and another that results in this conditional being false. Clause coverage requires us to use a test set that causes each of the four clauses C1 through C4 to evaluate to true at least once and to false at least once.

We can further strengthen clause coverage to require testing for all combinations of clause values. In the case of the conditional ((C1 && C2)|| (C3 && C4)), this strengthening requires the use of 16 sets of test data: one for each truth combination of the four conditions. However, several of these combinations may not be possible.

If we sequence the statements of a program in their order of execution by a certain set of test data, we get an execution path. Different test data may yield different execution paths. Program 1.36 has only four execution paths—lines 1 through 7 (lines are numbered beginning with the line double d = $\cdots$); 1, 2, 8 through 12; and lines 1, 2, 8, 13 through 19. The number of execution paths of Program 1.37 grows as n increases. When n < 0, there is just one execution path— 1, 2 (line 1 is the first if statement and line 3 is a blank line); when n = 0, there is again just one path—lines 1, 4, 5, 8; when n = 1, there are two paths—lines 1, 4, 5, 6, 5, 8 and 1, 4, 5, 6, 7, 5, 8; and when n = 2, there are four paths—1, 4, 5, 6, 5, 6, 5, 8; 1, 4, 5, 6, 7, 5, 6, 5, 8; 1, 4, 5, 6, 5, 6, 7, 5, 8; and 1, 4, 5, 6, 7, 5, 6, 7, 5, 8. For a general n, n $\geq$ 0, the number of execution paths is 2^n.

Execution path coverage requires the use of a test set that causes all execution paths to be executed. For the quadratic roots code, statement coverage, decision coverage, clause coverage, and execution path coverage are equivalent requirements. But for Program 1.37, statement coverage, decision coverage, and execution path coverage are different, and decision and clause coverage are equivalent.

Of the white box coverage criteria we have discussed, execution path coverage is generally the most demanding. A test set that results in total execution path coverage also results in statement and decision coverage. It may, however, not result in clause coverage. Total execution path coverage often requires an infinite number of test data or at least a prohibitively large number of test data. Hence total path coverage is often impossible in practice.

Many exercises in this book ask you to test the correctness of your codes. The test data you use should at least provide statement coverage. Additionally, you should test for special cases that could cause your program to malfunction. For example, a program designed to sort $n \geq 0$ elements should be tested with $n = 0$ and 1 in addition to other values of n. If such a program uses an array a[0:99], it should also be tested with $n = 100$. $n = 0$, 1, and 100 represent the **boundary conditions** empty, singleton, and full.

1.9.3   Debugging

Testing exposes the presence of errors in a program. Once a test run produces a result different from the one expected, we know that something is wrong with the program. The process of determining and correcting the cause of the discrepancy between the desired and observed behaviors is called **debugging**. Although a thorough study of debugging methods is beyond the scope of this book, we do provide some suggestions for debugging.

- Try to determine the cause of an error by logical reasoning. If this method fails, then you may wish to perform a program trace (using a debugger such as the one that comes with Microsoft Visual C++ .NET) to determine when the program started performing incorrectly. This approach becomes infeasible when the program executes many instructions with that test data and the program trace becomes too long to examine manually. In this case you must try to isolate the part of the code that is suspect and obtain a trace of this part.

- Do not attempt to correct errors by creating special cases. The number of special cases will soon become very large, and your code will look like a dish of spaghetti. Errors should be corrected by first determining their cause and then redesigning your solution as necessary.

- When correcting an error, be certain that your correction does not result in errors where there were none before. Run your corrected program on the test data on which it originally worked correctly to ensure that it still works correctly on these data.

- When testing and debugging a multimethod program, begin with a single method that is independent of the others. This method would typically be an input or output method. Then introduce additional methods one at a time, testing and debugging the larger program for correctness. This strategy is called **incremental testing and debugging**. When this strategy is used, the cause of a detected error can reasonably be expected to lie in the most recently introduced method.

EXERCISES

45. Show that test sets that provide statement coverage for Program 1.36 also provide decision and execution path coverage.

46. Develop a test set for Program 1.37 that provides execution path coverage for the for loop when n = 3.

47. How many execution paths are in Program 1.30?

48. How many execution paths are in method rSum of Program 1.31?

1.10   REFERENCES AND SELECTED READINGS

A good introduction to programming in C++ can be found in the texts *C++ Program Design: An Introduction to Programming and Object-Oriented Design* by J. Cohoon and J. Davidson, 3rd Edition, McGraw Hill, NY, 2002 and *C++ How to Program*, 4th Edition, by H. Deitel and P. Deitel, Prentice Hall, Englewood Cliffs, NJ, 2002.

You can find a description of all components of the STL at the Web site http://codeguru.earthweb.com/spp/stlguide.

The Art of Software Testing by G. Myers, John Wiley, New York, NY, 1979 and *Software Testing Techniques* by B. Beizer, Second Edition, Van Nostrand Reinhold, New York, NY, 1990 have more thorough treatments of software testing and debugging techniques.

CHAPTER 2

PERFORMANCE ANALYSIS

BIRD'S-EYE VIEW

The most important attribute of a program is correctness. A program that does not correctly perform the task it was designed to do is of little use. However, correct programs may also be of little use. This is the case, for example, when a correct program takes more memory than is available on the computer it is to run on as well as when a correct program takes more time than the user is willing to wait. We use the term *program performance* to refer to the memory and time requirements of a program. To appreciate the need for good data structures and algorithm design methods, you must be able to evaluate the performance of a program.

This chapter focuses on paper-and-pencil methods to determine the memory and time requirements of a program. The operation count and step-count approaches to estimate run time are developed, and the notions of best-case, worst-case, and average run time are introduced. A more advanced measure of run time—amortized complexity—is developed in the Web site for this book. You should not attempt to read the material on amortized complexity until you have completed Chapter 9.

Chapter 3 reviews asymptotic notations such as big oh, omega, theta, and little oh, which make up the lingua franca for performance analysis. The use of asymptotic notation often simplifies the analysis. Chapter 4 shows you how to measure the actual run time of a program by using a clocking method.

Many application codes are developed in this chapter. These applications, which will prove useful in later chapters, include

- Searching an array of elements for an element with a specified characteristic.

- Sorting an array of elements. Codes for the rank (or count) sort, selection sort, bubble sort, and insertion sort methods are developed.

- Evaluating a polynomial using Horner's rule.

- Performing matrix operations such as add, transpose, and multiply.

2.1 WHAT IS PERFORMANCE?

By the **performance of a program**, we mean the amount of computer memory and time needed to run a program. We use two approaches to determine the performance of a program. One is analytical, and the other experimental. In **performance analysis** we use analytical methods, while in **performance measurement** we conduct experiments.

The **space complexity** of a program is the amount of memory it needs to run to completion. We are interested in the space complexity of a program for the following reasons:

- If the program is to be run on a multiuser computer system, then we may need to specify the amount of memory to be allocated to the program.

- For any computer system, we would like to know in advance whether or not sufficient memory is available to run the program.

- A problem might have several possible solutions with different space requirements. For instance, one C++ compiler for your computer might need only 1 MB of memory, while another might need 4 MB. The 1 MB compiler is the only choice if your computer has less than 4 MB of memory. Even users whose computers have the extra memory will prefer the smaller compiler if its capabilities are comparable to those of the bigger compiler. The smaller compiler leaves the user with more memory for other tasks.

- We can use the space complexity to estimate the size of the largest problem that a program can solve. For example, we may have a circuit simulation program that requires $10^6 + 100(c + w)$ bytes of memory to simulate circuits with c components and w wires. If the total amount of memory available is $5.01 * 10^8$ bytes, then we can simulate circuits with $c + w \leq 5,000,000$.

The **time complexity** of a program is the amount of computer time it needs to run to completion. We are interested in the time complexity of a program for the following reasons:

- Some computer systems require the user to provide an upper limit on the amount of time the program will run. Once this upper limit is reached, the program is aborted. An easy way out is to simply specify a time limit of a few thousand years. However, this solution could result in serious fiscal problems if the program runs into an infinite loop caused by some discrepancy in the data and you actually get billed for the computer time used. We would like to provide a time limit that is just slightly above the expected run time.

- The program we are developing might need to provide a satisfactory real-time response. For example, all interactive programs must provide such a response. A text editor that takes a minute to move the cursor one page down or one page up will not be acceptable to many users. A spreadsheet program that takes several minutes to reevaluate the cells in a sheet will be satisfactory only to very patient users. A database management system that allows its users adequate time to drink two cups of coffee while it is sorting a relation will not find too much acceptance. Programs designed for interactive use must provide satisfactory real-time response. From the time complexity of the program or program module, we can decide whether or not the response time will be acceptable. If not, we need to either redesign the algorithm or give the user a faster computer.

- If we have alternative ways to solve a problem, then the decision on which to use will be based primarily on the expected performance difference among these solutions. We will use some weighted measure of the space and time complexities of the alternative solutions.

EXERCISES

1. Give two more reasons why analysts are interested in the space complexity of a program.

2. Give two more reasons why analysts are interested in the time complexity of a program.

2.2   SPACE COMPLEXITY

2.2.1   Components of Space Complexity

The space needed by a program has the following components:

- *Instruction space*
  Instruction space is the space needed to store the compiled version of the program instructions.

- *Data space*
  Data space is the space needed to store all constant and variable values. Data space has two components:

  1. Space needed by constants (for example, the numbers 0 and 1 in Programs 1.29 and 1.30) and simple variables (such as a, b, and c in Program 1.1).

  2. Space needed by dynamically allocated objects such as arrays and class instances.

- *Environment stack space*

  The environment stack is used to save information needed to resume execution of partially completed functions and methods. For example, if function `foo` invokes function `goo`, then we must at least save a pointer to the instruction of `foo` to be executed when `goo` terminates.

Instruction Space

The amount of instruction space that is needed depends on factors such as

- The compiler used to compile the program into machine code.

- The compiler options in effect at the time of compilation.

- The target computer.

The compiler is a very important factor in determining how much space the resulting code needs. Figure 2.1 shows three possible codes for the evaluation of `a+b+b*c+(a+b-c)/(a+b)+4`. These codes need a different amount of space, and the compiler in use determines exactly which code will be generated.

Even with the same compiler, the size of the generated program code can vary. For example, a compiler might provide the user with optimization options. These could include code-size optimization as well as execution-time optimization. In Figure 2.1, for instance, the compiler might generate the code of Figure 2.1(b) in nonoptimization mode. In optimization mode, the compiler might use the knowledge that `a+b+b*c = b*c+(a+b)` and generate the shorter and more time-efficient code of Figure 2.1(c). The use of the optimization mode will generally increase the time needed to compile the program.

The example of Figure 2.1 brings to light an additional contribution to the space requirements of a program. Space is needed for temporary variables such as `t1`, `t2`, $\cdots$, `t6`.

Another option that can have a significant effect on program space is the overlay option in which space is assigned only to the program module that is currently executing. When a new module is invoked, it is read in from a disk or other device, and the code for the new module overwrites the code of the old module. So program space corresponding to the size of the largest module (rather than the sum of the module sizes) is needed.

The configuration of the target computer also can affect the size of the compiled code. If the computer has floating-point hardware, then floating-point operations will translate into one machine instruction per operation. If this hardware is not installed, then code to simulate floating-point computations will be generated.

Data Space

The C++ language does not specify the space to be allocated for the various C++ data types. Figure 2.2 gives the space allocation used by most C++ compilers. The

```
    LOAD  a              LOAD  a              LOAD  a
    ADD   b              ADD   b              ADD   b
    STORE t1             STORE t1             STORE t1
    LOAD  b              SUB   c              SUB   c
    MULT  c              DIV   t1             DIV   t1
    STORE t2             STORE t2             STORE t2
    LOAD  t1             LOAD  b              LOAD  b
    ADD   t2             MUL   c              MUL   c
    STORE t3             STORE t3             ADD   t2
    LOAD  a              LOAD  t1             ADD   t1
    ADD   b              ADD   t3             ADD   4
    SUB   c              ADD   t2
    STORE t4             ADD   4
    LOAD  a
    ADD   b
    STORE t5
    LOAD  t4
    DIV   t5
    STORE t6
    LOAD  t3
    ADD   t6
    ADD   4
       (a)                  (b)                  (c)
```

Figure 2.1 Three equivalent codes

data type `int` is typically assigned as many bytes (1 byte = 8 bits) as there are in a word. So, on a 4-byte per word computer, an `int` is 4 bytes long while on a 2-byte per word computer, an `int` is typically 2 bytes. We shall use the data of Figure 2.2 when computing the space required by variables and constants.

We can obtain the space requirement for a structured variable by adding up the space requirements of all its components. Similarly, we can obtain the space requirement of an array by multiplying the array size and the space needs of a single array element.

Consider the following array declarations:

```
double a[100];
int maze[rows][cols];
```

When computing the space allocated to an array, we shall be concerned only with the space allocated for the array elements. The array `a` has space for 100 elements of type `double`, each taking 8 bytes. The total space allocated to the array is therefore

Type	Space (bytes)	Range
bool	1	{true, false}
char	1	$[-128, -127]$
unsigned char	1	$[0, 255]$
short	2	$[-32768, 32767]$
unsigned short	2	$[0, 65535]$
long	4	$[-2^{31}, 2^{31} - 1]$
unsigned long	4	$[0, 2^{32} - 1]$
int	4	$[-2^{31}, 2^{31} - 1]$
unsigned int	4	$[0, 2^{32} - 1]$
float	4	$\pm 3.4E \pm 38$ (7 digits)
double	8	$\pm 1.7E \pm 308$ (15 digits)
long double	10	$\pm 1.2E \pm 4932$ (19 digits)
pointer	2	(near, _cs, _ds, _es, _ss pointers)
pointer	4	(far, huge pointers)

Figure 2.2 Space typically allocated to C++ data types on a 32-bit/word computer

800 bytes. The array maze has space for rows*cols elements of type int. The total space taken by this array is 4*rows*cols bytes.

Environment Stack

Beginning performance analysts often ignore the space needed by the environment stack because they don't understand how functions (and in particular recursive ones) are invoked and what happens on termination. Each time a function is invoked the following data are saved on the environment stack:

- The return address.

- The values of all local variables and formal parameters in the function being invoked (necessary for recursive functions only).

Each time the recursive function rSum (Program 1.31) is invoked, whether from outside the function or from within, the current values of a and n and the program location to return to on completion are saved in the environment stack.

It is worth noting that some compilers may save the values of the local variables and formal parameters for both recursive and nonrecursive methods, while others may do so for recursive methods alone. So the compiler in use will affect the amount of space needed by the environment stack.

Summary

The space needed by a program depends on several factors. Some of these factors are not known at the time the program is conceived or written (e.g., the computer or the compiler that will be used). Until these factors have been determined, we cannot make an accurate analysis of the space requirements of a program.

We can, however, determine the contribution of those components that depend on characteristics of the problem instance to be solved. These characteristics typically include factors that determine the size of the problem instance (e.g., the number of inputs and outputs or magnitude of the numbers involved) being solved. For example, if we have a program that sorts n elements, we can determine space requirements as a function of n. For a program that adds two $n \times n$ matrices, we may use n as the instance characteristic, and for one that adds two $m \times n$ matrices, we may use m and n as the instance characteristics.

The size of the instruction space is relatively insensitive to the particular problem instance being solved. The contribution of the constants and simple variables to the data space is also independent of the characteristics of the problem instance to be solved except when the magnitude of the numbers involved becomes too large for the chosen data type. At this time we will need to either change the data type or rewrite the program using multiprecision arithmetic and then analyze the new program.

The space needed by some of the dynamically allocated memory may also be independent of the problem size. The environment stack space is generally independent of the instance characteristics unless recursive functions are in use. When recursive functions are in use, the instance characteristics will generally (but not always) affect the amount of space needed for the environment stack.

The amount of stack space needed by recursive functions is called the **recursion stack space**. For each recursive function this space depends on the space needed by the local variables and the formal parameters, the maximum depth of recursion (i.e., the maximum number of nested recursive calls), and the compiler being used. For Program 1.31 recursive calls get nested until n equals 0. At this time the nesting resembles Figure 2.3. The maximum depth of recursion for this program is therefore n+1. A smart compiler would replace a recursive call that is the last statement of a method (known as tail recursion) by equivalent iterative code. This technique could reduce, even eliminate, the recursion stack space.

We can divide the total space needed by a program into two parts:

- A fixed part that is independent of the instance characteristics. This part typically includes the instruction space (i.e., space for the code), space for simple variables, space for constants, and so on.

- A variable part that consists of the dynamically allocated space (to the extent that this space depends on the instance characteristics); and the recursion stack space (insofar as this space depends on the instance characteristics).

```
rSum(a,n)
    rSum(a,n-1)
        rSum(a,n-2)
            .
            .
            .
            rSum(a,1)
                rSum(a,0)
```

Figure 2.3 Nesting of recursive calls for Program 1.31

The space requirement of any program P may therefore be written as

$$c + S_P(\text{instance characteristics})$$

where c is a constant that denotes the fixed part of the space requirements and S_P denotes the variable component. An accurate analysis should also include the space needed by temporary variables generated during compilation (refer to Figure 2.1). This space is compiler dependent and, except in the case of recursive functions, independent of the instance characteristics. We will ignore the space needs of these compiler-generated variables.

When analyzing the space complexity of a program, we will concentrate solely on estimating S_P (instance characteristics). For any given problem we need to first determine which instance characteristics to use to measure the space requirements. The choice of instance characteristics is very problem specific, and we will resort to examples to illustrate the various possibilities. Generally speaking, our choices are limited to quantities related to the number and magnitude of the inputs to and outputs from the program. At times we also use more complex measures of the interrelationships among the data items.

2.2.2   Examples

Example 2.1 Consider Program 1.1. Before we can determine S_P, we must select the instance characteristics to be used for the analysis. Suppose we use the magnitudes of a, b, and c as the instance characteristic. Since a, b, and c are of type int, 4 bytes are allocated to each of the formal parameters. In addition, space is needed for the code. Neither the data space nor the instruction space is affected by the magnitudes of a, b, and c. Therefore, $S_{abc}(\text{instance characteristics}) = 0$.   ∎

Example 2.2 [Sequential Search] Program 2.1 examines the elements of the array a from left to right to see whether one of these elements equals x. If an element

```
template<class T>
int sequentialSearch(T a[], int n, const T& x)
{// Search the unordered list a[0:n-1] for x.
 // Return position if found; return -1 otherwise.
   int i;
   for (i = 0; i < n && a[i] != x; i++);
   if (i == n) return -1;
   else return i;
}
```

Program 2.1 Sequential search

equal to x is found, the function returns the position of the first occurrence of x. If the array has no element equal to x, the function of Program 2.1 returns -1.

We wish to obtain the space complexity of Program 2.1 in terms of the instance characteristic n. Although we need space for the formal parameters a, x and n, the constants 0 and -1, and the code, the space needed is independent of n. Therefore, $S_{\text{sequentialSearch}}(n) = 0$.

Note that the array a must be large enough to hold the n elements being searched. The space needed by this array ($n * s$ bytes, where s is the number of bytes needed by an object of type T). This space is, however, allocated in the function where the actual parameter corresponding to a is declared. As a result, we do not add the space requirements of this array into the space requirements of the function sequentialSearch. ∎

Example 2.3 For method sum (Program 1.30), suppose we are interested in measuring space requirements as a function of the number of elements to be summed. Space is required for the formal parameters a and n, the local variables i and theSum, the constant 0, and the instructions. The amount of space needed does not depend on the value of n, so $S_{\text{sum}}(n) = 0$. ∎

Example 2.4 Consider the function rSum (Program 1.31). As in the case of sum, assume that the instances are characterized by n. The recursion stack space includes space for the formal parameters a and n and the return address. In the case of a, a reference (4 bytes) is saved, while in the case of n, a value of type int (also 4 bytes) is saved on the recursion stack. If we assume that the return address also takes 4 bytes, we determine that each call to rSum requires 12 bytes of recursion stack space. Since the depth of recursion is n+1, the recursion stack space needed is 12(n+1) bytes. So $S_{\text{rSum}}(n) = 12(n+1)$.

Program 1.30 has a smaller space requirement than does Program 1.31. ∎

Example 2.5 [Factorial] The space complexity of Program 1.29, which computes the factorial function, is analyzed as a function of n rather than as a function of the number of inputs (one) or outputs (one). The recursion depth is max{n,1}. The recursion stack saves a return address (4 bytes) and the value of n (4 bytes) each time factorial is invoked. No additional space that is dependent on n is used, so $S_{\text{factorial}}(n) = 8 * \max\{n,1\}$. ■

Example 2.6 [Permutations] Program 1.32 outputs all permutations of a list of elements. With the initial invocation permutations(list,0,n-1), the depth of recursion is n. Since each recursive call requires 20 bytes of recursion stack space (4 for each of return address, list, k, m, and i), the recursion stack space needed is 20n bytes, so $S_{\text{permutations}}(n) = 20n$. ■

EXERCISES

3. Compile a sample C++ program using two C++ compilers. Is the code length the same or different?

4. List additional factors that may influence the space complexity of a program.

5. Using the data provided in Figure 2.2, determine the number of bytes needed by the following arrays:

   (a) double y[3]

   (b) int matrix[10][100]

   (c) double x[100][5][20]

   (d) float z[10][10][10][5]

   (e) bool a[2][3][4]

   (f) long b[3][3][3][3]

6. Program 2.2 gives a recursive function rSequentialSearch that searches the elements of the array a[0:n-1] for the element x. If x is found, the function returns the position of x in a. Otherwise, the function returns −1. Determine $S_P(n)$. Determine $S_{\text{rSequentialSearch}}(n)$.

7. Write a nonrecursive function to compute n! (see Example 1.1). Compare the space requirements of your nonrecursive function and those of the recursive version (Program 1.29).

```
template<class T>
int rSequentialSearch(T a[], int n, const T& x)
{// Search the unordered list a[0:n-1] for x.
 // Return position if found; return -1 otherwise.
   if (n < 1) return -1;
   if (a[n-1] == x) return n - 1;
   return rSequentialSearch(a, n-1, x);
}
```

Program 2.2 Recursive sequential search

2.3   TIME COMPLEXITY

2.3.1   Components of Time Complexity

The time complexity of a program depends on all the factors that the space complexity depends on. A program will run faster on a computer capable of executing 10^9 instructions per second than on one that can execute only 10^7 instructions per second. The code of Figure 2.1(c) will require less execution time than the code of Figure 2.1(a). Some compilers will take less time than others to generate the corresponding computer code. Smaller problem instances will generally take less time than larger instances.

The time taken by a program P is the sum of the compile time and the run (or execution) time. The compile time does not depend on the instance characteristics. Also, we can assume that a compiled program will be run several times without recompilation. Consequently, we will concern ourselves with just the run time of a program. This run time is denoted by t_P(instance characteristics).

Because many of the factors t_P depends on are not known when a program is conceived, it is reasonable to only estimate t_P. If we knew the characteristics of the compiler to be used, we could determine the number of additions, subtractions, multiplications, divisions, compares, loads, stores, and so on that the code for P would make. Then we could obtain a formula for t_P. Letting n denote the instance characteristics, we might have an expression for $t_P(n)$ of the form

$$t_P(n) = c_a ADD(n) + c_s SUB(n) + c_m MUL(n) + c_d DIV(n) + \cdots \qquad (2.1)$$

where c_a, c_s, c_m, and c_d respectively denote the time needed for an addition, subtraction, multiplication, and division, and ADD, SUB, MUL, and DIV are functions whose value is the number of additions, subtractions, multiplications, and divisions that will be performed when the code for P is used on an instance with characteristic n.

Since the time needed for an arithmetic operation depends on the type (int, float, double, etc.) of the numbers in the operation, an exact formula for run time must separate the operation counts by data type. Fine-tuning Equation 2.1 in this way still does not give us an accurate formula to predict run time because today's computers do not necessarily perform arithmetic operations in sequence. For example, computers can perform an integer operation and a floating-point operation at the same time. Further, the capability to pipeline arithmetic operations and the fact that modern computers have a memory hierarchy (Section 4.5) means that the time to perform m additions isn't necessarily m times the time to perform one.

Since the analytical approach to determine the run time of a program is fraught with complications, we attempt only to estimate run time. Two more manageable approaches to estimating run time are (1) identify one or more key operations and determine the number of times these are performed and (2) determine the total number of steps executed by the program.

2.3.2   Operation Counts

One way to estimate the time complexity of a program or method is to select one or more operations, such as add, multiply, and compare, and to determine how many of each is done. The success of this method depends on our ability to identify the operations that contribute most to the time complexity. Several examples of this method follow.

Example 2.7 [Max Element] Program 1.37 returns the position of the largest element in the array a[0:n-1]. The time complexity of Program 1.37 can be estimated by determining the number of comparisons made between elements of the array a. When n $\leq$ 0, an exception is thrown and the number of comparisons is 0. When n = 1, the for loop is not entered. So no comparisons between elements of a are made. When n > 1, each iteration of the for loop makes one comparison between two elements of a, and the total number of element comparisons is n-1. Therefore, the number of element comparisons is max{n-1, 0}. The function indexOfMax performs other comparisons (for example, each iteration of the for loop is preceded by a comparison between i and n) that are not included in the estimate. Other operations such as initializing indexOfMax and incrementing the for loop index i are also not included in the estimate. If we included these other operations into our count, the count would increase by a constant factor.   ∎

Example 2.8 [Polynomial Evaluation] Consider the polynomial $P(x) = \sum_{i=0}^{n} c_i x^n$. If $c_n \neq 0$, $P(x)$ is a polynomial of degree n. Program 2.3 gives one way to compute $P(x)$ for a given value of x. It's time complexity can be estimated by determining the number of additions and multiplications performed inside the for loop. We will use the degree n as the instance characteristic. The for loop is entered a total of n times, and each time we enter the for loop one addition and two multiplications are done. (This operation count excludes the add performed each time the loop variable i is incremented.) The number of additions is n, and the number of multiplications is $2n$.

```
template<class T>
T polyEval(T coeff[], int n, const T& x)
{// Evaluate the degree n polynomial with
 // coefficients coeff[0:n] at the point x.
   T y = 1, value = coeff[0];
   for (int i = 1; i <= n; i++)
   {// add in next term
      y *= x;
      value += y * coeff[i];
   }
   return value;
}
```

Program 2.3 Evaluating a polynomial

Horner's rule evaluates $P(x)$ as shown below.

$$P(x) = (\cdots (c_n * x + c_{n-1}) * x + c_{n-2}) * x + c_{n-3}) * x \cdots) * x + c_0$$

So $P(x) = 5 * x^3 - 4 * x^2 + x + 7$ is computed as $((5 * x - 4) * x + 1) * x + 7$. The corresponding C++ function is given in Program 2.4. Using the same measure as used for Program 2.3, we estimate the complexity of Program 2.4 as n additions and n multiplications. Since Program 2.3 performs the same number of additions but twice as many multiplications as does Program 2.4, we expect Program 2.4 to be faster.   ∎

Example 2.9 [Ranking] The **rank** of an element in a sequence is the number of smaller elements in the sequence plus the number of equal elements that appear to its left. For example if the sequence is given as the array a = [4, 3, 9, 3, 7], then the ranks are r = [2. 0, 4, 1, 3]. Function **rank** (Program 2.5) computes the ranks of the elements in the array a. We can estimate the complexity of **rank** by counting the number of comparisons between elements of a. These comparisons are done in the **if** statement. For each value of i, the number of element comparisons is i. So the total number of element comparisons is $1 + 2 + 3 + \cdots + n - 1 = (n-1)n/2$ (see Equation 1.3).

Note that our complexity estimate excludes the overhead associated with the **for** loops, the cost of initializing the array **r**, and the cost of incrementing **r** each time two elements of a are compared.   ∎

```
template<class T>
T horner(T coeff[], int n, const T& x)
{// Evaluate the degree n polynomial with
 // coefficients coeff[0:n] at the point x.
   T value = coeff[n];
   for (int i = 1; i <= n; i++)
      value = value * x + coeff[n - i];
   return value;
}
```

Program 2.4 Horner's rule for polynomial evaluation

```
template<class T>
void rank(T a[], int n, int r[])
{// Rank the n elements a[0:n-1].
 // Element ranks returned in r[0:n-1]
   for (int i = 0; i < n; i++)
      r[i] = 0;  // initialize

   // compare all element pairs
   for (int i = 1; i < n; i++)
      for (int j = 0; j < i; j++)
         if (a[j] <= a[i]) r[i]++;
         else r[j]++;
}
```

Program 2.5 Computing ranks

Example 2.10 [Rank Sort] Once the elements have been ranked using Program 2.5, they may be rearranged in increasing order so that $a[0] \leq a[1] \leq \cdots \leq a[n-1]$ by moving elements to positions corresponding to their ranks. If we have space for an additional array u, we can use the function **rearrange** given in Program 2.6.

Assume that the invocation of **new** succeeds in allocating space to the array u. The number of element moves performed during the execution of function **rearrange** is $2n$. The complete sort requires $(n-1)n/2$ comparisons and $2n$ element moves. This method of sorting is known as **rank** or **count** sort. An alternative method to rearrange the elements is considered later (Program 2.11). This alternative method does not use an additional array such as u. ∎

```
template<class T>
void rearrange(T a[], int n, int r[])
{// Rearrange the elements of a into sorted order
 // using an additional array u.
   T *u = new T [n]; // create additional array

   // move to correct place in u
   for (int i = 0; i < n; i++)
      u[r[i]] = a[i];

   // move back to a
   for (i = 0; i < n; i++)
      a[i] = u[i];

   delete [] u;
}
```

Program 2.6 Rearranging elements using an additional array

Example 2.11 [Selection Sort] Example 2.10 examined one way to rearrange the elements in an array a so that a[0] $\leq$ a[1] $\leq \cdots \leq$ a[n-1]. An alternative strategy is to determine the largest element and move it to a$[n-1]$, then determine the largest of the remaining $n-1$ elements and move it to a$[n-2]$, and so on. Figure 2.4(a) shows an example in which selection sort is used to sort the six-element array a[0:5] = [6, 5, 8, 4, 3, 1]. Shaded array positions designate the, as yet, unsorted part of the array. A heavy bar over an array position marks the maximum element, and a light bar marks the position into which the maximum element is to move.

Line 1 of the figure shows the initial configuration; the entire array is considered unsorted, the maximum element is in a[2], and this maximum element is to be moved to a[5]. The move is accomplished by swapping the elements at the positions designated by the bars. Following the swap, we need concern ourselves only with sorting the elements a[0:4] because a[5] is known to contain the maximum element. Line 2 shows the configuration after the swap; the maximum element of a[0:4] is a[0], and this element is to be swapped with a[4]. Line 3 shows the result. Line 6 shows the result following three more stages of find the max and swap. At this time the unsorted part of the array (a[0:0]) has a single element that is known to be less than or equal to the other elements in the array. So the entire array is sorted.

Program 2.7 gives the C++ function, selectionSort, which implements the above strategy. Program 1.37 gave the function indexOfMax. We can estimate the complexity of selectionSort by counting the number of element comparisons

Figure 2.4 Selection and bubble sort

made. From Example 2.7 we know that each invocation `indexOfMax(a,size)`, `size` ≥ 1, results in `size-1` comparisons being made. So the total number of comparisons is $n-1+n-2+\cdots+1=(n-1)n/2$. The number of element moves is $3(n-1)$. Selection sort uses the same number of comparisons rank sort uses (Example 2.10) but requires 50 percent more element moves. We consider another version of selection sort in Example 2.16. ∎

```
template<class T>
void selectionSort(T a[], int n)
{// Sort the n elements a[0:n-1].
   for (int size = n; size > 1; size--)
   {
      int j = indexOfMax(a, size);
      swap(a[j], a[size - 1]);
   }
}
```

Program 2.7 Selection sort

Example 2.12 [Bubble Sort] Bubble sort is another simple way to sort elements. This sort employs a "bubbling strategy" to get the largest element to the right. In a bubbling pass, pairs of adjacent elements are compared. The elements are swapped in case the one on the left is greater than the one on the right. Suppose we have six integers in the order [6, 5, 8, 4, 3, 1] (see line 1 of Figure 2.4(b)). First the 6 and the 5 are compared and swapped to get the sequence shown in line 2. Next the 6 and 8 are compared, and no swap takes place. Then 8 and 4 are compared (line 3) and swapped; line 4 shows the result. The next comparison is between 8 and 3, and the two are swapped. The last comparison is between 8 and 1; these are swapped to get the configuration shown in line 6. The bubbling pass is now complete. At the end of the bubbling pass, we are assured that the largest element is in the right-most position.

The function bubble (Program 2.8) performs a bubbling pass over a[0:n-1]. The number of comparisons between pairs of elements of a is n-1.

```
template<class T>
void bubble(T a[], int n)
{// Bubble largest element in a[0:n-1] to right.
   for (int i = 0; i < n - 1; i++)
      if (a[i] > a[i+1]) swap(a[i], a[i + 1]);
}
```

Program 2.8 A bubbling pass

Since bubble causes the largest element to move to the right-most position, it can be used in place of indexOfMax in selectionSort (Program 2.7) to obtain a new sorting function (Program 2.9). The number of element comparisons is $(n-1)n/2$ as it is for selectionSort. Figure 2.4(c) shows an initial array configuration as well as the array configuration after each bubbling pass. ∎

```
template<class T>
void bubbleSort(T a[], int n)
{// Sort a[0:n - 1] using bubble sort.
   for (int i = n; i > 1; i--)
      bubble(a, i);
}
```

Program 2.9 Bubble sort

2.3.3   Best, Worst, and Average Operation Counts

In the examples so far, the operation counts were nice functions of fairly simple instance characteristics like the number of inputs and/or outputs. Some of our examples would have been more complicated if we had chosen to count some other operations. For example, the number of swaps performed by `bubble` (Program 2.8) depends not only on the instance characteristic n but also on the particular values of the elements in the array `a`. The number of swaps varies from a low of 0 to a high of $n - 1$. Since the operation count isn't always uniquely determined by the chosen instance characteristics, we ask for the best, worst, and average counts. The average operation count is often quite difficult to determine. As a result, in several of the following examples we limit our analysis to determining the best and worst counts.

Example 2.13 [Sequential Search] We are interested in determining the number of comparisons between x and the elements of a during an execution of the sequential search code of Program 2.1. A natural instance characteristic to use is n. Unfortunately, the number of comparisons isn't uniquely determined by n. For example, if $n = 100$ and x = a[0], then only 1 comparison is made. However, if x isn't equal to any of the a[]s, then 100 comparisons are made.

A search is **successful** when x is one of the a[]s. All other searches are **unsuccessful**. Whenever we have an unsuccessful search, the number of comparisons is n. For successful searches the best comparison count is 1, and the worst is n. For the average count assume that all array elements are distinct and that each is searched for with equal frequency. The average count for a successful search is

$$\frac{1}{n}\sum_{i=1}^{n} i = (n+1)/2$$ ∎

Example 2.14 [Insertion into a Sorted Array] You are to insert a new element into a sorted array so that the result is also a sorted array. For example, when you insert 3 into a[0:4] = [2,4,6,8,9], the result is a[0:5] = [2,3,4,6,8,9]. The insertion may be done by beginning at the right end and successively moving array elements one position right until we find the location for the new element. Figure 2.5(a) illustrates the process. In our example we moved 9, 8, 6, and 4 one position right and inserted 3 into the now-vacant spot a[1].

Program 2.10 implements the above strategy to insert an element x into a sorted array a[0:n-1].

We wish to determine the number of comparisons made between x and the elements of a. The natural instance characteristic to use is the number n of elements initially in a. The best or minimum number of comparisons is 1, which happens when the new element x is to be inserted at the right end. The maximum number of comparisons is n, which happens when x is to be inserted at the left end. For

(a) Insert   (b) In-place rearrange   (c) In-place rearrange

Figure 2.5 Insert and rearrange

```
template<class T>
void insert(T a[], int& n, const T& x)
{// Insert x into the sorted array a[0:n-1].
 // Assume a is of size > n
   int i;
   for (i = n-1; i >= 0 && x < a[i]; i--)
      a[i+1] = a[i];
   a[i+1] = x;
   n++; // one element added to a
}
```

Program 2.10 Inserting into a sorted array

the average assume that x has an equal chance of being inserted into any of the possible n+1 positions. If x is eventually inserted into position i+1 of a, i $\geq$ 0, then the number of comparisons is n-i. If x is inserted into a[0], the number of comparisons is n. So the average count is

$$\frac{1}{n+1}(\sum_{i=0}^{n-1}(n-i)+n) \;=\; \frac{1}{n+1}(\sum_{j=1}^{n}j+n)$$

$$= \frac{1}{n+1}\left(\frac{n(n+1)}{2}+n\right)$$

$$= \frac{n}{2}+\frac{n}{n+1}$$

So the average count is almost 1 more than half the worst-case count.   ∎

Example 2.15 [Rank Sort Revisited] Suppose the elements of an array have been ranked using method `rank` (Program 2.5, Example 2.9). We can perform an in-place rearrangement of elements into sorted order by examining the array positions one at a time beginning with position 0. If we are currently examining position i and r[i] = i, then we may advance to the next position. If r[i] ≠ i, then we swap the elements in positions i and r[i]. This swap moves the element previously in position i into its correct sorted position. The swap operation is repeated at position i until the element that belongs in position i in the sorted order is swapped into position i. Then we advance i to the next position.

Parts (b) and (c) of Figure 2.5 show how the above rearrangement strategy works. The initial array is a[0:5] = [d,a,e,f,c,b]. Element ranks are shown above the elements. So the initial rank array is r[0:5] = [3,0,4,5,2,1]. We begin at array position 0. Since r[0] ≠ 0, a[0] and a[r[0]] = a[3] are to be swapped. The configurations of parts (b) and (c) of Figure 2.5 have a heavy bar above the position a[i] being examined (initially, i = 0) and a light bar above the position a[r[i]] where a[i] is to move to. When r[a[i]] = i, the figure has only a heavy bar above a[i]. Shaded array positions denote elements that are not in their proper place (i.e., elements with r[i] ≠ i).

We begin with i = 0 and swap elements a[i] and a[r[i]] = a[3]; r[0] and r[3] are also swapped. This process results in the second configuration. Notice that a[3] now contains the proper element and r[3] = 3. Next elements a[0] and a[r[0]] = a[5]) together with their ranks are swapped to get the third config-uration of Figure 2.5(b). When a[0] and a[r[0]] = a[1] (and their ranks) are swapped, we get the fourth configuration. Now r[0] = 0, and we increment i to the next position 1. The new configuration is shown at the top of Figure 2.5(c). Since r[i] = r[1] = 1, we advance i to the next position 2 (see the second con-figuration of Figure 2.5(c)). Now a[i] = a[2] and a[r[2]] = a[4] (as well as their ranks) are swapped. Following the swap, r[2] = 2. Even though the rear-rangement is complete at this time, our code will not be able to detect this and we continue to advance i to the right, making sure that each element is in its proper position. So i is advanced to the next position 3 (see the third configuration of Figure 2.5(c)). Then i is advanced to positions 4 and 5.

Program 2.11 gives the in-place rearrangement function `rearrange`.

The number of swaps performed varies from a low of 0 (when the elements are initially in sorted order) to a high of 2(n − 1). Notice that each swap involving the a[]s moves at least one element into its sorted position (i.e., element a[i]).

```
template<class T>
void rearrange(T a[], int n, int r[])
{// In-place rearrangement into sorted order.
    for (int i = 0; i < n; i++)
        // get proper element to a[i]
        while (r[i] != i)
        {
            int t = r[i];
            swap(a[i], a[t]);
            swap(r[i], r[t]);
        }
}
```

Program 2.11 In-place rearrangement of elements

So after at most $n - 1$ swaps, all n elements must be in sorted order. Exercise 20 establishes that this many element swaps may be needed on certain inputs. Hence the number of swaps is 0 in the best case and $2(n - 1)$ in the worst case (includes rank swaps). When this in-place rearrangement function is used in place of the one in Program 2.6, the worst-case execution time increases because we need more element moves (each swap requires three moves). However, the space requirements are reduced. ∎

Example 2.16 [Selection Sort Revisited] A shortcoming of the selection sort code of Program 2.7 is that it continues to work even after the elements have been sorted. For example, the for loop iterates $n-1$ times, even though the array may be sorted after the second iteration. To eliminate the unnecessary iterations, during the scan for the largest element we can check to see whether the array is already sorted. Program 2.12 gives the resulting selection sort function. Here we have incorporated the loop to find the largest element directly into selectionSort, rather than write it as a separate method.

Figure 2.6(a) shows the progress of Program 2.12 when started with a[0:5] = [6,5,4,3,2,1]. In the first iteration of the outer for loop, size = 6 and the line sorted = false is executed when i = 1, 2, 3, 4, and 5. So following the swap of a[0] and a[5], which results in the configuration of line 2, the outer for loop is reentered with size = 5. This time the line sorted = false is executed when i = 2, 3, and 4. Therefore, following the swap of a[1] and a[4], the outer for loop is reentered; this time size = 4. Now the line sorted = false is executed when i = 4, and following the swap of a[2] and a[3], the outer for loop is reentered. This time we are working with the array configuration of line 4; the line sorted = false is not executed, and execution of the outer for loop terminates. On the initial data of line 1 of Figure 2.6(a), the early terminating version makes one less

```
template<class T>
void selectionSort(T a[], int n)
{// Early-terminating version of selection sort.
   bool sorted = false;
   for (int size = n; !sorted && (size > 1); size--)
   {
       int indexOfMax = 0;
       sorted = true;
       // find largest
       for (int i = 1; i < size; i++)
          if (a[indexOfMax] <= a[i]) indexOfMax = i;
          else sorted = false; // out of order
          swap(a[indexOfMax], a[size - 1]);
   }
}
```

Program 2.12 Early-terminating version of selection sort

pass than it does when started with the data shown in line 1 of Figure 2.4(a).

| | (a) Early selection sort | (b) Early bubble sort | (c) Insertion sort |

Figure 2.6 Sorting examples

The best case for the early-terminating version of selection sort arises when the array a is sorted to begin with. Now the outer for loop iterates just once, and the number of comparisons between elements of a is $n - 1$. In the worst case the outer for loop is iterated until size $= 1$ and the number of comparisons is $(n - 1)n/2$. The best- and worst-case number of swaps remains the same as for Program 2.7. Notice that in the worst case we expect the early-terminating version to be slightly slower because of the additional work to maintain the variable sorted.   ■

Example 2.17 [Bubble Sort Revisited] As in the case of selection sort, we can devise an early-terminating version of bubble sort. If a bubbling pass results in no swaps, then the array is in sorted order and no further bubbling passes are necessary. Program 2.13 gives the early-terminating version of bubble sort.

```
template<class T>
bool bubble(T a[], int n)
{// Bubble largest element in a[0:n-1] to right.
   bool swapped = false; // no swaps so far
   for (int i = 0; i < n - 1; i++)
      if (a[i] > a[i+1])
      {
         swap(a[i], a[i + 1]);
         swapped = true; // swap was done
      }
   return swapped;
}

template<class T>
void bubbleSort(T a[], int n)
{// Early-terminating version of bubble sort.
   for (int i = n; i > 1 && bubble(a, i); i--);
}
```

Program 2.13 Early-terminating bubble sort

Line 1 of Figure 2.6(b) shows an instance on which at least one swap is done when going from line 1 to line 2 (the invocation bubble(a,6)) and in going from line 2 to line 3 (the invocation bubble(a,5)). No swaps are done in the invocation bubble(a,4), and so the sort terminates following this invocation.

The worst-case number of comparisons made by Program 2.13 is unchanged from the original version (Program 2.9). The best-case number of comparisons is $n - 1$.   ■

Example 2.18 [Insertion Sort] Program 2.10 can be used as the basis of a method to sort n elements. Since an array with one element is a sorted array, we start with an array that contains just the first of the n elements to be sorted. By inserting the second element into this one-element array, we get a sorted array of size 2. The insertion of the third element yields a sorted array of size 3. Continuing in this way, we obtain a sorted array of size n.

Line 1 of Figure 2.6(c) shows the unsorted array a[0:5]. We start with a sorted segment a[0:0]; the remaining elements a[1:5] define the unsorted segment. The unsorted segment is the shaded segment in Figure 2.6(c). First a[i] is inserted into the sorted segment a[0:0] to get the configuration of line 2; a[0:1] is now the sorted segment, and a[2:5] is the unsorted segment. Next a[2] is inserted into the sorted segment, and we get line 3 of the figure. a[0:2] becomes the sorted segment, and a[3:5] is the unsorted segment. After three more inserts, the entire array is sorted.

Function insertionSort (Program 2.14) implements this strategy. We have rewritten function insert for this application, as the original version (Program 2.10) performs some unnecessary operations. Actually, we could have embedded the code of the new insert function directly into the sort function to get the insertion sort version of Program 2.15. Equivalently, we could make insert an inline function.

```
template<class T>
void insert(T a[], int n, const T& x)
{// Insert x into the sorted array a[0:n-1].
   int i;
   for (i = n-1; i >= 0 && x < a[i]; i--)
      a[i+1] = a[i];
   a[i+1] = x;
}

template<class T>
void insertionSort(T a[], int n)
{// Sort a[0:n-1] using the insertion sort method.
   for (int i = 1; i < n; i++)
   {
      T t = a[i];
      insert(a, i, t);
   }
}
```

Program 2.14 Insertion sort

Both versions of insertion sort perform the same number of comparisons. In the best case the number of comparisons is $n - 1$, and in the worst case it is $(n-1)n/2$.

∎

```
template<class T>
void insertionSort(T a[], int n)
{// Sort a[0:n-1] using the insertion sort method.
   for (int i = 1; i < n; i++)
   {// insert a[i] into a[0:i-1]
      T t = a[i];
      int j;
      for (j = i-1; j >= 0 && t < a[j]; j--)
         a[j+1] = a[j];
      a[j+1] = t;
   }
}
```

Program 2.15 Another version of insertion sort

2.3.4   Step Counts

As noted in some of the examples on operation counts, the operation-count method of estimating time complexity omits accounting for the time spent on all but the chosen operations. In the **step-count** method, we attempt to account for the time spent in all parts of the program/method. As was the case for operation counts, the step count is a function of the instance characteristics. Although any specific instance may have several characteristics (e.g., the number of inputs, the number of outputs, the magnitudes of the inputs and outputs), the number of steps is computed as a function of some subset of these. Usually we choose the characteristics that are of interest to us. For example, we might wish to know how the computing (or run) time (i.e., time complexity) increases as the number of inputs increases. In this case the number of steps will be computed as a function of the number of inputs alone. For a different program we might want to determine how the computing time increases as the magnitude of one of the inputs increases. In this case the number of steps will be computed as a function of the magnitude of this input alone. Thus before the step count of a program can be determined, we need to know exactly which characteristics of the problem instance are to be used. These characteristics define not only the variables in the expression for the step count but also how much computing can be counted as a single step.

After the relevant instance characteristics have been selected, we can define a step. A **step** is any computation unit that is independent of the selected character-istics. Thus 10 additions can be one step; 100 multiplications can also be one step; but n additions, where n is an instance characteristic, cannot be one step. Nor can $m/2$ additions or $p + q$ subtractions, where m, p, and q are instance characteristics, be counted as one step.

Definition 2.1 *A* **program step** *is loosely defined to be a syntactically or seman-tically meaningful segment of a program for which the execution time is independent of the instance characteristics.* ∎

The amount of computing represented by one program step may be different from that represented by another. For example, the entire statement

```
return a+b+b*c+(a+b-c)/(a+b)+4;
```

can be regarded as a single step if its execution time is independent of the instance characteristics we are using. We may also count a statement such as

```
x = y;
```

as a single step.

We can determine the number of steps that a program or method takes to complete its task by creating a global variable `stepCount` with initial value 0. Next we introduce statements into the program to increment `stepCount` by the appropriate amount. Therefore, each time a statement in the original program or method is executed, `stepCount` is incremented by the step count of that statement. The value of `stepCount` when the program or method terminates is the number of steps taken.

Example 2.19 When statements to increment `stepCount` are introduced into Program 1.30, the result is Program 2.16. The change in the value of `stepCount` by the time this program terminates is the number of steps executed by Program 1.30.

```
template<class T>
T sum(T a[], int n)
{// Return sum of numbers a[0:n - 1].
   T theSum = 0;
   stepCount++;     // for theSum = 0
   for (int i = 0; i < n; i++)
   {
      stepCount++; // for the for statement
      theSum += a[i];
      stepCount++; // for assignment
   }
   stepCount++;    // for last execution of for statement
   stepCount++;    // for return
   return theSum;
}
```

Program 2.16 Counting steps in Program 1.30

Program 2.17, which is a simplified version of Program 2.16, determines only the change in the value of stepCount. We see that for every initial value of stepCount, both Programs 2.16 and 2.17 compute the same final value for stepCount. In the for loop of Program 2.17, the value of stepCount increases by a total of 2n. If stepCount is 0 to start with, then stepCount will be 2n+3 on termination. Therefore, each invocation of sum (Program 1.30) executes a total of 2n+3 steps.   ∎

```
template<class T>
T sum(T a[], int n)
{// Return sum of numbers a[0:n - 1].
   for (int i = 0; i < n; i++)
      stepCount += 2;
   stepCount += 3;
   return 0;
}
```

Program 2.17 Simplified version of Program 2.16

Example 2.20 When we introduce statements to increment stepCount into function rSum (Program 1.31), we obtain Program 2.18. Note that since Program 1.31 is a recursive function, it requires space for the recursion stack. Thus the function may fail to complete its task for lack of sufficient memory for the recursion stack. For the step-count analysis, we will assume that sufficient memory is available for the function rSum to successfully complete its task.

```
template<class T>
T rSum(T a[], int n)
{// Return sum of numbers a[0:n - 1].
   stepCount++; // for if conditional
   if (n > 0) {stepCount++; // for return and rSum invocation
               return rSum(a, n-1) + a[n-1];}
   stepCount++; // for return
   return 0;
}
```

Program 2.18 Counting steps in Program 1.31

Let $t_{rSum}(n)$ be the increase in the value of stepCount between the time rSum is initially invoked and the time it terminates. We see that $t_{rSum}(0) = 2$. When n

> 0, stepCount increases by 2 plus whatever increase results from the invocation of rSum from within the **then** clause. From the definition of t_{rSum}, it follows that this additional increase is t_{rSum}(n-1). So if the value of stepCount is 0 initially, its value at the time of termination is $2 + t_{rSum}$(n-1), n > 0.

When analyzing a recursive program for its step count, we often obtain a recursive formula for the step count (such as t_{rSum}(n) $= 2 + t_{rSum}$(n-1), n > 0 and t_{rSum}(0) $= 2$). This recursive formula is referred to as a **recurrence equation** (or simply as a **recurrence**). We can solve this recurrence by repeatedly substituting for t_{rSum} as shown:

$$
\begin{aligned}
t_{rSum}(n) &= 2 + t_{rSum}(n-1) \\
&= 2 + 2 + t_{rSum}(n-2) \\
&= 4 + t_{rSum}(n-2) \\
&\vdots \\
&= 2n + t_{rSum}(0) \\
&= 2n + 2, \quad n \geq 0
\end{aligned}
$$

So the step count for function rSum (Program 1.31) is 2n+2.   ∎

Comparing the step counts of Programs 1.30 and 1.31, we see that the count for Program 1.31 is less than that for Program 1.30. However, we cannot conclude that Program 1.30 is slower than Program 1.31, because a step doesn't correspond to a definite time unit. A step of rSum may take more time than a step of sum, so rSum might well be (and we expect it to be) slower than sum.

The step count is useful in that it tells us how the run time for a program changes with changes in the instance characteristics. From the step count for sum, we see that if n is doubled, the run time will also double (approximately); if n increases by a factor of 10, we expect the run time to increase by a factor of 10; and so on. So we expect the run time to grow *linearly* in n.

Rather than introduce statements to increment stepCount, we can build a table in which we list the total number of steps that each statement contributes to stepCount. We can arrive at this figure by first determining the number of steps per execution (s/e) of the statement and the total number of times (i.e., frequency) each statement is executed. Combining these two quantities gives us the total contribution of each statement. We can then add the contributions of all statements to obtain the step count for the entire program. This approach to obtaining the step count is called **profiling**.

The s/e of a statement is the amount by which stepCount *changes as a result of the execution of that statement.* An important difference between the step count of a statement and its s/e is illustrated by the following example. The statement

```
x = sum(a,m);
```

has a step count of 1, while the total change in stepCount resulting from the execution of this statement is actually 1 plus the change resulting from the invocation of sum (i.e., 2m+3). Therefore, the s/e of the above statement is 1+2m+3 = 2m+4.

Figure 2.7 lists the number of steps per execution and the frequency of each of the statements in function sum (Program 1.30). The total number of steps required by the program is 2n+3. Note that the frequency of the for statement is n+1 and not n because i has to be incremented to n before the for loop can terminate.

Statement	s/e	Frequency	Total steps
T sum(T a[], int n)	0	0	0
{	0	0	0
T theSum = 0;	1	1	1
for (int i = 0; i < n; i++)	1	$n+1$	$n+1$
theSum += a[i];	1	n	n
return theSum;	1	1	1
}	0	0	0
Total			$2n+3$

Figure 2.7 Step count for Program 1.30

Program 2.19 transposes a rows × rows matrix a[0:rows-1][0:rows-1]. Recall that b is the transpose of a iff (if and only if) b[i][j] = a[j][i] for all i and j.

```
template<class T>
void transpose(T **a, int rows)
{// In-place transpose of matrix a[0:rows-1][0:rows-1].
   for (int i = 0; i < rows; i++)
      for (int j = i+1;  j < rows; j++)
         swap(a[i][j], a[j][i]);
}
```

Program 2.19 Matrix transpose

Figure 2.8 gives the step-count table. Let us derive the frequency of the second for statement. For each value of i, this statement is executed rows-i times. So its frequency is

$$\sum_{i=0}^{rows-1} (rows - i) = \sum_{q=1}^{rows} q = rows(rows + 1)/2$$

Statement	s/e	Frequency	Total steps
void transpose(T **a, int rows)	0	0	0
{	0	0	0
for (int i = 0; i < rows; i++)	1	$rows + 1$	$rows + 1$
for (int j = i+1; j < rows; j++)	1	$rows(rows + 1)/2$	$rows(rows + 1)/2$
swap(a[i][j], a[j][i]);	1	$rows(rows - 1)/2$	$rows(rows - 1)/2$
}	0	0	0
Total			$rows^2 + rows + 1$

Figure 2.8 Step count for Program 2.19

The frequency for the swap statement is

$$\sum_{i=0}^{rows-1} (rows - i - 1) = \sum_{q=0}^{rows-1} q = rows(rows-1)/2$$

In some cases the number of steps per execution of a statement varies from one execution to the next, for example, for the assignment statement of function inef (Program 2.20). Function inef is a very inefficient way to compute the prefix sums $b[j]$.

$$b[j] = \sum_{i=0}^{j} a[i] \text{ for } j = 0, 1, \cdots, n - 1$$

```
template <class T>
void inef(T a[], T b[], int n)
{// Compute prefix sums.
    for (int j = 0; j < n; j++)
        b[j] = sum(a, j + 1);
}
```

Program 2.20 Inefficient prefix sums

The step count for sum(a,m) has already been determined to be 2m+3 (see Example 2.19). Therefore, the number of steps per execution of the assignment statement b[j] = sum(a, j + 1) of inef is 2j+6. To arrive at this step count, we have added 1 to the step count of sum to account for the cost of invoking the function sum and of assigning the function value to b[j]. The frequency of this assignment statement is n. But the total number of steps resulting from this statement is not $(2j+6)n$. Instead, the number of steps is

$$\sum_{j=0}^{n-1}(2j+6) = n(n+5)$$

Figure 2.9 gives the complete analysis for this function.

Statement	s/e	Frequency	Total steps
void inef(T a[], T b[], int n)	0	0	0
{	0	0	0
for (int j = 0; j < n; j++)	1	$n+1$	$n+1$
b[j] = sum(a, j + 1);	$2j+6$	n	$n(n+5)$
}	0	0	0
Total			n^2+6n+1

Figure 2.9 Step count for Program 2.20

The notions of best, worst, and average operation counts are easily extended to the case of step counts. Examples 2.21 and 2.22 illustrate these notions.

Example 2.21 [Sequential Search] Figures 2.10 and 2.11 show the best- and worst-case step-count analyses for function sequentialSearch (Program 2.1).

Statement	s/e	Frequency	Total steps
int sequentialSearch(T a[], int n, const T& x)	0	0	0
{	0	0	0
int i;	1	1	1
for (i = 0; i < n && a[i] != x; i++);	1	1	1
if (i == n) return -1;	1	1	1
else return i;	1	1	1
}	0	0	0
Total			4

Figure 2.10 Best-case step count for Program 2.1

For the average step-count analysis for a successful search, we assume that the n values in a are distinct and that in a successful search, x has an equal probability of being any one of these values. Under these assumptions the average step count for a successful search is the sum of the step counts for the n possible successful searches divided by n. To obtain this average, we first obtain the step count for the case x = a[j] where j is in the range $[0, n-1]$ (see Figure 2.12).

Now we obtain the average step count for successful searches:

Statement	s/e	Frequency	Total steps
int sequentialSearch(T a[], int n, const T& x)	0	0	0
{	0	0	0
int i;	1	1	1
for (i = 0; i < n && a[i] != x; i++);	1	$n+1$	$n+1$
if (i == n) return -1;	1	1	1
else return i;	1	0	0
}	0	0	0
Total			$n+3$

Figure 2.11 Worst-case step count for Program 2.1

Statement	s/e	Frequency	Total steps
int sequentialSearch(T a[], int n, const T& x)	0	0	0
{	0	0	0
int i;	1	1	1
for (i = 0; i < n && a[i] != x; i++);	1	$j+1$	$j+1$
if (i == n) return -1;	1	1	1
else return i;	1	1	1
}	0	0	0
Total			$j+4$

Figure 2.12 Step count for Program 2.1 when x = a[j]

$$\frac{1}{n}\sum_{j=0}^{n-1}(j+4) = (n+7)/2$$

This value is a little more than half the step count for an unsuccessful search.

Now suppose that successful searches occur only 80 percent of the time and that each a[i] still has the same probability of being searched for. The average step count for sequentialSearch is

.8 * (average count for successful searches) + .2 * (count for an unsuccessful search)

= $.8(n+7)/2 + .2(n+3)$

= $.6n + 3.4$ ∎

Example 2.22 [Insertion into a Sorted Array] The best- and worst-case step counts for function insert (Program 2.10) are obtained in Figures 2.13 and 2.14, respectively.

Statement	s/e	Frequency	Total steps
`void insert(T a[], int& n, const T& x)`	0	0	0
`{`	0	0	0
`    int i;`	1	1	1
`    for (i = n - 1; i >= 0 && x < a[i]; i--)`	1	1	1
`        a[i+1] = a[i];`	1	0	0
`    a[i+1] = x;`	1	1	1
`    n++; // one element added to a`	1	1	1
`}`	0	0	0
Total			4

Figure 2.13 Best-case step count for Program 2.10

Statement	s/e	Frequency	Total steps
`void insert(T a[], int& n, const T& x)`	0	0	0
`{`	0	0	0
`    int i;`	1	1	1
`    for (i = n - 1; i >= 0 && x < a[i]; i--)`	1	$n+1$	$n+1$
`        a[i+1] = a[i];`	1	n	n
`    a[i+1] = x;`	1	1	1
`    n++; // one element added to a`	1	1	1
`}`	0	0	0
Total			$2n+4$

Figure 2.14 Worst-case step count for Program 2.10

For the average step count, assume that x has an equal chance of being inserted into any of the possible n+1 positions. If x is eventually inserted into position j, $j \geq 0$, then the step count is 2n−2j+4. So the average count is

$$
\begin{aligned}
\frac{1}{n+1}\sum_{j=0}^{n}(2n-2j+4) &= \frac{1}{n+1}[2\sum_{j=0}^{n}(n-j)+\sum_{j=0}^{n}4] \\
&= \frac{1}{n+1}[2\sum_{k=0}^{n}k+4(n+1)] \\
&= \frac{1}{n+1}[n(n+1)+4(n+1)] \\
&= \frac{(n+4)(n+1)}{n+1} \\
&= n+4
\end{aligned}
$$

The average count is 2 more than half the worst-case count.   ■

EXERCISES

8. According to the analysis in Example 2.8, Program 2.3 makes four additions and eight multiplications when evaluating the polynomial $3x^4+4x^3+5x^2+6x+7$, and Program 2.4 makes four additions and four multiplications. Identify these additions and multiplications for the case $x = 2$. Do this by showing the precise numbers that are being added or multiplied.

9. Give the rank array r for the case when a[0:8] = [3, 2, 6, 5, 9, 4, 7, 1, 8] (see Example 2.9).

10. Consider the selection sort function of Program 2.7. Draw a figure similar to Figure 2.4(a) for the case when a[0:6] = [3, 2, 6, 5, 9, 4, 8].

11. Consider the bubbling pass function of Program 2.8. Draw a figure similar to Figure 2.4(b) for the case when a[0:6] = [3, 2, 6, 5, 9, 4, 8].

12. For the bubble sort function of Program 2.9, draw a figure similar to Figure 2.4(c) for the case when a[0:6] = [3, 2, 6, 5, 9, 4, 8].

13. Suppose that we are to insert 3 into the sorted array a[0:6] = [1, 2, 4, 6, 7, 8, 9]. Draw a figure similar to Figure 2.5(a). Your figure should show the progress of Program 2.10.

14. The array a[0:8] = [g, h, i, f, c, a, d, b, e] is to be sorted using a rank sort. The ranks are determined to be r[0:8] = [6, 7, 8, 5, 2, 0, 3, 1, 4]. Draw a figure similar to Figures 2.5(b) and (c) to show the progress of the in-place rearrangement function of Program 2.11.

15. (a) Suppose that the array a[0:9] = [9, 8, 7, 6, 5, 4, 3, 2, 1, 0] is sorted using the early-terminating version of selection sort (Program 2.12). Draw a figure similar to Figure 2.6(a) to show the progress of the sort.

    (b) Do part (a) for the case when a[0:8] = [8, 4, 5, 2, 1, 6, 7, 3, 0].

16. The array a[0:9] = [4, 2, 6, 7, 1, 0, 9, 8, 5, 3] is sorted using the early-terminating version of bubble sort (Program 2.13). Draw a figure similar to Figure 2.6(b) to show the progress of the sort.

17. The array a[0:9] = [4, 2, 6, 7, 1, 0, 9, 8, 5, 3] is to be sorted using insertion sort (Program 2.14). Draw a figure similar to Figure 2.6(c) to show the progress of the sort.

18. How many additions (i.e., invocations of increment) are done in the for loop of function sum (Program 1.30)?

19. How many multiplications are performed by the function `factorial` (Program 1.29)?

20. Create an input array `a` that causes function `rearrange` (Program 2.11) to do $n - 1$ element reference swaps and $n - 1$ rank swaps.

21. How many additions are performed between pairs of array elements by function `matrixAdd` (Program 2.21)?

```
template<class T>
void matrixAdd( T **a, T **b, T **c, int numberOfRows,
                                     int numberOfColumns)
{// Add matrices a and b to obtain matrix c.
   for (int i = 0; i < numberOfRows; i++)
      for (int j = 0;  j < numberOfColumns; j++)
         c[i][j] = a[i][j] + b[i][j];
}
```

Program 2.21 Matrix addition

22. How many swap operations are performed by function `transpose` (Program 2.19)?

23. Determine the number of multiplications done by function `squareMatrixMultiply` (Program 2.22), which multiplies two n × n matrices.

```
template<class T>
void squareMatrixMultiply(T **a, T **b, T **c, int n)
{// Multiply the n x n matrices a and b to get c.
   for (int i = 0; i < n; i++)
      for (int j = 0; j < n; j++)
      {
         T sum = 0;
         for (int k = 0; k < n; k++)
            sum += a[i][k] * b[k][j];
         c[i][j] = sum;
      }
}
```

Program 2.22 Multiply two n × n matrices

24. Determine the number of multiplications done by function `matrixMultiply` (Program 2.23), which multiplies an m × n matrix and an n × p matrix.

```
template<class T>
void matrixMultiply(T **a, T **b, T **c, int m, int n, int p)
{// Multiply the m x n matrix a and the n x p matrix b
 // to get c.
   for (int i = 0; i < m; i++)
      for (int j = 0; j < p; j++)
      {
         T sum = 0;
         for (int k = 0; k < n; k++)
            sum += a[i][k] * b[k][j];
         c[i][j] = sum;
      }
}
```

Program 2.23 Multiply an m × n and an n × p matrix

25. Determine the number of **swap** operations performed by function **permutations** (Program 1.32).

26. Method **minmax** (Program 2.24) determines the locations of the minimum and maximum elements in an array a. Let n be the instance characteristic. What is the number of comparisons between elements of a? Program 2.25 gives an alternative function to determine the locations of the minimum and maximum elements. What are the best-case and worst-case numbers of comparisons between elements of a? What can you say about the expected relative performance of the two functions?

27. How many comparisons between the a[]s and x are made by the recursive function **rSequentialSearch** (Program 2.2)?

28. Program 2.26 gives an alternative iterative sequential search function. What is the worst-case number of comparisons between x and the elements of a? Compare this number with the corresponding number for Program 2.1. Which function should run faster? Why?

29. (a) Introduce statements to increment **stepCount** at all appropriate points in Program 2.27.

    (b) Simplify the resulting program by eliminating statements. Both the simplified program and the program of part (a) should compute the same value for **stepCount**.

    (c) What is the exact value of **stepCount** when the program terminates? You may assume that the initial value of **stepCount** is 0.

```
template<class T>
bool minmax(T a[], int n, int& indexOfMin, int& indexOfMax)
{// Locate min and max elements in a[0:n-1].
 // Return false if less than one element.
   if (n < 1) return false;
   indexOfMin = indexOfMax = 0; // initial guess
   for (int i = 1; i < n; i++)
   {
      if (a[indexOfMin] > a[i]) indexOfMin = i;
      if (a[indexOfMax] < a[i]) indexOfMax = i;
   }
   return true;
}
```

Program 2.24 Finding the minimum and maximum

```
template<class T>
bool minmax(T a[], int n, int& indexOfMin, int& indexOfMax)
{// Locate min and max elements in a[0:n-1].
 // Return false if less than one element.
   if (n < 1) return false;
   indexOfMin = indexOfMax = 0; // initial guess
   for (int i = 1; i < n; i++)
      if (a[indexOfMin] > a[i]) indexOfMin = i;
      else if (a[indexOfMax] < a[i]) indexOfMax = i;
   return true;
}
```

Program 2.25 Another function to find the minimum and maximum

(d) Use the frequency method to determine the step count for Program 2.27. Clearly show the step-count table.

30. Do Exercise 29 for each of the following functions:

(a) indexOfMax (Program 1.37).

(b) minmax (Program 2.24).

(c) minmax (Program 2.25). Determine the worst-case step count.

(d) factorial (Program 1.29).

(e) polyEval (Program 2.3).

```
template<class T>
int sequentialSearch(T a[], int n, const T& x)
{// Search the unordered list a[0:n-1] for x.
 // Return position if found; return -1 otherwise.
   a[n] = x; // assume extra position available
   int i;
   for (i = 0; a[i] != x; i++);
   if (i == n) return -1;
   return i;
}
```

Program 2.26 Another sequential search function

```
void d(int x[], int n)
{
   for (int i = 0; i < n; i += 2)
      x[i] += 2;

   i = 1;
   while (i <= n/2)
   {
      x[i] += x[i+1];
      i++;
   }
}
```

Program 2.27 Method for Exercise 29

    (f) horner (Program 2.4).

    (g) rank (Program 2.5).

    (h) permutations (Program 1.32).

    (i) sequentialSearch (Program 2.26). Determine the worst-case step count.

    (j) selectionSort (Program 2.7). Determine the best- and worst-case step counts.

    (k) selectionSort (Program 2.12). Determine the best- and worst-case step counts.

    (l) insertionSort (Program 2.14). Determine the worst-case step count.

    (m) insertionSort (Program 2.15). Determine the worst-case step count.

    (n) bubbleSort (Program 2.9). Determine the worst-case step count.

  (o) bubbleSort (Program 2.13). Determine the worst-case step count.

  (p) matrixAdd (Program 2.21).

  (q) squareMatrixMultiply (Program 2.22).

31. Do Exercise 29 parts (a), (b), and (c) for the following functions:

  (a) transpose (Program 2.19).

  (b) inef (Program 2.20).

32. Determine the average step counts for the following functions:

  (a) rSequentialSearch (Program 2.2).

  (b) sequentialSearch (Program 2.26).

  (c) insert (Program 2.10).

33. (a) Do Exercise 29 for Program 2.23.

  (b) Under what conditions will it be profitable to interchange the two out-ermost for loops?

34. Compare the worst-case number of element reference moves made by functions selectionSort (Program 2.12), insertionSort (Program 2.15), bubbleSort (Program 2.13), and rank sort using Program 2.11.

35. Must a program exhibit its worst-case time behavior and worst-case space behavior at the same time (i.e., for the same input)? Prove your answer.

36. Use repeated substitution to solve the following recurrences (see Example 2.20).

  (a) $t(n) = \begin{cases} 2 & n = 0 \\ 2 + t(n-1) & n > 0 \end{cases}$

  (b) $t(n) = \begin{cases} 0 & n = 0 \\ 1 & n = 1 \\ 1 + t(n-2) & n > 0 \end{cases}$

  (c) $t(n) = \begin{cases} 0 & n = 0 \\ 2n + t(n-1) & n > 0 \end{cases}$

  (d) $t(n) = \begin{cases} 1 & n = 0 \\ 2 * t(n-1) & n > 0 \end{cases}$

  (e) $t(n) = \begin{cases} 1 & n = 0 \\ 3 * t(n-1) & n > 0 \end{cases}$

CHAPTER 3

ASYMPTOTIC NOTATION

BIRD'S-EYE VIEW

Chapter 2 showed you how to analyze the space and time complexities of a program. The methods of that chapter are somewhat cumbersome because they attempt to obtain exact counts, rather than estimates. In this chapter we review asymptotic notation, which is used to make statements about program performance when the instance characteristics are large. When we use this notation, we need only estimate the step count. Although the big oh notation is the most popular asymptotic notation used in the performance analysis of programs, the omega, theta, and little oh notations also are in common use.

Asymptotic notation is first introduced in an informal manner in Section 3.2. The informal treatment of this section is adequate to follow all the analyses done in this book. A more rigorous treatment is presented in Section 3.3. You may omit Section 3.3 and not face any dire consequences.

The use of asymptotic notation is illustrated through the applications developed in Chapters 1 and 2. Additionally, an important and efficient search method—binary search of a sorted array—is developed and analyzed in this chapter. This search method is also available as the STL algorithm binary_Search.

3.1   INTRODUCTION

Two important reasons to determine operation and step counts are (1) to predict the growth in run time as the instance characteristics increase and (2) to compare the time complexities of two programs that perform the same task. When using operation counts, we focus on certain "key" operations and ignore all others. Therefore, you must be very cautious when using an operation count for either of the above purposes. For example, a program may do $2n$ comparisons, but the total number of computation steps could be $6n^2 + 8n$. It would be incorrect to use the comparison count of $2n$ to conclude that the run time grows linearly in n. It would also be incorrect to conclude that a program that makes $2n$ comparisons is faster than a program, for the same task, that makes $3n$ comparisons; the $3n$ comparison program may actually do less total work than is done by the $2n$ comparison program.

The operation count method accounts for only some of the work that is done in a program. Step counts attempt to overcome this deficiency by accounting for all work. However, the notion of a step is inexact. Both the instructions x = y and x = y+z+(x/y) count as one step. Therefore, two analysts may arrive at $4n^2 + 6n + 2$ and $7n^2 + 3n + 4$ as the step count for the same program. We cannot conclude that the run time will grow as either $4n^2 + 6n + 2$ or $7n^2 + 3n + 4$, because any step count of the form $c_1 n^2 + c_2 n + c_3$, where $c_1 > 0$, c_2, and c_3 are constants, could be a correct step count for the program. Because of the inexactness of what a step stands for, the exact step count isn't very useful for comparative purposes either. However, when the difference in the step counts of two programs is very large as in $3n + 3$ versus $900n + 10$. We might feel quite safe in predicting that the program with step count $3n + 3$ will run in less time than the one with step count $900n + 10$.

We can use the step count to accurately predict the growth in run time for large instance sizes (i.e., in the asymptote as n approaches infinity) and to predict the relative performance of two programs when the instance size becomes large. Suppose that the step count of a program is determined to be $c_1 n^2 + c_2 n + c_3$, $c_1 > 0$. When n becomes large, the $c_1 n^2$ term will be much larger than the remaining terms $c_2 n + c_3$. The ratio of these two expressions is $r(n) = (c_2 n + c_3)/(c_1 n^2) = c_2/(c_1 n) + c_3/(c_1 n^2)$. Figure 3.1 plots $r(n)$ for the case $c_1 = 1$, $c_2 = 2$, and $c_3 = 3$. Even though $r(n)$ never equals 0 for any finite n, $r(n)$ gets closer and closer to 0 as we make n bigger and bigger.

Regardless of the values of $c_1 > 0$, c_2, and c_3, the ratio $r(n)$ approaches 0 as n approaches infinity; that is,

$$\lim_{n \to \infty} \left(\frac{c_2}{c_1 n} + \frac{c_3}{c_1 n^2} \right) = 0$$

So for large n, $c_2 n + c_3$ is insignificant when compared to $c_1 n^2$, and run time may be approximated by the $c_1 n^2$ term. Let n_1 and n_2 be two large values of n. We conclude that

Figure 3.1 Plot of $r(n) = 2/n + 3/n^2$

$$\frac{t(n_1)}{t(n_2)} \approx \frac{c_1 n_1^2}{c_1 n_2^2} = \left(\frac{n_1}{n_2}\right)^2$$

Therefore, the run time is expected to increase by a factor of 4 (approximately) when the instance size is doubled; the run time increases by a factor of 9 when the instance size is tripled; and so on. To make this conclusion, all we need to know is that the biggest term in the step count is an n^2 term; the value of the coefficient c_1 is irrelevant to the conclusion.

Suppose that programs A and B perform the same task. Assume that John has determined the step counts of these programs to be $t_A(n) = n^2 + 3n$ and $t_B(n) = 43n$. It is entirely possible that Mary's analysis of the same programs yields $t_A(n) = 2n^2 + 3n$ and $t_B(n) = 83n$. In fact, assuming that John's analysis is correct, all other correct analyses would result in $t_A(n) = c_1 n^2 + c_2 n + c_3$ and $t_B(n) = c_4 n$, where c_1, c_2, c_3, and c_4 are constants, $c_1 > 0$, and $c_4 > 0$.

To see what conclusion we can draw about the relative performance of programs A and B knowing that the constant coefficients may vary from analyst to analyst, examine the plot of Figure 3.2. First, look at the curves for John's analysis, $t_A(n) = n^2 + 3n$ and $t_B(n) = 43n$. We conclude that for $n < 40$, program A is faster; for

$n > 40$, program B is faster; and $n = 40$ is the break-even point between the two programs. Now suppose that the analysis had instead concluded that $t_B(n) = 83n$. In this case we would conclude that for $n < 80$, program A is faster; for $n > 80$, program B is faster; and $n = 80$ is the break-even point between the two programs. Our conclusion that program B is faster than program A for large n does not change; only the break-even point changes.

Figure 3.2 Comparing run time functions

What if John's analysis had concluded $t_A(n) = 2n^2 + 3n$? From Figure 3.2, we see that regardless of whether $t_B(n) = 43n$ or $83n$, program B remains faster than program A when n is suitably large ($n > 20$ when $t_B(n) = 43n$ and $n > 40$ when $t_B(n) = 83n$).

To arrive at the conclusion that program B is faster than program A when n is large, all we need to know is that the biggest term in the step count for program A is an n^2 term while that for program B is an n term; the values of the coefficients c_1 through c_4 are irrelevant to this conclusion. Asymptotic analysis focuses on determining the biggest terms (but not their coefficients) in the complexity function.

3.2   ASYMPTOTIC NOTATION

3.2.1   Big Oh Notation (O)

Definition 3.1 *Let $p(n)$ and $q(n)$ be two nonnegative functions. $p(n)$ is* **asymptotically bigger** *($p(n)$ asymptotically dominates $q(n)$) than the function $q(n)$ iff*

$$\lim_{n \to \infty} \frac{q(n)}{p(n)} = 0 \qquad (3.1)$$

$q(n)$ is **asymptotically smaller** *than $p(n)$ iff $p(n)$ is asymptotically bigger than $q(n)$. $p(n)$ and $q(n)$ are* **asymptotically equal** *iff neither is asymptotically bigger than the other.* ∎

Example 3.1 Since

$$\lim_{n \to \infty} \frac{10n + 7}{3n^2 + 2n + 6} = \frac{10/n + 7/n^2}{3 + 2/n + 6/n^2} = 0/3 = 0$$

$3n^2 + 2n + 6$ is asymptotically bigger than $10n + 7$ and $10n + 7$ is asymptotically smaller than $3n^2 + 2n + 6$. A similar derivation shows that $8n^4 + 9n^2$ is asymptotically bigger than $100n^3 - 3$, and that $2n^2 + 3n$ is asymptotically bigger than $83n$. $12n + 6$ is asymptotically equal to $6n + 2$. ∎

   In the following discussion the function $f(n)$ denotes the time or space complexity of a program as a function of the instance characteristic n. Since the time or space requirements of a program are nonnegative quantities, we assume that the function f has a nonnegative value for all values of n. Further, since n denotes an instance characteristic, we assume that $n \geq 0$. The function $f(n)$ will, in general, be a sum of terms. For example, the terms of $f(n) = 9n^2 + 3n + 12$ are $9n^2$, $3n$, and 12. We may compare pairs of terms to determine which is bigger (see Definition 3.1). The biggest term in the example $f(n)$ is $9n^2$.

   Figure 3.3 gives the terms that occur frequently in a step-count analysis. Although all the terms in Figure 3.3 have a coefficient of 1, in an actual analysis, the coefficients of these terms may have a different value.

   We do not associate a logarithmic base with the functions in Figure 3.3 that include $\log n$ because for any constants a and b greater than 1, $\log_a n = \log_b n / \log_b a$. So $\log_a n$ and $\log_b n$ are asymptotically equal.

   Using Definition 3.1, we obtain the following ordering for the terms of Figure 3.3 ($<$ is to be read as "is asymptotically smaller than"):

$$1 < \log n < n < n \log n < n^2 < n^3 < 2^n < n!$$

Term	Name
1	constant
$\log n$	logarithmic
n	linear
$n \log n$	$n \log n$
n^2	quadratic
n^3	cubic
2^n	exponential
$n!$	factorial

Figure 3.3 Commonly occurring terms

Asymptotic notation describes the behavior of the time or space complexity for large instance characteristics. Although we will develop asymptotic notation with reference to step counts alone, our development also applies to space complexity and operation counts. The terms *time complexity* and *step count* are used as synonyms. When the instance characteristic is described by a single variable, say n, asymptotic notation describes the complexity using a single term, the asymptotically biggest term in the step count.

The notation $f(n) = O(g(n))$ (read as "$f(n)$ is big oh of $g(n)$") means that $f(n)$ is asymptotically smaller than or equal to $g(n)$. Therefore, in an asymptotic sense $g(n)$ is an upper bound for $f(n)$. You may use this as a working definition of "big oh"; a formal definition is provided in Section 3.3.1.

Example 3.2 From Example 3.1 and the working definition of big oh, it follows that $10n + 7 = O(3n^2 + 2n + 6)$; $100n^3 - 3 = O(8n^4 + 9n^2)$; $12n + 6 = O(6n + 2)$; $3n^2 + 2n + 6 \neq O(10n + 7)$; and $8n^4 + 9n^2 \neq O(100n^3 - 3)$.   ∎

Although Example 3.2 uses the big oh notation in a correct way, it is customary to use $g(n)$ functions that are **unit terms** (i.e., $g(n)$ is a single term whose coefficient is 1) except when $f(n) = 0$. In addition, it is customary to use, for $g(n)$, the smallest unit term for which the statement $f(n) = O(g(n))$ is true. When $f(n) = 0$, it is customary to use $g(n) = 0$.

Example 3.3 The customary way to describe the asymptotic behavior of the functions used in Example 3.2 is $10n + 7 = O(n)$; $100n^3 - 3 = O(n^3)$; $12n + 6 = O(n)$; $3n^2 + 2n + 6 \neq O(n)$; and $8n^4 + 9n^2 \neq O(n^3)$.   ∎

In asymptotic complexity analysis, we determine the biggest term in the complexity; the coefficient of this biggest term is set to 1. The unit terms of a step-count function are step-count terms with their coefficients changed to 1. For example, the unit terms of $3n^2 + 6n \log n + 7n + 5$ are n^2, $n \log n$, n, and 1; the biggest unit term is n^2. So when the step count of a program is $3n^2 + 6n \log n + 7n + 5$, we say that its asymptotic complexity is $O(n^2)$.

Example 3.4 In Example 2.19, we determined that $t_{\text{sum}}(n) = 2n + 3$. Since the biggest unit term in $t_{\text{sum}}(n)$ is n, $t_{\text{sum}}(n) = O(n)$.

Since $t_{\text{rSum}}(n) = 2n + 2$ (see Example 2.20), $t_{\text{rSum}}(n) = O(n)$.

The step count for Program 2.19 is $rows^2 + rows + 1$ (see Figure 2.8). The biggest unit term is $rows^2$. Therefore, $t_{\text{transpose}}(rows) = O(rows^2)$. ∎

Notice that $f(n) = O(g(n))$ is not the same as $O(g(n)) = f(n)$. In fact, saying that $O(g(n)) = f(n)$ is meaningless. The use of the symbol $=$ is unfortunate, as this symbol commonly denotes the equals relation. We can avoid some of the confusion that results from the use of this symbol (which is standard terminology) by reading the symbol $=$ as "is" and not as "equals."

Definition 3.2 *Let $t(m, n)$ and $u(m, n)$ be two terms. $t(m, n)$ is asymptotically bigger than $u(m, n)$ (equivalently, $u(m, n)$ is asymptotically smaller than $t(m, n)$) iff either*

$$\lim_{n \to \infty} \frac{u(m, n)}{t(m, n)} = 0 \ and \ \lim_{m \to \infty} \frac{u(m, n)}{t(m, n)} \neq \infty$$

or

$$\lim_{n \to \infty} \frac{u(m, n)}{t(m, n)} \neq \infty \ and \ \lim_{m \to \infty} \frac{u(m, n)}{t(m, n)} = 0$$ ∎

We may obtain a working definition of big oh for the case of functions in more than one variable as follows.

- Let $f(m, n)$ be the step count of a program. From $f(m, n)$ remove all terms that are asymptotically smaller than at least one other term in $f(m, n)$.

- Change the coefficients of all remaining terms to 1.

Example 3.5 Consider $f(m, n) = 3m^2n + m^3 + 10mn + 2n^2$. $10mn$ is smaller than $3m^2n$ because

$$\lim_{n \to \infty} \frac{10mn}{3m^2n} = \frac{10}{3m} \neq \infty \ and \ \lim_{m \to \infty} \frac{10mn}{3m^2n} = \lim_{m \to \infty} \frac{10}{3m} = 0$$

None of the remaining terms is smaller than another. Dropping the $10mn$ term and changing the coefficients of the remaining terms to 1, we get $f(m, n) = O(m^2n + m^3 + n^2)$. ∎

3.2.2   Omega (Ω) and Theta (Θ) Notations

Although the big oh notation is the most frequently used asymptotic notation, the omega and theta notations are sometimes used to describe the asymptotic complexity of a program. We provide a working definition of these notations in this section. See Sections 3.3.2 and 3.3.3 for a more formal definition.

The notation $f(n) = \Omega(g(n))$ (read as "$f(n)$ is omega of $g(n)$") means that $f(n)$ is asymptotically bigger than or equal to $g(n)$. Therefore, in an asymptotic sense, $g(n)$ is a lower bound for $f(n)$. The notation $f(n) = \Theta(g(n))$ (read as "$f(n)$ is theta of $g(n)$") means that $f(n)$ is asymptotically equal to $g(n)$.

Example 3.6 $10n+7 = \Omega(n)$ because $10n+7$ is asymptotically equal to n; $100n^3 - 3 = \Omega(n^3)$; $12n+6 = \Omega(n)$; $3n^3+2n+6 = \Omega(n)$; $8n^4+9n^2 = \Omega(n^3)$; $3n^3+2n+6 \neq \Omega(n^5)$; and $8n^4 + 9n^2 \neq \Omega(n^5)$.

$10n+7 = \Theta(n)$ because $10n+7$ is asymptotically equal to n; $100n^3 - 3 = \Theta(n^3)$; $12n + 6 = \Theta(n)$; $3n^3 + 2n + 6 \neq \Theta(n)$; $8n^4 + 9n^2 \neq \Theta(n^3)$; $3n^3 + 2n + 6 \neq \Theta(n^5)$; and $8n^4 + 9n^2 \neq \Theta(n^5)$.

Since $t_{sum}(n) = 2n + 3$ (see Example 2.19) and $2n + 3$ is asymptotically equal to n, $t_{sum}(n) = \Theta(n)$.

Since $t_{rSum}(n) = 2n + 2$ (see Example 2.20) and $2n + 2$ asymptotically equals n, $t_{rSum}(n) = \Theta(n)$.

The step count for Program 2.19 is $rows^2 + rows + 1$ (see Figure 2.8), and $rows^2 + rows + 1$ asymptotically equals $rows^2$. Therefore, $t_{transpose}(rows) = \Theta(rows^2)$.

The best-case step count for sequentialSearch (Program 2.1) is 4 (Figure 2.10), the worst-case step count is $n + 3$, and the average step count is $0.6n + 3.4$. So the best-case asymptotic complexity of sequentialSearch is $\Theta(1)$, and the worst-case and average complexities are $\Theta(n)$. It is also correct to say that the complexity of sequentialSearch is $\Omega(1)$ and $O(n)$ because 1 is a lower bound (in an asymptotic sense) and n is an upper bound (in an asymptotic sense) on the step count.

From Figures 2.13 and 2.14, it follows that $4 \leq t_{insert}(n) \leq 2n + 4$. Therefore, $t_{insert}(n)$ is both $\Omega(1)$ and $O(n)$.   ∎

At times it is useful to interpret $O(g(n))$, $\Omega(g(n))$, and $\Theta(g(n))$ as being the following sets:

$O(g(n)) = \{f(n) | f(n) = O(g(n))\}$

$\Omega(g(n)) = \{f(n) | f(n) = \Omega(g(n))\}$

$\Theta(g(n)) = \{f(n) | f(n) = \Theta(g(n))\}$

Under this interpretation, statements such as $O(g_1(n)) = O(g_2(n))$ and $\Theta(g_1(n)) = \Theta(g_2(n))$ are meaningful. When using this interpretation, it is also convenient to read $f(n) = O(g(n))$ as "f of n is in (or is a member of) big oh of g of n" and so on.

The working definitions of big oh, omega, and theta are all you need to understand the analyses done in this book. The next section contains a more formal treatment of asymptotic notation that will help you with more complex analyses.

EXERCISES

1. Use Equation 3.1 to show that $p(n)$ is asymptotically bigger than $q(n)$ for the following functions:

    (a) $p(n) = 3n^4 + 2n^2$, $q(n) = 100n^2 + 6$

    (b) $p(n) = 6n^{1.5} + 12$, $q(n) = 100n$

    (c) $p(n) = 7n^2 \log n$, $q(n) = 10n^2$

    (d) $p(n) = 17n^2 2^n$, $q(n) = 100n2^n + 33n$

2. Express the following step counts using big oh notation. Your $g(n)$ function should be the smallest possible unit term.

    (a) $2n^3 - 6n + 30$

    (b) $44n^{1.5} + 33n - 200$

    (c) $16n^2 \log n + 5n^2$

    (d) $31n^3 + 17n^2 \log n$

    (e) $23n2^n - 3n^3$

3. Use the working definition of big oh and Equation 3.1 to show the following:

    (a) $2n + 7 \neq O(1)$

    (b) $12n^2 + 8n + 7 \neq O(n)$

    (c) $5n^3 + 6n^2 \neq O(n^2)$

    (d) $15n^3 \log n + 16n^2 \neq O(n^3)$

4. Express the step counts of Exercise 2 using omega notation.

5. Use the working definition of omega and Equation 3.1 to show the following:

    (a) $2n + 7 \neq \Omega(n^2)$

    (b) $12n^2 + 8n + 7 \neq \Omega(n^3)$

    (c) $5n^3 + 6n^2 \neq \Omega(n^3 \log n)$

    (d) $15n^3 \log n + 16n^2 \neq \Omega(n^4)$

6. Express the step counts of Exercise 2 using theta notation.

7. Let $t(n)$ be the step count of a program. Express the following step-count information using asymptotic notation. Use the most appropriate $g(n)$ functions.

    (a) $6 \leq t(n) \leq 20$

    (b) $6 \leq t(n) \leq 2n$

    (c) $3n^2 + 1 \leq t(n) \leq 4n^2 + 3n + 9$

    (d) $3n^2 + 1 \leq t(n) \leq 4n^2 \log n + 3n^2 + 9$

    (e) $t(n) \geq 5n^3 + 7$

    (f) $t(n) \geq 32n \log n + 77n - 6$

    (g) $t(n) = 17n^2 + 3n$

8. Express the following step counts using big oh notation. m and n are instance characteristics.

    (a) $7m^2n^2 + 2m^3n + mn + 5mn^2$

    (b) $2m^2 \log n + 3mn + 5m \log n + m^2n^2$

    (c) $m^4 + n^3 + m^3n^2$

    (d) $3mn^2 + 7m^2n + 4mn + 8m + 2n + 16$

3.3   ASYMPTOTIC MATHEMATICS (OPTIONAL)

3.3.1   Big Oh Notation (O)

The big oh notation describes an upper bound on the asymptotic growth rate of the function f.

Definition 3.3 [Big oh] $f(n) = O(g(n))$ *iff positive constants c and n_0 exist such that $f(n) \leq cg(n)$ for all n, $n \geq n_0$.* ∎

    The definition states that the function f is at most c times the function g except possibly when n is smaller than n_0. Here c is some positive constant. Thus g is an upper bound (up to a constant factor c) on the value of f for all suitably large n (i.e., $n \geq n_0$). Figure 3.4 illustrates what it means for a function $g(n)$ to upper bound (up to a constant factor c) another function $f(n)$. Although $f(n)$ may be less than, equal to, or greater than $cg(n)$ for several values of n, there must exist a value m of n beyond which $f(n)$ is never greater than $cg(n)$. The n_0 in the definition of big oh could be any integer $\geq m$.

    When providing an upper-bound function g for f, we will normally use only simple functional forms. These typically contain a single term in n with a multiplicative constant of 1.

Example 3.7 [Linear Function] Consider $f(n) = 3n + 2$. When n is at least 2, $3n + 2 \leq 3n + n \leq 4n$. So $f(n) = O(n)$. Thus $f(n)$ is bounded from above by a linear function. We can arrive at the same conclusion in other ways. For example,

Figure 3.4 $g(n)$ is an upper bound (up to a constant factor c) on $f(n)$

$3n + 2 \leq 10n$ for $n > 0$. Therefore, we can also satisfy the definition of big oh by selecting $c = 10$ and n_0 equal to any integer greater than 0. Alternatively, $3n + 2 \leq 3n + 2n = 5n$ for $n \geq 1$, so we can satisfy the definition of big oh by setting $c = 5$ and $n_0 = 1$. The values of c and n_0 used to satisfy the definition of big oh are not important because we will be saying only that $f(n)$ is big oh of $g(n)$ and in this statement neither c nor n_0 play a role.

For $f(n) = 3n + 3$, we note that for $n \geq 3$, $3n + 3 \leq 3n + n \leq 4n$. So $f(n) = O(n)$. Similarly, $f(n) = 100n + 6 \leq 100n + n = 101n$ for $n \geq n_0 = 6$. Therefore, $100n + 6 = O(n)$. As expected, $3n + 2$, $3n + 3$, and $100n + 6$ are all big oh of n; that is, they are bounded from above by a linear function (for suitably large n).   ∎

Example 3.8 [Quadratic Function] Suppose that $f(n) = 10n^2 + 4n + 2$. We see that for $n \geq 2$, $f(n) \leq 10n^2 + 5n$. Now we note that for $n \geq 5$, $5n \leq n^2$. Hence for $n \geq n_0 = 5$, $f(n) \leq 10n^2 + n^2 = 11n^2$. Therefore, $f(n) = O(n^2)$.

As another example of a quadratic complexity, consider $f(n) = 1000n^2 + 100n - 6$. We easily see that $f(n) \leq 1000n^2 + 100n$ for all n. Furthermore, $100n \leq n^2$ for $n \geq 100$. Hence $f(n) < 1001n^2$ for $n \geq n_0 = 100$. So $f(n) = O(n^2)$.   ∎

Example 3.9 [Exponential Function] As an example of exponential complexity, consider $f(n) = 6 * 2^n + n^2$. Observe that for $n \geq 4$, $n^2 \leq 2^n$. So $f(n) \leq 6 * 2^n + 2^n = 7 * 2^n$ for $n \geq 4$. Therefore, $6 * 2^n + n^2 = O(2^n)$.   ∎

Example 3.10 [Constant Function] When $f(n)$ is a constant, as in $f(n) = 9$ or $f(n) = 2033$, we write $f(n) = O(1)$. The correctness of this is easily established. For example, $f(n) = 9 \leq 9 * 1$; setting $c = 9$ and $n_0 = 0$ satisfies the definition of big oh. Similarly, $f(n) = 2033 \leq 2033 * 1$, and the definition of big oh is satisfied by setting $c = 2033$ and $n_0 = 0$.   ∎

Example 3.11 [Loose Bounds] $3n + 3 = O(n^2)$ as $3n + 3 \leq 3n^2$ for $n \geq 2$. Although n^2 is an upper bound for $3n + 3$, it is not a tight upper bound; we can find a smaller function (in this case linear) that also satisfies the big oh relation.

$10n^2 + 4n + 2 = O(n^4)$ as $10n^2 + 4n + 2 \leq 10n^4$ for $n \geq 2$. Once again, n^4 does not provide a tight upper bound for $100n^2 + 4n + 2$.

Similarly, $6n2^n + 20 = O(n^2 2^n)$, but it is not a tight upper bound because we can find a smaller function, namely, $n2^n$, for which the definition of big oh is satisfied. That is, $6n2^n + 20 = O(n2^n)$.   ∎

Note that the strategy in each of the preceding derivations is to replace the low-order terms by higher-order terms until only a single term remains.

Example 3.12 [Incorrect Bounds] $3n + 2 \neq O(1)$, as there is no $c > 0$ and n_0 such that $3n + 2 \leq c$ for all n, $n \geq n_0$. We can use contradiction to prove this condition formally. Suppose that such a c and n_0 exist. Then $n \leq (c - 2)/3$ for all n, $n \geq n_0$. This is not true for $n > \max\{n_0, (c - 2)/3\}$.

To prove $10n^2 + 4n + 2 \neq O(n)$, suppose the equality holds. That is, $10n^2 + 4n + 2 = O(n)$. There exists a positive c and an n_0 such that $10n^2 + 4n + 2 \leq cn$ for all $n \geq n_0$. Dividing both sides of the relation by n, we get $10n + 4 + 2/n \leq c$ for $n \geq n_0$. This relation cannot be true because the left side increases as n increases, whereas the right side does not change. In particular, we get a contradiction for $n \geq \max\{n_0, (c - 4)/10\}$.

$f(n) = 3n^2 2^n + 4n 2^n + 8n^2 \neq O(2^n)$. To prove this inequality, suppose that $f(n) = O(2^n)$. Then a $c > 0$ and an n_0 exist such that $f(n) \leq c * 2^n$ for $n \geq n_0$. Dividing both sides by 2^n, we get $3n^2 + 4n + 8n^2/2^n \leq c$ for $n \geq n_0$. Once again, the left side of the relation is an increasing function of n while the right side is constant. So the relation cannot hold for "large" n.   ∎

As illustrated in Example 3.11, the statement $f(n) = O(g(n))$ states only that $cg(n)$ is an upper bound on the value of $f(n)$ for all n, $n \geq n_0$. It doesn't say anything about how good or tight this bound is. Notice that $n = O(n^2)$, $n = O(n^{2.5})$, $n = O(n^3)$, and $n = O(2^n)$. For the statement $f(n) = O(g(n))$ to be informative, $g(n)$ should be as small a function of n as possible for which $f(n) = O(g(n))$. So although we often say $3n + 3 = O(n)$, we almost never say $3n + 3 = O(n^2)$, even though the latter statement is correct.

Theorem 3.1 obtains a very useful result concerning the order of $f(n)$ (i.e., the $g(n)$ in $f(n) = O(g(n))$) when $f(n)$ is a polynomial in n.

Theorem 3.1 *If $f(n) = a_m n^m + \cdots + a_1 n + a_0$ and $a_m > 0$, then $f(n) = O(n^m)$.*

Proof $f(n) \le \sum_{i=0}^m |a_i| n^i \le n^m \sum_0^m |a_i| n^{i-m} \le n^m \sum_0^m |a_i|$ for $n \ge 1$. So $f(n) = O(n^m)$. ∎

Example 3.13 Let us apply Theorem 3.1 to the functions of Examples 3.7, 3.8, and 3.10. For the three linear functions of Example 3.7, $m = 1$, and so these functions are $O(n)$. For the functions of Example 3.8, $m = 2$, and so all are $O(n^2)$. For the constants of Example 3.10, $m = 0$, so both constants are $O(1)$. ∎

We can extend the strategy used in Example 3.12 to show that an upper bound is incorrect to the case when an upper bound is correct, as shown in the following theorem. *It is usually easier to show $f(n) = O(g(n))$ by using this theorem than by using the definition of big oh.*

Theorem 3.2 [Big oh ratio theorem] *Let $f(n)$ and $g(n)$ be such that $\lim_{n \to \infty} f(n)/g(n)$ exists. $f(n) = O(g(n))$ iff $\lim_{n \to \infty} f(n)/g(n) \le c$ for some finite constant c.*

Proof If $f(n) = O(g(n))$, then positive c and an n_0 exist such that $f(n)/g(n) \le c$ for all $n \ge n_0$. Hence $\lim_{n \to \infty} f(n)/g(n) \le c$. Suppose that $\lim_{n \to \infty} f(n)/g(n) \le c$. It follows that an n_0 exists for which $f(n) \le \max\{1, c\} * g(n)$ for all $n \ge n_0$. ∎

Example 3.14 $3n + 2 = O(n)$ as $\lim_{n \to \infty} (3n+2)/n = 3$. $10n^2 + 4n + 2 = O(n^2)$ as $\lim_{n \to \infty} (10n^2 + 4n + 2)/n^2 = 10$. $6 * 2^n + n^2 = O(2^n)$ as $\lim_{n \to \infty} (6 * 2^n + n^2)/2^n = 6$. $2n^2 - 3 = O(n^4)$ as $\lim_{n \to \infty} (2n^2 - 3)/n^4 = 0$. $3n^2 + 5 \ne O(n)$ as $\lim_{n \to \infty} (3n^2 + 5)/n = \infty$. ∎

3.3.2   Omega Notation (Ω)

The omega notation, which is the lower-bound analog of the big oh notation, permits us to bound the asymptotic growth rate of f from below.

Definition 3.4 [Omega] *$f(n) = \Omega(g(n))$ iff positive constants c and n_0 exist such that $f(n) \ge cg(n)$ for all n, $n \ge n_0$.* ∎

When we write $f(n) = \Omega(g(n))$, we are saying that f is at least c times the function g except possibly when n is smaller than n_0. Here c is some positive constant. Thus g is a lower bound (up to a constant factor c) on the value of f for all suitably large n (i.e., $n \ge n_0$). Figure 3.5 illustrates what it means for a function $g(n)$ to lower bound (up to a constant factor c) another function $f(n)$. Although $f(n)$ may be less than, equal to, or greater than $cg(n)$ for several values of n, there must exist a value m of n beyond which $f(n)$ is never less than $cg(n)$. The n_0 in the definition of omega could be any integer $\ge m$.

As in the case of the big oh notation, we normally use only simple functional forms for g.

Figure 3.5 $g(n)$ is a lower bound (up to a constant factor c) on $f(n)$

Example 3.15 $f(n) = 3n + 2 > 3n$ for all n. So $f(n) = \Omega(n)$. Also, $f(n) = 3n + 3 > 3n$, and so $f(n) = \Omega(n)$. Since $f(n) = 100n + 6 > 100n$, $100n + 6 = \Omega(n)$. So $3n + 2$, $3n + 3$, and $100n + 6$ are all bounded from below by a linear function.

$f(n) = 10n^2 + 4n + 2 > 10n^2$ for $n \geq 0$. So $f(n) = \Omega(n^2)$. Similarly, $1000n^2 + 100n - 6 = \Omega(n^2)$. Furthermore, since $6 * 2^n + n^2 > 6 * 2^n$, $6 * 2^n + n^2 = \Omega(2^n)$.

Observe also that $3n + 3 = \Omega(1)$; $10n^2 + 4n + 2 = \Omega(n)$; $10n^2 + 4n + 2 = \Omega(1)$; $6 * 2^n + n^2 = \Omega(n^{100})$; $6 * 2^n + n^2 = \Omega(n^{50.2})$; $6 * 2^n + n^2 = \Omega(n^2)$; $6 * 2^n + n^2 = \Omega(n)$; and $6 * 2^n + n^2 = \Omega(1)$.

To see that $3n + 2 \neq \Omega(n^2)$, suppose that $3n + 2 = \Omega(n^2)$. Then positive c and n_0 exist such that $3n + 2 \geq cn^2$ for all $n \geq n_0$. So $cn^2/(3n + 2) \leq 1$ for all $n \geq n_0$. This relation cannot be true because its left side increases to infinity as n becomes large. ∎

As in the case of the big oh notation, there are several functions $g(n)$ for which $f(n) = \Omega(g(n))$. $g(n)$ is only a lower bound (up to a constant factor) on $f(n)$. For the statement $f(n) = \Omega(g(n))$ to be informative, $g(n)$ should be as large a function of n as possible for which the statement $f(n) = \Omega(g(n))$ is true. So although we say that $3n + 3 = \Omega(n)$ and that $6 * 2^n + n^2 = \Omega(2^n)$, we almost never say that $3n + 3 = \Omega(1)$ or that $6 * 2^n + n^2 = \Omega(1)$, even though both these statements are correct.

Theorem 3.3 is the analog of Theorem 3.1 for the omega notation.

Theorem 3.3 *If* $f(n) = a_m n^m + \cdots + a_1 n + a_0$ *and* $a_m > 0$, *then* $f(n) = \Omega(n^m)$.

Proof See Exercise 12. ∎

Example 3.16 From Theorem 3.3, it follows that $3n + 2 = \Omega(n)$, $10n^2 + 4n + 2 = \Omega(n^2)$, and $100n^4 + 3500n^2 + 82n + 8 = \Omega(n^4)$. ∎

Theorem 3.4 is the analog of Theorem 3.2, and it is usually easier to show $f(n) = \Omega(g(n))$ by using Theorem 3.4 than by using the definition of omega.

Theorem 3.4 [Omega ratio theorem] *Let $f(n)$ and $g(n)$ be such that $\lim_{n \to \infty} g(n)/f(n)$ exists. $f(n) = \Omega(g(n))$ iff $\lim_{n \to \infty} g(n)/f(n) \leq c$ for some finite constant c.*

Proof See Exercise 13. ∎

Example 3.17 $3n + 2 = \Omega(n)$ as $\lim_{n \to \infty} n/(3n + 2) = 1/3$. $10n^2 + 4n + 2 = \Omega(n^2)$ as $\lim_{n \to \infty} n^2/(10n^2 + 4n + 2) = 0.1$. $6 * 2^n + n^2 = \Omega(2^n)$ as $\lim_{n \to \infty} 2^n/(6 * 2^n + n^2) = 1/6$. $6n^2 + 2 = \Omega(n)$ as $\lim_{n \to \infty} n/(6n^2 + 2) = 0$. $3n^2 + 5 \neq \Omega(n^3)$ as $\lim_{n \to \infty} n^3/(3n^2 + 5) = \infty$. ∎

3.3.3   Theta Notation (Θ)

The theta notation is used when the function f can be bounded both from above and below by the same function g.

Definition 3.5 [Theta] *$f(n) = \Theta(g(n))$ iff positive constants c_1 and c_2 and an n_0 exist such that $c_1 g(n) \leq f(n) \leq c_2 g(n)$ for all n, $n \geq n_0$.* ∎

When we write $f(n) = \Theta(g(n))$, we are saying that f lies between c_1 times the function g and c_2 times the function g except possibly when n is smaller than n_0. Here c_1 and c_2 are positive constants. Thus g is both a lower and upper bound (up to a constant factor c) on the value of f for all suitably large n (i.e., $n \geq n_0$). Another way to view the theta notation is that it says $f(n)$ is both $\Omega(g(n))$ and $O(g(n))$.

Figure 3.6 illustrates what it means for a function $g(n)$ to both upper and lower bound (up to a constant factor) another function $f(n)$. There must exist a value m of n beyond which $f(n)$ lies between $c_1 g(n)$ and $c_2 g(n)$. The n_0 in the definition of theta could be any integer $\geq m$.

As in the case of the big oh and omega notations, we normally use only simple functional forms for g.

Example 3.18 From Examples 3.7, 3.8, 3.9, and 3.15, it follows that $3n + 2 = \Theta(n)$; $3n + 3 = \Theta(n)$; $100n + 6 = \Theta(n)$; $10n^2 + 4n + 2 = \Theta(n^2)$; $1000n^2 + 100n - 6 = \Theta(n^2)$; and $6 * 2^n + n^2 = \Theta(2^n)$.

$10 * \log_2 n + 4 = \Theta(\log_2 n)$ as $\log_2 n < 10 \log_2 n + 4 \leq 11 \log_2 n$ for $n \geq 16$. As remarked earlier, $\log_a n$ is $\log_b n$ times a constant, and we write $\Theta(\log_a n)$ simply as $\Theta(\log n)$.

Figure 3.6 $g(n)$ is a lower and upper bound (up to a constant factor) on $f(n)$

In Example 3.12 we showed that $3n + 2 \neq O(1)$. So $3n + 2 \neq \Theta(1)$. Similarly, we may show that $3n + 3 \neq \Theta(1)$ and $100n + 6 \neq \Theta(1)$. Since $3n + 3 \neq \Omega(n^2)$, $3n + 3 \neq \Theta(n^2)$. Since $10n^2 + 4n + 2 \neq O(n)$, $10n^2 + 4n + 2 \neq \Theta(n)$. Also, since $10n^2 + 4n + 2 \neq O(1)$, it is not $\Theta(1)$.

Since $6 * 2^n + n^2$ is not $O(n^2)$, it is not $\Theta(n^2)$. Similarly, $6 * 2^n + n^2 \neq \Theta(n^{100})$; and $6 * 2^n + n^2 \neq \Theta(1)$. ∎

As mentioned earlier it is common practice to use only g functions with a multiplicative factor of 1. We almost never say that $3n + 3 = O(3n)$ or $10 = O(100)$ or $10n^2 + 4n + 2 = \Omega(4 * n^2)$ or $6 * 2^n + n^2 = \Omega(6 * 2^n)$ or $6 * 2^n + n^2 = \Theta(4 * 2^n)$, even though each of these statements is true.

Theorem 3.5 If $f(n) = a_m n^m + \cdots + a_1 n + a_0$ and $a_m > 0$, then $f(n) = \Theta(n^m)$.

Proof See Exercise 12. ∎

Example 3.19 From Theorem 3.5 it follows that $3n + 2 = \Theta(n)$, $10n^2 + 4n + 2 = \Theta(n^2)$, and $100n^4 + 3500n^2 + 82n + 8 = \Theta(n^4)$. ∎

Theorem 3.6 is the analog of Theorems 3.2 and 3.4.

Theorem 3.6 [Theta ratio theorem] Let $f(n)$ and $g(n)$ be such that $\lim_{n\to\infty} f(n)/g(n)$ and $\lim_{n\to\infty} g(n)/f(n)$ exist. $f(n) = \Theta(g(n))$ iff $\lim_{n\to\infty} f(n)/g(n) \leq c$ and $\lim_{n\to\infty} g(n)/f(n) \leq c$ for some finite constant c.

Proof See Exercise 13.   ∎

Example 3.20 $3n + 2 = \Theta(n)$ as $\lim_{n\to\infty}(3n + 2)/n = 3$ and $\lim_{n\to\infty} n/(3n + 2)$
$= 1/3 < 3$; $10n^2 + 4n + 2 = \Theta(n^2)$ as $\lim_{n\to\infty}(10n^2 + 4n + 2)/n^2 = 10$; and
$\lim_{n\to\infty} n^2/(10n^2 + 4n + 2) = 0.1 < 10$. $6*2^n + n^2 = \Theta(2^n)$ as $\lim_{n\to\infty}(6*2^n + n^2)/2^n$
$= 6$ and $\lim_{n\to\infty} 2^n/(6*2^n + n^2) = 1/6 < 6$. $6n^2 + 2 \neq \Theta(n)$ as $\lim_{n\to\infty}(6n^2 + 2)/n$
$= \infty$.   ∎

3.3.4 Little Oh Notation (*o*)

The little oh notation describes a strict upper bound on the asymptotic growth
rate of the function f. Informally, $f(n)$ is little oh of $g(n)$ iff $f(n)$ is asymptotically
smaller than $g(n)$ (recall that $f(n)$ is big oh of $g(n)$ iff $f(n)$ is asymptotically smaller
than or equal to $g(n)$).

Definition 3.6 [Little oh] $f(n) = o(g(n))$ *(read as "f of n is little oh of g of n")*
iff $f(n) = O(g(n))$ *and* $f(n) \neq \Omega(g(n))$.   ∎

Example 3.21 [Little oh] $3n + 2 = o(n^2)$ as $3n + 2 = O(n^2)$ and $3n + 2 \neq \Omega(n^2)$.
However, $3n + 2 \neq o(n)$. Similarly, $10n^2 + 4n + 2 = o(n^3)$, but is not $o(n^2)$.   ∎

The little oh notation is often used in step-count analyses. A step count of $3n$
$+ o(n)$ would mean that the step count is $3n$ plus terms that are asymptotically
smaller than n. When performing such an analysis, one can ignore portions of the
program that are known to contribute less than $\Theta(n)$ steps.

3.3.5 Properties

The following theorem is useful in computations involving asymptotic notation.

Theorem 3.7 *These statements are true for every real number* x, $x > 0$ *and for
every real* ϵ, $\epsilon > 0$:

1. *An* n_0 *exists such that* $(\log n)^x < (\log n)^{x+\epsilon}$ *for every* n, $n \geq n_0$.

2. *An* n_0 *exists such that* $(\log n)^x < n^\epsilon$ *for every* n, $n \geq n_0$.

3. *An* n_0 *exists such that* $n^x < n^{x+\epsilon}$ *for every* n, $n \geq n_0$.

4. *For every real* y, *an* n_0 *exists such that* $n^x(\log n)^y < n^{x+\epsilon}$ *for every* n, $n \geq$
   n_0.

5. *An* n_0 *exists such that* $n^x < 2^n$ *for every* n, $n \geq n_0$.

Proof Follows from the definition of the individual functions.   ∎

Example 3.22 From Theorem 3.7 we obtain the following: $n^3 + n^2 \log n = \Theta(n^3)$; $2^n/n^2 = \Omega(n^k)$ for every natural number k; $n^4 + n^{2.5} \log^{20} n = \Theta(n^4)$; $2^n n^4 \log^3 n + 2^n n^4/\log n = \Theta(2^n n^4 \log^3 n)$. ∎

Figure 3.7 lists some of the more useful identities involving the big oh, omega, and theta notations. In this table all symbols other than n are positive constants. Figure 3.8 lists some useful inference rules for sums and products.

	$f(n)$	Asymptotic
E1	c	$\oplus(1)$
E2	$\sum_{i=0}^{k} c_i n^i$	$\oplus(n^k)$
E3	$\sum_{i=1}^{n} i$	$\oplus(n^2)$
E4	$\sum_{i=1}^{n} i^2$	$\oplus(n^3)$
E5	$\sum_{i=1}^{n} i^k,\ k > 0$	$\oplus(n^{k+1})$
E6	$\sum_{i=0}^{n} r^i,\ r > 1$	$\oplus(r^n)$
E7	$n!$	$\oplus(\sqrt{n}(n/e)^n)$
E8	$\sum_{i=1}^{n} 1/i$	$\oplus(\log n)$

$\oplus$ can be any one of O, Ω, and Θ

Figure 3.7 Asymptotic identities

Figures 3.7 and 3.8 prepare you to use asymptotic notation to describe the time complexity (or step count) of a program.

The definitions of O, Ω, Θ, and o can be extended to include functions of more than one variable. For example, $f(n,m) = O(g(n,m))$ iff positive constants c, n_0, and m_0 exist such that $f(n,m) \leq cg(n,m)$ for all $n \geq n_0$ and all $m \geq m_0$.

EXERCISES

9. Show that the following equalities are correct, using the definitions of O, Ω, Θ, and o only. Do not use Theorems 3.1 through 3.6, or Figures 3.7 and 3.8.

   (a) $5n^2 - 6n = \Theta(n^2)$.

I1 $\{f(n) = \oplus(g(n))\} \to \sum_{n=a}^{b} f(n) = \oplus(\sum_{n=a}^{b} g(n))$.

I2 $\{f_i(n) = \oplus(g_i(n)), 1 \le i \le k\} \to \sum_{i=1}^{k} f_i(n) = \oplus(\max_{1 \le i \le k}\{g_i(n)\})$.

I3 $\{f_i(n) = \oplus(g_i(n)), 1 \le i \le k\} \to \prod_{i=1}^{k} f_i(n) = \oplus(\prod_{i=1}^{k} g_i(n))$.

I4 $\{f_1(n) = O(g_1(n)), f_2(n) = \Theta(g_2(n))\} \to f_1(n) + f_2(n) = O(g_1(n) + g_2(n))$.

I5 $\{f_1(n) = \Theta(g_1(n)), f_2(n) = \Omega(g_2(n))\} \to f_1(n) + f_2(n) = \Omega(g_1(n) + g_2(n))$.

I6 $\{f_1(n) = O(g(n)), f_2(n) = \Theta(g(n))\} \to f_1(n) + f_2(n) = \Theta(g(n))$.

Figure 3.8 Inference rules for $\oplus \in \{O, \Omega, \Theta\}$

(b) $n! = O(n^n)$.

(c) $2n^2 2^n + n \log n = \Theta(n^2 2^n)$.

(d) $\sum_{i=0}^{n} i^2 = \Theta(n^3)$.

(e) $\sum_{i=0}^{n} i^3 = \Theta(n^4)$.

(f) $n^{2^n} + 6 * 2^n = \Theta(n^{2^n})$.

(g) $n^3 + 10^6 n^2 = \Theta(n^3)$.

(h) $6n^3/(\log n + 1) = O(n^3)$.

(i) $n^{1.001} + n \log n = \Theta(n^{1.001})$.

(j) $n^{k+\epsilon} + n^k \log n = \Theta(n^{k+\epsilon})$ for all k and ϵ, $k \ge 0$, and $\epsilon > 0$.

10. Do Exercise 9 using Theorems 3.2, 3.4, and 3.6.

11. Show that the following equalities are incorrect:

(a) $10n^2 + 9 = O(n)$.

(b) $n^2 \log n = \Theta(n^2)$.

(c) $n^2/\log n = \Theta(n^2)$.

(d) $n^3 2^n + 6n^2 3^n = O(n^3 2^n)$.

12. Prove Theorems 3.3 and 3.5.

13. Prove Theorems 3.4 and 3.6.

14. Prove that $f(n) = o(g(n))$ iff $\lim_{n \to \infty} f(n)/g(n) = 0$.

15. Prove that equivalences E5 to E8 (Figure 3.7) are correct.

16. Prove the correctness of inference rules I1 to I6 (Figure 3.8).

17. Which of the following inferences are true? Why?

    (a) $\{f(n) = O(F(n)), g(n) = O(G(n))\} \rightarrow f(n)/g(n) = O(F(n)/G(n))$.

    (b) $\{f(n) = O(F(n)), g(n) = O(G(n))\} \rightarrow f(n)/g(n) = \Omega(F(n)/G(n))$.

    (c) $\{f(n) = O(F(n)), g(n) = O(G(n))\} \rightarrow f(n)/g(n) = \Theta(F(n)/G(n))$.

    (d) $\{f(n) = \Omega(F(n)), g(n) = \Omega(G(n))\} \rightarrow f(n)/g(n) = \Omega(F(n)/G(n))$.

    (e) $\{f(n) = \Omega(F(n)), g(n) = \Omega(G(n))\} \rightarrow f(n)/g(n) = O(F(n)/G(n))$.

    (f) $\{f(n) = \Omega(F(n)), g(n) = \Omega(G(n))\} \rightarrow f(n)/g(n) = \Theta(F(n)/G(n))$.

    (g) $\{f(n) = \Theta(F(n)), g(n) = \Theta(G(n))\} \rightarrow f(n)/g(n) = \Theta(F(n)/G(n))$.

    (h) $\{f(n) = \Theta(F(n)), g(n) = \Theta(G(n))\} \rightarrow f(n)/g(n) = \Omega(F(n)/G(n))$.

    (i) $\{f(n) = \Theta(F(n)), g(n) = \Theta(G(n))\} \rightarrow f(n)/g(n) = O(F(n)/G(n))$.

3.4 COMPLEXITY ANALYSIS EXAMPLES

In Section 3.2 we saw several examples in which we started with the step count of a program and then arrived at its asymptotic complexity. Actually, we can determine the asymptotic complexity quite easily without determining the exact step count. The procedure is to first determine the asymptotic complexity of each statement (or group of statements) in the program and then add up these complexities. Figures 3.9 to 3.12 determine the asymptotic complexity of several methods without performing an exact step-count analysis. These figures use the following fact that when $f_1(n) = \Theta(g_1(n))$ and $f_2(n) = \Theta(g_2(n))$, then $f_1(n) + f_2(n) = \Theta(\max\{g_1(n), g_2(n)\})$.

Statement	s/e	Frequency	Total Steps
`T sum(T a[], int n)`	0	0	$\Theta(0)$
`{`	0	0	$\Theta(0)$
`T theSum = 0;`	1	1	$\Theta(1)$
`for (int i = 0; i < n; i++)`	1	$n+1$	$\Theta(n)$
`theSum += a[i];`	1	n	$\Theta(n)$
`return theSum;`	1	1	$\Theta(1)$
`}`	0	0	$\Theta(0)$

$$t_{\text{sum}}(n) = \Theta(\max\{g_i(n)\}) = \Theta(n)$$

Figure 3.9 Asymptotic complexity of `sum` (Program 1.30)

While the analyses of Figures 3.9 through 3.12 are actually carried out in terms of step counts, it is correct to interpret $t_P(n) = \Theta(g(n))$, $t_P(n) = O(g(n))$, or $t_P(n) = \Omega(g(n))$ as a statement about the computing time of program P because each step takes only $\Theta(1)$ time to execute.

Statement	s/e	Frequency	Total Steps
void transpose(T **a, int rows)	0	0	$\Theta(0)$
{	0	0	$\Theta(0)$
for (int i = 0; i < rows; i++)	1	$rows + 1$	$\Theta(rows)$
for (int j = i+1; j < rows; j++)	1	$rows(rows + 1)/2$	$\Theta(rows^2)$
swap(a[i][j], a[j][i]);	1	$rows(rows - 1)/2$	$\Theta(rows^2)$
}	0	0	$\Theta(0)$

$$t_{\text{transpose}}(rows) = \Theta(rows^2)$$

Figure 3.10 Asymptotic complexity of transpose (Program 2.19)

Statement	s/e	Frequency	Total Steps
void inef(T a[], T b[], int n)	0	0	$\Theta(0)$
{	0	0	$\Theta(0)$
for (int j = 0; j < n; j++)	1	$n + 1$	$\Theta(n)$
b[j] = sum(a, j + 1);	$2j + 6$	n	$\Theta(n^2)$
}	0	0	$\Theta(0)$

$$t_{\text{inef}}(n) = \Theta(n^2)$$

Figure 3.11 Asymptotic complexity of inef (Program 2.20)

Statement	s/e	Frequency	Total Steps
int sequentialSearch(T a[], int n, const T& x)	0	0	$\Theta(0)$
{	0	0	$\Theta(0)$
int i;	1	1	$\Theta(1)$
for (i = 0; i < n && a[i] != x; i++);	1	$\Omega(1), O(n)$	$\Omega(1), O(n)$
if (i == n) return -1;	1	1	$\Theta(1)$
else return i;	1	$\Omega(0), O(1)$	$\Omega(0), O(1)$
}	0	0	$\Theta(0)$

$$t_{\text{sequentialSearch}}(n) = \Omega(1) \qquad t_{\text{sequentialSearch}}(n) = O(n)$$

Figure 3.12 Asymptotic complexity of sequentialSearch (Program 2.1)

After you have had some experience using the table method, you will be in a position to arrive at the asymptotic complexity of a program by taking a more global approach. We elaborate on this method in the following examples.

Example 3.23 [Permutations] Consider the permutation generation code of Program 1.32. Assume that $m = n-1$. When $k = m$, the time taken is cn, where c is a constant. When $k < m$, the else clause is entered. At this time the for loop is entered m-k+1 times. Each iteration of this loop takes $dt_{\text{permutations}}$(k+1,m) time, where d is a constant. So $t_{\text{permutations}}$(k,m) $= d$(m-k+1)$t_{\text{permutations}}$(k+1,m) when k<m. Using the substitution method, we obtain $t_{\text{permutations}}$(0,m) $= \Theta$((m+1)*(m+1)!) $= \Theta$(n*n!). ∎

Example 3.24 [Binary Search] Program 3.1 is a method to search a sorted array a for the element x. The STL algorithm binary_Search is quite similar. The variables left and right keep track of the two ends of the array segment to be searched. Initially we are to search between positions 0 and n-1. So left and right are, respectively, initialized to these values. We maintain the following invariant throughout:

x is one of a[0:n-1] iff x is one of a[left:right]

```
template<class T>
int binarySearch(T a[], int n, const T& x)
{// Search a[0] <= a[1] <= ... <= a[n-1] for x.
 // Return position if found; return -1 otherwise.
   int left = 0;                        // left end of segment
   int right = n - 1;                   // right end of segment
   while (left <= right) {
      int middle = (left + right)/2;    // middle of segment
      if (x == a[middle]) return middle;
      if (x > a[middle]) left = middle + 1;
      else right = middle - 1;
      }
   return -1; // x not found
}
```

Program 3.1 Binary search

The search begins by comparing x with the element in the middle of the segment to be searched. If x equals this element, the search terminates. If x is smaller than this element, then we need only search the left half and so right is updated to middle-1. If x is bigger than the middle element, only the right half needs to be searched and left is updated to middle+1.

Each iteration of the while loop—except the last one—results in a decrease in the size of the segment of a that has to be searched by a factor of about 2. So this loop iterates $\Theta(\log n)$ times in the worst case. As each iteration takes $\Theta(1)$ time, the overall worst-case complexity is $\Theta(\log n)$. ∎

Example 3.25 [Insertion Sort] Program 2.15 uses the insertion sort method to sort n elements. For each value of i, the innermost for loop has a worst-case complexity $\Theta(i)$. As a result, the worst-case time complexity of Program 2.15 is $\Theta(1 + 2 + 3 + \cdots + n - 1) = \Theta(n^2)$. The best-case time complexity of Program 2.15 is $\Theta(n)$. ∎

EXERCISE

18. Determine the asymptotic time complexity of the following methods. Set up a frequency table similar to Figures 3.9 through 3.12.

    (a) factorial (Program 1.29).

    (b) minmax (Program 2.24).

    (c) minmax (Program 2.25).

    (d) matrixAdd (Program 2.21).

    (e) squareMatrixMultiply (Program 2.22).

    (f) matrixMultiply (Program 2.23).

    (g) indexOfMax (Program 1.37).

    (h) polyEval (Program 2.3).

    (i) horner (Program 2.4).

    (j) rank (Program 2.5).

    (k) permutations (Program 1.32).

    (l) selectionSort (Program 2.7).

    (m) selectionSort (Program 2.12).

    (n) insertionSort (Program 2.14).

    (o) insertionSort (Program 2.15).

    (p) bubbleSort (Program 2.9).

    (q) bubbleSort (Program 2.13).

3.5   PRACTICAL COMPLEXITIES

We have seen that the time complexity of a program is generally some function of the instance characteristics. This function is very useful in determining how the time requirements vary as the instance characteristics change. We can also use the complexity function to compare two programs P and Q that perform the same task. Assume that program P has complexity $\Theta(n)$ and that program Q has complexity $\Theta(n^2)$. We can assert that program P is faster than program Q is for "sufficiently large" n. To see the validity of this assertion, observe that the actual computing time of P is bounded from above by cn for some constant c and for all n, $n \geq n_1$, while that of Q is bounded from below by dn^2 for some constant d and all n, $n \geq n_2$. Since $cn \leq dn^2$ for $n \geq c/d$, program P is faster than program Q whenever $n \geq \max\{n_1, n_2, c/d\}$.

One should always be cautiously aware of the presence of the phrase *sufficiently large* in the assertion of the preceding discussion. When deciding which of the two programs to use, we must know whether the n we are dealing with is, in fact, sufficiently large. If program P actually runs in $10^6 n$ milliseconds while program Q runs in n^2 milliseconds and if we always have $n \leq 10^6$, then program Q is the one to use.

To get a feel for how the various functions grow with n, you should study Figures 3.13 and 3.14 very closely. These figures show that 2^n grows very rapidly with n. In fact, if a program needs 2^n steps for execution, then when $n \doteq 40$, the number of steps needed is approximately $1.1*10^{12}$. On a computer performing $1,000,000,000$ steps per second, this program would require about 18.3 minutes. If $n = 50$, the same program would run for about 13 days on this computer. When $n = 60$, about 310.56 years will be required to execute the program, and when $n = 100$, about $4*10^{13}$ years will be needed. We can conclude that the utility of programs with exponential complexity is limited to small n (typically $n \leq 40$).

$\log n$	n	$n \log n$	n^2	n^3	2^n
0	1	0	1	1	2
1	2	2	4	8	4
2	4	8	16	64	16
3	8	24	64	512	256
4	16	64	256	4096	65,536
5	32	160	1024	32,768	4,294,967,296

Figure 3.13 Value of various functions

Programs that have a complexity that is a high-degree polynomial are also of limited utility. For example, if a program needs n^{10} steps, then our $1,000,000,000$ steps per second computer needs 10 seconds when $n = 10$; 3171 years when $n = 100$; and $3.17*10^{13}$ years when $n = 1000$. If the program's complexity had been n^3 steps instead, then the computer would need 1 second when $n = 1000$, 110.67 minutes when $n = 10,000$, and 11.57 days when $n = 100,000$.

Figure 3.15 gives the time that a $1,000,000,000$ instructions per second computer needs to execute a program of complexity $f(n)$ instructions. One should note that currently only the fastest computers can execute about $1,000,000,000$ instructions per second. From a practical standpoint, it is evident that for reasonably large n (say $n > 100$) only programs of small complexity (such as n, $n \log n$, n^2, and n^3)

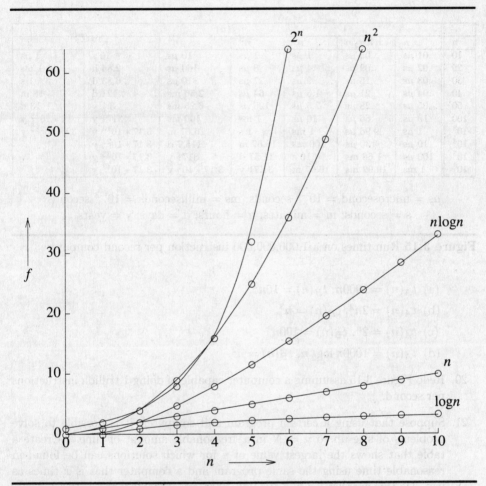

Figure 3.14 Plot of various functions

are feasible. Further, this is the case even if we could build a computer capable of executing 10^{12} instructions per second. In this case the computing times of Figure 3.15 would decrease by a factor of 1000. Now when $n = 100$, it would take 3.17 years to execute n^{10} instructions and $4 * 10^{10}$ years to execute 2^n instructions.

EXERCISES

19. Let A and B be two programs that perform the same task. Let $t_A(n)$ and $t_B(n)$, respectively, denote their run times. For each of the following pairs, find the range of n values for which program A is faster than program B.

				$f(n)$			
n	n	$n\log_2 n$	n^2	n^3	n^4	n^{10}	2^n
10	.01 μs	.03 μs	.1 μs	1 μs	10 μs	10 s	1 μs
20	.02 μs	.09 μs	.4 μs	8 μs	160 μs	2.84 h	1 ms
30	.03 μs	.15 μs	.9 μs	27 μs	810 μs	6.83 d	1 s
40	.04 μs	.21 μs	1.6 μs	64 μs	2.56 ms	121 d	18 m
50	.05 μs	.28 μs	2.5 μs	125 μs	6.25 ms	3.1 y	13 d
100	.10 μs	.66 μs	10 μs	1 ms	100 ms	3171 y	$4 * 10^{13}$ y
10^3	1 μs	9.96 μs	1 ms	1 s	16.67 m	$3.17 * 10^{13}$ y	$32 * 10^{283}$ y
10^4	10 μs	130 μs	100 ms	16.67 m	115.7 d	$3.17 * 10^{23}$ y	
10^5	100 μs	1.66 ms	10 s	11.57 d	3171 y	$3.17 * 10^{33}$ y	
10^6	1 ms	19.92 ms	16.67 m	31.71 y	$3.17 * 10^7$ y	$3.17 * 10^{43}$ y	

μs = microsecond = 10^{-6} seconds; ms = milliseconds = 10^{-3} seconds
s = seconds; m = minutes; h = hours; d = days; y = years

Figure 3.15 Run times on a 1,000,000,000 instruction per second computer

(a) $t_A(n) = 1000n$, $t_B(n) = 10n^2$.

(b) $t_A(n) = 2n^2$, $t_B(n) = n^3$.

(c) $t_A(n) = 2^n$, $t_B(n) = 100n$.

(d) $t_A(n) = 1000n\log_2 n$, $t_B(n) = n^2$.

20. Redo Figure 3.15 assuming a computer capable of doing 1 trillion instructions per second.

21. Suppose that using a certain program and computer, it is possible to solve problems of size up to $n = N$ in a "reasonable amount of time." Create a table that shows the largest value of n for which solutions can be found in reasonable time using the same program and a computer that is x times as fast. Do this exercise for $x = 10$, 100, 1000, and 1,000,000 and $t_A(n) = n$, n^2, n^3, n^5, and 2^n

3.6 REFERENCES AND SELECTED READINGS

The following books provide asymptotic analyses for several programs: *Fundamentals of Computer Algorithms* by E. Horowitz, S. Sahni, and S. Rajasekaran, W. H. Freeman and Co., New York, NY, 1998; *Introduction to Algorithms*, Second Edition, by T. Cormen, C. Leiserson, and R. Rivest, McGraw-Hill, New York, NY, 2002; and *Compared to What: An Introduction to the Analysis of Algorithms* by G. Rawlins, W. H. Freeman and Co., New York, NY, 1992.

CHAPTER 4

PERFORMANCE MEASUREMENT

BIRD'S-EYE VIEW

You can analyze and dissect all you like, but the proof of the pudding lies in the tasting. When you try to market an application code, your customer will want to know how many megabytes and seconds it's going to take to solve his/her problem on his/her computer. We can get a good handle on the memory requirements from the size of the compiled code and the size of the data space needed. The size of the data space is usually easy to figure out once you know what size instances the user is interested in solving. Determining the number of seconds the program will run requires you to actually perform experiments and measure run times. This chapter goes through the steps required to perform such an experiment.

The performance of your program depends not only on the number and type of operations you perform but also on the memory access pattern for the data and instructions in your program. Your computer has different kinds of memory—L1 cache, L2 cache, and main memory (for example)—and the time needed to access data from each is quite different. So a program with a large operation count and a small number of accesses to slow memory may take less time than a program with a small operation count and a large number of accesses to slow memory. This phenomenon is demonstrated using the matrix multiplication problem.

121

4.1   INTRODUCTION

Performance measurement is concerned with obtaining the actual space and time requirements of a program. As noted in earlier sections, these quantities are very dependent on the particular compiler and options used as well as on the specific computer on which the program is run. Unless otherwise stated, all performance values in this book were obtained using a 1.7 GHz Intel Pentium 4 PC with 512MB RAM and Microsoft Visual Studio .NET 2003. Time optimized code was generated using the statement

```
#pragma optimize(' _", on)
```

We ignore the space and time needed for compilation because each program (after it has been fully debugged) will be compiled once and then executed several times. However, the space and time needed for compilation are important during program testing when more time may be spent on this task than in actually running the compiled code.

We do not explicitly consider measuring the run-time space requirements of a program for the following reasons:

- The size of the instruction and statically allocated data space is the size of the compiled code created by the compiler. This size may be determined using operating system commands to obtain the size of the file that contains the executable code. ·

- We can get a fairly accurate estimate of the recursion stack space and the space needed by dynamically allocated variables using the analytical methods of the earlier sections.

To obtain the execution (or run) time of a program, we need a clocking mechanism. In this book, we shall use the C++ function clock(), which measures time in ticks. The constant CLOCKS_PER_SEC, which is defined in the header file time.h, gives us the number of ticks in one second. This constant is used to convert from ticks to seconds. For our system, CLOCKS_PER_SEC = 1000. So, 1 tick equals 1 millisecond. Although more accurate time measurements are possible using system functions such as QueryPerformanceCounter, the C++ function clock() is adequate for our purposes.

Suppose we wish to measure the worst-case time requirements of function insertionSort (Program 2.15). First we need to

1. Decide on the values of n for which the times are to be obtained.

2. Determine, for each of the above values of n, the data that exhibit the worst-case behavior.

4.2 CHOOSING INSTANCE SIZE

We decide on which values of n to use according to two factors: the amount of timing we want to perform and what we expect to do with the times. Suppose we want to predict how long it will take, in the worst case, to sort an array **a** of n objects using insertionSort. From Example 3.25 we know that the worst-case complexity of insertionSort is $\Theta(n^2)$; that is, it is quadratic in n. In theory, if we know the times for any three values of n, we can determine the quadratic function that describes the worst-case run time of insertionSort and we can obtain the time for all other values of n from this quadratic function. In practice, we need the times for more than three values of n for the following two reasons:

1. Asymptotic analysis tells us the behavior only for sufficiently large values of n. For smaller values of n, the run time may not follow the asymptotic curve. To determine the point beyond which the asymptotic curve is followed, we need to examine the times for several values of n.

2. Even in the region where the asymptotic behavior is exhibited, the times may not lie exactly on the predicted curve (quadratic in the case of insertionSort) because of the effects of low-order terms that are discarded in the asymptotic analysis. For instance, a program with asymptotic complexity $\Theta(n^2)$ can have an actual complexity that is $c_1 n^2 + c_2 n \log n + c_3 n + c_4$—or any other function of n in which the highest order term is $c_1 n^2$ for some constant c_1, $c_1 > 0$.

We expect the asymptotic behavior of Program 2.15 to begin for some n that is smaller than 100. So for $n > 100$ we will obtain the run time for just a few values. A reasonable choice is $n = 200, 300, 400, \cdots, 1000$. There is nothing magical about this choice of values. We can just as well use $n = 500, 1000, 1500, \cdots, 10{,}000$ or $n = 512, 1024, 2048, \cdots, 2^{15}$. The latter choices will cost us more in terms of computer time and probably will not provide any better information about the run time of our method.

For n in the range $[0, 100]$, we will carry out a more refined measurement, as we aren't quite sure where the asymptotic behavior begins. Of course, if our measurements show that the quadratic behavior doesn't begin in this range, we will have to perform a more detailed measurement in the range $[100, 200]$ and so on until we detect the onset of this behavior. Times in the range $[0, 100]$ will be obtained in steps of 10 beginning at $n = 0$.

4.3 DEVELOPING THE TEST DATA

For many programs we can generate manually or by computer the data that exhibit the best- and worst-case time complexity. The average complexity, however, is usually quite difficult to demonstrate. For insertionSort the worst-case data for any n are a decreasing sequence such as $n, n-1, n-2, \cdots, 1$. The best-case data are a sorted sequence such as 0, 1, 2, $\cdots$, $n - 1$. It is difficult to envision the data that would cause insertionSort to exhibit its average behavior.

When we are unable to develop the data that exhibit the complexity we want to measure, we can pick the least (maximum, average) measured time from some randomly generated data as an estimate of the best (worst, average) behavior.

4.4   SETTING UP THE EXPERIMENT

Having selected the instance sizes and developed the test data, we are ready to write a program that will measure the desired run times. For our insertion sort example this program takes the form given in Program 4.1. The measured times are given in Figure 4.1.

```
int main()
{
   int a[1000], step = 10;
   double clocksPerMillis = double(CLOCKS_PER_SEC) / 1000;
                    // clock ticks per millisecond

   cout << "The worst-case time, in milliseconds, are" << endl;
   cout << "n \t Time" << endl;

   // times for n = 0, 10, 20, ..., 100, 200, 300, ..., 1000
   for (int n = 0; n <= 1000; n += step)
   {
      // initialize with worst-case data
      for (int i = 0; i < n; i++)
         a[i] = n - i;

      clock_t startTime = clock( );
      insertionSort(a, n);
      double elapsedMillis = (clock( ) - startTime) / clocksPerMillis;

      cout << n << '\t' << elapsedMillis << endl;

      if (n == 100) step = 100;
   }
   return 0;
}
```

Program 4.1 Program to obtain worst-case run times for insertion sort

n	Time	n	Time
0	0	100	0
10	0	200	0
20	0	300	0
30	0	400	0
40	0	500	0
50	0	600	0
60	0	700	0
70	0	800	15
80	0	900	0
90	0	1000	0

Times are in milliseconds

Figure 4.1 Times using Program 4.1

Figure 4.1 suggests that no time is needed to sort n elements for any of the tested values of n other than $n = 800$. Furthermore, to sort 800 numbers we need 15 milliseconds in the worst case while we can sort 1000 numbers in no time. This conclusion, of course, isn't true. The problem is that the time needed for our worst-case sorts is too small for clock() to measure. Although the C++ language does not specify the accuracy of clock(), let us assume that this function is accurate to within 100 ticks, which equals 100 milliseconds on our system. Therefore, if the method returns a time of t, the actual time lies between $\max\{0, t - 100\}$ and $t + 100$. The reported time (see Figure 4.1) for $n = 1000$ is 0 milliseconds. So the actual time could be anywhere between 0 and 100 milliseconds. If we wish our measurements to be accurate to within 10 percent, clock() - startTime should be at least 1000 ticks, which equals 1 second for our system. The times in Figure 4.1 do not meet this criterion.

To improve the accuracy of our measurements, we need to repeat the sort several times for each value of n. Since the sort changes the array a, we need to initialize this array before each sort. Program 4.2 gives the new timing program. Notice that now the measured time is the time to sort plus the time to initialize a and the overhead associated with the while loop. Figure 4.2 gives the measured times, and Figure 4.3 is a plot of these times.

We can determine the overhead associated with the while loop and the initialization of the array a by running Program 4.2 without the statement

```
insertionSort(a, n);
```

Figure 4.4 gives the output from this run for selected values of n. Subtracting the overhead time from the time per sort (Figure 4.2) gives us the worst-case time for

```
int main()
{
    int a[1000], step = 10;
    double clocksPerMillis = double(CLOCKS_PER_SEC) / 1000;
                        // clock ticks per millisecond

    cout << "The worst-case time, in milliseconds, are" << endl;
    cout << "n \tRepetitions \t Total Ticks \tTime per Sort" << endl;

    // times for n = 0, 10, 20, ..., 100, 200, 300, ..., 1000
    for (int n = 0; n <= 1000; n += step)
    {
        // get time for size n
        long numberOfRepetitions = 0;
        clock_t startTime = clock( );
        do
        {
            numberOfRepetitions++;

            // initialize with worst-case data
            for (int i = 0; i < n; i++)
                a[i] = n - i;

            insertionSort(a, n);
        } while (clock( ) - startTime < 1000);
            // repeat until enough time has elapsed

        double elapsedMillis = (clock( ) - startTime) / clocksPerMillis;
        cout << n << '\t' << numberOfRepetitions << '\t' << elapsedMillis
            << '\t' << elapsedMillis / numberOfRepetitions
            << endl;

        if (n == 100) step = 100;
    }
    return 0;
}
```

Program 4.2 Program to obtain times with an accuracy of 10 percent

insertionSort as a function of n. Notice how for larger n the times of Figure 4.2 almost quadruple each time n is doubled. We expect this pattern, because the

n	Repetitions	Total Time	Time per Sort
0	6605842	1000	0.00015
10	2461486	1000	0.00041
20	1020396	1000	0.00098
30	585217	1000	0.00171
40	384720	1000	0.00260
50	262557	1000	0.00381
60	200216	1000	0.00499
70	150964	1000	0.00662
80	126457	1000	0.00791
90	99776	1000	0.01002
100	80252	1000	0.01246
200	20849	1000	0.04796
300	9527	1000	0.10497
400	5537	1000	0.18060
500	3576	1000	0.27964
600	2466	1000	0.40552
700	1870	1000	0.53476
800	1393	1000	0.71788
900	1156	1000	0.86505
1000	918	1000	1.08932

Times are in milliseconds

Figure 4.2 Output from Program 4.2

worst-case complexity is $\Theta(n^2)$.

EXERCISES

1. Why does Program 4.3 not measure run times to an accuracy of 10 percent?

2. Use Program 4.2 to obtain the worst-case run times for the two versions of insertion sort given in Programs 2.14 and 2.15. Use the same values of n as used in Program 4.2. Evaluate the relative merits of using the **insert** function versus incorporating the code for an insert directly into the sort function.

3. Use Program 4.2 to obtain the worst-case run times for the versions of bubble sort given in Programs 2.9 and 2.13. Use the same values of n as used in Program 4.2. However, you will need to verify that the worst-case data used by Program 4.2 is, in fact, worst-case data for the two bubble sort functions. Present your results as a table with three columns: n, Program 2.9, and

Figure 4.3 Plot of worst-case insertion sort times

n	Repetitions	Total Time	Overhead
0	6588805	1000	0.00015
10	6129343	1000	0.00016
50	3014729	1000	0.00033
100	2985688	1000	0.00033
500	909538	1000	0.00110
1000	482291	1000	0.00207

Times are in milliseconds

Figure 4.4 Overhead in measurements of Figure 4.2

Program 2.13. What can you say about the worst-case performance of the two bubble sorts?

4. (a) Devise worst-case data for the two versions of selection sort given in Programs 2.7 and 2.12.

   (b) Use a suitably modified version of Program 4.2 to determine the worst-case times for the two selection sort functions. Use the same values of n

```
int main()
{
   long numberOfRepetitions = 0;
   clock_t elapsedTime = 0;
   do
   {
      numberOfRepetitions++;
      clock_t startTime = clock( );

      doSomething();

      elapsedTime += clock( ) - startTime;
   } while (elapsedTime < 1000);
      // repeat until enough time has elapsed

   cout << "Time is (in ticks) "
        << ((double) elapsedTime) / numberOfRepetitions
        << endl;
   return 0;
}
```

Program 4.3 Inaccurate way to time doSomething

        as used in Program 4.2.

    (c) Present your results as a single table with three columns: n, Program 2.7, and Program 2.12.

    (d) What can you say about the worst-case performance of the two selection sorts?

5. This exercise compares the worst-case run times of insertion sort (Program 2.15) and the early-terminating versions of selection sort (Program 2.12) and bubble sort (Program 2.13). To level the playing field, rewrite Program 2.13 as a single function.

    (a) Devise data that show the worst-case behavior of each function.

    (b) Using the data of (a) and the timing program of Program 4.2, obtain worst-case run times.

    (c) Provide these times both as a single table with columns labeled n, selection sort, bubble sort, and insertion sort and as a single graph showing three curves (one for each function). The x-axis of the graph is labeled by n values, and the y-axis by time values.

(d) What conclusions can you draw about the relative worst-case performance of the three sort functions?

(e) Measure the overheads for each value of n and report these in a table as in Figure 4.4. Subtract this overhead from the times obtained in (b) and present a new table of times and a new graph.

(f) Are there any changes to your conclusions about relative performance as a result of subtracting the overhead?

(g) Using the data you have obtained, estimate the worst-case time to sort 2000; 4000; and 10,000 numbers using each sort function.

6. Modify Program 4.2 so that it obtains an estimate of the average run time of insertionSort (Program 2.15). Do the following:

(a) Sort a random permutation of the numbers 0, 1, ⋯, n-1 on each iteration of the while loop. This permutation is generated using a random permutation generator. In case you don't have such a function available, try to write one using a random number generator, or simply generate a random sequence of n numbers.

(b) Set the while loop so that at least 20 random permutations are sorted and so that at least 1 second has elapsed.

(c) Estimate the average sort time by dividing the elapsed time by the number of permutations sorted.

Present the estimated average times as a table.

7. Use the strategy of Exercise 6 to estimate the average run times of the bubble sort functions given in Programs 2.9 and 2.13. Use the same values of n as in Program 4.2. Present your results as a table and as a graph.

8. Use the strategy of Exercise 6 to estimate the average run times of the selection sort functions given in Programs 2.7 and 2.12. Use the same values of n as in Program 4.2. Present your results as a table and as a graph.

9. Use the strategy of Exercise 6 to estimate and compare the average run times of the functions of Programs 2.12, 2.13, and 2.15. Use the same values of n as in Program 4.2. Present your results as a table and as a graph.

10. Devise experiments to determine the average time taken by sequential search (Program 2.1) and binary search (Program 3.1) to perform a successful search. Assume that each element of the array being searched is looked for with equal probability. Present your results as a table and as a graph.

11. Devise experiments to determine the worst-case time taken by sequential search (Program 2.1) and binary search (Program 3.1) to perform a successful search. Present your results as a table and as a graph.

12. Determine the run time of function `matrixAdd` (Program 2.21) for `rows` = 10, 20, 30, $\cdots$, 100. Present your measured times as a table and as a graph.

13. C++ has a sort function `sort(begin,end)` that may be used to sort the array `a[0:n-1]` using the invocation `sort(a, a+n)`. This sort function, which is defined in the header `algorithm`, uses a combination of the insertion sort, quick sort (Section 18.2.3) and heap sort (Section 12.6.1) methods. The complexity of the C++ function `sort` is $O(n \log n)$. Measure the time C++'s sort function takes on best- and worst-case insertion sort data. Compare these times with those for Program 2.15.

14. Determine the run time of function `transpose` (Program 2.19) for `rows` = 10, 20, 30, $\cdots$, 100. Present your measured times as a table and as a graph.

15. Determine the run time of function `squareMatrixMultiply` (Program 2.22) for `rows` = 10, 20, 30, $\cdots$, 100. Present your measured times as a table and as a graph.

4.5   YOUR CACHE AND YOU

4.5.1   A Simple Computer Model

Consider a simple computer model in which the computer's memory consists of an L1 (level 1) cache, an L2 cache, and main memory. Arithmetic and logical operations are performed by the arithmetic and logic unit (ALU) on data resident in registers (R). Figure 4.5 gives a block diagram for our simple computer model.

Figure 4.5 A simple computer model

Typically, the size of main memory is tens or hundreds of megabytes; L2 cache sizes are typically a fraction of a megabyte; L1 cache is usually in the tens of kilobytes; and the number of registers is between 8 and 32. When you start your program, all your data are in main memory.

To perform an arithmetic operation such as an add, in our computer model, the data to be added are first loaded from memory into registers, the data in the registers are added, and the result is written to memory.

Let one cycle be the length of time it takes to add data that are already in registers. The time needed to load data from L1 cache to a register is two cycles in our model. If the required data are not in L1 cache but are in L2 cache, we get an L1 cache miss and the required data are copied from L2 cache to L1 cache and the register in 10 cycles. When the required data are not in L2 cache either, we have an L2 cache miss and the required data are copied from main memory into L2 cache, L1 cache, and the register in 100 cycles. The write operation is counted as one cycle even when the data are written to main memory because we do not wait for the write to complete before proceeding to the next operation.

4.5.2   Effect of Cache Misses on Run Time

For our simple model, the statement `a = b + c` is compiled into the computer instructions

```
load a; load b; add; store c;
```

where the `load` operations load data into registers and the `store` operation writes the result of the `add` to memory. The `add` and the `store` together take two cycles. The two `load`s may take anywhere from 4 cycles to 200 cycles depending on whether we get no cache miss, L1 misses, or L2 misses. So the total time for the statement `a = b + c` varies from 6 cycles to 202 cycles. In practice, the variation in time is not as extreme because we can overlap the time spent on successive cache misses.

Suppose that we have two algorithms that perform the same task. The first algorithm does 2000 adds that require 4000 `load`, 2000 add, and 2000 `store` operations and the second algorithm does 1000 adds. The data access pattern for the first algorithm is such that 25 percent of the `load`s result in an L1 miss and another 25 percent result in an L2 miss. For our simplistic computer model, the time required by the first algorithm is $2000 * 2$ (for the 50 percent `load`s that cause no cache miss) $+ 1000 * 10$ (for the 25 percent `load`s that cause an L1 miss) $+ 1000 * 100$ (for the 25 percent `load`s that cause an L2 miss) $+ 2000 * 1$ (for the adds) $+ 2000 * 1$ (for the stores) $= 118,000$ cycles. If the second algorithm has 100 percent L2 misses, it will take $2000 * 100$ (L2 misses) $+ 1000 * 1$ (adds) $+ 1000 * 1$ (stores) $= 202,000$ cycles. So the second algorithm, which does half the work done by the first, actually takes 76 percent more time than is taken by the first algorithm.

Computers use a number of strategies (such as preloading data that will be needed in the near future into cache, and when a cache miss occurs, the needed data as well as data in some number of adjacent bytes are loaded into cache) to reduce the number of cache misses and hence reduce the run time of a program. These strategies are most effective when successive computer operations use adjacent bytes of main memory.

Although our discussion has focused on how cache is used for data, computers also use cache to reduce the time needed to access instructions.

4.5.3   Matrix Multiplication

This section is for the skeptics among you who do not believe that on a commercial computer, a program that performs more operations may actually take less time than another program that performs fewer operations. We are about to make a believer out of you.

Program 2.22 is the real program we start with. This program multiplies two square matrices that are represented as two-dimensional arrays. It performs the following computation:

$$c[i][j] = \sum_{k=1}^{n} a[i][k] * b[k][j], \ 1 \le i \le n, \ 1 \le j \le n \qquad (4.1)$$

(You don't need to understand matrix multiplication to follow this demonstration. Matrix multiplication is motivated in Section 7.2.1.) Program 2.22 is a fairly standard piece of code that you can find in many books. Program 4.4 is an alternative code that produces the same two-dimensional array c as is produced by Program 2.22. We observe that Program 4.4 has two nested **for** loops that are not present in Program 2.22 and does more work than is done by Program 2.22 with respect to indexing into the array c. The remainder of the work is the same.

```
void fastSquareMatrixMultiply(int ** a, int ** b, int ** c, int n)
{
    for (int i = 0; i < n; i++)
        for (int j = 0; j < n; j++)
            c[i][j] = 0;

    for (int i = 0; i < n; i++)
        for (int j = 0; j < n; j++)
            for (int k = 0; k < n; k++)
                c[i][j] += a[i][k] * b[k][j];
}
```

Program 4.4 Less efficient way than Program 2.22 to multiply square matrices

You will notice that if you permute the order of the three nested **for** loops in Program 4.4, you do not affect the result array c. We refer to the loop order in Program 4.4 as ijk order. When we swap the second and third **for** loops, we get ikj order. In all, there are 3! = 6 ways in which we can order the three nested **for** loops. All six orderings result in functions that perform exactly the same number of operations of each type. So you might think all six take the same time. Not so. By changing the order of the loops, we change the data access pattern and so change the number of cache misses. This in turn affects the run time.

In ijk order, we access the elements of a and c by rows; the elements of b are accessed by column. Since elements in the same row are in adjacent memory and elements in the same column are far apart in memory, the accesses of b are likely to result in many L2 cache misses when the matrix size is too large for the three arrays to fit into L2 cache. In ikj order, the elements of a, b, and c are accessed by rows. Therefore, ikj order is likely to result in fewer L2 cache misses and so has the potential to take much less time than taken by ijk order.

Figure 4.6 gives the run time for Program 4.4 using ijk and ikj order as well as for Program 2.22. Figure 4.7 shows the normalized run times (i.e., the time taken by a method divided by the time taken by ikj order).

| | Program 2.22 | Program 4.4 | |
n	mult	ijk order	ikj order
500	1.5	2.6	0.9
1000	16.1	26.5	6.7
2000	719.8	844.6	54.2

Figure 4.6 Run times (in seconds) for matrix multiplication

What a surprise: ikj order runs much faster than both ijk order and Program 2.22! In fact, when $n = 500$, ikj order takes about 1/3rd the time taken by ijk order and about 1/2 that taken by Program 2.22. When $n = 1000$, these ratios are approximately 7/16 and 1/4; and when $n = 2000$, the ratios are approximately 1/13 and 1/16. Recall that ikj order does more work (as measured by the operation count) than is done by Program 2.22 and the same as is done by ijk order. Only the run time for ikj order grows at the $\Theta(n^3)$ rate predicted by an asymptotic analysis. The run time for ijk order and Program 2.22, for the tested values of n, is dominated by effects (such as cache misses) other than the operation count. Are you still skeptical?

The effect that memory hierarchy has on the performance of your code varies with the programming language, compiler, compiler options, and computer configuration. For example, when our matrix multiply codes were run on a 2.4 GHz Intel Pentium IV PC that has twice as much L2 cache as does the 1.7 GHz PC used in the experiment of Figures 4.6 and 4.7, the ratios for $n = 500$ were about 9/16 and 2/5. For $n = 1000$, the ratios were about 1/2 and 1/3; and for $n = 2000$, the ratios were about 1/4 and 1/5.

Figure 4.7 Normalized run times for matrix multiplication

EXERCISES

16. Repeat the experiment of Figure 4.6 using all six orderings of the three nested `for` loops of Program 4.4. Present your results as a table and as a bar chart.

17. In an alternative implementation of matrix multiplication, we first compute the transpose array $bt[j][k] = b[k][j]$. Equation 4.1 becomes

$$c[i][j] = \sum_{k=1}^{n} a[i][k] * bt[j][k], \ 1 \le i \le m, \ 1 \le j \le p \qquad (4.2)$$

(a) Write functions to compute the two-dimensional array `c` by first computing `bt` and then using Equation 4.2. You should have seven functions: one for each of the six permutations of the three nested `for` loops and one that corresponds to Program 2.22.

(b) Measure the time taken by these seven functions for the cases $n = 500$, 1000, and 2000.

(c) Present your results as a table and as a bar chart. Compare these times with those of Exercise 16.

18. Write a function to transpose an $n \times n$ array by blocks. That is, imagine that the array is partitioned into $k \times k$ subarrays (or blocks) and transpose one subarray at a time. Measure the run time of your transpose code for large n; use $k = 2, 4, 8, 16, 32,$ and 64; assume that n is a power of 2. How does the performance of your code compare with that of the transpose code of Program 2.19. Can you explain the relative performance?

4.6   REFERENCES AND SELECTED READINGS

To learn more about how a cache works, see *Computer Organization and Design*, by J. Hennessey and D. Patterson, Second Edition, Morgan Kaufmann Publishers, Inc., San Francisco, CA, 1998, Chapter 7.

CHAPTER 5

LINEAR LISTS—ARRAY REPRESENTATION

BIRD'S-EYE VIEW

We are now ready to begin the study of data structures, which continues through Chapter 16 of this book. Although Chapters 5 and 6 focus on the data structure *linear list*, their primary purpose is to introduce the different ways in which data may be represented or stored in a computer's memory as well as on a disk. In succeeding chapters we study the representation of other popular data structures such as matrices, stacks, queues, dictionaries, priority queues, tournament trees, search trees, and graphs.

The common data representation methods used by C++ programs are array based and linked (or pointer based). The data structure *linear list* is used to illustrate these representation methods. The current chapter develops the array representation of a linear list and Chapter 6 develops the linked representation of a linear list.

The STL's containers—`vector` and `list`—are roughly equivalent to our array and (doubly) linked representations of a linear list; the STL classes have many additional methods though. In our development of the array and linked representations of a linear list, we have used the same function/method names and similar signatures as used by the STL implementations. This approach will enable you to switch easily to the STL implementations.

137

In an array representation, elements are stored in an array; a mathematical formula is used to determine where to store each element. This formula gives the array index where the element resides. In the simplest cases the formula stores successive elements of a list in successive memory locations, and we obtain what is commonly known as the sequential representation of a list.

The data structure concepts introduced in this chapter are

- Abstract data types and their specification as C++ abstract classes.

- Linear lists.

- Changing array length (i.e., number of positions in the array) and array doubling.

- Array representation.

- Data structure iterators.

The C++ concepts developed in this chapter are

- Abstract classes.

- Iterators.

No new array applications are introduced in this chapter because several array applications were developed in Chapters 1 through 3.

5.1   DATA OBJECTS AND STRUCTURES

A **data object** is a set of *instances* or *values*. Some examples are

1. *boolean* = {*false, true*}

2. *digit* = {0, 1, 2, 3, 4, 5, 6, 7, 8, 9}

3. *letter* = {A, B, C, ⋯, Z, a, b, ⋯, z}

4. *naturalNumber* = {0, 1, 2, ⋯}

5. *integer* = {0, ±1, ±2, ±3, ⋯}

6. *string* = {a, b, ⋯, aa, ab, ac, ⋯}

boolean, digit, letter, naturalNumber, integer, and *string* are data objects. *true* and *false* are the instances of *boolean*, while 0, 1, ⋯, and 9 are the instances of *digit*. We may regard the individual instances of a data object as being either **primitive** (or **atomic**) or composed of instances of another (possibly the same) data object. In the latter case we use the term **element** to refer to the individual components of an instance of an object.

For example, each instance of the data object *NaturalNumber* can be regarded as atomic. In this case we are not concerned with a further decomposition of the instances of this data object. Another view is to regard each instance of a *naturalNumber* as being composed of several instances of the data object *digit*. In this view the number 675 comprises the digits 6, 7, and 5 (in that order).

The data object *string* is the set of all possible string instances. Each instance of a string is composed of characters. Some examples of instances are *good, a trip to Hawaii, going down hill,* and *abcabcdabcde*. The first string has the four elements *g, o, o,* and *d* (in that order). Each element is an instance of the data object *Letter*.

The instances of a data object as well as the elements that constitute individual instances are generally related in some way. For example, the natural number 0 is the smallest natural number; 1 is the next; and 2 is the next. In the natural number 675, the most significant digit is 6, the next is 7, and 5 is the least significant digit. In the string *good*, *g* is the first letter, *o* the second and third, and *d* the last.

In addition to interrelationships, a set of operations (or functions) is generally associated with any data object. These operations may transform one instance of an object into another instance of that object, or into an instance of another data object, or do both these transformations. The operation could simply create a new instance without transforming the instances from which the new one is created. For example, the operation *add* defined on the natural numbers creates a new natural number that is the sum of the two numbers to be added; the two numbers that get added are unaltered.

A **data structure** is a data object together with the relationships that exist among the instances and among the individual elements that compose an instance. These relationships are provided by specifying the operations of interest.

When we study data structures, we are concerned with the representation of data objects (actually of the instances) as well as the implementation of the operations of interest for the data objects. The representation of each data object should facilitate an efficient[1] implementation of the operations.

The most frequently used data objects together with their frequently used operations are already implemented in C++ as primitive data types. The data objects *integer* (int) and *boolean* (bool), defined above, fall into this category. All other data objects can be represented using the primitive data types and the grouping ability provided by the class, array, and pointer features of C++. Many of the data objects we shall study in this text (for example, linear list, stack, queue, and priority queue) have been implemented as classes in the STL.

5.2   THE LINEAR LIST DATA STRUCTURE

Each instance of the data structure **linear list** (or **ordered list**) is an ordered collection of elements. Each instance is of the form $(e_0, e_1, \cdots, e_{n-1})$ where n is a finite natural number; the e_i items are the elements of the list; the **index** of e_i is i; and n is the list **length** or **size**. The elements may be viewed as atomic, as their individual structure is not relevant to the structure of the list. When $n = 0$, the list is **empty**. When $n > 0$, e_0 is the **zeroth** (or **front**) element and e_{n-1} is the **last** element of the list. We say that e_0 **comes before** (or precedes) e_1, e_1 comes before e_2, and so on. Other than this precedence relation, no other structure exists in a linear list.

Some examples of linear lists are (1) an alphabetized (i.e., ordered by name) list of students in a class; (2) a list of exam scores in nondecreasing order; (3) an alphabetized list of members of Congress; and (4) a list of gold-medal winners in the Olympics men's basketball event ordered by year. With these examples in mind, we see the need to perform the following operations on a linear list:

- Create a linear list.

- Destroy a linear list.

- Determine whether the list is empty.

- Determine the size of the list.

- Find the element with a given index.

- Find the index of a given element.

- Delete, erase or remove an element given its index.

- Insert a new element so that it has a given index.

---

[1]The term *efficient* is used here in a very liberal sense. It includes performance efficiency as well as measures of the complexity of development and maintenance of associated software.

• Output the list elements in order, left to right.

5.2.1   The Abstract Data Type *linearList*

A linear list may be specified as an **abstract data type** (ADT) in which we provide a specification of the instances as well as of the operations that are to be performed (see ADT 5.1). The ADT specification is independent of any representation and programming language we have in mind. All representations of the ADT must satisfy the specification, and the specification becomes a way to validate the representation. In addition, all representations that satisfy the specification may be used interchangeably in applications of the data type. In ADT 5.1 we have omitted specifying operations to create and destroy instances of the data type. All ADT specifications implicitly include an operation to create an empty instance and, optionally, an operation to destroy an instance.

AbstractDataType *linearList*
{

   instances
       ordered finite collections of zero or more elements

   operations
       empty() : return **true** if the list is empty, **false** otherwise

       size() : return the list size (i.e., number of elements in the list)

       get(index): return the *index*th element of the list

       indexOf(x): return the index of the first occurrence of *x* in the list,
                   return −1 if *x* is not in the list

       erase(index): remove/delete the *index*th element, elements with higher index have their index reduced by 1

       insert(index, x): insert *x* as the *index*th element, elements with index ≥ *index* have their index increased by 1

       output(): output the list elements from left to right

}

ADT 5.1 Abstract data type specification of a linear list

5.2.2   The Abstract Class `LinearList`

C++ supports two types of classes—abstract and concrete. An abstract class is a class that contains a member function for which no implementation has been specified. Such a function, called a *pure virtual function*, is specified using the zero initializer as in

```
virtual int myPureVirtualFunction(int x) = 0;
```

A concrete class contains no pure virtual function. Only concrete classes may be instantiated. That is, we may create an instance or object only of a concrete class. However, we can create pointers to objects of an abstract class.

Rather than use the informal English approach to specify an ADT as in ADT 5.1, we may use a C++ abstract class as in Program 5.1.

```cpp
template<class T>
class linearList
{
    public:
        virtual ~linearList() {}
        virtual bool empty() const = 0;
                // return true iff list is empty
        virtual int size() const = 0;
                // return number of elements in list
        virtual T& get(int theIndex) const = 0;
                // return element whose index is theIndex
        virtual int indexOf(const T& theElement) const = 0;
                // return index of first occurence of theElement
        virtual void erase(int theIndex) = 0;
                // remove the element whose index is theIndex
        virtual void insert(int theIndex, const T& theElement) = 0;
                // insert theElement so that its index is theIndex
        virtual void output(ostream& out) const = 0;
                // insert list into stream out
};
```

Program 5.1 Abstract class specification of a linear list

Although the specification of Program 5.1 is quite similar to that of ADT 5.1, this specification is programming-language dependent. In particular, many of the keywords we have used are defined only in C++. Since a class that derives from or extends an abstract class is itself abstract (and so cannot be instantiated) unless it provides an implementation for all pure virtual functions of the base class, by requiring that every ADT implementation be derived from the abstract class for that ADT, we ensure a complete and consistent (i.e., with the same public functions) implementation of the ADT.

We provide a virtual destructor for our abstract class so that when a reference to a linear list goes out of scope, the default destructor for linear list isn't invoked; rather the destructor for the true data type of the referenced object is invoked.

EXERCISE

1. Let $L = (a, b, c, d)$ be a linear list. What is the result of each of the following operations?

   (a) $empty()$

   (b) $size()$

   (c) $get(0)$, $get(2)$, $get(6)$, $get(-3)$

   (d) $indexOf(a)$, $indexOf(c)$, $indexOf(q)$

   (e) $erase(0)$, $erase(2)$, $erase(3)$

   (f) $insert(0, e)$, $insert(2, f)$, $insert(3, g)$, $insert(4, h)$, $insert(6, h)$, $insert(-3, h)$

5.3   ARRAY REPRESENTATION

5.3.1   The Representation

In an **array representation**, we use an array to store the list elements. Although we can pack several list instances into a single array (see Section 5.5), it is easier to use a different array for each instance. Individual elements of an instance are located in the array using a mathematical formula.

Suppose we decide to use a one-dimensional `element` to store the elements of a linear list. The array `element` has positions (or locations) `element[0]` $\cdots$ `element[arrayLength-1]`, where `arrayLength` is the length or capacity of the array. Each array position can be used to store a single list element. We need to map the elements of the list to positions in the array. Where does the zeroth element reside? Where does the last element reside? The most natural mapping uses the formula

$$location(i) = i \tag{5.1}$$

Equation 5.1 states that the ith element of the list (if it exists) is stored in position i of the array. Figure 5.1(a) shows how the list [5, 2, 4, 8, 1] is stored in the array `element` using the mapping of Equation 5.1. The length of the array is 10, and the size of the list is 5.

(a) *location* $(i)=i$

(b) *location* $(i)=9-i$

(c) *location* $(i)=(7+i)\%10$

Figure 5.1 Different ways to map [5, 2, 4, 8, 1] into a one-dimensional array

Although Equation 5.1 is a natural choice for a formula to map list elements into array positions, other choices are possible. For example, the formula

$$location(i) = \texttt{arrayLength} - i - 1 \tag{5.2}$$

stores the list elements backwards beginning at the right end of the array element, and the formula

$$location(i) = (location(0) + i)\%\texttt{arrayLength} \tag{5.3}$$

stores elements beginning at any position in the array and wraps around to the front of the array, if necessary, to store the remaining elements. Figure 5.1(b) shows how the list [5, 2, 4, 8, 1] is stored when Equation 5.2 is used, and Figure 5.1(c) shows how this list is stored using Equation 5.3 and $location(0) = 7$. Equation 5.3 is used in Chapter 9 to map a queue into a one-dimensional array.

In our array representation of a linear list, we use a one-dimensional array element that holds the list elements as per Equation 5.1, a variable listSize that keeps track of the number of elements currently in the list, and a variable array-Length that keeps track of the capacity of the array element. We may remove element e_i from the list by moving elements to its right down by 1. For example, to remove the element $e_1 = 2$ from the list of Figure 5.1(a), we have to move the elements $e_2 = 4$, $e_3 = 8$, and $e_4 = 1$, which are to the right of e_1, to positions 1, 2, and 3 of the array `element`. Figure 5.2(a) shows the result. The shaded elements were moved.

(a) 2 removed from `element[1]`, `listSize` = 4

(b) 7 inserted at `element[2]`, `listSize` = 5

Figure 5.2 Removing and inserting an element

To insert an element so that it becomes element i of a list, we must first move the existing element e_i (if any) and all elements to its right one position right and then put the new element into position i of the array. For example, to insert 7 as the second element of the list of Figure 5.2(a), we first move elements e_2 and e_3 to the right by 1 and then put 7 into position 2 of the array. Figure 5.2(b) shows the result. The shaded elements were moved.

Before we can write an array class that implements the ADT *linearList*, we must decide on the data type of the array `element` and the length of this array. By making our linear list class a template class, we avoid having to make the first decision. For the second decision, we note that the array `element` must be large enough to hold the maximum number of elements that might be in the list at any time. This maximum number is often difficult to estimate. To overcome this hurdle, we can ask the user to provide an estimate and then dynamically increase the length of the array `element` in case the user underestimated.

5.3.2 Changing the Length of a One-Dimensional Array

To increase or decrease the length of a one-dimensional array `a` that contains elements in positions `a[0:n-1]`, we first define an array of the new length, then copy the `n` elements from `a` to the new array, and finally change the value of `a` so that it references the new array. Program 5.2 gives the method `changeLength1D`, which performs these three tasks.

It takes $\Theta(1)$ time to create an array of length m. Notice that the invocation of `new` to create the new array may cause a `bad_alloc` exception to be thrown. If `new` is successful in creating the new array, Program 5.2 spends $\Theta(n)$ time copying elements from the source array into the destination array. Therefore, the complexity of Program 5.2 is $O(n) = O(n)$.

```
template<class T>
void changeLength1D(T*& a, int oldLength, int newLength)
{
   if (newLength < 0)
      throw illegalParameterValue("new length must be >= 0");

   T* temp = new T[newLength];              // new array
   int number = min(oldLength, newLength);  // number to copy
   copy(a, a + number, temp);
   delete [] a;                             // deallocate old memory
   a = temp;
}
```

Program 5.2 Changing the length of a one-dimensional array

When an array is used to represent a data structure whose size increases dynamically, the array length is often doubled whenever the array becomes full. This process is referred to as **array doubling**. When array doubling is used, the total time spent changing the array length is (in an asymptotic sense) no more than the total time spent inserting elements into the data structure (see Theorem 5.1).

5.3.3   The Class arrayList

Class Definition for arrayList

We define a C++ class arrayList that implements the ADT *linearList* using Equation 5.1. Program 5.3 gives the class header, the data members, and the function/method prototypes. Since arrayList is to be a concrete class that extends the abstract class linearList, it must provide an implementation of all the methods of the abstract class linearList. The class arrayList may, however, contain methods that are not declared in linearList. Our class, for example, contains the methods capacity and checkIndex that are not declared in linearList. The method capacity, gives the current length of the array element while the method checkIndex verifies that a specified element index is in the permissible range 0 through listSize − 1.

Constructor and Copy Constructor for arrayList

Program 5.4 gives the class constructor as well as the copy constructor. The constructor creates an array whose length is initialCapacity; the default value for this length is 10. Also, it sets arrayLength to initialCapacity and listSize to 0. The copy constructor makes a copy or clone of an object. This constructor is invoked, for example, when an object is passed by value to a function as well as

```
template<class T>
class arrayList : public linearList<T>
{
   public:
      // constructor, copy constructor and destructor
      arrayList(int initialCapacity = 10);
      arrayList(const arrayList<T>&);
      ~arrayList() {delete [] element;}

      // ADT methods
      bool empty() const {return listSize == 0;}
      int size() const {return listSize;}
      T& get(int theIndex) const;
      int indexOf(const T& theElement) const;
      void erase(int theIndex);
      void insert(int theIndex, const T& theElement);
      void output(ostream& out) const;

      // additional method
      int capacity() const {return arrayLength;}

   protected:
      void checkIndex(int theIndex) const;
            // throw illegalIndex if theIndex invalid
      T* element;              // 1D array to hold list elements
      int arrayLength;         // capacity of the 1D array
      int listSize;            // number of elements in list
};
```

Program 5.3 Class definition for arrayList

when a function returns an object. Our code for this constructor employs the STL algorithm copy (see Section 1.8).

Program 5.4 also gives the code for the empty, size, and capacity functions. If we assume that the complexity of the new operator is $O(1)$, we see that the complexity of the constructor is $O(1)$ when T is a primitive data type of C++ (e.g., int, float, and so on). When T is a user-defined data type, the complexity of the constructor is $O(\text{initialCapacity})$. This is so because when the array element is created, the constructor for the user-defined data type T is invoked for each position of the array. The complexity of empty, size, and capacity methods is $O(1)$ and that of the copy constructor is $O(n)$, where n is the size of the list that is to be

```
template<class T>
arrayList<T>::arrayList(int initialCapacity)
{// Constructor.
   if (initialCapacity < 1)
   {ostringstream s;
    s << "Initial capacity = " << initialCapacity << " Must be > 0";
    throw illegalParameterValue(s.str());
   }
   arrayLength = initialCapacity;
   element = new T[arrayLength];
   listSize = 0;
}

template<class T>
arrayList<T>::arrayList(const arrayList<T>& theList)
{// Copy constructor.
   arrayLength = theList.arrayLength;
   listSize = theList.listSize;
   element = new T[arrayLength];
   copy(theList.element, theList.element + listSize, element);
}
```

Program 5.4 Constructors for `arrayList`

copied.

Instantiating `arrayList`

Linear lists that are represented as arrays may be created/instantiated using statements similar to those given below.

```
// create two linear lists with initial capacity 100
linearList *x = (linearList) new arrayList<int>(100);
arrayList<double> y(100);

// create a linear list with the default initial capacity
arrayList<char> z;

// create a linear list that is a copy of the list y
arrayList<double> w(y);
```

Elementary Methods of `arrayList`

Program 5.5 gives the implementation of the `checkIndex`, `get` and `indexOf` methods. The code for the `indexOf` method uses the STL function `find` that searches a range for the first occurrence of a matching element.

```
template<class T>
void arrayList<T>::checkIndex(int theIndex) const
{// Verify that theIndex is between 0 and listSize - 1.
   if (theIndex < 0 || theIndex >= listSize)
   {ostringstream s;
    s << "index = " << theIndex << " size = " << listSize;
    throw illegalIndex(s.str());
   }

}

template<class T>
T& arrayList<T>::get(int theIndex) const
{// Return element whose index is theIndex.
 // Throw illegalIndex exception if no such element.
   checkIndex(theIndex);
   return element[theIndex];
}

template<class T>
int arrayList<T>::indexOf(const T& theElement) const
{// Return index of first occurrence of theElement.
 // Return -1 if theElement not in list.

   // search for theElement
   int theIndex = (int) (find(element, element + listSize, theElement)
                          - element);

   // check if theElement was found
   if (theIndex == listSize)
     // not found
     return -1;
   else return theIndex;
}
```

Program 5.5 `checkIndex`, `get` and `indexOf`

The complexity of checkIndex and get is $\Theta(1)$ and that of indexOf is $O(\max\{$listSize, $1\})$. For simplicity, we will often write complexities of this latter form as $O($listSize$)$.

Removing an Element

To remove or delete the theIndexth element from a list, we need to first ascertain that the list contains an element with this index and then delete this element. If the list does not have a theIndexth element, an exception occurs because the ADT *linearList* (ADT 5.1) doesn't tell us what to do at this time. Therefore, we throw an exception of type illegalIndex.

When there is a theIndexth element, we can perform the deletion by using the copy algorithm to move elements theIndex+1, theIndex+2, $\cdots$, listSize-1 down (left) one position and reducing the value of listSize by 1. Function erase (Program 5.6) implements the delete/remove operation.

```
template<class T>
void arrayList<T>::erase(int theIndex)
{// Delete the element whose index is theIndex.
 // Throw illegalIndex exception if no such element.
   checkIndex(theIndex);

   // valid index, shift elements with higher index
   copy(element + theIndex + 1, element + listSize,.
                                element + theIndex);

   element[--listSize].~T(); // invoke destructor
}
```

Program 5.6 Remove the theIndexth element

When there is no theIndexth element, an exception is thrown and the time taken by erase is $\Theta(1)$. When the list has a theIndexth element, listSize-theIndex elements are moved, taking $\Theta($listSize-theIndex$)$ time (assuming each element move takes $O(1)$ time). Hence the overall complexity is $O($listSize-theIndex$)$.

Inserting an Element

To insert a new element as the theIndexth element in the list, we need to first move elements theIndex through listSize-1 one position up (right), then insert the new element in position theIndex, and finally increment listSize by 1. This upward move of elements is accomplished using the copy_backward STL function rather than the copy function. The copy_backward function moves elements beginning with the rightmost one that is to be moved. Program 5.7 gives the complete C++ code to insert an element. As you can see, the method doubles the length of the array **element** in case the array has no space to accommodate the new element that is to be inserted.

```
template<class T>
void arrayList<T>::insert(int theIndex, const T& theElement)
{// Insert theElement so that its index is theIndex.
   if (theIndex < 0 || theIndex > listSize)
   {// invalid index
      ostringstream s;
      s << "index = " << theIndex << " size = " << listSize;
      throw illegalIndex(s.str());
   }

   // valid index, make sure we have space
   if (listSize == arrayLength)
      {// no space, double capacity
         changeLength1D(element, arrayLength, 2 * arrayLength);
         arrayLength *= 2;
      }

   // shift elements right one position
   copy_backward(element + theIndex, element + listSize,
                 element + listSize + 1);

   element[theIndex] = theElement;

   listSize++;
}
```

Program 5.7 Insert theElement as theIndexth element

It takes $\Theta(1)$ time to determine whether an exception is to be thrown, $\Theta(\text{array-Length}) = \Theta(\text{listSize})$ time to double the array length if this doubling is necessary, and $\Theta(\text{listSize-theIndex})$ time to shift elements. Therefore, the total time taken by insert is $O(\text{listSize})$.

Why do we double the array length in Program 5.7 and not simply increase the length by 1 or 2 (say)? Although increasing the array length by 1 or 2 every time does not affect the worst-case complexity of an insert (this worst-case complexity remains $\Theta(\text{listSize})$), increasing array length in this way can affect the asymptotic complexity of a sequence of inserts. Suppose we start with an empty list with initial capacity 1 and perform $n = 2^k + 1$ inserts. Assume that the inserts are performed at the end of the list. Therefore, no insert requires a shift of previously inserted elements and the time required to make the n inserts is $\Theta(n)$ plus the time spent increasing the array length. When the array length is always increased by 1, the time spent increasing the array length is $\Theta(\sum_{i=1}^{n-1} i) = \Theta(n^2)$. Therefore, the total time needed for the n inserts is $\Theta(n^2)$.

If we double the array length as is done in Program 5.7, the total time spent changing the array length is $\Theta(\sum_{i=0}^{k} 2^i) = \Theta(2^{k+1} - 1) = \Theta(n)$. Therefore, the complexity of the n inserts is $\Theta(n)$. In fact, a simple generalization of this analysis shows that when the array length is always increased by a multiplicative factor (from arrayLength to $c*$arrayLength, where $c > 1$ is a constant), the total time spent increasing the array length is O(number of inserts) even if erase and other operations are mixed in with the insert operations. This analysis leads to Theorem 5.1.

Theorem 5.1 *If we always increase the array length by a constant factor (which is 2 in Program 5.7), the time spent on any sequence of linear list operations increases by at most a constant factor when compared to the time taken for the same set of operations under the assumption that the initial capacity is not an underestimate (note that when this assumption is valid, no time is spent increasing the array length).*

The Function output and Overloading <<

Program 5.8 gives the code for output. The complexity of this code is $O(\text{listSize})$ under the assumption that the time to needed to insert a single element into the output stream is $O(1)$. Program 5.8 also gives the code to overload the stream insertion operator <<.

```
template<class T>
void arrayList<T>::output(ostream& out) const
{// Put the list into the stream out.
    copy(element, element + listSize, ostream_iterator<T>(cout, "  "));
}

// overload <<
template <class T>
ostream& operator<<(ostream& out, const arrayList<T>& x)
    {x.output(out); return out;}
```

Program 5.8 Inserting a linear list into an output stream

Decreasing the Length of `element`

Although our implementation of a linear list increases the length of `element` as needed, it never reduces its length. Therefore, an array linear list whose element array has grown to a length of 1,000,000 (say) will hold on to this much array space until the linear list is destroyed. This status continues even though the list may never again have more than 10 elements in it.

To enable the linear list to free some of the array space when the list size becomes small, we can modify the method `erase` so that it reduces the array length to max{`initialCapacity`, `length/2`} whenever `size` < `length/4` (say). This strategy is considered in Exercise 20.

Using the Class `arrayList`

A sample `main` method and the generated output can be found on the Web site for this book.

5.3.4   Iterators in C++

An **iterator** is a pointer to an element of an object (for example, a pointer to an element of an array). As the name suggests, an iterator permits you to go (or iterate) through the elements of the object one by one. Program 5.9 shows how to use a pointer `y` to an array element to iterate through the array's elements. The datatype of the pointer `y` is `int*`, which indicates that `y` points to elements of type `int`. In the `for` loop header, `y` is initialized to point to the first element in the array `x[]` (technically, the variable `x` is a pointer to the first element of the array). The expression `y++` increments the pointer so that it advances to the next element of the array. Similarly, `x + 3` is a pointer 3 positions from `x`; that is, it points one position past the last element `x[2]` of the array. So in the `for` loop of Program 5.9 the pointer (or iterator) `y` iterates through elements in the range [x, x + 3). The expression `*y` dereferences the pointer `y` so as to get the element pointed to by `y`. The program outputs `x[0:2]`.

The following code is equivalent to the `for` loop of Program 5.9.

```
for (int i = 0; i != 3; i++)
   cout << x[i] << "   ";
```

Although you may find this code more transparent than that of Program 5.9, the code of Program 5.9 is generalized easily to output the elements of any object for which an iterator is defined. The code

```
for (iterator i = start; i != end; i++)
   cout << *i << "   ";
```

outputs all elements in the range [start, end). In this code `iterator` is the datatype of the iterator, `start` is the iterator value for the first element in the range and

```
int main()
{
    int x[3] = {0, 1, 2};

    // use a pointer y to iterate through the array x
    for (int* y = x; y != x + 3; y++)
        cout << *y << "   ";
    cout << endl;
    return 0;
}
```

Program 5.9 Using an array iterator

end is the value the iterator has when incremented one past the last element to be output.

The concept of an iterator is fundamental to writing generic code in C++. Program 5.10 gives a possible code for the STL copy function, for example. This code may be used to copy elements of any object that has an iterator for which the operators !=, *, and ++ (postincrement) as well as the dereferenced assignment (*to =) are defined. Different generic codes we write require our iterator to have different capabilities. For example, the copy_backward function requires us to decrement the value of the iterator.

```
template <class iterator>
void copy(iterator start, iterator end, iterator to)
{// copy from [start, end) to [to, to + end - start)
    while (start != end)
    {*to = *start; start++; to++;}
}
```

Program 5.10 Possible code for STL copy function

To simplify iterator development and categorization of generic iterator-based codes, the C++ STL defines five categories of iterators: input, output, forward, bidirectional and random access. All iterators support the equality operators == and != as well as the dereference operator *. Input iterators additionally provide read access to the elements pointed at and support the pre- and post-increment operator ++. Output iterators provide write access to the elements and also permit iterator advancement via the ++ operator. Forward iterators may be advanced using the increment operator ++ while bidirectional iterators may be incremented as well as decremented (--). Random access iterators are the most general. They permit pointer jumps by arbitrary amounts as well as pointer arithmetic. C++ array iterators such as y in Program 5.9 are random access iterators.

5.3.5   An Iterator for `arrayList`

We shall define a C++ class `iterator` that will serve as a bidirectional iterator for `arrayList`. This class will, itself, be a public member of the class `arrayList`. Additionally, we shall add two public methods `begin()` and `end()` to `arrayList`. These methods, respectively, return iterators whose value is a pointer to the first element of the list (i.e., `element[0]`) and a pointer to one position past the last element (i.e., `element[listSize]`). The code for these two methods of `arrayList` is

```
class iterator;
iterator begin() {return iterator(element);}
iterator end() {return iterator(element + listSize);}
```

Program 5.11 gives the code for the class `iterator`. The five `typedef` statements are required by C++ to recognize our iterator class as a bidirectional iterator and to generate proper code for STL algorithms that employ bidirectional iterators. The complexity of each method of our iterator class is $\Theta(1)$.

An instance of our list iterator may be created and initialized using a statement such as

```
arrayList<int>::iterator x = y.begin();
```

where y is of type `arrayList`. With the addition of the iterator to our linear list class, we can use STL algorithms to perform tasks that require only the capabilities of a bidirectional iterator. For example, we can reverse the elements in a list y using the STL function `reverse` and we can sum the list elements using the STL function `accumulate`. The code for these two tasks is

```
reverse(y.begin(), y.end());
int sum = accumulate(y.begin(), y.end(), 0);
```

However, we cannot use the STL algorithm `sort` as this algorithm requires a random access iterator.

EXERCISES

2. Let L = (a, b, c, d, e) be a linear list that is represented in an array `element` using Equation 5.1. Assume that `arrayLength` = 10. Draw figures similar to Figure 5.2 showing the contents of the array `element` and the value of `listSize` following each operation in the operation sequence: initial state, $insert(0, f)$, $insert(3, g)$, $insert(7, h)$, $erase(0)$, $erase(4)$.

```
class iterator
{
   public:
      // typedefs required by C++ for a bidirectional iterator
      typedef bidirectional_iterator_tag iterator_category;
      typedef T value_type;
      typedef ptrdiff_t difference_type;
      typedef T* pointer;
      typedef T& reference;

      // constructor
      iterator(T* thePosition = 0) {position = thePosition;}

      // dereferencing operators
      T& operator*() const {return *position;}
      T* operator->() const {return &*position;}

      // increment
      iterator& operator++()   // preincrement
             {++position; return *this;}
      iterator operator++(int) // postincrement
            {iterator old = *this;
             ++position;
             return old;
             }

      // decrement
      iterator& operator--()   // predecrement
             {--position; return *this;}
      iterator operator--(int) // postdecrement
            {iterator old = *this;
             --position;
             return old;
             }

      // equality testing
      bool operator!=(const iterator right) const
            {return position != right.position;}
      bool operator==(const iterator right) const
            {return position == right.position;}
   protected:
      T* position;  // pointer to a list element
};
```

Program 5.11 An iterator for the class arrayList

3. Write a function **changeLength2D** to change the length of a two-dimensional array. You must allow for a change in both dimensions of the array. Test your code.

4. To the class **arrayList** add a constructor that allows you to specify the amount by which the list capacity (or array length) is to be increased whenever array resizing is needed. When no capacity increment is specified, array doubling is done. Modify **insert** to work in this way. Test your code.

5. Write the method **arrayList<T>::trimToSize**, which makes the array length equal to max{**listSize**, 1}. What is the complexity of your method? Test your code.

6. Write the method **arrayList<T>::setSize**, which makes the list size equal to the specified size. If the original list size was less than the new one, NULL elements are added, and if the original size was more than the new one, the extra elements are removed. What is the complexity of your method? Test your code.

7. Overload the operator [] so that the expression x[i] returns a reference to the ith element of the list. If the list doesn't have an ith element, an **illegalIndex** exception is to be thrown. The statements x[i] = y and y = x[i] should work as expected. Test your code.

8. Overload the operator == so that the expression x == y returns true iff the two array lists x are y are equal (i.e., the ith elements of both lists are equal for all i). Test your code.

9. Overload the operator != so that the expression x != y returns true iff the two array lists x are y are not equal (see Exercise 8). Test your code.

10. Overload the operator < so that the expression x < y returns true iff the array list x is lexically smaller than the array list y (see Exercise 8). Test your code.

11. Write the method **arrayList<T>::push_back**, which inserts **theElement** at the right end of the list. Do not use the **insert** method. What is the time complexity of your method? Test your code.

12. Write the method **arrayList<T>::pop_back**, which erases the element at the right end of the list. Do not use the **erase** method. What is the time complexity of your method? Test your code.

13. Write the method **arrayList<T>::swap(theList)**, which swaps the elements of the lists *this and **theList**. What is the time complexity of your method? Test your code.

14. Write the method `arrayList<T>::reserve(theCapacity)`, which changes the capacity of the list to the larger of its current capacity and `theCapacity`. Test your code.

15. Write the method `arrayList<T>::set(theIndex, theElement)`, which replaces the element whose index is `theIndex` with `theElement`. Throw an exception in case `theIndex` is out of range. You should return the old element with the specified index. Test your code.

16. Write the method `arrayList<T>::clear`, which makes the list empty. What is the complexity of your method? Test your code.

17. Write the method `arrayList<T>::removeRange`, which removes all elements in the specified index range. What is the complexity of your method? Test your code.

18. Write the method `arrayList<T>::lastIndexOf`, which returns the index of the right-most occurrence of the specified object. A −1 is returned in case the specified object is not in the list. What is the complexity of your method? Test your code.

19. Prove Theorem 5.1.

20. A shortcoming of the class `arrayList` (Program 5.1) is that it never decreases the length of the array `element`.

    (a) Write a new version of this class so that if, following a deletion, the list size drops below `arrayLength/4`, a smaller array of length max{`arrayLength/2, initialCapacity`} is allocated and the elements are copied from the old array into the new one.

    (b) (Optional) Consider any sequence of n linear list operations beginning with an empty list. Suppose that the total step count is $f(n)$ when the initial capacity equals or exceeds the maximum list size. Show that if we start with an initial capacity of 1 and use array resizing during inserts and removes as described above and in Section 5.3, the new step count is at most $cf(n)$ for some constant c.

21. Prove a theorem analogous to Theorem 5.1 for the case when array length is increased by a constant factor $c > 1$ whenever the array gets full and is reduced by the factor c whenever array occupancy falls below $1/(2c)$ (subject, of course, to the constraint that array length never falls below its initial length).

22. (a) Write the method `arrayList<T>::reverse`, which reverses the order of the elements in the list. The reversal is to be done in place (i.e., within the array `element` and without the creation of a new array). Note that before the reversal, the kth element (if it exists) of the list is in `element[k]`; following the reversal the kth element is in `element[listSize-k-1]`. Do not use the STL function `reverse`.

(b) The complexity of your method should be linear in `listSize`. Show that this is the case.

(c) Test the correctness of your code, using your own test data.

(d) Now write another in-place method to reverse an object of type `array-List`. This method is not a member of `arrayList` and should not access the data members of `arrayList`. Rather, your method should use the member methods of `arrayList` to produce the reversed list.

(e) What is the time complexity of your new method?

(f) Compare the run-time performance of the two reversal methods using linear lists of size 1000; 5000; and 10,000.

23. (a) Write the method `arrayList<T>::leftShift(i)` that shifts the list elements left by i positions. If x = [0, 1, 2, 3, 4], then x.`leftShift(2)` results in x = [2, 3, 4].

(b) What is the time complexity of your method?

(c) Test your code.

24. In a circular shift operation, the elements of a linear list are rotated clockwise by a given amount. For example, when the elements of x = [0, 1, 2, 3, 4] are shifted circularly by 2, the result is x = [2, 3, 4, 0, 1].

(a) Describe how you can perform a circular shift using three reversal operations. Each reversal may reverse a portion of the list or reverse the entire list.

(b) Write the method `arrayList<T>::circularShift(i)`, which performs a circular shift by i positions. The complexity of your method should be linear in the list length.

(c) Test your code.

25. The invocation x.`half()` eliminates every other element of x. So if x.`size()` is initially 7 and x.`element[]` = [2, 13, 4, 5, 17, 8, 29], then following the execution of x.`half()`, x.`size()` is 4 and x.`element[]` = [2, 4, 17, 29]. If x.`size()` is initially 4 and x.`element[]` = [2, 13, 4, 5], then following the execution of x.`half()`, x.`size()` is 2 and x.`element[]` = [2, 4]. If x is initially empty, then it is empty following the execution of x.`half()`.

(a) Write code for the method `arrayList<T>::half()`. You should not use any of the other methods of `arrayList`. The complexity of your code should be $O(\text{size})$.

(b) Show that the complexity of your code is, in fact, $O(\text{listSize})$.

(c) Test your code.

26. Write a function equivalent to the method **half** of Exercise 25. Your function should not be a member of **arrayList** and should not access any of the data members of this class either. Rather, accomplish your task by using public methods of **arrayList**. What is the complexity of your method? Test your code.

27. Extend the iterator class **arrayList::iterator** (Program 5.11) so that it is a random access iterator. Test your iterator by using the STL **sort** function to sort the elements of a linear list.

28. Let a and b be two objects of type **arrayList**.

    (a) Write the method **arrayList<T>::meld(a,b)**, which creates a linear list that contains elements alternately from a and b, beginning with the zeroth element of a. If you run out of elements in one list, then append the remaining elements of the other list to the list being created. The invocation c.meld(a,b) should make c the melded list. The complexity of your code should be linear in the sizes of the two input lists.

    (b) Show that the complexity of your code is linear in the sum of the sizes of a and b.

    (c) Test your code.

29. Let a and b be objects of type **arrayList**. Assume that the elements of a and b are in sorted order (i.e., nondecreasing from left to right).

    (a) Write the method **arrayList<T>::merge(a,b)**, which creates a new sorted linear list that contains all the elements in a and b. The merged list is assigned to the invoking object ***this**. Do not use the STL function **merge**.

    (b) What is the complexity of your method?

    (c) Test your code.

30. (a) Write the method **arrayList<T>::split(a,b)**, which creates two linear lists a and b. a contains the elements of ***this** that have an even index, and b contains the remaining elements.

    (b) What is the complexity of your method?

    (c) Test your code.

31. Suppose that we are to represent a linear list using Equation 5.3. Rather than store the list size explicitly, we keep variables **first** and **last** that give the locations of the first and last elements of the list.

    (a) Develop a class similar to **arrayList** for this representation. Name your class **circularArrayList**. Write code for all methods. You can make the **erase** and **insert** codes more efficient by properly choosing to move either elements to the left or right of the removed/inserted element.

(b) What is the time complexity of each of your methods?

(c) Test your code.

32. Write a bidirectional iterator for `circularArrayList` class of Exercise 31.

33. Do Exercise 22 using Equation 5.3 instead of 5.1.

34. Do Exercise 28 using Equation 5.3 instead of 5.1.

35. Do Exercise 29 using Equation 5.3 instead of 5.1.

36. Do Exercise 30 using Equation 5.3 instead of 5.1.

5.4   VECTOR REPRESENTATION

The STL provides a class `vector` that uses an array and provides all of the functionality of the class `arrayList` (plus many additional methods). The length of the array used to implement a `vector` is dynamically increased as needed. Typically an insertion into a full vector will result in increasing the vector capacity by the larger of 1 and 50% of current capacity. The class `vector` doesn't have a constructor equivalent to that of `arrayList`; nor does it have methods with names `get`, `indexOf`, and `output`. However, `vector` has the methods `empty` and `size` that are equivalent to the corresponding methods of `arrayList`. Although `vector` has the methods `erase` and `insert` that respectively delete and add an element, the `vector` methods need to know the memory address (rather than element index) where the operation is to be performed. Another difference between `vector` and `arrayList` is that the two classes throw different types of exceptions when something goes wrong. To account for these differences, we define a class `vectorList` that uses a `vector` to represent a linear list and whose methods have the same signatures and behavior as those of `linearList`. Consequently, the classes `arrayList` and `vectorList` may be used interchangeably.

Programs 5.12 through 5.14 give the codes for some of the methods of the class `vectorList`.

EXERCISES

37. Write code for the method `vectorList<T>::half` (see Exercise 25). The complexity of your code should be linear in the size of the list. Test your code.

38. Write code for the method `vectorList<T>::meld(a,b)` (see Exercise 28). The complexity of your code should be linear in the sizes of the two input lists. Test your code.

```
template<class T>
class vectorList : public linearList<T>
{
   public:
      // constructor, copy constructor and destructor
      vectorList(int initialCapacity = 10);
      vectorList(const vectorList<T>&);
      ~vectorList() {delete element;}

      // ADT methods
      bool empty() const {return element->empty();}
      int size() const {return (int) element->size();}
      T& get(int theIndex) const;
      int indexOf(const T& theElement) const;
      void erase(int theIndex);
      void insert(int theIndex, const T& theElement);
      void output(ostream& out) const;

      // additional method
      int capacity() const {return (int) element->capacity();}

      // iterators to start and end of list
      typedef typename vector<T>::iterator iterator;
      iterator begin() {return element->begin();}
      iterator end() {return element->end();}

   protected:  // additional members of vectorList
      void checkIndex(int theIndex) const;
      vector<T>* element;       // vector to hold list elements
};
```

Program 5.12 An array linear list implemented using a vector

39. Write code for the method vectorList<T>::merge(a,b) (see Exercise 29). Test your code.

40. Write code for the method vectorList<T>::split(a,b) (see Exercise 30). Test your code.

```
template<class T>
vectorList<T>::vectorList(int initialCapacity)
{// Constructor.
   if (initialCapacity < 1)
   {ostringstream s;
    s << "Initial capacity = " << initialCapacity << " Must be > 0";
    throw illegalParameterValue(s.str());
   }

   element = new vector<T>;
            // create an empty vector with capacity 0
   element->reserve(initialCapacity);
            // increase vector capacity from 0 to initialCapacity
}

template<class T>
vectorList<T>::vectorList(const vectorList<T>& theList)
{// Copy constructor.
   element = new vector<T>(*theList.element);
}
```

Program 5.13 Constructors for vectorList

5.5 MULTIPLE LISTS IN A SINGLE ARRAY

Before accepting the array representation of a linear list, let us reflect on its merits. Certainly, the operations to be performed on a linear list can be implemented as very simple C++ methods. The methods indexOf, remove, and add have a worst complexity that is linear in the size of the individual list. We might regard this complexity as quite satisfactory. (In Chapter 15 we will see representations that allow us to perform these operations even faster.)

A negative aspect of the array representation is its inefficient use of space. Consider the following situation. We are to maintain three lists. We know that the three lists together will never have more than 4097 elements in them at any time. However, it is quite possible for a particular list to have 4097 elements at one time and for another list to have 4097 elements at another time. If we create three instances of arrayList, each with an initial array length of 4097, we will need space for a total of 12,291 elements even though we will never have more than 4097 elements at any time. However, using an initial length of 4097 for each array ensures that array resizing will not be required and our program will run as fast as possible. On the other hand, if we create three arrays with initial length 1, then when the length of one of these arrays is to increase from 4096 to 4097, we will need to first

```
template<class T>
void vectorList<T>::erase(int theIndex)
{// Delete the element whose index is theIndex.
 // Throw illegalIndex exception if no such element.
   checkIndex(theIndex);
   element->erase(begin() + theIndex);
}


template<class T>
void vectorList<T>::insert(int theIndex, const T& theElement)
{// Insert theElement so that its index is theIndex.
   if (theIndex < 0 || theIndex > size())
   {// invalid index
      ostringstream s;
      s << "index = " << theIndex << " size = " << size();
      throw illegalIndex(s.str());
   }

   element->insert(element->begin() + theIndex, theElement);
            // may throw an uncaught exception if insufficient
            // memory to resize vector
}
```

Program 5.14 Delete and insert for vectorList

create an array of length 8192 and copy 4096 elements into the new array. During the copy, both the 4096 and 8192 length arrays are needed. Therefore, space for at least 12,288 elements is needed.

In many applications of linear lists, the amount of memory used is not an issue because our computer has enough memory for the application to run to completion using the single-list-in-a-single-array representation. However, in applications that use very large lists, the list representations of this chapter may cause the application to fail (for insufficient memory) even though the total number of elements we have is small enough that all elements can be accommodated in the available memory. The application fails because excess memory has been allocated to a particular array or because array doubling fails.

One way to overcome this space requirement problem is to buy more memory. Another possibility is to map all of our lists into a single array element whose length is the maximum possible. In addition, we use two other arrays, front and last, to index into the array list. Figure 5.3 shows three lists represented in the single array element. We adopt the convention that the lists are numbered 1 through m if

there are m lists and that front[i] is actually one less than the actual position of
the zeroth element in list i. This convention on front[i] makes it easier to use the
representation. last[i] is the actual position of the last element in list i. Notice
that with this convention, last[i] > front[i] whenever the ith list is not empty.
We shall have front[i] = last[i] whenever list i is empty. So in the example of
Figure 5.3, list 2 is empty. The lists are represented in the array in the order 1, 2,
3, $\cdots$, m from left to right.

Figure 5.3 Three lists in a single array

To avoid having to handle the first and last lists differently from others, we define
two boundary lists 0 and m+1 with front[0] = last[0] = −1 and front[m+1] =
last[m+1] = list.length-1. To insert an element as the indexth element of list
i, we need to first create space for the new element. If last[i] = front[i+1],
then there is no space between lists i and i+1 and we cannot move elements index
through the last one up one position. At this time we can check whether it is
possible to move elements 0 through index-1 of the ith list one position down by
checking the relation last[i-1] < front[i]. If this relation does not hold, then
we need to either shift some of the lists 1 through i-1 down or some of the lists i+1
through m up and create space for list i to grow. This shifting is possible when the
total number of elements in all the lists is fewer than list.length.

Figure 5.4 is a pseudo-C++ version of the method to insert an element into list
i. This pseudocode may be refined into compilable C++ code.

Although representing several lists in a single array uses space more efficiently
than using a separate array for each list, insertions take more time in the worst
case. In fact, a single insertion could require us to move as many as arrayLength-1
elements, where arrayLength is the length of the array list. The multiple-list-
in-a-single-array representation is also quite cumbersome to implement. A much
simpler solution whose space requirement equals that for the elements in all the
lists plus that for one pointer per element is the subject of the next chapter.

EXERCISES

41. Refine Figure 5.4 into a C++ method and test its correctness.

```
void insert(int i, int index, Object element)
{// Insert y as the index'th element in list i.
   size = last[i] - front[i]; // number of elements in list i
   if (index < 0 || index > size)
   throw an exception;
   // Is there space on the right?
```
Find the least j, j ≥ i such that last[j] < front[j+1];
If such a j exists, then move lists i+1 through j and elements index through
   the last one of list i up one position and insert element into list i;
   This move should update appropriate last and first values;

```
   // Is there space on the left?
```
If no j was found above, then find the largest j, j < i such that
last[j] < front[j+1];
If such a j is found, then move lists j through i-1
and elements 1 through index-1 of list i one position left and insert element;
This move should update appropriate last and first values;

```
   // Success?
   if (no j was found above) throw an exception;
}
```

Figure 5.4 Pseudocode to insert an element in the many lists per array representation

42. Write a C++ method to insert an element as the *index*th element in list *i*. Assume that a single array represents *m* lists. If you have to move lists to accommodate the new element, your should first determine the amount of available space and then move the lists so that each has about the same amount of space available for future growth. Test your code.

43. Write a C++ method to remove the *index*th element from list *i*. Assume that a single array represents *m* lists. Test the correctness of your code by compiling and executing it.

5.6 PERFORMANCE MEASUREMENT

In this chapter we have developed two array classes that implement the data structure *linear list*—arrayList and vectorList. Both classes are equally good as far as their space complexity is concerned. Even though both classes offer the same asymptotic time complexity, their actual run times are likely to be different.

To obtain the actual run times, we must design an experiment. We wish to measure the time taken by the operations `get`, `indexOf`, `erase`, and `insert`. For the `get` and `indexOf` operations, we measure the total time required for the sequences `get(i)`, $0 \leq i <$ `listSize` and `indexOf(e`$_i$`)`, $0 \leq i <$ `listSize`, where e_i is the ith element of the list. Figure 5.5 gives the measured times for `listSize` = 50,000, and Figure 5.6 shows these times as bar graphs.

operation	arrayList	vectorList
get	1.0 ms	1.4 ms
indexOf	2.3 s	2.3 s
best-case inserts	4.0/2.1 ms	7.5/5.3 ms
average inserts	1.5/1.5 s	1.5/1.5 s
worst-case inserts	2.5/2.5 s	2.7/2.5 s
best-case erases	2.0 ms	2.9 ms
average erases	1.5 s	1.5 s
worst-case erases	2.5 s	2.4 s

Times for 50,000 operations

Figure 5.5 Time taken by different array linear list implementations

For the `insert` operation, we do a sequence of $n = 50,000$ inserts beginning with an empty list and report the total time for the 50,000 inserts. The best case for the insert sequence is when each new element is inserted at the right end of the list; the worst case is when each new element is inserted at the left end. To estimate average behavior, we do the inserts at randomly generated positions of the list. Figure 5.5 gives the insert times in the format TA/TB, where TA is the time when the list is constructed with the default initial capacity of 10 and TB is the time when the initial capacity is $50,000$. For best-case inserts, array doubling increases run time by about 90 percent for `arrayList` when compared with the case when no array resizing is done. Increasing array size by a factor of 50 percent whenever array resizing is needed increases the run time of a best-case insert in `vectorList` by about 42 percent when compared to the case when no array resizing is done. The total time spent resizing the element array was 1.9 ms in the case of `arrayList` and 2.2 ms in the case of `vectorList`. For the average and worst-case tests, the array resizing time is a negligible part of the total cost. This result is to be expected because both array doubling and increasing array size by 50 percent add $\Theta(n)$ to the cost of n inserts; the cost of n best-case inserts is $\Theta(n)$, and the cost of n average- and worst-case inserts is $\Theta(n^2)$.

Notice the colossal increase in run time from the best-case inserts to the worst-case inserts—the run time for `arrayList` jumped from 4.0 ms to 2.5 seconds, a 625-fold increase. This 625-fold increase isn't altogether surprising given that n best-case inserts take $\Theta(n)$ time, whereas n worst-case inserts take $\Theta(n^2)$ time. If

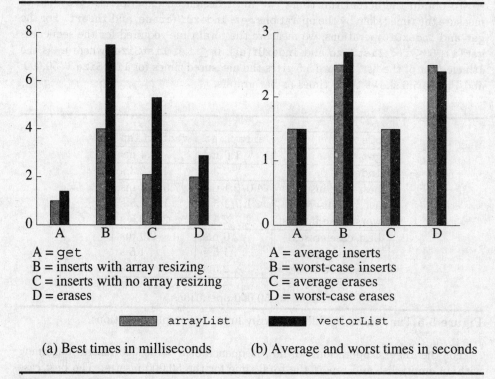

A = get
B = inserts with array resizing
C = inserts with no array resizing
D = erases

A = average inserts
B = worst-case inserts
C = average erases
D = worst-case erases

arrayList   vectorList

(a) Best times in milliseconds   (b) Average and worst times in seconds

Figure 5.6 Plot of run times

the constant factors in the best-case and worst-case time expressions are the same (and they are not), we would expect to see the time go up by a factor of almost $n = 50,000$.

The average insert time is approximately half the worst-case insert time. This result is to be expected because, on average, half the elements have to be moved during an insert; in the worst-case, all elements are moved.

For the erase operation, we start with a list that has $n = 50,000$ elements and do a sequence of n removes. The best case for the remove sequence is when each remove operation removes the element at the right end of the list; the worst case is when each remove operation removes the element at the left end. To estimate average behavior, we do the removes from randomly generated positions of the list.

For the get operation as well as for best-case inserts and erases, arrayList is considerably faster than vectorList. However, for the indexOf as well as for average- and worst-case inserts and erases the two classes perform about the same. This result is to be expected, because of the significantly larger overheads associated with the vector class relative to those associated with an array. For $O(1)$ time operations such as get and best-case inserts and erases, this overhead dominates the run time and causes vectorList to perform poorly. But for the $O(n)$ operations such as indexOf and average- and worst-case inserts and deletes, the overhead is dwarfed by the time spent searching for or moving elements.

So which class should you use? If your primary operation is get or if you are doing inserts and erases primarily from the right end of the list (as is the case for the stack data structure of Chapter 8), use arrayList. For other applications of a linear list, either arrayList or vectorList may be used. But wait; we have yet to see other linear list implementations. These might be even faster!

EXERCISE

44. Develop the class arrayListNoSTL, which implements a linear list using an array. However, unlike the class arrayList, the class arrayListNoSTL doesn't use any STL function. So, for example, STL functions such as copy, copy_backward, and find should not be used. Repeat the experiment described in this section obtaining run times for arrayList, vectorList, and arrayListNoSTL. Present your results in both tabular and bar chart forms.

5.7   REFERENCES AND SELECTED READINGS

Additional material on data structures in C++ may be found in the texts *C++ Plus Data Structures*, Third Edition, by N. Dale, Jones and Bartlett, Sudbury, MA, 2003; *Data Structures and Algorithm Analysis in C++*, Second Edition, by M. Weiss, Addison-Wesley, Menlo Park, CA, 1998; *Data Structures and Algorithms in C++* by M. Goodrich, R. Tamassia, and D. Mount, John Wiley & Sons, New York, NY, 2002; and *Fundamentals of Data Structures in C++* by E. Horowitz, S. Sahni and D. Mehta, Computer Science Press, New York, NY, 1995.

CHAPTER 6

LINEAR LISTS—LINKED REPRESENTATION

BIRD'S-EYE VIEW

The array representation of a linear list is so natural that you may think there is no other reasonable way to represent a linear list. This chapter will dispel any such thought you may have.

In a linked representation, the elements of a list may be stored in any arbitrary set of memory locations. Each element has an explicit pointer or link (the terms *pointer* and *link* are synonyms) that tells us the location (i.e., the address) of the next element in the list.

In an array representation, the element addresses are determined by using a mathematical formula; and in a linked representation, the element addresses are distributed across the list elements.

The data structure concepts introduced in this chapter are

- Linked representation.

- Chains, circular lists, and doubly linked lists.

- Header nodes.

The STL container class `list` uses a doubly linked circular list with a header node to represent its instances. The methods of `list` have the same signatures and behavior as do those of the class `vector`. Hence the `list` methods `erase` and `insert` don't have the same signatures as required by our ADT *linearList*. However, as was the case for `vector`, `list` may be used in the development of a concrete linear list class that derives from the abstract class `linearList`.

The applications developed in this chapter are bin sort (also known as bucket sort), radix sort, convex hulls, and the union-find problem. Bin sort, radix sort and the union-find problem use chains; the convex hull application uses a doubly linked list. Using either a bin sort or a radix sort, you can sort n elements in $O(n)$ time provided the keys are in an "appropriate range." Although the sort methods developed in Chapter 2 take $O(n^2)$ time, they do not require the keys to lie in a particular range. Bin sort and radix sort are considerably faster than the sort methods of Chapter 2 when the keys lie in an appropriate range. The union-find problem illustrates how linked lists may be built using integers as pointers.

6.1   SINGLY LINKED LISTS AND CHAINS

6.1.1   The Representation

In a linked representation each element of an instance of a data object is represented in a cell or node. The nodes, however, need not be components of an array, and no formula is used to locate individual elements. Instead, each node keeps explicit information about the location of other relevant nodes. This explicit information about the location of another node is called a **link** or **pointer**.

Let $L = (e_0, e_1, \cdots, e_{n-1})$ be a linear list. In one possible linked representation for this list, each element e_i is represented in a separate node. Each node has exactly one link field that is used to locate the next element in the linear list. So the node for e_i links to that for e_{i+1}, $0 \le i < n - 1$. The node for e_{n-1} has no node to link to and so its link field is NULL. The variable firstNode locates the first node in the representation. Figure 6.1 shows the linked representation of the list $L = (e_0, e_1, ..., e_{n-1})$. Links are shown as arrows. To locate the element e_2, for example, we must start at firstNode; follow the pointer in firstNode to the next node; follow one more pointer to get to the node with e_2. In general, to locate the element with index *theIndex*, we must follow a sequence of *theIndex* pointers beginning at firstNode.

Figure 6.1 Linked representation of a linear list

Since each node in the linked representation of Figure 6.1 has exactly one link, the structure of this figure is called a **singly linked list**. Since the nodes are ordered from left to right with each node (other than the last one) linking to the next, and the last node has a NULL link, the structure is also called a **chain**.

To remove the element e_2 whose index is 2 from the chain of Figure 6.2, we do the following (note that e_2 is in the third node of the chain):

- Locate the second node (i.e., the node with e_1) in the chain.

- Link the second node to the fourth node.

firstNode

e_0 e_1 e_2 e_3 e_4 NULL

Figure 6.2 Removing e_2 from a 5-node chain

Notice that the removal of the third node from Figure 6.2 automatically decrements the index of the succeeding nodes by 1 (i.e., what were previously the fourth and fifth nodes of the chain become the third and fourth nodes). Because the nodes on a chain are always defined to be those nodes that can be reached following a sequence of pointers beginning at firstNode, we do not bother to change the pointer in the removed node (i.e., the former third node of the chain). Since the removed node is no longer reachable from firstNode, it is no longer part of the chain.

To insert a new element as the indexth element in a chain, we need to first locate the index-1th element and then insert a new node just after it. Figure 6.3 shows the link changes needed for the two cases index = 0 and 0 < index ≤ listSize. Solid pointers exist prior to the insert, and those shown as broken (or dashed) lines exist following the insert.

firstNode

index - 1th
element

index = 0   0 < index ≤ listSize

Figure 6.3 Insertion into a chain

6.1.2   The Struct `chainNode`

To represent a linear list as a chain, we define a struct `chainNode` and a class `chain`. Program 6.1 gives the struct `chainNode`, which defines the data type of the nodes used in Figure 6.1. The data member `element` holds a list element and is the data field of the node; the data member `next` holds a pointer to the next node in the chain and is the node's link field.

```
template <class T>
struct chainNode
{
   // data members
   T element;
   chainNode<T> *next;

   // methods
   chainNode() {}
   chainNode(const T& element)
      {this->element = element;}
   chainNode(const T& element, chainNode<T>* next)
      {this->element = element;
       this->next = next;}
};
```

Program 6.1 Struct definition for a chain node

Notice that two of the constructors of `chainNode` use the syntax `this->element` and `this->next` to access the data members of the constructed instance. This syntax is necessary to distinguish between the data members of the constructed instance and the formal parameters of the constructors because the data members and formal parameters have the same names.

6.1.3   The Class `chain`

Header, `empty`, and `size`

The class `chain` implements a linear list as a singly linked list of nodes in which the last node has the pointer NULL; that is, it implements a linear list as a chain of nodes. Program 6.2 gives the class header, data members and code for the `empty`, and `size` methods.

The data members are `firstNode` and `listSize`. `firstNode` is a pointer to the first node (i.e., the node for the zeroth element of the list) in the chain. When the chain has no first node, that is, when the chain is empty, `firstNode` is NULL.

```
template<class T>
class chain : public linearList<T>
{
   public:
      // constructor, copy constructor and destructor
      chain(int initialCapacity = 10);
      chain(const chain<T>&);
      ~chain();

      // ADT methods
      bool empty() const {return listSize == 0;}
      int size() const {return listSize;}
      T& get(int theIndex) const;
      int indexOf(const T& theElement) const;
      void erase(int theIndex);
      void insert(int theIndex, const T& theElement);
      void output(ostream& out) const;

   protected:
      void checkIndex(int theIndex) const;
            // throw illegalIndex if theIndex invalid
      chainNode<T>* firstNode;  // pointer to first node in chain
      int listSize;             // number of elements in list
};
```

Program 6.2 Header for the class `chain`

`listSize` gives the number of elements in the list, which equals the number of nodes in the chain.

Constructor and copy constructor

Program 6.3 gives the constructor and copy constructor for `chain`.

To create an empty chain, we need merely set the first node pointer `firstNode` to NULL. Unlike the case when a linear list is represented by an array, we do not allocate space for the expected maximum number of elements at the time the chain is created. Therefore, the user does not need to specify an estimate of this maximum size or provide an initial capacity for the list. Nevertheless, we have provided a constructor which has `initialCapacity` as a formal parameter in order to be compatible with the class `arrayList`. In particular, an application can create an array of type `linearList` and initialize the array components using either form of constructor as is shown below.

```
template<class T>
chain<T>::chain(int initialCapacity)
{// Constructor.
   if (initialCapacity < 1)
   {ostringstream s;
    s << "Initial capacity = " << initialCapacity << " Must be > 0";
    throw illegalParameterValue(s.str());
   }
   firstNode = NULL;
   listSize = 0;
}


template<class T>
chain<T>::chain(const chain<T>& theList)
{// Copy constructor.
   listSize = theList.listSize;

   if (listSize == 0)
   {// theList is empty
      firstNode = NULL;
      return;
   }

   // non-empty list
   chainNode<T>* sourceNode = theList.firstNode;
                   // node in theList to copy from
   firstNode = new chainNode<T>(sourceNode->element);
                   // copy first element of theList
   sourceNode = sourceNode->next;
   chainNode<T>* targetNode = firstNode;
                   // current last node in *this
   while (sourceNode != NULL)
   {// copy remaining elements
      targetNode->next = new chainNode<T>(sourceNode->element);
      targetNode = targetNode->next;
      sourceNode = sourceNode->next;
   }
   targetNode->next = NULL; // end the chain
}
```

Program 6.3 Constructor and copy constructor for chain

```
linearList<int>* list[10];
list[0] = new arrayList<int>(20);
list[1] = new arrayList<int>();
list[2] = new chain<int>(5);
list[3] = new chain<int>;
```

The complexity of the constructor is $\Theta(1)$. The copy constructor makes a clone of the chain theChain by copying the nodes of theChain one node at a time. The complexity of the copy constructor is $O(\text{theList.listSize})$.

The destructor

Program 6.4 gives the destructor for chain. The destructor deletes the nodes of the chain one by one. The strategy used in our destructor code is to repeatedly delete the first node in the chain until the remaining chain has no first node. Note that we must save the pointer to the second node in a variable such as nextNode before we delete the first node. The complexity of the destructor is $O(\text{listSize})$.

```
template<class T>
chain<T>::~chain()
{// Chain destructor. Delete all nodes in chain.
   while (firstNode != NULL)
   {// delete firstNode
      chainNode<T>* nextNode = firstNode->next;
      delete firstNode;
      firstNode = nextNode;
   }
}
```

Program 6.4 Destructor for chain

The method get

When an array representation is used, we locate a list element by evaluating a (usually simple) formula. To find the theIndexth element of a chain, however, we must start at the first node and follow the next links until we reach the desired node; that is, we must follow theIndex number of links. *We cannot access the desired node by performing arithmetic on the value of* firstNode. Program 6.5 gives the code. The method checkIndex is the same as that defined for arrayList. The complexity of chain<T>::get is $O(\text{theIndex})$, while that of arrayList<T>::get is $\Theta(1)$.

```
template<class T>
T& chain<T>::get(int theIndex) const
{// Return element whose index is theIndex.
 // Throw illegalIndex exception if no such element.
   checkIndex(theIndex);

   // move to desired node
   chainNode<T>* currentNode = firstNode;
   for (int i = 0; i < theIndex; i++)
      currentNode = currentNode->next;

   return currentNode->element;
}
```

Program 6.5 Method to return the theIndexth element

The method indexOf

Program 6.6 gives the code for the method chain<T>::indexOf. This code differs from the code for arrayList<T>::indexOf primarily in the mechanism used to go from one list element to the next. In the case of an array list, we go from one element to the next by performing some arithmetic on the location of the current, element (when Equation 5.1 is used, we add 1 to the current location to get to the next location). When a chain is used, the only way to go from one node to the next is to follow the link or pointer in the current node. The complexity of chain<T>::indexOf is $O(\text{listSize})$.

The method erase

Program 6.7 gives the code for the erase operation. There are three cases to consider:

- theIndex < 0 or theIndex ≥ listSize. In this case the erase operation fails because there is no theIndexth element to erase. This case implicitly covers the case when the chain is empty.

- The zeroth element is to be erased from a nonempty chain.

- An element other that the zeroth element is to be erased.

To get a feel for Program 6.7, manually try it on an initially empty list as well as on lists that contain at least one node. In addition, try out values of theIndex such as theIndex < 0, theIndex = 0 (erase the zeroth element), theIndex = listSize-1 (erase the last element), theIndex ≥ listSize, and 0 < theIndex < listSsize-1 (erase an interior element).

```
template<class T>
int chain<T>::indexOf(const T& theElement) const
{// Return index of first occurrence of theElement.
 // Return -1 if theElement not in list.

   // search the chain for theElement
   chainNode<T>* currentNode = firstNode;
   int index = 0;  // index of currentNode
   while (currentNode != NULL &&
          currentNode->element != theElement)
   {
      // move to next node
      currentNode = currentNode->next;
      index++;
   }

   // make sure we found matching element
   if (currentNode == NULL)
      return -1;
   else
      return index;
}
```

Program 6.6 Method to return the index of the first occurrence of `theElement`

The complexity of `chain<T>::erase` is $O(\text{theIndex})$, whereas the complexity of `arrayList<T>::erase` is $O(\text{listSize-theIndex})$. Therefore, the linked implementation of a linear list is expected to perform better than the array implementation for erases that are done from near the front of the list.

The method `insert`

Insertion and erasing work in a similar way. To insert a new element as the `theEndex`th one in a chain, we need to first locate the `theIndex-1`th element and then insert a new node just after it. Program 6.8 gives the code. Its complexity is $O(\text{theIndex})$.

Outputting a chain

Program 6.9 gives the code for the `output` method as well as for the overloading of the stream insertion operator `<<`. The code for `chain<T>::output` differs from that for `arrayList<T>::output` primarily in its use of the `next` pointer to go from

```
template<class T>
void chain<T>::erase(int theIndex)
{// Delete the element whose index is theIndex.
 // Throw illegalIndex exception if no such element.
   checkIndex(theIndex);

   // valid index, locate node with element to delete
   chainNode<T>* deleteNode;
   if (theIndex == 0)
   {// remove first node from chain
      deleteNode = firstNode;
      firstNode = firstNode->next;
   }
   else
   {  // use p to get to predecessor of desired node
      chainNode<T>* p = firstNode;
      for (int i = 0; i < theIndex - 1; i++)
         p = p->next;

      deleteNode = p->next;
      p->next = p->next->next; // remove deleteNode from chain
   }
   listSize--;
   delete deleteNode;
}
```

Program 6.7 Erase the theIndexth element

one node to the next. The complexity of chain<T>::output is the same as that of arrayList<T>::output, $O(\text{listSize})$.

The member class iterator

By using **next** pointers, we can efficiently move from a node to its successor node in the chain. However, in a chain, there is no efficient way to move from a node to its predecessor. Therefore, for a chain, we define only a forward iterator. Recall that for an **arrayList** we defined a bidirectional iterator that enabled us to move from any list element to both its successor element and its predecessor element in $O(1)$ time. Program 6.10 gives the code for some of the methods of he forward iterator for a chain. The complete code may be found at the Web site for this book.

The methods chain<T>::begin and chain<T>::end are defined as

```
template<class T>
void chain<T>::insert(int theIndex, const T& theElement)
{// Insert theElement so that its index is theIndex.
   if (theIndex < 0 || theIndex > listSize)
   {// invalid index
      ostringstream s;
      s << "index = " << theIndex << " size = " << listSize;
      throw illegalIndex(s.str());
   }

   if (theIndex == 0)
      // insert at front
      firstNode = new chainNode<T>(theElement, firstNode);
   else
   {  // find predecessor of new element
      chainNode<T>* p = firstNode;
      for (int i = 0; i < theIndex - 1; i++)
         p = p->next;

      // insert after p
      p->next = new chainNode<T>(theElement, p->next);
   }
   listSize++;
}
```

Program 6.8 Insert theElement as the theIndexth element of the chain

```
iterator begin() {return iterator(firstNode);}
iterator end() {return iterator(NULL);}
```

The difference in run times between using the get method and the iterator method to access the linear list elements in left-to-right order is quite dramatic when the list is represented as a chain. The time needed to access the ith element using get is $\Theta(i)$. Therefore, the get method to examine the list elements one at a time takes $\Theta(\texttt{listSize}^2)$ time, whereas the iterator method takes only $\Theta(\texttt{listSize})$ time.

6.1.4   Extensions to the ADT *linearList*

In some applications of linear lists, we wish to perform operations in addition to those that are part of the abstract data type *linearList* (ADT 5.1). So it is useful to

```
template<class T>
void chain<T>::output(ostream& out) const
{// Put the list into the stream out.
   for (chainNode<T>* currentNode = firstNode;
                      currentNode != NULL;
                      currentNode = currentNode->next)
      out << currentNode->element << "  ";
}

// overload <<
template <class T>
ostream& operator<<(ostream& out, const chain<T>& x)
   {x.output(out); return out;}
```

Program 6.9 The method output

extend the ADT to include additional functions such as *clear* (remove all elements
from the list) and *push_back*(*theElement*) (insert *theElement* at the end of the
list). Program 6.11 gives the abstract class that corresponds to the extended ADT.

6.1.5 The Class extendedChain

We will develop a class extendedChain that provides a linked implementation of
the abstract class extendedLinearList. The easiest way to arrive at the class
extendedChain is to derive it from chain.

To efficiently insert an element at the end of a chain, we add a new data member lastNode that points to the last node in the chain. Using this pointer, we can
append an element to a chain in $\Theta(1)$ time. However, the addition of this new data
member requires us to make changes in the implementation of the methods erase
and insert because these methods may change the last node in the chain. When
these methods change the last node, they must also update the new data member lastNode. Therefore, the class extendedChain will declare the data member
lastNode; provide modified implementations of the methods erase and insert;
define the remaining pure virtual functions of linearList as invocations of the
corresponding methods in the class chain; and provide implementations for the
new methods clear and push_back.

Program 6.12 gives the code for the methods clear and push_back. The full
code for extendedChain may be found at the Web site for this book.

```
class iterator
{
   public:
      // typedefs required by C++ for a forward iterator omitted

      // constructor
      iterator(chainNode<T>* theNode = NULL)
         {node = theNode;}

      // dereferencing operators
      T& operator*() const {return node->element;}
      T* operator->() const {return &node->element;}

      // increment
      iterator& operator++()    // preincrement
               {node = node->next; return *this;}
      iterator operator++(int) // postincrement
            {iterator old = *this;
             node = node->next;
             return old;
            }

      // equality testing
      bool operator!=(const iterator right) const
            {return node != right.node;}
      bool operator==(const iterator right) const
            {return node == right.node;}
   protected:
      chainNode<T>* node;
};
```

Program 6.10 The class chain<T>::iterator

6.1.6 Performance Measurement

Memory Comparison

In an array implementation of a linear list, we typically use array doubling when
the array gets full and array halving when the array occupancy falls below 25
percent (note, however, that the STL container class **vector** increases array length
by a factor of 1.5 and never decreases array length; our array list classes use array
doubling and do not decrease array length when usage falls below 25 percent of

```
template<class T>
class extendedLinearList : linearList<T>
{
   public:
      virtual ~extendedLinearList() {}
      virtual void clear() = 0;
               // empty the list
      virtual void push_back(const T& theElement) = 0;
               // insert theElement at end of list
};
```

Program 6.11 Abstract class for extended linear list

```
template<class T>
void extendedChain<T>::clear()
{// Delete all nodes in chain.
   while (firstNode != NULL)
   {// delete firstNode
      chainNode<T>* nextNode = firstNode->next;
      delete firstNode;
      firstNode = nextNode;
   }
   listSize = 0;
}

template<class T>
void extendedChain<T>::push_back(const T& theElement)
{// Insert theElement at the end of the chain.
   chainNode<T>* newNode = new chainNode<T>(theElement, NULL);
   if (firstNode == NULL)
      // chain is empty
         firstNode = lastNode = newNode;
   else
   {  // attach next to lastNode
      lastNode->next = newNode;
      lastNode = newNode;
   }
   listSize++;
}
```

Program 6.12 The methods clear and push_back of extendedChain<T>

array capacity). Therefore, a linear list with n elements may reside in an array whose length is between n and $4n$. So space for between n and $4n$ elements is needed. When a chain is used, exactly n nodes, each with two fields, are alloted to the list. Therefore, the chain representation uses space for n elements and n pointers. Let s be the number of bytes required by an element and assume that a pointer requires 4 bytes. Ignoring the space required by class data members such as `size` and `firstNode`, the array representation of a linear list requires between ns and $4ns$ bytes while a singly-linked representation requires $n(s + 4)$ bytes. For most applications this difference in the space requirements will not be a deciding factor in selecting the representation to use.

Run-Time Comparison

For the time requirements we expect `chain<T>::get` to be much slower than `array-List<T>::get`, because the complexity of `chain<T>::get` is $O(\text{listSize})$, whereas the complexity of the `arrayList<T>::get` is $\Theta(1)$. This expectation is borne out by experiment. We constructed a 50,000-node chain by making successive inserts at the left end of an initially empty chain. Then we measured the total time required to perform the 50,000 get operations `get(i)`, $0 \le \text{i} < 50000$. `chain<T>::get` took 13.2 seconds to perform this sequence of operations, while `arrayList<T>::get` took 1.0 ms—not a commendable showing for the `chain` class. Things do not get any better when we compare the times for the `indexOf`, `insert` and `erase` methods.

Figures 6.4 and 6.5 show the times taken by `arrayList` and `chain` for operation sequences as described in Section 5.6. The time for 50,000 `indexOf` operations using `chain<T>::indexOf` is approximately 6 times that when `arrayList<T>::indexOf` is used. The average-case insert and erase times for the class `chain` are about 33 and 46 times that for for the corresponding methods of `arrayList`.

operation	arrayList	chain
get	1.0 ms	13.2 s
indexOf	2.3 s	13.0 s
best-case inserts	2.1 ms	45.1 ms
average inserts	1.5 s	49.3 s
worst-case inserts	2.5 s	12.9 s
best-case erases	2.0 ms	2.1 ms
average erases	1.5 s	68.8 s
worst-case erases	2.5 s	12.9 s

Times for 50,000 operations

Figure 6.4 Time taken by different linear list implementations

Even though the insert and erase sequences (insert and erase from the right

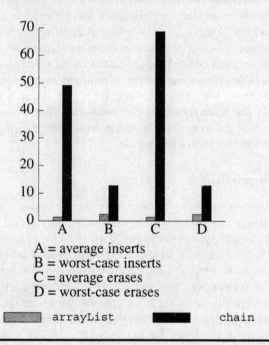

A = average inserts
B = worst-case inserts
C = average erases
D = worst-case erases

 arrayList   ▮ chain

Figure 6.5 Average- and worst-case times, in seconds, for 50,000 operations

end of a chain) used in our worst-case test for chains cause our methods to do the maximum work, these sequences do not ensure maximum run time because of the cache effect (Section 4.5). In fact, you will notice that the measured worst-case times are smaller than the measured average times!

The average-case insert times were obtained by inserting into random positions of the linear list. Consequently, nodes that are adjacent in the chain are randomly located in memory. Hence when you move down the chain from left to right, you need to access random memory locations. This results in many cache misses. The same is true for the average-case erase experiment, which uses a randomly constructed chain. For the worst-case experiment, successive inserts are made at the right end of the chain. Since, for our experimental setup, successive calls to **new** return nodes that are adjacent in memory, nodes that are adjacent in the chain also are adjacent in memory. So when you move down the chain from left to right, you access adjacent memory; a memory access pattern that is favored by the cache management scheme. So the number of cache misses is reduced. This reduction in cache misses results in the anomalous run time measurements for worst-case inserts and erases relative to the average times.

The reported times for **chain<T>::get** and **chain<T>::indexOf** were obtained from a chain constructed by making inserts at the front of the chain (best-case inserts). Since, in our experimental setup, successive calls to new return nodes that are adjacent in memory, adjacent nodes in the chain used to measure the times for the get and indexOf sequences occupy adjacent memory. So expect that performing the same sequence of get and indexOf operations in a chain created by making random inserts would take much more time. In fact, in a separate experiment, we determined this time to be 167 seconds and 165 seconds, respectively. So the time needed for our sequence of 50,000 gets in a randomly constructed chain is about 13 times that in the chain constructed for best-case inserts. This ratio is about the same for the indexOf operation. The linked representation gets a thumbs down as far as standard linear list operations are concerned!

Note that cache effects did not play a role in our comparison of best-case, average, and worst-case times for array representation (Section 5.6) because in all tests, the array elements are accessed from left to right and an array occupies a contiguous block of memory.

Are Pointers Any Good?

You are probably wondering whether you have just wasted a lot of time studying pointers. In Chapter 15 we develop balanced binary tree structures such as AVL and red-black trees. Indexed versions of these structures (e.g., the indexed AVL tree) may be used to represent a linear list (see Exercise 15.20). These structures use pointers and knock the socks off of arrayList as far as worst-case inserts and erases are concerned.

Despite the poor showing of chains in the linear list timing experiments we conducted, chains are more efficient than array linear list representations in several linear list applications. Section 6.5 gives a few of these applications. These applications require us to combine multiple lists into one or to remove and insert elements when the node just before the node to be removed or inserted is known because of other work done on the chain.

Two chains may be combined into one by linking the last node of one chain to the first node of the second. If we know both the first and last nodes of a chain, this combining is done in $O(1)$ time. To combine two array linear lists into one, we must copy the second into the array used by the first. This copying takes $\Theta($size of second list$)$ time. When we know the "just before node," the remove and insert operations of a chain run in $O(1)$ time; the complexity of these operations remains $O($list size$)$ when an array representation is used.

EXERCISES

1. Let L $= (a, b, c, d, e)$ be a linear list that is represented as a chain. Draw figures similar to Figure 6.1 showing the chain following each operation in the operation sequence: initial state, $insert(0, f)$, $insert(3, g)$, $insert(7, h)$, $erase(0)$, $erase(4)$.

2. Write code for the method `chain<T>::setSize(int theSize)` that makes the list size equal to `theSize`. If the original list size was less than the new one, `NULL` elements are added at the right end, and if the original size was more than the new one, the extra elements are removed from the right end. What is the complexity of your method? Test your code.

3. Write code for the method `chain<T>::set(theIndex, .theElement)` that sets the element whose index is `theIndex` to `theElement`. Throw an exception in case `theIndex` is out of range. What is the complexity of your method? Test your code.

4. Write code for the method `chain<T>::removeRange(fromIndex, toIndex)` that removes all elements in the specified index range. What is the complexity of your method? Test your code.

5. Write code for the method `chain<T>::lastIndexOf(theElement)` that returns the index of the rightmost occurrence of `theElement`. A −1 is returned in case `theElement` is not in the list. What is the complexity of your method? Test your code.

6. Overload the operator `[]` so that the expression `x[i]` returns a reference to the `i`th element of the chain `x`. If the chain doesn't have an `i`th element, an `illegalIndex` exception is to be thrown. The statements `x[i] = y` and `y = x[i]` should work as expected. Test your code.

7. Overload the operator `==` so that the expression `x == y` returns true iff the two chains `x` are `y` are equal (i.e., the `i`th elements of both chains are equal for all `i`). Test your code.

8. Overload the operator `!=` so that the expression `x != y` returns true iff the two chains `x` are `y` are not equal (see Exercise 7). Test your code.

9. Overload the operator `<` so that the expression `x < y` returns true iff the chain `x` is lexically smaller than the chain `y` (see Exercise 7). Test your code.

10. Write code for the method `chain<T>::swap(theChain)`, which swaps the elements of the chains `*this` and `theChain`. What is the time complexity of your method? Test your code.

11. Write a method to convert an array linear list into a chain. Your method is a member of neither `arrayList` nor `chain`. Use the `get` method of `arrayList` and the `insert` method of `chain`. What is the time complexity of your method? Test the correctness of your code.

12. Write a method to convert a linear list that is an instance of `chain` into an equivalent list that is an instance of `arrayList`. Your method is a member of neither `arrayList` nor `chain`.

(a) First use only the **get** and **listSize** methods of **chain** and the **insert** method of **arrayList**. What is the time complexity of your method? Test the correctness of your code.

(b) Now use a chain iterator. What is the time complexity of the new code? Test your code using your own test data.

13. Add methods to **chain** to convert an **arrayList** to a **chain** and vice versa. Specifically, write a method **fromList(theList)** to convert the array linear list **theList** into a chain and another method **toList(theList)** to convert the chain ***this** into an array linear list **theList**. What is the time complexity of each method? Test the correctness of your code.

14. (a) Write code for the method **chain<T>::leftShift(i)** that shifts the list elements left by i positions. If $1 = [0, 1, 2, 3, 4]$, then **l.leftShift(2)** results in $1 = [2, 3, 4]$.

(b) What is the time complexity of your method?

(c) Test your code.

15. (a) Write code for the method **chain<T>::reverse**, which reverses the order of the elements in ***this**. Do the reversal in-place and do not allocate any new nodes.

(b) What is the complexity of your method?

(c) Test the correctness of your method by compiling and then executing the code. Use your own test data.

16. Write a nonmember method to reverse a chain. Use the member methods of **chain** to accomplish the reversal. What is the complexity of your method? Test the correctness of your method.

17. Let a and b be of type **extendedChain**.

(a) Write a method **meld** to create a new extended chain c that contains elements alternately from a and b, beginning with the first element of a. If you run out of elements in one of a and b, then append the remaining elements of the other extended chain to c. The complexity of your code should be linear in the lengths of the a and b. Note that **meld** is not a member method of the class **extendedChain**.

(b) Show that your code has linear complexity.

(c) Test the correctness of your method by compiling and then executing the code. Use your own test data.

18. Write code for the method **chain<T>::meld**. This method is similar to the method **meld** of Exercise 17. However, a and b as well as the result are of type **chain<T>**. You should use the same physical nodes used by the chains a and b to create the resulting melded chain. Following a call to **meld**, the input chains a and b are empty.

(a) Write the code for `meld`. The complexity of your code should be linear in the lengths of initial chains.

(b) Show that your code has linear complexity.

(c) Test the correctness of your code by compiling and then executing the code. Use your own test data.

19. Let `a` and `b` be of type `extendedChain`. Assume that the elements of `a` and `b` are of a type for which the relational operators <, >, <=, >=, ==, and != are defined. Further, assume that both `a` and `b` and are in sorted order (i.e., nondecreasing from left to right).

(a) Write a nonmember method `merge` to create a new sorted linear list `c` that contains all the elements in `a` and `b`.

(b) What is the complexity of your method?

(c) Test the correctness of your method by compiling and then executing the code. Use your own test data.

20. Redo Exercise 19 but this time write code for the method `chain<T>::merge`. You should use the same nodes as the two input chains use. Following the merge, the input chains are empty.

21. Let `c` be of type `extendedChain`.

(a) Write a nonmember method `split` to create two extended chains `a` and `b`. `a` contains all elements in odd positions of `c`, and `b` contains the remaining elements. Your method should not change the extended chain `c`.

(b) What is the complexity of your code?

(c) Test the correctness of your method by compiling and then executing the code. Use your own test data.

22. Write code for the method `chain<T>::split` that is similar to the method `split` of Exercise 21. However, the new method `split` destroys the input chain `*this` and uses its nodes to construct the chains `a` and `b`.

23. In a circular shift operation, the elements of a linear list are rotated clockwise by a given amount. For example, when the elements of L = [0, 1, 2, 3, 4] are shifted circularly by 2, the result is L = [2, 3, 4, 0, 1].

(a) Write code for the method `extendedChain<T>::circularShift(i)`, which performs a circular shift by i positions.

(b) Test your code.

24. Let `theChain` be a chain. Suppose that as we move to the right, we reverse the direction of the chain pointers; therefore, when we are at node p, the chain is split into two chains. One is a chain that begins at p and goes to the last node of `theChain`. The other begins at the node l that precedes p in `theChain` and goes back to the first node of `theChain`. Initially, p = `theChain.firstNode` and l = NULL.

   (a) Draw a chain with six nodes and show the configuration when p is at the third node and l is at the second.

   (b) Develop the class `moveLeftAndRightOnAChain`. The class constructor initializes the data members l and p. The public methods of `move-LeftAndRightOnAChain` are `moveRight`—move l and p one node right, `moveLeft`—move l and p one node left, `currentElement`—return the element at node p, and `previousElement`—return the element at node l.

   (c) Test your codes using suitable data.

25. Use the ideas of Exercise 24 to obtain a new version of the class `chain` of Program 6.2. The new version should permit you to move back and forth on a chain efficiently and to perform the methods of `linearList` even though the chain may be split into two chains as described in Exercise 24. For this version, add the data members l and p as in Exercise 24 and add the following public methods:

   (a) `reset`—Set p to `firstNode` and l to NULL.

   (b) `current()`—Return the element pointed to by p; throw an exception if the operation fails.

   (c) `atEnd`—Return `true` if p is at the last element of the list; return `false` otherwise.

   (d) `atFront`—Return `true` if p is at the first element of the list; return `false` otherwise.

   (e) `moveToNext`—Move p and l one position right; throw an exception if the operation fails.

   (f) `moveToPrevious`—Move p and l one position back; throw an exception if the operation fails.

   To implement the `insert`, `erase`, and `indexOf` methods efficiently, it will be useful to have another data member `currentElement` that gives you the index of the element to which p points (i.e., is it element 0, 1, 2, etc., of the list?). Test the correctness of your code using suitable test data.

26. Write code for the method `chain<T>::insertionSort`, which uses insertion sort (see Program 2.15) to reorder the chain elements into nondecreasing order.

Do not create new nodes or delete old ones. You may assume that the elements being sorted are of type for which the relational operators (<, >, etc.) are defined.

   (a) What is the worst-case time complexity of your method? How much time does your method need if the elements are already in sorted order?

   (b) Test the correctness of your method by compiling and then executing the code. Use your own test data.

27. Do Exercise 26 for the following sort methods (see Chapter 2 for descriptions):

   (a) Bubble sort.

   (b) Selection sort.

   (c) Count or rank sort.

6.2   CIRCULAR LISTS AND HEADER NODES

Application codes that result from the use of chains can often be simplified and made to run faster by doing one or both of the following: (1) represent the linear list as a **singly linked circular list** (or simply **circular list**), rather than as a chain, and (2) add an additional node, called the **header node**, at the front. A circular list is obtained from a chain by linking the last node back to the first as in Figure 6.6(a). Figure 6.6(b) shows a nonempty circular list with a header node, and Figure 6.6(c) shows an empty circular list with a header node.

   The use of header nodes is a very common practice when linked lists are used, as their presence generally leads to simpler and faster programs. Program 6.13 gives the constructor and `indexOf` methods for the class `circularListWithHeader`, which represents a linear list as a circular list with a header node. The constructor creates the configuration for an empty list (Figure 6.6(c)). The complexity of the constructor is $\Theta(1)$ and that of `indexOf` is $O(\text{listSize})$. Although `chain<T>::indexOf` and `circularListWithHeader<T<::indexOf` have the same complexity, the code for the latter method is slightly simpler. Since `circularList-WithHeader<T>::indexOf` avoids the check `currentNode != NULL` that is made by `chain<T>::indexOf` on each iteration of its `while` loop, `circularListWithHeader<T>::indexOf` will run slightly faster than `chain<T>::indexOf` except possibly when we are looking for an element near the left end of the chain.

EXERCISES

28. Compare the run-time performance of the `indexOf` methods of Programs 6.6 and 6.13. Do this for both worst-case and average run times using linear lists of size 100; 1000; 10,000; and 100,000. Present your times in tabular form and in graph form.

(a) Circular list

(b) Circular list with header node   (c) Empty list

Figure 6.6 Circular linked lists

29. Develop the class `circularList`. Objects of this type are circular linked lists, as in Figure 6.6, except the lists do not have a header node. You must implement all the methods defined for the classes `chain` (Section 6.1.3) and `extendedChain` (Section 6.1.5). What is the time complexity of each method? Test the correctness of your code.

30. Do Exercise 15 using circular lists instead of chains.

31. Do Exercise 16 using circular lists instead of chains.

32. Do Exercise 17 using circular lists instead of chains.

33. Do Exercise 19 using circular lists instead of chains.

34. Do Exercise 20 using circular lists instead of chains.

35. Do Exercise 21 using circular lists instead of chains.

36. Do Exercise 22 using circular lists instead of chains.

37. Let x point to an arbitrary node in a circular list.

    (a) Write a method to remove the element in node x. *Hint:* Since we do not know which node precedes x, it is difficult to remove the node x from the list; however, to remove the element in x, it is sufficient to replace the

```
template<class T>
circularListWithHeader<T>::circularListWithHeader()
{// Constructor.
   headerNode = new chainNode<T>();
   headerNode->next = headerNode;
   listSize = 0;
}


template<class T>
int circularListWithHeader<T>::indexOf(const T& theElement) const
{// Return index of first occurrence of theElement.
 // Return -1 if theElement not in list.

   // Put theElement in header node
   headerNode->element = theElement;

   // search the chain for theElement
   chainNode<T>* currentNode = headerNode->next;
   int index = 0;  // index of currentNode
   while (currentNode->element != theElement)
   {
      // move to next node
      currentNode = currentNode->next;
      index++;
   }

   // make sure we found matching element
   if (currentNode == headerNode)
      return -1;
   else
      return index;
}
```

Program 6.13 Searching a circular linked list that has a header node

data field (i.e., element) of x by the data field of the node y that follows it and then remove the node y. When the element in the last node is removed, the element in the first node becomes the last element.

(b) What is the complexity of your method?

(c) Test the correctness of your method by compiling and then executing the code. Use your own test data.

38. Complete the class `circularListWithHeader` by writing code for the remaining methods of `extendedLinearList`. What is the time complexity of each method? Test the correctness of your code.

39. Do Exercises 15 and 16 using circular lists with header nodes instead of chains.

40. Do Exercises 17 and 18 using circular lists with header nodes instead of chains.

41. Do Exercises 19 and 20 using circular lists with header nodes instead of chains.

42. Do Exercises 21 and 22 using circular lists with header nodes instead of chains.

6.3   DOUBLY LINKED LISTS

For most applications of linear lists, the chain and/or circular list representations are adequate. However, in some applications it is useful to have a pointer from each element to both the next and previous elements. A **doubly linked list** is an ordered sequence of nodes in which each node has two pointers: `next` and `previous`. The `previous` pointer points to the node (if any) on the left, and the `next` pointer points to the node (if any) on the right. Figure 6.7 shows the doubly linked list representation of the linear list $(1, 2, 3, 4)$.

Figure 6.7 A doubly linked list

When defining the class `doublyLinkedList`, we use two data members `firstNode` and `lastNode` that, respectively, point to the left-most and right-most nodes of the doubly linked list (see Figure 6.7). A doubly linked list with just one element or node p has `firstNode` = `lastNode` = p, whereas `firstNode` = `lastNode` = NULL for an empty doubly linked list. These conventions are similar to those used for an extended chain (Program 6.12). When a doubly linked list is used, we find the `index`th element by moving from left to right when `index` < `listSize`/2 and from right to left otherwise. Exercise 43 asks you to develop the code for the class `doublyLinkedList`.

We can enhance doubly linked lists by adding a header node at the left and/or right ends and by making them circular lists. In a nonempty circular doubly linked list, `firstNode.previous` is a pointer to the right-most node (i.e., `firstNode.-previous` = `lastNode`), and `lastNode.next` is a pointer to the left-most node. So we can dispense with one of the variables `firstNode` and `lastNode` and simply keep track of the list using the remaining variable.

EXERCISES

43. Develop the class `doublyLinkedList`. Objects of this type are doubly linked lists with no header node. You must implement all the methods defined for the class `extendedChain` (Section 6.1.5). What is the time complexity of each method? Test the correctness of your code.

44. Write a method to join two doubly linked lists into a single doubly linked list. In a join the elements of the second list are appended to the end of those of the first list; the join is destructive in the sense that following the join, the second list becomes empty. Test your code.

45. Do Exercises 15 and 16 using doubly linked lists instead of chains.

46. Do Exercises 17 and 18 using doubly linked lists instead of chains.

47. Do Exercises 19 and 20 using doubly linked lists instead of chains.

48. Do Exercises 21 and 22 using doubly linked lists instead of chains.

49. Develop the class `doubleCircularList`. Objects of this type are doubly linked circular lists with no header node. You must implement all the methods defined for the class `extendedChain` (Section 6.1.5). What is the time complexity of each method? Test the correctness of your code.

50. Do Exercises 15 and 16 using doubly linked circular lists.

51. Do Exercise 44 using doubly linked circular lists.

52. Do Exercises 17 and 18 using doubly linked circular lists.

53. Do Exercises 19 and 20 using doubly linked circular lists.

54. Do Exercises 21 and 22 using doubly linked circular lists.

55. Do Exercise 49 using a header node for the doubly linked circular list. Compare the run time of your class with that of an equivalent class that uses the STL container class `list` much in the same way that `vectorList` (Program 5.12) uses a vector to implement an array linear list. Perform an experiment similar to that done in Section 6.1.6.

56. Do Exercises 15 and 16 using doubly linked circular lists with header nodes.

57. Do Exercise 44 using doubly linked circular lists with header nodes.

58. Do Exercises 17 and 18 using doubly linked circular lists with header nodes.

59. Do Exercises 19 and 20 using doubly linked circular lists with header nodes.

60. Do Exercises 21 and 22 using doubly linked circular lists with header nodes.

61. For the doubly linked circular list with header node class of Exercise 55, develop a bidirectional iterator. Test the correctness of your code using suitable test data.

6.4   GLOSSARY OF LINKED LIST TERMS

This chapter introduced the following important concepts:

- *chain.* A chain is a singly linked list of nodes. Let x be a chain. x is empty iff x.firstNode = NULL. If x is not empty, then x.firstNode points to the first node in the chain. The first node links to the second; the second to the third; and so on. The link (i.e., next) field of the last node is NULL.

- *Singly linked circular list.* This type of list differs from a chain only in that now the last node links back to the first. When the circular list x is empty, x.firstNode = NULL.

- *Header node.* A header node is an additional node introduced into a linked list. The use of this additional node generally results in simpler programs, as we can often avoid treating the empty list as a special case. When a header node is used, every list (including the empty list) contains at least one node, (i.e., the header node).

- *Doubly linked list.* A doubly linked list consists of nodes ordered from left to right. Nodes are linked from left to right using a pointer field (say) next. The right-most node has this field set to NULL. Nodes are also linked from right to left using a pointer field (say) previous. The left-most node has this field set to NULL.

- *Circular doubly linked list.* This type of list differs from a doubly linked list only in that now the left-most node uses its previous field to point to the right-most node and the right-most node uses its next field to point to the left-most node.

6.5   APPLICATIONS

6.5.1   Bin Sort

Suppose that a chain is used to maintain a list of students in a class. Each node has fields for the student's name, Social Security number, score on each assignment and test, and weighted aggregate score of all assignments and tests. Assume that all scores are integers in the range 0 through 100. We are to sort the nodes in order of the aggregate score. This sort takes $O(n^2)$ time (n is the number of students in the class) if we use one of the sort methods of Chapter 2. A faster way to accomplish the sort is to use **bin sort**. In a bin sort the nodes are placed into bins, each bin containing nodes with the same score. Then we combine the bins to create a sorted chain.

Figure 6.8(a) shows a sample chain with 10 nodes. This figure shows only the name and score fields of each node. The first field is the name, and the second is the score. For simplicity, we assume that each name is a single character and that the scores are in the range 0 through 5.

(a) Input chain

(b) Nodes in bins

(c) Sorted chain

Figure 6.8 Bin sort example

We will need six bins, one for each of the possible score values 0 through 5. Figure 6.8(b) shows the 10 nodes distributed into bins by score. We can obtain this distribution by moving down the chain and examining the nodes one at a time. When a node is examined. it is placed into the bin that corresponds to its score. So the first node is placed into bin 2. the second into bin 4. and so forth. Now if we collect the nodes from the bins, beginning with those in bin 0. we will have a sorted list as shown in Figure 6.8(c).

To implement the bins, we note that each bin is a linear list of nodes. The number of nodes in a bin may vary from 0 to as many as n. Before we begin the node distribution step, all bins are empty.

For bin sort we need to be able to (1) move down the input chain deleting nodes from this chain and adding them to the list for the appropriate bin and (2) collect and concatenate lists from the bins into a single sorted chain. If the input chain is of type chain (Program 6.2), we can do (1) by successively deleting the first element from the chain and inserting it as the first element in the appropriate bin list; we can do (2) by deleting the elements from the bins (beginning with the last bin) and inserting them at the front of an initially empty chain.

Program 6.14 gives a possible struct definition for student records. Our intent is to use chains of type chain<studentRecord>. In a realistic situation, studentRecord would contain several additional data members. The operators != and << have been overloaded, as these operators are used by the class chain.

```
struct studentRecord
{
   int score;
   string* name;
   int operator !=(studentRecord x) const
      {return (score != x.score);}
};

ostream& operator<<(ostream& out, const studentRecord& x)
   {out << x.score << ' ' << *x.name << endl; return out;}
```

Program 6.14 Possible struct for bin sort chain elements

An alternative to overloading != is to provide a conversion from the type studentRecord to a numeric type that can be used for comparison and other purposes. For example, we can overload the type conversion operator int() as shown in Program 6.15. Operators such as the arithmetic and relational operators +, /, <= and != that are not explicitly defined on the type studentRecord now can complete successfully by first performing a conversion to the type int. This solution is somewhat more general than our earlier one in which we explicitly overloaded the operator !=, as now the code works even when the class chain includes methods that perform other operations on this->element.

We can combine both overloading approaches so that type conversion to int occurs only when the operator will fail without the type conversion. So we may, for example, use the definition of Program 6.16. Type conversion to int now will take place only for operators other than != and <<.

Program 6.17 gives the code for the bin sort method. This code uses a chain for each bin. Although we could have represented each bin as an array list, we have used a chain because we plan to develop another bin sort method that is a member

```
struct studentRecord
{
   int score;
   string* name;

   operator int() const {return score;}
     // type conversion from studentRecord to int
};

ostream& operator<<(ostream& out, const studentRecord& x)
   {out << x.score << ' ' << *x.name << endl; return out;}
```

Program 6.15 An alternative definition of studentRecord

```
struct studentRecord
{
   int score;
   string* name;

   int operator !=(studentRecord x) const
   {return (score != x.score || name != x.name);}
   operator int() const {return score;}
};

ostream& operator<<(ostream& out, const studentRecord& x)
   {out << x.score << ' ' << *x.name << endl; return out;}
```

Program 6.16 Yet another definition of studentRecord

of chain. In this new method, it is more efficient to use chains rather than array lists because the input and output for the sort is a chain.

For the complexity analysis, we first note that binSort (Program 6.17) could terminate prematurely because of an exception. For example, the statement

```
bin = new chain<studentRecord> [range + 1];
```

could fail for lack of sufficient memory. If this statement fails, the method terminates in $\Theta(1)$ time. Assume that no exception occurs while the method executes. Now the first for loop takes $\Theta(range)$ time. Each get, insert and erase performed in the remaining two for loops takes $\Theta(1)$ time. Therefore, the complexity of the second for loop is $\Theta(n)$ where n is the size of the input chain, the complexity of the third

```
void binSort(chain<studentRecord>& theChain, int range)
{// Sort by score.

   // initialize the bins
   chain<studentRecord> *bin;
   bin = new chain<studentRecord> [range + 1];

   // distribute student records from theChain to bins
   int numberOfElements = theChain.size();
   for (int i = 1; i <= numberOfElements; i++)
   {
      studentRecord x = theChain.get(0);
      theChain.erase(0);
      bin[x.score].insert(0,x);
   }

   // collect elements from bins
   for (int j = range; j >= 0; j--)
      while (!bin[j].empty())
      {
         studentRecord x = bin[j].get(0);
         bin[j].erase(0);
         theChain.insert(0,x);
      }

   delete [] bin;
}
```

Program 6.17 Bin sort using the methods of chain

for loop is $\Theta(n+\text{range})$, and the overall complexity of binSort (when no exception is thrown) is $\Theta(n+\text{range})$. Accounting for the possibility of an exception or error, the overall complexity is $O(n+\text{range})$.

Bin Sort as a Method of a chain

Efficiency-conscious readers have probably noticed that we can avoid much of the work done by the method binSort (Program 6.17) by developing binSort as a method of chain. This approach enables us to avoid the calls to new made by the invocations of insert in Program 6.17; the calls to delete made by the invocations of erase also may be avoided. Further, by keeping track of the front and end of each bin chain, we can concatenate the bin chains in the "collection phase," as shown in

Program 6.18.

The chain for each bin begins with the node at the bottom of the bin and goes to the node at the top of the bin. Each chain has two pointers, `bottom` and `top`, to it. `bottom[theBin]` points to the node at the bottom of bin `theBin`, while `top[theBin]` points to the node at the top of this bin. The initial configuration of empty bins is represented by `bottom[theBin]` = `NULL` for all bins. As chain nodes are examined, they are added to the top of the required bin (first `for` loop of Program 6.18). The second `for` loop examines the bins beginning with bin 0 and concatenates the chains in the nonempty bins to form the sorted chain.

For the time complexity of `binSort`, assume that no exception is thrown. The creation and initialization of the arrays `bottom` and `top` as well as the second `for` loop take $\Theta(\text{range})$ time, and the first `for` loop takes $\Theta(n)$ time. Allowing for the possibility that an exception or error is thrown, the overall complexity is $O(n+\text{range})$.

Notice that `binSort` (Program 6.18) does not change the relative order of elements that have the same score. For example, suppose that E, G, and H all have the score 3 and that E comes before G, which comes before H in the input chain. In the sorted chain, too, E comes before G, which comes before H. A sort method that preserves the relative order of elements with the same value is called a **stable sort**.

6.5.2   Radix Sort

The bin sort method of Section 6.5.1 may be extended to sort, in $\Theta(n)$ time, n integers in the range 0 through $n^c - 1$ where $c \geq 0$ is an integer constant. Notice that if we use `binSort` with `range` = n^c, the sort complexity will be $\Theta(n + \text{range})$ = $\Theta(n^c)$. Instead of using `binSort` directly on the numbers to be sorted, we will decompose these numbers using some radix r. For example, the number 928 decomposes into the digits 9, 2, and 8 using the radix 10 (i.e., $928 = 9*10^2+2*10^1+8*10^0$). The most significant digit is 9, and the least significant digit is 8; the ones digit is 8, the tens digit is 2, and the hundreds digit is 9. The number 3725 has the radix 10 decomposition 3, 7, 2, and 5; using the radix 60 instead, the decomposition is 1, 2, and 5 (i.e., $(3725)_{10} = (125)_{60}$). In a **radix sort** we decompose the numbers into digits using some radix r and then sort by digits.

Example 6.1 Suppose that we are sorting 10 integers in the range 0 through 999. If we use `binSort` with `range` = 1000, then the bin initialization takes 1000 steps, the node distribution takes 10 steps, and collecting from the bins takes 1000 steps. The total step count is 2010. Another approach is

1. Use `binSort` to sort the 10 numbers by their least significant digit (i.e., the ones digit). Since each digit ranges from 0 through 9, we have `range` = 10. Figure 6.9(a) shows a sample 10-number chain, and Figure 6.9(b) shows the chain sorted by least significant digit.

```
template<class T>
void chain<T>::binSort(int range)
{// Sort the nodes in the chain.
   // create and initialize the bins
   chainNode<T> **bottom, **top;
   bottom = new chainNode<T>* [range + 1];
   top = new chainNode<T>* [range + 1];
   for (int b = 0; b <= range; b++)
      bottom[b] = NULL;

   // distribute to bins
   for (; firstNode != NULL; firstNode = firstNode->next)
   {// add firstNode to proper bin
      int theBin = firstNode->element; // type conversion to int
      if (bottom[theBin] == NULL) // bin is empty
        bottom[theBin] = top[theBin] = firstNode;
      else
      {// bin not empty
        top[theBin]->next = firstNode;
        top[theBin] = firstNode;
      }
   }

   // collect from bins into sorted chain
   chainNode<T> *y = NULL;
   for (int theBin = 0; theBin <= range; theBin++)
      if (bottom[theBin] != NULL)
      {// bin not empty
         if (y == NULL) // first nonempty bin
             firstNode = bottom[theBin];
         else // not first nonempty bin
             y->next = bottom[theBin];
         y = top[theBin];
      }
   if (y != NULL)
      y->next = NULL;

   delete [] bottom;
   delete [] top;
}
```

Program 6.18 Bin sort as a method of chain

2. Use `binSort` to sort the chain from (1) by the next digit (i.e., the tens digit). Again, `range` = 10. Since bin sort is a stable sort, elements that have the same second digit remain sorted by the least significant digit. As a result, the chain is now sorted by the two least significant digits. Figure 6.9(c) shows our chain following this sort.

3. Use `binSort` to sort the chain from (2) by the next digit (i.e., the hundreds digit). (For numbers smaller than 100, the hundreds digit is 0.) Since the sort on the hundreds digit is stable, elements with the same hundreds digit remain sorted on the remaining two digits. As a result, the chain is sorted on the three least significant digits. Figure 6.9(d) shows the chain following this sort.

(a) Input chain

(b) Chain after sorting on least significant digit

(c) Chain after sorting on second-least significant digit

(d) Chain after sorting on most significant digit

Figure 6.9 Radix sort with $r = 10$ and $d = 3$

The preceding sorting scheme describes a radix 10 sort. The numbers to be sorted are decomposed into their decimal (or base 10) digits, and the numbers are sorted on these digits. Since each number has at most three digits, three sort passes are made. Each sort pass uses a bin sort with `range` = 10. In each of these three bin sorts, we spend 10 steps in initializing the bins, 10 in distributing the records, and 10 in bin collection. The total number of steps is 90, which is less than when the 10 numbers are sorted using a single bin sort with `range` = 1000. The single bin sort scheme is really a radix sort with $r = 1000$. ∎

Example 6.2 Suppose that 1000 integers in the range 0 through $10^6 - 1$ are to be sorted. Using a radix of $r = 10^6$ corresponds to using binSort directly on the numbers and takes 10^6 steps to initialize the bins, 1000 steps to distribute the numbers into bins, and another 10^6 to collect from the bins. The total number of steps is therefore 2,001,000. With $r = 1000$, the sort proceeds as follows:

1. Sort using the three least significant decimal digits of each number and use range = 1000.

2. Sort the result of (1) using the next three decimal digits of each number.

Each of the preceding sorts takes 3000 steps, so the sort is accomplished in a total of 6000 steps. When $r = 100$ is used, three bin sorts on pairs of decimal digits are performed. Each of these sorts takes 1200 steps, and the total number of steps needed for the sort becomes 3600. If we use $r = 10$, six bin sorts will be done, one on each decimal digit. The total number of steps will be $6(10 + 1000 + 10) = 6120$. For our example we expect radix sort with $r = 100$ to be most efficient. ∎

We can decompose a number into digits by using the division and mod operators. If we are performing a radix 10 decomposition, then the radix 10 digits may be computed (from least significant to most significant) using the following expressions:

$$x\%10; \quad (x\%100)/10; \quad (x\%1000)/100; \quad \cdots$$

When $r = 100$, these expressions become

$$x\%100; \quad (x\%10000)/100; \quad (x\%1000000)/10000; \quad \cdots$$

For a general radix r, the expressions are

$$x\%r; \quad (x\%r^2)/r; \quad (x\%r^3)/r^2; \quad \cdots$$

When we use the radix $r = n$ to decompose n integers in the range 0 through $n^c - 1$, the number of digits is c. So the n numbers can be sorted using c bin sort passes with range = n. The time needed for the sort is $\Theta(cn) = \Theta(n)$, as c is a constant.

6.5.3   Convex Hull

A **polygon** is a closed planar figure with three or more straight edges. The polygon of Figure 6.10(a) has six edges, and that of Figure 6.10(b) has eight. A polygon **contains** all points that are either on its edges or inside the region it encloses. A polygon is **convex** iff all line segments that join two points on or in the polygon include no point that is outside the polygon. The polygon of Figure 6.10(a) is convex, while that of Figure 6.10(b) is not. Figure 6.10(b) shows two line segments (broken lines) whose endpoints are on or in the polygon. Both of these segments contain points that are outside the polygon.

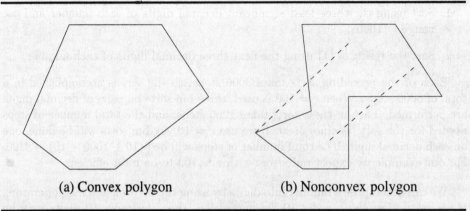

(a) Convex polygon   (b) Nonconvex polygon

Figure 6.10 Convex and nonconvex polygons

The **convex hull** of a set S of points in the plane is the smallest convex polygon that contains all these points. The vertices (i.e., corners) of this polygon are the **extreme points** of S. Figure 6.11 shows 13 points in the plane. The convex hull is the polygon defined by the solid lines. The extreme points have been identified by circles. When all points of S lie on a straight line (i.e., they are collinear), we have a degenerate case for which the convex hull is defined to be the smallest straight line that includes all the points.

The problem of finding the convex hull of a set of points in the plane is a fundamental problem in computational geometry. The solutions to several other problems in computational geometry (e.g., find the smallest rectangle that encloses a set of points in the plane) require the computation of the convex hull. In addition, the convex hull finds application in image processing and statistics.

Suppose we pick a point X in the interior of the convex hull of S and draw a vertical line downwards from X (Figure 6.12(a)). Exercise 67 describes how we can select the point X. Let a_i be the (polar) angle made by this line and the line from X to the ith point of S. a_i is measured by going counterclockwise from a point on the vertical line to the line from X to the ith point. Figure 6.12(a) shows a_2. Now let us arrange the points of S into nondecreasing order of a_i. Points with the same polar angle are ordered by distance from X. In Figure 6.12(a) the points have been numbered 1 through 13 in the stated order.

A counterclockwise sweep of the vertical line downwards from X encounters the extreme points of S in order of the polar angle a_i. If u, v, and w are three consecutive extreme points in counterclockwise order, then the counterclockwise

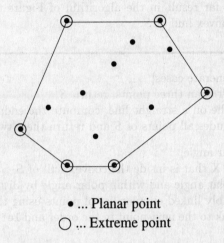

• ... Planar point

◯ ... Extreme point

Figure 6.11 Convex hull of planar points

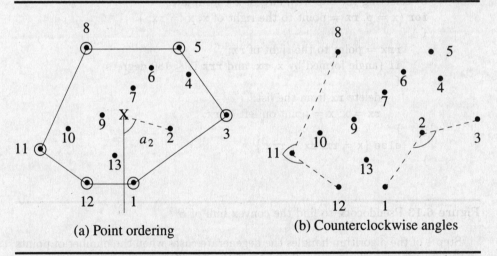

(a) Point ordering

(b) Counterclockwise angles

Figure 6.12 Identifying extreme points

angle made by the line segments from u to v and w to v is more than 180 degrees. (Figure 6.12(b) shows the counterclockwise angle made by points 8, 11, and 12.) When the counterclockwise angle made by three consecutive points in the polar order is less than or equal to 180 degrees, then the second of these points is not an extreme point. Notice that when the angle made by u, v, and w is less than 180 degrees, if we walk from u to v to w, we make a right turn at v. When we walk counterclockwise around a convex polygon, all our turns are left turns. The observations made so far result in the algorithm of Figure 6.13, which finds the extreme points and convex hull of S.

Step 1: [Handle degenerate cases]
    If S has fewer than three points, return S.
    If all points lie on a straight line, compute the endpoints of the smallest line that includes all points of S and return these two points.

Step 2: [Sort by polar angle]
    Find a point X that is inside the convex hull of S.
    Sort S by polar angle and within polar angle by distance from X.
    Create a doubly linked circular list of points using the above order.
    Let `right` link to the next point in the order and `left` link to the previous point.

Step 3: [Eliminate nonextreme points]
    Let p be the point that has the smallest y-coordinate (break a tie, if any, by selecting the one with largest x-coordinate).

```
for (x = p, rx = point to the right of x; x != rx; )
{
    rrx = point to the right of rx;
    if (angle formed by x, rx, and rrx is ≤ 180 degrees)
    {
        delete rx from the list;
        rx = x; x = point on left of rx;
    }
    else {x = rx; rx = rrx;}
}
```

Figure 6.13 Pseudocode to find the convex hull of S

Step 1 of the algorithm handles the degenerate cases when the number of points in S is 0 or 1, as well as when all points of S are collinear. This step can be done in $O(n)$ time where n is the number of points in S. For the collinearity test, we select any two points and compute the equation of the line through them. Next we examine the remaining $n - 2$ points and determine whether they lie on this line. During this process we can also determine the endpoints of the shortest line that includes all points in case they are collinear.

In step 2 the points are ordered by polar angle and collected into a doubly linked list because in step 3 we will be eliminating points that are not extreme points and also moving backwards on the list. Both operations are straightforward in a doubly linked list. Exercise 67 asks you to explore the use of a singly linked list. Because of the sort, this step takes $O(n^2)$ time if we use any of the sorts from Chapter 2. In Chapters 9 and 14, we will see that we can sort in $O(n \log n)$ time. As a result, the complexity of step 2 is counted as $O(n \log n)$.

In step 3 we repeatedly examine sets of three consecutive points in counter-clockwise order and check whether the angle they make is less than or equal to 180 degrees. If it is, then the middle point rx is not an extreme point and is eliminated. If the angle exceeds 180 degrees, rx may or may not be an extreme point and we advance x to the next vertex rx. When the for loop is exited, every point x on the doubly linked circular list satisfies the property that the angle made by x, rx, and rrx exceeds 180 degrees. Hence all of these points are extreme points. By going around the list using the right fields, we traverse the boundary of the convex hull in counterclockwise order. We begin at the point with lowest y, as this point must be in the convex hull.

For the complexity of step 3, we note that following each angle check in the for loop either (1) a vertex rx is eliminated and x is moved back one node on the list or (2) x is moved forward on the list. Since the number of eliminated vertices is $O(n)$, x can be moved back at most a total of $O(n)$ nodes. Hence we can be in case (2) only $O(n)$ times. So the for loop is iterated $O(n)$ times. Since an angle check takes $\Theta(1)$ time, the complexity of step 3 is $O(n)$. As a result, we can find the convex hull of n points in $O(n \log n)$ time.

6.5.4   Union-Find Problem

Equivalence Classes

Suppose we have a set $U = 1, 2, \cdots, n$ of n elements and a set $R = (i_1, j_1)$, $(i_2, j_2), \cdots, (i_r, j_r)$ of r relations. The relation R is an **equivalence relation** iff the following conditions are true:

- $(a, a) \in R$ for all $a \in U$ (the relation is reflexive).

- $(a, b) \in R$ iff $(b, a) \in R$ (the relation is symmetric).

- $(a, b) \in R$ and $(b, c) \in R$ imply that $(a, c) \in R$ (the relation is transitive).

Often when we specify an equivalence relation R, we omit some of the pairs in R. The omitted pairs may be obtained by applying the reflexive, symmetric, and transitive properties of an equivalence relation.

Example 6.3 Suppose $n = 14$ and $R = \{(1,11), (7,11), (2,12), (12,8), (11,12), (3,13), (4,13), (13,14), (14,9), (5,14), (6,10)\}$. We have omitted all pairs of the form (a, a) because these pairs are implied by the reflexive property. Similarly, we have omitted all symmetric pairs. Since $(1,11) \in R$, the symmetric property requires $(11,1) \in R$. Other omitted pairs are obtained by applying the transitive property. For example, $(7,11)$ and $(11,12)$ imply $(7,12)$. ∎

Two elements a and b are equivalent if $(a, b) \in R$. An **equivalence class** is defined to be a maximal set of equivalent elements. *Maximal* means that no element outside the class is equivalent to an element in the class. Since it is not possible for an element to be in more than one equivalence class, an equivalence relation partitions the universe U into disjoint classes.

Example 6.4 Consider the equivalence relation of Example 6.3. Since elements 1 and 11, and 11 and 12 are equivalent, elements 1, 11, and 12 are equivalent. They are therefore in the same class. These three elements do not, however, form an equivalence class, as they are equivalent to other elements (e.g., 7). So {1, 11, 12} is not a maximal set of equivalent elements. The set {1, 2, 7, 8, 11, 12} is an equivalence class. The relation R defines two other equivalence classes: {3, 4, 5, 9, 13, 14} and {6, 10}. Notice that the three equivalence classes are disjoint.   ∎

In the **offline equivalence class** problem, we are given n and R and we need to determine the equivalence classes. From the definition of an equivalence class, it follows that each element is in exactly one equivalence class. In the **online equivalence class** problem, we begin with n elements, each in a separate equivalence class. We are to process a sequence of the operations: (1) combine(a,b) ··· combines the equivalence classes that contain elements a and b into a single class and (2) find(theElement) ··· determines the class that currently contains element theElement. The purpose of the find operation is to determine whether two elements are in the same class. Hence the find operation is to be implemented to return the same answer for elements in the same class and different answers for elements in different classes.

We can write the combine operation in terms of two finds and a unite (or union) that actually takes two different classes and makes one. So combine(a,b) is equivalent to

```
classA = find(a);
classB = find(b);
if (classA != classB)
   unite(classA, classB);
```

Notice that with the find and union operations, we can add new relations to R. For instance, to add the relation (a, b), we determine whether a and b are already in the same class. If they are, then the new relation is redundant. If they aren't, then we perform a unite on the two classes that contain a and b.

In this section we are concerned primarily with the online equivalence problem, which is more commonly known as the **union-find** problem. Although the solutions developed in this section are rather simple, they are not the most efficient. Faster solutions are developed in Section 11.9.2. A fast solution for the offline equivalence problem is developed in Section 8.5.5.

Applications

The following examples show how a machine-scheduling problem and a circuit-wiring problem may be modeled as online equivalence class problems. A version of the circuit wiring problem may be modeled as an offline equivalence class problem.

Example 6.5 A certain factory has a single machine that is to perform n tasks. Task i has an integer release time r_i and an integer deadline d_i. The completion of each task requires one unit of time on this machine. A **feasible schedule** is an assignment of tasks to time slots on the machine such that task i is assigned to a time slot between its release time and deadline and no slot has more than one task assigned to it.

Consider the following four tasks:

Task	A	B	C	D
Release time	0	0	1	2
Deadline	4	4	2	3

Tasks A and B are released at time 0, task C is released at time 1, and task D is released at time 2. The following task-to-slot assignment is a feasible schedule: do task A from 0 to 1; task C from 1 to 2; task D from 2 to 3; and task B from 3 to 4 (see Figure 6.14).

Figure 6.14 A schedule for four tasks

An intuitively appealing method to construct a schedule is

1. Sort the tasks into nonincreasing order of release time.

2. Consider the tasks in this nonincreasing order. For each task determine the free slot nearest to, but not after, its deadline. If this free slot is before the task's release time, fail. Otherwise, assign the task to this slot.

Exercise 74 asks you to prove that the strategy just described fails to find a feasible schedule only when such a schedule does not exist.

The online equivalence class problem can be used to implement step (2). For this step, let d denote the latest deadline of any task. The usable time slots are of the form "from $i - 1$ to i" where $1 \leq i \leq d$. We will refer to these usable slots as slots 1 through d. For any slot a, define $near(a)$ as the largest i such that $i \leq a$

and slot i is free. If no such i exists, define $near(a) = near(0) = 0$. Two slots a and b are in the same equivalence class iff $near(a) = near(b)$.

Prior to the scheduling of any task, $near(a) = a$ for all slots, and each slot is in a separate equivalence class. When slot a is assigned a task in step (2), $near$ changes for all slots b with $near(b) = a$. For these slots the new value of $near$ is $near(a - 1)$. Hence when slot a is assigned a task, we need to perform a unite on the equivalence classes that currently contain slots a and $a - 1$. If with each equivalence class e we retain, in $nearest[e]$, the value of $near$ of its members, then $near(a)$ is given by $nearest[\text{find}(a)]$. (Assume that the equivalence class name is taken to be whatever the find operation returns.)   ∎

Example 6.6 [From Wires to Nets] An electronic circuit consists of components, pins, and wires. Figure 6.15 shows a circuit with the three components A, B, and C. Each wire connects a pair of pins. Two pins a and b are **electrically equivalent** iff they are either connected by a wire or there is a sequence $i_1, i_2, \ldots i_k$ of pins such that $a, i_1; i_1, i_2; i_2, i_3; \cdots; i_{k-1}, i_k;$ and i_k, b are all connected by wires. A **net** is a maximal set of electrically equivalent pins. *Maximal* means that no pin outside the net is electrically equivalent to a pin in the net.

Figure 6.15 A three-chip circuit on a printed circuit board

Consider the circuit shown in Figure 6.16. In this figure only the pins and wires have been shown. The 14 pins are numbered 1 through 14. Each wire may be described by the two pins that it connects. For instance, the wire connecting pins 1 and 11 is described by the pair $(1,11)$, which is equivalent to the pair $(11,1)$. The set of wires is $\{(1,11), (7,11), (2,12), (12,8), (11,12), (3,13), (4,13), (13,14), (14,9), (5,14), (6,10)\}$. The nets are $\{1, 2, 7, 8, 11, 12\}$, $\{3, 4, 5, 9, 13, 14\}$ and $\{6, 10\}$.

In the **offline net finding problem**, we are given the pins and wires and are to determine the nets. This problem is modeled by the offline equivalence problem with each pin being a member of U and each wire a member of R.

Figure 6.16 Circuit with pins and wires shown

In the **online** version we begin with a collection of pins and no wires and are to perform a sequence of operations of the form (1) add a wire to connect pins a and b and (2) find the net that contains pin a. The purpose of the find operation is to determine whether two pins are in the same net or in different nets. This version of the net problem may be modeled by the online equivalence class problem. Initially, there are no wires, and we have $R = \phi$. The net find operation corresponds to the equivalence class **find** operation and adding a new wire (a, b) corresponds to combine(a, b), which is equivalent to **unite(find(a), find(b))**.   ∎

First Union-Find Solution

A simple solution to the online equivalence class problem is to use an array **equiv-Class** and let **equivClass[i]** be the class that currently contains element **i**. The methods to initialize, union, and find take the form given in Program 6.19. **n** is the number of elements. **n** and **equivClass** are global variables. To unite two different classes, we arbitrarily pick one of these classes and change the **equivClass** values of all elements in this class to correspond to the **equivClass** values of the elements of the other class. Note that the inputs to **unite** are **equivClass** values (i.e., the results of a **find** operation) and not element indexes. Even though **unite** works correctly when a redundant union (i.e., one in which **classA = classB**), we make the assumption that redundant unions are not performed. The **initialize** and **unite** methods have complexity $\Theta(n)$ (we assume that **new** does not throw an exception when invoked by **initialize**), and the complexity of **find** is $\Theta(1)$. From Examples 6.5 and 6.6, we see that in any application of these methods, we will perform one initialization, u unites, and f finds. The time needed for all of these operations is $\Theta(n+u*n+f) = \Theta(u*n+f)$.

```
int *equivClass,    // equivalence class array
    n;              // number of elements

void initialize(int numberOfElements)
{// Initialize numberOfElements classes with one element each.
   n = numberOfElements;
   equivClass = new int [n + 1];
   for (int e = 1; e <= n; e++)
      equivClass[e] = e;
}


void unite(int classA, int classB)
{// Unite the classes classA and classB.
 // Assume classA != classB
   for (int k = 1; k <= n; k++)
      if (equivClass[k] == classB)
         equivClass[k] = classA;
}

int find(int theElement)
{// Find the class that contains theElement.
   return equivClass[theElement];
}
```

Program 6.19 Union-find solution using arrays

Second Union-Find Solution

The time complexity of the union operation can be reduced by keeping a chain for each equivalence class because now we can find all elements in a given equivalence class by going down the chain for that class, rather than by examining all equivClass values. In fact, if each equivalence class knows its size, we can choose to change the equivClass values of the smaller equivalence class and perform the union operation even faster. By using integer pointers (also known as simulated pointers), we get quick access to the node that represents element e. We adopt the following conventions:

- equivNode is a struct with data members equivClass, size, and next. Program 6.20 gives the code for this struct.

- An array node[1:n] of type equivNode is used to represent the n elements together with the equivalence class chains.

```
struct equivNode
{
    int equivClass,  // element class identifier
        size,        // number of elements in class
        next;        // pointer to next element in class
};
```

Program 6.20 The struct equivNode

- node[e].equivClass is both the value to be returned by find(e) and an integer pointer to the first node in the chain for the equivalence class node[e].equivClass.

- node[e].size is defined only if e is the first node on a chain. In this case node[e].size is the number of nodes on the chain that begins at node[e].

- node[e].next gives the next node on the chain that contains node e. Since the nodes in use are numbered 1 through n, a NULL pointer can be simulated by the integer 0.

Program 6.21 gives the new code for initialize, unite, and find.

Since an equivalence class is of size $O(n)$, the complexity of the union operation is $O(n)$ when chains are used. The complexity of the initialization and find operations remain $O(n)$ and $\Theta(1)$, respectively. To determine the complexity of performing one initialization and a sequence of u unions and f finds, we will use the following lemma.

Lemma 6.1 *If we start with n classes that have one element each and perform u nonredundant unions, then*

1. *No class has more than $u + 1$ elements.*

2. *At least $n - 2u$ singleton classes remain.*

3. *$u < n$.*

Proof See Exercise 72.   ∎

The complexity of the initialize and f finds is $O(n+f)$. For the u nonredundant unions, we note that the cost of each union is Θ(size of smaller class). During the union elements are moved from the smaller class to the bigger one. The complexity of a single union is O(number of elements moved), and the complexity of all u unions is O(total number of element moves). Following a union operation, each element that is moved to a new class ends up in a class whose size is at least twice that of the class the element was in before the union operation (because elements move from an

```
equivNode *node; // array of nodes
int n;            // number of elements

void initialize(int numberOfElements)
{// Initialize numberOfElements classes with one element each.
   n = numberOfElements;
   node = new equivNode [n + 1];

   for (int e = 1; e <= n; e++)
   {
      node[e].equivClass = e;
      node[e].next = 0;    // no next node on chain
      node[e].size = 1;
   }
}

void unite(int classA, int classB)
{// Unite the classes classA and classB.
 // Assume classA != classB
 // classA and classB are first elements in their chains

   // make classA smaller class
   if (node[classA].size > node[classB].size)
      swap(classA, classB);

   //  change equivClass values of smaller class
   int k;
   for (k = classA; node[k].next != 0; k = node[k].next)
      node[k].equivClass = classB;
   node[k].equivClass = classB; // last node in chain

   // insert chain classA after first node in chain classB
   // and update new chain size
   node[classB].size += node[classA].size;
   node[k].next = node[classB].next;
   node[classB].next = classA;
}

int find(int theElement)
{// Find the class that contains theElement.
   return node[theElement].equivClass;
}
```

Program 6.21 Union-find solution using chains and integer pointers initially smaller class into an initially bigger class). Therefore, since at the end no class has more than $u+1$ elements (Lemma 6.1(1)), no element can be moved more than $\log_2(u+1)$ times during the u unions. Furthermore, from Lemma 6.1(2), at most $2u$ elements can move (because the elements left in singleton classes have never moved). So the total number of element moves cannot exceed $2u\log_2(u+1)$. As a result, the time needed to perform the u unions is $O(u\log u)$. The complexity of the initialization and the sequence of u unions and f finds is therefore $O(\text{n}+u\log u+f)$.

EXERCISES

62. Is Program 6.17 a stable sort program?

63. Compare the run times of the bin sort methods given in Programs 6.17 and 6.18. Use $n = 10,000$; $50,000$; and $100,000$. What can you say about the overhead introduced by using the class **chain**?

64. In this exercise we shall develop a method to sort a chain using the radix sort technique.

    (a) Write code for the method **chain<T>::radixSort(r, d)**, which sorts a chain into ascending order using the radix sort technique. The radix r and number of digits d in the radix r decomposition are inputs to your method. You my assume that a type conversion from the data type **T** to **int** is defined. The complexity of your method should be $O(d(r + n))$. Show that this is the case.

    (b) Test the correctness of your method by compiling and executing it with your own test data.

    (c) Compare the performance of your method with one that performs a linked insertion sort. Do so for $n = 100$; 1000; and $10,000$; $r = 10$; and $d = 3$.

65. (a) Write a method to sort n integers in the range 0 through $n^c - 1$ using the radix sort method and $r = n$. The complexity of your method should be $O(cn)$. Show that this is the case. Assume the integers are in a chain; the element type is **int**.

    (b) Test the correctness of your method.

    (c) Measure the run time of your method for $n \doteq 10$; 100; 1000; and $10,000$ and $c = 2$. Present your results in tabular form and in graph form.

66. You are given a pile of n card decks. Each card has three fields: deck number, suit, and face value. Since each deck has at most 52 cards (some cards may be missing from a deck), the pile has at most $52n$ cards. You may assume there is at least one card from each deck. So the number of cards in the pile is at least n.

(a) Explain how to sort this pile by deck number, within deck number by suit, and within suit by face value. You should make three bin sort passes over the pile to accomplish the sort.

(b) Write a program to input n and a card pile and to output the sorted pile. You should represent the card pile as a chain. Each card has the fields: `deck`, `suit`, `face`, and `link`. The complexity of your program should be $O(n)$. Show that this is the case.

(c) Test the correctness of your program.

67. [Convex Hull]

(a) Let u, v, and w be three points in the plane. Assume that they are not collinear. Write a method to find a point inside the triangle formed by these three points.

(b) Let S be a set of points in the plane. Write a method to determine whether all the points are collinear. In case they are, your method should compute the endpoints of the shortest line that includes all the points. In case the points are not collinear, then you should find three noncollinear points from the given point set. You can use these three points together with your method for part (a) to determine a point inside the convex hull of S. The complexity of your method should be $O(n)$. Show that this is the case.

(c) Use the codes of (a) and (b) to refine Figure 6.13 into a Java program that inputs S and outputs the convex hull of S. During input the points may be collected into a doubly linked list that is later sorted by polar angle. For the sort step you may use one of the sort methods of Chapter 2, or if you have access to an $O(n \log n)$ sort, you may use it.

(d) Write additional convex hull programs that replace the use of a doubly linked list with (i) a chain and (ii) an array linear list.

(e) Test the correctness of your convex hull programs.

68. Do Exercise 67 using a singly linked list. Use the ideas of Exercise 24 to ensure that the `for` loop of step 3 of Figure 6.13 has complexity $O(n)$.

69. Develop a representation for integers that is suitable for performing arithmetic on arbitrarily large integers. The arithmetic is to be performed with no loss of accuracy. Write Java methods to input and output large integers and to perform the arithmetic operations add, subtract, multiply, and divide. The method for division will return two integers: the quotient and the remainder.

70. [Polynomials] A **univariate polynomial** of degree d has the form

$$c_d x^d + c_{d-1} x^{d-1} + c_{d-2} x^{d-2} + \cdots + c_0$$

where $c_d \neq 0$. The c_is are the coefficients, and $d, d-1, \cdots$ are the exponents. By definition d is a nonnegative integer. For this exercise you may assume that the coefficients are also integers. Each $c_i x^i$ is a term of the polynomial. We wish to develop a Java class to support arithmetic involving polynomials. For this exercise we will represent each polynomial as a linear list $(c_0, c_1, c_2, \cdots, c_d)$ of coefficients.

Develop a C++ class `polynomial` that should have an instance data member `degree`, which is the degree of the polynomial. It may have other instance data members also. Your polynomial class should support the following operations:

(a) `polynomial()`—Create the zero polynomial. The degree of this polynomial is 0 and it has no terms. `polynomial()` is the class constructor.

(b) `degree()`—Return the degree of the polynomial.

(c) `input(inStream)`—Read in a polynomial from the input stream `inStream`. You may assume the input consists of the polynomial degree and a list of coefficients in ascending order of exponents.

(d) `output(outStream)`—Output the polynomial to the output stream `outStream`. The output format should be the same as the input format.

(e) `add(b)`—Add to polynomial b and return the result polynomial.

(f) `subtract(b)`—Subtract the polynomial b and return the result.

(g) `multiply(b)`—Multiply with polynomial b and return the result.

(h) `divide(b)`—Divide by polynomial b and return the quotient.

(i) `valueOf(x)`—Return the value of the polynomial at point x.

Test your code.

71. [Polynomials] Design and code a linked class to represent and manipulate univariate polynomials (see Exercise 70). Assume that the coefficients are integers. Use circular linked lists with header nodes. Each node should have the fields `exp` (exponent), `coeff` (coefficient), and `next` (pointer to next node). In addition to the header node, the circular list representation of a polynomial has one node for each term that has a nonzero coefficient. Terms whose coefficient is 0 are not represented. The terms are in decreasing order of exponent, and the header node has its exponent field set to -1. Figure 6.17 gives some examples.

The external (i.e., for input or output) representation of a univariate polynomial will be assumed to be a sequence of numbers of the form $n, e_1, c_1, e_2, c_2, e_3, c_3, \cdots, e_n, c_n$, where the e_i represent the exponents and the c_i the coefficients; n gives the number of terms in the polynomial. The exponents are in decreasing order; that is, $e_1 > e_2 > \cdots > e_n$.

Your class should support all the methods of Exercise 70. Test the correctness of your code using suitable polynomials.

(a) $A(x) = 99x^{87} + 5x^{30} - 25x$

(b) $B(x) = -3x^{17} + 2x^{10} + 7x^4 - 2$

(c) $C(x) = 0$

Figure 6.17 Sample polynomials

72. Prove Lemma 6.1.

73. Write a C++ program for the online net finding problem of Example 6.6. Model the problem as the online equivalence class problem and use the chain method. Test the correctness of your program.

74. Prove that the strategy outlined in Example 6.5 fails to find a feasible schedule only when such a schedule does not exist.

75. Compare the run-time performance of Programs 6.19 and 6.21.

76. Develop a version of Program 6.21 in which the chains are replaced by array linear lists.

    (a) Test your code.

    (b) What is the time complexity of your new implementation?

    (c) Compare the performance of Program 6.21 and your new implementation.

77. Develop a version of Program 6.21 in which the chains use C++ pointers rather than integer pointers. To access the node for element i in $O(1)$ time, keep an array *theNode* such that *theNode*[i] is a pointer to the node that represents element i.

(a) Test your code.

(b) What is the time complexity of your new implementation?

(c) Compare the performance of Program 6.21 and your new implementation.

78. Write a C++ program for the scheduling problem of Example 6.5. Model the problem as the online equivalence class problem and use the chain method. Test the correctness of your program.

CHAPTER 7

ARRAYS AND MATRICES

BIRD'S-EYE VIEW

In practice, data are often available in tabular form. Although arrays are the most natural way to represent tabular data, we can often reduce both the space and time requirements of our programs by using a customized representation. This reduction is possible, for example, when a large portion of the table entries are 0.

This chapter begins by examining the row-major and column-major representations of a multidimensional array. These representations map a multidimensional array into a one-dimensional array.

The data object matrix is often represented as a two-dimensional array. However, matrices are normally indexed beginning at 1 rather than 0. Matrices also support operations such as add, multiply, and transpose, which are not supported by C++'s two-dimensional arrays. Therefore, we develop the class `matrix` that conforms more closely to the data object matrix.

We consider also the representation of matrices with special structures—diagonal, tridiagonal, triangular, and symmetric matrices. Using customized array representations, we can reduce the space requirements of these matrices considerably when compared to the space used by the natural two-dimensional array representation. The customized representations also result in reduced run times for most operations.

The final section of this chapter develops array and linked representations for sparse matrices (i.e., matrices with a large number of 0s) in which the positions of the 0s do not necessarily define a regular pattern.

222

7.1 ARRAYS

7.1.1 The Abstract Data Type

Each instance of an array is a set of pairs of the form (index, value). No two pairs
in this set have the same index. The operations performed on the array follow.

- *Get an element*—Gets the value of the pair that has a given index.

- *Set an element*—Adds a pair of the form (index, value) to the set, and if a
  pair with the same index already exists, deletes the old pair.

These two operations define the abstract data type *array* (ADT 7.1).

AbstractDataType *array*
{

    instances
        set of (index, value) pairs, no two pairs have the same index

    operations
        get(index) : return the value of the pair with this index

  set(index, value) : add this pair to set of pairs, overwrite existing pair (if any) with
             the same index

}

ADT 7.1 Abstract data type specification of an array

Example 7.1 The high temperature (in degrees Fahrenheit) for each day of last
week may be represented by the following array:

$high$ = {(Sunday, 82), (Monday, 79), (Tuesday, 85), (Wednesday, 92),
(Thursday, 88), (Friday, 89), (Saturday, 91)}

Each pair of the array is composed of an index (day of week) and a value (the high
temperature for that day). The name of the array is *high*. We can change the high
temperature recorded for Monday to 83 by performing the following operation:

$set(Monday, 83)$

We can determine the high temperature for Friday by performing this operation:

$$get(\text{Friday})$$

An alternative array to represent the daily high temperature is

$$high = \{(0,82),(1,79),(2,85),(3,92),(4,88),(5,89),(6,91)\}$$

In this array the index is a number rather than the name of the day. The numbers $(0, 1, 2, \cdots)$ replace the names of the days of the week (Sunday, Monday, Tuesday, $\cdots$). ∎

7.1.2   Indexing a C++ Array

An array is a standard data structure in C++. The index (also called **subscript**) of an array in C++ must be of the form

$$[i_1][i_2][i_3]\cdots[i_k]$$

where each i_j is a nonnegative integer. If k is one, the array is a one-dimensional array, and if k is two, it is a two-dimensional array. i_1 is the first coordinate of the index, i_2 the second, and i_k the kth. A 3-dimensional array `score`, whose values are of type integer, may be *created* in C++ using the statement

$$\texttt{int score}[u_1][u_2][u_3]$$

where the u_is are positive constants or positive expressions derived from constants. With such a declaration, indexes with i_j in the range $0 \leq i_j < u_j$, $1 \leq j \leq 3$ are permitted. So the array can hold a maximum of $n = u_1 u_2 u_3$ values. Since each value in the array `score` is of type `int`, 4 bytes are needed for each. The memory, `sizeOf(score)`, needed for the entire array is therefore $4n$ bytes. The C++ compiler reserves this much memory for the array. This memory begins at byte *start* (say) and extends up to and including byte *start* + `sizeOf(score)` -1.

7.1.3   Row- and Column-Major Mappings

Some applications of arrays require us to arrange the array elements into a serial or one-dimensional order. For example, the elements of an array can be output or input only one element at a time. Therefore, we must decide on the order in which the array elements are output or input. In Sections 7.3 and 7.4, we will see several types of two-dimensional tables (matrices) that we will map into a one-dimensional array. To accomplish this mapping, we convert the two-dimensional arrangement of the table elements into a one-dimensional arrangement.

Let n be the number of elements in a k-dimensional array. The serialization of the array is done using a mapping function, which maps the array index $[i_1][i_2][i_3] \cdots [i_k]$ into a number $map(i_1, i_2, \cdots, i_k)$ in the range $[0, \ n-1]$ such that array element with index $[i_1][i_2][i_3] \cdots [i_k]$ is mapped to position $map(i_1, i_2, \cdots, i_k)$ in the serial order.

When the number of dimensions is 1 (i.e., $k = 1$), the function

$$map(i_1) = i_1 \tag{7.1}$$

is used. When the number of dimensions is 2, the indexes may be arranged into a table with indexes that have the same first coordinate forming a row of the table and those with the same second coordinate forming a column (see Figure 7.1).

$[0][0]$	$[0][1]$	$[0][2]$	$[0][3]$	$[0][4]$	$[0][5]$
$[1][0]$	$[1][1]$	$[1][2]$	$[1][3]$	$[1][4]$	$[1][5]$
$[2][0]$	$[2][1]$	$[2][2]$	$[2][3]$	$[2][4]$	$[2][5]$

Figure 7.1 Tabular arrangement of indexes for `int score[3][6]`

The mapping is obtained by numbering the indexes by row beginning with those in the first (i.e., top) row. Within each row, numbers are assigned from left to right. The result is shown in Figure 7.2(a). This way of mapping the positions in a two-dimensional array into a number in the range 0 through $n-1$ is called **row major**. The numbers are assigned in row-major order. Figure 7.2(b) shows an alternative scheme, called **column major**. In column-major order the numbers are assigned by column beginning with the left column. Within a column the numbers are assigned from top to bottom.

0	1	2	3	4	5		0	3	6	9	12	15
6	7	8	9	10	11		1	4	7	10	13	16
12	13	14	15	16	17		2	5	8	11	14	17

(a) Row-major mapping	(b) Column-major mapping

Figure 7.2 Mapping a two-dimensional array

When row-major order is used, the mapping function is

$$map(i_1, i_2) = i_1 u_2 + i_2 \tag{7.2}$$

where u_2 is the number of columns in the array. To verify the correctness of Equation 7.2, note that by the time the index $[i_1][i_2]$ is numbered in the row-major scheme, $i_1 u_2$ elements from the rows $0, \cdots, i_1 - 1$ as well as i_2 elements from row i_1 have been numbered.

Let us try out the row-major mapping function on the sample 3×6 array of Figure 7.2(a). Since the number of columns, u_2, is 6, the formula becomes

$$map(i_1, i_2) = 6i_1 + i_2$$

So $map(1,3) = 6 + 3 = 9$, and $map(2,5) = 6 * 2 + 5 = 17$. Both agree with the numbers given in Figure 7.2(a).

The row-major scheme may be extended to obtain mapping functions for arrays with more than two dimensions. Notice that in row-major order, we list first all indexes with the first coordinate equal to 0, then those with this coordinate equal to 1, and so on. Indexes with the same first coordinate are listed in increasing order of the second coordinate; that is, the indexes are listed in lexicographic order. For a three-dimensional array, we list first all indexes with the first coordinate equal to 0, then those with this coordinate equal to 1, and so on. Indexes with the same first coordinate are listed in order of the second coordinate, and indexes that agree on the first two coordinates are listed in order of the third. For example, the indexes of score[3][2][4] in row-major order are

[0][0][0]	[0][0][1]	[0][0][2]	[0][0][3]	[0][1][0]	[0][1][1]	[0][1][2]	[0][1][3]
[1][0][0]	[1][0][1]	[1][0][2]	[1][0][3]	[1][1][0]	[1][1][1]	[1][1][2]	[1][1][3]
[2][0][0]	[2][0][1]	[2][0][2]	[2][0][3]	[2][1][0]	[2][1][1]	[2][1][2]	[2][1][3]

The mapping function for a three-dimensional array is

$$map(i_1, i_2, i_3) = i_1 u_2 u_3 + i_2 u_3 + i_3$$

To see that this mapping function is correct, observe that the elements with the first coordinate i_1 are preceded by all elements whose first coordinate is less than i_1. There are $u_2 u_3$ elements that have the same first coordinate. So there are $i_1 u_2 u_3$ elements with the first coordinate less than i_1. The number of elements with the first coordinate equal to i_1 and the second coordinate less than i_2 is $i_2 u_3$, and the number with the first coordinate equal to i_1, the second equal to i_2, and the third less than i_3 is i_3.

7.1.4   Array of Arrays Representation

C++ uses the so-called array-of-arrays representation to represent a multidimensional array. In this representation, a two-dimensional array is represented as a one-dimensional array in which each element is, itself, a one-dimensional array. To represent the two-dimensional array

```
int x[3][5];
```

we actually create a one-dimensional array x whose length is 3; each element of x is a one-dimensional array whose length is 5. Figure 7.3 shows the memory structure. Four separate memory blocks are used. One block (the lightly shaded block) is large enough for three pointers and each of the remaining blocks is large enough for 5 ints. At 4 bytes per pointer and int, a total of 72 bytes is used.

Figure 7.3 Memory structure for a two-dimensional array

C++ finds the element x[i][j] by using the mapping function for one-dimensional arrays (Equation 7.1) to get to the pointer in x[i]. This pointer gives us the address, in memory, of the zeroth element of row i. The mapping function for one-dimensional arrays is used once again to find the [j]th element of row i.

A three-dimensional array is represented as a one-dimensional array, each of whose elements is a two-dimensional array. Each of these two-dimensional arrays is represented as shown in Figure 7.3.

7.1.5   Row-Major and Column-Major Representation

An alternative representation, not used by C++, is to actually create a one-dimensional array and then map our multidimensional array into this one-dimensional array using either a row- or column-major mapping. The two-dimensional array x[3][5] of ints that was considered above could be mapped into a 15-element array

```
int y[15];
```

using either a row-major or column-major mapping. In this case a single contiguous block of memory large enough to hold 15 ints is used. The total memory required drops from 72 bytes to 60 bytes.

To access x[i][j], we must use the two-dimensional mapping function (Equation 7.2 in case a row-major mapping is used) to compute an index u and then access y[u] using the one-dimensional mapping function. Depending on whether it takes more or less time to use the one-dimensional mapping function to fetch a pointer and then follow this pointer or to compute the two-dimensional mapping function, C++'s array representation scheme could be slower or faster than using a row- or column-major mapping.

7.1.6   Irregular Two-Dimensional Arrays

A two-dimensional array is regular in the sense that every row has the same number of elements. For example, every row of the 3×6 array score of Figure 7.1 has six elements. When two or more rows of an array have a different number of elements, we call the array **irregular**. Irregular arrays may be created and used as illustrated in Program 7.1. Notice that the only difference between regular and irregular arrays in that an irregular array may have rows whose length is different, whereas in a regular array all rows have the same length. The elements in regular and irregular arrays are accessed in the same way.

EXERCISES

1. (a) List the indexes of score[2][3][2][2] in row-major order.

   (b) Develop the row-major mapping function for a four-dimensional array.

2. Develop the row-major mapping function for a five-dimensional array.

3. Develop the row-major mapping function for a k-dimensional array.

4. (a) List the indexes of score[2][3][4] in column-major order. Note that now all indexes with the third coordinate equal to 0 are listed first, then those with this coordinate equal to 1, and so on. Indexes with the same third coordinate are listed in order of the second, and those with the same last two coordinates in order of the first.

   (b) Develop the column-major mapping function for a three-dimensional array.

5. (a) List the indexes of score[2][3][2][2] in column-major order.

   (b) Develop the column-major mapping function for a four-dimensional array (see Exercise 4).

6. Develop the column-major mapping function for a k-dimensional array.

7. We wish to map the elements of a two-dimensional array beginning with the bottom row and within a row from left to right.

   (a) List the indexes of score[3][5] in this order.

```
int main(void)
{
    int numberOfRows = 5;

    // define the length of each of the five rows
    int length[5] = {6, 3, 4, 2, 7};

    // declare a two-dimensional array variable
    // and allocate the desired number of rows
    int **irregularArray = new int* [numberOfRows];

    // now allocate space for the elements in each row
    for (int i = 0; i < numberOfRows; i++)
        irregularArray[i] = new int [length[i]];

    // use the array like any regular array
    irregularArray[2][3] = 5;
    irregularArray[4][6] = irregularArray[2][3] + 2;
    irregularArray[1][1] = 3;

    // output selected elements
    cout << irregularArray[2][3] << endl;
    cout << irregularArray[4][6] << endl;
    cout << irregularArray[1][1] << endl;

    return 0;
}
```

Program 7.1 Creating and using an irregular two-dimensional array

      (b) Develop the mapping function for score$[u_1][u_2]$.

8. We wish to map the elements of a two-dimensional array beginning with the right column and within a column from top to bottom.

      (a) List the indexes of score[3][5] in this order.

      (b) Develop the mapping function for score$[u_1][u_2]$.

9. A two-dimensional $m \times n$ array has mn elements.

      (a) Determine the amount of memory used when these mn elements are stored using a two-dimensional C++ array and when they are stored in a one-dimensional array using row-major mapping. Assume that the elements are of type int. First do this exercise for the case $m = 10$ and $n = 2$ and then for general m and n.

(b) How large can the ratio of the two memory requirements get?

10. A three-dimensional $m \times n \times p$ array has mnp elements.

(a) Determine the amount of memory used when these mnp elements are stored using a three-dimensional C++ array and when they are stored in a one-dimensional array using row-major mapping. Assume that the elements are of type int. First do this exercise for the case $m = 10$, $n = 4$, and $p = 2$ and then for general m, n, and p.

(b) How large can the ratio of the two memory requirements get?

(c) When is one scheme expected to provide faster element access than the other?

11. A four-dimensional $m \times n \times p \times q$ array has $mnpq$ elements.

(a) Determine the amount of memory used when these $mnpq$ elements are stored using a four-dimensional C++ array and when they are stored in a one-dimensional array using row-major mapping. Assume that the elements are of type int.

(b) How large can the ratio of the two memory requirements get?

12. A k-dimensional $u_1 \times u_2 \times \cdots \times u_k$ array has $u_1 u_2 \cdots u_k$ elements.

(a) Determine the amount of memory used when these $u_1 u_2 \cdots u_k$ elements are stored using a k-dimensional C++ array and when they are stored in a one-dimensional array using row-major mapping. Assume that the elements are of type int.

(b) How large can the ratio of the two memory requirements get?

(c) When is one scheme expected to provide faster element access than the other?

7.2   MATRICES

7.2.1   Definitions and Operations

An $m \times n$ **matrix** is a table with m rows and n columns (Figure 7.4). m and n are the **dimensions** of the matrix.

Example 7.2 Matrices are often used to organize data. For instance, in an effort to document the assets of the world, we might first produce a list of asset types of interest. This list could include mineral deposits (silver, gold, etc.); animals (lions, elephants, etc.); people (physicians, engineers, etc.); and so on. We can determine

$$\begin{array}{c} \text{col 1 col 2 col 3 col 4} \\ \begin{array}{c} \text{row 1} \\ \text{row 2} \\ \text{row 3} \\ \text{row 4} \\ \text{row 5} \end{array} \begin{bmatrix} 7 & 2 & 0 & 9 \\ 0 & 1 & 0 & 5 \\ 6 & 4 & 2 & 0 \\ 8 & 2 & 7 & 3 \\ 1 & 4 & 9 & 6 \end{bmatrix} \end{array}$$

Figure 7.4 A 5×4 matrix

the amount of each asset type present in the country. The data can be presented as a table with one column for each country and one row for each asset type. The result is an asset matrix with a number of columns n equal to the number of countries and a number of rows m equal to the number of asset types. We use the notation $M(i,j)$ to refer to the element in row i and column j of matrix M, $1 \le i \le m$, $1 \le j \le n$. If row i represents cats and column j represents the United States, then $asset(i,j)$ would be the number of cats in the United States.

Figure 7.5(a) shows an asset matrix for four countries; the assets listed in this matrix are platinum, gold, and silver. Country B has $asset(1,2) = 5$ units of platinum, $asset(2,2) = 2$ units of gold, and $asset(3,2) = 10$ units of silver.

asset	country			
	A	B	C	D
platinum	2	5	1	0
gold	6	2	3	8
silver	0	10	50	30

(a) *asset*

asset	scenario		
	1	2	3
platinum	20	15	50
gold	15	12	40
silver	1	1	2

(b) *value*

Figure 7.5 Asset and value matrices

Figure 7.5(b) shows a matrix that gives the value of one unit of each asset type for three different economic scenarios. Under scenario 3 a unit of platinum is worth

$value(1,3) = \$50$; a unit of gold is worth $value(2,3) = \$40$; and a unit of silver is worth $value(3,3) = \$2$. ∎

The operations most commonly performed on matrices are transpose, addition or sum, and multiplication or product. The transpose of an $m \times n$ matrix M is an $n \times m$ matrix M^T with the property

$$M^T(i,j) = M(j,i), \; 1 \leq i \leq n, \; 1 \leq j \leq m$$

The sum of two matrices is defined only when the two matrices have the same dimensions (i.e., the same number of rows and the same number of columns). The sum of two $m \times n$ matrices A and B is a third $m \times n$ matrix C such that

$$C(i,j) = A(i,j) + B(i,j), \; 1 \leq i \leq n, \; 1 \leq j \leq m \tag{7.3}$$

The product $A * B$ of an $m \times n$ matrix A and a $q \times p$ matrix B is defined only when the number of columns in A equals the number of rows in B, that is, $n = q$. When $n = q$, the product is an $m \times p$ matrix C with the property

$$C(i,j) = \sum_{k=1}^{n} A(i,k) * B(k,j), \; 1 \leq i \leq m, \; 1 \leq j \leq p$$

Example 7.3 Consider the asset matrix described in Example 7.2. Suppose that the data are being accumulated by two agencies and neither duplicates the work of the other. The result is two $m \times n$ matrices: $asset1$ and $asset2$. To get the desired asset matrix, we add the two matrices $asset1$ and $asset2$.

Next suppose we have another matrix $value$ (as in Figure 7.5(b)) that is an $m \times s$ matrix. $value(i,j)$ is the value of one unit of asset i under scenario j. Let $CV(i,j)$ be the value of the assets of country i under scenario j. Using the data of Figure 7.5, we see that the value of the assets held by country B under scenario 3 is

$$
\begin{aligned}
CV(2,3) \;=\; & \text{(amount of platinum} * \text{value of platinum)} \\
& + \text{(amount of gold} * \text{value of gold)} \\
& + \text{(amount of silver} * \text{value of silver)} \\
=\; & asset(1,2) * value(1,3) + asset(2,2) * value(2,3) \\
& + asset(3,2) * value(3,3) \\
=\; & 5 * 50 + 2 * 40 + 10 * 2 \\
=\; & 350
\end{aligned}
$$

We see that CV is an $n \times s$ matrix and that

$$CV(i,j) = \sum_{k=1}^{m} asset(k,i) * value(k,j) = \sum_{k=1}^{m} asset^T(i,k) * value(k,j)$$

So CV satisfies the equation

$$CV = asset^T * value$$

Figure 7.6(a) gives the transpose of the asset matrix of Figure 7.5(a), and Figure 7.6(b) gives the CV matrix that corresponds to the asset and value matrices of Figure 7.5. ∎

	p	g	s
A	2	6	0
B	5	2	10
C	1	3	50
D	0	8	30

(a) $asset^T$

	1	2	3
A	130	102	340
B	140	109	350
C	115	101	270
D	150	126	380

(b) $CV = asset^T * value$

Figure 7.6 Example for matrix transpose and product

C++ functions to compute the transpose of a matrix and to add and multiply two matrices represented as two-dimensional arrays were considered in Chapter 2 (Programs 2.21, 2.19, 2.22, and 2.23, respectively).

7.2.2   The Class matrix

A rows × cols matrix M, all of whose elements are integer, may be represented as a two-dimensional integer array

```
int x[rows][cols];
```

with $M(i,j)$ being stored as x[i-1][j-1]. This representation requires the user to write applications using array indexes that differ from matrix indexes by 1. Alternatively, we may define the array x as

```
int x[rows + 1][cols + 1];
```

and not use the array positions [0][*] and [*][0]. In this section we develop a representation in which the elements of matrix M are mapped into a one-dimensional array in row-major order.

The class matrix uses a one-dimensional array element to store, in row-major order, the rows * cols elements of a rows × cols matrix. Program 7.2 gives the class header. Notice that we intend to overload the () operator so that matrices may be indexed in a program the same way they are indexed in mathematics. Additionally we intend to overload the arithmetic operators so that they work with objects of type matrix.

```
template<class T>
class matrix
{
   friend ostream& operator<<(ostream&, const matrix<T>&);
   public:
      matrix(int theRows = 0, int theColumns = 0);
      matrix(const matrix<T>&);
      ~matrix() {delete [] element;}
      int rows() const {return theRows;}
      int columns() const {return theColumns;}
      T& operator()(int i, int j) const;
      matrix<T>& operator=(const matrix<T>&);
      matrix<T> operator+() const; // unary +
      matrix<T> operator+(const matrix<T>&) const;
      matrix<T> operator-() const; // unary minus
      matrix<T> operator-(const matrix<T>&) const;
      matrix<T> operator*(const matrix<T>&) const;
      matrix<T>& operator+=(const T&);
   private:
      int theRows,    // number of rows in matrix
          theColumns; // number of columns in matrix
      T *element;      // element array
};
```

Program 7.2 Header for the class matrix

Program 7.3 gives the constructor and copy constructor for the class. Notice that the constructor allows you to create a 0×0 matrix as well as matrices for which both `theRows` > 0 and `theColumns` > 0.

```
template<class T>
matrix<T>::matrix(int theRows, int theColumns)
{// matrix constructor.
   // validate theRows and theColumns
   if (theRows < 0 || theColumns < 0)
      throw illegalParameterValue("Rows and columns must be >= 0");
   if ((theRows == 0 || theColumns == 0)
               && (theRows != 0 || theColumns != 0))
      throw illegalParameterValue
      ("Either both or neither rows and columns should be zero");

   // create the matrix
   this->theRows = theRows;
   this->theColumns = theColumns;
   element = new T [theRows * theColumns];
}

template<class T>
matrix<T>::matrix(const matrix<T>& m)
{// Copy constructor for matrices.
   // create matrix
   theRows = m.theRows;
   theColumns = m.theColumns;
   element = new T [theRows * theColumns];

   // copy each element of m
   copy(m.element,
        m.element + theRows * theColumns,
        element);
}
```

Program 7.3 Constructor and copy constructor for `matrix`

Program 7.4 gives the code to overload the assignment operator =.

To index a matrix using left and right parenthesis (), we overload the C++ function operator (), which can take any number of parameters. In our case, we use two parameters of type `int` with the overloaded (), because to index a matrix we need two integer parameters. Program 7.5 gives the code to overload (). This code returns a reference to the (i,j)th element of a matrix and this reference may

```
template<class T>
matrix<T>& matrix<T>::operator=(const matrix<T>& m)
{// Assignment. (*this) = m.
   if (this != &m)
   {// not copying to self
      delete [] element;
      theRows = m.theRows;
      theColumns = m.theColumns;
      element = new T [theRows * theColumns];
      // copy each element
      copy(m.element,
           m.element + theRows * theColumns,
           element);
   }
   return *this;
}
```

Program 7.4 Overloading the = operator for `matrix`

be used to either set or get the value of the (i,j)th element using statements such
as $a(i,j) = 2$ and $x = a(i,j)$, where a is of type `matrix`.

```
template<class T>
T& matrix<T>::operator()(int i, int j) const
{// Return a reference to element (i,j).
   if (i < 1 || i > theRows
       || j < 1 || j > theColumns)
      throw matrixIndexOutOfBounds();
   return element[(i - 1) * theColumns + j - 1];
}
```

Program 7.5 Overloading the () operator for `matrix`

Program 7.6 gives the code for matrix addition. Since matrices have been
mapped into one-dimensional arrays, we can add two matrices using a single **for**
loop rather than two nested **for** loops as were used in Program 2.21. The codes
for matrix operations such as increment (increase the value of each matrix entry by
the same amount) and subtraction are similar to that for matrix addition.

The loop structure of the matrix multiplication code (Program 7.7) is similar to
that of Program 2.23. There are three nested **for** loops. The innermost loop uses

```
template<class T>
matrix<T> matrix<T>::operator+(const matrix<T>& m) const
{// Return w = (*this) + m.
   if (theRows != m.theRows
       || theColumns != m.theColumns)
      throw matrixSizeMismatch();

   // create result matrix w
   matrix<T> w(theRows, theColumns);
   for (int i = 0; i < theRows * theColumns; i++)
      w.element[i] = element[i] + m.element[i];

   return w;
}
```

Program 7.6 Matrix addition

Equation 7.3 to compute the (i,j)th element of the product matrix. When we enter the innermost loop, `element[ct]` is the first element of row i and `m.element[cm]` is the first of column j. To go to the next element of row i, ct is to be incremented by 1 because in row-major order the elements of a row occupy consecutive positions. To go to the next element of column j, cm is to be incremented by `m.theColumns`, as consecutive elements of a column are `m.theColumns` positions apart in row-major order. When the innermost loop completes, ct is positioned at the end of row i and cm is at the end of column j. For the next iteration of the for j loop, ct needs to be at the start of row i and cm at the start of the next column of m. The resetting that occurs after the innermost loop completes positions ct. When the for j loop completes, ct should be set to the position of the first element of the next row and cm to that of the first element of the first column.

The matrix multiplication code can be made more efficient by reducing the number of cache misses as in the ikj order version of Program 4.4. The code for the remaining methods of `matrix` may be found at the Web site for this book.

Complexity

The complexity of the matrix constructor and destructor is $O(1)$ when T is a primitive data type of C++ (e.g., int, double). When T is a user-defined data type, the complexity of the constructor (destructor) is $O(\text{theRows} * \text{theColumns})$ because the constructor (destructor) for the data type T is invoked for every position in the array `element` when this array is created (deleted).

The asymptotic complexity of the copy constructor and the add method is $O(\text{theRows} * \text{theColumns})$ if we assume that the times to copy a matrix term

```
template<class T>
matrix<T> matrix<T>::operator*(const matrix<T>& m) const
{// matrix multiply.  Return w = (*this) * m.
   if (theColumns != m.theRows)
      throw matrixSizeMismatch();

   matrix<T> w(theRows, m.theColumns);  // result matrix

   // define cursors for *this, m, and w
   // and initialize to location of (1,1) element
   int ct = 0, cm = 0, cw = 0;

   // compute w(i,j) for all i and j
   for (int i = 1; i <= theRows; i++)
   {// compute row i of result
      for (int j = 1; j <= m.theColumns; j++)
      { // compute first term of w(i,j)
         T sum =  element[ct] * m.element[cm];

         // add in remaining terms
         for (int k = 2; k <= theColumns; k++)
         {
            ct++;  // next term in row i of *this
            cm += m.theColumns;  // next in column j of m
            sum += element[ct] * m.element[cm];
         }
         w.element[cw++] = sum;  // save w(i,j)

         // reset to start of row and next column
         ct -= theColumns - 1;
         cm = j;
      }

      // reset to start of next row and first column
      ct += theColumns;
      cm = 0;
   }

   return w;
}
```

Program 7.7 Matrix multiplication

and add two matrix terms are both $\Theta(1)$. The matrix multiplication code has the complexity $O(\texttt{theRows} * \texttt{theColumns} * \texttt{m.theColumns})$.

EXERCISES

13. (a) What is the transpose of the matrix of Figure 7.4?

(b) What is the product of the matrix of Figure 7.4 and the transpose?

14. Do Exercise 13 using the matrix of Figure 7.2(b).

15. Add code for the methods `-=` (decrease each matrix entry by a specified amount), `<<` (input a matrix), `*=` (multiply each matrix entry by a specified value), and `/=` to the class `matrix`. Test your methods.

16. To the class `matrix` add the method `transpose()`, which returns the transpose of `*this`. Test your code.

17. (a) Develop the class `matrixAs2DArray` in which a matrix is represented as a two-dimensional array. Your class should include all methods of `matrix` as well as a method to transpose a matrix.

(b) Test your methods.

(c) Compare the performance of the matrix addition and multiplication methods of the classes `matrix` and `matrixAs2DArray`. Do this comparison by making actual run-time measurements. What can you say about the merits of using the row-major mapping instead of a two-dimensional array?

7.3 SPECIAL MATRICES

7.3.1 Definitions and Applications

A **square** matrix has the same number of rows and columns. Some special forms of square matrices that arise frequently are

- **Diagonal.** M is diagonal iff $M(i,j) = 0$ for $i \neq j$; see Figures 7.7(a) and 7.8(a).

- **Tridiagonal.** M is tridiagonal iff $M(i,j) = 0$ for $|i-j| > 1$; see Figures 7.7(b) and 7.8(b).

- **Lower triangular.** M is lower triangular iff $M(i,j) = 0$ for $i < j$; see Figures 7.7(c) and 7.8(c).

- **Upper triangular.** M is upper triangular iff $M(i,j) = 0$ for $i > j$; see Figures 7.7(d) and 7.8(d).

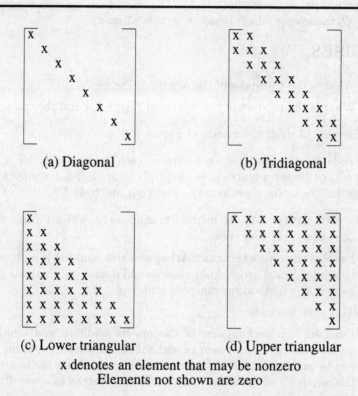

(a) Diagonal   (b) Tridiagonal

(c) Lower triangular   (d) Upper triangular

x denotes an element that may be nonzero
Elements not shown are zero

Figure 7.7 Location of nonzero elements in special matrices

- **Symmetric.** Matrix M is symmetric iff $M(i,j) = M(j,i)$ for all i and j; see Figure 7.8(e).

Example 7.4 Consider the six cities Gainesville, Jacksonville, Miami, Orlando, Tallahassee, and Tampa, which are all in Florida. We may number these cities 1 through 6 in the listed order. The distance between pairs of these cities may be represented using a 6×6 matrix $distance$. The ith row and column of this matrix represent the ith city, and $distance(i,j)$ is the distance between city i and city j. Figure 7.9 shows the distance matrix. Since $distance(i,j) = distance(j,i)$ for all i and j, the distance matrix is symmetric. ∎

Example 7.5 Suppose we have a stack of n cartons with carton 1 at the bottom and carton n at the top. Each carton has width w and depth d. The height of the ith carton is h_i. The volume occupied by the stack is $w * d * \sum_{i=1}^{n} h_i$. In the **stack folding** problem, we are permitted to create substacks of cartons by selecting a fold point i and creating two adjacent stacks. One has cartons 1 through i and the other

```
2  0  0  0          2  1  0  0          2  0  0  0
0  1  0  0          3  1  3  0          5  1  0  0
0  0  4  0          0  5  2  7          0  3  1  0
0  0  0  6          0  0  9  0          4  2  7  0
```

   (a) Diagonal   (b) Tridiagonal   (c) Lower triangular

```
        2  1  3  0          2  4  6  0
        0  1  3  8          4  1  9  5
        0  0  1  6          6  9  4  7
        0  0  0  0          0  5  7  0
```

     (d) Upper triangular   (e) Symmetric

Figure 7.8 4 × 4 special matrices

	GN	JX	MI	OD	TL	TM
GN	0	73	333	114	148	129
JX	73	0	348	140	163	194
MI	333	348	0	229	468	250
OD	114	140	229	0	251	84
TL	148	163	468	251	0	273
TM	129	194	250	84	273	0

GN = Gainesville	OD = Orlando
JX = Jacksonville	TL = Tallahassee
MI = Miami	TM = Tampa

Distance in miles

Figure 7.9 A distance matrix (source: Rand McNally Road Atlas)

cartons $i + 1$ through n. By repeating this folding process, we may obtain several stacks of cartons. If we create s stacks, the width of the arrangement is $s * w$, its depth is d, and the height h is the height of the tallest stack. The volume of the space needed for the stacks is $s * w * d * h$. Since h is the height of a stack of boxes i through j for some i and j, $i \leq j$, the possible values for h are given by the $n \times n$ matrix H where $H(i,j)$ is 0 for $i > j$ and is $\sum_{k=i}^{j} h_k$ for $i \leq j$. Since the height of each carton is > 0, an $H(i,j)$ value of 0 indicates an infeasible stack height. Figure 7.10(a) shows a five-carton stack. The numbers inside each rectangle give the carton height. Figure 7.10(b) shows a folding of the five-carton stack into three stacks. The height of the largest stack is 7. The matrix H is an upper-triangular matrix, as shown in Figure 7.10(c). One application of the stack folding problem is to the folding of a stack of electronic components so as to minimize the area occupied by the folded stack (see Web site).   ∎

(a) Stack   (b) Three-stack folding   (c) H matrix

Figure 7.10 Stack folding

7.3.2   Diagonal Matrices

One way to represent a rows $\times$ rows diagonal matrix D is to use a two-dimensional array element[rows][rows] and use element[i-1][j-1] to represent $D(i,j)$. This representation requires space for rows^2 objects of type T. However, since a diagonal matrix contains at most rows nonzero entries, we may use a one-dimensional array element[rows] and use element[i-1] to represent $D(i,i)$. The elements of the matrix D that are not represented in the array are all known to be zero. This representation, which requires space for only rows objects of type T, leads to the C++ class diagonalMatrix (Programs 7.8 through 7.10).

The complexity of the constructor is $O(1)$ when T is a primitive data type and $O(\text{rows})$ when T is a user-defined data type. The complexity of the methods get and set is $\Theta(1)$.

```
template<class T>
class diagonalMatrix
{
   public:
      diagonalMatrix(int theN = 10);
      ~diagonalMatrix() {delete [] element;}
      T get(int, int) const;
      void set(int, int, const T&);
   private:
      int n;          // matrix dimension
      T *element;     // 1D array for diagonal elements
};

template<class T>
diagonalMatrix<T>::diagonalMatrix(int theN)
{// Constructor.
   // validate theN
   if (theN < 1)
      throw illegalParameterValue("Matrix size must be > 0");

   n = theN;
   element = new T [n];
}
```

Program 7.8 Header and constructor for diagonalMatrix

```
template <class T>
T diagonalMatrix<T>::get(int i, int j) const
{// Return (i,j)th element of matrix.
   // validate i and j
   if (i < 1 || j < 1 || i > n || j > n)
      throw matrixIndexOutOfBounds();

   if (i == j)
      return element[i-1];    // diagonal element
   else
      return 0;               // nondiagonal element
}
```

Program 7.9 Get method for diagonalMatrix

```
template<class T>
void diagonalMatrix<T>::set(int i, int j, const T& newValue)
{// Store newValue as (i,j)th element.
   // validate i and j
   if (i < 1 || j < 1 || i > n || j > n)
      throw matrixIndexOutOfBounds();

   if (i == j)
      // save the diagonal value
      element[i-1] = newValue;
   else
      // nondiagonal value, newValue must be zero
      if (newValue != 0)
         throw illegalParameterValue
               ("nondiagonal elements must be zero");
}
```

Program 7.10 Set method for `diagonalMatrix`

7.3.3   Tridiagonal Matrix

In a `rows` × `rows` tridiagonal matrix, the nonzero elements lie on one of the three diagonals:

1. Main diagonal—for this, $i = j$.

2. Diagonal below main diagonal—for this, $i = j + 1$.

3. Diagonal above main diagonal—for this, $i = j - 1$.

The number of elements on these three diagonals is $3*rows-2$. We can use a one-dimensional array `element` with $3*rows-2$ positions to represent the tridiagonal matrix. Only the elements on the three diagonals are explicitly stored. Consider the 4×4 tridiagonal matrix of Figure 7.8(b). There are 10 elements on the main diagonal and the diagonals just above and below the main diagonal. If these elements are mapped into `element` by rows, then `element[0:9]` = [2, 1, 3, 1, 3, 5, 2, 7, 9, 0]; if the mapping is by columns, `element` = [2, 3, 1, 1, 5, 3, 2, 9, 7, 0]; and if the mapping is by diagonals beginning with the lowest, then `element` = [3, 5, 9, 2, 1, 2, 0, 1, 3, 7]. As we can see, there are several reasonable choices for the mapping of T into `element`. Each requires a different code for the `get` and `set` methods. Suppose that the class `tridiagonalMatrix` maps by diagonals. The data members and constructor are quite similar to those of the class `diagonal`. Program 7.11 gives the code for `get`; the code for `set` is similar and is on the Web site.

```
template <class T>
T tridiagonalMatrix<T>::get(int i, int j) const
{// Return (i,j)th element of matrix.

   // validate i and j
   if ( i < 1 || j < 1 || i > n || j > n)
      throw matrixIndexOutOfBounds();

   // determine lement to return
   switch (i - j)
   {
      case 1: // lower diagonal
              return element[i - 2];
      case 0: // main diagonal
              return element[n + i - 2];
      case -1: // upper diagonal
              return element[2 * n + i - 2];
      default: return 0;
   }
}
```

Program 7.11 The method get for a tridiagonal matrix

An alternative space-efficient representation of a tridiagonal array is considered in Exercise 25. This alternative representation uses an irregular array (see Section 7.1.6).

7.3.4 Triangular Matrices

In an n-row lower-triangular matrix (Figure 7.7(c)), the nonzero region has one element in row 1, two in row 2, $\cdots$, and n in row n; and in an n-row upper-triangular matrix, the nonzero region has n elements in row 1, $n-1$ in row 2, $\cdots$, and one in row n. In both cases the total number of elements in the nonzero region is

$$\sum_{i=1}^{n} i = n(n+1)/2$$

Both kinds of triangular matrices may be represented by using a one-dimensional array of size $n(n+1)/2$. Consider a lower-triangular matrix L mapped into a one-dimensional array element. Two possible ways to do the mapping are by rows and by columns. If the mapping is done by rows, then the 4×4 lower-triangular matrix of Figure 7.8(c) has the mapping element[0:9] $= [2, 5, 1, 0, 3, 1, 4, 2, 7, 0]$. The column mapping results in element $= [2, 5, 0, 4, 1, 3, 2, 1, 7, 0]$.

Consider element $L(i, j)$ of a lower-triangular matrix. If $i < j$, the element is in the zero region. If $i \geq j$, the element is in the nonzero region. In a row mapping, the element $L(i, j)$, $i \geq j$, is preceded by $\sum_{k=1}^{i-1} k$ nonzero region elements that are in rows 1 through $i - 1$ and $j - 1$ such elements from row i. The total number of nonzero region elements that precede $L(i, j)$ in a row mapping is $i(i-1)/2 + j - 1$. This expression also gives the position of $L(i, j)$ in element. Using this expression, we arrive at the set method given in Program 7.12; the method to get a value is similar. Both methods have time complexity $\Theta(1)$.

```
template<class T>
void lowerTriangularMatrix<T>::set(int i, int j, const T& newValue)
{// Store newValue as (i,j)th element.
   // validate i and j
   if ( i < 1 || j < 1 || i > n || j > n)
       throw matrixIndexOutOfBounds();


   // (i,j) in lower triangle iff i >= j
   if (i >= j)
      element[i * (i - 1) / 2 + j - 1] = newValue;
   else
      if (newValue != 0)
         throw illegalParameterValue
               ("elements not in lower triangle must be zero");
}
```

Program 7.12 The method lowerTriangularMatrix<T>::set

An alternative space-efficient representation of a triangular array is considered in Exercise 26. This alternative representation uses an irregular array (see Section 7.1.6).

7.3.5   Symmetric Matrices

An $n \times n$ symmetric matrix can be represented using a one-dimensional array of size $n(n+1)/2$ by storing either the lower or upper triangle of the matrix using one of the schemes for a triangular matrix. The elements that are not explicitly stored may be computed from those that are explicitly stored.

EXERCISES

18. Tubing down Sleepy River is a pleasant activity that thousands of folks participate in during the summer. Sleepy River has seven places where you can get into or out of the river. These places are numbered 1 through 7; 2 is downstream from 1, 3 is downstream from 2, and so on. A different tube rental vendor does business at each location. The vendor that rents tubes at 1 will retrieve you and your tube at places 1, 3, 6, and 7; the vendor that rents tubes at 2 has a pickup service at 3, 5, and 6. The pickup services for the vendors that rent tubes at 3, 4, 5, 6, and 7 are, respectively, at 3, 5, 7; 5, 6, 7; 7; 6, 7; and 7.

   (a) Write a 7×7 matrix in which the (i, j) entry is 1 if it is possible to rent a tube at i and be picked up at j and is 0 otherwise. Is your matrix symmetric, upper triangular, or lower triangular?

   (b) Write a 7×7 matrix in which the (i, j) entry is 1 if it is possible to be picked up at i when you rent your tube at j and is 0 otherwise. Is your matrix symmetric, upper triangular, or lower triangular?

   (c) Renumber the seven tube rental places in the order downstream to upstream. For this numbering scheme write a 7×7 matrix in which the (i, j) entry is 1 if it is possible to rent a tube at i and be picked up at j and is 0 otherwise. Is your matrix symmetric, upper triangular, or lower triangular?

19. There are five equally spaced kennels in a row. Each kennel has a dog that is chained to the kennel post, and the length of each chain equals the distance between two adjacent kennels. Assume that dog i is chained to kennel i.

   (a) Which kennels can dog 3 visit?

   (b) Write a 5×5 matrix in which the (i, j) entry is 1 if dog i can visit kennel j and is 0 otherwise.

   (c) Is your matrix symmetric, upper triangular, lower triangular, tridiagonal, or diagonal?

20. (a) To the class `diagonalMatrix` (Program 7.8) add methods to input, output, add, subtract, multiply, and transpose diagonal matrices represented as one-dimensional arrays. Note that in each case the result is a diagonal matrix represented as a one-dimensional array.

   (b) Test the correctness of your codes.

   (c) What is the time complexity of each of your methods?

21. (a) To the class `tridiagonalMatrix` (Program 7.11) add methods to input, output, add, subtract, and transpose tridiagonal matrices.

   (b) Test the correctness of your codes.

(c) What is the time complexity of each method?

22. (a) Develop a C++ class `tridiagonalByColumns` that maps a tridiagonal $n \times n$ matrix into a one-dimensional array of size $3n - 2$ by columns. Include methods for the input, output, get, set, add, subtract, and transpose operations.

(b) Test the correctness of your codes.

(c) What is the time complexity of each method?

23. Do Exercise 22 for the class `tridiagonalByRows` in which the $n \times n$ tridiagonal matrix is mapped into a one-dimensional array of size $3n - 2$ by rows.

24. Is the product of two tridiagonal matrices neccessarily tridiagonal?

25. Develop the class `tridiagonalAsIrregularArray` in which a tridiagonal matrix is represented using a two-dimensional array `element`. When representing an $n \times n$ matrix, rows 0 and $n - 1$ of `element` have two positions each; the remaining rows have three positions each. See Section 7.1.6 to determine how to create such an array. Your class must include all methods included in the class `tridiagonalMatrix`.

(a) Test your code.

(b) Comment on the relative merits of the one-dimensional array representation as used in the class `tridiagonalMatrix` and the irregular array representation as used in `tridiagonalAsIrregularArray`.

26. Develop the class `lowerTriangleAsIrregularArray` in which a lower-triangular matrix is represented using a two-dimensional array `element`. When representing an $n \times n$ matrix, row i of element has i positions. See Section 7.1.6 to determine how to create such an array. Your class must include all methods included in the class `lowerTriangularMatrix`.

(a) Test your code.

(b) Comment on the relative merits of the one-dimensional array representation as used in the class `lowerTriangularMatrix` and the irregular array representation as used in `lowerTriangleAsIrregularArray`.

27. Develop the C++ class `upperTriangularMatrix` analogous to Program 7.12 for the case of an upper-triangular matrix. Include constructor, get, and set methods.

28. To the class `lowerTriangularMatrix` add methods to input, output, add, and subtract lower-triangular matrices. What is the time complexity of each method?

29. To the class `lowerTriangularMatrix` add the method `transpose`, which returns the transpose of the lower-triangular matrix `*this`. The transpose is an instance of the class `upperTriangularMatrix`. What is the time complexity of your code?

30. Let A and B be two $n \times n$ lower-triangular matrices. The total number of elements in the lower triangles of the two matrices is $n(n+1)$. Devise a scheme to represent both triangles in an array `element[n+1][n]`. [Hint: If you join the lower triangle of A and the upper triangle of B^T, you get an $(n+1) \times n$ matrix.] Write the get and set functions for both A and B. The complexity of each should be $\Theta(1)$.

31. Write a method to multiply two lower-triangular matrices that are members of the class `lowerTriangularMatrix` (Program 7.12). The result matrix is to be stored in a two-dimensional array. What is the time complexity of your method?

32. Write a method to multiply a lower-triangular and an upper-triangular matrix mapped into one-dimensional arrays by rows. The result matrix is in a two-dimensional array. What is the time complexity of your method?

33. Suppose that symmetric matrices are stored by mapping the lower-triangular region into one-dimensional arrays by rows. Develop a C++ class `lowerSymmetricMatrix` that includes methods for the get and set operations. The complexity of your methods should be $\Theta(1)$.

34. In an $n \times n$ **C-matrix**, all terms other than those in row 1, row n, and column 1 (see Figure 7.11)) are zero. A C-matrix has at most $3n-2$ nonzero terms. A C-matrix may be compactly stored in a one-dimensional array by first storing row 1, then row n, and then the remaining column 1 elements.

x denotes a possible nonzero
All other terms are zero

Figure 7.11 A C-matrix

(a) Give a sample 4×4 C-matrix and its compact representation.

(b) Show that an $n \times n$ C-matrix has at most $3n - 2$ nonzero terms.

(c) Develop a class cMatrix that represents an $n \times n$ C-matrix in a one-dimensional array element as above. You should include the constructor and get and set methods.

35. An $n \times n$ square matrix M is an **antidiagonal** matrix iff all entries $M(i, j)$ with $i + j \neq n + 1$ equal zero.

(a) Give a sample of a 4×4 antidiagonal matrix.

(b) Show that the antidiagonal matrix M has at most n nonzero entries.

(c) Devise a way to represent an antidiagonal matrix in a one-dimensional array of size n.

(d) Use the representation of (c) to arrive at the code for the C++ class antidiagonalMatrix that includes methods for the get and set operations.

(e) What is the time complexity of your get and set codes?

(f) Test your code.

36. An $n \times n$ matrix T is a **Toeplitz matrix** iff $T(i, j) = T(i - 1, j - 1)$ for all i and j, $i > 1$ and $j > 1$.

(a) Show that a Toeplitz matrix has at most $2n - 1$ distinct elements.

(b) Develop a mapping of a Toeplitz matrix into a one-dimensional array of size $2n - 1$.

(c) Use the mapping of (b) to obtain a C++ class toeplitzMatrix in which a Toeplitz matrix is mapped into a one-dimensional array of size $2n - 1$. Include methods for the get and store operations. The complexity of each should be $\Theta(1)$.

(d) Write a method to multiply two Toeplitz matrices stored as in (b). The result is stored in a two-dimensional array. What is the time complexity of your code?

37. A **square band matrix** $D_{n,a}$ is an $n \times n$ matrix in which all the nonzero terms lie in a band centered around the main diagonal. The band includes the main diagonal and $a - 1$ diagonals below and above the main diagonal (Figure 7.12).

(a) How many elements are in the band matrix $D_{n,a}$?

(b) What is the relationship between i and j for elements $d_{i,j}$ in the band of $D_{n,a}$?

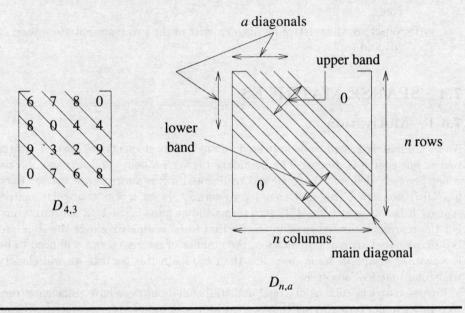

$D_{4,3}$

$D_{n,a}$

Figure 7.12 Square band matrix

b[0]	b[1]	b[2]	b[3]	b[4]	b[5]	b[6]	b[7]	b[8]	b[9]	b[10]	b[11]	b[12]	b[13]
9	7	8	3	6	6	0	2	8	7	4	9	8	4
d_{20}	d_{31}	d_{10}	d_{21}	d_{32}	d_{00}	d_{11}	d_{22}	d_{33}	d_{01}	d_{12}	d_{23}	d_{02}	d_{13}

Figure 7.13 Representation for matrix $D_{4,3}$ of Figure 7.12

(c) Assume that the band of $D_{n,a}$ is mapped into a one-dimensional array b by diagonals, starting with the lowest diagonal. Figure 7.13 shows the representation for band matrix $D_{4,3}$ of Figure 7.12.

Develop a formula for the location of an element $d_{i,j}$ in the lower band of $D_{n,a}$ (location(d_{10}) = 2 in the example above).

(d) Develop the C++ class `squareBandMatrix` that uses the mapping of (c); include methods for the get and set operations. What is the time complexity of each method? Test your code.

(e) Develop the class `squareBandAsIrregularArray` that uses a two-dimensional array `element` in which each row has as many positions as the width of the band at that row. For example, `element[0]` is a one-dimensional array with a positions; include methods for the get and set operations. What is the time complexity of each method? Test your code.

(f) What are the relative merits/demerits of the two representations used in (d) and (e)?

7.4   SPARSE MATRICES

7.4.1   Motivation

An $m \times n$ matrix is said to be **sparse** if "many" of its elements are zero. A matrix that is not sparse is **dense**. The boundary between a dense and a sparse matrix is not precisely defined. Diagonal and tridiagonal $n \times n$ matrices are sparse. Each has $O(n)$ nonzero terms and $O(n^2)$ zero terms. Is an $n \times n$ triangular matrix sparse? It has at least $n(n-1)/2$ zero terms and at most $n(n+1)/2$ nonzero terms. For the representation schemes in this section to be competitive over the standard two-dimensional array representation, the number of nonzero terms will need to be less than $n^2/3$ and in some cases less than $n^2/5$. In this context we will classify triangular matrices as dense.

Sparse matrices such as diagonal and tridiagonal matrices have sufficient structure in their nonzero regions that we can devise a simple representation scheme whose space requirements equal the size of the nonzero region. In this section we are concerned with sparse matrices with an irregular or unstructured nonzero region.
Example 7.6 A supermarket is conducting a study of the mix of items purchased by its customers. For this study, data are gathered for the purchases made by 1000 customers. These data are organized into a matrix, *purchases*, with $purchases(i,j)$ being the quantity of item i purchased by customer j. Suppose that the supermarket has an inventory of 10,000 different items. The *purchases* matrix is therefore a $10,000 \times 1000$ matrix. If the average customer buys 20 different items, only about 20,000 of the 10,000,000 matrix entries are nonzero. However, the distribution of the nonzero entries does not fall into any well-defined structure.

The supermarket has a $10,000 \times 1$ matrix, *price*. $price(i)$ is the selling price of one unit of item i. The matrix $spent = purchases^T * price$ is a 1000×1 matrix that gives the amount spent by each customer. If a two-dimensional array is used to represent the matrix *purchases*, an unnecessarily large amount of memory is used and the time required to compute *spent* is also unnecessarily large.   ∎

7.4.2   Representation Using a Single Linear List

The nonzero entries of an irregular sparse matrix may be mapped into a linear list in row-major order. For example, the nonzero entries of the 4×8 matrix of Figure 7.14(a) in row-major order are 2, 1, 6, 7, 3, 9, 8, 4, 5.

To reconstruct the matrix structure, we need to record the originating row and column for each nonzero entry. So each element of the array into which the sparse

	0 0 0 2 0 0 1 0
	0 6 0 0 7 0 0 3
	0 0 0 9 0 8 0 0
	0 4 5 0 0 0 0 0

terms	0	1	2	3	4	5	6	7	8
row	1	1	2	2	2	3	3	4	4
col	4	7	2	5	8	4	6	2	3
value	2	1	6	7	3	9	8	4	5

(a) A 4×8 matrix   (b) Its linear list representation

Figure 7.14 A sparse matrix and its linear list representation

matrix is mapped needs to have three fields: `row` (the row of the matrix entry), `col` (the column of the matrix entry), and `value` (the value of the matrix entry). For this purpose we define the struct `matrixTerm` that has these three data members. The data type of `row` and `col` is `int` and that of `value` is `T`.

The nonzero entries of the matrix of Figure 7.14(a) may be stored in a linear list `terms` in row-major order as shown in Figure 7.14(b). The row labeled `terms` gives the list index of a matrix term. In addition to storing the nonzero entries of the matrix, we need to store the number of rows and columns in the matrix.

Suppose that our linear list `terms` is an instance of `arrayList`. If we assume that the nine nonzero elements of Figure 7.14(a) are stored as `int`s, the linear list representation requires 8 (for number of rows and columns) + 9 * 12 (each nonzero element requires the storage of its row, column, and value; 4 bytes each) + 8 (for the size and capacity of the linear list `terms`) + 4 (for a reference to the array `terms.elements`) = 128 bytes. If we had represented our matrix using a 4×8 array `theArray`, the space used would have been 32 * 4 (for the array entries) + 4 * 4 (for the pointers in `thearray[]`) + 4 (for a reference to `theArray`) = 148 bytes. The space saving achieved by the linear list representation isn't much in this example. However, for the matrix *purchase* (see our supermarket example, Example 7.6), the array representation takes approximately $20,000 * 12 = 240,000$ bytes, whereas the two-dimensional array representation needs approximately $10,000,000 * 4 = 40,000,000$ bytes. The space saving is about 39,760,000 bytes! A corresponding amount of time is saved creating the linear list representation over initializing a two-dimensional array.

The linear list representation of a sparse matrix does not lead to efficient implementations of the get and set operations. The get operation takes $O(\log [\text{number of nonzero entries}])$ time when an array linear list and binary search are used. The set operation takes $O(\text{number of nonzero entries})$ time because we may need to move this many entries to make room for the new term. Both operations take $O(\text{number of nonzero entries})$ time when a linked linear list is used. Each of these operations takes $\Theta(1)$ time using the standard two-dimensional array representation. However, matrix operations such as transpose, add, and multiply can be performed efficiently using the linear list representation.

The Class sparseMatrix

Based on our experiments of Section 6.1.6, we are motivated to use an array representation for **terms**. We use the class **arrayList** with the following methods added to it.

1. **reSet(newSize)** $\cdots$ change the size of the list to **newSize** increasing the capacity of the array if necessary.

2. **set(theIndex, theElement)** $\cdots$ make **theElement** the list element whose index is **theIndex**.

3. **clear()** $\cdots$ make the list size zero

Program 7.13 gives the header for the class **sparseMatrix** which uses the row-major mapping of a sparse matrix into an **arrayList**. Notice that the only constructor this class has is the default constructor.

```
template<class T>
class sparseMatrix
{
   public:
      void transpose(sparseMatrix<T> &b);
      void add(sparseMatrix<T> &b, sparseMatrix<T> &c);
   private:
      int rows,     // number of rows in matrix
          cols;     // number of columns in matrix
      arrayList<matrixTerm<T> > terms;
                    // list of nonzero terms
};
```

Program 7.13 Header for sparseMatrix

Program 7.14 gives the code to overload the output operator <<. Notice that this codes employs an iterator to sequence through the elements in the **arrayList** in left-to-right order. This order gets the nonzero matrix elements in row-major order. If the output is printed or displayed on a screen we will see one matrix term per line.

Program 7.15 inputs the sparse matrix entries in row-major order and sets up the internal representation. Exercise 42 considers refinements of this code.

```
template <class T>
ostream& operator<<(ostream& out, sparseMatrix<T>& x)
{// Put x in output stream.

   // put matrix characteristics
   out << "rows = " << x.rows << " columns = "
       << x.cols  << endl;
   out << "nonzero terms = " << x.terms.size() << endl;

   // put terms, one per line
   for (arrayList<matrixTerm<T> >::iterator i = x.terms.begin();
        i != x.terms.end(); i++)
      out << "a(" << (*i).row << ',' << (*i).col
          << ") = " << (*i).value << endl;

   return out;
}
```

Program 7.14 Overloading the output operator <<

Matrix Transpose .

Program 7.16 gives the code for the **transpose** method. We first set the number of rows and columns in the result matrix b and also make the size of the linear list b.terms equal to the number of terms in the transpose. Even though the list b.terms has none of the terms of the transpose yet, we set its size equal to the number of nonzero entries it will eventually have. This step is necessary so that we can use the method **arrayList<T>::set** to place entries into arbitrary positions in b.terms. If we do not change the size of b.terms in this manner, then we must grow the linear list one element at a time. As we will see, when we transpose a sparse matrix, the zeroth element of the matrix being transposed may be the sixth (say) element of the transpose. We cannot insert an element at position 6 of a linear list unless the list size is currently 6 or more. By beginning with a list whose size equals the final desired size (even though no element is defined or correct), we can essentially use the list as a one-dimensional array. The element in any position of the list can be assigned a new value using the method **set**.

Next we create two arrays colSize and rowNext. colSize[i] is the number of nonzero entries of the input matrix *this that are in column i, and rowNext[i] denotes the index in b for the next nonzero term that is in row i of the transpose. For the sparse matrix of Figure 7.14(a), colSize[1:8] = [0, 2, 1, 2, 1, 1, 1, 1]. Prior to the generation of any entries in the transpose matrix, rowNext[1:8] = [0, 0, 2, 3, 5, 6, 7, 8].

```
template<class T>
istream& operator>>(istream& in, sparseMatrix<T>& x)
{// Input a sparse matrix.

   // input matrix characteristics
   int numberOfTerms;
   cout << "Enter number of rows, columns, and #terms"
        << endl;
   in >> x.rows >> x.cols >> numberOfTerms;

   // should validate input values here, left as an exercise

   // set size of x.terms and ensure enough capacity
   x.terms.reSet(numberOfTerms);

   // input terms
   matrixTerm<T> mTerm;
   for (int i = 0; i < numberOfTerms; i++)
   {
      cout << "Enter row, column, and value of term "
           << (i + 1) << endl;
      in >> mTerm.row >> mTerm.col >> mTerm.value;
      // should validate input, left as an exercise

      x.terms.set(i, mTerm);
   }

   return in;
}
```

Program 7.15 Overloading the input operator >>

colSize is computed in the first two **for** loops by simply examining each term of the input matrix using an iterator. rowNext is computed in the next **for** loop. In this **for** loop, rowNext[i] is set to be the number of entries in rows 0 through i-1 of the transpose matrix b, which is equal to the number of entries in columns 0 through i-1 of the input matrix *this. Finally, in the last **for** loop, the nonzero entries are copied from the input matrix to their correct positions in b.

Although Program 7.16 is more complex than its counterpart for matrices stored as two-dimensional arrays (see Program 2.19), for matrices with many zero entries, Program 7.16 is faster. It is not too difficult to see that computing the transpose of

```
template<class T>
void sparseMatrix<T>::transpose(sparseMatrix<T> &b)
{// Return transpose of *this in b.

   // set transpose characteristics
   b.cols = rows;
   b.rows = cols;
   b.terms.reSet(terms.size());

   // initialize to compute transpose
   int* colSize = new int[cols + 1];
   int* rowNext = new int[cols + 1];

   // find number of entries in each column of *this
   for (int i = 1; i <= cols; i++) // initialize
      colSize[i] = 0;
   for (arrayList<matrixTerm<T> >::iterator i = terms.begin();
        i != arms.end(); i++)
      colSize[(*i).col]++;

   // find the starting point of each row of b
   rowNext[1] = 0;
   for (int i = 2; i <= cols; i++)
      rowNext[i] = rowNext[i - 1] + colSize[i - 1];

   // perform the transpose copying from *this to b
   matrixTerm<T> mTerm;
   for (arrayList<matrixTerm<T> >::iterator i = terms.begin();
        i != terms.end(); i++)
   {
      int j = rowNext[(*i).col]++; // position in b
      mTerm.row = (*i).col;
      mTerm.col = (*i).row;
      mTerm.value = (*i).value;
      b.terms.set(j, mTerm);
   }
}
```

Program 7.16 Transpose a sparse matrix

the *purchases* matrix of Example 7.6 using the linear list representation and method `transpose` is much faster than using a two-dimensional array representation and the transpose function of Program 2.19. The time complexity of `transpose` is $O(\text{cols+terms.size()})$.

Adding Two Matrices

The code of Program 7.17 computes `c = *this + b`. The result matrix `c` is produced by scanning the non-zero terms of `*this` and `b` from left to right. This scan is done using two iterators—`it` (for the matrix `*this`) and `ib` (for the matrix `b`). On each iteration of the `while` loop, we need to determine whether the position in `b` of the term `*it` is before, at the same place as, or after that of `*ib`. We can make this determination by comparing the row-major index of these two terms. However, it is actually simpler to compute and compare the row-major index plus the number of columns in the matrix, as we do (`tIndex` and `bIndex`).

The `while` loop of `add` is iterated at most `terms.size() + b.terms.size()` times, as on each iteration the iterator `it` for `*this` or the iterator `ib` for `b` or both advance by one. The first `for` loop is iterated at most `terms.size()` times, while the second is iterated $O(\text{b.terms.size()})$ times. Also, each iteration of each loop takes constant time. So the complexity of `add` is $O(\text{terms.size()+b.terms.size()})$. If the two matrices `*this` and `b` were represented as two-dimensional arrays, it would take $O(\text{rows*cols})$ time to add them. When `terms.size()+b.terms.size()` is much less than `rows*cols`, the sparse matrix representation results in a faster implementation.

7.4.3   Representation Using Many Linear Lists

An alternative sparse matrix representation results when we store the nonzero entries in each row in a separate linear list. In exploring this alternative, we use linked lists; array lists may be used instead (Exercise 52).

The Representation

We link together the nonzero entries in each row to form a chain (called a row chain) as shown by the unshaded nodes of Figure 7.15.

Each unshaded node represents a nonzero term of the sparse matrix. Each node in a row chain has the fields (data members) `element` and `next`. The `element` field of a node in a row chain has two subfields—`col` (the column number for the term) and `value` (the value of the term). Figure 7.16(a) shows the structure of a node on a row chain. Subfields of `element` are not shaded.

Row chains are created only for rows that have at least one nonzero term. The nodes on a row chain are linked in ascending order of their `col` value. The row chains (i.e., unshaded chains) are collected together by using another chain (called the header-node chain) as shown by the shaded nodes of Figure 7.15. Like a node

```
template<class T>
void sparseMatrix<T>::add(sparseMatrix<T> &b, sparseMatrix<T> &c)
{// Compute c = (*this) + b.

   // verify compatibility
   if (rows != b.rows || cols != b.cols)
      throw matrixSizeMismatch(); // incompatible matrices

   // set characteristics of result c
   c.rows = rows;
   c.cols = cols;
   c.terms.clear();
   int cSize = 0;

   // define iterators for *this and b
   arrayList<matrixTerm<T> >::iterator it = terms.begin();
   arrayList<matrixTerm<T> >::iterator ib = b.terms.begin();
   arrayList<matrixTerm<T> >::iterator itEnd = terms.end();
   arrayList<matrixTerm<T> >::iterator ibEnd = b.terms.end();

   // move through *this and b adding like terms
   while (it != itEnd && ib != ibEnd)
   {
      // row-major index plus cols of each term
      int tIndex = (*it).row * cols + (*it).col;
      int bIndex = (*ib).row * cols + (*ib).col;

      if (tIndex < bIndex)
      {// b term comes later
      c.terms.insert(cSize++, *it);
         it++;
      }
```

Program 7.17 Adding two sparse matrices (continues)

on a row chain, a node on the header-node chain has two fields—element and next. The element field of a node on the header-node chain has two subfields—row (row number for corresponding row chain) and rowChain (the chain of unshaded nodes; rowChain.firstNode points to the first unshaded node). Figure 7.16(b) shows the structure of a node on the header-node chain.

The nodes on the header-node chain are linked together in ascending order of

```
    else {if (tIndex == bIndex)
        {// both in same position

            // append to c only if sum not zero
            if ((*it).value + (*ib).value != 0)
            {
                matrixTerm<T> mTerm;
                mTerm.row = (*it).row;
                mTerm.col = (*it).col;
                mTerm.value = (*it).value + (*ib).value;
                c.terms.insert(cSize++, mTerm);
            }

            it++;
            ib++;
        }
        else
        {// a term comes later
            c.terms.insert(cSize++, *ib);
            ib++;
        }
        }
    }

// copy over remaining terms
for (; it != itEnd; it++)
    c.terms.insert(cSize++, *it);
for (; ib != ibEnd; ib++)
    c.terms.insert(cSize++, *ib);
}
```

Program 7.17 Adding two sparse matrices (concluded)

their row value. Each node on the header-node chain may be viewed as the header node of a row chain. An empty header-node chain represents a matrix with no nonzero terms.

Element Types

The struct rowElement defines a data type suitable for the elements of a row chain. Its data members are col (column index of the term) and value (value of the term). The struct headerElement defines a corresponding struct for elements in

N = NULL

Figure 7.15 Linked representation of matrix of Figure 7.14(a)

element	next
col	value

next	element
	row	rowChain

(a) Node for nonzero term

(b) Node for header-node chain

Figure 7.16 Node structures in linked sparse matrix representation

the header-node chain. Its data members are `row` (index of row) and `rowChain` (the actual chain, data type is `extendedChain`).

The Class `linkedMatrix`

The class that uses the representation of Figure 7.15 is called `linkedMatrix`. The row chains and header-node chain of Figure 7.15 are actually represented as instances of `extendedChain` because we will need to append (i.e., add at the right end) elements to these chains. In an `extendedChain` (Program 6.12) an element can be appended in $\Theta(1)$ time, whereas it takes Θ(size of chain) time to append to an instance of `chain` (Program 6.2). For our sparse matrix application we have added the method `zero()` to `extendedChain`. This method makes the chain size 0 but does not delete the chain nodes (unlike `clear` which makes the chain size 0 and also deletes all chain nodes).

The data members for `linkedMatrix` are almost the same as those for `sparse-Matrix`; the exception is that the data member `terms` is replaced by `headerChain`, which is of type `extendedChain`. The codes to overload `<<` and `>>` are on the Web site.

The Method `linkedMatrix<T>::transpose`

For the transpose operation, we use bins to collect the terms of the input matrix `*this` that belong in the same row of the result. `bin[i]` is a chain for the terms of row `i` of the result matrix `b`. In the nested `while` loops of Program 7.18, we examine the terms of `*this` in row-major order by going down the header-node chain of the input matrix and making a left-to-right traversal of each row chain. We move along the header-node and row chains by using an iterator `ih` for the header-node chain and another iterator `ir` for the row chain. Each term encountered in this ordered traversal of the matrix `*this` is appended to the bin chain for its row in the result. The bin chains are collected together in the `for` loop to create the header-node chain of the result.

The time spent in the `while` loops is O(number of nonzero terms), and the time spent in the `for` loop is $O(\text{this}->\text{cols})$. Therefore, the overall time is O(number of nonzero terms + $\text{this}->\text{cols}$).

Exercise 51 asks you to implement the `add` method as well as other basic methods.

7.4.4   Performance Measurement

The space requirements of `sparseMatrix` and `linkedMatrix` are approximately the same. However, we can modify the former representation to use 33 percent less space (see Exercise 47); this modification does not reduce run-time efficiency. Although Exercise 53 considers an alternative linked representation for sparse matrices, this alternative representation takes 66 percent more space than does `linkedMatrix`.

Figures 7.17 and 7.18 give the measured run times for matrix addition and transpose using two-dimensional arrays as in Programs 2.21 and 2.19 (2DArray, 2DA), `sparseMatrix` (SM) and `linkedMatrix` (LM). The `add` used two 500×500 sparse matrices; one had 1994 nonzero terms, and the other had 999 nonzero terms. For `transpose` a 500×500 matrix with 1994 nonzero terms was used.

The linked sparse matrix implementation, while slower than the array implementation of a sparse matrix, is faster than 2DArray. The reduction in time obtained by the array sparse matrix implementation `sparseMatrix` (relative to the nonsparse implementation 2DArray) is quite striking—matrix addition and transpose times are reduced by a factor of about 20.

```
template<class T>
void linkedMatrix<T>::transpose(linkedMatrix<T> &b)
{// Return transpose of *this as matrix b.
   b.headerChain.clear(); // delete all nodes from b

   // create bins to collect rows of b
   extendedChain<rowElement<T> > *bin;
   bin = new extendedChain<rowElement<T> > [cols + 1];

   // head node iterator
   extendedChain<headerElement<T> >::iterator
      ih = headerChain.begin(),
      ihEnd = headerChain.end();

   // copy terms of *this into bins
   while (ih != ihEnd)
   {// examine all rows
      int r = ih->row; // row number for row chain

      // row chain iterator
      extendedChain<rowElement<T> >::iterator
         ir = ih->rowChain.begin(),
         irEnd = ih->rowChain.end();

      rowElement<T> x;
      // terms from row r of *this go to column r of b
      x.col = r;

      while (ir != irEnd)
      {// copy a term from the row chain into a bin
         x.value = ir->value;
         // x will eventually be in row ir->col of transpose
         bin[ir->col].push_back(x);
         ir++;  // next term in row
      }

      ih++; // go to next row
   }
```

Program 7.18 Transpose a sparse matrix (continues)

```
    // set dimensions of transpose
    b.rows = cols;
    b.cols = rows;

    // assemble header chain of transpose
    headerElement<T> h;
    // scan bins
    for (int i = 1; i <= cols; i++)
       if (!bin[i].empty())
       {// row i of transpose
          h.row = i;
          h.rowChain = bin[i];
          b.headerChain.push_back(h);
          bin[i].zero(); // save from destructor
       }

    h.rowChain.zero();    // save from destructor

    delete [] bin;
}
```

Program 7.15 Transpose a sparse matrix (concluded)

Class	add	transpose
2DArray	2.69	1.97
sparseMatrix	0.13	0.09
linkedMatrix	***	1.57

*** Time not measured
Times are in milliseconds

Figure 7.17 Time taken by different matrix implementations

EXERCISES

38. (a) Draw figures similar to Figure 7.14(b) for the matrices of Figure 7.8.

     (b) Manually work out a sparse matrix transpose as implemented by **sparse-Matrix<T>::transpose** using the matrix of Figure 7.8(b).

     (c) Manually work out a sparse matrix add as implemented by **sparse-Matrix<T>::add** using the matrices of Figures 7.8(b) and (c).

Figure 7.18 Sparse matrix run times in milliseconds

39. (a) Suppose that a 500×500 matrix that has 2000 nonzero terms is to be represented. How much space is needed when a 500×500 two-dimensional array of type **int** is used? How much space is needed when **sparseMatrix** is used?

   (b) How many nonzero elements must an $m \times n$ matrix have before the space required by **sparseMatrix** exceeds that required by an $m \times n$ two-dimensional array? You may assume that **T** is **int**.

40. Develop the formula for the row-major index of element (i, j) of a *rows* $\times$ *cols* matrix. Why is it easier to compute the value *index* = row-major index + *cols* than it is to compute the row-major index? Show that if $index_1$ and $index_2$ are the indexes of two matrix elements, then $index_1 < index_2$ iff the first element precedes the second element in row-major order.

41. Write the methods **get(theRow,theColumn)** and **set(theRow,theColumn, theValue)** for the class **sparseMatrix**. What is the time complexity of your methods?

42. Refine the input code of Program 7.15 so that it verifies that the terms are, in fact, input in row-major order; that the row and column indexes of each term are valid; and that each term is nonzero.

43. Write a copy constructor for the class **sparseMatrix**.

44. Suppose that a sparse matrix is mapped into an arrayList (with the additional methods indicated in this chapter) in column-major order of the nonzero terms.

    (a) Develop the representation of the sparse matrix of Figure 7.14(a).

    (b) Write the get and set methods for sparse matrices stored in this way.

    (c) What is the time complexity of your methods?

45. Write a method to multiply two sparse matrices represented using an array linear list. Assume that both matrices are mapped in row-major order. The result matrix is similarly represented.

46. Do Exercise 45 using a column-major mapping.

47. We can reduce the space required by the linear list representation of a sparse matrix by eliminating the data member row from matrixTerm and using an array rowStart such that rowStart[i] is the index of the first term in row i. The terms of row i have the indexes rowStart[i] ··· rowStart[i+1].

    (a) Draw a figure similar to Figure 7.14(b) for the sparse matrix of Figure 7.14(a). Use the representation of this exercise and show the terms in row-major order. Also give the values of rowStart[1:5].

    (b) Write the struct newMatrixTerm to represent a nonzero term. This struct differs from the struct matrixTerm only in that newMatrixTerm does not have the data member row.

    (c) Write the class newSparseMatrix to implement a sparse matrix using the representation of this exercise. Your class must include all methods implemented for sparseMatrix as well as the methods get and set (see Exercise 41).

    (d) Test your code.

    (e) Make a qualitative comparison of the classes newSparseMatrix and sparseMatrix.

    (f) Compare the run times of the add and transpose methods of the two classes using 500 × 500 sparse matrices with approximately 6000 nonzero terms.

48. Write a matrix multiply method for the representation of Exercise 47. Test your code.

49. (a) Draw figures similar to Figure 7.15 for the matrices of Figure 7.8.

    (b) Manually work out a sparse matrix transpose as implemented by linkedMatrix<T>::transpose using the matrix of Figure 7.8(b).

50. (a) Suppose that a 500×500 matrix that has 2000 nonzero terms is to be represented. How much space is needed when a 500×500 two-dimensional array of type int is used? How much space is needed when linkedMatrix is used?

    (b) How many nonzero elements must an $m \times n$ matrix have before the space required by linkedMatrix exceeds that required by an $m \times n$ two-dimensional array?

51. Extend the class linkedMatrix by adding methods for the following operations:

    (a) Set a term given the row index, column index, and value of the term.

    (b) Get a term given its row and column indexes.

    (c) Add two sparse matrices.

    (d) Subtract two sparse matrices.

    (e) Multiply two sparse matrices.

    Also, refine the code for >> as described in Exercise 42. Test your code.

52. Develop the class arrayMatrix in which each row of nonzero terms is represented as a separate array linear list. The representation differs from that of Section 7.4.3 in that the linked lists of the figure are replaced by array lists. Implement methods to input, output, add, transpose, and multiply. Test your code.

53. [Orthogonal Linked List Representation] An alternative linked representation for sparse matrices uses nodes that have the fields down, right, row, col, and value. Each nonzero entry of the sparse matrix is represented by a node. The zero terms are not explicitly stored. The nodes are linked together to form two circular lists. The first list, the row list, is made up by linking nodes by rows and within rows by columns using the right field. The second list, the column list, is made up by linking nodes via the down field. In this list, nodes are linked by columns and within columns by rows. These two lists share a common header node. In addition, a node is added to contain the dimensions of the matrix.

    (a) Write down any 5×8 matrix that has exactly nine nonzero terms such that at least one nonzero term appears in each row and each column. For this sparse matrix draw the linked representation.

    (b) Suppose that an $m \times n$ matrix with t nonzero terms is represented as above. How small must t be so that the above linked scheme uses less space than an $m \times n$ array uses?

(c) Design a suitable external (i.e., one that can be used for input and output) representation for a sparse matrix. Your representation should not require explicit input of the zero terms.

(d) Develop a class that uses the representation of this exercise. Include all the methods of **sparseMatrix**.

(e) For each public method of the class, obtain its asymptotic time complexity. How do these complexities compare with the corresponding complexities for the methods of **sparseMatrix**?

CHAPTER 8
STACKS

BIRD'S-EYE VIEW

Stacks and queues are, perhaps, the most frequently used data structures. Both are restricted versions of the linear or ordered list data structure studied extensively in Chapters 5 and 6. In fact, stacks and queues are so widely used that the C++ STL provides the classes **stack** and **queue**, which are array implementations of these data structures. We will study stacks in this chapter and queues in the next. Even though C++ provides an implementation of a stack and a queue, we obtain our own stack and queue implementations just to learn how to implement these data structures.

The stack data structure is obtained from a linear list by restricting the insertions and removals to take place from the same end. As a result, a stack is a last-in-first-out (LIFO) structure. Since a stack is a special kind of linear list, it is natural to derive stack classes from corresponding linear list classes. Therefore, we may derive an array-stack class from any of the array linear list representations of Chapter 5; a linked-stack class may be derived from the class **chain** (Program 6.2). Although these derivations simplify the programming task, they result in code that incurs a significant run-time penalty. Since a stack is a very basic data structure that many applications employ, we also develop array- and linked-stack classes from scratch (i.e., not derived from any other class). These latter classes provide improved run-time performance over their derived counterparts.

269

Six application codes that make use of stacks are also developed. The first is a simple program to match left and right parentheses in an expression. The second is the classical Towers of Hanoi problem in which we move disks one at a time from a source tower to a destination tower using one intermediary tower; each tower operates as a stack. The third application uses stacks to represent shunting tracks in a railroad yard. The objective is to rearrange the cars in a train into the desired order. The fourth application is from the computer-aided design of circuits field. In this application we use a stack to determine whether a switch box can be feasibly routed. The fifth application revisits the offline equivalence class problem introduced in Section 6.5.4. A stack enables us to determine the equivalence classes in linear time. The final application considered in this chapter is the classical rat-in-a-maze problem in which we are to find a path from the entrance of a maze to its exit. You are urged to go through this application very carefully, as its treatment in this chapter illustrates many software-engineering principles. Additional stack applications appear in later chapters.

8.1   DEFINITION AND APPLICATIONS

Definition 8.1 *A* **stack** *is a linear list in which insertions (also called additions and pushes) and removals (also called deletions and pops) take place at the same end. This end is called the* **top**; *the other end of the list is called the* **bottom**.   ■

Figure 8.1(a) shows a stack with four elements. Suppose we wish to add element E to the stack of Figure 8.1(a). This element will have to be placed on top of element D, giving us the configuration of Figure 8.1(b). If we are to delete an element from the stack of Figure 8.1(b), it will be element E. Following the deletion, the configuration of Figure 8.1(a) results. If we perform three successive deletions on the stack of Figure 8.1(b), the stack of Figure 8.1(c) results.

Figure 8.1 Stack configurations

From the preceding discussion, we see that a stack is a LIFO list. Lists of this type appear frequently in computing.

Example 8.1 [Stacks in the Real World]

- If you examine the paper tray of your printer (or copy machine), you will see that the next sheet that gets used is the one at the top; when you add a sheet to the paper tray, you add it to the top. So the paper tray maintains a stack of paper; the paper tray works in a LIFO manner. This LIFO behavior of the paper tray is quite convenient when you want to do that occasional letter on a preprinted letterhead sheet or you want to print the next page on a preprinted form—you simply put the letterhead sheet or form at the top of the paper tray and smile when the printer prints on the desired sheet.

- Walk into a cafeteria, and you'll see a stack of trays. When you get into the food line, you pick up a tray from the top of this stack (unless, of course, you spot a new tray not too far from the top); when the tray stack is replenished, trays are added at the top of the stack. So barring anomalous behavior (like picking up a new tray that is not at the stack top), the tray stack in a cafeteria operates just like the stack data structure we have defined—the tray stack works in a LIFO manner.

- The next time you are in a college bookstore at the start of a term, observe any pile of heavy text books. Each student who needs the book removes and purchases the book at the top of the pile. When the pile gets sufficiently low, a bookstore employee mysteriously appears and adds books to the top of the pile. The book pile works in a LIFO manner—the pile is a stack.   ∎

Example 8.2 [Recursion] How does your computer run a recursive method? Recursive methods are correctly executed using a **recursion stack**. When a method is invoked, a return address (i.e., the location of the program instruction to execute once the invoked method completes) and the values of all local variables and formal parameters of the invoked method are stored on the recursion stack. When a `return` is executed, the values of local variables and formal parameters are restored to their values prior to the method invocation (these prior values are at the top of the recursion stack) and program execution resumes from the return address, which is also at the top of the stack.

Suppose the recursive sum function (Program 1.31) is invoked from the function `outerFunction` using the statement   .

```
y = rSum(x,2);
```

This statement is compiled into code to invoke `rSum` and is followed by code to store the value returned by `rSum` into y. Let l_1 be the address of the first instruction in the code to store the returned value into y. The `return rSum` statement of Program 1.31 is compiled into code to invoke `rSum`, followed by code to add the returned value to `a[n - 1]`, followed by code to return the result of this addition. Let l_2 be the address of the first instruction in the code to add the returned value to `a[n - 1]`.

When the invocation `rSum(x,2)` is made from `outerFunction`, the return address (l_1) and the the values of the formal parameters and local variables of `rSum` are saved on the recursion stack as a tuple of the form

(return address, values of formal parameters, values of local variables)

Since a and n have unspecified values at this time, the tuple $(l_1, *, *)$ (* denotes an unspecified value) is added to the recursion stack (note that `rSum` has no local variables) and the formal parameters of `rSum` are assigned their new values. The parameter a is assigned the value of x, which is a reference to element 0 of the array `x[]`, and n is assigned the value 2. Execution continues with the first instruction of `rSum`.

When `rSum` is invoked from within `rSum`, the tuple $(l_2, x, 2)$ is added to the stack; the formal parameters of `rSum` are assigned their new values $(x$ and $1)$; and we continue with the first instruction of `rSum`. The function `rSum` is invoked again from within `rSum`, and $(l_2, x, 1)$ is added to the stack; the formal parameters are assigned their new values $(x$ and $0)$; and we proceed to the first instruction of `rSum`. Now since n equals 0, the value 0 is to be returned by `rSum`. How do we know whether we should return to l_1 or to l_2? This determination is made by removing the top tuple from the stack. The stack contents (from bottom to top) are

$$[(l_1, *, *), (l_2, x, 2), (l_2, x, 1)]$$

The top tuple $(l_2, x, 1)$ is removed from the stack, the values of the formal parameters and local variables of the function we are exiting (i.e., rSum) are reset (a is reset to x and n is reset to 1), and we continue with the instruction at l_2. The sum 0 + x[0] is computed, and another return executed. At this time the recursion stack looks like this:

$$[(l_1, *, *), (l_2, x, 2)]$$

The top tuple $(l_2, x, 2)$ is removed from the stack, a is reset to x, n is reset to 2, the computed sum 0 + a[0] is to be returned, and we continue with the instruction at l_2. This time a[1] is added to 0 + a[0], the top tuple $(l_1, *, *)$ is removed from the stack, a is set to *, n is set to *, the value 0 + a[0] + a[1] is to be returned, and we continue at l_1.   ■

EXERCISES

1. The following sequence of operations is done on an initially empty stack: push A, push B, pop, push T, push T, push U, pop, pop, push A, push D. Draw figures similar to those of Figure 8.1 to show the stack configuration after each operation.

2. Do Exercise 1 for the operation sequence: push S, push S, push T, push U, pop, pop, push A, push L, push G, pop, push C, push A, push B, pop, pop.

3. Identify three additional real-world applications of a stack.

4. Show the contents of the recursion stack following each invocation of and each return from the method rSum (Program 1.31). The initial invocation is rSum(x,3).

5. Show the contents of the recursion stack following each invocation of and each return from the method **factorial** (Program 1.29). The initial invocation is factorial(3).

6. Show the contents of the recursion stack following each invocation of and each return from the method **perm** (Program 1.32). The initial invocation is perm(x, 0, 2).

8.2   THE ABSTRACT DATA TYPE

The ADT stack is specified in ADT 8.1. We have chosen the stack operation names to be the same as the method names used in the STL class `stack`.

AbstractDataType *stack*
{
    instances
        linear list of elements; one end is called the *bottom*; the other is the *top*;

    operations
        empty() : Return **true** if the stack is empty, return **false** otherwise;

          size() : Return the number of elements in the stack;

           top() : Return the top element of the stack;

          pop() : Remove the top element from the stack;

        push(x) : Add element x at the top of the stack;
}

ADT 8.1 The abstract data type stack

Program 8.1 gives the C++ abstract class that corresponds to the *stack* abstract data type.

8.3   ARRAY REPRESENTATION

Since a stack is a linear list with the restriction that additions and deletions take place at the same end, we may use any of the linear list representations of Section 5.3.3. When we identify the stack top with the right end of the array linear list, the `push` and `pop` operations correspond to the best case for linear list inserts and erases. Consequently, both operations take $O(1)$ time.

8.3.1   Implementation as a Derived Class

Program 8.2 gives the class `derivedArrayStack`, whose base classes are `arrayList` and `stack`.

    The constructor for `derivedArrayStack` simply invokes the constructor for the base `arrayList`, which allocates a one-dimensional array whose capacity (length) is `initialCapacity`. The default value for `initialCapacity` is 10. The codes for the remaining methods of `derivedArrayStack` are also straightforward.

```
template<class T>
class stack
{
   public:
      virtual ~stack() {}
      virtual bool empty() const = 0;
               // return true iff stack is empty
      virtual int size() const = 0;
               // return number of elements in stack
      virtual T& top() = 0;
               // return reference to the top element
      virtual void pop() = 0;
               // remove the top element
      virtual void push(const T& theElement) = 0;
               // insert theElement at the top of the stack
};
```

Program 8.1 The C++ abstract class stack

Complexity of derivedArrayStack Methods

The complexity of the constructor is $O(1)$ when T is a primitive data type and is $O(\text{initialCapacity})$ when T is a user-defined type. The complexity of push is $\Theta(1)$ except when we need to increase the capacity of the stack. In this latter case the complexity is $O(\text{stack size})$. The complexity of each of the remaining methods is $\Theta(1)$.

Comments on derivedArrayStack

The codes for top and pop check whether the stack is empty before they, respectively, invoke the base class methods get and erase. Since the invoked base-class methods will throw an exception when invoked with an empty stack, we can eliminate the stack empty check from top and pop without affecting the program outcome. However, since the get and remove methods of arrayList throw an exception of type illegalIndex, the user of our derived stack class will be bewildered upon having an exception of this type thrown when he/she invokes top and pop. An alternative is to replace the check for an empty stack by a try-catch construct in which the catch block catches the exception thrown by the base-class method and throws a new and meaningful exception in its place. Program 8.3 shows the code for the method top when we use this alternative. The corresponding class is called derivedArrayStackWithCatch.

The derivation from arrayList has the access modifier private. Consequently,

```
template<class T>
class derivedArrayStack : private arrayList<T>,
                          public stack<T>
{
   public:
      derivedArrayStack(int initialCapacity = 10)
        : arrayList<T> (initialCapacity) {}
      bool empty() const
          {return arrayList<T>::empty();}
      int size() const
          {return arrayList<T>::size();}
      T& top()
      {
          if (arrayList<T>::empty())
             throw stackEmpty();
          return get(arrayList<T>::size() - 1);
      }
      void pop()
      {
          if (arrayList<T>::empty())
             throw stackEmpty();
          erase(arrayList<T>::size() - 1);
      }
      void push(const T& theElement)
          {insert(arrayList<T>::size(), theElement);}
};
```

Program 8.2 An array stack class derived from `arrayList`

```
T& top()
{
    try {return get(arrayList<T>::size() - 1);}
    catch (illegalIndex)
        {throw stackEmpty();}
}
```

Program 8.3 Implementation of `top` using the `try-catch` construct

the public and protected methods and data members of `arrayList` are accessible
only from within the code for `derivedArrayStack`. In particular, users of the de-

fined stack class are unable to access `arrayList` methods such as `get`, `insert`, and `erase`. Hence the LIFO stack discipline is enforced on instances of type `derived-ArrayStack`.

An alternative, but very similar, implementation of an array stack would use a data member `stack` of type `arrayList` and define the stack methods in terms of operations on the linear list `stack`. The code would be quite similar to that of Program 8.2. Alternatively, the data member `stack` could be an array of type `T`, and the code for the `stack` methods would not employ any method of `linearList`. We explore this alternative in the next subsection.

8.3.2   The Class `arrayStack`

When we obtain a stack class by extending a linear list class as was done in Program 8.2, we pay a performance penalty. For example, whenever we add an element to a stack, the `push` method invokes `arrayList<T>::insert`, which does an index check, a possible array doubling, and a `copy_backward` prior to actually inserting the new element. The index check and `copy_backward` are unnecessary because when we add an element to a stack, the element is always added to the right end of the linear list.

One way to arrive at a faster implementation of an array stack is to develop a class that employs an array `stack` to hold the stack elements. Program 8.4 gives the class `arrayStack` that does just this. The bottom element of the stack is stored in `stack[0]`, and the top element in `stack[top]`. The codes for the methods of `array-Stack` may be arrived at from those of `arrayList` by eliminating the redundant code in `arrayList`. The asymptotic complexity of each method of `arrayStack` is the same as that of the corresponding method of `derivedArrayStack`.

8.3.3   Performance Measurement

Even though the array stack classes `arrayStack` (AS), `derivedArrayStack` (DAS), and the C++ STL container class `stack` (STL) implement all methods of the stack ADT so as to have the same asymptotic complexity, the observed performance of the methods is expected to be different for each class.

Define an n-sequence to be a sequence of n `push` operations followed by an alternating sequence of n `top` and n `pop` operations. Figure 8.2 gives the measured times to perform a 50,000,000-sequence, and Figure 8.3 shows these time as a bar chart. For all stack classes except the STL stack class, we obtained the run times for the cases: (1) start with a stack having the default capacity and (2) start with a stack whose initial capacity is 50,000,000. We did not try (2) for the STL stack class because this class does not have a constructor that allows us to specify an initial capacity.

The STL class `stack` took 2 times the time taken by `arrayStack` to perform a 50,000,000-sequence when the initial stack capacity is the default capacity. The performance ratio jumps to 3.7 when we start with an `arrayStack` whose capacity

```
template<class T>
class arrayStack : public stack<T>
{
    public:
        arrayStack(int initialCapacity = 10);
        ~arrayStack() {delete [] stack;}
        bool empty() const {return stackTop == -1;}
        int size() const
            {return stackTop + 1;}
        T& top()
        {
            if (stackTop == -1)
                throw stackEmpty();
            return stack[stackTop];
        }
        void pop()
        {
            if (stackTop == -1)
                throw stackEmpty();
            stack[stackTop--].~T();  // destructor for T
        }
        void push(const T& theElement);
    private:
        int stackTop;        // current top of stack
        int arrayLength;     // stack capacity
        T *stack;            // element array
};
```

Program 8.4 The class `arrayStack` (continues)

	initialCapacity	
Class	default	50,000,000
arrayStack	2.7	1.5
derivedArrayStack	7.5	6.3
stack	5.6	-

Times are in seconds

Figure 8.2 Time taken by different array stack implementations

```
template<class T>
arrayStack<T>::arrayStack(int initialCapacity)
{// Constructor.
   if (initialCapacity < 1)
   {ostringstream s;
    s << "Initial capacity = " << initialCapacity << " Must be > 0";
    throw illegalParameterValue(s.str());
   }
   arrayLength = initialCapacity;
   stack = new T[arrayLength];
   stackTop = -1;
}

template<class T>
void arrayStack<T>::push(const T& theElement)
{// Add theElement to stack.
   if (stackTop == arrayLength - 1)
      {// no space, double capacity
         changeLength1D(stack, arrayLength, 2 * arrayLength);
         arrayLength *= 2;
      }

   // add at stack top
   stack[++stackTop] = theElement;
}
```

Program 8.4 The class `arrayStack` (concluded)

is 50,000,000 (this jump is due mainly to the fact that `stack` does not allow you to specify an initial capacity and so array resizing cannot be avoided). It is more appropriate to compare the performance of the STL class with that of `derived-ArrayStack` because both of these classes derive from other concrete linear list classes. The STL class `stack` derives from the STL class `deque` (Exercise 9.9) while `derivedArrayStack` derives from `arrayList`. `stack` has a better performance than `derivedArrayStack` primarily because `deque` does no index checking while `array-List` does index checking.

An interesting (and expected) observation is that the time spent resizing the array (this is just the difference in the time taken when the initial capacity is 10 and when it is 500,000) is approximately the same for both of stack implementations developed in this section (approximately 1.2 seconds). The time spent on array resizing is about 44 percent of the total time taken by `arrayStack` when we start

A = default initial capacity
B = initial capacity is 50,000,000

AS   DAS   STL

Figure 8.3 Stack run times in seconds

with an array having the default length 10.

EXERCISES

7. (a) Extend the stack ADT by adding functions to
    i. Input a stack.
    ii. Convert a stack into a string suitable for output.
    iii. Split a stack in two. The first contains the bottom half elements, and the second the remaining elements.
    iv. Combine two stacks by placing all elements of the second stack on top of those in the first. The relative order of elements from the second stack is unchanged.
    (b) Define the abstract class extendedStack that extends the abstract class stack (Program 8.1) and includes the methods that correspond to the functions of (a).
    (c) Develop the concrete classes extendedDerivedArrayStack and extended-ArrayStack whose base class is extendedStack and which also are, respectively, derived from derivedArrayStack and arrayStack.

(d) Test the correctness of your codes.

8. Consider the class `arrayStack`. Show that even though it is possible for an individual `push` operation to take $\Theta(\text{stack size})$ time, the time taken by any sequence of n stack operations is $O(n)$.

9. Consider the class `arrayStack`.

   (a) As implemented in Program 8.4, the capacity of a stack (i.e., the length of the array `stack`) can increase but not decrease. To use space more efficiently, modify the implementation of `pop` so that you decrease the capacity to one-half of the current capacity whenever a `pop` reduces the stack occupancy below one-fourth of capacity.

   (b) Show that even though it is possible for an individual `push` and `pop` operation to take $\Theta(\text{capacity})$ time, the time taken by any sequence of n stack operations is $O(n)$.

10. Develop the concrete class `stackWithArrayList` that derives from the abstract class `stack`. This class has the single data member `list` whose datatype is `arrayList<T>`. Comment on the relative merits of the classes `derivedArrayStack` and `stackWithArrayList`.

11. Develop the C++ class `twoStacks` in which a single array is used to represent two stacks. Peg the bottom of one stack at position 0 and the bottom of the other at position `arrayLength-1`. The two stacks grow toward the middle of the array (see Figure 8.4). Your class must contain methods to perform all operations of the ADT *stack* on each of the two stacks. Further the complexity of each method should be $O(1)$ excluding the time for array resizing.

Figure 8.4 Two stacks in an array

8.4   LINKED REPRESENTATION

When using a chain to represent a stack, we must decide which end of the chain corresponds to the stack top. If we associate the right end of the chain with the stack top, then the stack operations `top`, `push`, and `pop` are implemented using invocations to the chain methods `get(size() - 1)`, `insert(size(), theElement)`, and `erase(size() - 1)`. Each of these chain operations takes $O(\text{size}())$ time. On the other hand, if we associate the left end of the chain with the stack top, then the chain operations to use are `get(0)`, `insert(0, theElement)`, and `erase(0)`. Each of these operations takes $\Theta(1)$ time. This analysis shows that we should use the left end of the chain to represent the stack top.

8.4.1   The Class `derivedLinkedStack`

The code for the class `derivedLinkedStack`, which derives from `chain` (Program 6.2) and which implements the abstract class `stack`, may be obtained from the code for `derivedArrayStack` (Program 8.2) by replacing the clause `private array-List<T>` with the clause `private chain<T>`; replacing all occurrences of the name `derivedArrayStack` with the name `derivedLinkedStack`; and changing the index actual parameter to all uses of the methods `get`, `insert`, and `erase` to 0 so that these operations take place at the left end of the chain. What could be easier? By using the object-oriented programming principles of information hiding and encapsulation, we have greatly simplified program development. The complexity of each method of `derivedLinkedStack` (including the constructor and `push` methods) is $\Theta(1)$.

8.4.2   The Class `linkedStack`

As was the case with the class `arrayStack` (Program 8.4), we can improve the run-time performance by customizing the code and not deriving our linked-stack class from the class `chain`. Program 8.5 gives the customized code.

8.4.3   Performance Measurement

`derivedLinkedStack` and `linkedStack` took 41 and 40.5 seconds, respectively, to perform a 50,000,000-sequence (these times were obtained by measuring the times for a 10,000,000-sequence and multiplying by 5). Comparing with the times reported in Figure 8.2, we see that `linkedStack` takes 15 times the time `arrayStack` takes when started with a capacity of 10 and 27 times the time taken when the array stack's initial capacity is 50,000,000.

EXERCISES

12. In some stack applications the elements to be put on a stack are already in nodes of type `chainNode`. For these applications it is desirable to have the

```
template<class T>
class linkedStack : public stack<T>
{
   public:
      linkedStack(int initialCapacity = 10)
            {stackTop = NULL; stackSize = 0;}
      ~linkedStack();
      bool empty() const
            {return stackSize == 0;}
      int size() const
          {return stackSize;}
      T& top()
         {
            if (stackSize == 0)
               throw stackEmpty();
            return stackTop->element;
         }
      void pop();
      void push(const T& theElement)
         {
             stackTop = new chainNode<T>(theElement, stackTop);
             stackSize++;
         }
   private:
      chainNode<T>* stackTop;   // pointer to stack top
      int stackSize;            // number of elements in stack
};
```

Program 8.5 Customized linked stack (continues)

methods pushNode(chainNode* theNode), which adds theNode to the top of the stack (notice that no call to new is made), and popNode, which removes and returns the top node of the stack.

(a) Write code for these methods

(b) Test your code.

(c) Compare the performance of a 10,000,000-sequence that uses pushNode and popNode with a 10,000,000-sequence that uses push and pop.

13. Develop the concrete class extendedLinkedStack that derives from both linkedStack and the abstract class extendedStack (see Exercise 7).

```
template<class T>
linkedStack<T>::~linkedStack()
{// Destructor.
   while (stackTop != NULL)
   {// delete top node
      chainNode<T>* nextNode = stackTop->next;
      delete stackTop;
      stackTop = nextNode;
   }
}

template<class T>
void linkedStack<T>::pop()
{// Delete top element.
   if (stackSize == 0)
      throw stackEmpty();

   chainNode<T>* nextNode = stackTop->next;
   delete stackTop;
   stackTop = nextNode;
   stackSize--;
}
```

Program 8.5 Customized linked stack (concluded)

14. Compare the performance of the array stack classes used in Figure 8.2 and the
linked classes derivedLinkedStack and linkedStack. Do this by performing
an alternating sequence of 10,000,000 push and pop operations. For the array
classes start with the default initial capacity. Does array doubling occur in
your experiment? Why?

8.5   APPLICATIONS

8.5.1   Parenthesis Matching

Problem Description

In this problem we are to match the left and right parentheses in a character string.
For example, the string (a*(b+c)+d) has left parentheses at positions 0 and 3 and
right parentheses at positions 7 and 10. The left parenthesis at position 0 matches
the right at position 10, while the left parenthesis at position 3 matches the right
parenthesis at position 7. In the string (a+b))(, the right parenthesis at position

5 has no matching left parenthesis, and the left parenthesis at position 6 has no matching right parenthesis. Our objective is to write a C++ program that inputs a string and outputs the pairs of matched parentheses as well as those parentheses for which there is no match. Notice that the parenthesis matching problem is equivalent to the problem of matching braces ({ and }) in a C++ program.

Solution Strategy

We observe that if we scan the input expression from left to right, then each right parenthesis is matched to the most recently seen unmatched left parenthesis. This observation motivates us to save the position of left parentheses on a stack as they are encountered in a left-to-right scan. When a right parenthesis is encountered, it is matched to the left parenthesis (if any) at the top of the stack. The matched left parenthesis is deleted from the stack.

C++ Implementation

Program 8.6 gives the C++ code.

Complexity

The time complexity of Program 8.6 is $O(n)$ where n is the length of the input expression. To see this, note that the program performs $O(n)$ **push** and $O(n)$ **pop** operations. Even though the complexity of an individual **push** operation is $O(\text{capacity})$ (because of array doubling), the complexity of $O(n)$ **push** operations is $O(n)$. The complexity of each **pop** operation is $O(1)$. Therefore, the complexity of $O(n)$ **pop** operations is $O(n)$.

8.5.2   Towers of Hanoi

Problem Description

The **Towers of Hanoi** problem is fashioned after the ancient Tower of Brahma ritual. According to legend, when the world was created, there was a diamond tower (tower 1) with 64 golden disks (Figure 8.5). The disks were of decreasing size and were stacked on the tower in decreasing order of size from bottom to top. Next to this tower are two other diamond towers (towers 2 and 3). Since the time of creation, Brahman priests have been attempting to move the disks from tower 1 to tower 2, using tower 3 for intermediate storage. As the disks are very heavy, they can be moved only one at a time. In addition, at no time can a disk be on top of a smaller disk. According to legend, the world will come to an end when the priests have completed their task.

In the Towers of Hanoi problem, we are given n disks and three towers. The disks are initially stacked on tower 1 in decreasing order of size from bottom to top. We are to move the disks to tower 2, one disk at a time, such that no disk is ever

```
void printMatchedPairs(string expr)
{// Parenthesis matching.
   arrayStack<int> s;
   int length = (int) expr.size();

   // scan expression expr for ( and )
   for (int i = 0; i < length; i++)
      if (expr.at(i) == '(')
         s.push(i);
      else
         if (expr.at(i) == ')')
      try
         {// remove location of matching '(' from stack
            cout << s.top() << ' ' << i << endl;
            s.pop();  // unstack match
         }
         catch (stackEmpty)
         {// stack was empty, no match exists
            cout << "No match for right parenthesis"
                 << " at " << i << endl;
         }

   // remaining '(' in stack are unmatched
   while (!s.empty())
   {
      cout << "No match for left parenthesis at "
           << s.top() << endl;
      s.pop();
   }
}
```

Program 8.6 Program to output matched parentheses

on top of a smaller one. You may wish to attempt a solution to this problem for $n = 2, 3,$ and 4 before reading further.

Solution Strategy

A very elegant solution results from the use of recursion. To get the largest disk to the bottom of tower 2, we move the remaining $n - 1$ disks to tower 3 and then move the largest to tower 2. Now we are left with the task of moving the $n - 1$ disks from tower 3 to tower 2. To perform this task, we can use towers 1 and 2. We can

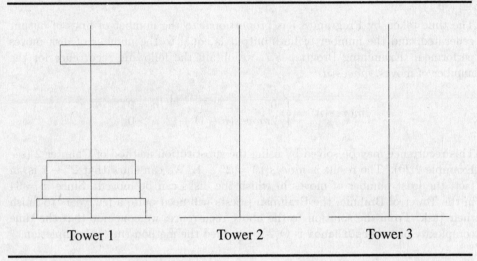

Figure 8.5 Towers of Hanoi

safely ignore the fact that tower 2 has a disk on it because this disk is larger than the disks being moved from tower 3. Therefore, we can place any disk on top of the disk on tower 2.

First Implementation

Program 8.7 gives recursive C++ code for this solution. The initial invocation is towersOfHanoi(n, 1, 2, 3). The correctness of Program 8.7 is easily established.

```
void towersOfHanoi(int n, int x, int y, int z)
{// Move the top n disks from tower x to tower y.
 // Use tower z for intermediate storage.
   if (n > 0)
   {
      towersOfHanoi(n-1, x, z, y);
      cout << "Move top disk from tower " << x
           << " to top of tower " << y << endl;
      towersOfHanoi(n-1, z, y, x);
   }
}
```

Program 8.7 Recursive method for Towers of Hanoi

Complexity

The time taken by Program 8.7 is proportional to the number of lines of output generated, and the number of lines output is equal to the number of disk moves performed. Examining Program 8.7, we obtain the following recurrence for the number of moves, $moves(n)$:

$$moves(n) = \begin{cases} 0 & n = 0 \\ 2moves(n-1)+1 & n > 0 \end{cases}$$

This recurrence may be solved by using the substitution method of Chapter 2 (see Example 2.20). The result is $moves(n) = 2^n - 1$. We can show that $2^n - 1$ is, in fact, the least number of moves in which the disks can be moved. Since $n = 64$ in the Tower of Brahma, the Brahman priests will need quite a few years to finish their task. From the solution to the above recurrence, we conclude that the time complexity of `towersOfHanoi` is $\Theta(2^n)$ provided the method runs to completion.

Second Implementation

The output from Program 8.7 gives us the disk-move sequence needed to move the disks from tower 1 to tower 2. Suppose we wish to show the state (i.e., the disks together with their order bottom to top) of the three towers following each move. To show this state, we must store the state of the towers in memory and change the state of each as disks are moved. Following each move, we can output the tower states to an output device such as the computer screen, printer, or video recorder.

Since disks are removed from each tower in a LIFO manner, each tower may be represented as a stack. The three towers together contain exactly n disks at any time. Using linked stacks, we can get by with space for n elements. If array stacks are used, towers 1 and 2 must have a capacity of n disks each, while tower 3 must have a capacity of $n-1$. Therefore, we need space for a total of $3n-1$ disks. As our earlier analysis has shown, the time complexity of the Towers of Hanoi problem is exponential in n. So using a reasonable amount of computer time, the problem can be solved only for small values of n (say $n \leq 30$). For these small values of n, the difference in space required by the array and linked representations is sufficiently small that either may be used. Since the array implementations of a stack run faster than the linked implementations, we use an array implementation.

The code of Program 8.8 uses array stacks. `towersOfHanoi(n)` is just a preprocessor for the recursive method `moveAndShow`, which is modeled after the method of Program 8.7. The preprocessor creates the three stacks `tower[1:3]` that will store the states of the three towers. The disks are numbered 1 (smallest) through n (largest). Since the disks are modeled as integers, the data type for the stack elements is `int`. The initial configuration has all n disks in `tower[1]`; the remaining two towers have no disk. After constructing this initial configuration, the preprocessor invokes the method `moveAndShow`.

```
// global variable, tower[1:3] are the three towers
arrayStack<int> tower[4];

void moveAndShow(int, int, int, int);

void towersOfHanoi(int n)
{// Preprocessor for moveAndShow.
   for (int d = n; d > 0; d--) // initialize
      tower[1].push(d); // add disk d to tower 1

   // move n disks from tower 1 to 3 using 2 as
   // intermediate tower
   moveAndShow(n, 1, 2, 3);
}


void moveAndShow(int n, int x, int y, int z)
{// Move the top n disks from tower x to tower y showing states.
 // Use tower z for intermediate storage.
   if (n > 0)
   {
      moveAndShow(n-1, x, z, y);
      int d = tower[x].top();    // move a disk from top of
      tower[x].pop();            // tower x to top of
      tower[y].push(d);          // tower y
      showState();               // show state of 3 towers
      moveAndShow(n-1, z, y, x);
   }
}
```

Program 8.8 Towers of Hanoi using stacks

8.5.3   Rearranging Railroad Cars

Problem Description

A freight train has n railroad cars. Each is to be left at a different station. Assume that the n stations are numbered 1 through n and that the freight train visits these stations in the order n through 1. The railroad cars are labeled by their destination. To facilitate removal of the railroad cars from the train, we must reorder the cars so that they are in the order 1 through n from front to back. When the cars are in this order, the last car is detached at each station. We rearrange the cars at a shunting yard that has an *input track*, an *output track*, and k holding tracks between the input and output tracks. Figure 8.6(a) shows a shunting yard with $k = 3$ holding tracks $H1$, $H2$, and $H3$. The n cars of the freight train begin in the input track and are to end up in the output track in the order 1 through n from right to left. In Figure 8.6(a), $n = 9$; the cars are initially in the order 5, 8, 1, 7, 4, 2, 9, 6, 3 from back to front. Figure 8.6(b) shows the cars rearranged in the desired order.

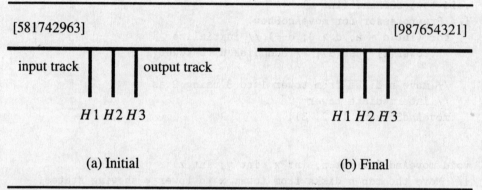

[581742963]   [987654321]

input track   output track

H1 H2 H3   H1 H2 H3

(a) Initial   (b) Final

Figure 8.6 A three-track example

Solution Strategy

To rearrange the cars, we examine the cars on the input track from front to back. If the car being examined is the next one in the output arrangement, we move it directly to the output track. If not, we move it to a holding track and leave it there until it is time to place it in the output track. The holding tracks operate in a LIFO manner as cars enter and leave these tracks from the top. When rearranging cars, only the following moves are permitted:

- A car may be moved from the front (i.e., right end) of the input track to the top of one of the holding tracks or to the left end of the output track.

- A car may be moved from the top of a holding track to the left end of the output track.

Consider the input arrangement of Figure 8.6(a). Car 3 is at the front and cannot be output yet, as it is to be preceded by cars 1 and 2. So car 3 is detached and moved to the holding track $H1$. The next car, car 6, is also to be moved to a holding track. If car 6 is moved to $H1$, the rearrangement cannot be completed because car 3 will be below car 6. However, car 3 is to be output before car 6 and so must leave $H1$ before car 6 does. So car 6 is put into $H2$. The next car, car 9, is put into $H3$ because putting it into either $H1$ or $H2$ will make it impossible to complete the rearrangement. *Notice that whenever the car labels in a holding*

Figure 8.7 Track states

track are not in increasing order from top to bottom, the rearrangement cannot be completed. The current state of the holding tracks is shown in Figure 8.7(a).

Car 2 is considered next. It can be moved into any of the holding tracks while satisfying the requirement that car labels in any holding track be in increasing order, but moving it to $H1$ is preferred. If car 2 is moved to $H3$, then we have no place to move cars 7 and 8. If we move it to $H2$, then the next car, car 4, will have to be moved to $H3$ and we will have no place for cars 5, 7, and 8. *The least restrictions on future car placement arise when the new car u is moved to the holding track that has at its top a car with smallest label v such that v > u.* We will use this **assignment rule** to select the holding track.

When car 4 is considered, the cars at the top of the three holding tracks are 2, 6, and 9. Using our assignment rule, car 4 is moved to $H2$. Car 7 is then moved to $H3$. Figure 8.7(b) shows the current state of the holding tracks. The next car, car 1, is moved to the output track. It is now time to move car 2 from $H1$ to the output track. Next car 3 is moved from $H1$, and then car 4 is moved from $H2$. No other cars can be moved to the output at this time.

The next input car, car 8, is moved to $H1$. Then car 5 is moved from the input track to the output track. Following this move, car 6 is moved from $H2$. Then car 7 is moved from $H3$, car 8 from $H1$, and car 9 from $H3$.

While three holding tracks are sufficient to rearrange the cars from the initial ordering of Figure 8.6(a), other initial arrangements may need more tracks. For example, the initial arrangement $1, n, n - 1, ..., 2$ requires $n - 1$ holding tracks.

C++ Implementation

We use k array stacks, `track[1:k]`, to represent the k holding tracks. Array stacks are used because they are faster than linked stacks. Program 8.9 gives the global variables we use.

The function `railroad` (Program 8.10) determines a sequence of moves that results in rearranging cars with initial ordering `inputOrder[1:theNumberOfCars]`

```
arrayStack<int> *track; // array of holding tracks
int numberOfCars;
int numberOfTracks;
int smallestCar; // smallest car in any holding track
int itsTrack;    // holding track with car smallestCar
```

Program 8.9 Global variables for railroad car problem

using at most `theNumberOfTracks` holding tracks. If such a sequence does not exist, `railroad` returns `false`. Otherwise, it returns `true`.

Function `railroad` begins by creating an array `track` of stacks. `track[i]` represents holding track i, $1 \leq i \leq$ `numberOfTracks`. The `for` loop maintains the invariant: *at the start of this loop, the car with label* `nextCarToOutput` *is not in a holding track.*

In iteration i of the `for` loop, car `inputOrder[i]` is moved from the input track. This car is to move to the output track only if `inputOrder[i]` equals `nextCarToOutput`. If car `inputOrder[i]` is moved to the output track, `nextCarToOutput` increases by one, and it may be possible to move one or more of the cars in the holding tracks. These cars are moved to the output by the `while` loop. If car `inputOrder[i]` cannot be moved to the output, then no car can be so moved. Consequently, car `inputOrder[i]` is added to a holding track using the stated track assignment rule.

Programs 8.11 and 8.12, respectively, give the functions `outputFromHolding-Track` and `putInHoldingTrack` utilized by `railroad`. `outputFromHoldingTrack` outputs instructions to move a car from a holding track to the output track. It also updates `smallestCar` and `itsTrack`. The method `putInHoldingTrack` puts car c into a holding track using the stated track assignment rule. It also outputs instructions to move the car to the chosen holding track and updates `smallestCar` and `itsTrack` if necessary.

Complexity

For the time complexity of `railroad` (Program 8.10), we first observe that both `outputFromHoldingTrack` and `putInHoldingTrack` have complexity $O(\text{numberOf-}$ $\text{Tracks})$. Since at most `numberOfCars-1` cars can be output from the `while` loop of `railroad` and at most `numberOfCars-1` put into holding tracks from the `else` clause, the total time spent in the functions `outputFromHoldingTrack` and `put-InHoldingTrack` is $O(\text{numberOfTracks} * \text{numberOfCars})$. The remainder of the `for` loop of `railroad` takes $\Theta(\text{numberOfCars})$ time. So the overall complexity of Program 8.10 is $O(\text{numberOfTracks} * \text{numberOfCars})$. This complexity can be reduced to $O(\text{numberOfCars} * \log(\text{numberOfTracks}))$ by using a balanced binary search tree (such as an AVL tree) to store the labels of the cars at the top of

```
bool railroad(int inputOrder[],
             int theNumberOfCars, int theNumberOfTracks)
{// Rearrange railroad cars beginning with the initial order.
 // Return true if successful, false if impossible.

   numberOfCars = theNumberOfCars;
   numberOfTracks = theNumberOfTracks;

   // create stacks for use as holding tracks
   track = new arrayStack<int> [numberOfTracks + 1];

   int nextCarToOutput = 1;
   smallestCar = numberOfCars + 1;  // no car in holding tracks

   // rearrange cars
   for (int i = 1; i <= numberOfCars; i++)
      if (inputOrder[i] == nextCarToOutput)
      {// send car inputOrder[i] straight out
         cout << "Move car " << inputOrder[i]
              << " from input track to output track" << endl;
         nextCarToOutput++;

         // output from holding tracks
         while (smallestCar == nextCarToOutput)
         {
            outputFromHoldingTrack();
            nextCarToOutput++;
         }
      }
      else
      // put car inputOrder[i] in a holding track
         if (!putInHoldingTrack(inputOrder[i]))
            return false;

   return true;
}
```

Program 8.10 The function `railroad`

the holding tracks (see Chapter 15). When a balanced binary search tree is used in this way, the functions outputFromHoldingTrack and putInHoldingTrack can

```
void outputFromHoldingTrack()
{// Output the smallest car from the holding tracks.

   // remove smallestCar from itsTrack
   track[itsTrack].pop();
   cout << "Move car "  << smallestCar  << " from holding "
       << "track "  << itsTrack  << " to output track" << endl;

   // find new smallestCar and itsTrack by checking top of all stacks
   smallestCar = numberOfCars + 2;
   for (int i = 1; i <= numberOfTracks; i++)
      if (!track[i].empty() && (track[i].top() < smallestCar))
      {
          smallestCar = track[i].top();
          itsTrack = i;
      }
}
```

Program 8.11 The function outputFromHoldingTrack

be rewritten to have complexity $O(\log(\texttt{numberOfTracks}))$. The use of a balanced binary search tree for this application is recommended only when numberOfTracks is large.

8.5.4   Switch Box Routing

Problem Description

In the switch box routing problem, we are given a rectangular routing region with pins at the periphery. Pairs of pins are to be connected together by laying a metal path between the two pins. This path is confined to the routing region and is called a wire. If two wires intersect, an electrical short occurs. So wire intersections are forbidden. Each pair of pins that is to be connected is called a **net**. We are to determine whether the given nets can be routed with no intersections. Figure 8.8(a) shows a sample switch box instance with eight pins and four nets. The nets are (1, 4), (2, 3), (5, 6), and (7, 8). The wire routing of Figure 8.8(b) has a pair of intersecting wires (those for nets (1, 4) and (2, 3)), whereas the routing of Figure 8.8(c) has no intersections. Since the four nets can be routed with no intersections, the given switch box is a **routable switch box**. (In practice, we also require a minimum separation between adjacent wires. We ignore this additional requirement here.) Our problem is to input a switch box routing instance and determine whether it is routable.

```
bool putInHoldingTrack(int c)
{// Put car c into a holding track. Return false iff there is
 // no feasible holding track for this car.

   // find best holding track for car c
   // initialize
   int bestTrack = 0,                 // best track so far
       bestTop = numberOfCars + 1;    // top car in bestTrack

   // scan tracks
   for (int i = 1; i <= numberOfTracks; i++)
      if (!track[i].empty())
      {// track i not empty
          int topCar = track[i].top();
          if (c < topCar && topCar < bestTop)
          {// track i has smaller car at top
             bestTop = topCar;
             bestTrack = i;
          }
      }
      else // track i empty
         if (bestTrack == 0) bestTrack = i;

   if (bestTrack == 0) return false; // no feasible track

   // add c to bestTrack
   track[bestTrack].push(c);
   cout << "Move car " << c << " from input track "
        << "to holding track " << bestTrack << endl;

   // update smallestCar and itsTrack if needed
   if (c < smallestCar)
   {
       smallestCar = c;
       itsTrack = bestTrack;
   }

   return true;
}
```

Program 8.12 The function putInHoldingTrack

Figure 8.8 Sample switch box

While the wires in both Figures 8.8(b) and (c) are composed of straight line segments parallel to the x- and y-axes, segments that are not parallel to these axes as well as segments that are not straight lines are permissible.

Solution Strategy

To solve the switch box routing problem, we note that when a net is connected, the wire partitions the routing region into two regions. The pins that fall on the boundary of a partition·do not depend on the wire path, but only on the pins of the net that was routed. For instance, when net (1, 4) is routed, we get two regions. One contains the pins 2 and 3, and the other contains the pins 5 through 8. If there is now a net with one pin in one region and the other in a different region, this new net cannot be routed and the routing instance is unroutable. If there is no net with this property, then since the wires cannot cross between regions, we can attempt to determine whether each region is independently routable. To make this determination, we pick a net in one of the regions; this net partitions its region into two regions, and none of the remaining nets should have a pin in one partition and another in the other partition.

We can implement this strategy by moving around the periphery of the switch box in either clockwise or counterclockwise order, beginning at any pin. If we traverse the pins of Figure 8.8(a) in clockwise order, beginning at pin 1, the pins are examined in the order, 1, 2, $\cdots$, 8. The pins that lie between pin 1 and its net partner, pin 4, define one region of the first partition, and those that lie between pins 4 and 1 define the other. We will place pin 1 on a stack and continue processing pins until pin 4 is encountered. This procedure allows us to process one of the regions before going on to the other. The next pin, pin 2, and its net partner, pin 3, partition the current region into two regions. As before, pin 2 is placed on the stack, and we proceed to pin 3. Since pin 3's partner, pin 2, is at the top of the stack, we have completed a region and pin 2 is deleted from the stack. Next we encounter pin 4 whose partner is now at the top of the stack. The processing of a region is now complete, and pin 1 is deleted from the stack. Proceeding in this way, we are able to complete the processing of all created regions, and the stack is empty after pin 8 is examined.

What happens on a nonroutable instance? Suppose the nets for Figure 8.8(a) are (1, 5), (2, 3), (4, 7), and (6, 8). Pins 1 and 2 are put on the stack initially. When pin 3 is examined, pin 2 is deleted from the stack. Next pin 4 is added to the stack, as pin 4 and the pin at the stack top do not define a region boundary. When pin 5 is examined, it is also added to the stack. Even though pins 1 and 5 have both been seen, we are unable to complete the processing of the first region defined by this net, as pin 4's routing has to cross the boundary. As a result, when we complete the examination of all pins, the stack will not be empty.

C++ Implementation and Complexity

Program 8.13 gives a C++ function that implements this strategy. This function assumes that the number of pins is even and that each pin has a net number. So for the example in Figure 8.8(c), the input array **net** is [1, 2, 2, 1, 3, 3, 4, 4]. The complexity of the program is $O(n)$ where n is the number of pins.

8.5.5   Offline Equivalence Class Problem

Problem Description

The offline equivalence problem was defined in Section 6.5.4. The inputs to this problem are the number of elements n, the number of relation pairs r, and the r relation pairs. We are to partition the n elements into equivalence classes.

Solution Strategy

The solution is in two phases. In the first phase we input the data and set up n lists to represent the relation pairs. For each relation pair (i, j), i is put on $list[j]$ and j is put on $list[i]$.

Example 8.3 Suppose that $n = 9$, $r = 11$, and the 11 relation pairs are (1, 5), (1, 6), (3, 7), (4, 8), (5, 2), (6, 5), (4, 9), (9, 7), (7, 8), (3, 4), and (6, 2). The nine lists are

$$list[1] = [5, 6]$$
$$list[2] = [5, 6]$$
$$list[3] = [7, 4]$$
$$list[4] = [8, 9, 3]$$
$$list[5] = [1, 2, 6]$$

```
bool checkBox(int net[], int n)
{// Determine whether the switch box is routable.
 // net[0..n-1] is array of pin to net assignments.
 // n is number of pins.

   arrayStack<int>* s = new arrayStack<int>(n);

   // scan nets clockwise
   for (int i = 0; i < n; i++)
      // process pin i
      if (!s->empty())
         // check with top net
         if (net[i] == net[s->top()])
            // net[i] is routable, delete from stack
            s->pop();
         else s->push(i);
      else s->push(i);

   // any unrouted nets left?
   if (s->empty())
   {// no nets remain
      cout << "Switch box is routable" << endl;
      return true;
   }

   cout << "Switch box is not routable" << endl;
   return false;
}
```

Program 8.13 Switch box routing

$$
\begin{aligned}
list[6] &= [1,2,5] \\
list[7] &= [3,9,8] \\
list[8] &= [4,7] \\
list[9] &= [4,7]
\end{aligned}
$$

Element order within a list is not important.   ∎

In the second phase, the equivalence classes are identified by first locating an element that has not been output as part of an equivalence class. This element becomes the **seed** for the next equivalence class. The seed is output as the first member of the next equivalence class. From the seed we identify all other members of the class as follows. The seed is put onto a list, *unprocessedList*, of elements that are in the same equivalence class as the seed and whose lists have yet to be processed. We remove an element i from *unprocessedList* and process $list[i]$. All elements on $list[i]$ are in the same equivalence class as the seed; elements on $list[i]$ that haven't already been identified as class members are output and added to *unprocessedList*. This process of removing an element i from *unprocessedList* and then outputting and adding elements in $list[i]$ that haven't already been output to *unprocessedList* continues until the *unprocessedList* becomes empty. At this time we have completed a class, and we proceed to find a seed for the next class.

Example 8.4 Consider the data of Example 8.3. Let 1 be the first seed; 1 is output as part of a new class and is also added to *unprocessedList*. Next 1 is removed from *unprocessedList*, and $list[1]$ is processed. The elements 5 and 6 that are in $list[1]$ are output as part of the same class as element 1; 5 and 6 are also added to *unprocessedList*. Either 5 or 6 is removed from *unprocessedList*, and its list is processed. Suppose that 5 is removed. The elements 1, 2, and 6 that are in $list[5]$ are examined. Since 1 and 6 have already been output, we ignore them. Element 2 is output and added to *unprocessedList*. When the remaining elements (6 and 2) that are in *unprocessedList* are removed and processed, no additional element is output or added to *unprocessedList*; this list becomes empty, and we have identified an equivalence class.

To find another equivalence class, we search for a seed—an element not yet output. Element 3 has not been output and is used as the seed for the next class. Elements 3, 4, 7, 8, and 9 are output as part of this next class. Since no seeds remain, we have found all the classes.   ∎

C++ Implementation

To proceed with an implementation, we must select a representation for *list* and *unprocessedList*. The operations performed on *list* are to insert and examine all elements. Since it doesn't matter where elements are inserted in *list*, any linear list or stack representation may be used. We select a specific linear list or stack representation based on which is expected to provide the best space and time performance.

The total number of elements in all n of the lists $list[1 : n]$ is $2r$. Therefore, as far as space requirements go, all our array linear list and stack classes require space for between $2r$ and $4r$ elements (because of array doubling, the allocated array length may be up to two times the number of elements). Our linked classes require space for $2r$ elements and $2r$ pointers. Our run-time performance studies of linear list and stack implementations (see Sections 5.6, 6.1.6, 8.3.3, and 8.4.3) show that the linked implementations of these data structures are slower than their array counterparts. So we eliminate the linked representations from further consideration as far the offline equivalence class problem is concerned.

By inserting new elements at the right end of a list, our application will exhibit the best-case time performance for arrayList (Section 5.3). However, if we use an arrayStack, we will do slightly better. For performance reasons *unprocessedList* is also implemented as an arrayStack.

Program 8.14 gives a two-part program for the offline equivalence problem. In the first part, n, r, and the r pairs are input, and the stack (list) for each of the n elements constructed. The stack list[i] for element i contains all elements j such that (i,j) or (j,i) is an input relation pair. Our code can be made more robust by verifying that every pair (a, b) that is input has both a and b in the range [1, n]. Exercise 31 asks you to modify the code so as to validate the input relations.

The second part of the program outputs the equivalence classes. For the second part we maintain an array out such that out[i] = true iff element i has been output as a member of some equivalence class. A stack unprocessedList assists in locating all elements of an equivalence class. This stack holds all elements that have been output as part of the current class and that may lead to additional elements of the class. To find the seed for the next equivalence class, we scan the array out for an element not yet output. If there is no such element, then there is no next class. If such an element is found, it begins the next class.

Complexity

For the complexity analysis, we assume that no exceptions are thrown during execution (in particular, the input pairs (a, b) are valid). Part 1 of the program (input and initialize the array list[] of relation pairs) takes $\Theta(n+r)$ time. For part 2, we note that since each of the n elements is output exactly once, each is added to unprocessedList once and deleted from unprocessedList once. So the total time spent pushing and popping elements from unprocessedList is $\Theta(n)$. Finally, when an element j is removed from unprocessedList, all elements on list[j] are examined by popping then off of list[j]. Each element in each list[j] is popped exactly once. So the time required to pop and examine all elements on all lists list[1:n] is $\Theta(r)$ (note that the total number of elements on all lists list[1:n] is 2 * r following the input phase). Allowing for the possibility that an exception may occur, we conclude that the overall complexity of Program 8.14 is $O(n+r)$. The complexity when no exception occurs is $\Theta(n+r)$.

Since every program for the offline equivalence class problem must examine each relation and element at least once, it is not possible to solve the offline equivalence problem in less than $O(n+r)$ time.

8.5.6   Rat in a Maze

Problem Description

A **maze** (Figure 8.9) is a rectangular area with an entrance and an exit. The interior of the maze contains walls or obstacles that one cannot walk through. In

```
int main()
{
   int n,    // number of elements
       r;    // number of relations

   cout << "Enter number of elements" << endl;
   cin >> n;
   if (n < 2)
   {
      cout << "Too few elements" << endl;
      return 1;   // terminate with error
   }

   cout << "Enter number of relations" << endl;
   cin >> r;
   if (r < 1)
   {
      cout << "Too few relations" << endl;
      return 1;   // terminate with error
   }

   // create an array of empty stacks, stack[0] not used
   arrayStack<int>* list = new arrayStack<int> [n+1];

   // input the r relations and put on lists
   int a, b;  // (a, b) is a relation
   for (int i = 1; i <= r; i++)
   {
      cout << "Enter next relation/pair" << endl;
      cin >> a >> b;
      list[a].push(b);
      list[b].push(a);
   }
```

Program 8.14 Offline equivalence class program (continues)

our mazes these obstacles are placed along rows and columns that are parallel to the rectangular boundary of the maze. The entrance is at the upper-left corner, and the exit is at the lower-right corner.

Suppose that the maze is to be modeled as an $n \times m$ matrix with position (1,1) of the matrix representing the entrance and position (n, m) representing the

```
   // initialize to output equivalence classes
   arrayStack<int> unprocessedList;
   bool* out = new bool[n + 1];
   for (int i = 1; i <= n; i++)
      out[i] = false;

   // output equivalence classes
   for (int i = 1; i <= n; i++)
      if (!out[i])
      {// start of a new class
         cout << "Next class is: " << i << " ";
         out[i] = true;
         unprocessedList.push(i);
         // get rest of class from unprocessedList
         while (!unprocessedList.empty())
         {
            int j = unprocessedList.top();
            unprocessedList.pop();

            // elements on list[j] are in the same class
            while (!list[j].empty())
            {
               int q = list[j].top();
               list[j].pop();
               if (!out[q])  // q not yet output
               {
                  cout << q << " ";
                  out[q] = true;
                  unprocessedList.push(q);
               }
            }
         }
         cout << endl;
      }

   cout << "End of list of equivalence classes" << endl;

   return 0;
}
```

Program 8.14 Offline equivalence class program (concluded)

Figure 8.9 A maze

$$
\begin{array}{cccccccccc}
0 & 1 & 1 & 1 & 1 & 1 & 0 & 0 & 0 & 0 \\
0 & 0 & 0 & 0 & 0 & 1 & 0 & 1 & 0 & 0 \\
0 & 0 & 0 & 1 & 0 & 1 & 0 & 0 & 0 & 0 \\
0 & 1 & 0 & 1 & 0 & 1 & 0 & 1 & 1 & 0 \\
0 & 1 & 0 & 1 & 0 & 1 & 0 & 1 & 0 & 0 \\
0 & 1 & 1 & 1 & 0 & 1 & 0 & 1 & 0 & 1 \\
0 & 1 & 0 & 0 & 0 & 1 & 0 & 1 & 0 & 1 \\
0 & 1 & 0 & 1 & 1 & 1 & 0 & 1 & 0 & 0 \\
1 & 0 & 0 & 0 & 0 & 0 & 0 & 1 & 0 & 0 \\
0 & 0 & 0 & 0 & 1 & 1 & 1 & 1 & 0 & 0 \\
\end{array}
$$

Figure 8.10 Matrix representation of maze of Figure 8.9

exit. n and m are, respectively, the number of rows and columns in the maze. Each maze position is described by its row and column intersection. The matrix has a 1 in position (i, j) iff there is an obstacle at the corresponding maze position. Otherwise, there is a 0 at this matrix position. Figure 8.10 shows the matrix representation of the maze of Figure 8.9. The **rat-in-a-maze** problem is to find a path from the entrance to the exit of a maze. A **path** is a sequence of positions, none of which is blocked, and such that each (other than the first) is the north, south, east, or west neighbor of the preceding position (Figure 8.11).

Figure 8.11 The four options for a move from any position in the maze

You are to write a program to solve the rat-in-a-maze problem. You may assume that the mazes for which your program is to work are square (i.e., $m = n$) and are sufficiently small so that the entire maze can be represented in the memory of the target computer. Your program will be a stand-alone product that will be used directly by persons wishing to find a path in a maze of their choice.

Design

We will use the top-down modular methodology to design the program. It is not too difficult to see the three aspects to the problem: input the maze, find a path, and output the path. We will use one program module for each task. A fourth module that displays a welcome message and identifies the program and its author is also desirable. While this module is not directly related to the problem at hand, the use of such a module enhances the user-friendliness of the program.

The module that finds the path does not interact directly with the user and will therefore contain no help facility and will not be menu driven. The remaining three modules interact with the user, and we need to expend some effort designing their user interface. The user interface should make the user want to use your program rather than competing programs.

Let us begin with the welcome module. We wish to display a message such as

Welcome To
RAT IN A MAZE
©Joe Bloe, 2000

While displaying this message might seem like a trivial task, we can use various design elements to obtain a pleasing effect. For example, the message can be multi-colored to take advantage of the user's color display. The three lines of the welcome display need to be positioned on the screen, and we can change the character size from one line to the next (or even from character to character). The welcome message can be introduced on the display with a reasonable time lapse between the introduction of one character and the next. Alternatively, the time lapse can be very small. In addition, we might consider the use of sound effects. We also need to determine the duration for which the message is to be displayed. It should be displayed long enough so that the user can read it, but not long enough to leave the user yawning. As you can see, the design of the welcome message (and the whole user interface in general) requires strong artistic skills.

For the input module we must decide whether we want the input as a matrix of 0s and 1s or whether we will display a maze of the desired size and then ask the user to click a mouse at the squares that contain an obstacle. We must also decide on the colors to use, whether we will have audio during input, and so on.

The input module can also verify that the entrance and exit of the maze are not blocked. If they are, then no path exists. In all likelihood the user made an error in input. The following discussion assumes that the input module performs this verification and that the entrance and exit are not blocked.

Once again, we see that what initially appeared to be a simple task (read in a matrix) is actually quite complex if we want to do it in a user-friendly way.

The output module design involves essentially the same considerations as the design of the input module.

Program Plan

The design phase has already pointed out the need for four program modules. We also need a root (or main) module that invokes these four modules in the following sequence: welcome module, input module, find path module, and output module.

Our program will have the modular structure of Figure 8.12. Each program module can be coded independently. The root module will be coded as the method main; the welcome, input, find path, and output path modules will each be a single private method.

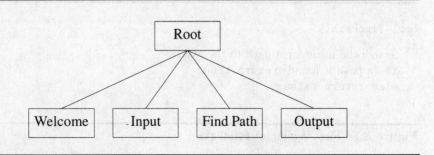

Figure 8.12 Modular structure of rat-in-a-maze program

At this point we see that our program is going to have the form given in Figure 8.13.

```
// function welcome comes here
// function inputMaze comes here
// function findPath comes here
// function outputPath comes here

void main()
{
    welcome();
    inputMaze();
    if (findPath())
        outputPath();
    else
        cout << No path" << endl;
}
```

Figure 8.13 Form of rat-in-a-maze program

Program Development

Substantial data structure and algorithm issues arise in the development of the path-finding module only. Consequently, we will develop just this module here. Exercise 33 asks you to develop the remaining modules. Without thinking too much about the coding of the path-finding module, we can arrive at the C++ pseudocode given in Figure 8.14. This code is readily seen to be correct. Unfortunately, we cannot present it to a computer in this form, and we need to refine the pseudocode into pure C++ code.

```
bool findPath()
{
    Search the maze for a path to the exit;
    if (a path is found) return true;
    else return false;
}
```

Figure 8.14 First version of findPath

Before attempting a refinement of Figure 8.14 that will get us closer to C++

code, let us figure out how we are to search the maze for a path. We begin with the entrance as our present position. If the present position is the exit, then we have found a path and we are done. If we are not at the exit, then we block the present position (i.e., place an obstacle there) so as to prevent the search from returning here. Next we see whether there is an adjacent maze position that is not blocked. If so, we move to this new adjacent position and attempt to find a path from there to the exit. If we are unsuccessful, we attempt to move to some other unblocked adjacent maze position and try to find a path from there. To facilitate this move, we save the current position on a stack before advancing to a new adjacent position. If all adjacent unblocked positions have been tried and no path is found, there is no path from entrance to exit in the maze.

Let us use the above strategy on the maze of Figure 8.9. We begin with the position (1,1) on the stack and move to its only unblocked neighbor (2,1). The position (1,1) is blocked to prevent the search path from moving through this position later. From (2,1) we can move to (3,1) or (2,2). Suppose we decide to move to (3,1). Prior to the move, we block (2,1) and add it to the stack. From (3,1) we may move to either (4,1) or (3,2). If we move to (4,1), (4,1) gets blocked and added to the stack. From (4,1) we move to (5,1), (6,1), (7,1), and (8,1). The path cannot be extended from (8,1). Our stack now contains the path from (1,1) to (8,1). To try another path, we back up to (7,1) by deleting this position from the stack. As there are no unblocked positions adjacent to (7,1), we back up to (6,1) by deleting this position from the stack. In this way we back up to position (3,1) from which we are again able to move forward (i.e , move to (3,2)). Notice that the stack always contains the path from the entrance to the current position. If we reach the exit, the entrance-to-exit path will be on the stack.

To refine Figure 8.14, we need representations for the maze, which is a matrix of zeros and ones, each maze position, and the stack. Let us consider the maze first. The maze is naturally represented as a two-dimensional array `maze` of type `int`. (Since each array position can take on only one of the values 0 and 1, we could use the data type `bool` and represent the value 1 by `true` and the value 0 by `false`. This approach would reduce the space required for the array `maze`.) Position (i,j) of the maze matrix corresponds to position `[i][j]` of the array `maze`.

From interior (i.e., nonboundary) positions of the maze, four moves are possible: right, down, left, and up. From positions on the boundary of the maze, either two or three moves are possible. To avoid having to handle positions on the boundaries of the maze differently from interior positions, we will surround the maze with a wall of obstacles. For an $m \times m$ maze, this wall will occupy rows 0 and $m + 1$ and columns 0 and $m + 1$ of the array `maze` (see Figure 8.15).

All positions in the maze are now within the boundary of the surrounding wall, and we can move to four possible positions from each position (some of these four positions may have obstacles). By surrounding the maze with our own boundary, we have eliminated the need for our program to handle boundary conditions, which significantly simplifies the code. This simplification is achieved at the cost of a

```
1 1 1 1 1 1 1 1 1 1 1 1 1
1 0 1 1 1 1 1 0 0 0 0 1
1 0 0 0 0 0 1 0 1 0 0 1
1 0 0 0 1 0 1 0 0 0 0 1
1 0 1 0 1 0 1 0 1 1 0 1
1 0 1 0 1 0 1 0 1 0 0 1
1 0 1 1 1 0 1 0 1 0 1 1
1 0 1 0 0 0 1 0 1 0 1 1
1 0 1 0 1 1 1 0 1 0 0 1
1 1 0 0 0 0 0 0 1 0 0 1
1 0 0 0 0 1 1 1 1 0 0 1
1 1 1 1 1 1 1 1 1 1 1 1
```

Figure 8.15 Maze of Figure 8.9 with wall of 1s around it

slightly increased space requirement for the array **maze**.

Each maze position is described by its row and column index, which are, respectively, called the row and column coordinates of the position. We may define a class **position** with data members **row** and **col** and use objects of type **position** to keep track of maze positions. The stack, **path**, that maintains the path from the entrance to the current position may be represented as an array stack. An $m \times m$ maze with no blockages can have paths with as many as m^2 positions (see Figure 8.16(a)).

(a) A long path   (b) A short path

Figure 8.16 Paths in a maze with no blockages

Since no path repeats a position and the maze has only m^2 positions, no path can have more than m^2 positions. Further, as the last position on a path is not stored on the stack, at most $m^2 - 1$ positions can get stacked. Notice that a maze with no blockages always has a path with at most $2m$ positions between any two points (see, for example, Figure 8.16(b)). However, we have no assurance at this time that our path finder will find the shortest path.

We can now refine Figure 8.14 and obtain Figure 8.17, which is closer to being a C++ program.

Now we need to tackle the problem of determining a neighbor of position **here** that can be moved to. The task of trying out alternative moves is simplified if we select from the options available at any position in some systematic way. For example, we may first attempt to move right, then down, then left, and finally up. Once an option has been selected, we need to know the coordinates of the position to move to. These coordinates are easily computed by maintaining a table of offsets as in Figure 8.18. The moves right, down, left, and up have, respectively, been numbered 0, 1, 2, and 3. In the table of Figure 8.18, **offset[i].row** and **offset[i].col**, respectively, give the amounts to be added to the **row** and **col** coordinates of the present position to move to the adjacent position in direction **i**. For example, if we are at position (3, 4), then the position on the right has row coordinate 3+**offset[0].row** = 3 and column coordinate 4+**offset[0].col** = 5.

To avoid moving to positions that we have been through before, we place an obstacle (i.e., set **maze[i][j]** = 1) at each position **maze[i][j]** that we move to.

Incorporating these refinements into the code of Figure 8.17 results in the C++ code of Program 8.15. In the code of Program 8.15, the variable **size** contains the number m of rows and columns in the maze.

The method **findPath** begins by creating an empty stack **path**. It then initializes the array of offsets and builds a wall of obstacles around the maze. In the **while** loop we attempt to advance the path forward from the current position **here** by trying the move options in the following order: right, down, left, and up. If we are able to move forward, the present location is stored on the stack **path** and a forward move is made. If a forward move isn't possible, we try to back up to a previous position. If there is no position to back up to (i.e., the stack is empty), there is no path to the exit. Otherwise, we can back up. Once we back up to the top position on the stack (**next**), we need to move forward by trying the next move option. This option can be computed from the positions **next** and **here**. Notice that **here** is a neighbor of **next**. In fact, at some previous time in the program, we moved from **next** to **here**, and this move was the last move made from **next**. The next move option to try is correctly computed by the following code:

```
if (next.row == here.row)
    option = 2 + next.col - here.col;
else option = 3 + next.row - here.row;
```

```
bool findPath()
{// Find a path from (1,1) to the exit (size, size).
 // Return true if successful, false if impossible.

   path = new arrayStack<position>;

   // initialize offsets
   position offset[4];
   offset[0].row = 0; offset[0].col = 1;    // right
   offset[1].row = 1; offset[1].col = 0;    // down
   offset[2].row = 0; offset[2].col = -1;   // left
   offset[3].row = -1; offset[3].col = 0;   // up

   // initialize wall of obstacles around maze
   for (int i = 0; i <= size + 1; i++)
   {
      maze[0][i] = maze[size + 1][i] = 1; // bottom and top
      maze[i][0] = maze[i][size + 1] = 1; // left and right
   }

   position here;
   here.row = 1;
   here.col = 1;
   maze[1][1] = 1; // prevent return to entrance
   int option = 0; // next move
   int lastOption = 3;

   // search for a path
   while (here.row != size || here.col != size)
   {// not exit
      // find a neighbor to move to
      int r, c;
      while (option <= lastOption)
      {
         r = here.row + offset[option].row;
         c = here.col + offset[option].col;
         if (maze[r][c] == 0) break;
         option++; // next option
      }
```

Program 8.15 Code to find a path in a maze (continues)

```
bool findPath()
{// Find a path from (1,1) to the exit (m,m).
   Initialize wall of obstacles around maze;

   // initialize variable to keep track of
   // our current position in the maze
   here.row = 1;
   here.col = 1;

   maze[1][1] = 1;  // prevent return to entrance

   // search for a path to the exit
   while (not at exit) do
   {
      find a neighbor to move to;
      if (there is such a neighbor)
      {
         add position here to path stack;
         // move to and block neighbor
         here = neighbor;
         maze[here.row][here.col] = 1;
      }
      else
      {
         // cannot move forward, backup
         if (path empty) return false;
         back up to position here, which is at top of path stack;
      }
   }
   return true;
}
```

Figure 8.17 Refined version of Figure 8.14

For the time complexity analysis, we see that in the worst case we may move to each unblocked position of the input maze. Each such position may get added to the stack at most three times. (Each time we move forward from a position, it is added to the stack; at most three forward moves are possible from any position.) Hence each position may be removed from the stack at most three times. Further, at each position $\Theta(1)$ time is spent examining its neighbors. So the time complexity

Move	Direction	offset[move].row	offset[move].col
0	right	0	1
1	down	1	0
2	left	0	−1
3	up	−1	0

Figure 8.18 Table of offsets

```
    // was a neighbor found?
    if (option <= lastOption)
    {// move to maze[r][c]
       path->push(here);
       here.row = r;
       here.col = c;
       maze[r][c] = 1; // set to 1 to prevent revisit
       option = 0;
    }
    else
    {// no neighbor to move to, back up
       if (path->empty())
          return false;   // no place to back up to
       position next = path->top();
       path->pop();
       if (next.row == here.row)
          option = 2 + next.col - here.col;
       else option = 3 + next.row - here.row;
       here = next;
    }
  }

  return true;  // at exit
}
```

Program 8.15 Code to find a path in a maze (concluded)

is $O(unblocked)$ where *unblocked* is the number of unblocked positions in the input maze. This complexity is $O(\text{size}^2) = O(m^2)$.

When you get to Section 16.8.4 you'll see that the strategy used by findPath is really a depth-first search, which is just a special case of a more general strategy called backtracking. So findPath is really an application of depth-first search, backtracking, and stacks.

EXERCISES

15. Write a program to determine whether or not a character string has an unmatched parenthesis. You should not use a stack. Test your code. What is the time complexity of your program?

16. Write a version of Program 8.6 that looks for matched pairs of parentheses and matched pairs of brackets ([and]). In the string (a+[b*(c-d)+f]), the matched pairs are (0,14), (3,13), and (6,10); and in the string (a+[b*(c-d]+f)), there is a nesting problem because the left parenthesis at 6 should be matched by a right parenthesis before a left bracket is encountered. Test your code.

17. Do Exercise 16 for the case when you have parentheses, brackets, and braces ({ and }).

18. Manually determine the sequence of disk moves for the four-disk Tower of Hanoi problem.

19. Establish the correctness of Program 8.7 by induction on the number of disks.

20. Assume that the Towers of Hanoi disks are labeled 1 through n with the smallest disk being disk 1. Modify Program 8.7 so that it also outputs the label of the disk that is being moved. This modification requires a simple change to the output statement. Do not make any other changes.

21. Write code for the showState method of Program 8.8 assuming that the output device is a computer screen. If necessary, add methods to arrayStack so that you can access the disks on a tower in a convenient manner. You will need to introduce a time delay so that the display does not change too rapidly. Show each disk in a different color.

22. The Towers of HaHa problem is like the Towers of Hanoi problem. However, the disks are numbered 1 through n; odd-numbered disks are red, and even-numbered ones are yellow. The disks are initially on tower 1 in the order 1 through n from top to bottom. The disks are to be moved to tower 2, and at no time should a disk sit on top of a disk that has the same color. The initial and final disk order are the same.

    (a) Write a program to move the disks from tower 1 to tower 2 using tower 3 for intermediate storage.

    (b) How many disk moves does your program make?

23. Investigate the Towers of Hanoi problem under the assumption that you have $k > 1$ intermediate towers. The availability of more towers reduces the number

of moves needed. For example, when the number of intermediate towers is $n-1$, a total of $2n-1$ disk moves suffices. A good place to start is the case when two intermediate towers are available.

24. (a) You have a railroad shunting yard with three shunting tracks that operate as stacks. The initial ordering of cars is 3, 1, 6, 7, 2, 8, 5, 4. Draw figures similar to Figures 8.6 and 8.7 to show the configuration of the shunting tracks, the input track, and the output track following each car move made by the solution of Section 8.5.3.

    (b) Do part (a) for two shunting tracks.

25. In our solution to the railroad car rearrangement problem (Section 8.5.3), we use k array stacks to represent k holding tracks. How large can each stack get? What is the total stack space required?

26. (a) Does Program 8.10 succeed in rearranging the cars whenever it is possible to do this rearrangement using k tracks?

    (b) The total number of car moves required is n + (number of cars moved to a holding track). Suppose that the initial car arrangement can be rearranged using k tracks and Program 8.10. Does Program 8.10 perform the rearrangement using the minimum number of moves? Prove your answer.

27. Develop a program for the railroad car rearrangement problem under the assumption that holding track i can hold at most s_i cars, $1 \le i \le k$.

28. Walk through Program 8.13 for the case when the nets are (1, 6), (2, 5), (3, 4), (7, 10), (8, 9), (12, 13), and (11, 14). Show the stack configuration after the examination of each pin.

29. In the switch box routing application, we noted that processing can stop when two pins of the same net get on to the stack. Write a new version of checkBox that does this. The time complexity of your new method should be $O(n)$ where n is the number of pins. You may assume that the net numbers are 1 through $n/2$. How large a stack do you need?

30. Do the following for the offline equivalence class problem:

    (a) Give the lists $list[1:n]$ for the case when $n = 9$, $r = 9$, and the input relation pairs are (1, 3), (4, 2), (3, 8), (6, 7), (5, 8), (6, 2), (1, 5), (4, 7), and (9, 7).

    (b) Walk through the second phase of the solution strategy using the lists of part (a). Provide an explanation of your progress as is done in Example 8.4.

31. Program 8.14 does not validate the relations as they are input. Modify this program so that it makes sure that each a and b that is input is in the range [1, n] and throws an exception of type myInputException whenever this is not the case.

32. (a) Modify Program 8.14 so that list [] is an array of type arrayList rather than arrayStack. Use a linear list iterator to examine the elements on a linear list in phase 2 of the program.

    (b) Experimentally compare the performance of Program 8.14 and your new code.

33. Complete the rat-in-a-maze code. Write a pleasing C++ program by doing the following:

    (a) Write a welcome function that incorporates graphics and audio.

    (b) Write a robust inputMaze function that validates the data that is input. Also provide user prompts for input.

    (c) Write the outputPath function to output the path from the maze to the exit (not from the exit to the entrance).

    Test your codes using sample mazes.

34. Modify the code for the rat-in-a-maze problem so that the code works for mazes in which you are allowed to move to the north, northeast, east, southeast, south, southwest, west, and northwest neighbors of a position. Test the correctness of the modified code using suitable mazes.

35. Develop a better bound than $m^2 - 1$ for the maximum size of the stack path.

36. The strategy used to find a path in a maze is really a recursive one. From the present position we find a neighbor to move to and then determine whether there is a path from this neighbor to the exit. If so, we are done. If not, we find another neighbor to move to. Use recursion to find a path in a maze. Test the correctness of your code using suitable mazes.

37. Study the rat-in-a-maze animation that is on the Web site for this book.

    (a) Identify heuristics you could program into the rat-in-a-maze program to select the next move in a more intelligent fashion than is done in Program 8.15. For example, should you preferentially follow along a wall of blocked positions looking for a break in the wall?

    (b) Modify Program 8.15 to incorporate your heuristics.

    (c) Test the correctness of the new code.

    (d) Compare the run-time performance of the new code and that of Program 8.15.

38. You are given an array, data[], of integers. Your task is to compute another integer array lastAsBig[]. Informally, lastAsBig[i] gives you the nearest position to the left where the data value is at least as big. For example, when data[] = [6, 2, 3, 1, 7, 5], lastAsBig[] = [−1, 0, 0, 2, −1, 4]. More formally, lastAsBig[i] is the largest integer j such that j < i and data[j] ≥ data[i]. In case no there is no such j, then lastAsBig[i] = −1.

One application of lastAsBig is in weather reporting. Let data[i] be the high temperature recorded in Gainesville in day i of the current year. If lastAsBig[i] is −1, then we have not seen a temperature this high earlier in the year. When lastAsBig[i] ≠ −1, lastAsBig[i] gives the last time this year that the temperature was this high; i − lastAsBig[i] gives the number of days since the temperature was this high (this year).

(a) Give two more applications for lastAsBig.

(b) Write a method to compute lastAsBig that uses a stack. The time complexity of your method should be $O(\texttt{data.length})$.

(c) Test your method.

8.6   REFERENCES AND SELECTED READINGS

The switch box routing algorithm is from Hsu and Pinter. It is described in the papers "General River Routing Algorithm" by C. Hsu, *ACM/IEEE Design Automation Conference*, pages 578–583, 1983 and "River-Routing: Methodology and Analysis" by R. Pinter, *Third Caltech Conference on VLSI*, March 1983.

CHAPTER 9

QUEUES

BIRD'S-EYE VIEW

A queue, like a stack, is a special kind of linear list. In a queue insertions and deletions take place from different ends of the linear list. Consequently, a queue is a first-in-first-out (FIFO) list. Another variety of queue—a priority queue—from which deletions are made in order of element priority is developed in Chapter 12. The C++ STL class `queue` is an array implementation of the queue data structure. This class derives from the STL class `deque`, which is an array implementation of the double-ended queue data structure (Exercise 9).

Although queue classes may be derived easily from any of the linear list classes developed in Chapters 5 and 6, we do not do so in this chapter. For run-time efficiency reasons, the array and linked classes for a queue are developed from scratch.

In the applications section we develop four sample codes that use a queue. The first is for the railroad-switching problem considered initially in Section 8.5.3. In this chapter the problem has been modified so that the shunting tracks at the railroad yard are FIFO rather than LIFO. The second application is the classical Lee's algorithm to find the shortest path for a wire that is to connect two given points. This application may also be viewed as a variant of the rat-in-a-maze problem of Section 8.5.6. In this variant we must find the shortest path between the maze entrance and exit. Notice that the code developed in Section 8.5.6 does not guarantee to find a shortest path. That code simply guarantees to find a path

317

(of unspecified length) whenever the maze has at least one entrance-to-exit path. The third application, from the computer-vision field, labels the pixels of a binary image so that two pixels have the same label iff they are part of the same image component. The final application is a machine shop simulation. The machine shop has several machines, each capable of performing a different task. Each job in the shop requires one or more tasks to be performed. We provide a program to simulate the flow of jobs through the machine shop. Our program determines the total time each job spends waiting to be processed as well as the total wait at each machine. We can use this information to improve the machine shop. Although the machine shop simulator developed in this chapter uses FIFO queues, real-world machine shops may require some or all of these FIFO queues be replaced by priority queues. Additional queue applications appear in later chapters.

9.1 DEFINITION AND APPLICATIONS

Definition 9.1 *A* **queue** *is a linear list in which insertions (also called additions and puts) and deletions (also called removals) take place at different ends. The end at which new elements are added is called the* **back** *or* **rear** *, and that from which old elements are deleted is called the* **front**. ∎

A queue with three elements is shown in Figure 9.1(a). The first element we delete from the queue of Figure 9.1(a) is *A*. Following the deletion, the configuration of Figure 9.1(b) results. To add element *D* to the queue of Figure 9.1(b), we must place it after element *C*. The new configuration is shown in Figure 9.1(c).

Figure 9.1 Sample queues

So a queue is a FIFO list, whereas a stack is a LIFO list.

Example 9.1 [Queues in the Real World]

- Although the stack of trays in a cafeteria works in a LIFO manner (see Example 8.1), the food line you stand in works in a FIFO manner. Customers exit at the checkout register in the order in which they entered the food line—the food line is a queue. Most other lines you find yourself in—the check-out line at a store, the line in front of a bank teller, the line of cars waiting at a car wash, the line at the postal center—also work in a FIFO manner.

- In a soda vending machine, you have a column of soda cans for each variety of soda dispensed. In each column cans are piled one on top of another. When you buy a can of soda, the can at the bottom of a column is given; when the stock is replenished, cans are added to the top of the column. The vending machine dispenses soda cans in a FIFO manner; the machine maintains a queue for each variety of soda dispensed.

- In a distributed system a single queue often feeds a bank of queues. A distributed system that has *m* servers has a bank of *m* server queues, one for each server. In addition, there is a queue called the broker or trader queue. Requests for service are first queued in the broker queue; a broker (or trader or dispatcher) examines the service requests in the broker queue in a FIFO order and sends each request to the queue for the most appropriate server; servers handle the service requests in their queues in a FIFO order. Two specific examples follow.

1. In a distributed file system, computer files are replicated across file servers so as to provide a better level of service. All requests for a file are first queued in a broker queue; a broker dispatches each request to the least loaded server that has a copy of the requested file; the dispatched request waits its turn in the queue for the file server to which it is dispatched.

2. Voter polling stations provide a rather interesting application of queues. When you arrive at the polling station, you join a broker queue. When you get to the front of the broker queue, a polling volunteer directs you to a server queue based on the first letter of your surname. At the head of each server queue is a volunteer who checks your ID, gets your signature, and issues a ballot card. Once you have a card, you get into another queue and wait for a booth where you can punch holes in the ballot card to select your desired candidates.   ■

EXERCISES

1. The following sequence of operations is done on an initially empty queue: add X, add Y, remove, add D, add A, remove, add T, add A. Draw figures similar to those of Figure 9.1 to show the queue configuration after each operation.

2. Identify three additional real-world applications of a queue. Do not include applications that involve people in a single line or vending machines. Distributed systems that involve people are okay.

3. Identify three real-world applications in which a stack is used sometimes and a queue is used at other times. For example, if you examine napkin dispensers, you will notice that some work as a stack and others work as a queue.

4. Which applications from Section 8.5 can use a queue instead of a stack without affecting the correctness of the program?

9.2   THE ABSTRACT DATA TYPE

The ADT queue is specified in ADT 9.1. The ADT function names are the same as those used in the C++ STL container class queue.

Program 9.1 gives the C++ abstract class that corresponds to ADT 9.1.

AbstractDataType *queue*
{

    instances
        ordered list of elements; one end is called the front; the other is the back;

    operations
     empty() : Return **true** if the queue is empty, return **false** otherwise;

      size() : Return the number of elements in the queue;

   front() : Return the front element of the queue;

    back() : Return the back element of the queue;

      pop() : Remove an element from the front of the queue;

  push(x) : Add element x at the back of the queue;

}

ADT 9.1 The abstract data type queue

```
template<class T>
class queue
{
   public:
      virtual ~queue() {}
      virtual bool empty() const = 0;
                // return true iff queue is empty
      virtual int size() const = 0;
                // return number of elements in queue
      virtual T& front() = 0;
                // return reference to the front element
      virtual T& back() = 0;
                // return reference to the back element
      virtual void pop() = 0;
                // remove the front element
      virtual void push(const T& theElement) = 0;
                // add theElement at the back of the queue
};
```

Program 9.1 The abstract class queue

9.3   ARRAY REPRESENTATION

9.3.1   The Representation

Suppose that the queue elements are mapped into an array **queue** using Equation 9.1.

$$location(i) = i \qquad (9.1)$$

This equation worked well for the array representation of linear lists and stacks. Element i of the queue is stored in **queue[i]**, $i \geq 0$. Let **arrayLength** be the length or capacity of the array **queue** and let **queueFront** and **queueBack**, respectively, be the locations of the front and back elements of the queue. When Equation 9.1 is used, **queueFront** equals 0 and the queue size is **queueBack+1**. An empty queue has **queueBack** $= -1$. Using Equation 9.1, the queues of Figure 9.1 are represented as in Figure 9.2.

Figure 9.2 Queues of Figure 9.1 using Equation 9.1

To push an element into a queue, we need to increase **queueBack** by 1 and place the new element at **queue[queueBack]**, which means that a **push** operation requires $\Theta(1)$ time. To pop an element, we must slide the elements in positions 1 through **queueBack** one position down the array. Sliding the elements takes $\Theta(n)$ time where n is the number of elements in the queue following the pop.

We can pop an element in $\Theta(1)$ time if we use Equation 9.2 instead of Equation 9.1.

$$location(i) = location(\text{front element}) + i \qquad (9.2)$$

Equation 9.2 does not require us to shift the queue one position left each time an element is popped from the queue. Instead, we simply increase $location$(front element) by 1. Figure 9.3 shows the representation of the queues of Figure 9.1 that results when Equation 9.2 is used. Notice that `queueFront` = *location*(front element), `queueBack` = *location*(last element), and an empty queue has `queueBack` < `queueFront`.

Figure 9.3 Queues of Figure 9.1 using Equation 9.2

As Figure 9.3(b) shows, each pop operation causes `queueFront` to move right by 1. Hence there will be times when `queueBack` = `arrayLength` - 1 and `queueFront` > 0. At these times the number of elements in the queue is less than `arrayLength`, and there is space for additional elements at the left end of the array. To continue inserting elements into the queue, we can shift all elements to the left end of the queue (as in Figure 9.4) and create space at the right end. This shifting increases the worst-case time for a push operation from $\Theta(1)$, when Equation 9.1 is used, to $\Theta(\texttt{arrayLength})$. So the trade-off for improved efficiency of the pop operation is a loss of efficiency for the push operation.

Figure 9.4 Shifting a queue

The worst-case push and pop times (assuming no array resizing is needed) become $\Theta(1)$ when we permit the queue to wrap around the end of the array. At this time it is convenient to think of the array positions as arranged in a circle (Figure 9.5) rather than in a straight line (Figure 9.4).

When the array is viewed as a circle, each array position has a next and a previous position. The position next to position `arrayLength` − 1 is 0, and the

Figure 9.5 Circular queues

position that precedes 0 is `arrayLlength − 1`. When the back of the queue is at `arrayLength − 1`, the next element is put into position 0. The circular array representation of a queue uses the following mapping function:

$$location(i) = (location(\text{front element}) + i)\%\texttt{arrayLength} \qquad (9.3)$$

In Figure 9.5 we have changed the convention for the variable `queueFront`. This variable now points one position counterclockwise from the location of the front element in the queue. The convention for `queueBack` is unchanged. This change simplifies the codes.

Pushing an element into the queue of Figure 9.5(a) results in the queue of Figure 9.5(b). Popping an element from the queue of Figure 9.5(b) results in the queue of Figure 9.5(c).

A queue is empty iff `queueFront` = `queueBack`. The initial condition `queueFront` = `queueBack` = 0 defines an initially empty queue. If we push elements into the queue of Figure 9.5(b) until the number of elements in the array `queue` equals `arrayLength` (i.e., the queue becomes full), we obtain the configuration of Figure 9.6. This configuration has `queueFront` = `queueBack`, which is the same condition as when the queue is empty! Therefore, we cannot distinguish between an empty and a full queue. To avoid this difficulty, we will not permit a queue to get full. Before pushing an element into a queue, we verify whether this push will cause the queue to get full. If so, we double the length of the array `queue` and then proceed with the push. Using this strategy, the array `queue` can have at most `arrayLength-1` elements in it.

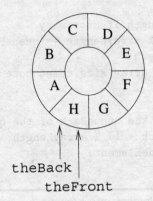

theBack
theFront

Figure 9.6 A circular queue with `arrayLength` elements

9.3.2   The Class `arrayQueue`

The class `arrayQueue` uses Equation 9.3 to map a queue into a one-dimensional array `queue`. The data members of `arrayQueue` are `queueFront`, `queueBack`, and `queue`; the codes for all methods other than `push` and `pop` are similar to those for the corresponding methods of `arrayStack`. These similar codes are available from the Web site. The method `push` (Program 9.2) uses customized code (Program 9.3) to double the array length.

To visualize array doubling when a circular queue is used, it is better to flatten out the array as in Figure 9.7(a). This figure shows a queue with seven elements in an array whose length is 8. Figure 9.7(b) shows the the flattened view of the same queue. Figure 9.7(c) shows the array after array doubling by `changeLength1D` (Program 5.2).

To get a proper circular queue configuration, we must slide the elements in the right segment (i.e., elements A and B) to the right end of the array as in Figure 9.7(d). The array doubling copies `arrayLength` (this is the capacity of the array `queue` prior to array doubling) elements, and when the second segment is slid right, up to `arrayLength-2` additional elements are copied. The number of elements copied can be limited to `arrayLength-1` by customizing the array doubling code. Figure 9.7(e) shows an alternative configuration for the array after doubling. This configuration may be obtained as follows:

- Create a new array `newQueue` of twice the length.

```
template<class T>
void arrayQueue<T>::push(const T& theElement)
{// Add theElement to queue.

   // increase array length if necessary
   if ((queueBack + 1) % arrayLength == queueFront)
   {// double array length
      // code to double array size comes here
   }

   // put theElement at the queueBack of the queue
   queueBack = (queueBack + 1) % arrayLength;
   queue[queueBack] = theElement;
}
```

Program 9.2 Pushing an element into a queue

- Copy the second segment (i.e., the elements `queue[queueFront+1]` through `queue[arrayLength - 1]`) to positions in `newQueue` beginning at 0.

- Copy the first segment (i.e., the elements `queue[0]` through `queue[queueBack]`) to positions in `newQueue` beginning at `arrayLength-queueFront-1`.

The code of Program 9.3 obtains the configuration of Figure 9.7(e). The segment copying is done using the STL function `copy`. Program 9.4 gives the code for the pop method.

The complexity of the queue constructor is $O(1)$ when the T is a primitive datatype and is $O(\text{initialCapacity})$ when T is a user-defined type. The complexity of `empty`, `size`, `front`, `back`, and `pop` is $\Theta(1)$; and the complexity of `push` is $\Theta(1)$ when no array doubling is done and is $\Theta(\text{queue size})$ when array doubling is done. From the analysis used to establish Theorem 5.1, it follows that the complexity of m invocations of `push` is $O(m)$.

EXERCISES

5. (a) Extend the queue ADT by adding functions to

      i. Input a queue.
      ii. Output a queue.
      iii. Split a queue into two queues. The first of the resulting queues contains the first, third, fifth, $\cdots$ elements of the original queue; the second contains the remaining elements.

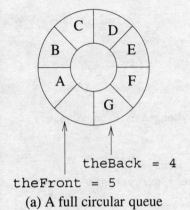

queue   [0]   [1]   [2]   [3]   [4]   [5]   [6]   [7]

| C | D | E | F | G | | A | B |

theFront = 5, theBack = 4

(b) flattened view of circular full queue

theBack = 4

theFront = 5

(a) A full circular queue

[0]   [1]   [2]   [3]   [4]   [5]   [6]   [7]   [8]   [9]   [10] [11] [12] [13] [14] [15]

theFront = 5, theBack = 4

(c) after array doubling

[0]   [1]   [2]   [3]   [4]   [5]   [6]   [7]   [8]   [9]   [10] [11] [12] [13] [14] [15]

theFront = 13, theBack = 4

(d) after shifting right segment

[0]   [1]   [2]   [3]   [4]   [5]   [6]   [7]   [8]   [9]   [10] [11] [12] [13] [14] [15]

theFront = 15, theBack = 6

(e) alternative configuration

Figure 9.7 Doubling array length

iv. Combine two queues by selecting elements alternately from the two queues beginning with queue 1. When a queue exhausts, append the remaining elements from the other queue to the combined queue. The relative order of elements from each queue is unchanged.

```
// allocate a new array
T* newQueue = new T[2 * arrayLength];

// copy elements into new array
int start = (theFront + 1) % arrayLength;
if (start < 2)
   // no wrap around
   copy(queue + start, queue + start + arrayLength - 1, newQueue);
else
{ // queue wraps around
   copy(queue + start, queue + arrayLength, newQueue);
   copy(queue, queue + theBack + 1, newQueue + arrayLength - start);
}

// switch to newQueue and set theFront and theBack
theFront = 2 * arrayLength - 1;
theBack = arrayLength - 2;    // queue size arrayLength - 1
arrayLength *= 2;
queue = newQueue;
```

Program 9.3 Doubling the length of the array `queue`

```
void pop()
     {// remove queueFront element
        if (queueFront == queueBack)
           throw queueEmpty();
        queueFront = (queueFront + 1) % arrayLength;
        queue[queueFront].~T();  // destructor for T
     }
```

Program 9.4 Popping an element from a queue

(b) Define the abstract class `extendedQueue` that derives from the abstract class `queue` and includes methods that correspond to the functions of (a).

(c) Develop code for the concrete class `extendedarrayQueue` that derives from the classes `arrayQueue` and `extendedQueue`.

(d) Test your code.

6. Develop the concrete class `slowArrayQueue` that derives from `queue` and use

the mapping of Equation 9.2 Test your code and compare its performance with that of `arrayQueue`.

7. Modify the representation used in the class `arrayQueue` so that a queue can hold as many elements as the length of the array `queue`. For this modification replace the variable `queueBack` with the variable `queueSize`, which equals the size of the queue. Use the convention that the front element is at `queue[queueFront]`. Note that the location of the back element may be computed from `queueSize` and `queueFront`. Test the correctness of your modified code.

8. Modify the representation used in the class `arrayQueue` so that a queue can hold as many elements as the length of the array `queue`. For this modification introduce another data member `lastOp` that keeps track of the last operation (from among the operations `push` and `pop`) performed on the queue. Notice that if the last operation performed was `push`, the queue cannot be empty. Also, if the last operation was `pop`, the queue cannot be full. So `lastOp` can be used to distinguish between an empty and full queue when `queueFront = queueBack`. Test the correctness of your modified code.

9. A **deque** (pronounced *deck*) is an ordered list to/from which we can make pushes and pops at/from either end. Therefore, we can call it a double-ended queue.

   (a) Define the ADT *deque*. Include the operations *empty, size, front, back, push_front, push_back, pop_front,* and *pop_back*.

   (b) Define an abstract C++ class `deque` that includes methods for each function of the ADT *deque*.

   (c) Use Equation 9.3 to represent a deque. Develop a concrete C++ class `arrayDeque` that derives from `deque`. Note that the C++ STL has a concrete class `deque` that is an array implementation of the data structure *deque*.

   (d) Test your code using suitable test data.

10. (a) Develop the concrete class `dequeStack` that derives from `stack` (Program 8.1) and `arrayDeque` (see Exercise 9).

    (b) What is the time complexity of each method of `dequeStack`?

    (c) Comment on the expected performance of the methods of `dequeStack` relative to their counterparts in `arrayStack`.

11. (a) Develop the concrete class `dequeQueue` that derives from `queue` (Program 9.1) and `arrayDeque` (see Exercise 9).

    (b) What is the time complexity of each method of `dequeQueue`?

    (c) Comment on the expected performance of the methods of `dequeQueue` relative to their counterparts in `arrayQueue`.

9.4   LINKED REPRESENTATION

A queue, like a stack, can be represented as a chain. We need two variables, `queueFront` and `queueBack`, to keep track of the two ends of a queue. There are two possibilities for binding these two variables to the two ends of a chain. The nodes can be linked from front to back (Figure 9.8(a)) or from back to front (Figure 9.8(b)). The relative difficulty of performing pushes and pops determines the direction of linkage. Figures 9.9 and 9.10, respectively, illustrate the mechanics of a push and a pop. We can see that both linkage directions are well suited for pushes, but the front-to-back linkage is more efficient for pops. Hence we will link the nodes in a queue from front to back.

Figure 9.8 Linked queues

We can use the initial values `queueFront` = `queueBack` = NULL and the boundary value `queueFront` = NULL iff the queue is empty. The class `linkedQueue` may be defined as a derived class of `extendedChain` (Program 6.12). Exercise 12 considers this way of developing `linkedQueue`. In this section we develop the class `linkedQueue` from scratch.

Program 9.5 gives the `push` and `pop` methods of `linkedQueue`. You should run through these codes by hand using an empty queue, a queue with one element, and a queue with many elements as examples. The complexity of each of the linked queue methods is $\Theta(1)$.

EXERCISES

12. Develop the class `linkedQueueFromExtendedChain`, which implements a linked queue by deriving from `extendedChain` (Section 6.1.5) and `queue`.

13. Do Exercise 5 using a linked queue.

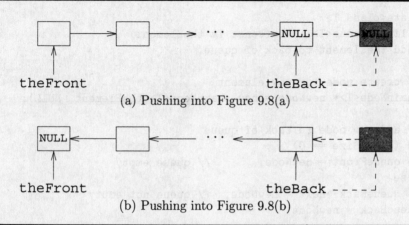

(a) Pushing into Figure 9.8(a)

(b) Pushing into Figure 9.8(b)

Figure 9.9 Pushing an element into a linked queue

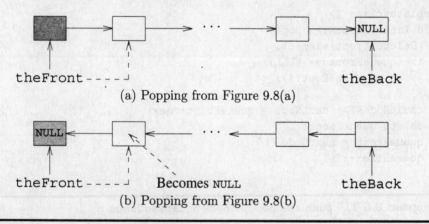

(a) Popping from Figure 9.8(a)

(b) Popping from Figure 9.8(b)

Figure 9.10 Popping an element from a linked queue

14. Compare the performance of `arrayQueue` and `linkedQueue` by performing a sequence of 1,000,000 `push` operations followed by 1,000,000 `pop` operations.

15. In some queue applications the elements to be put on a queue are already in nodes of type `chainNode`. For these applications it is desirable to have the methods `pushNode(chainNode theNode)`, which adds `theNode` at the back of the queue (notice that no call to `new` is made), and `popNode`, which removes and returns the front node of the queue.

    (a) Write code for these methods.

```
template<class T>
void linkedQueue<T>::push(const T& theElement)
{// Add theElement to back of queue.

   // create node for new element
   chainNode<T>* newNode = new chainNode<T>(theElement, NULL);

   // add new node to back of queue
   if (queueSize == 0)
      queueFront = newNode;        // queue empty
   else
      queueBack->next = newNode;   // queue not empty
   queueBack = newNode;

   queueSize++;
}

template<class T>
void linkedQueue<T>::pop()
{// Delete front element.
   if (queueFront == NULL)
      throw queueEmpty();

   chainNode<T>* nextNode = queueFront->next;
   delete queueFront;
   queueFront = nextNode;
   queueSize--;
}
```

Program 9.5 The push and pop methods of linkedQueue

    (b) Test your code.

    (c) Compare the time required by a sequence of 1,000,000 push operations followed by 1,000,000 pop operations with that required by 1,000,000 pushNodes followed by 1,000,000 popNodes.

16. See Exercise 9 for the definition of a deque.

    (a) Develop a concrete C++ class doublyLinkedDeque that derives from the abstract class deque of Exercise 9 and uses a doubly linked list. Your class should not derive from any other class.

    (b) What is the complexity of each method of your class?

(c) Test your code using suitable test data.

17. Do Exercise 16 using a singly linked list (i.e., a chain) rather than a doubly linked list. Name your class `linkedDeque`.

18. Do Exercise 16 using a singly linked circular list rather than a doubly linked list. Name your class `circularDeque`.

9.5   APPLICATIONS

9.5.1   Railroad Car Rearrangement

Problem Description and Solution Strategy

We will reconsider the railroad car rearrangement problem of Section 8.5.3. This time the holding tracks lie between the input and output track as in Figure 9.11. These tracks operate in a FIFO manner and so may be regarded as queues. As in the case of Section 8.5.3, moving a car from a holding track to the input track or from the output track to a holding track is forbidden. All car motion is in the direction indicated by the arrowheads of Figure 9.11.

Figure 9.11 A three-track example

We reserve track Hk for moving cars directly from the input track to the output track. So only $k-1$ tracks are available to hold cars that are not ready to be output. Consider rearranging nine cars that have the initial ordering 5, 8, 1, 7, 4, 2, 9, 6, 3. Assume that $k = 3$ (Figure 9.11). Car 3 cannot be moved directly to the output track, as cars 1 and 2 must come before it. So car 3 is moved to $H1$. Car 6 can be placed behind car 3 in $H1$, as car 6 is to be output after car 3. Car 9 can now be placed after car 6 in $H1$. Car 2 cannot be placed after car 9, as car 2 is to be output before car 9. So it is placed at the front of $H2$. Car 4 can now be placed after car 2 in $H2$, and car 7 can be placed after it. Car 1 can be moved to the output using $H3$. Next car 2 is moved from $H2$ to the output. Then car 3 is moved from $H1$ to the output, and car 4 is moved from $H2$ to the output. Car 5 is to be output next.

It is still in the input track. So car 8 is moved from the input track to $H2$. Then car 5 is moved to the output track. Now cars 6, 7, 8, and 9 are moved from their holding tracks to the output track.

When a car is to be moved to a holding track, we can use the following track selection method. *Move car c to a holding track that contains only cars with a smaller label; if several such tracks exist, select one with the largest label at its left end; otherwise, select an empty track (if one remains).*

First Implementation

We can implement the car rearrangement algorithm by using queues for the $k - 1$ holding tracks that can hold cars. We can model the code after Programs 8.9 through 8.12. Program 9.6 gives the new code for outputFromHoldingTrack, and Program 9.7 gives the new code for putInHoldingTrack. The method railroad of Program 8.10 needs to be modified. The changes are (1) decrease the number of tracks by 1 and (2) change the type of track to arrayQueue. The time needed to perform the rearrangement is $O(\text{numberOfCars} * k)$. We can use AVL trees (see Chapter 15) to reduce this time to $O(\text{numberOfCars} * \log k)$.

```
void outputFromHoldingTrack()
{// output the smallest car from the holding tracks
   // pop smallestCar from itsTrack
   track[itsTrack].pop();
   cout << "Move car " << smallestCar << " from holding track "
        << itsTrack << " to output track" << endl;

   // find new smallestCar and itsTrack by checking all queue fronts
   smallestCar = numberOfCars + 2;
   for (int i = 1; i <= numberOfTracks; i++)
      if (!track[i].empty() && track[i].front() < smallestCar)
      {
         smallestCar = track[i].front();
         itsTrack = i;
      }
}
```

Program 9.6 Function to output a railroad car

Second Implementation

To animate the progress of the rearrangement algorithm, it is useful to keep the queues used in our first implementation. In an animation we wish to move all cars

```
bool putInHoldingTrack(int c)
{// Put car c into a holding track.
 // Return false iff there is no feasible holding track for this car.

   // find best holding track for car c
   // initialize
   int bestTrack = 0,   // best track so far
       bestLast =  0;   // last car in bestTrack

   // scan tracks
   for (int i = 1; i <= numberOfTracks; i++)
      if (!track[i].empty())
      {// track i not empty
          int lastCar = track[i].back();
          if (c > lastCar && lastCar > bestLast)
          {
              // track i has bigger car at its rear
              bestLast = lastCar;
              bestTrack = i;
          }
      }
      else // track i empty
         if (bestTrack == 0)
             bestTrack = i;

   if (bestTrack == 0)
      return false; // no feasible track

   // add c to bestTrack
   track[bestTrack].push(c);
   cout << "Move car " << c << " from input track "
        << "to holding track " << bestTrack << endl;

   // update smallestCar and itsTrack if needed
   if (c < smallestCar)
   {
       smallestCar = c;
       itsTrack = bestTrack;
   }

   return true;
}
```

Program 9.7 Function to put a railroad car into a holding track in a holding track one position right after the front car has been removed from the holding track. This is relatively easy to do when we have a list (in our case a queue) of the remaining cars in the holding track.

If our objective is simply to output the sequence of moves necessary to accomplish the rearrangement, then we need to know only the last member of each holding track (or queue) and the current track of each car. If holding track i is empty, let lastCar[i] be 0; otherwise let it be the label/number of the last car in track i. If car i is in the input track, let whichTrack[i] be 0; otherwise let it be the holding track car i is (was) in. Initially lastCar[i] = 0, $1 \leq i < k$, and whichTrack[i] = 0, $1 \leq i \leq n$. Using these variables and no queues, we can produce the same output as our first implementation produced. The code for the no-queue implementation is available from the Web site file railroadWithNoQueues.cpp.

9.5.2   Wire Routing

Problem Description

As noted in Section 8.5.6, our solution to the rat-in-a-maze problem does not always find a shortest path from maze entrance to exit. The problem of finding a shortest path in a grid has many applications (besides the rat-in-a-maze problem). For example, a common approach to the wire-routing problem for electrical circuits is to impose a grid over the wire-routing region. The grid divides the routing region into an $n \times m$ array of squares much like a maze (Figure 9.12(a)). A wire runs from the midpoint of one square a to the midpoint of another b. In doing so, the wire may make right-angle turns (Figure 9.12(b)). Grid squares that already have a wire through them are blocked. To minimize signal delay, we wish to route the wire using a shortest path between a and b.

(a) A 7 × 7 grid   (b) A wire between a and b

Figure 9.12 Wire-routing example

Solution Strategy

The following discussion assumes that you are familiar with the rat-in-a-maze development of Section 8.5.6. If not, you should review this development before proceeding. The shortest path between grid positions a and b is found in two passes—a distance-labeling pass and a path-identification pass. In the distance-labeling pass, we begin at position a and label its reachable neighbors 1 (i.e., they are distance 1 from a). Next the reachable neighbors of squares labeled 1 are labeled 2. This labeling process is continued until we either reach b or have no more reachable neighbors. Figure 9.13(a) shows the result of the distance-labeling pass for the case $a = (3,2)$ and $b = (4,6)$. The shaded squares are blocked squares.

(a) Distance labeling   (b) Wire path

Figure 9.13 Wire routing

Once we have reached b, we can label it with its distance (9 in the case of Figure 9.13(a)). The distance-labeling pass is followed by the path-identification pass in which we begin at b and move to any one its neighbors labeled 1 less than b's label. Such a neighbor must exist as each grid's label is 1 more than that of at least one of its neighbors. In the case of Figure 9.13(a), we move from b to $(5, 6)$. From here we move to one of its neighbors whose label is 1 less and so on until we reach a. In the example of Figure 9.13(a), from $(5, 6)$ we move to $(6, 6)$ and then to $(6, 5), (6, 4), (5, 4)$, and so on. Figure 9.13(b) shows the constructed path, which is a shortest path between $(3, 2)$ and $(4, 6)$. Notice that the shortest path between $(3, 2)$ and $(4, 6)$ is not unique; $(3, 2), (3, 3), (4, 3), (5, 3), (5, 4), (6, 4), (6, 5), (6, 6), (5, 6), (4, 6)$ is another shortest path.

C++ Implementation

Now let us take the strategy outlined above and obtain C++ code to find a shortest path in a grid. We will use many ideas from the rat-in-a-maze solution of Section 8.5.6. An $m \times m$ grid is represented as a two-dimensional array grid with a 0 representing an open position and a 1 a blocked position, The grid is surrounded by a "wall" of 1s; the array offsets helps us move from a position to its neighbors; and a queue keeps track of labeled grid positions whose neighbors have not been examined.

To implement the distance-labeling pass, we can either use an additional two-dimensional array for the distances or we can overload the use of the array grid. In practice, wire-routing grids do get large enough to tax the memory of even the most memory-rich computers. Therefore, the use of a second array is not recommended. When we overload the use of the array grid, we have a conflict between our use of the label 1 to designate a blocked grid position and our use of the label 1 for a position that is a unit distance from the start position a. To resolve this conflict, we increase all distance labels by 2. So grid[i][j] = 1 for a blocked position; grid[i][j] > 1 for a position whose distance from the start position is grid[i][j] − 2; and grid[i][j] = 0 for an unblocked and unreached position.

Program 9.8 gives the code. grid, size, pathLength, q, start, finish and path are global variables.

Our code assumes that the positions start and finish are not blocked. The code begins with a check to see whether the start and finish positions are the same. In this case the path length is 0, and the code terminates. Otherwise, we set up a wall of blocked positions around the grid, initialize the offset array, and label the start position with a distance of 2. Using the queue q and beginning at position start, we move to reachable grid positions that are distance 1 from the start and then to those that are distance 2, and so on until we either reach the finish position or are unable to move to a new, unblocked position. In the latter case there is no path to the finish position. In the former case the finish position is labeled by its distance value.

If we reach the finish position, the path is reconstructed using the distance labels. The positions on the path (except for start) are stored in the array path.

Complexity

Since no grid position can get on the queue more than once, it takes $O(m^2)$ time (for an $m \times m$ grid) to complete the distance-labeling phase. The time needed for the path-construction phase is O(length of the shortest path).

```
bool findPath()
{// Find a shortest path from start to finish.
 // Return true if successful, false if impossible.

   if ((start.row == finish.row) && (start.col == finish.col))
   {// start == finish
       pathLength = 0;
       return true;
   }

   // initialize offsets
   position offset[4];
   offset[0].row = 0; offset[0].col = 1;    // right
   offset[1].row = 1; offset[1].col = 0;    // down
   offset[2].row = 0; offset[2].col = -1;   // left
   offset[3].row = -1; offset[3].col = 0;   // up

   // initialize wall of blocks around the grid
   for (int i = 0; i <= size + 1; i++)
   {
      grid[0][i] = grid[size + 1][i] = 1; // bottom and top
      grid[i][0] = grid[i][size + 1] = 1; // left and right
   }

   position here = start;
   grid[start.row][start.col] = 2; // block
   int numOfNbrs = 4; // neighbors of a grid position

   // label reachable grid positions
   arrayQueue<position> q;
   position nbr;
   do
   {// label neighbors of here
       for (int i = 0; i < numOfNbrs; i++)
       {// check out neighbors of here
          nbr.row = here.row + offset[i].row;
          nbr.col = here.col + offset[i].col;
          if (grid[nbr.row][nbr.col] == 0)
          {// unlabeled nbr, label it
             grid[nbr.row][nbr.col]
                 = grid[here.row][here.col] + 1;
```

Program 9.8 Find a wire route (continues)

```
           if ((nbr.row == finish.row) &&
               (nbr.col == finish.col)) break; // done
            // put on queue for later expansion
          q.push(nbr);
        }
    }

    // have we reached finish?
    if ((nbr.row == finish.row) &&
      (nbr.col == finish.col)) break;        // done

    // finish not reached, can we move to a nbr?
    if (q.empty())
       return false;            // no path
    here = q.front();           // get next position
    q.pop();
} while(true);

// construct path
pathLength = grid[finish.row][finish.col] - 2;
path = new position [pathLength];

// trace backwards from finish
here = finish;
for (int j = pathLength - 1; j >= 0; j--)
{
   path[j] = here;
   // find predecessor position
   for (int i = 0; i < numOfNbrs; i++)
   {
      nbr.row = here.row + offset[i].row;
      nbr.col = here.col + offset[i].col;
      if (grid[nbr.row][nbr.col] == j + 2) break;
   }
   here = nbr;  // move to predecessor
}

return true;
}
```

Program 9.8 Find a wire route (concluded)

9.5.3   Image-Component Labeling

Problem Description

A digitized image is an $m \times m$ matrix of pixels. In a binary image each pixel is either 0 or 1. A 0 pixel represents image background, while a 1 represents a point on an image component. We will refer to pixels whose value is 1 as component pixels. Two pixels are adjacent if one is to the left, above, right, or below the other. Two component pixels that are adjacent are pixels of the same image component. The objective of component labeling is to label the component pixels so that two pixels get the same label iff they are pixels of the same image component.

Consider Figure 9.14(a) that shows a 7×7 image. The blank squares represent background pixels, and the 1s represent component pixels. Pixels (1, 3) and (2, 3) are pixels of the same component because they are adjacent. Since component pixels (2, 3) and (2, 4) are adjacent, they are also of the same component. Hence the three pixels (1, 3), (2, 3), and (2, 4) are from the same component. Since no other image pixels are adjacent to these three pixels, these three define an image component. The image of Figure 9.14(a) has four components. The first component is defined by the pixel set (1, 3), (2, 3), (2, 4); the second is (3, 5), (4, 4), (4, 5), (5, 5); the third is (5, 2), (6, 1), (6, 2), (6, 3), (7, 1), (7, 2), (7, 3); and the fourth is (5, 7), (6, 7), (7, 6), (7, 7). In Figure 9.14(b) the component pixels have been given labels so that two pixels have the same label iff they are part of the same component. We use the numbers 2, 3, 4, ... as component identifiers; there is no component numbered 1 because 1 designates an unlabeled component pixel.

(a) A 7×7 image

(b) Labeled components

Figure 9.14 Image-component labeling

Solution Strategy

The components are determined by scanning the pixels by rows and within rows by columns. When an unlabeled component pixel is encountered, it is given a component identifier/label. This pixel forms the seed of a new component. We determine the remaining pixels in the component by identifying and labeling all component pixels that are adjacent to the seed. Call the pixels that are adjacent to the seed the distance 1 pixels. Then unlabeled component pixels that are adjacent to the distance 1 pixels are identified and labeled. These newly labeled pixels are the distance 2 pixels. Then unlabeled component pixels adjacent to the distance 2 pixels are identified and labeled. This process continues until no new unlabeled adjacent component pixels are found.

C++ Implementation

Our program to label component pixels uses much of the development used for the wire-routing problem. To move around the image with ease, we surround the image with a wall of blank (i.e., 0) pixels. We use the `offset` array to determine the pixels adjacent to a given pixel.

The labeling process used in the component-labeling problem is very similar to the process used to label squares in a wiring grid by their distance from the start square. This similarity results in a component-labeling code (Program 9.9) that is similar to Program 9.8.

Program 9.9 begins by setting up a wall of background (0) pixels around the image and initializing the array of neighbor/adjacent pixel offsets. The next two `for` loops scan the image for a seed for the next component. The seed is an unmarked component pixel. For such a pixel, `pixel[r][c]` is 1. The seed is assigned a component label by changing `pixel[r][c]` from 1 to a component identifier/label (`id`). Then with the help of a queue (a stack can be used instead), the remaining pixels in this component are identified. By the time the method `labelComponents` terminates, all component pixels have been assigned a label.

Complexity

It takes $\Theta(m)$ time to initialize the wall of background pixels and $\Theta(1)$ time to initialize `offsets`. Although the condition `pixel[r][c] == 1` is checked m^2 times, it is true only as many times as the number of components in the image. For each component O(number of pixels in component) time is spent identifying and labeling its pixels (other than the component seed). Since no pixel is in two or more components, the total time spent identifying and labeling nonseed component pixels is O(number of component pixels in image). Since the number of component pixels equals the number of pixels with value 1 in the input image and since this number is at most m^2, the overall time complexity of `labelComponents` is $O(m^2)$.

```
void labelComponents()
{// Label the components.

   // initialize offsets
   position offset[4];
   offset[0].row = 0; offset[0].col = 1;    // right
   offset[1].row = 1; offset[1].col = 0;    // down
   offset[2].row = 0; offset[2].col = -1;   // left
   offset[3].row = -1; offset[3].col = 0;   // up

   // initialize wall of 0 pixels
   for (int i = 0; i <= size + 1; i++)
   {
      pixel[0][i] = pixel[size + 1][i] = 0; // bottom and top
      pixel[i][0] = pixel[i][size + 1] = 0; // left and right
   }

   int numOfNbrs = 4; // neighbors of a pixel position

   // scan all pixels labeling components
   arrayQueue<position> q;
   position here, nbr;
   int id = 1;  // component id
   for (int r = 1; r <= size; r++)        // row r of image
      for (int c = 1; c <= size; c++)     // column c of image
         if (pixel[r][c] == 1)
         {// new component
            pixel[r][c] = ++id; // get next id
            here.row = r;
            here.col = c;

            while (true)
            {// find rest of component
               for (int i = 0; i < numOfNbrs; i++)
               {// check all neighbors of here
                  nbr.row = here.row + offset[i].row;
                  nbr.col = here.col + offset[i].col;
                  if (pixel[nbr.row][nbr.col] == 1)
                  {// pixel is part of current component
                     pixel[nbr.row][nbr.col] = id;
                     q.push(nbr);
                  }
               }
```

Program 9.9 Component labeling (continues)

```
                // any unexplored pixels in component?
                if (q.empty()) break;
                here = q.front(); // a component pixel
                q.pop();
        }

    } // end of if, for c, and for r
}
```

Program 9.9 Component labeling (concluded)

9.5.4   Machine Shop Simulation

Problem Description

A machine shop (or factory or plant) comprises m machines or workstations. The machine shop works on jobs, and each job comprises several tasks. Each machine can process one task of one job at any time, and different machines perform different tasks. Once a machine begins to process a task, it continues processing that task until the task completes.

Example 9.2 A sheet metal plant might have one machine (or station) for each of the following tasks: design; cut the sheet metal to size; drill holes; cut holes; trim edges; shape the metal; and seal seams. Each of these machines/stations can work on one task at a time.

Each job includes several tasks. For example, to fabricate the heating and air-conditioning ducts for a new house, we would need to spend some time in the design phase, and then some time cutting the sheet metal stock to the right size pieces. We need to drill or cut the holes (depending on their size), shape the cut pieces into ducts, seal the seams, and trim any rough edges.   ∎

For each task of a job, there is a task time (i.e., how long does it take) and a machine on which it is to be performed. The tasks of a job are to be performed in a specified order. So a job goes first to the machine for its first task. When this first task is complete, the job goes to the machine for its second task, and so on until its last task completes. When a job arrives at a machine, the job may have to wait because the machine might be busy. In fact, several jobs may already be waiting for that machine.

Each machine in our machine shop can be in one of three states: active, idle, and change over. In the active state the machine is working on a task of some job; in the idle state it is doing nothing; and in the change-over state the machine has completed a task and is preparing for a new task. In the change-over state, the machine operator might, for example, clean the machine, put away tools used for the last task, and take a break. The time each machine must spend in its change-over state depends on the machine.

When a machine becomes available for a new job, it will need to pick one of the waiting jobs to work on. We assume that each machine serves its waiting jobs in a FIFO manner, and so the waiting jobs at each machine form a (FIFO) queue. Other assumptions for the selection of the next job are possible. For example, the next job may be selected by priority. Each job has a priority, and when a machine becomes free, the waiting job with highest priority is selected.

The time at which a job's last task completes is called its **finish time**. The **length** of a job is the sum of its task times. If a job of length l arrives at the machine shop at time 0 and completes at time f, then it must have spent exactly $f - l$ amount of time waiting in machine queues. To keep customers happy, it is desirable to minimize the time a job spends waiting in machine queues. Machine shop performance can be improved if we know how much time jobs spend waiting and which machines are contributing most to this wait.

How the Simulation Works

When simulating a machine shop, we follow the jobs from machine to machine without physically performing the tasks. We simulate time by using a simulated clock that is advanced each time a task completes or a new job enters the machine shop. As tasks complete, new tasks are scheduled. Each time a task completes or a new job enters the shop, we say that an **event** has occurred. In addition, a **start event** initiates the simulation. When two or more events occur at the same time, we arbitrarily order these events. Figure 9.15 describes how a simulation works.

Example 9.3 Consider a machine shop that has $m = 3$ machines and $n = 4$ jobs. We assume that all four jobs are available at time 0 and that no new jobs become available during the simulation. The simulation will continue until all jobs have completed.

The three machines, $M1$, $M2$, and $M3$, have a change-over time of 2, 3, and 1, respectively. So when a task completes, machine 1 must wait two time units before starting another, machine 2 must wait three time units, and machine 3 must wait one time unit. Figure 9.16(a) gives the characteristics of the four jobs. Job 1, for example, has three tasks. Each task is specified as a pair of the form (machine, time). The first task of job 1 is to be done on $M1$ and takes two time units, the second is to be done on $M2$ and takes four time units, the third is to be done on $M1$ and takes one time unit. The job lengths (i.e., the sum of their task times) are 7, 6, 8, and 4, respectively.

Figure 9.16(b) shows the machine shop simulation. Initially, the four jobs are placed into queues corresponding to their first tasks. The first task for jobs 1 and 3 are to be done on $M1$, so these jobs are placed on the queue for $M1$. The first tasks for jobs 2 and 4 are to be done on $M3$. Consequently, these jobs begin on the queue for $M3$. The queue for $M2$ is empty. At the start all three machines are idle.

```
// initialize
input the data;
create the job queues at each machine;
schedule first job in each machine queue;

// do the simulation
while (an unfinished job remains)
{
    determine the next event;
    if (the next event is the completion of a machine change over)
        schedule the next job (if any) from this machine's queue;
    else
      {// a job task has completed
        put the machine that finished the job task into its change-over state;
        move the job whose task has finished to the machine for its next task
        (if any);
      }
}
```

Figure 9.15 The mechanics of simulation

We use the symbol I to indicate that the machines have no active job at this time. Since no machine is active, the time at which they will finish their current active task is undefined and denoted by the symbol L (large time).

The simulation begins at time 0. That is, the first event, the start event, occurs at time 0. At this time the first job in each machine queue is scheduled on the corresponding machine. Job 1's first task is scheduled on $M1$, and job 2's first task on $M3$. The queue for $M1$ now contains job 3 only, while that for $M3$ contains job 4 only. The queue for $M2$ remains empty. Job 1 becomes the active job on $M1$, and job 2 the active job on $M3$. $M2$ remains idle. The finish time for $M1$ becomes 2 (current time of 0 plus task time of 2), and the finish time for $M3$ becomes 4.

The next event occurs at time 2. This time is determined by finding the minimum of the machine finish times. At time 2 machine $M1$ completes its active task. This task is a job 1 task. Job 1 is moved to machine $M2$ for the next task. Since $M2$ is idle, the processing of job 1's second task begins immediately. This task will complete at time 6 (current time of 2 plus task time of 4). $M1$ goes into its change-over state and will remain in this state for two time units. Its active job is set to C (change over), and its finish time is set to 4.

At time 4 both $M1$ and $M3$ complete their active tasks. As machine $M1$ completes a change-over task, that machine begins a new job; selecting the first job, job 3, from its queue. Since the task length for job 3's next task is 4, the task will complete at time 8 and the finish time for $M1$ becomes 8. The next task for job 2,

Job#	#Tasks	Tasks	Length
1	3	(1,2) (2,4) (1,1)	7
2	2	(3,4) (1,2)	6
3	2	(1,4) (2,4)	8
4	2	(3,1) (2,3)	4

(a) Job characteristics

Time	Machine Queues			Active Jobs			Finish Times		
	$M1$	$M2$	$M3$	$M1$	$M2$	$M3$	$M1$	$M2$	$M3$
Init	1,3	–	2,4	I	I	I	L	L	L
0	3	–	4	1	I	2	2	L	4
2	3	–	4	C	1	2	4	6	4
4	2	–	4.	3	1	C	8	6	5
5	2	–	–	3	1	4	8	6	6
6	2,1	4	–	3	C	C	8	9	7
7	2,1	4	–	3	C	I	8	9	L
8	2,1	4,3	–	C	C	I	10	9	L
9	2,1	3	–	C	4	I	10	12	L
10	1	3	–	2	4	I	12	12	L
12	1	3	–	C	C	I	14	15	L
14	–	3	–	1	C	I	15	15	L
15	–	–	–	C	3	I	17	19	L
16	–	–	–	C	3	I	17	19	L
17	–	–	–	I	3	I	L	19	L

(b) Simulation

Job#	Finish Time	Wait Time
1	15	8
2	12	6
3	19	11
4	12	8
Total	58	33

(c) Finish and wait times

Figure 9.16 Machine shop simulation example

which just completed its first task on machine $M3$, needs to be done on $M1$. Since
$M1$ is busy, job 2 is added to $M1$'s job queue. $M3$ moves into its change-over state
and completes this change-over task at time 5. You should now be able to follow

the remaining sequence of events.

Figure 9.16(c) gives the finish and wait times. Since the length of job 2 is 6 and its finish time 12, job 2 must have spent a total of $12 - 6 = 6$ time units waiting in machine queues. Similarly, job 4 must have spent $12 - 4 = 8$ time units waiting in queues.

We may determine the distribution of the 33 units of total wait time across the three machines. For example, job 4 joined the queue for $M3$ at time 0 and did not become active until time 5. So this job waited at $M3$ for five time units. No other job experienced a wait at $M3$. The total wait time at $M3$ was, therefore, five time units. Going through Figure 9.16(b), we can compute the wait times for $M1$ and $M2$. The numbers are 18 and 10, respectively. As expected the sum of the job wait times (33) equals the sum of the machine wait times.   ∎

Benefits of Simulating a Machine Shop

Why do we want to simulate a machine shop? Here are some reasons:

- By simulating the shop, we can identify bottleneck machines/stations. If we determine that the paint station is going to be a bottleneck for the current mix of jobs, we can increase the number of paint stations in operation for the next few shifts. Similarly, if our simulation determines that the wait time at the drill station will be excessive in the next shift, we can schedule more drill station operators and put more drilling machines to work. Therefore, the simulator can be used for short-term operator-scheduling decisions.

- Using a machine shop simulator, we can answer questions such as, How is average wait time affected if we replace a certain machine with a more expensive but more effective machine? So the simulator can be used to help make expansion/modernization decisions at the factory.

- When customers arrive at the plant, they would like a fairly accurate estimate of when their jobs will complete. Such an estimate may be obtained by using a machine shop simulator.

High-Level Simulator Design

In designing our simulator, we will assume that all jobs are available initially (i.e., no jobs enter the shop during the simulation). Further, we assume that the simulation is to be run until all jobs complete.

The simulator is implemented as the class `machineShopSimulator`. Since the simulator is a fairly complex program, we break it into modules. The tasks to be performed by the simulator are input the data and put the jobs into the queues for their first tasks; perform the start event (i.e., do the initial loading of jobs onto the machines); run through all the events (i.e., perform the actual simulation); and output the machine wait times. We will have one C++ function for each task. Program 9.10 gives the main function. The variable `largeTime` is a global variable that denotes a time that is larger than any permissible simulated time; that is all tasks of all jobs must complete before the time `largeTime`.

```
void main()
{
    inputData();          // get machine and job data
    startShop();          // initial machine loading
    simulate();           // run all jobs through shop
    outputStatistics();   // output machine wait times
}
```

Program 9.10 Main function for machine shop simulation

The Struct Task

Before we can develop the code for the four functions invoked by Program 9.10, we must develop representations for the data objects that are needed. These objects include tasks, jobs, machines, and an event list. We define a struct for the first three of these data object and a class for the third.

Each task has two components: `machine` (the machine on which it is to be performed) and `time` (the time needed to complete the task). Program 9.11 gives the struct `task`. Since machines are assumed to be have integer labels, `machine` is of type `int`. We will assume that all times are integral.

```
struct task
{
    int machine;
    int time;

    task(int theMachine = 0, int theTime = 0)
    {
        machine = theMachine;
        time = theTime;
    }
};
```

Program 9.11 The struct task

The Struct job

Each job has a list of associated tasks that are performed in list order. Consequently, the task list may be represented as a queue taskQ. To determine the total wait time experienced by a job, we need to know its length and finish time. The finish time is determined by the event clock, while the job length is the sum of task times. To determine a job's length, we associate a data member length with it. Program 9.12 gives the struct job.

```
struct job
{
   arrayQueue<task> taskQ;    // this job's tasks
   int length;               // sum of scheduled task times
   int arrivalTime;          // arrival time at current queue
   int id;                   // job identifier

   job(int theId = 0)
   {
      id = theId;
      length = 0;
      arrivalTime = 0;
   }

   void addTask(int theMachine, int theTime)
   {
      task theTask(theMachine, theTime);
      taskQ.push(theTask);
   }

   int removeNextTask()
   {// Remove next task of job and return its time.
    // Also update length.

      int theTime =  taskQ.front().time;
      taskQ.pop();
      length += theTime;
      return theTime;
   }
};
```

Program 9.12 The struct job

The data member arrivalTime records the time at which a job enters its current machine queue and determines the time the job waits in this queue. The job identifier is stored in `id` and is used only when outputting the total wait time encountered by this job.

The method `addTask` adds a task to the job's task queue. The task is to be performed on machine `theMachine` and takes `theTime` time. This method is used only during data input. The method `removeNextTask` is used when a job is moved from a machine queue to active status. At this time the job's first task is removed from the task queue (the task queue maintains a list of tasks yet to be scheduled on machines), the job length is incremented by the task time, and the task time is returned. The data member `length` becomes equal to the job length when we schedule the last task for the job.

The Struct `machine`

Each machine has a change-over time, an active job, and a queue of waiting jobs. Since each job can be in at most one machine queue at any time, the total space needed for all queues is bounded by the number of jobs. However, the distribution of jobs over the machine queues changes as the simulation proceeds. It is possible to have a few very long queues at one time. These queues might become very short later, and some other queues become long. By using linked queues, we limit the space required for the machine queues to that required for n nodes where n is the number of jobs.

Program 9.13 gives the struct `machine`. The data members `jobQ`, `changeTime`, `totalWait`, `numTasks`, and `activeJob`, respectively, denote the queue of waiting jobs, the change-over time for the machine, the total time jobs have spent waiting at this machine, the number of tasks processed by the machine, and the currently active job. The currently active job is `NULL` whenever the machine is idle or in its change-over state.

The Class `eventList`

We store the finish times of all machines in an event list. To go from one event to the next, we need to determine the minimum of these finish times. Our simulator also needs an operation that sets the finish time of a particular machine. This operation has to be done each time a new job is scheduled on a machine. When a machine becomes idle, its finish time is set to the large number `largeTime`. Program 9.14 gives the class `eventList` that implements the event list as a one-dimensional array `finishTime`, with `finishTime[p]` being the finish time of machine `p`.

The method `nextEventMachine` returns the machine that completes its active task first. The time at which machine `p` finishes its active task can be determined by invoking the method `nextEventTime(p)`. For a machine shop with m machines, it takes $\Theta(m)$ time to find the minimum of the finish times, so the complexity of `nextEventMachine` is $\Theta(m)$. The method to set the finish time of a machine, `setFinishTime`, runs in $\Theta(1)$ time. In Chapter 13 we will see two data

```
struct machine
{
   arrayQueue<job*> jobQ;
                     // queue of waiting jobs for this machine
   int changeTime;   // machine change-over time
   int totalWait;    // total delay at this machine
   int numTasks;     // number of tasks processed on this machine
   job* activeJob;   // job currently active on this machine

   machine()
   {
      totalWait = 0;
      numTasks = 0;
      activeJob = NULL;
   }
};
```

Program 9.13 The struct machine

structures—heaps and leftist trees—that may also represent an event list. When we use either of these data structures, the complexity of both nextEventMachine and setFinishTime becomes $O(\log m)$. If the total number of tasks across all jobs is $numTasks$, then, in a successful simulation run, our simulator will invoke nextEventMachine and setFinishTime $\Theta(numTasks)$ times each. Using the event list implementation of Program 9.14, these invocations take a total of $\Theta(numTasks * m)$ time; using one of the data structures of Chapter 13, the invocations take $O(numTasks * \log m)$ time. Even though the data structures of Chapter 13 are more complex, they result in a faster simulation when the number of machines m is suitably large.

Global Variables

Program 9.15 gives the global variables used by our code. The significance of most of these variables is self-evident. timeNow is the simulated clock and records the current time. Each time an event occurs, it is updated to the event time. largeTime is a time that exceeds the finish time of the last job and denotes the finish time of an idle machine.

The Function inputData

The code for the function inputData (Program 9.16) begins by inputting the number of machines and jobs in the shop. Next we create the initial event list eList,

```
class eventList
{
   public:
      eventList(int theNumMachines, int theLargeTime)
      {// Initialize finish times for m machines.
         if (theNumMachines < 1)
            throw illegalParameterValue
                  ("number of machines must be >= 1");
         numMachines = theNumMachines;
         finishTime = new int [numMachines + 1];

         // all machines are idle, initialize with
         // large finish time
         for (int i = 1; i <= numMachines; i++)
            finishTime[i] = theLargeTime;
      }

      int nextEventMachine()
      {// Return machine for next event.

         // find first machine to finish, this is the
         // machine with smallest finish time
         int p = 1;
         int t = finishTime[1];
         for (int i = 2; i <= numMachines; i++)
            if (finishTime[i] < t)
            {// i finishes earlier
               p = i;
               t = finishTime[i];
            }
         return p;
      }

      int nextEventTime(int theMachine)
      {return finishTime[theMachine];}

      void setFinishTime(int theMachine, int theTime)
      {finishTime[theMachine] = theTime;}
   private:
      int* finishTime;    // finish time array
      int numMachines;    // number of machines
};
```

Program 9.14 The class eventList

```
// global variables
int timeNow;              // current time
int numMachines;          // number of machines
int numJobs;              // number of jobs
eventList* eList;         // pointer to event list
machine* mArray;          // array of machines
int largeTime = 10000;    // all machines finish before this
```

Program 9.15 Global variables for machine shop simulation

```
void inputData()
{// Input machine shop data.

    cout << "Enter number of machines and jobs" << endl;
    cin >> numMachines >> numJobs;
    if (numMachines < 1 || numJobs < 1)
        throw illegalInputData
            ("number of machines and jobs must be >= 1");

    // create event and machine queues
    eList = new eventList(numMachines, largeTime);
    mArray = new machine [numMachines + 1];

    // input the change-over times
    cout << "Enter change-over times for machines" << endl;
    int ct;
    for (int j = 1; j <= numMachines; j++)
    {
        cin >> ct;
        if (ct < 0)
            throw illegalInputData("change-over time must be >= 0");
        mArray[j].changeTime = ct;
    }
```

Program 9.16 Code to input machine shop data (continues)

with finish times equal to largeTime for each machine, and the array mArray of machines. Then we input the change-over times for the machines. Next we input the jobs one by one. For each job we first input the number of tasks it has, and then we input the tasks as pairs of the form (machine, time). The machine for the

```
// input the jobs
job* theJob;
int numTasks, firstMachine, theMachine, theTaskTime;
for (int i = 1; i <= numJobs; i++)
{
   cout << "Enter number of tasks for job " << i << endl;
   cin >> numTasks;
   firstMachine = 0;    // machine for first task
   if (numTasks < 1)
      throw illegalInputData("each job must have > 1 task");

   // create the job
   theJob = new job(i);
   cout << "Enter the tasks (machine, time)"
        << " in process order" << endl;
   for (int j = 1; j <= numTasks; j++)
   {// get tasks for job i
      cin >> theMachine >> theTaskTime;
      if (theMachine < 1 || theMachine > numMachines
         || theTaskTime < 1)
      throw illegalInputData("bad machine number or task time");
      if (j == 1)
         firstMachine = theMachine;    // job's first machine
      theJob->addTask(theMachine, theTaskTime);   // add to
   }                                              // task queue
   mArray[firstMachine].jobQ.push(theJob);
}
}
```

Program 9.16 Code to input machine shop data (concluded)

first task of the job is recorded in the variable `firstMachine`. When all tasks of a job have been input, the job is added to the queue for the first task's machine.

The Functions `startShop` and `changeState`

To start the simulation, we need to move the first job from each machine's job queue to the machine and commence processing. Since each machine is initialized in its idle state, we perform the initial loading in the same way as we change a machine from its idle state, which may happen during simulation, to an active state. The method `changeState(i)` performs this change over for machine i. The method to start the shop, Program 9.17, needs merely invoke `changeState` for each machine.

```
void startShop()
{// Load first jobs onto each machine.
   for (int p = 1; p <= numMachines; p++)
      changeState(p);
}
```

Program 9.17 Initial loading of machines

Program 9.18 gives the code for changeState. If machine theMachine is idle or in its change-over state, changeState returns NULL. Otherwise, it returns the job that theMachine has been working on. Additionally, changeState(theMachine) changes the state of machine theMachine. If machine theMachine was previously idle or in its change-over state, then it begins to process the next job on its queue. If that queue is empty, the machine's new state is "idle." If machine theMachine was previously processing a job, machine theMachine moves into its change-over state.

If mArray[theMachine].activeJob is NULL, then machine theMachine is either in its idle or change-over state; the job, lastJob, to return is NULL. If the job queue is empty, the machine moves into its idle state and its finish time is set to largeTime. If its job queue is not empty, the first job is removed from the queue and becomes machine theMachine's active job. The time this job has spent waiting in machine theMachine's queue is added to the total wait time for this machine, and the number of tasks processed by the machine incremented by 1. Next the task that this machine is going to work on is deleted from the job's task list, and the finish time of the machine is set to the time at which the new task will complete.

If mArray[theMachine].activeJob is not NULL, the machine has been working on a job whose task has just completed. Since this job is to be returned, we save it in lastJob. The machine should now move into its change-over state and remain in that state for changeTime time units.

The Functions simulate and moveToNextMachine

The function simulate, Program 9.19, cycles through all shop events until the last job completes. numJobs is the number of incomplete jobs, so the while loop of Program 9.19 terminates when no incomplete jobs remain. In each iteration of the while loop, the time for the next event is determined, and the clock time timeNow updated to this event time. A change-job operation is performed on the machine nextToFinish on which the event occurred. If this machine has just finished a task of a job (theJob is not NULL), job theJob moves to the machine on which its next task is to be performed. The function moveToNextMachine performs this move. If there is no next task for job theJob, the job has completed, function moveToNextMachine returns false, and numJobs is decremented by 1.

```
job* changeState(int theMachine)
{// Task on theMachine has finished, schedule next one.
 // Return last job run on this machine.
   job* lastJob;
   if (mArray[theMachine].activeJob == NULL)
   {// in idle or change-over state
      lastJob = NULL;
      // wait over, ready for new job
      if (mArray[theMachine].jobQ.empty()) // no waiting job
           eList->setFinishTime(theMachine, largeTime);
      else
      {// take job off the queue and work on it
         mArray[theMachine].activeJob =
              mArray[theMachine].jobQ.front();
         mArray[theMachine].jobQ.pop();
         mArray[theMachine].totalWait +=
              timeNow - mArray[theMachine].activeJob->arrivalTime;
         mArray[theMachine].numTasks++;
         int t = mArray[theMachine].activeJob->removeNextTask();
         eList->setFinishTime(theMachine, timeNow + t);
      }
   }
   else
   {// task has just finished on theMachine
    // schedule change-over time
      lastJob = mArray[theMachine].activeJob;
      mArray[theMachine].activeJob = NULL;
      eList->setFinishTime(theMachine, timeNow +
                         mArray[theMachine].changeTime);
   }

   return lastJob;
}
```

Program 9.18 Code to change the active job at a machine

The function moveToNextMachine (Program 9.20) first checks to see whether any unprocessed tasks remain for the job theJob. If not, the job has completed and its finish time and wait time are output. The method returns **false** to indicate there was no next machine for this job.

When the job theJob to be moved has a next task, the machine p for this task

```
void simulate()
{// Process all jobs to completion.
   while (numJobs > 0)
   {// at least one job left
      int nextToFinish = eList->nextEventMachine();
      timeNow = eList->nextEventTime(nextToFinish);
      // change job on machine nextToFinish
      job* theJob = changeState(nextToFinish);
      // move theJob to its next machine
      // decrement numJobs if theJob has finished
      if (theJob != NULL && !moveToNextMachine(theJob))
         numJobs--;
   }
}
```

Program 9.19 Run all jobs through their machines

is determined and the job is added to this machine's queue of waiting jobs. In case machine p is idle, **changeState** is invoked to change the state of machine p so that machine p begins immediately to process the next task of **theJob**.

The Function outputStatistics

Since both the time at which a job finishes and the time a job spends waiting in machine queues are output by **moveToNextMachine**, **outputStatistics** needs to output only the time at which the machine shop completes all jobs (this time is also the time at which the last job completed and has been output by **moveToNextMachine**) and the statistics (total wait time and number of tasks processed) for each machine. Program 9.21 gives the code.

EXERCISES

19. Which applications from this section can use a stack instead of a queue without affecting the correctness of the program?

20. (a) You have a railroad shunting yard with three shunting tracks that operate as queues. The initial ordering of cars is 3, 1, 7, 6, 2, 8, 5, 4. Draw figures similar to Figures 9.11 to show the configuration of the shunting tracks, the input track, and the output track following each car move made by the solution of Section 9.5.1.

     (b) Do part (a) for the case when the number of shunting tracks is 2.

```
bool moveToNextMachine(job* theJob)
{// Move theJob to machine for its next task.
 // Return false iff no next task.

   if (theJob->taskQ.empty())
   {// no next task
      cout << "Job " << theJob->id << " has completed at "
           << timeNow << " Total wait was "
           << (timeNow - theJob->length) << endl;
      return false;
   }
   else
   {// theJob has a next task
    // get machine for next task
      int p = theJob->taskQ.front().machine;
      // put on machine p's wait queue
      mArray[p].jobQ.push(theJob);
      theJob->arrivalTime = timeNow;
      // if p idle, schedule immediately
      if (eList->nextEventTime(p) == largeTime)
          // machine is idle
          changeState(p);

      return true;
   }
}
```

Program 9.20 Move a job to the machine for the next task

21. Does Program 9.6 successfully rearrange all input car permutations that can be rearranged using k holding tracks that operate as queues? Prove your answer.

22. Rewrite Program 9.6 under the assumption that at most s_i cars can be in holding track i at any time. Reserve the track with smallest s_i for direct input to output moves.

23. Can you eliminate the use of queues and, instead, use the strategy of the second implementation of the railroad car problem when you have to display the state of the holding tracks following each move of a railroad car? Justify your answer.

24. Is it possible to solve the problem of Section 8.5.3 without the use of a stack

```
void outputStatistics()
{// Output wait times at machines.
   cout << "Finish time = " << timeNow << endl;
   for (int p = 1; p <= numMachines; p++)
   {
      cout << "Machine " << p << " completed "
           << mArray[p].numTasks << " tasks" << endl;
      cout << "The total wait time was "
           << mArray[p].totalWait << endl;
      cout << endl;
   }
}
```

Program 9.21 Output the wait times at each machine

(see second implementation of Section 9.5.1)? If so, develop and test such a program.

25. Consider the wire-routing grid of Figure 9.13(a). You are to route a wire between (1, 4) and (2, 2). Label all grid positions that are reached in the distance-labeling pass by their distance value. Now use the methodology of the path-identification pass to mark the shortest wire path.

26. Develop a complete C++ program for wire routing. Your program should include a **welcome** method that displays the program name and functionality; a method to input the wire grid size, blocked and unblocked grid positions, and wire endpoints; the method **findPath** (Program 9.8); and a method to output the input grid with the wire path shown. Test your code.

27. In a typical wire-routing application, several wires are routed in sequence. After a path has been found for one wire, the grid positions used by this path are blocked and we proceed to find a path for the next wire. When the array **grid** is overloaded to designate both blocked and unblocked positions as well as distances, we must clean the grid (i.e., set all grid positions that are on the wire path to 1 and all remaining positions with a label > 1 to 0) before we can begin on the next wire. Write a method to clean the grid. Do so by first restoring the grid to its initial state, using a process similar to that used in the distance-labeling pass. Then write code to block the positions on the wire path just found. This way the complexity of the cleanup pass is the same as that of the distance-labeling pass.

28. Develop a complete C++ program for image-component labeling. Your program should include a **welcome** function that displays the program name and

functionality; a function to input the image size and binary image; the function `labelComponents` (Program 9.9); and a function to output the image using a different color for pixels that are in different components. Test your code.

29. Rewrite function `labelComponents` using a stack. What are the relative merits/demerits of using a stack rather than a queue for this method?

30. Can we replace the stack in Program 8.6 with a queue? Why?

31. Can we replace the stack in Program 8.13 with a queue? Why?

32. Can we replace the stack in Program 8.14 with a queue? Why?

33. Can we replace the stack in Program 8.15 with a queue? Why?

34. Write an enhanced machine shop simulator that allows you to specify a minimum wait time between successive tasks of the same job. Your simulator must move a job into a wait state following the completion of each task (including the last one). Therefore, a job is placed on its next queue as soon as a task is complete. Upon arriving in this queue, the job enters its wait state. When a machine is ready to start a new task, it must bypass jobs at the front of the queue that are still in a wait state. The bypassed jobs could, for example, be moved to the end of the queue.

35. Write an enhanced machine shop simulator that allows jobs to enter the shop during simulation. The simulation stops at a specified time. Jobs that have not been completed by this time remain incomplete.

9.6 REFERENCES AND SELECTED READINGS

The wire-routing algorithm of Section 9.5.2 is known as Lee's router. The book *Algorithms for VLSI Physical Design Automation*, 2nd edition, by N. Sherwani, Kluwer Academic Publishers, Boston, 1995, contains a detailed discussion of this and other routing algorithms.

CHAPTER 10

SKIP LISTS AND HASHING

BIRD'S-EYE VIEW

Although a sorted array of n elements can be searched in $O(\log n)$ time with the binary search method, the search operation on a sorted chain takes $O(n)$ time. We can improve the expected performance of a sorted chain by placing additional pointers in some or all of the chain nodes. These pointers permit us to skip over several nodes of the chain during a search. Thus it is no longer necessary to examine all chain nodes from left to right during a search.

Chains augmented with additional forward pointers are called **skip lists**. Skip lists employ a randomization technique to determine which chain nodes are to be augmented by additional forward pointers and how many additional pointers are to be placed in the node. Using this randomization technique, skip lists deliver an expected performance of $O(\log n)$ for the search, insert, and delete operations. However, the worst-case performance is $\Theta(n)$.

Hashing is another randomization scheme that may be used to search, insert, and delete elements. It provides improved expected performance, $\Theta(1)$, over skip lists but has the same worst-case performance, $\Theta(n)$. Despite this performance, skip lists have an advantage over hashing in applications where we need to frequently output all elements in sorted order and/or search by element rank (e.g., find the 10th-smallest element). These latter two operations can be performed more efficiently with skip lists.

The asymptotic performance of sorted arrays, sorted chains, skip lists, and hash tables is summarized in the following table.

Method	Worst Case			Expected		
	Search	Insert	Erase	Search	Insert	Erase
sorted array	$\Theta(\log n)$	$\Theta(n)$	$\Theta(n)$	$\Theta(\log n)$	$\Theta(n)$	$\Theta(n)$
sorted chain	$\Theta(n)$	$\Theta(n)$	$\Theta(n)$	$\Theta(n)$	$\Theta(n)$	$\Theta(n)$
skip lists	$\Theta(n)$	$\Theta(n)$	$\Theta(n)$	$\Theta(\log n)$	$\Theta(\log n)$	$\Theta(\log n)$
hash tables	$\Theta(n)$	$\Theta(n)$	$\Theta(n)$	$\Theta(1)$	$\Theta(1)$	$\Theta(1)$

The C++ STL has several container classes that employ hashing—hash_map, hash_multimap, hash_multiset, and hash_set.

One application of hashing is developed in this chapter. This application is text compression and decompression. The program we develop is based on the popular Lempel-Ziv-Welch algorithm.

10.1   DICTIONARIES

A **dictionary** is a collection of pairs of the form (k, v), where k is a **key** and v is the **value** associated with the key k (equivalently, v is the value whose key is k). No two pairs in a dictionary have the same key.

The following operations are performed on a dictionary:

- Determine whether or not the dictionary is empty.

- Determine the dictionary size (i.e., number of pairs).

- Find the pair with a specified key.

- Insert a pair into the dictionary.

- Delete or erase the pair with a specified key.

Example 10.1 The class list for the data structures course is a dictionary with as many pairs as students registered for the course. When a new student registers, a pair/record corresponding to this student is inserted into the dictionary; when a student drops the course, his/her record may be deleted. During the course the instructor may query the dictionary to determine the record corresponding to a particular student and make changes to the record (for example, add/change test or assignment scores). The student name may be used as the key; the remaining information in a record is the value associated with the key.   ■

A **dictionary with duplicates** is similar to a dictionary as defined above. However, it permits two or more $(key, value)$ pairs to have the same key.

Example 10.2 A word dictionary is a collection of pairs; each pair comprises a word and its value. The value of a word includes the meaning of the word, the pronunciation, etymologies, and so on. Webster's dictionary contains a pair (or entry) for the word *date*. Part of this pair reads "date, the point of time at which a transaction or event takes place." For this pair *date* is the key. Webster's dictionary actually has several pairs with the key *date*. Abbreviated forms of these pairs are "date, the oblong fruit of a palm" and "date, to assign a chronology record." The dictionary publisher inserts new pairs into the word dictionary as new words are created and as words take on new meanings; the publisher also deletes pairs that are no longer required. Users of a word dictionary, that is you and I, generally only search the dictionary for pairs with a given key. Occasionally, we might jot down a new entry into our copy of a dictionary. In data structures terminology a word dictionary is a dictionary with duplicates—it is a collection of pairs, each pair has a key, the keys need not be distinct, and the operations you perform on the pair collection are find, insert, and erase. Although the printed form of a word dictionary lists the pairs in alphabetical order of the keys, this arrangement is not required by an electronic dictionary. In a computer you can store the pairs any way you like.

A telephone directory is another example of a dictionary with duplicates.   ∎

In a dictionary with duplicates, we need a rule to eliminate the ambiguity in the find and erase operations. That is, if we are to find (or erase) a pair with a specified key, then which of the several pairs with this key is to be returned (or erased)? Two possibilities for the find operation are (1) find any pair that has the specified key and (2) find all pairs that have the specified key. For the erase operation, we may require that the user be presented with all pairs that have the specified key; the user must select which pair(s) to erase. Alternatively, we may arbitrarily erase any one pair that has the specified key or erase all pairs with the specified key.

In the case of both dictionaries and dictionaries with duplicates, some applications require a different form of the erase operation in which all pairs inserted after a particular time are to be removed.

Example 10.3 A compiler uses a dictionary with duplicates, called the **symbol table**, of user-defined identifiers. When an identifier is defined, a pair (*key*, *value*) is created for it and inserted into the symbol table. The identifier is the *key* and information such as identifier type (`int`, `float`, etc.) and (relative) memory address for the value of the identifier comprise the *value* component of the pair. Since the same identifier name may be defined more than once (in different program blocks), the symbol table must be able to hold multiple pairs with the same key. A search should return the most recently inserted pair with the given key. Deletions are done only when the end of a program block is reached. All pairs inserted after the start of that block are to be deleted.   ∎

The find operation allows you to retrieve dictionary pairs **randomly**, by providing the key of the pair you want. Some dictionary applications require an additional access mode—**sequential access**—in which pairs are retrieved one by one in ascending order of keys. Sequential access requires an iterator that can sequence through the pairs in the dictionary in ascending order of their keys. All dictionary implementations developed in this chapter (other than hash tables) are suitable for both random and sequential access.

EXERCISES

1. Look in a word dictionary and find a word (other than *date*) for which there are multiple entries. Try to find a word that has more than three entries.

2. Give three real-world applications of dictionaries and/or dictionaries with duplicates. Do not repeat the ones given in this section. Explain which dictionary operations are used in each of your applications.

3. Give an application of a dictionary or dictionary with duplicates in which sequential access is desired.

10.2   THE ABSTRACT DATA TYPE

The abstract data type *Dictionary* is specified in ADT 10.1. In this specification, *p.first* and *p.second*, respectively, refer to the first and second components of the pair *p*. The first component of a pair is its key, and the second is the value. When the dictionary contains no pair with key *p.first*, *insert(p)* inserts the pair *p* into the dictionary; when the dictionary already contains a pair with key *p.first*, the old value associated with *p.first* is replaced by the new value *p.second*. This behavior of the *insert* operation agrees with the behavior of the **insert** operation of the STL class **hash_map**.

AbstractDataType *Dictionary*
{

   instances
      collection of pairs with distinct keys

   operations
      empty() : return true iff the dictionary is empty;

      size() : return the number of pairs in the dictionary;

      find(k) : return the pair with key *k*;

      insert(p) : insert the pair *p* into the dictionary;

      erase(k) : delete the pair with key *k*;

}

ADT 10.1 Dictionary abstract data type

Program 10.1 gives the C++ abstract class that corresponds to ADT 10.1. We require the **find** method to return a pointer to the matching pair rather than the pair itself. This behavior conforms to that of the **find** method of the STL container class **hash_map**.

In this chapter we do not explicitly develop representations for dictionaries with duplicates. However, the representations developed for dictionaries without duplicates may be adapted to the case when duplicate entries are permitted. The STL class **hash_multimap** represents a dictionary with duplicates.

EXERCISE

4. List the methods included in the C++ STL class **hash_map** that are not included in our abstract class **dictionary**? What does each new method do?

```
template<class K, class E>
class dictionary
{
   public:
      virtual ~dictionary() {}
      virtual bool empty() const = 0;
                  // return true iff dictionary is empty
      virtual int size() const = 0;
                  // return number of pairs in dictionary
      virtual pair<const K, E>* find(const K&) const = 0;
                  // return pointer to matching pair
      virtual void erase(const K&) = 0;
                  // remove matching pair
      virtual void insert(const pair<const K, E>&) = 0;
                  // insert a (key, value) pair into the dictionary
};
```

Program 10.1 The abstract class `dictionary`

10.3   LINEAR LIST REPRESENTATION

A dictionary may be maintained as an ordered linear list $(p_0, p_1, \cdots)$ where the p_is are the dictionary pairs in ascending order of key. To facilitate this representation, we may define two classes `sortedArrayList` and `sortedChain`. The first uses an array representation of a linear list (see Section 5.3), while the latter uses a linked representation (see Section 6.1).

Exercise 5 asks you to develop the class `sortedArrayList`. We note that you can search a `sortedArrayList` using the binary search method. So the *find* operation takes $O(\log n)$ time for an n-pair dictionary. To make an insertion, we need to verify that the dictionary doesn't already contain a pair with the same key. This verification is done by performing a search (i.e., a `find`). Following this search, the insertion may be done in $O(n)$ additional time, as $O(n)$ pairs must be moved to make room for the new pair. Each erase is done by first searching for the pair to be erased and then erasing it. Following the search, the erasing takes $O(n)$ time as $O(n)$ pairs must be moved to fill up the vacancy left by the erased pair.

Programs 10.2, 10.3, and 10.4 give the `find`, `insert`, and `erase` methods of the class `sortedChain`. The nodes in `sortedChain` are instances of `pairNode`. Each instance of `pairNode`, like each instance of `chainNode` (Program 6.1), has an `element` and `next` field; the datatype of these fields are, respectively, `pair<const K, E>` and `pairNode<K,E>*`.

Using either the class `sortedArrayList` or `sortedChain` and the corresponding iterator methods, we can provide sequential access to the dictionary pairs; pairs can

```
template<class K, class E>
pair<const K,E>* sortedChain<K,E>::find(const K& theKey) const
{// Return pointer to matching pair.
 // Return NULL if no matching pair.
   pairNode<K,E>* currentNode = firstNode;

   // search for match with theKey
   while (currentNode != NULL &&
          currentNode->element.first != theKey)
     currentNode = currentNode->next;

   // verify match
   if (currentNode != NULL && currentNode->element.first == theKey)
     // yes, found match
     return &currentNode->element;

   // no match
   return NULL;
}
```

Program 10.2 The method sortedChain<K,E>::find

be examined in ascending order of keys at a cost of $\Theta(1)$ time per pair.

EXERCISES

5. Develop the C++ class sortedArrayList that uses an array representation. Provide the same member methods as provided in the class sortedChain. Write and test code for all methods.

6. Modify the class sortedChain to use a chain that has both a header node and a tail node. Use the tail node to simplify your code by placing the key being searched for, inserted, or erased into the tail node at the start of the operation.

10.4 SKIP LIST REPRESENTATION (OPTIONAL)

10.4.1 The Ideal Case

A search in an n-pair dictionary that is represented as a sorted chain requires up to n key comparisons. The number of comparisons can be reduced to $n/2 + 1$ if we

```
template<class K, class E>
void sortedChain<K,E>::insert(const pair<const K, E>& thePair)
{// Insert thePair into the dictionary. Overwrite existing
 // pair, if any, with same key.
   pairNode<K,E> *p = firstNode,
                 *tp = NULL; // tp trails p

   // move tp so that thePair can be inserted after tp
   while (p != NULL && p->element.first < thePair.first)
   {
      tp = p;
      p = p->next;
   }

   // check if there is a matching pair
   if (p != NULL && p->element.first == thePair.first)
   {// replace old value
      p->element.second = thePair.second;
      return;
   }

   // no match, set up node for thePair
   pairNode<K,E> *newNode = new pairNode<K,E>(thePair, p);

   // insert newNode just after tp
   if (tp == NULL) firstNode = newNode;
   else tp->next = newNode;

   dSize++;
   return;
}
```

Program 10.3 The method `sortedChain<K,E>::insert`

keep a pointer to the middle pair. Now to search for a pair, we first compare with the middle one. If we are looking for a pair with smaller key, we need search only the left half of the sorted chain. If we are looking for a larger key, we need compare only the right half of the chain.

Example 10.4 Consider the seven-pair sorted chain of Figure 10.1(a). This sorted chain has been augmented by a header node and a tail node. The number inside a node is its key. A search of this chain may involve up to seven key comparisons. We

```
template<class K, class E>
void sortedChain<K,E>::erase(const K& theKey)
{// Delete the pair, if any, whose key equals theKey.
   pairNode<K,E> *p = firstNode,
                 *tp = NULL; // tp trails p

   // search for match with theKey
   while (p != NULL && p->element.first < theKey)
   {
      tp = p;
      p = p->next;
   }

   // verify match
   if (p != NULL && p->element.first == theKey)
   {// found a match
      // remove p from the chain
      if (tp == NULL) firstNode = p->next;  // p is first node
      else tp->next = p->next;

      delete p;
      dSize--;
   }
}
```

Program 10.4 The method sortedChain<K,E>::erase

can reduce this worst-case number of comparisons to 4 by keeping a pointer to the middle pair as in Figure 10.1(b). Now to search for a key, we first compare with the key of the middle pair and then, depending on the outcome, compare with either the left or right half of the chain. If we are looking for a pair with key 26, then we begin by comparing 26 with the middle key 40. Since 26 < 40, we need not examine the pairs to the right of 40. If we are searching for a pair with key 75, then we can limit the search to the pairs that follow 40.   ■

We can reduce the worst-case number of key comparisons by keeping pointers to the middle pairs of each half as in Figure 10.1(c). The level 0 chain is essentially that of Figure 10.1(a) and includes all seven pairs of the dictionary. The level 1 chain includes the second, fourth, and sixth pairs, while the level 2 chain includes only the fourth pair. To search for a pair with key 30, we begin with a comparison against the middle key. This key is found in $\Theta(1)$ time using the level 2 chain. Since 30 < 40, the search continues by examining the middle key of the left half. This

(a) A sorted chain with header and tail nodes

headerNode

tailNode

(b) Pointer to middle added

(c) Pointers to every second node added

(d) Last pointers encountered when searching for 77

(e) 77 inserted

Figure 10.1 Fast searching of a sorted chain

key is also found in $\Theta(1)$ time using the level 1 chain. Since $30 > 24$, we continue the search by dropping into the level 0 chain and comparing with the next key in this chain.

As another example, consider the search for a pair with key 77. The first comparison is with 40. Since $77 > 40$, we drop into the level 1 chain and compare with the key (75) in this chain that comes just after 40. Since $77 > 75$, we drop into the level 0 chain and compare with the key (80) in this chain that comes just after 75.

At this time we know that 77 is not in the dictionary. Using the three-chain structure of Figure 10.1(c), we can perform all searches using at most three comparisons. The three-chain structure allows us to perform a binary search in the sorted chain.

For general n the level 0 chain includes all pairs; the level 1 chain includes every second pair; the level 2 chain every fourth pair; and the level i chain every 2^ith pair. We will say that a pair is a **level i pair** iff it is in the chains for levels 0 through i and it is not on the level $i+1$ chain (in case this chain exists). In Figure 10.1(c), 40 is the (key of the) only level 2 pair; 24 and 75 are the level 1 pairs; and 20, 30, 60, and 80 are the level 0 pairs.

We will use the term **skip list** to refer to a structure such as that of Figure 10.1(c). In such a structure we have a hierarchy of chains. The level 0 chain is a sorted chain of all pairs. The level 1 chain is also a sorted chain that comprises some subset of the pairs on the level 0 chain. In general, the level i chain comprises a subset of the pairs in the level $i-1$ chain. The skip list of Figure 10.1(c) has a very regular structure in that the level i chain comprises every other pair of the level $i-1$ chain.

10.4.2   Insertions and Deletions

When insertions and deletions occur, we cannot maintain the regular structure of Figure 10.1(c) without doing $O(n)$ work. We can attempt to approximate this structure in the face of insertions by noting that in the regular structure, $n/2^i$ pairs are level i pairs. When an insertion is made, the pair level is i with probability $1/2^i$. We can actually allow for any probability to be used when making this determination. Therefore, we can assign the newly inserted pair at level i with probability p^i. Figure 10.1(c) corresponds to the case $p = 0.5$. For general p the number of chain levels is $\lfloor \log_{1/p} n \rfloor + 1$. In this case a regular skip list structure has the property that the level i chain comprises every $1/p$th pair of the level $i-1$ chain.

Suppose we are to insert a pair with key 77. We first search to make sure that no pair with this key is present. During this search the last level 2 pointer seen is associated with key 40, the last level 1 pointer seen is associated with key 75, and the last level 0 pointer seen is associated with key 75. These pointers are cut by the broken line of Figure 10.1(d). The new pair is to be inserted between the pairs with keys 75 and 80 at the position shown by the broken line of Figure 10.1(d).

To make the insertion, we need to assign a level to the new pair. This assignment can be made by using a random number generator as described later. If the new pair is a level i pair, then only the level 0 through level i pointers cut by the broken line are affected. Figure 10.1(e) shows the list structure following the insertion of 77 as a level 1 pair.

We have no control over the structure that is left following a deletion. To delete the 77 from the skip list structure of Figure 10.1(e), we first search for 77. The last pointers encountered in the chains are the level 2 pointer in the node with 40 and the level 1 and level 0 pointers in the node with 75. Of these pointers only the level 0 and level 1 pointers are to be changed, as 77 is a level 1 pair. When these pointers are changed to point to the pair after 77 in their respective chains, we get the structure of Figure 10.1(d).

10.4.3   Assigning Levels

The basis of level assignment is the observation that in a regular skip list structure, a fraction p of the pairs on the level $i-1$ chain are also on the level i chain. Therefore, the probability that a pair that is on the level $i-1$ chain is also on the level i chain is p. Suppose we have a uniform random number generator that generates real numbers between 0 and 1. Then the probability that the next random number is $\leq p$ is p. Consequently, if the next random number is $\leq p$, then the new pair should be on the level 1 chain. Now we need to decide whether it should also be on the level 2 chain. To make this decision, we simply generate another random number. If the new random number is $\leq p$, then the pair is also on the level 2 chain. We can continue this process until a random number $> p$ is generated.

A potential shortcoming of this way of assigning levels is that some pairs may be assigned a very large level, resulting in a number of chains far in excess of $\log_{1/p} N$ where N is the maximum number of pairs expected in the dictionary. To prevent this possibility, we can set an upper limit to the assignable level number. In a regular skip list structure with N pairs, the maximum level maxLevel is

$$\lceil \log_{1/p} N \rceil - 1 \tag{10.1}$$

We can use this value as the upper limit.

Another shortcoming is that even with the use of an upper limit as above, we may find ourselves in a situation where, for example, we have 3 chains just before the insertion and 10 just after. In this case the new pair was assigned the level 9 even though there were no pairs at levels 3 through 8 prior to the insertion. In other words, prior to and following the insertion, there are no level 3, 4, $\cdots$, 8 pairs. Since there is no immediate benefit to having these empty levels, we may alter the level assignment of the pair to 3.

Example 10.5 We are using a skip list to represent a dictionary that will have no more than 1024 pairs. We have decided to use $p = 0.5$, so maxLevel is $\log_2 1024 - 1 = 9$.

Suppose we start with an empty dictionary that is represented by a skip list structure that has a header and a tail. The header has 10 pointers, one for each of the 10 chains we might have. Each pointer goes from the header to the tail.

When the first pair is inserted, it is assigned a level. The permissible levels are 0 through 9 (maxLevel). If the level assigned is 9, then to insert the first pair, we will need to change nine chain pointers. On the other hand, as we have no level 0, level 1, $\cdots$, level 8 pairs, we may alter the level assignment to 0 and change only one chain pointer. ∎

An alternative way to assign levels is to divide the range of values the random number generator outputs into segments. The first segment contains $1 - 1/p$ of the range, the second $1/p - 1/p^2$ of the range, and so on. If the random number generated falls in the ith segment, the pair to be inserted is a level $i - 1$ pair.

10.4.4   The Struct skipNode

The header node of a skip list structure needs sufficient pointer fields for the maximum number of level chains that might be constructed. The tail node needs no pointer field. Each node that contains a dictionary pair needs an element field for the pair and a number of pointer fields that is one more than its level number. The struct skipNode of Program 10.5 can meet the needs of all kinds of nodes.

```
template <class K, class E>
struct skipNode
{
    typedef pair<const K, E> pairType;

    pairType element;
    skipNode<K,E> **next;    // 1D array of pointers

    skipNode(const pairType& thePair, int size)
            :element(thePair){next = new skipNode<K,E>* [size];}
};
```

Program 10.5 The struct skipNode

The pointer fields are represented by the array next with next[i] being the pointer for the level i chain. The constructor places the dictionary pair into element and allocates space for the array of pointers. When the constructor is invoked, the value of size should be lev + 1 for a level lev pair.

10.4.5   The Class skipList

The Data Members of skipList

Program 10.6 gives the data members of the class skipList. The significance of each data member should be clear from its name and the attached comment.

The Constructor for skipList

Program 10.7 gives the constructor. largeKey is a value larger than the key of any pair to be kept in the dictionary. The value largeKey is used in the tail node. maxPairs is the maximum number of pairs the dictionary is to hold. Although our

```
float cutOff;              // used to decide level number
int levels;                // max current nonempty chain
int dSize;                 // number of pairs in dictionary
int maxLevel;              // max permissible chain level
K tailKey;                 // a large key
skipNode<K,E>* headerNode; // header node pointer
skipNode<K,E>* tailNode;   // tail node pointer
skipNode<K,E>** last;      // last[i] = last node seen on level i
```

Program 10.6 The data members of skipList

```
template<class K, class E>
skipList<K,E>::skipList(K largeKey, int maxPairs, float prob)
{// Constructor for skip lists with keys smaller than largeKey and
 // size at most maxPairs. 0 < prob < 1.
   cutOff = prob * RAND_MAX;
   maxLevel = (int) ceil(logf((float) maxPairs) / logf(1/prob)) - 1;
   levels = 0;  // initial number of levels
   dSize = 0;
   tailKey = largeKey;

   // create header & tail nodes and last array
   pair<K,E> tailPair;
   tailPair.first = tailKey;
   headerNode = new skipNode<K,E> (tailPair, maxLevel + 1);
   tailNode = new skipNode<K,E> (tailPair, 0);
   last = new skipNode<K,E> *[maxLevel+1];

   // header points to tail at all levels as lists are empty
   for (int i = 0; i <= maxLevel; i++)
       headerNode->next[i] = tailNode;
}
```

Program 10.7 Constructor

codes permit more pairs than maxPairs, the expected performance is better if the number of pairs does not exceed maxPairs, as the number of chains is limited by substituting maxPairs for N in Equation 10.1. prob is the probability that a pair in the level $i - 1$ chain is also in the level i chain. The constructor initializes the data members of skipList to the values stated earlier. The constructor also allocates space for the header and tail nodes and the array last that is used to keep track of the last node encountered in each chain during the search phase that precedes an insert and erase; the skip list is initialized to the empty configuration in which we have maxLevel+1 pointers from the header node to the tail node. The complexity of the constructor is $O(\texttt{maxLevel})$.

The Method skipList<K,E>::find

Program 10.8 gives the code for the method find. The method returns NULL in case no pair with key theKey is in the dictionary. When the dictionary contains a pair with key theKey, a pointer to this pair is returned.

```
template<class K, class E>
pair<const K,E>* skipList<K,E>::find(const K& theKey) const
{// Return pointer to matching pair.
 // Return NULL if no matching pair.
   if (theKey >= tailKey)
     return NULL;  // no matching pair possible

   // position beforeNode just before possible node with theKey
   skipNode<K,E>* beforeNode = headerNode;
   for (int i = levels; i >= 0; i--)            // go down levels
     // follow level i pointers
     while (beforeNode->next[i]->element.first < theKey)
        beforeNode = beforeNode->next[i];

   // check if next node has theKey
   if (beforeNode->next[0]->element.first == theKey)
     return &beforeNode->next[0]->element;

   return NULL;  // no matching pair
}
```

Program 10.8 The method skipList<K,E>::find

find begins with the highest level chain—the level levels chain—that contains a pair and works its way down to the level 0 chain. At each level we advance as close to the pair being searched as possible without advancing to the right of the pair. Although we can terminate the search at level i if we reach a pair whose key equals theKey, the additional comparison needed to test for equality isn't justified because most pairs are expected to be only in the level 0 chain. When we exit from the for loop, we are positioned just to the left of the pair we seek. Comparing with

the next pair on the level 0 chain permits us to determine whether or not the pair
we seek is in the structure.

The Method skipList<K,E>::insert

Before we can write code for the method to insert a pair into a skip list, we must
write methods to assign a level number to a new pair and to search the skip list as
is done by find but saving a pointer to the last node encountered at each level of
the search. Programs 10.9 and 10.10 give these two methods.

```
template<class K, class E>
int skipList<K,E>::level() const
{// Return a random level number <= maxLevel.
   int lev = 0;
   while (rand() <= cutOff)
      lev++;
   return (lev <= maxLevel) ? lev : maxLevel;
}
```

Program 10.9 Method to assign a level number

Program 10.11 gives the code to insert the pair **thePair** into a skip list. **thePair**
is not inserted if largeKey $\leq$ thePair.first. Also, if the skip list already has a
pair whose key is thePair.first, the second component of this existing pair is
changed to thePair.second.

The Method skipList<K,E>::erase

Program 10.12 gives the code to erase the dictionary pair, if any, with key **theKey**.
The while loop updates levels so that there is at least one level levels pair unless
the skip list is empty. In the latter case levels is set to 0.

Other Methods

The codes for other methods such as **size** and **empty**, and the iterator methods are
similar to the codes for the corresponding methods of **chain**. Recall that the pairs
in the chain for each level (excluding the header node, which has no key) are in
ascending order from left to right. In particular, the level 0 chain contains all pairs
in the dictionary in ascending order of their key. Therefore the **skipList** iterator
is able to provide sequential access to the dictionary pairs in sorted order in $\Theta(1)$
time per pair accessed.

```
template<class K, class E>
pair<const K,E>* skipList<K,E>::find(const K& theKey) const
{// Return pointer to matching pair.
 // Return NULL if no matching pair.
   if (theKey >= tailKey)
      return NULL;  // no matching pair possible

   // position beforeNode just before possible node with theKey
   skipNode<K,E>* beforeNode = headerNode;
   for (int i = levels; i >= 0; i--)              // go down levels
      // follow level i pointers
      while (beforeNode->next[i]->element.first < theKey)
         beforeNode = beforeNode->next[i];

   // check if next node has theKey
   if (beforeNode->next[0]->element.first == theKey)
      return &beforeNode->next[0]->element;

   return NULL;  // no matching pair
}
```

Program 10.10 Method to search a skip list and save the last node encountered at each level

10.4.6   Complexity of skipList Methods

The complexity of methods find, insert, and erase is $O(n+\text{maxLevel})$ where n is the number of pairs in the dictionary. In the worst case there may be only one level maxLevel pair, and the remaining pairs may all be level 0 pairs. Now $O(\text{maxLevel})$ time is spent on the level i chains for $i > 0$, and $O(n)$ time on the level 0 chain. Despite this poor worst-case performance, skip lists are a valuable representation method, as the expected complexity of methods find, insert, and erase is $O(\log n)$.

As for the space complexity, we note that in the worst case each pair might be a level maxLevel pair requiring maxLevel+1 pointers. Therefore, in addition to the space needed to store the n pairs, we need space for $O(n*\text{MaxLevel})$ pointers. On the average, however, only $n*p$ of the pairs are expected to be on the level 1 chain, $n*p^2$ on the level 2 chain, and $n*p^i$ on the level i chain. So the expected number of pointer fields (excluding those in the header and tail nodes) is $n\sum_i p^i = n/(1-p)$. So while the worst-case space requirements are large, the expected requirements are not. When $p = 0.5$, the expected space requirements (in addition to that for the dictionary pairs) is that for approximately $2n$ pointers!

```
template<class K, class E>
void skipList<K,E>::insert(const pair<const K, E>& thePair)
{// Insert thePair into the dictionary. Overwrite existing
 // pair, if any, with same key.
   if (thePair.first >= tailKey) // key too large
   {ostringstream s;
    s << "Key = " << thePair.first << " Must be < " << tailKey;
    throw illegalParameterValue(s.str());
   }

   // see if element with theKey already present
   skipNode<K,E>* theNode = search(thePair.first);
   if (theNode->element.first == thePair.first)
   {// update theNode->element.second
      theNode->element.second = thePair.second;
      return;
   }

   // not present, determine level for new node
   int theLevel = level(); // level of new node
   // fix theLevel to be <= levels + 1
   if (theLevel > levels)
   {
      theLevel = ++levels;
      last[theLevel] = headerNode;
   }

   // get and insert new node just after theNode
   skipNode<K,E>* newNode = new skipNode<K,E>(thePair, theLevel + 1);
   for (int i = 0; i <= theLevel; i++)
   {// insert into level i chain
      newNode->next[i] = last[i]->next[i];
      last[i]->next[i] = newNode;
   }

   dSize++;
   return;
}
```

Program 10.11 Skip list insertion

```
template<class K, class E>
void skipList<K,E>::erase(const K& theKey)
{// Delete the pair, if any, whose key equals theKey.
   if (theKey >= tailKey) // too large
      return;

   // see if matching element present
   skipNode<K,E>* theNode = search(theKey);
   if (theNode->element.first != theKey) // not present
      return;

   // delete node from skip list
   for (int i = 0; i <= levels &&
                   last[i]->next[i] == theNode; i++)
      last[i]->next[i] = theNode->next[i];

   // update levels
   while (levels > 0 && headerNode->next[levels] == tailNode)
      levels--;

      delete theNode;
      dSize--;
}
```

Program 10.12 Erasing a pair from a skip list

EXERCISES

7. Write a level allocation program that divides the range of random number values into segments as described in the text and then determines the level on the basis of which segment a random number falls into.

8. Modify the class `skipList` to allow for the presence of pairs that have the same key. Each chain is now in nondecreasing order of key from left to right. Test your code.

9. Extend the class `skipList` by including methods to erase the pair with smallest key and to erase the pair with largest key. What is the expected complexity of each method?

10.5   HASH TABLE REPRESENTATION

10.5.1   Ideal Hashing

Another possibility for the representation of a dictionary is to use **hashing**. This method uses a **hash function** to map dictionary pairs into positions in a table called the **hash table**. In the ideal situation, if pair p has the key k and f is the hash function, then p is stored in position $f(k)$ of the table. Assume for now that each position of the table can store at most one pair. To search for a pair with key k, we compute $f(k)$ and see whether a pair exists at position $f(k)$ of the table. If so, we have found the desired pair. If not, the dictionary contains no pair with the specified key k. In the former case the pair may be deleted (if desired) by making position $f(k)$ of the table empty. In the latter case the pair may be inserted by placing it in position $f(k)$.

Example 10.6 Consider the student records dictionary of Example 10.1. Suppose that instead of using student names as the key, we use student ID numbers, which are six-digit integers. For our class assume we will have at most 100 students and their ID numbers will be in the range 951000 and 952000. The function $f(k)$ $= k - 951,000$ maps student IDs into table positions 0 through 1000. We may use an array table[1001] to store pointers to our dictionary pairs. This array is initialized so that table[i] is NULL for $0 \leq i \leq 1000$. To search for a pair with key k, we compute $f(k) = k - 951,000$. The pair (or more accurately, a pointer to the pair) is at table$[f(k)]$ provided table$[f(k)]$ is not NULL. If table$[f(k)]$ is null, the dictionary contains no pair with key k. In the latter case the pair may be inserted at this position. In the former case the pair may be removed by setting table$[f(k)]$ to NULL. ∎

In the ideal situation just described, it takes $O(b)$ time to initialize an empty dictionary (b is the number of positions in the hash table) and $\Theta(1)$ time to perform a find, insert, or erase operation.

Although the ideal hashing solution just described may be used in many applications of a dictionary, in many other applications the range in key values is so large that a table either doesn't make sense or is impractical (or both).

Example 10.7 Suppose that in the class list example (Example 10.1) the student IDs are in the range [100000, 999999] and we are to use the hash function $f(k) = k - 100,000$. Since the value of $f()$ is in the range [0, 899,999], we need a table with 900,000 positions. It doesn't make sense to use a table this large for a class with only 100 students. Besides being terribly wasteful of space, it takes quite a bit of time to initialize the 900,000 array entries to NULL. ∎

Example 10.8 [Converting Strings to Unique Numbers] Imagine you are maintaining a dictionary in which the keys are exactly three characters long. For example, each key may be the initials in a name; the key for Mohandas Karamchand Gandhi would be MKG.

Since each character in C++ is 1 byte long, we could convert a three-character string into a long integer using the code of Program 10.13.

```
long threeToLong(string s)
{// Assume s.length() >= 3.
    // leftmost char
    long answer = s.at(0);

    // shift left 8 bits and add in next char
    answer = (answer << 8) + s.at(1);

    // shift left 8 bits and add in next char
    return (answer << 8) + s.at(2);
}
```

Program 10.13 Converting a three-character string to a long integer

When s = abc, s.charAt(0) = a, s.charAt(1) = b, and s.charAt(2) = c. If each of the characters a, b, and c is typecast into an integer, you get the numbers 97, 98, and 99, respectively. The left shifts (in Program 10.13) by 8 are done so that the bits of one character do not interfere with the bits of another character. Because of this shifting, different three-character strings convert to different long integers and it is possible to reconstruct s from threeToLong(s) (see Exercise 12).

Since a left shift by 8 is equivalent to multiplying by $2^8 = 256$, the computation performed by Program 10.13 when s = abc is equivalent to computing $((97 * 256 + 98) * 256) + 99 = 6,382,179$.

Although Program 10.13 converts each three-character key into a unique long integer, the range of these long integers is $[0, 2^{24} - 1]$. ∎

10.5.2   Hash Functions and Tables

Buckets and Home Buckets

When the key range is too large to use the ideal method described above, we use a hash table that has a number of positions that is smaller than the key range and a hash function $f(k)$ that maps several different keys into the same position of the hash table. Each position of the table is a **bucket**; $f(k)$ is the **home bucket** for the pair whose key is k; and the number of buckets in a table equals the table length. Since a hash function may map several keys into the same bucket, we may consider designing buckets that can hold more than one pair. We consider two extremes in this chapter. In the first, each bucket may hold just one pair and in the second, each bucket is a linear list of all pairs for which this bucket is the home bucket.

The Division Hash Function

Of the many hash functions that have been proposed, hashing by division is most common. In hashing by division, the hash function has the form

$$f(k) = k\%D \tag{10.2}$$

where k is the key, D is the length (i.e., number of buckets) of the hash table, and % is the modulo operator. The positions in the hash table are indexed 0 through $D-1$. When $D = 11$, the home buckets for the keys 3, 22, 27, 40, 80, and 96 are $f(3) = 3$, $f(22) = 0$, $f(27) = 5$, 7, 3, and 8, respectively.

Other hash functions are described in this book's Web site.

Collisions and Overflows

Figure 10.2(a) shows a hash table with 11 buckets numbered 0 through 10, and each bucket has space for one pair. The figure shows only the key for each pair in the table. The divisor D that has been used is 11. The 80 is in position 3 because 80 % 11 = 3; the 40 is in position 40 % 11 = 7; and the 65 is in position 65 % 11 = 10. Each pair is in its home bucket. The remaining buckets in the hash table are empty.

Now suppose we wish to enter the key 58 into the table. The home bucket is $f(58) = 58 \% 11 = 3$. This bucket is already occupied by a different key. We say that a **collision** has occurred. A collision occurs whenever two different keys have the same home bucket. Since a bucket may be able to accommodate more than one pair, a collision may not be a problem. All pairs that have the same home bucket can be stored in their home bucket provided enough space is available in the home bucket. An **overflow** occurs when there isn't room in the home bucket for the new pair.

In our example each bucket can accommodate only one pair. So collisions and overflows occur at the same time. If we cannot put 58 into its home bucket, where should we put it? This question is answered by the overflow-handling mechanism in use. The most popular overflow-handling mechanism is linear probing (Section 10.5.3). Other mechanisms such as quadratic probing and double hashing are described in the Web site.

I Want a Good Hash Function

Although collisions may not give you a headache, they lead to overflows, which are guaranteed to cause a headache (unless a bucket can hold an unlimited number of pairs) as far as the insertion operation is concerned. The expected occurrence of

Figure 10.2 Hash tables

collisions and overflows is minimized when approximately the same number of keys from the key range hashes into any bucket of the table. A **uniform hash function** provides such a distribution of home buckets.

Example 10.9 [Uniform Hash Function] Assume that our hash table has $b > 1$ buckets numbered 0 through $b - 1$. The hash function $f(k) = 0$ for all k is not a uniform hash function because all keys hash into the same bucket, bucket 0. When this hash function is used, we get the maximum number of collisions and overflows that are possible. Suppose $b = 11$ and the key range is [0, 98]. A uniform hash function will hash approximately 9 of these keys into each bucket; when the key range is [0, 999], approximately 91 keys are hashed into each bucket.

The function $f(k) = k\%b$ is a uniform hash function for every key range [0, r] where r is a positive integer. When $r = 20$ and $b = 11$, for example, some buckets get two keys and others get one; and when $r = 50$ and $b = 11$, some buckets get five keys and others get four. No matter what r and $b > 1$ are, when division is used, some buckets get $\lfloor r/b \rfloor$ keys and the remaining buckets get $\lceil r/b \rceil$ keys. Division yields a uniform hash function.   ∎

If people would select the set of keys in their dictionary uniformly from the key range, the use of a uniform hash function would result in a uniform assignment of dictionary keys to home buckets. Unfortunately, we haven't figured out how to make people select keys in this manner. In practice, dictionary applications have keys that show some degree of correlation. For example, when the keys are integers, you might have a preponderance of odd keys or even keys, rather than an equal number of odd and even keys; when the keys are alphanumeric, you may have clusters of keys that have the same prefix or the same suffix. Because keys in real-world applications are not selected uniformly from the key range, some uniform hash functions work better than others in providing an approximately equal distribution of keys to home buckets. These uniform hash functions that actually give a good distribution of keys in practice are called **good hash functions**.

Example 10.10 [Selecting the Hash Function Divisor D] When using the hash function $f(k) = k\%D$ $(D = b)$, some choices of D result in a good hash function and other choices result in a bad hash function. As noted above, all choices of D, $D > 1$, result in a uniform hash function.

Suppose that D is an even integer. Now $f(k)$ is even whenever k is even, and $f(k)$ is odd whenever k is odd. For example, $k\%20$ is even whenever k is even and is odd whenever k is odd. If your application has a preponderance of even keys, then many more keys get even home buckets than get odd home buckets. We do not get a uniform assignment of home buckets. The same is true when your application has a preponderance of odd keys. This time many more keys get an odd home bucket than get an even home bucket. So choosing D to be even gives us a bad hash function.

When D is divisible by small odd numbers such as 3, 5, and 7, hashing by division does not distribute the use of home buckets uniformly in real-world dictionaries. Therefore, for division by hashing to be a good hash function, we must choose a divisor D that is neither even nor divisible by small odd numbers. *The ideal choice for D is a prime number. When you cannot find a prime number close to the table length you have in mind, you should choose D so that it is not divisible by any number between 2 and 19.* Other considerations for the choice of D are discussed in Sections 10.5.3 and 10.5.4.   ∎

Because of the correlation among keys in a dictionary application, you should choose uniform hash functions whose value depends on all bits of the key (as opposed to just the first few, last few, or middle few). The hash functions described in this book's Web site have this property. Therefore, these hash functions are good hash functions. When using the division hash function, dependence on all bits is obtained by using an odd value for D. Best results are obtained when D (and therefore the number of buckets b) is either a prime number or has *no prime factors less than* 20.

Division and Nonintegral Keys

To use the division hash function, keys need to be converted to nonnegative integers before $f(k)$ can be computed. Since all hash functions hash several keys into the same home bucket, it is not necessary for us to convert keys into unique nonnegative integers. It is ok for us to convert the strings *data*, *structures*, and *algorithms* into the same integer (say, 199).

Example 10.11 [Converting Strings to Integers] Program 10.13 cannot be extended to convert strings with more than four characters into a number because a long integer has only 32 bits. Since it is not necessary to convert strings into unique nonnegative integers, we can map every string, no matter how long, into a 16-bit integer. Program 10.14 shows you one way to do this.

```
int stringToInt(string s)
{// Convert s into a nonnegative int that depends on all
 // characters of s.
   int length = (int) s.length();    // number of characters in s
   int answer = 0;
   if (length % 2 == 1)
   {// length is odd
      answer = s.at(length - 1);
      length--;
   }

   // length is now even
   for (int i = 0; i < length; i += 2)
   {// do two characters at a time
      answer += s.at(i);
      answer += ((int) s.at(i + 1)) << 8;
   }

   return (answer < 0) ? -answer : answer;
}
```

Program 10.14 Converting a string into a nonunique integer

Program 10.14 converts pairs of characters into a unique integer, using the technique of Program 10.13, and then sums these unique integers. Although it would have been easier to simply add all the characters together (rather than shift every other one by 16 bits), doing so would give us integers that are not much more than 8 bits long; strings that are eight characters long would produce integers up to 11 bits long. Shifting by 16 bits allows us to cover the entire range of integers even with strings that are two characters long. ∎

The C++ STL provides specializations of the template class hash<T> that transform instances of type T into a nonnegative integer of type size_t. Program 10.15 shows a possible specialization of hash<T> for the case when T is the STL class string. This specialization is identical to that used in the SGI STL specialization hash<char*>.

```
template<>
class hash<string>
{
   public:
      size_t operator()(const string theKey) const
      {// Convert theKey to a nonnegative integer.
         unsigned long hashValue = 0;
         int length = (int) theKey.length();
         for (int i = 0; i < length; i++)
            hashValue = 5 * hashValue + theKey.at(i);

         return size_t(hashValue);
      }
};
```

Program 10.15 The specialization hash<string>

10.5.3   Linear Probing

The Method

The easiest way to find a place to put 58 into the table of Figure 10.2(a) is to search the table for the next available bucket and then put 58 into it. This method of handling overflows is called **linear probing** (also referred to as linear open addressing).

The 58 gets inserted into position 4. Suppose that the next key to be inserted is 24. 24 % 11 is 2. This bucket is empty, and so the 24 is placed there. Our hash table now has the form shown in Figure 10.2(b). Let us attempt to insert the key 35 into this table. Its home bucket (2) is full. Using linear probing, this key is placed in the next available bucket, and the table of Figure 10.2(c) results. As a final example, consider inserting 98 into the table. Its home bucket (10) is full. The next available bucket is 0, and the insertion is made into this bucket. So the search for the next available bucket is made by regarding the table as circular!

Having seen how insertions are made when linear probing is used, we can devise a method to search such a table. The search begins at the home bucket $f(k)$ of the key k we are searching for and continues by examining successive buckets in the table (regarding the table as circular) until one of the following happens: (1) a bucket containing a pair with key k is reached, in which case we have found the pair we were searching for; (2) an empty bucket is reached; and (3) we return to the home bucket. In the latter two cases, the table contains no pair with key k.

The deletion of a pair must leave behind a table on which the search method just described works correctly. If we are to delete the pair with key 58 from the table of Figure 10.2(c), we cannot simply make position 4 of the table NULL. Doing so will result in the search method failing to find the pair with key 35. A deletion may require us to move several pairs. The search for pairs to move begins just after the bucket vacated by the deleted pair and proceeds to successive buckets until we either reach an empty bucket or we return to the bucket from which the deletion took place. When pairs are moved up the table following a deletion, we must take care not to move a pair to a position before its home bucket because making such a pair move would cause the search for this pair to fail.

An alternative to this rather cumbersome deletion strategy is to introduce the field neverUsed in each bucket. When the table is initialized, this field is set to true for all buckets. When a pair is placed into a bucket, its neverUsed field is set to false. Now condition (2) for search termination is replaced by: a bucket with its neverUsed field equal to true is reached. We accomplish a removal by setting the table position occupied by the removed pair to NULL. A new pair may be inserted into the first empty bucket encountered during a search that begins at the pair's home bucket. Notice that in this alternative scheme, neverUsed is never reset to true. After a while all (or almost all) buckets have this field equal to false, and unsuccessful searches examine all buckets. To improve performance, we must reorganize the table when many empty buckets have their neverUsed field equal to false. This reorganization could, for example, involve reinserting all remaining pairs into an empty hash table.

C++ Implementation of Linear Probing

Program 10.16 gives the data members and the constructor for our hash table class hashTable that uses linear probing. Notice that the hash table is defined as a one-dimensional array table[] of type pair<const K, E>*.

Program 10.17 gives the method search of hashTable. This method returns a bucket b in the table that satisfies exactly one of the following: (1) table[b] points to a pair whose key is theKey; (2) no pair in the table has the key theKey, table[b] is NULL, and the pair with key theKey may be inserted into bucket b if desired; and (3) no pair in the table has the key theKey, table[b] has a key other than theKey, and the table is full.

Program 10.18 implements the method hashTable<K,E>::find.

Program 10.19 gives the implementation of the method insert. This code begins by invoking the method search. From the specification of search, if the returned bucket b is empty, then there is no pair in the table with key thePair.first and the pair thePair may be inserted into this bucket. If the returned bucket is not empty, then it either contains a pair with key thePair.first or the table is full. In the former case we change the second component of the pair stored in the bucket to thePair.second; in the latter, we throw an exception (increasing the table size is an alternative to throwing an exception; this alternative is considered in Exercise 25). Exercise 26 asks you to write code for the method erase.

```
// data members of hashTable
pair<const K, E>** table;    // hash table
hash<K> hash;                // maps type K to nonnegative integer
int dSize;                   // number of pairs in dictionary
int divisor;                 // hash function divisor

// constructor
template<class K, class E>
hashTable<K,E>::hashTable(int theDivisor)
{
   divisor = theDivisor;
   dSize = 0;

   // allocate and initialize hash table array
   table = new pair<const K, E>* [divisor];
   for (int i = 0; i < divisor; i++)
      table[i] = NULL;
}
```

Program 10.16 Data members and constructor for hashTable

```
template<class K, class E>
int hashTable<K,E>::search(const K& theKey) const
{// Search an open addressed hash table for a pair with key theKey.
 // Return location of matching pair if found, otherwise return
 // location where a pair with key theKey may be inserted
 // provided the hash table is not full.

   int i = (int) hash(theKey) % divisor;  // home bucket
   int j = i;    // start at home bucket
   do
   {
      if (table[j] == NULL || table[j]->first == theKey)
         return j;
      j = (j + 1) % divisor;  // next bucket
   } while (j != i);          // returned to home bucket?

   return j;  // table full
}
```

Program 10.17 The method hashTable<K,E>::search

```
template<class K, class E>
pair<const K,E>* hashTable<K,E>::find(const K& theKey) const
{// Return pointer to matching pair.
 // Return NULL if no matching pair.
   // search the table
   int b = search(theKey);

   // see if a match was found at table[b]
   if (table[b] == NULL || table[b]->first != theKey)
      return NULL;                 // no match

   return table[b];  // matching pair
}
```

Program 10.18 The method `hashTable<K,E>::find`

Performance Analysis

We will analyze the time complexity only. Let b be the number of buckets in the hash table. When division with divisor D is used as the hash function, $b = D$. The time needed to initialize the table is $O(b)$. The worst-case insert and find time is $\Theta(n)$ when n pairs are present in the table. The worst case happens, for instance, when all n key values have the same home bucket. Comparing the worst-case complexity of hashing to that of the linear list method to maintain a dictionary, we see that both have the same worst-case complexity.

For average performance, however, hashing is considerably superior. Let U_n and S_n, respectively, denote the average number of buckets examined during an unsuccessful and a successful search when n is large. This average is defined over all possible sequences of n key values being inserted into the table. For linear probing, it can be shown that

$$U_n \approx \frac{1}{2}\left(1 + \frac{1}{(1-\alpha)^2}\right) \tag{10.3}$$

$$S_n \approx \frac{1}{2}\left(1 + \frac{1}{1-\alpha}\right) \tag{10.4}$$

where $\alpha = n/b$ is the **loading factor**. Although Equation 10.3 is rather difficult to derive, Equation 10.4 can be derived from Equation 10.3 with modest effort (Exercise 21a).

From Equations 10.3 and 10.4, it follows that when $\alpha = 0.5$, an unsuccessful search will examine 2.5 buckets on the average and an average successful search

```
template<class K, class E>
void hashTable<K,E>::insert(const pair<const K, E>& thePair)
{// Insert thePair into the dictionary. Overwrite existing
 // pair, if any, with same key.
 // Throw hashTableFull exception in case table is full.
   // search the table for a matching element
   int b = search(thePair.first);

   // check if matching element found
   if (table[b] == NULL)
   {
      // no matching element and table not full
      table[b] = new pair<const K,E> (thePair);
      dSize++;
   }
   else
   {// check if duplicate or table full
      if (table[b]->first == thePair.first)
      {// duplicate, change table[b]->second
         table[b]->second = thePair.second;
      }
      else // table is full
         throw hashTableFull();
   }
}
```

Program 10.19 The method hashTable<K,E>::insert

will examine 1.5 buckets. When $\alpha = 0.9$, these figures are 50.5 and 5.5. These figures, of course, assume that n is much larger than 51. When it is possible to work with small loading factors, the average performance of hashing with linear probing is significantly superior to that of the linear list method. Generally, when linear probing is used, we try to keep $\alpha \leq 0.75$.

Analysis of Random Probing

To give you a taste of what is involved in determining U_n and S_n, we derive U_n and S_n formulas for the random probing method to handle overflows. In random probing, when an overflow occurs, the search for a free bucket in which the new key is inserted is done in a random manner (in practice, a pseudorandom number generator is used so we can reproduce the bucket search sequence and use this sequence in subsequent searches for the inserted pair).

Our derivation of the formula for U_n makes use of the following result from probability theory.

Theorem 10.1 *Let p be the probability that a certain event occurs. The expected number of independent trials needed for that event to occur is $1/\alpha$.*

To get a feel for the validity of Theorem 10.1, suppose that you flip a coin. The probability that the coin lands heads up is $p = 1/2$. The number of times you expect to flip the coin before it lands heads up is $1/p = 2$. A die has six sides labeled 1 through 6. When you throw a die, the probability of drawing an odd number is $p = 1/2$. You expect to throw the die $1/p = 2$ times before drawing an odd number. The probability that a die throw draws a 6 is $p = 1/6$, so you expect to throw the die $1/p = 6$ times before drawing a 6.

The formula for U_n is derived as follows. When the loading density is α, the probability that any bucket is occupied is also α. Therefore, the probability that a bucket is empty is $p = 1 - \alpha$. In random probing an unsuccessful search looks for an empty bucket, using a sequence of independent trials. Therefore, the expected number of buckets examined is

$$U_n \approx \frac{1}{p} = \frac{1}{1-\alpha} \tag{10.5}$$

The equation for S_n may be derived from that for U_n. Number the n pairs in the table $1, 2, \cdots, n$ in the order they were inserted. When the ith pair is inserted, an unsuccessful search is done and the pair is inserted into the empty bucket where the unsuccessful search terminates. At the time the ith pair is inserted, the loading factor is $(i-1)/b$ where b is the number of buckets. From Equation 10.5 it follows that the expected number of buckets that are to be examined when searching for the ith pair is

$$\frac{1}{1 - \frac{i-1}{b}}$$

Assuming that each pair in the table is searched for with equal probability, we get

$$\begin{aligned}
S_n &\approx \frac{1}{n} \sum_{i=1}^{n} \frac{1}{1 - \frac{i-1}{b}} \\
&= \frac{1}{n} \sum_{i=0}^{n-1} \frac{1}{1 - \frac{i}{b}} \\
&\approx \frac{1}{n} \int_{i=0}^{n-1} \frac{1}{1 - \frac{i}{b}} di
\end{aligned}$$

$$\approx \quad \frac{1}{n} \int_{i=0}^{n} \frac{1}{1 - \frac{i}{b}} di$$

$$= \quad -\frac{b}{n} \log_e (1 - i/b) \Big]_0^n$$

$$= \quad -\frac{1}{\alpha} \log_e (1 - \alpha) \tag{10.6}$$

Linear probing incurs a performance penalty relative to random probing as far as the number of examined buckets is concerned. For example, when $\alpha = 0.9$, an unsuccessful search using linear probing is expected to examine 50.5 buckets; when random probing is used, this expected number drops to 10. So why do we not use random probing? Here are two reasons:

- Our real interest is run time, not number of buckets examined. It takes more time to compute the next random number than it does to examine several buckets.

- Since random probing searches the table in a random fashion, it pays a run-time penalty because of the cache effect (Section 4.5). Therefore, even though random probing examines a smaller number of buckets than does linear probing, examining this smaller number of buckets actually takes more time except when the loading factor is close to 1.

Choosing a Divisor D

To determine D, we first determine what constitutes acceptable performance for unsuccessful and successful searches. Using the formulas for U_n and S_n, we can determine the largest α that can be used. From the value of n (or an estimate) and the computed value of α, we obtain the smallest permissible value for b. Next we find the smallest integer that is at least as large as this value of b and that either is a prime or has no factors smaller than 20. This integer is the value of D and b to use.

Example 10.12 We are to design a hash table for up to 1000 pairs. Successful searches should require no more than four bucket examinations on average, and unsuccessful searches should examine no more than 50.5 buckets on average. From the formula for U_n, we obtain $\alpha \le 0.9$, and from that for S_n, we obtain $4 \ge 0.5 + 1/(2(1-\alpha))$ or $\alpha \le 6/7$. Therefore, we require $\alpha \le \min\{0.9, 6/7\} = 6/7$. Hence b should be at least $\lceil 7n/6 \rceil = 1167$. $b = D = 1171$ is a suitable choice. ∎

Another way to compute D is to begin with a knowledge of the largest possible value for b as determined by the maximum amount of space available for the hash table. Now we find the largest D no larger than this largest value that is either a prime or has no factors smaller than 20. For instance, if we can allot at most 530 buckets to the table, then $23 * 23 = 529$ is the right choice for D and b.

10.5.4   Hashing with Chains

The Method

We may eliminate the overflow problem altogether if each position of the hash table is able to hold an unlimited number of pairs. One way to accomplish this is to place a linear list in each position of the hash table. Now each pair may be stored in its home-bucket linear list. We consider the case when each bucket of the hash table is a sorted chain. Figure 10.3 shows an example of such a hash table. As in our earlier example, the hash function divisor is 11.

Figure 10.3 A chained hash table

To search for a pair with key k, we first compute the home bucket, $k\%D$, for the key and then search the chain in this bucket. To insert a pair, we need to first verify that the table does not already have a pair with the same key. This search can, of course, be limited to the chain in the home bucket of the new pair. Finally, to erase the pair with key k, we access the home bucket chain, search this chain for the pair with the given key, and then erase the pair.

C++ Implementation of Chained Hash Tables

The class hashChains implements a dictionary using a one-dimensional array table-[0:divisor-1] of type sortedChain<K,E> (see Section 10.3). Program 10.20 gives the important methods of hashChains.

```
template<class K, class E>
pair<const K, E>* find(const K& theKey) const
   {return table[hash(theKey) % divisor].find(theKey);}

void insert(const pair<const K, E>& thePair)
{
   int homeBucket = (int) hash(thePair.first) % divisor;
   int homeSize = table[homeBucket].size();
   table[homeBucket].insert(thePair);
   if (table[homeBucket].size() > homeSize)
      dSize++;
}

void erase(const K& theKey)
   {table[hash(theKey) % divisor].erase(theKey);}
```

Program 10.20 Some methods of hashChains

An Improved Implementation

We can get slightly improved performance by adding a tail node to the end of each chain as in Figure 10.4. The tail node has a key that is at least as large as that of any pair to be inserted into the table. In Figure 10.4 this large key is denoted by the symbol ∞. In practice, when the keys are integer, we can use the constant INT_MAX, which is defined in th file limits.h. With the use of a tail node, we can eliminate most of the checks against NULL that are used in the codes for the methods of sortedChain. Also, notice that although Figure 10.4 has been drawn so as to use a separate tail for each chain, in practice, we may use the same tail node for all chains.

Comparison with Linear Probing

We will explicitly compare linear probing with chaining for the case where the chains do not have a tail node. First, let us consider the space requirements for linear probing and chaining. Our implementation of linear probing uses $2b$ bytes for the b-bucket hash table and sn bytes for the n pairs. This analysis assumes

∞ denotes large key

Figure 10.4 Hash table with tail nodes

that a pointer takes 2 bytes and that a dictionary pair takes s bytes. When sorted chains are used, we need space for b firstNode pointers, b dSize values, n pairs, and n next pointers. Assuming that an int is 2 bytes, the total space works out to $4b + (s + 2)n$ bytes. Both analyses ignore the space required by those data members of hashTable and hashChains whose size is independent of b and n. The space $2b + sn$ required by linear probing is less than the space required when sorted chains are used.

As far as the worst-case time complexities are concerned, a search can require the examination of all n keys in both cases. For the expected performance of a search when chaining is used, we use the notation U_n and S_n. These are defined as for linear probing except that now we count the number of nodes rather than the number of buckets. U_n and S_n may be derived in the following way. An unsuccessful search of a sorted chain with i nodes on it will examine either one, two, three, $\cdots$, or i nodes, for $i \geq 1$. Consider the chain table[3] of Figure 10.3. A search for a key that is less than 36 examines one node; a search for a key greater than 36 and less than 69 examines two nodes; and a search for a key greater than 69 examines 2 nodes. For an i-node chain, there are $i + 1$ possibilities for the range in which the search key falls. If each of these possibilities happens with equal probability, then the average number of nodes that get examined in an unsuccessful search is

$$\frac{1}{i+1}(i + \sum_{j=1}^{i} j) = \frac{1}{i+1}(i + \frac{i(i+1)}{2}) = \frac{i(i+3)}{2(i+1)}$$

when $i \geq 1$. When $i = 0$, the average number of nodes examined is 0. For chained hash tables we expect the length of a chain to be $n/b = \alpha$ on average. When $\alpha \geq 1$, we may substitute α for i in the above expression to get

$$U_n \approx \frac{\alpha(\alpha+3)}{2(\alpha+1)}, \ \alpha \geq 1 \qquad (10.7)$$

When $\alpha < 1$, $U_n \leq \alpha$ because the average chain length is α and no search requires us to examine more nodes than on a chain.

For S_n we need to know the expected distance of each of the n identifiers from the head of its chain. To determine this distance, assume that the identifiers are inserted in increasing order. This assumption does not affect the positioning of identifiers on their respective chains. When the ith identifier is inserted, its chain is expected to have a length of $(i-1)/b$. The ith identifier gets added to the end of the chain as identifiers are inserted in increasing order. Hence a search for this identifier will require us to examine $1 + (i - 1)/b$ nodes. Note also that when identifiers are inserted in increasing order, their distance from the chain head does not change as a result of further insertions. Assuming that each of the n identifiers is searched for with equal probability, we get

$$S_n = \frac{1}{n} \sum_{i=1}^{n} \{1 + (i-1)/b\} = 1 + \frac{n-1}{2b} \approx 1 + \frac{\alpha}{2} \qquad (10.8)$$

Comparing the formulas for chaining with those for linear and random probing, we see that, on average, the number of nodes examined when chaining is used is smaller than the number of buckets examined when linear and random probing are used. For instance, when $\alpha = 0.9$, an unsuccessful search in a chained hash table is expected to examine 0.9 node and a successful search, 1.45 nodes. On the other hand, when linear probing is used, 50.5 buckets are expected to be examined if the search is unsuccessful and 5.5 if it is successful!

Comparison with Skip Lists

Both skip lists and hashing utilize a randomization process to improve the expected performance of the dictionary operations. In the case of skip lists, randomization is used to assign a level to a pair at the time of insertion. This level assignment is done without examining the key of the pair being inserted. In the case of hashing, the hash function assigns a bucket so as to randomly distribute the bucket assignments for the different pairs being inserted. The hash function does utilize the key of the pair being inserted.

By using randomization, skip lists and hashing, respectively, obtain logarithmic and constant time expected performance. However, the worst-case complexity of the skip list method is $\Theta(n+\texttt{maxLevel})$, while that of hashing is $\Theta(n)$. When skip lists are used, the expected space required for the pointers is approximately $\texttt{maxLevel}+n/(1-p)$; in the worst case, space for $\texttt{maxLevel}*(n+1)$ pointers is required. The worst-case space requirements are considerably larger for skip lists than for a chained hash table; a chained hash table requires space for $D+n$ pointers.

The skip list structure is, however, more versatile than a hash table. For example, we can output the pairs in ascending order of key in linear time by simply going down the level 0 chain. When a chained hash table is used, it takes $\Theta(D)$ time to collect the, at most, D nonempty chains and an additional $O(n \log D)$ to combine the sorted chains in ascending order of key. The combining process is done as follows: (1) put the chains on a queue; (2) extract a pair of chains from the queue, merge the pair of chains into a single sorted chain, and put the resulting chain into the queue; and (3) repeat (2) until only one chain remains. Other operations, such as find or remove the pair with largest or smallest key, are also more expensive (in terms of expected complexity) when a hash table is used.

EXERCISES

10. Use ideal hashing to implement a C++ class for dictionaries. Assume that keys are integers in the range 0 through `maxKey` where `maxKey` is specified by the user at the time the dictionary is created. Test your code.

11. Let u and v be two different three-character strings. Prove that Program 10.13 converts u and v into different numbers.

12. Write a method to take the value returned by Program 10.13 and convert it into the three-character string from which it came.

13. In which of the following cases is the specified hash function a uniform hash function (b is the number of buckets in the hash table)? Explain.

    (a) The keys are integers in the range [0, 999], $b = 50$, and $f(k) = k\%47$.

    (b) The keys are even numbers in the range [0, 999], $b = 70$, and $f(k) = k\%70$.

    (c) The keys are odd numbers in the range [0, 999], $b = 70$, and $f(k) = k\%70$.

    (d) The keys are three lowercase letters from the English alphabet, $b = 70$, and $f(k) =$ first letter in the key k.

14. You have a hash table with b buckets; the hash function is $f(k) = k\%b$. Which of the following b values satisfies the recommendation made for the

hash function divisor is Example 10.10? That is, which of the following values gives a good hash function?

(a) $b = 93$

(b) $b = 37$

(c) $b = 1024$

(d) $b = 529$

15. Use the recommendation made at the end of Example 10.11 and write a method to convert a string into an integer. Your method should cover the range of positive integers even when most string characters are ASCII and the string length is small.

16. Write a method to convert a **double** into an integer suitable for use by the division hash function.

17. Use linear probing, a hash table with $b = 13$ buckets, and the hash function $f(k) = k\%b$. Start with an empty hash table and insert pairs whose keys are 7, 42, 25, 70, 14, 38, 8, 21, 34, 11. The pairs are inserted in this order.

   (a) Draw the hash table following each insert.

   (b) What is the loading factor of your table after the last insert?

   (c) What is the maximum and average number of buckets examined in an unsuccessful search of your table?

   (d) What is the maximum and average number of buckets examined in a successful search?

   (e) Compute U_n and S_n using your loading factor and the formulas for linear probing (Equations 10.3 and 10.4). How do these numbers compare with the numbers you computed in parts (c) and (d). Explain any discrepancy.

18. Do Exercise 17 for the case when $b = 17$.

19. Do Exercise 17 for the case when $b = 27$.

20. Design an experiment to determine the accuracy of the formulas for U_n and S_n for linear probing. Conduct the experiment and present your results as a table in which you give both the measured and computed values.

21. (a) Derive Equation 10.4 from Equation 10.3. Use the same approach as used to derive Equation 10.6 from Equation 10.5.

   (b) Can this approach be used to derive Equation 10.8 from Equation 10.7? Why?

22. Develop a table of U_n and S_n values for $\alpha = 0.1, 0.2, 0.3, \cdots, 0.9$ for both linear probing and random probing.

23. Determine a suitable value for the hash function divisor D when linear probing is used. Do this for each of the following situations:

   (a) $n = 50$, $S_n \leq 3$, $U_n \leq 20$.
   (b) $n \doteq 500$, $S_n \leq 5$, $U_n \leq 60$.
   (c) $n = 10$, $S_n \leq 2$, $U_n \leq 10$.

24. For each of the following conditions, obtain a suitable value for the hash function divisor D. For this value of D determine S_n and U_n as a function of n. Assume that linear probing is used.

   (a) $MaxElements \leq 530$.
   (b) $MaxElements \leq 130$.
   (c) $MaxElements \leq 150$.

25. Write a version of the method hashTable<K,E>::insert (Program 10.19) in which the table size is approximately doubled whenever the loading density exceeds a user-specified amount. This loading density is specified along with the initial capacity when the hash table is constructed. Specifically, we limit ourselves to odd table sizes (and so to odd divisors); and each time the loading density is exceeded, the new table size is 2 * (oldtablesize) + 1. Although this method does not pick divisors according to the rule we have specified, this approach avoids even divisors and is easy to implement.

26. Write code for the method hashTable<K,E>::erase. Do not change any existing members of hashTable. What is the worst-case time complexity of your code to erase a pair? Use suitable data to test its correctness.

27. Develop a class for hash tables using linear probing and the neverUsed concept to handle an erase operation. Write complete C++ code for all methods. Include a method to reorganize the table when (say) 60 percent of the empty buckets have neverUsed equal to false. The reorganization should move pairs around as necessary and leave a properly configured hash table in which neverUsed is true for every empty bucket. Test the correctness of your code.

28. (a) Implement a hash table class that uses quadratic probing instead of linear probing. You need not implement a method to erase pairs. See the Web site for a description of quadratic probing.

   (b) Compare the performance of your class with that of the class hash-Table that was developed in Section 10.5.3. Do this comparison by experimentally measuring the average number of key comparisons made in successful and unsuccessful searches as well as by measuring the actual run time.

29. Do Exercise 28 using double hashing rather than quadratic probing. See the Web site for a description of double hashing.

30. Comment on the difficulty of providing sequential access when (a) linear probing is used and (b) when a chained hash table is used.

31. Do Exercise 17 for a chained hash table.

32. Do Exercise 20 for a chained hash table.

33. Develop a new class `sortedChainWithTail` in which the sorted chain has a tail node. Use the tail node to simplify your code by placing the pair or key being searched for, inserted, or deleted into the tail at the start of the operation. Compare the run-time performance of sorted chains with and without tail nodes.

34. Develop the class `chainedHashTable` that implements all methods of `dictionary`. The class should be developed from scratch and should make insertions and removals from its chains without invoking any method of any chain class. Test your code.

35. Develop a chained hash table class `hashChainsWithTails` in which the chains are instances of the class `sortedChainWithTail` (see Exercise 33). Compare the run-time performance of hash tables that are instances of `hashChains` and those that are instances of `hashChainsWithTails`.

36. Develop a class `hashChainsWithTail` in which each hash table chain is a sorted chain with a tail node. The tail node for all chains is the same physical node. The class should be developed from scratch and should make insertions and removals from its chains without invoking any method of any chain class. Compare the run-time performance of this class with that of `hashChains` (Program 10.20).

37. In an effort to simplify the insert and erase codes for chained hash tables, we might consider adding a header node to each chain. The header node is in addition to a tail node as discussed in the text. All insertions and removals now take place between the header and tail of a chain. As a result, the case of insertion and erase at/from the front of a chain is eliminated.

    (a) Is it possible to use the same header node for all chains? Why?

    (b) Is it desirable to set the key field(s) of the header node(s) to a particular value? Why?

    (c) Develop and test the class `hashChainsWithHeadersAndTail` in which each chain has a header node and a tail node. The class should be developed from scratch and should make insertions and removals from its chains without invoking any method of any chain class. Include all methods included in `hashChains`.

(d) State the merits and demerits of using header and tail nodes versus using only tail nodes versus using neither header nor tail nodes. Of these options which do you recommend? Why?

38. (a) Implement a hash table class that uses a vector of iterators into a list of pairs. The list of pairs is an instance of the STL class `list`. All pairs whose home bucket is 0 appear first in this list. These pairs are followed by those whose home bucket is 1 and so on. The ith iterator in the vector of iterators points to the first pair on the list whose home bucket is i. Test your code.

(b) Compare the performance of your class with that of the class `hash-Chains` that was developed in Section 10.5.4. Do this comparison by experimentally measuring the average number of key comparisons made in successful and unsuccessful searches as well as by measuring the actual run time.

39. Do Exercise 25 for `hashChains<K,E>::insert`.

40. (a) Design an experiment to compare the expected run-time performance of `sortedChain`, `skipList`, `hashTable`, `hashChains`, and `hash_map`. Since we have not implemented `hashTable<K,E>::erase` in the text, your experiment should include only the `find` and `insert` methods.

(b) Perform your experiment of part (a) and measure the run times. Present your times both as a table and as a bar chart.

(c) Which class do you recommend for dictionary applications?

41. Derive formulas for U_n and S_n for a chained hash table in which the chains are not sorted; whenever a pair is inserted into a chain, it is appended to the right end of the chain.

10.6   AN APPLICATION—TEXT COMPRESSION

We can often reduce the disk storage needed to store a text file by storing a coded version of the file. For example, a text file that is a string of 1000 xs followed by a string of 2000 ys will take 3002 bytes of space (1 byte for each x and y and 2 bytes to denote the string end) when stored as an uncoded text file. The same file can be coded, using *run-length coding*, as the string $1000x2000y$, which is 10 characters long and can be stored in 12 bytes of space. The space can be further reduced by storing the run lengths (1000 and 2000) in their binary representation. With 2 bytes per run length, the maximum run length is 2^{16}. Our example string can now be stored using 8 bytes. When the coded file is read back from storage, it needs to be decoded into the original file. File coding is done by a **compressor** and decoding by a **decompressor**.

In this section we will develop C++ code to compress and decompress text files using a technique developed by Lempel, Ziv, and Welch. Hence we will refer to the technique as the LZW method.

10.6.1   LZW Compression

The LZW compression method maps strings of text characters into numeric codes 0, 1, 2, and so on. To begin with, all characters that may occur in the string are assigned a code. For example, suppose that the string S = aaabbbbbbaabaaba is to be compressed. This string is composed of the characters a and b. a is assigned the code 0, and b the code 1.

The mapping between character strings and their codes is stored in a dictionary of pairs. Each pair is of the form $(key, value)$, where key is a character string and $value$ is the code for this character string. Figure 10.5(a) gives the initial dictionary for our example.

Beginning with the configuration of Figure 10.5, the LZW compressor repeatedly finds the longest prefix, p, of the unencoded part of S (the unencoded part of S is shaded in Figure 10.5) that is in the dictionary and outputs its code. If there is a next character c in S, then pc (pc is the prefix string p followed by the character c) is assigned the next code and inserted into the dictionary. This strategy is called the **LZW rule**.

Let us try the LZW method on our sample string. The longest prefix of the input that is in the initial dictionary is a. Its code, 0, is output, and the string aa is assigned the code 2 and entered into the dictionary. Figure 10.5(b) shows the new configuration for the dictionary and string S. aa is the longest prefix of the remaining string that is in the dictionary. Its code, 2, is output; the string aab is assigned the code 3 and entered into the dictionary (Figure 10.5(c)). *Notice that even though aab has the code 3 assigned to it, only the code 2 for aa is output. The suffix b will be part of the next code output. The reason for not outputting 3 is that the code table is not part of the compressed file. Instead, the code table is reconstructed during decompression using the compressed file. This reconstruction is possible only if we adhere strictly to the LZW rule.*

Following the output of code 2, the code for b is output; bb is assigned code 4 and entered into the code dictionary (Figure 10.5(d)). Then the code for bb is output, and bbb is entered into the table with code 5 (Figure 10.5(e)). Next code 5 is output, and bbba is entered with code 6 (Figure 10.5(f)). Then code 3 is output for aab, and aaba is entered into the dictionary with code 7 (Figure 10.5(g)). Finally, code 7 is output for the remaining string aaba. Our 16-character sample string S is encoded as the string 0214537.

10.6.2   Implementation of LZW Compression

The LZW compression program comprises functions to open the input and output files (`setFiles`), output a byte of the compressed file (`output`), read bytes of the

code	0	1
key	a	b

0	1	2
a	b	aa

`aaabbbbbbaabaaba`

Compressed string = null

(a) Initial configuration

`a``aabbbbbbaabaaba`

Compressed string = 0

(b) a has been compressed

0	1	2	3
a	b	aa	aab

0	1	2	3	4
a	b	aa	aab	bb

`aaa``bbbbbbaabaaba`

Compressed string = 02

(c) aaa has been compressed

`aaab``bbbbbaabaaba`

Compressed string = 021

(d) aaab has been compressed

0	1	2	3	4	5
a	b	aa	aab	bb	bbb

0	1	2	3	4	5	6
a	b	aa	aab	bb	bbb	bbba

`aaabbb``bbbaabaaba`

Compressed string = 0214

(e) aaabbb has been compressed

`aaabbbbbb``aabaaba`

Compressed string = 02145

(f) aaabbbbbb has been compressed

0	1	2	3	4	5	6	7
a	b	aa	aab	bb	bbb	bbba	aaba

`aaabbbbbbaab``aaba`

Compressed string = 021453

(g) aaabbbbbbaab has been compressed

Figure 10.5 LZW compression

input file and determine their output code (`compress`), and a main function (`main`).

Establish Input and Output Streams

The input to the compressor is a text file, and the output is a binary file. If the input file name is `inputFile`, then the output file name is to be `inputFile.zzz`. We further assume that the user is to have the option of providing the input file name on the command line. So if the compression program is called `compress`, then the command line

```
compress foo
```

should result in the compressed version of the file `foo` being saved as the file `foo.zzz`. If the user does not specify the file name on the command line, then we are to prompt the user for this name.

Function `setFiles` (Program 10.21) establishes the input and output streams `in` and `out`, which are global variables of type `ifstream` and `ostream`, respectively. This function assumes that the `main` function has the prototype

```
void main(int argc, char* argv[])
```

`argc` is set to the number of parameters in the command line, and `argv[i]` points to the `i`th argument. If the command line is

```
compress foo
```

then `argc` is 2, `argv[0]` points to the character string `compress`, and `argv[1]` points to `foo`.

Dictionary Organization

Each pair of the dictionary has the form (*key*, *value*) where *key* is a string and *value* is an integer code for this string. Although, *key* is a potentially long sequence of characters, we can transform it into a compact fixed-length version. Notice that each *key* of length $l > 1$ has the property that its first $l - 1$ characters (called the key prefix) are the key of some other pair in the dictionary. Since each dictionary pair has a unique code (in addition to having a unique key), we may replace the key prefix by its code. So in the example of Figure 10.5, the key aa may be represented as 0a and aaba as 3a. The dictionary now takes the form given in Figure 10.6.

code	0	1	2	3	4	5	6	7
key	a	b	0a	2b	1b	4b	5a	3a

Figure 10.6 Modified LZW compression dictionary for aaabbbbbbaabaaba

```
void setFiles(int argc, char* argv[])
{// Create input and output streams.
   char outputFile[50], inputFile[54];
   // see if file name provided
   if (argc >= 2)
      strcpy(inputFile, argv[1]);
   else
   {// name not provided, ask for it
      cout << "Enter name of file to compress" << endl;
      cin >> inputFile;
   }

   // open files in binary mode
   in.open(inputFile, ios::binary);
   if (in.fail())
   {
      cerr << "Cannot open " << inputFile << endl;
      exit(1);
   }
   strcpy(outputFile, inputFile);
   strcat(outputFile, ".zzz");
   out.open(outputFile, ios::binary);
}
```

Program 10.21 Establish input and output streams

To simplify decoding the compressed file, we will write each code using a fixed number of bits. In further development we will assume that each code is 12 bits long. Hence we can assign at most $2^{12} = 4096$ codes. Under this assumption, the encoding 0214537 for our 16-character sample string S is written out as $12 * 7 = 84$ bits, which rounds to 11 bytes.

Since each character is 8 bits long (we are assuming each character is one of the 256 ASCII characters), a key is 20 bits long (12 bits for the code of the prefix and 8 bits for the last character in the key) and can be represented using a long integer (32 bits). The least significant 8 bits are used for the last character in the key, and the next 12 bits for the code of its prefix. The dictionary itself may be represented as a chained hash table. If the prime number DIVISOR = 4099 is used as the hash function divisor, the loading density will be less than 1, as we can have at most 4096 pairs in the dictionary. The declaration

hashChains<long, int> h(DIVISOR);

suffices to create the table.

Output of Codes

Since each code is 12 bits long and each byte is 8 bits, we can output only part of a code as a byte. Eight bits of the first code are output, and the remaining four are saved for later output. When the next code is to be output, we have 4 bits from before, resulting in a total of 16 bits. These 16 bits can be output as 2 bytes. Program 10.22 gives the C++ code for the output function. MASK1 is 255, MASK2 is 15, EXCESS is 4, and BYTE_SIZE is 8. bitsLeftOver is true iff 4 bits of the previous code remain to be output. When bitsLeftOver is true, the 4 bits that remain to be output are in the variable leftOver.

```
void output(long pcode)
{// Output 8 bits, save rest in leftOver.
   int c, d;
   if (bitsLeftOver)
   {// half byte remains from before
      d = int(pcode & MASK1); // right ByteSize bits
      c = int((leftOver << EXCESS) | (pcode >> BYTE_SIZE));
      out.put(c);
      out.put(d);
      bitsLeftOver = false;
   }
   else
   {// no bits remain from before
      leftOver = pcode & MASK2; // right EXCESS bits
      c = int(pcode >> EXCESS);
      out.put(c);
      bitsLeftOver = true;
   }
}
```

Program 10.22 Output a code

Compression

Program 10.23 gives the code for the LZW compression algorithm. We begin by initializing the dictionary with all 256 (ALPHA = 256) 8-bit bytes (these correspond to the 256 ASCII characters) and their codes. The variable codesUsed keeps track of the number of codes used so far. With 12 bits per code, at most MAX_CODES = 4096 codes may be assigned. To find the longest prefix that is in the dictionary, we examine prefixes of length 1, 2, 3, $\cdots$, in this order until we reach the first one that is not in the table. At this time a code is output, and a new code is created (unless we have used all 4096 codes).

```
void compress()
{// Lempel-Ziv-Welch compressor.
   // define and initialize the code dictionary
   hashChains<long, int> h(DIVISOR);
   for (int i = 0; i < ALPHA; i++)
      h.insert(pairType(i, i));
   int codesUsed = ALPHA;

   // input and compress
   int c = in.get(); // first character of input file
   if (c != EOF)
   {// input file is not empty
      long pcode = c; // prefix code
      while ((c = in.get()) != EOF)
      {// process character c
         long theKey = (pcode << BYTE_SIZE) + c;
         // see if code for theKey is in the dictionary
         pairType* thePair = h.find(theKey);
         if (thePair == NULL)
         {// theKey is not in the table
            output(pcode);
            if (codesUsed < MAX_CODES) // create new code
               h.insert(pairType((pcode << BYTE_SIZE) | c, codesUsed++));
            pcode = c;
         }
         else pcode = thePair->second;  // theKey is in table
      }

      // output last code(s)
      output(pcode);
      if (bitsLeftOver)
         out.put(leftOver << EXCESS);
   }

   out.close();
   in.close();
}
```

Program 10.23 LZW compressor

Constants, Global Variables and the Function main

Program 10.24 gives the constants and global variables as well as the function main.

```
// constants
const DIVISOR = 4099,      // hash function DIVISOR
      MAX_CODES = 4096,    // 2^12
      BYTE_SIZE = 8,
      EXCESS = 4,          // 12 - BYTE_SIZE
      ALPHA = 256,         // 2^BYTE_SIZE
      MASK1 = 255,         // ALPHA - 1
      MASK2 = 15;          // 2^EXCESS - 1

typedef pair<const long, int> pairType ;
   // pair.first = key, pair.second = code

// globals
int leftOver;              // code bits yet to be output
bool bitsLeftOver = false; // false means no bits in leftOver
ifstream in;               // input file
ofstream out;              // output file

void main(int argc, char* argv[])
{
   setFiles(argc, argv);
   compress();
}
```

Program 10.24 Constants, global variables, and main

10.6.3   LZW Decompression

For decompression we input the codes one at a time and replace them by the texts they denote. The code-to-text mapping can be reconstructed in the following way. The codes assigned for single-character texts are entered into the dictionary. As before, the dictionary entries are code-text pairs. This time, however, the dictionary is searched for an entry with a given code (rather than with a given text). Therefore the dictionary pairs $(key, value)$ are constructed so that key is a code and $value$ is the text denoted by the code. The first code in the compressed file corresponds to a single character and so may be replaced by the corresponding character. For all other codes p in the compressed file, we have two cases to consider: (1) the code p is in the dictionary, and (2) it is not.

Case When Code p Is in the Dictionary

When p is in the dictionary, the text $text(p)$ to which it corresponds is extracted from the dictionary and output. Also, from the working of the compressor, we know that if the code that precedes p in the compressed file is q and $text(q)$ is the corresponding text, then the compressor would have created a new code for the text $text(q)$ followed by the first character $fc(p)$ of $text(p)$. So we enter the pair (next code, $text(q)fc(p)$) into the directory.

Case When Code p Is Not in the Dictionary

This case arises only when the current text segment has the form $text(q)text(q)fc(q)$ and $text(p) = text(q)fc(q)$. The corresponding compressed file segment is qp. During compression, $text(q)fc(q)$ is assigned the code p, and the code p is output for the text $text(q)fc(q)$. During decompression, after q is replaced by $text(q)$, we encounter the code p. However, there is no code-to-text mapping for p in our table. We are able to decode p by knowing that this situation arises only when the decompressed text segment is $text(q)text(q)fc(q)$. So when we encounter a code p for which the code-to-text mapping is undefined, the code-to-text mapping for p is $text(q)fc(q)$ where q is the code that precedes p.

An Example

Let us try this decompression scheme on our earlier sample string

aaabbbbbbaabaaba

which was compressed into the coded string 0214537. To begin, we initialize the dictionary with the pairs (0, a) and (1, b) and obtain the first two entries in the dictionary of Figure 10.5. The first code in the compressed file is 0. It is replaced by the text a. The next code 2 is undefined. Since the previous code, 0, has $text(0)$ = a, $fc(0)$ = a and $text(2) = text(0)fc(0)$ = aa. So the code 2 is replaced by aa, and (2, aa) is entered into the dictionary. The next code, 1, is replaced by $text(1)$ = b, and (3, $text(2)fc(1)$) = (3, aab) is entered into the dictionary. The next code, 4, is not in the dictionary. The code preceding it is 1, and so $text(4)$ = $text(1)fc(1)$ = bb. The pair (4, bb) is entered into the dictionary, and bb is output to the decompressed file. When the next code, 5, is encountered, (5, bbb) is entered into the directory; bbb is output to the decompressed file. The next code is 3. $text(3)$ = aab is output to the decompressed file, and the pair (6, $text(5)fc(3)$) = (6, bbba) is entered into the dictionary. Finally, when the code 7 is encountered, (7, $text(3)fc(3)$) = (7, aaba) is entered into the dictionary and aaba output.

10.6.4   Implementation of LZW Decompression

As was the case for the implementation of the compression algorithm, the decompression task is decomposed into several subtasks, and each is implemented by a different function. Since the decompression function setFiles, which establishes the input and output streams, is very similar to the corresponding function for compression, we do not discuss this function further.

Dictionary Organization

Because we will be querying the dictionary by providing a code and since the number of codes is 4096, we can use an array ht[4096] and store $text(p)$ in ht[p]. Using array ht in this way corresponds to ideal hashing with $f(k) = k$. $text(p)$ may be compactly stored by using the code for the prefix of $text(p)$ and the last character (suffix) of $text(p)$ as in Figure 10.6. For our decompression application it is convenient to store the prefix code and suffix using the two fields of a pair. The prefix code is stored in first field of a pair and the suffix is stored in the second field. The declaration

```
typedef pair<int, char> pairType;
pairType ht[MAX_CODES];
```

may be used to define our dictionary. So if $text(p) = text(q)c$, then ht[p].second equals the character c and ht[p].first equals q.

When this dictionary organization is used, $text(p)$ may be constructed from right to left beginning with the last character ht[p].second, as is shown in Program 10.25. This code obtains suffix values of codes $\geq$ ALPHA from the table ht, and for codes $<$ ALPHA it uses the knowledge that the code is just the integer representation of the corresponding character. $text(p)$ is assembled into the array s[] and then output. Since $text(p)$ is assembled from right to left, the first character of $text(p)$ is in s[size].

Input of Codes

Since the sequence of 12-bit codes is represented as a sequence of 8-bit bytes in the compressed file, we need to reverse the process employed by the output function of the LZW compressor (Program 10.22). This reversal is done by the function get-Code (Program 10.26). The only new constant here is MASK. Its value, 15, enables us to extract the low-order 4 bits of a byte.

Decompression

Program 10.27 gives the LZW decompressor. The first code in the compressed file is decoded outside the while loop by doing a type conversion to the type char, and the remaining codes are decoded inside this loop. *At the start of each iteration of*

```
void output(int code)
{// Output string corresponding to code.
   size = -1;
   while (code >= ALPHA)
   {// suffix in dictionary
      s[++size] = ht[code].second;
      code = ht[code].first;
   }
   s[++size] = code;   // code < ALPHA

   // decompressed string is s[size] ... s[0]
   for (int i = size; i >= 0; i--)
      out.put(s[i]);
}
```

Program 10.25 Compute *text*(code)

```
bool getCode(int& code)
{// Put next code in compressed file into code.
 // Return false if no more codes.
   int c, d;
   if ((c = in.get()) == EOF)
      return false;   // no more codes

   // see if any left over bits from before
   // if yes, concatenate with left over 4 bits
   if (bitsLeftOver)
      code = (leftOver << BYTE_SIZE) | c;
   else
   {// no left over bits, need four more bits
    // to complete code
    d = in.get();   // another 8 bits
    code = (c << EXCESS) | (d >> EXCESS);
    leftOver = d & MASK;   // save 4 bits
   }
   bitsLeftOver = !bitsLeftOver;
   return true;
}
```

Program 10.26 Extracting codes from a compressed file

the while *loop,* s[size] *contains the first character of the last decoded text that was output.* To establish this condition for the first iteration, we set size to 0 and s[0] to the first and only character corresponding to the first code in the compressed file.

The while loop repeatedly obtains a code ccode from the compressed file and decodes it. There are two cases for ccode—(1) ccode is in the dictionary, and (2) it is not. ccode is in the dictionary iff ccode < codesUsed where ht[0:codesUsed-1] is the defined part of table h. In this case the code is decoded using the decompression function output, and following the LZW rule, a new code is created with suffix being the first character of the text just output for ccode. When ccode is not defined, we are in the special case discussed at the beginning of this section and ccode is *text*(pcode)s[size]. This information is used to create a table entry for code and to output the decoded text to which it corresponds.

Constants, Global Variables, and the Function main

Program 10.28 gives the constants, global variables, and main function for LZW decompression.

10.6.5   Performance Evaluation

Well, how good is our compressor compared to, say, the popular compression program zip? Our program compressed a 33,772-byte ASCII file to 18,765 bytes, achieving a compression ratio of 33,772/18,765 = 1.8; zip did much better—it compressed the same file to 11,041 bytes, achieving a compression ratio of 3.1. This disappointing showing by our compression program should not be a cause for concern, since commercial compression programs such as zip couple methods such as LZW compression with good coding techniques such as Huffman coding (see Section 12.6.3) to obtain a higher compression ratio. So we should not expect a raw LZW compressor to match the performance of a commercial compressor.

EXERCISES

42. Start with an LZW compression dictionary that has the entries (a, 0) and (b, 1).

    (a) Draw figures similar to Figure 10.5 for the LZW compression dictionary following the processing of each character of the string babababbabba.

    (b) Give the code sequence for the compressed form of babababbabba.

    (c) Now decompress the code sequence of part (b). For each code encountered, explain how it is decoded. Draw the decode table following the decoding of each code.

```
void decompress()
{// Decompress a compressed file.
   int codesUsed = ALPHA; // codes codesUsed so far

   // input and decompress
   int pcode, // previous code
       ccode; // current code
   if (getCode(pcode))
   {// file is not empty
      s[0] = pcode;   // character for pcode
      out.put(s[0]);  // output string for pcode
      size = 0; // s[size] is first character of
                // last string output

      while(getCode(ccode))
      {// there is another code
         if (ccode < codesUsed)
         {// ccode is defined
            output(ccode);
            if (codesUsed < MAX_CODES)
            {// create new code
               ht[codesUsed].first = pcode;
             ht[codesUsed++].second = s[size];
             }
         }
         else
         {// special case, undefined code
            ht[codesUsed].first = pcode;
            ht[codesUsed++].second = s[size];
            output(ccode);
         }
         pcode = ccode;
      }
   }

   out.close();
   in.close();
}
```

Program 10.27 LZW decompressor

```
// constants
const MAX_CODES = 4096,     // 2^12
      BYTE_SIZE = 8,
      EXCESS = 4,           // 12 - BYTE_SIZE
      ALPHA = 256,          // 2^BYTE_SIZE
      MASK = 15;            // 2^EXCESS - 1

typedef pair<int, char> pairType;

// globals
pairType ht[MAX_CODES];     // dictionary
char s[MAX_CODES];          // used to reconstruct text
int size;                   // size of reconstructed text
int leftOver;               // code bits yet to be output
bool bitsLeftOver = false;  // false means no bits in leftOver
ifstream in;                // input file
ofstream out;               // output file

void main(int argc, char* argv[])
{
   setFiles(argc, argv);
   decompress();
}
```

Program 10.28 Constants, globals, and main for decompression

43. Do Exercise 42 for the string $A(10)$ = aaaaaaaaaa whose length is 10. This time start with a dictionary that has the single entry (a, 0). Can you predict the code sequence for the string $A(100)$ whose length is 100 and all of whose characters are the letter a?

44. Our LZW compressor code uses the class hashChains. Determine the effect of changing the hash table class to each of the classes sortedChain, hashTable, and hash_map. Do this exercise by measuring the time needed to compress the sample input file compress.input that is given in the Web site. Based on your experiment, which hash table class do you recommend for LZW compression? Why?

45. Is is possible for the compressed file generated by our LZW compressor to be longer than the original file? If so, by how much?

46. Write an LZW compressor and decompressor for files composed of the characters {a, b, ⋯, z, 0, 1, ⋯, 9, '.', ',', ';', ':'} and the end-of-line character.

Use 8 bits per code. Test the correctness of your program. Is it possible for the compressed file to be longer than the original file?

47. Modify the LZW compress and decompress programs so that the code table is reinitialized after every x kilobytes of the text file have been compressed / decompressed. Experiment with the modified compression code using text files that are 100K to 200K bytes long and $x = 10, 20, 30, 40$, and 50. Which value of x gives the best compression?

48. A **concordance** is an alphabetized list of all the words in a text. Together with each word is a sorted list of all the lines of the text that contain this word. That is, each entry of a concordance is a pair of the form (word, sorted list of all line numbers where this word occurs). Notice that a concordance is similar to a book index; however, unlike a book index, which lists the page numbers on which only some of the words in the book occur, a concordance includes every word and lists line numbers rather than page numbers. The objective of this exercise is to write a program that uses a hash table to create a concordance. Each hash table entry is a pair (**key, list**) = (word, sorted list of line numbers where this word occurs).

(a) Develop a C++ class for the hash table pairs. Justify your selection of data types for **key** and **list**. When selecting a data type for **list**, consider the types **vector**, **arrayList**, **chain**, **arrayQueue**, **linkedQueue**, and any customized type(s) that may be appropriate.

(b) Develop two C++ programs to input text and output its concordance. The first program should use the STL class **hash_map** to construct the concordance entries and then use a suitable sort method to sort these entries by their **key** fields. The second program should use the class **hashChains** to construct the concordance entries and then should merge the hash table chains to obtain a sorted list of concordance entries.

(c) Compare the run-time performance of the two programs you have developed.

10.7   REFERENCES AND SELECTED READINGS

Skip lists were proposed by William Pugh. An analysis of their expected complexity can be found in the paper "Skip Lists: A Probabilistic Alternative to Balanced Trees" by W. Pugh, *Communications of the ACM*, 33, 6, 1990, 668–676.

Visit this book's Web site to learn more about hash functions and overflow-handling mechanisms. To find out everything you ever wanted to know about hashing, see the book *The Art of Computer Programming: Sorting and Searching*, Volume 3, Second Edition, by D. Knuth, Addison-Wesley, Menlo Park, CA, 1998.

Our description of the Lempel-Ziv-Welch compression method is based on the paper "A Technique for High-Performance Data Compression" by T. Welch, *IEEE Computer*, June 1994, 8–19. For more on data compression, see the survey article "Data Compression" by D. Lelewer and D. Hirschberg, *ACM Computing Surveys*, 19, 3, 1987, 261–296.

CHAPTER 11

BINARY AND OTHER TREES

BIRD'S-EYE VIEW

Yes, it's a jungle out there. The jungle is populated with many varieties of trees, plants, and animals. The world of data structures also has a wide variety of trees, too many for us to discuss in this book. In the present chapter we study two basic varieties: general trees (or simply trees) and binary trees. Chapters 12 through 15 consider the more popular of the remaining varieties—heaps, leftist trees, tournament trees, binary search trees, AVL trees, red-black trees, splay trees, and B-trees. Chapters 12 through 14 are fairly independent and may be read in any order. However, Chapter 15 should be read only after you have assimilated Chapter 14. If you are still hungry for trees when you are done with these chapters, you can find additional tree varieties—pairing heaps, interval heaps, tree structures for double-ended priority queues, tries, and suffix trees—on the Web site for this book.

Two applications of trees are developed in the applications section. The first concerns the placement of signal boosters in a tree distribution network. The second revisits the online equivalence problem introduced in Section 6.5.4. This problem is also known as the union/find problem. By using trees to represent the sets, we can obtain improved run-time performance over the chain representation developed in Section 6.5.4.

418

In addition, this chapter covers the following topics:

- Tree and binary tree terminology such as height, depth, level, root, leaf, child, parent, and sibling.

- Array and linked representations of binary trees.

- The four common ways to traverse a binary tree: preorder, inorder, postorder, and level order.

11.1   TREES

So far in this text we have seen data structures for linear and tabular data. These data structures are generally not suitable for the representation of hierarchical data. In hierarchical data we have an ancestor-descendant, superior-subordinate, whole-part, or similar relationship among the data elements.

Example 11.1 [Joe's Descendants] Figure 11.1 shows Joe and his descendants arranged in a hierarchical manner, beginning with Joe at the top of the hierarchy. Joe's children (Ann, Mary, and John) are listed next in the hierarchy, and a line or edge joins Joe and his children. Ann has no children, while Mary has two and John has one. Mary's children are listed below her, and John's child is listed below him. There is an edge between each parent and his/her children. From this hierarchical representation, it is easy to identify Ann's siblings, Joe's descendants, Chris's ancestors, and so on.   ■

Figure 11.1 Descendants of Joe

Example 11.2 [Corporate Structure] As an example of hierarchical data, consider the administrative structure of the corporation of Figure 11.2. The person (in this case the president) highest in the hierarchy appears at the top of the diagram. Those who are next in the hierarchy (i.e., the vice presidents) are shown below the president and so on. The vice presidents are the president's subordinates, and the president is their superior. Each vice president, in turn, has his/her subordinates who may themselves have subordinates. In the diagram we have drawn a line or edge between each person and his/her direct subordinates or superior.   ■

Figure 11.2 Hierarchical administrative structure of a corporation

Example 11.3 [Governmental Subdivisions] Figure 11.3 is a hierarchical drawing of the branches of the federal government. At the top of the hierarchy, we have the entire federal government. At the next level of the hierarchy, we have drawn its major subdivisions (i.e., the different departments). Each department may be further subdivided. These subdivisions are drawn at the next level of the hierarchy. For example, the Department of Defense has been subdivided into the Army, Navy, Air Force, and Marines. A line runs between each element and its components. The data of Figure 11.3 are an example of whole-part relationships.   ∎

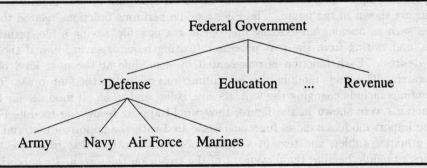

Figure 11.3 Modules of the federal government

Example 11.4 [Software Engineering] For another example of hierarchical data, consider the software-engineering technique referred to as modularization. In modularization we decompose a large and complex task into a collection of smaller, less complex tasks. The objective is to divide the software system into many functionally independent parts or **modules** so that each can be developed relatively independently. This decision reduces the overall software development time, as it is much easier to solve several small problems than one large one. Additionally, different programmers can develop different modules at the same time. If necessary, each module may be further decomposed so as to obtain a hierarchy of modules as shown by the tree of Figure 11.4. This tree represents a possible modular decomposition of a text processor.

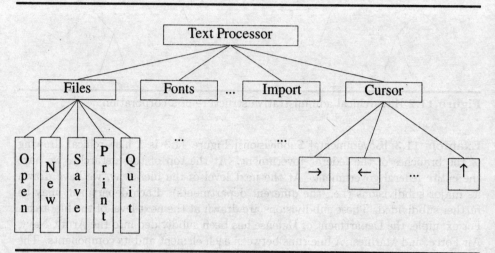

Figure 11.4 Module hierarchy for text processor

At the top level the text processor has been split into several modules. Only four are shown in the figure. The Files module performs functions related to text files such as opening an existing file, opening a new file, saving a file, printing a file, and exiting from the text processor (exiting requires saving files if the user so desires). Each function is represented by a module at the next level of the hierarchy. The Fonts module handles all functions related to the font in use. These functions include changing the font, its size, color, and so on. If modules for these functions were shown in the figure, they would appear below the module Fonts. The Import module handles functions associated with the import of material such as graphics, tables, and text in a format not native to this text processor. The Cursor module handles the movement of the cursor on the screen. Its subordinate modules correspond to various cursor motions. Programmers can carry out the specification, design, and development of each module in a relatively independent manner after the interfaces are fully specified.

When the software system is specified and designed in a modular fashion, it is natural to develop the system itself in this way. The resulting software system will have as many modules as there are nodes in the module hierarchy. Modularization improves the intellectual manageability of a problem. By systematically dividing a large problem into smaller relatively independent problems, we can solve the large problem with much less effort. The independent problems can be assigned to different persons for parallel solution. It is harder to share labor on a single module. Another advantage of developing modular software is that it is much easier to test and verify many small modules independently before testing them as a unit than to do so for one large module. The hierarchical organization clearly shows the relationship among the modules.   ∎

Definition 11.1 *A* **tree** *t is a finite nonempty set of elements. One of these elements is called the* **root***, and the remaining elements (if any) are partitioned into trees, which are called the* **subtrees** *of t.*   ∎

Let us see how this definition relates to our examples of hierarchical data. The element at the highest level of the hierarchy is the root. The elements at the next level are the roots of the subtrees formed by a partitioning of the remaining elements.

Example 11.5 In the descendants-of-Joe example (Example 11.1), the data set is {Joe, Ann, Mary, Mark, Sue, John, Chris}. So $n = 7$. The root of the collection is Joe. The remaining elements are partitioned into the three disjoint sets {Ann}; {Mary, Mark, Sue}; and {John, Chris}. {Ann} is a tree with a single element; its root is Ann. The root of {Mary, Mark, Sue} is Mary, and that of {John, Chris} is John. The remaining elements of {Mary, Mark, Sue} are partitioned into the disjoint sets {Mark} and {Sue}, which are both single-element (sub)trees, and the remaining element of {John, Chris} is also a single-element subtree.   ∎

When drawing a tree, each element is represented as a node. The tree root is drawn at the top, and its subtrees are drawn below. There is a line or edge from the tree root to the roots of its subtrees (if any). Each subtree is drawn similarly with its root at the top and its subtrees below. The edges in a tree connect an element node and its **children** nodes. In Figure 11.1, for example, Ann, Mary, and John are the children of Joe, and Joe is their **parent**. Children of the same parent are called **siblings**. Ann, Mary, and John are siblings in the tree of Figure 11.1, but Mark and Chris are not. The extension of this terminology to include the terms **grandchild**, **grandparent**, **ancestor**, **descendent**, and so forth is straightforward. In a tree, elements with no children are called **leaves**. So Ann, Mark, Sue, and Chris are the leaves of the tree of Figure 11.1. The tree root is the only tree element that has no parent.

Example 11.6 In the corporate-structure example (Example 11.2), the company employees are the tree elements. The president is the tree root. The remaining employees are partitioned into disjoint sets, which represent different divisions of the company. Each division has a vice president, who is the root of the subtree that represents the division. The remaining employees of a division are partitioned into disjoint sets representing departments. The department head will be the root of the department subtree. The remaining employees of a department could be partitioned into projects and so on.

The vice presidents are children of the president; department heads are children of their vice president, and so on. The president is the parent of the vice presidents, and each vice president is the parent of the department heads in his/her division.

In Figure 11.3 the root is the element Federal Government. Its subtrees have the roots Defense, Education, ···, and Revenue, which are the children of Federal Government. Federal Government is the parent of its children. Defense has the children Army, Navy, Air Force, and Marines. The children of Defense are siblings and are also leaves.   ■

Another commonly used tree term is **level**. By definition the tree root is at level 1; its children (if any) are at level 2; their children (if any) are at level 3; and so on.[1] In the tree of Figure 11.3, Federal Government is at level 1; Defense, Education, and Revenue are at level 2; and Army, Navy, Air Force, and Marines are at level 3.

The **height** (or **depth**) of a tree is the number of levels in it. The trees of Figures 11.1, 11.3, and 11.4 have a height of 3.

The **degree of an element** is the number of children it has. The degree of a leaf is 0. The degree of Files in Figure 11.4 is 5. The **degree of a tree** is the maximum of its element degrees.

EXERCISES

1. Explain why the diagram of Figure 11.1 is a tree. Label the root node and mark each node with its level number and degree. What is the depth of this tree?

2. Do Exercise 1 for the recursion diagram of Figure 1.3.

3. Develop a tree representation for the major elements (whole book, chapters, sections, and subsections) of this text.

   (a) What is the total number of elements in your tree?
   (b) Identify the leaf elements.
   (c) Identify the elements on level 3.
   (d) List the degree of each element.

4. Access the World Wide Web home page for your department. (Alternatively, access http://www.cise.ufl.edu.)

   (a) Follow some of the links to lower-level pages and draw the resulting structure. In your drawing the Web pages should be represented by nodes, and the links by edges that join pairs of nodes.

---

[1]Some authors number tree levels beginning at 0 rather than 1. In this case the root of a tree is at level 0.

(b) Is it necessary for the structure to be a tree? Why?

(c) In case your structure is a tree, identify the root and the leaves.

11.2   BINARY TREES

Definition 11.2 *A* **binary tree** *t is a finite (possibly empty) collection of elements. When the binary tree is not empty, it has a* **root** *element and the remaining elements (if any) are partitioned into two binary trees, which are called the left and right subtrees of t.* ∎

The essential differences between a binary tree and a tree are

- Each element in a binary tree has exactly two subtrees (one or both of these subtrees may be empty). Each element in a tree can have any number of subtrees.

- The subtrees of each element in a binary tree are ordered. That is, we distinguish between the left and the right subtrees. The subtrees in a tree are unordered.

Another difference between a tree and a binary tree—a binary tree can be empty, whereas a tree cannot—is largely a matter of definition. Some authors relax the definition of a tree to allow for an empty tree.

Like a tree, a binary tree is drawn with its root at the top. The elements in the left (right) subtree of the root are drawn below and to the left (right) of the root. Between each element and its children is a line or edge.

Figure 11.5 shows some binary trees that represent arithmetic expressions. Each operator $(+, -, *, /)$ may have one or two operands. The left operand (if any) is the left subtree of the operator. The right operand is its right subtree. The leaf elements in an expression tree are either constants or variables. Note that an expression tree contains no parentheses.

One application of expression trees is in the generation of optimal computer code to evaluate an expression. Although we do not study algorithms to generate optimal code from an expression tree, we will use these trees to illustrate some of the operations that are commonly performed on binary trees.

EXERCISES

5. (a) Identify the leaves of the binary trees of Figure 11.5.

    (b) Identify all level 3 nodes in Figure 11.5(b).

    (c) How many level 4 nodes are in Figure 11.5(c)?

(a) $(a * b) + (c / d)$

(b) $((a + b) + c) + d$

(c) $((-a) + (x + y)) / ((+b) * (c * a))$

Figure 11.5 Expression trees

6. Draw the binary expression trees corresponding to each of the following expressions:

   (a) $(a + b)/(c - d) + e + g * h/a$

   (b) $-x - y * z + (a + b + c/d * e)$

   (c) $((a + b) > (c - e))||a < b\&\&(x < y||y > z)$

11.3   PROPERTIES OF BINARY TREES

Property 11.1 *The drawing of every binary tree with n elements, $n > 0$, has exactly $n - 1$ edges.*

Proof Every element in a binary tree (except the root) has exactly one parent. There is exactly one edge between each child and its parent. So the number of edges is $n - 1$. ∎

Property 11.2 *A binary tree of height h, $h \geq 0$, has at least h and at most $2^h - 1$ elements in it.*

Proof Since each level has at least one element, the number of elements is at least h. As each element can have at most two children, the number of elements at level i is at most 2^{i-1}, $i > 0$. For $h = 0$, the total number of elements is 0, which equals $2^0 - 1$. For $h > 0$, the number of elements cannot exceed $\sum_{i=1}^{h} 2^{i-1} = 2^h - 1$. ∎

Property 11.3 *The height of a binary tree that contains n, $n \geq 0$, elements is at most n and at least $\lceil \log_2(n+1) \rceil$.*

Proof Since there must be at least one element at each level, the height cannot exceed n. From Property 11.2 we know that a binary tree of height h can have no more than $2^h - 1$ elements. So $n \leq 2^h - 1$. Hence $h \geq \log_2(n+1)$. Since h is an integer, we get $h \geq \lceil \log_2(n+1) \rceil$. ∎

A binary tree of height h that contains exactly $2^h - 1$ elements is called a **full binary tree**. The binary tree of Figure 11.5(a) is a full binary tree of height 3. The binary trees of Figures 11.5(b) and (c) are not full binary trees. Figure 11.6 shows a full binary tree of height 4.

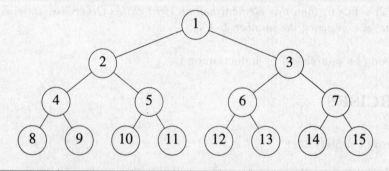

Figure 11.6 Full binary tree of height 4

Suppose we number the elements in a full binary tree of height h using the numbers 1 through $2^h - 1$. We begin at level 1 and go down to level h. Within levels the elements are numbered left to right. The elements of the full binary tree of Figure 11.6 have been numbered in this way. Now suppose we delete the k elements numbered $2^h - i$, $1 \leq i \leq k < 2^h$. The resulting binary tree is called a **complete binary tree**. Figure 11.7 gives some examples. Note that a full binary tree is a special case of a complete binary tree. Also, note that the height of a complete binary tree that contains n elements is $\lceil \log_2(n+1) \rceil$.

There is a very nice relationship among the numbers assigned to an element and its children in a complete binary tree, as given by Property 11.4.

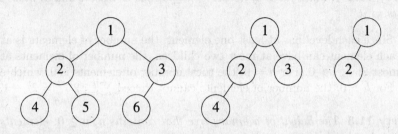

Figure 11.7 Complete binary trees

Property 11.4 *Let* i, $1 \le i \le n$, *be the number assigned to an element of a complete binary tree. The following are true:*

1. *If* $i = 1$, *then this element is the root of the binary tree. If* $i > 1$, *then the parent of this element has been assigned the number* $\lfloor i/2 \rfloor$.

2. *If* $2i > n$, *then this element has no left child. Otherwise, its left child has been assigned the number* $2i$.

3. *If* $2i + 1 > n$, *then this element has no right child. Otherwise, its right child has been assigned the number* $2i + 1$.

Proof Can be established by induction on i. ∎

EXERCISES

7. Prove Property 11.4.

8. In a k-ary tree, $k > 1$, each node may have up to k children. These children are called, respectively, the first, second, $\cdots$, kth child of the node. A 2-ary tree is a binary tree.

   (a) Determine the analogue of Property 11.1 for k-ary trees.

   (b) Determine the analogue of Property 11.2 for k-ary trees.

   (c) Determine the analogue of Property 11.3 for k-ary trees.

   (d) Determine the analogue of Property 11.4 for k-ary trees.

9. What is the maximum number of nodes in a binary tree that has m leaves?

11.4   REPRESENTATION OF BINARY TREES

11.4.1   Array-Based Representation

The array representation of a binary tree utilizes Property 11.4. The binary tree to be represented is regarded as a complete binary tree with some missing elements. Figure 11.8 shows two sample binary trees. The first binary tree has three elements (A, B, and C), and the second has five elements (A, B, C, D, and E). Neither is complete. Unshaded circles represent missing elements. All elements (including the missing ones) are numbered as described in the previous section.

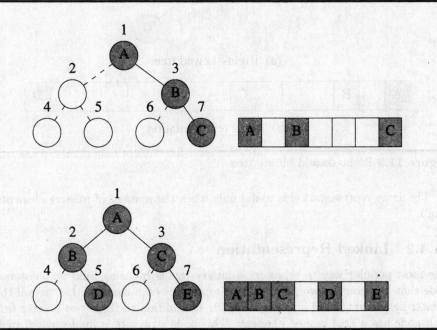

Figure 11.8 Incomplete binary trees

In an array representation, the binary tree is represented in an array by storing each element at the array position corresponding to the number assigned to it. Figure 11.8 also shows the array representations for its binary trees (position 0 of the array is not shown). Missing elements are represented by white boxes. As can be seen, this representation scheme is quite wasteful of space when many elements are missing. In fact, a binary tree that has n elements may require an array of size up to 2^n (including position 0) for its representation. This maximum size is needed when each element (except the root) of the n-element binary tree is the right child of its parent. Figure 11.9 shows such a binary tree with four elements. Binary trees of this type are called **right-skewed** binary trees. Note that the worst-case space required may be reduced to $2^n - 1$ by numbering the binary tree nodes beginning at 0 rather than at 1.

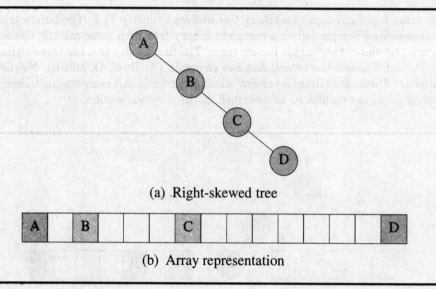

(a) Right-skewed tree

(b) Array representation

Figure 11.9 Right-skewed binary tree

The array representation is useful only when the number of missing elements is small.

11.4.2   Linked Representation

The most popular way to represent a binary tree is by using links or pointers. A node that has exactly two pointer fields represents each element. Let us call these pointer fields `leftChild` and `rightChild`. In addition to these two pointer fields, each node has a field named `element`. This node structure is implemented by the C++ struct `binaryTreeNode` (Program 11.1). We have provided three constructors for a binary tree node. The first takes no parameters and sets the two children fields to NULL; the second takes one parameter and uses it to initialize `element`, and the child fields are set to NULL; the third takes three parameters and uses these to initialize all three fields of the node.

Each pointer from a parent node to a child node represents an edge in the drawing of a binary tree. Since an n-element binary tree has exactly $n-1$ edges, we are left with $2n - (n-1) = n+1$ pointer fields that have no value. These pointer fields are set to NULL. Figure 11.10 shows the linked representations of the binary trees of Figure 11.8.

We can access all nodes in a binary tree by starting at the root and following `leftChild` and `rightChild` pointers. The absence of a parent pointer from the

```
template <class T>
struct binaryTreeNode
{
   T element;
   binaryTreeNode<T> *leftChild,    // left subtree
                     *rightChild;   // right subtree

   binaryTreeNode() {leftChild = rightChild = NULL;}
   binaryTreeNode(const T& theElement)
   {
      element = theElement;
      leftChild = rightChild = NULL;
   }
   binaryTreeNode(const T& theElement,
                  binaryTreeNode *theLeftChild,
                  binaryTreeNode *theRightChild)
   {
      element = theElement;
      leftChild = theLeftChild;
      rightChild = theRightChild;
   }
};
```

Program 11.1 Node struct for linked binary trees

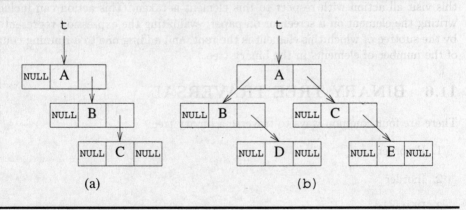

               (a)   (b)

Figure 11.10 Linked representations

linked representation of a binary tree generally causes no difficulties, as most of the functions we perform on a binary tree do not require this pointer. If some application needs this pointer, we can add another pointer field to each node.

EXERCISES

10. Draw the array representation of the binary trees that correspond to the expressions of Exercise 6.

11. Do Exercise 10 for the binary trees of Figure 11.5.

11.5   COMMON BINARY TREE OPERATIONS

Some of the operations that are commonly performed on binary trees are

- Determine its height.

- Determine the number of elements in it.

- Make a copy.

- Display the binary tree on a screen or on paper.

- Determine whether two binary trees are identical.

- Make the tree empty.

These operations can be performed by traversing the binary tree in a systematic manner. In a binary tree **traversal**, each element is **visited** exactly once. During this visit all action with respect to this element is taken. This action can include writing the element on a screen or on paper, evaluating the expression represented by the subtree of which this element is the root, and adding one to a running count of the number of elements in the binary tree.

11.6   BINARY TREE TRAVERSAL

There are four common ways to traverse a binary tree:

1. Preorder

2. Inorder

3. Postorder

4. Level order

```
template <class T>
void preOrder(binaryTreeNode<T> *t)
{// Preorder traversal of *t.
   if (t != NULL)
   {
      visit(t);                   // visit tree root
      preOrder(t->leftChild);     // do left subtree
      preOrder(t->rightChild);    // do right subtree
   }
}
```

Program 11.2 Preorder traversal

```
template <class T>
void inOrder(binaryTreeNode<T> *t)
{// Inorder traversal of *t.
   if (t != NULL)
   {
      inOrder(t->leftChild);   // do left subtree
      visit(t);                // visit tree root
      inOrder(t->rightChild);  // do right subtree
   }
}
```

Program 11.3 Inorder traversal

```
template <class T>
void postOrder(binaryTreeNode<T> *t)
{// Postorder traversal of *t.
   if (t != NULL)
   {
      postOrder(t->leftChild);    // do left subtree
      postOrder(t->rightChild);   // do right subtree
      visit(t);                   // visit tree root
   }
}
```

Program 11.4 Postorder traversal

The first three traversal methods are best described recursively as in Programs 11.2, 11.3, and 11.4. These codes assume that the binary tree being traversed is represented with the linked scheme of the previous section.

In the first three traversal methods, the left subtree of a node is traversed before the right subtree. The difference among the three orders comes from the difference in the time at which a node is visited. In the case of a preorder traversal, each node is visited before its left and right subtrees are traversed. In an inorder traversal, the root of each subtree is visited after its left subtree has been traversed but before the traversal of its right subtree begins. In a postorder traversal, each root is visited after its left and right subtrees have been traversed.

Figure 11.11 shows the output generated by Programs 11.2—11.4 when `visit(t)` is as shown in Program 11.5. The input binary trees are those of Figure 11.5.

```
template <class T>
void visit(binaryTreeNode<T> *x)
{// visit node *x, just output element field.
    cout << x->element;
}
```

Program 11.5 A `visit` function

Preorder	$+*ab/cd$	$+++abcd$	$/+-a+xy*+b*ca$
Inorder	$a*b+c/d$	$a+b+c+d$	$-a+x+y/+b*c*a$
Postorder	$ab*cd/+$	$ab+c+d+$	$a-xy++b+ca**/$
	(a)	(b)	(c)

Figure 11.11 Elements of a binary tree listed in pre-, in-, and postorder

When an expression tree is output in pre-, in-, or postorder, we get the prefix, infix, and postfix forms of the expression, respectively. The **infix** form of an expression is the form in which we normally write an expression. In this form each binary operator (i.e., operator with two operands) appears just after the infix form of its left operand and just before the infix form of its right operand. An expression presented as a binary tree is unambiguous in the sense that the association between operators and operands is uniquely determined by the representation. This association is not uniquely determined by the representation when the infix form is used. For example, is $x + y * z$ to be interpreted as $(x + y) * z$ or $x + (y * z)$? To resolve this ambiguity, one assigns priorities to operators and employs priority rules. Further, delimiters such as parentheses are used to override these rules if necessary. In a *fully parenthesized* infix representation, each operator and its operands are enclosed in a pair of parentheses. Furthermore, each of the operands of the operator are in fully parenthesized form. Some representations of this type are $((x) + (y))$, $((x) + ((y) * (z)))$, and $((((x) + (y)) * ((y) + (z))) * (w))$. This form of the expression is obtained by modifying inorder traversal as in Program 11.6.

```
template <class T>
void infix(binaryTreeNode<T> *t)
{// Output infix form of expression.
   if (t != NULL)
   {
      cout << '(';
      infix(t->leftChild);    // left operand
      cout << t->element;     // operator
      infix(t->rightChild);   // right operand
      cout << ')';
   }
}
```

Program 11.6 Output fully parenthesized infix form

In the **postfix form** each operator comes immediately after the postfix form of its operands. The operands themselves appear in left-to-right order. In the **prefix form** each operator comes immediately before the prefix form of its operands. The operands themselves appear in left-to-right order. Like the binary tree representation, the prefix and postfix representations are unambiguous. As a result, neither the prefix nor the postfix representation employs parentheses or operator priorities. The association between operators and operands is easily determined by scanning the expression from right to left or from left to right and by employing a stack of operands. If an operand is encountered during this scan, it is stacked. If an operator is encountered, it is associated with the correct number of operands from the top of the stack. These operands are deleted from the stack and replaced by an operand that represents the result produced by the operator.

In a level-order traversal, elements are visited by level from top to bottom. Within levels, elements are visited from left to right. It is quite difficult to write a recursive function for level-order traversal, as the correct data structure to use here is a queue and not a stack. Program 11.7 traverses a binary tree in level order.

Program 11.7 enters the **while** loop only if the tree is not empty. The root is visited, and its children, if any, are added to the queue. Following the addition of the children of t to the queue, we attempt to access the front element of the queue. When the queue is empty, **front()** throws an exception of type **queueEmpty**; and when the queue is not empty, **front** returns a pointer to the front element. This element is the next node that is to be visited.

```
template <class T>
void levelOrder(binaryTreeNode<T> *t)
{// Level-order traversal of *t.
   arrayQueue<binaryTreeNode<T>*> q;
   while (t != NULL)
   {
      visit(t);   // visit t

      // put t's children on queue
      if (t->leftChild != NULL)
         q.push(t->leftChild);
      if (t->rightChild != NULL)
         q.push(t->rightChild);

      // get next node to visit
      try {t = q.front();}
      catch (queueEmpty) {return;}
      q.pop();
   }
}
```

Program 11.7 Level-order traversal

Let n be the number of nodes in a binary tree. The space and time complexity of each of the four traversal programs is $O(n)$. To verify this claim, observe that the recursion stack space needed by pre-, in-, and postorder traversal is $\Theta(n)$ when the tree height is n (as is the case for a right-skewed binary tree (Figure 11.9)); the queue space needed by level-order traversal is $\Theta(n)$ when the tree is a full binary tree. For the time complexity observe that each of the traversal methods spends $\Theta(1)$ time at each node of the tree (assuming the time needed to visit a node is $\Theta(1)$).

EXERCISES

12. List the nodes of the binary trees of Figure 11.10 in pre-, in-, post-, and level order.

13. Do Exercise 12 for the full binary tree of Figure 11.6.

14. List the nodes of the binary trees for the expressions of Exercise 6 in pre-, in-, post-, and level order.

15. The nodes of a binary tree are labeled $a - h$. The preorder listing is *abcdefgh*, and the inorder listing is *cdbagfeh*. Draw the binary tree. Also, list the nodes of your binary tree in postorder and level order.

16. Do Exercise 15 for a binary tree with node labels $a - l$, preorder listing *abcdefghijkl*, and inorder listing *aefdcgihjklb*.

17. The nodes of a binary tree are labeled $a - h$. The postorder listing is *abcdefgh*, and the inorder listing is *aedbchgf*. Draw the binary tree. Also, list the nodes of your binary tree in preorder and level order.

18. Do Exercise 17 for a binary tree with node labels $a - l$, postorder listing *abcdefghijkl*, and inorder listing *backdejifghl*.

19. Draw two binary trees whose preorder listing is *abcdefgh* and whose postorder listing is *dcbgfhea*. Also, list the nodes of your binary trees in inorder and level order.

20. Write a function to perform a preorder traversal on a binary tree represented as an array. Assume that the elements of the binary tree are stored in array a and that `last` is the position of the last element of the tree. The array is of type `pair<bool, T>`, where `a[i].first` is `true` iff there is an element (`a[i].second`) at position i. What is the time complexity of your function?

21. Do Exercise 20 for inorder.

22. Do Exercise 20 for postorder.

23. Do Exercise 20 for level order.

24. Write a C++ function to make a copy of a binary tree represented as an array.

25. Write two C++ functions to make a copy of a binary tree that is represented using nodes of type `binaryTreeNode`. The first function should traverse the tree in postorder, and the second in preorder. What is the difference (if any) in the recursion stack space needed by these two functions?

26. Write a function to evaluate an expression tree that is represented using nodes of type `binaryTreeNode`. Develop a suitable data type for the elements in the tree.

27. Write a function to determine the height of a linked binary tree. What is the time complexity of your function?

28. Write a function to determine the number of nodes in a linked binary tree. What is the time complexity of your function?

29. Write a function to determine the level of a linked binary tree that has the maximum number of nodes (*Hint:* perform a level-order traversal). What is the time complexity of your function?

30. Write an iterative function to traverse a linked binary tree in inorder. Your function can use an array stack. Make your function as elegant as possible. How much stack space does the traversal need? Give this stack space as a function of the height of the binary tree.

31. Do Exercise 30 for preorder.

32. Do Exercise 30 for postorder.

33. Suppose you have a binary tree whose nodes have distinct data. Do the pre- and inorder listings of the data fields uniquely define the binary tree? If so, write a function to construct the binary tree. What is the time complexity of your function?

34. Do Exercise 33 for pre- and postorder.

35. Do Exercise 33 for post- and inorder.

36. Write a C++ function to accept an expression in postfix form and construct its binary tree representation. Assume that each operator may have either one or two operands.

37. Do Exercise 36 beginning with the prefix form.

38. Write a C++ function to transform a postfix expression into its fully parenthesized infix form.

39. Do Exercise 38 beginning with a prefix expression.

40. Wtite a function that begins with an infix expression (not necessarily fully parenthesized) and obtains its postfix form. For this exercise assume that the permissible operators are binary +, −, *, / and the permissible delimiters are (and). Notice that since the order of operands is the same in infix, prefix, and postfix, the translation from infix to prefix or postfix can be done by scanning the infix form from left to right and outputting operands as they are encountered. Operators are held in a stack until the right time to output them, which is determined by assigning priorities to the operators and to (. Use the priorities 1 (for + and −) and 2 (for * and /). Use priority 3 for a (that is outside the stack and 0 for a (that is in the stack.

41. Do Exercise 40 but this time generate the prefix form.

42. Do Exercise 40 but this time generate the binary tree form.

43. Write a function to evaluate an expression that is in its postfix form. Assume a suitable array representation for the expression.

11.7 THE ADT *BinaryTree*

Now that we have some understanding of what a binary tree is, we can specify it as an abstract data type (ADT 11.1). Since the number of operations we may wish to perform on a binary tree is quite large, we list only some of the commonly performed ones.

AbstractDataType *binaryTree*
{
    instances
        collection of elements; if not empty, the collection is partitioned into a root, left subtree, and right subtree; each subtree is also a binary tree;

    operations
            empty() : return **true** if empty, return **false** otherwise;

             size() : return number of elements/nodes in the tree;

    preOrder(*visit*) : preorder traversal of binary tree; *visit* is the visit function to use;

      inOrder(*visit*) : inorder traversal of binary tree;

    postOrder(*visit*) : postorder traversal of binary tree;

   levelOrder(*visit*) : level-order traversal of binary tree;
}

ADT 11.1 The abstract data type binary tree

Program 11.8 gives the C++ abstract class `binaryTree` that corresponds to the ADT *binaryTree*. The class T refers to the data type of the nodes in the binary tree. The data type

```
void (*) (T *)
```

used to specify the data type of the single parameter of the binary tree traversal methods specifies a function whose return type is `void` and which takes a single parameter of type T*.

11.8 THE CLASS `linkedBinaryTree`

The class `linkedBinaryTree` derives from the abstract class `binaryTree` and uses nodes of the type `binaryTreeNode` (Program 11.1). Program 11.9 gives the data members and some of the public and private methods of of `linkedBinaryTree`.

```
template<class T>
class binaryTree
{
   public:
       virtual ~binaryTree() {}
       virtual bool empty() const = 0;
       virtual int size() const = 0;
       virtual void preOrder(void (*) (T *)) = 0;
       virtual void inOrder(void (*) (T *)) = 0;
       virtual void postOrder(void (*) (T *)) = 0;
       virtual void levelOrder(void (*) (T *)) = 0;
};
```

Program 11.8 Binary tree abstract class

linkedBinaryTree has two instance data members root and treeSize. root is a pointer to the root node of the binary tre and treeSize is the number of nodes in the binary treee. The class linkedBinaryTree has a static data member visit, which is (a pointer to) a function whose return type is void and which has a single parameter that is a pointer to a binaryTreeNode. The static method dispose deletes a single node, and the method erase uses the static method dispose as the visit method for a postorder traversal to delete all nodes in a binary tree.

Program 11.10 gives the code for the preorder traversal method. The public method preOrder sets the class data member visit so that the desired function is used during the visit step. After setting the class data member visit, preOrder invokes the private recursive method preOrder, which does the actual preorder traversal. The corresponding inorder and postorder methods are similar.

The code for level-order traversal is quite similar to that given in Program 11.7. We may add a method to output a binary tree in preorder by adding the line

```
void preOrderOutput() {preOrder(output); cout << endl;}
```

to the public part of Program 11.9 and the lines

```
static void output(binaryTreeNode<E> *t)
            {cout << t->element << ' ';}
```

to the private part. Methods for inorder, postorder, and level-order output may be defined similarly.

Program 11.11 gives an additional public member method of linkedBinaryTree together with its accompanying private static recursive method. This recursive method determines the height of a binary tree by performing a postorder traversal of the binary tree. The method first determines the height of the left subtree, then

```
template<class E>
class linkedBinaryTree : public binaryTree<binaryTreeNode<E> >
{
   public:
      linkedBinaryTree() {root = NULL; treeSize = 0;}
      ~linkedBinaryTree(){erase();};
      bool empty() const {return treeSize == 0;}
      int size() const {return treeSize;}
      void preOrder(void(*theVisit)(binaryTreeNode<E>*))
         {visit = theVisit; preOrder(root);}
      void inOrder(void(*theVisit)(binaryTreeNode<E>*))
         {visit = theVisit; inOrder(root);}
      void postOrder(void(*theVisit)(binaryTreeNode<E>*))
         {visit = theVisit; postOrder(root);}
      void levelOrder(void(*)(binaryTreeNode<E> *));
      void erase()
         {
             postOrder(dispose);
             root = NULL;
             treeSize = 0;
         }
   private:
      binaryTreeNode<E> *root;               // pointer to root
      int treeSize;                          // number of nodes in tree
      static void (*visit)(binaryTreeNode<E>*);   // visit function
      static void preOrder(binaryTreeNode<E> *t);
      static void inOrder(binaryTreeNode<E> *t);
      static void postOrder(binaryTreeNode<E> *t);
      static void dispose(binaryTreeNode<E> *t) {delete t;}
};
```

Program 11.9 Data members and visit methods of `linkedBinaryTree`

determines the height of the right subtree, and finally (in the visit step) determines
the tree height by adding 1 to the larger of the left and right subtree heights.

EXERCISES

44. Write a copy constructor for `linkedBinaryTree`. Test your code. What is
    the complexity of your code?

45. Write the method `linkedBinaryTree<E>::compare(x)`, which compares the

```
template<class E>
void linkedBinaryTree<E>::preOrder(binaryTreeNode<E> *t)
{// Preorder traversal.
   if (t != NULL)
   {
      linkedBinaryTree<E>::visit(t);
      preOrder(t->leftChild);
      preOrder(t->rightChild);
   }
}
```

Program 11.10 Private preorder method of `linkedBinaryTree`

```
int height() const {return height(root);}

template <class E>
int linkedBinaryTree<E>::height(binaryTreeNode<E> *t)
{// Return height of tree rooted at *t.
   if (t == NULL)
      return 0;                        // empty tree
   int hl = height(t->leftChild);   // height of left
   int hr = height(t->rightChild);  // height of right
   if (hl > hr)
      return ++hl;
   else
      return ++hr;
}
```

Program 11.11 Determining the height of a binary tree

binary tree *this with the binary tree x. The method returns true iff the two binary trees are identical. Test your code. What is the complexity of your code?

46. Write the method `linkedBinaryTree<E>::swapTrees()`, which swaps the left and right subtrees of each node of a binary tree. Test your code. What is the complexity of your code?

47. Let $heightDifference(x)$ be the absolute value of the difference in heights of the left and right subtrees of node x. Let $maxHeightDifference(t)$ be $max\{heightDifference(x)|x$ is a node of the binary tree $t\}$. Write the method

linkedBinaryTree<E>::maxHeightDifference(), which computes the max height difference of a binary tree. Test your code. What is the complexity of your code?

48. Develop an inorder iterator for the class linkedBinaryTree (the solution to Exercise 30 should help you with this exercise). The time taken to enumerate all elements of an n-element binary tree should be $O(n)$. The complexity of no method should exceed $O(h)$, where h is the tree height, and the space requirements should be $O(h)$. Test your code.

49. Develop a preorder iterator for the class linkedBinaryTree. Excluding the time needed to double the stack size (in case you use arrayStack), the complexity of each method should be $O(1)$, and the space requirements should be $O(h)$. Test your code.

50. Develop a postorder iterator for the class linkedBinaryTree (the solution to Exercise 32 should help you with this exercise). The time taken to enumerate all elements of an n-element binary tree should be $O(n)$. The complexity of no method should exceed $O(h)$, where h is the tree height, and the space requirements should be $O(h)$. Test your code.

51. Develop a level-order iterator for the class linkedBinaryTree. Excluding the time needed to double the queue size (in case you use arrayQueue), the complexity of each method should be $O(1)$. Test your code.

52. Develop the class expression as a derived class of linkedBinaryTree. This class should permit the following operations:

   (a) Output the fully parenthesized infix form of the expression.
   (b) Output the prefix and postfix forms.
   (c) Convert from prefix to expression tree.
   (d) Convert from postfix to expression tree.
   (e) Convert from infix to expression tree.
   (f) Evaluate an expression tree.

   Test your code.

11.9   APPLICATIONS

11.9.1   Placement of Signal Boosters

Problem Descripton

In a distribution network a resource is distributed from its origin to several other sites. For example, petroleum or natural gas can be distributed through a network of pipes from the source of the petroleum/natural gas to the consumption sites. Similarly, electrical power may be distributed through a network of wires from the power plant to the points of consumption. We will use the term **signal** to refer to the resource (petroleum, natural gas, power, etc.) that is to be distributed. While the signal is being transported through the distribution network, it may experience a loss in or degradation of one or more of its characteristics. For example, there may be a pressure drop along a natural gas pipeline or a voltage drop along an electrical transmission line. In other situations noise may enter the signal as it moves along the network. Between the signal source and point of consumption, we can tolerate only a certain amount, *tolerance*, of signal degradation. To guarantee a degradation that does not exceed this amount, **signal boosters** are placed at strategic places in the network. A signal booster might, for example, increase the signal pressure or voltage so that it equals that at the source or may enhance the signal so that the signal-to-noise ratio is the same as that at the source. In this section we develop an algorithm to determine where to place signal boosters. Our objective is to minimize the number of boosters in use while ensuring that the degradation in signal (relative to that at the source) does not exceed the given tolerance.

To simplify the problem, we assume that the distribution network is a tree with the source as the root. Each node in the tree (other than the root) represents a substation where we can place a booster. Some of these nodes also represent points of consumption. The signal flows from a node to its children. Figure 11.12 shows a distribution network that is a tree. Each edge is labeled by the amount of signal degradation that takes place when a signal flows between the corresponding parent and child. The units of degradation are assumed to be additive. That is, when a signal flows from node p to node v in Figure 11.12, the degradation is 5; the degradation from node q to node x is 3. When a signal booster is placed at node r, the strength of the signal that arrives at r is three units less than that of the signal that leaves source p; however, the signal that leaves r has the same strength as the signal that left p. Therefore, the signal that arrives at v has degraded by two units relative to the signal at the source; and the signal that arrives at z is four units weaker than the signal that left p. Without the booster at r, the arriving signal at z will be seven units weaker than the signal that left p.

Solution Strategy

Let $degradeFromParent(i)$ denote the degradation between node i and its parent. Therefore, in Figure 11.12, $degradeFromParent(w) = 2$, $degradeFromParent(p) = 0$, and $degradeFromParent(r) = 3$. Since signal boosters can be placed only at nodes of the distribution tree, the presence of a node i with $degradeFromParent(i) > tolerance$ implies that no placement of boosters can prevent signal degradation from exceeding *tolerance*. For example, if *tolerance* = 2, then there is no way to place signal boosters so that the degradation between p and r is $\leq$ *tolerance* = 2 in Figure 11.12.

For any node i let $degradeToLeaf(i)$ denote the maximum signal degradation from node i to any leaf in the subtree rooted at i. If i is a leaf node, then

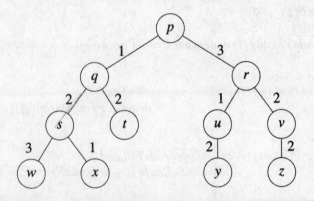

Figure 11.12 Tree distribution network

$degradeToLeaf(i) = 0$. For the example of Figure 11.12, $degradeToLeaf(i) = 0$ for $i \in \{w, x, t, y, z\}$. For the remaining nodes $degradeToLeaf(i)$ may be computed using the following equality:

$$degradeToLeaf(i) = \max_{j \text{ is a child of } i} \{degradeToLeaf(j) + degradeFromParent(j)\}$$

So $degradeToLeaf(s) = 3$. To use this equation, we must compute the $degradeToLeaf$ value of a node after computing that of its children. Therefore, we must traverse the tree so that we visit a node after we visit its children. We can compute the $degradeToLeaf$ value of a node when we visit it. This traversal order is a natural extension of postorder traversal to trees of degree (possibly) more than 2.

Suppose that during the computation of $degradeToLeaf$ as described above, we encounter a node i with a child j such that

$$degradeToLeaf(j) + degradeFromParent(j) > tolerance$$

If we do not place a booster at j, then the signal degradation from i to a leaf will exceed $tolerance$ even if a booster is placed at i. For example, in Figure 11.12, when computing $degradeToLeaf(q)$, we compute

$$degradeToLeaf(s) + degradeFromParent(s) = 5$$

If $tolerance = 3$, then placing a booster at q or at any of q's ancestors doesn't reduce signal degradation between q and its descendents. We need to place a booster at s. If a booster is placed at s, then $degradeToLeaf(q) = 3$.

```
degradeToLeaf(i) = 0;
for (each child j of i)
    if (degradeToLeaf(j) + degradeFromParent(j)) > tolerance)
    {
        place a booster at j;
        degradeToLeaf(i) = max{degradeToLeaf(i),
                                    degradeFromParent(j)};
    }
    else
        degradeToLeaf(i) = max{degradeToLeaf(i),
                                degradeToLeaf(j) + degradeFromParent(j)};
```

Figure 11.13 Pseudocode to place boosters and compute $degradeToLeaf$

Figure 11.13 gives the pseudocode to place boosters and compute $degradeToLeaf$.
Applying this computation method to the distribution tree of Figure 11.12 results in the placement of boosters at nodes r, s, and v (see Figure 11.14). The $degradeToLeaf$ values for nodes are given inside the node.

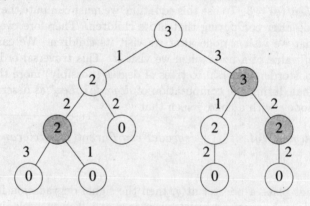

Signal boosters are at shaded nodes
Numbers inside nodes are $degradeToLeaf$ values

Figure 11.14 Distribution network with signal boosters

Theorem 11.1 *The procedure outlined above uses the minimum number of boosters.*

Proof The proof is by induction on the number n of nodes in the distribution tree. If $n = 1$, the theorem is trivially valid. Assume that the theorem is valid for $n \leq m$ where m is an arbitrary natural number. Let t be a tree with $n + 1$ nodes. Let X be the set of vertices at which the outlined procedure places boosters and let W be a minimum cardinality placement of boosters that satisfies the tolerance requirements. We need to show that $|X| = |W|$.

If $|X| = 0$, then $|X| = |W|$. If $|X| > 0$, then let z be the first vertex at which a booster is placed by the outlined procedure. Let t_z be the subtree of t rooted at z. Since $degradeToLeaf(z) + degradeFromParent(z) > tolerance$, W must contain at least one vertex u that is in t_z. If W contains more than one such u, then W cannot be of minimum cardinality because by placing boosters at $W - \{$all such $u\} + \{z\}$, we can satisfy the tolerance requirement. Hence W contains exactly one such u. Let $W' = W - \{u\}$. Let t' be the tree that results from the removal of t_z from t except z. We see that W' is a minimum cardinality booster placement for t' that satisfies the tolerance requirement. Also, $X' = X - \{z\}$ satisfies the tolerance requirement for t' and is the booster placement generated by our outlined procedure on the tree t'. Since the number of vertices in t' is less than $m + 1$, $|X'| = |W'|$. Hence $|X| = |X'| + 1 = |W'| + 1 = |W|$.   ∎

C++ Implementation

When no node of the distribution tree has more than two children, the distribution tree may be represented as a binary tree by using the class `linkedBinaryTree` (Program 11.9) and the struct `booster` (Program 11.12). The field `boosterHere` is used to differentiate between nodes at which a booster is placed and those where it is not. The `element` fields of our binary tree will be of type `booster`.

We can compute the $degradeToLeaf$ values for the nodes and the location of a minimum set of boosters by performing a postorder traversal of the binary distribution tree. During the visit step, we execute the code of Program 11.13. The code for `placeBoosters` assumes that `tolerance` is a global variable.

If t is a `linkedBinaryTree` whose `degradeFromParent` fields have been set to the degradation values and whose `boosterHere` fields have been set to `false`, then the invocation `t.postOrder(placeBoosters)` will reset the `degradeToLeaf` and `boosterHere` fields correctly. Since the complexity of `placeBoosters` is $\Theta(1)$, the invocation `t.postOrder(placeBoosters)` takes $O(n)$ time where n is the number of nodes in the distribution tree.

Binary Tree Representation of a Tree

When the distribution tree t contains nodes that have more than two children, we can still represent the tree as a binary tree. This time, for each node x of the tree t, we link its children into a chain using the `rightChild` fields of the children nodes. The `leftChild` field of x points to the first node in this chain. The `rightChild` field of x is used for the chain of x's siblings. Figure 11.15 shows a tree and its

```
struct booster
{
    int degradeToLeaf,              // degradation to leaf
        degradeFromParent;          // degradation from parent
    bool boosterHere;               // true iff booster here

    void output(ostream& out) const
    {out << boosterHere << ' ' << degradeToLeaf << ' '
        << degradeFromParent << ' ';}
};

// overload <<
ostream& operator<<(ostream& out, booster x)
    {x.output(out); return out;}
```

Program 11.12 The struct booster

binary tree representation. Solid lines represent left-child pointers, and right-child
pointers are shown as dotted lines.

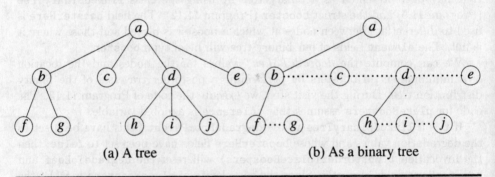

(a) A tree   (b) As a binary tree

Figure 11.15 A tree and its binary tree representation

When the binary tree representation of a tree is used, the invocation t.postOrder-
(placeBoosters) does not have the desired effect. The development of the new
function to compute degradeToLeaf and boosterHere is considered in Exercise 57.

```
void placeBoosters(binaryTreeNode<booster> *x)
{// Compute degradation at *x. Place booster(s) at children
 // of x if degradation exceeds tolerance.

   x->element.degradeToLeaf = 0;  // initialize degradation at x

   // compute degradation from left subtree of x and
   // place a booster at the left child of x if needed
   binaryTreeNode<booster> *y = x->leftChild;
   if (y != NULL)
   {// x has a nonempty left subtree
      int degradation = y->element.degradeToLeaf +
                        y->element.degradeFromParent;
      if (degradation > tolerance)
      {// place a booster at y
         y->element.boosterHere = true;
         x->element.degradeToLeaf = y->element.degradeFromParent;
      }
      else  // no booster needed at y
         x->element.degradeToLeaf = degradation;
   }

   // compute degradation from right subtree of x and
   // place a booster at the right child of x if needed
   y = x->rightChild;
   if (y != NULL)
   {// x has a nonempty right subtree
      int degradation = y->element.degradeToLeaf +
                        y->element.degradeFromParent;
      if (degradation > tolerance)
      {// place booster at y
         y->element.boosterHere = true;
         degradation = y->element.degradeFromParent;
      }
      if (x->element.degradeToLeaf < degradation)
         x->element.degradeToLeaf = degradation;
   }
}
```

Program 11.13 Place boosters and determine `degradeToLeaf` for binary distribution trees

11.9.2   Union-Find Problem

Problem Description

The union-find problem was introduced in Section 6.5.4. Basically, we begin with n elements numbered 1 through n; initially, each is in a class of its own, and we perform a sequence of find and combine operations. The operation find(the-Element) returns a unique characteristic of the class that theElement is in, and combine(a,b) combines the classes that contain the elements a and b. In Section 6.5.4 we saw that combine(a,b) is usually implemented by using the union operation unite(classA, classB) where classA = find(a), classB = find(b), and classA $\neq$ classB. The solution provided in Section 6.5.4 used chains and had a complexity $O(n + u \log u + f)$ where u is the number of union operations and f is the number of find operations performed. In this section we explore an alternative solution in which each set (or class) is represented as a tree.

Representing a Set as a Tree

Any set S may be represented as a tree with $|S|$ nodes, one node per element. Any element of S may be selected as the root element; any subset of the remaining elements could be the children of the root; any subset of the elements that remain could be the grandchildren of the root; and so on.

Figure 11.16 shows some sets represented as trees. Notice that each node that is not a root has a pointer to its parent in the tree. Our pointers go from a node to its parent because the find operation will require us to move up a tree. Neither the find nor union operations requires us to move down a tree.

We say that the elements 1, 2, 20, 30, and so on are in the set with root 20; the elements 11, 16, 25, and 28 are in the set with root 16; the element 15 is in the set with root 15; and the elements 26 and 32 are in the set with root 26 (or simply the set 26).

Solution Strategy

Our strategy to solve the union-find problem is to represent each set as a tree. For the find operation we use the element in the root as the set identifier. So find(3) returns the value 20 (see Figure 11.16); find(1) returns 20; and find(26) returns 26. Since each tree has a unique root, find(i) = find(j) iff i and j are in the same set. To find the set that contains theElement, we begin at the node for element theElement and move up the tree until we reach the root.

For the union operation we assume that the invocation unite(classA, classB) is done with classA and classB being the elements in the roots of two different trees (i.e., classA $\neq$ classB). To unite the two trees (or sets) of elements, we make one tree a subtree of the other. For instance, if classA = 16 and classB = 26 (Figure 11.16), the tree of Figure 11.17(a) results if classA is made a subtree of classB, whereas the result is Figure 11.17(b) if classB is made a subtree of classA.

Figure 11.16 Tree representation of disjoint sets

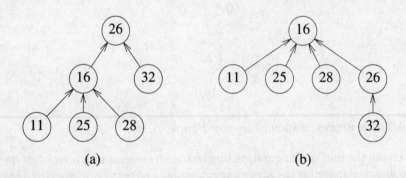

Figure 11.17 Union

C++ Implementation

The solution to the union-find problem is a good example of the use of simulated pointers. A linked representation of the trees is needed. Each node must have a **parent** field. Children fields are, however, not needed. We also have a need to make direct access to nodes. To find the set containing element 10, we need to determine which node represents the element 10 and then follow a sequence of **parent** pointers

to the root. This direct access is best obtained if the nodes are indexed 1 through
n (the number of elements) and if node *e* represents element *e*. Each `parent` field
gives the index of the parent node. Hence the `parent` fields are of type `int`.

Figure 11.18 represents the trees of Figure 11.16 using this representation. The
number inside a node is the value of its parent field. The number outside a node is
its index. This index is also the element it represents. The parent field for a root
node is set to 0. Since there is no node with index 0, a parent field of 0 is detected
as a link to no node (or a null link).

(a)   (b)

(c)

Figure 11.18 Representation of trees of Figure 11.16

To create the initial configuration in which each element is in a set of its own, we
need to allocate space for the array `parent` and set `parent[1:numberOfElements]`
to 0. This initialization is done by the function `initialize` (Program 11.14).

To find the set that contains `theElement`, we begin at node `theElement` and
follow `parent` pointers until we reach the root. For instance, if `theElement` = 4
and the status of the sets is as in Figure 11.16(a), we begin at 4. Following the
pointer `parent[4]` gets us to node 8, and `parent[8]` gets us to node 20 whose
`parent` is 0. Hence 20 is the root of the tree that contains element 4. The function
`find` of Program 11.14 implements this strategy. This function assumes that the
test 1 ≤ `theElement` ≤ `numberOfElements` (i.e., `theElement` is a valid element) is
performed externally.

The function `unite` of Program 11.14 performs a union. It assumes that the

```
void initialize(int numberOfElements)
{// Initialize numberOfElements trees, 1 element per set/class/tree.
   parent = new int[numberOfElements + 1];
   for (int e = 1; e <= numberOfElements; e++)
      parent[e] = 0;
}

int find(int theElement)
{// Return root of tree that contains theElement.
   while (parent[theElement] != 0)
      theElement = parent[theElement];   // move up one level
   return theElement;
}

void unite(int rootA, int rootB)
{// Combine trees with different roots rootA and rootB.
   parent[rootB] = rootA;
}
```

Program 11.14 Simple tree solution to the union-find problem

check rootA $\neq$ rootB is performed externally. rootB is always made a subtree of rootA.

Performance Analysis

The time complexity of the constructor is $O(\text{numberOfElements})$; the complexity of find(theElement) is $O(h)$ where h is the height of the tree that contains element theElement; and the complexity of unite(rootA, rootB) is $\Theta(1)$.

In a typical application of the union-find problem, many union and find operations are performed. Furthermore, in typical applications we do not care how much time an individual operation takes; we are concerned with the time taken for all operations collectively. Assume that u unions and f finds are to be performed. Since each union is necessarily preceded by two finds (these finds determine the roots of the trees to be united), we may assume that $f > u$. Each union takes $\Theta(1)$ time. The time for each find depends on the height of the trees that get created. In the worst case a tree with m elements can have a height of m. This worst case happens, for example, when the following sequence of unions is performed:

$$unite(2, 1), unite(3, 2), unite(4, 3), unite(5, 4), \cdots$$

Hence each find can take as much as $\Theta(q)$ time where q is the number of unions that have been performed before the find. Therefore, the time for a sequence of operations becomes $O(fu)$. The worst-case time needed for a sequence of operations can be reduced to almost $O(f+u) = O(f)$ by enhancing the union and find methods as described next.

Enhancing the Union Function

We can enhance the performance of the union-find algorithms by using either the **weight** or the **height** rule when performing a union of the trees with roots i and j.

Definition 11.3 [Weight rule] *If the number of nodes in the tree with root i is less than the number in the tree with root j, then make i a child of j; otherwise, make j a child of i.* ∎

Definition 11.4 [Height rule] *If the height of tree i is less than that of tree j, then make j the parent of i; otherwise, make i the parent of j.* ∎

If we perform a union on the trees of Figure 11.16 (a) and (b), then the tree with root 16 becomes a subtree of the tree with root 20 regardless of whether the weight or the height rule is used. When we perform a union on the trees of Figure 11.19 (a) and (b), the tree with root 16 becomes a subtree of the tree with root 20 in case the weight rule is used. However, when the height rule is used, the tree with root 20 becomes a subtree of the one with root 16.

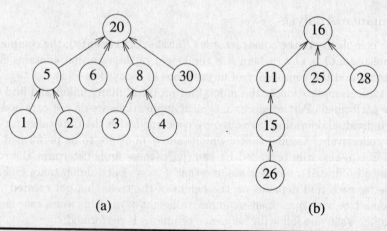

(a)   (b)

Figure 11.19 Two sample trees

To incorporate the weight rule into the function for a union, we add a Boolean field **root** to each node. The **root** field of a node is **true** iff the node is currently a root node. The **parent** field of each root node keeps a count of the total number of nodes in the tree. For the trees of Figure 11.16, we have **node[i].root = true** iff i = 20, 16, 15, or 26. Also, **node[i].parent** = 9, 4, 1, and 2 for i = 20, 16, 15, and 26, respectively. The remaining **parent** fields are unchanged.

To implement the weighting rule, we define the struct **unionFindNode** that defines the data type of the nodes in a tree. Program 11.15 gives the code for this struct.

```
struct unionFindNode
{
    int parent;   // if true then tree weight
                  // otherwise pointer to parent in tree
    bool root;    // true iff root

    unionFindNode()
        {parent = 1; root = true;}
};
```

Program 11.15 Struct used when implementing the weighting rule

The **initialize**, **find** and **unite** functions now take the form given in Program 11.16.

The time required to perform a union has increased somewhat but is still bounded by a constant; it is $\Theta(1)$. Lemma 11.1 determines the maximum time to perform a find.

Lemma 11.1 [Weight rule lemma] *Assume that we start with singleton sets and perform unions, using the weight rule (as in Program 11.16). Let t be a tree with p nodes created in this way. The height of t is at most $\lfloor \log_2 p \rfloor + 1$.*

Proof The lemma is clearly true for $p = 1$. Assume it is true for all trees with i nodes, $i \leq p - 1$. We will show that it is also true for $i = p$. Consider the last union operation, $union(k, j)$, performed to create tree t. Let m be the number of nodes in tree j and let $p - m$ be the number of nodes in k. Without loss of generality, we may assume $1 \leq m \leq p/2$. So j is made a subtree of tree k. Therefore, the height of t either is the same as that of k or is one more than that of j. If the former is the case, then the height of t is $\leq \lfloor \log_2(p - m) \rfloor + 1 \leq \lfloor \log_2 p \rfloor + 1$. If the latter is the case then the height of t is $\leq \lfloor \log_2 m \rfloor + 2 \leq \lfloor \log_2 p/2 \rfloor + 2 \leq \lfloor \log_2 p \rfloor + 1$. ∎

If we start with singleton sets and perform an intermixed sequence of u unions and f finds, no set will have more than $u + 1$ elements in it. From Lemma 11.1 it follows that when the weight rule is used, the cost of the sequence of union and find operations (excluding the initialization time) is $O(u + f \log u) = O(f \log u)$ (since we assume $f > u$).

```
void initialize(int numberOfElements)
{// Initialize numberOfElements trees, 1 element per set/class/tree.
   node = new unionFindNode[numberOfElements+1];
}

int find(int theElement)
{// Return root of tree containing theElement.
   while (!node[theElement].root)
      theElement = node[theElement].parent;   // move up one level
   return theElement;
}

void unite(int rootA, int rootB)
{// Combine trees with different roots rootA and rootB.
 // Use the weighting rule.
   if (node[rootA].parent < node[rootB].parent)
   {// rootA becomes subtree of rootB
      node[rootB].parent += node[rootA].parent;
      node[rootA].root = false;
      node[rootA].parent = rootB;
   }
   else
   {// rootB becomes subtree of rootA
      node[rootA].parent += node[rootB].parent;
      node[rootB].root = false;
      node[rootB].parent = rootA;
   }
}
```

Program 11.16 Functions using the weighting rule

When the weight rule is replaced by the height rule in Program 11.16, the bound of Lemma 11.1 still governs the height of the resulting trees. Exercises 60, 61, and 62 explore the use of the height rule.

Enhancing the Find Function

Further improvement in the worst-case performance is possible by modifying the find function of Program 11.14 so as to reduce the length of the path from the find element e to the root. This reduction in path length is obtained by using a process called **path compression**, which we can do in at least three different ways—path compaction, path splitting, and path halving.

In **path compaction** we change the pointers in all nodes on the path from the element being searched to the root so that these nodes point directly to the root. As an example, consider the tree of Figure 11.20. When we perform a `find(10)`, the nodes 10, 15, and 3 are determined to be on the path from 10 to the root. Their parent fields are changed to 2, and the tree of Figure 11.21 is obtained. (Since node 3 already points to 2, its field doesn't have to be changed; when writing the program, it turns out to be easier to include this node in the set of nodes whose parent field is to be changed.)

Figure 11.20 Sample tree

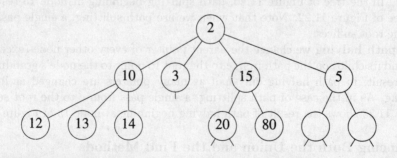

Figure 11.21 Path compaction

Although path compaction increases the time needed for an individual find, it reduces the cost of future finds. For instance, finding the elements in the subtrees of 10 and 15 is quicker in the compacted tree of Figure 11.21. Program 11.17 implements the compaction rule.

```
int find(int theElement)
{// Return root of tree containing theElement.
 // Compact path from theElement to root.

   // theRoot will eventually be the root of the tree
   int theRoot = theElement;
   while (!node[theRoot].root)
      theRoot = node[theRoot].parent;

   // compact pathe from theElement to theRoot
   int currentNode = theElement;  // start at theElement
   while (currentNode != theRoot)
   {
      int parentNode = node[currentNode].parent;
      node[currentNode].parent = theRoot;  // move to level 2
      currentNode = parentNode;            // moves to old parent
   }

   return theRoot;
}
```

Program 11.17 Find an element using path compaction

In **path splitting** we change the parent pointer in each node (except the root and its child) on the path from e to the root to point to the node's original grandparent. In the tree of Figure 11.20, path splitting beginning at node 13 results in the tree of Figure 11.22. Note that when we use path splitting, a single pass from e to the root suffices.

In **path halving** we change the parent pointer of every other node (except the root and its child) on the path from e to the root to point to the node's grandparent. As a result, in path halving only half as many pointers are changed as in path splitting. As in the case of path splitting, a single pass from e to the root suffices. Figure 11.23 shows the result of path halving beginning at node 13 of Figure 11.20.

Enhancing Both the Union and the Find Methods

Path compression may change the height of a tree, but not its weight. Determining the new tree height following path compression requires considerable effort. So while it is relatively easy to use any of the path-compression schemes in conjunction

Figure 11.22 Path splitting

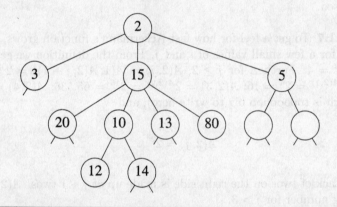

Figure 11.23 Path halving

with the weight rule, using path compression in conjunction with the height rule is difficult. We can, however, modify the height rule so as to use the tree height under the assumption that no path compression is done. With this modification the *modified tree height* changes only when two trees of equal modified height are united.

Worst-Case Complexity of Enhanced Union-Find Solution

When unions are done with either the weight or the modified height rule and finds are done with any of the three path-compression methods, the time needed to process an intermixed sequence of unions and finds is almost linear in the number of unions and finds. Not only is the complexity analysis exceptionally difficult, but stating the result is also quite difficult.

We first define the explosively growing Ackermann's function $A(i, j)$ and its inverse $\alpha(p, q)$ (which grows at a snail's pace) as follows:

$$A(i, j) = \begin{cases} 2^j & i = 1 \text{ and } j \geq 1 \\ A(i-1, 2) & i \geq 2 \text{ and } j = 1 \\ A(i-1, A(i, j-1)) & i, j \geq 2 \end{cases}$$

$$\alpha(p, q) = \min\{z \geq 1 | A(z, \lfloor p/q \rfloor) > \log_2 q\}, \ p \geq q \geq 1$$

Exercise 67 shows that $A(i, j)$ is an increasing function of i and j; that is, $A(i, j) > A(i-1, j)$, and $A(i, j) > A(i, j-1)$. Actually, $A(i, j)$ is a very rapidly growing function of i and j. Consequently, its inverse α grows very slowly as p and q are increased.

Example 11.7 To get a feel for how fast Ackermann's function grows, let us evaluate $A(i, j)$ for a few small values of i and j. From the definition we get $A(2, 1) = A(1, 2) = 2^2 = 4$. Further, for $j \geq 2$, $A(2, j) = A(1, A(2, j-1)) = 2^{A(2,j-1)}$. So $A(2, 2) = 2^{A(2,1)} = 2^4 = 16$; $A(2, 3) = 2^{A(2,2)} = 2^{16} = 65,536$; $A(2, 4) = 2^{A(2,3)} = 2^{65,536}$ (which is toooooooo big to write here); and

$$A(2, j) = 2^{2^{2^{2^{\cdot^{\cdot^{-}}}}}}$$

where the stack of twos on the right side is made up of $j + 1$ twos. $A(2, j)$ is quite a frightening number for $j > 3$.

$A(3, 1) = A(2, 2) = 16$ is not a number to be frightened by. But $A(4, 1) = A(3, 2) = A(2, A(3, 1)) = A(2, 16)$. If $A(2, 4)$ is toooooooo big, then how big is $A(4, 1) = A(2, 16)$?

The intent of this example is not to impress you with how fast $A(i, j)$ grows, but with how slow $\alpha(p, q)$ grows. When $q = 65,535 = 2^{16} - 1$, $\log q < 16$. Since $A(3, 1) = 16$, $\alpha(65, 535, 65, 535) = 3$ and $\alpha(p, 65, 535) \leq 3$ for $p \geq 65,535$. $\alpha(65, 536, 65, 536) = 4$ and $\alpha(p, 65, 536) \leq 4$ for $p \geq 65,536$. $\alpha(q, q)$ does not become 5 until $q = 2^{A(4,1)}$, an amazingly large number. Therefore, $\alpha(p, q)$, $p \geq q$, does not become 5 until $q = 2^{A(4,1)}$.

In the complexity analysis of the enhanced union-find algorithms, q is the number of elements, and p is the sum of the number of finds and the number of elements. Therefore, for all practical purposes, we can assume that $\alpha(p, q) \leq 4$. ∎

Theorem 11.2 [Tarjan and Van Leeuwen] *Let $T(f, u)$ be the maximum time required to process any intermixed sequence of f finds and u unions. Assume that $u \geq n/2$, where n is the number of elements.. Then*

$$k_1(n + f\alpha(f + n, n)) \leq T(f, u) \leq k_2(n + f\alpha(f + n, n))$$

for some positive constants k_1 and k_2. These bounds apply when we start with singleton sets and use either the weight or height rule for unions and any one of the three path-compression methods for a find.

The requirement that $u \geq n/2$ in Theorem 11.2 is really not significant because when $u < n/2$, some elements are not involved in union operations. These elements remain in singleton sets throughout the sequence of union and find operations, and we can eliminate them from consideration because find operations that involve these elements can be done in $O(1)$ time each. Even though the function $\alpha(f + n, n)$ is ≤ 4 for all practical purposes, the function remains a very slowly growing function and the complexity of a sequence of union and find operations is not linear in the number of elements and operations.

We have two choices for enhancing the union operation, and three for enhancing the union operation. In all, we have six possibilities for an implementation of a program to solve the union-find problem in the time bound given in Theorem 11.2. We can determine which of these six possibilities works best by experiment.

EXERCISES

53. You have a distribution network that is a full binary tree whose height is 4. The nodes are numbered 1–15 as in Figure 11.6 and $degradeFromParent(2 : 15) = [4, 3, 6, 2, 5, 2, 2, 4, 6, 4, 5, 3, 6, 2]$.

    (a) Draw the distribution network with each edge labeled by its *degradeFromParent* value (see Figure 11.12).

    (b) Label each node of your distribution tree by its *degradeToLeaf* value.

    (c) Use the method of Section 11.9.1 to determine the minimum number of signal boosters needed when *tolerance* = 8. Label each node and edge as in Figure 11.14.

54. Do Exercise 53 with $degradeFromParent(2 : 15) = [2, 4, 5, 6, 3, 4, 2, 6, 3, 1, 3, 2, 6, 3]$ and *tolerance* = 11.

55. (a) Draw the binary tree representations of the trees of Figures 11.16(a) and (b), Figures 11.17(a) and (b), and Figures 11.19(a) and (b).

    (b) Draw the binary tree representation of the tree of Figure 11.12. (Note that the binary tree representation of this tree is different from that obtained by using the left-child pointer of a node to point to one child and the right-child pointer to point to the other.)

56. A **forest** is a collection of zero or more trees. In the binary tree representation of a tree, the root has no right child. We may use this observation to arrive at a binary tree representation for a forest with m trees. First we obtain the binary tree representation of each tree in the forest. Next the ith tree is made the right subtree of the $(i-1)$th, $2 \le i \le m$. Draw the binary tree representation of the four-tree forest of Figure 11.16, the two-tree forest of Figure 11.17, and the two-tree forest of Figure 11.19.

57. Let t be an instance of `linkedBinaryTree`. Assume that t is the binary tree representation of a distribution tree (see Figure 11.15). Develop a program to compute the `degradeToLeaf` and `boosterHere` values of each node in t. Your program should also output these values by invoking `t.postOrderOutput()`. Use suitable distribution trees to test your program.

58. Suppose we start with n sets, each containing a distinct element.

   (a) Show that if u unions are peformed, then no set contains more than $u+1$ elements.

   (b) Show that at most $n-1$ unions can be performed before the number of sets becomes 1.

   (c) Show that if fewer than $\lceil n/2 \rceil$ unions are performed, then at least one set with a single element in it remains.

   (d) Show that if u unions are performed, then at least $\max\{n-2u, 0\}$ singleton sets remain.

59. Give an example of a sequence of unions that start with singleton sets and create trees whose height equals the upper bound given in Lemma 11.1. Assume that each union is performed with the weight rule.

60. Write a version of the method **union** (Program 11.14) that uses the height rule instead of the weight rule.

61. Prove Lemma 11.1 for the case when the height rule is used instead of the weight rule.

62. Give an example of a sequence of unions that start with singleton sets and create trees whose height equals the upper bound given in Lemma 11.1. Assume that each union is performed with the height rule.

63. Compare the average performance of the simple union/find solution of Programs 11.14 and the solution tht uses the weight rule as well as path compaction (Programs 11.16 and 11.17). Do this comparison for different values of n. For each value of n, generate a random sequence of pairs (i, j). Replace each pair by two finds (one for i and the other for j). If the two are in different sets, then a union is to be performed. Repeat the experiment with

many different random sequences. Measure the total time taken over these sequences. It is left to you to take this basic description of the experiment and plan a meaningful experiment to compare the average performance of the two sets of programs. Write a report that describes your experiment and your conclusions. Include program listings, a table of average times, and graphs in your report.

64. Write code for the find operation that uses path halving instead of path compaction (as used in Program 11.17).

65. Write code for the find operation that uses path splitting instead of path compaction (as used in Program 11.17).

66. Program the six ways in which you can achieve the performance stated in Theorem 11.2. Conduct experiments to evaluate these six solutions to determine which performs best.

67. Show that

(a) $A(i,j) > A(i-1,j)$ for $i > 1$ and $j \geq 1$.

(b) $A(i,j) > A(i,j-1)$ for $i \geq 1$ and $j > 1$.

(c) $\alpha(r,q) \geq \alpha(p,q)$ for $r > p \geq q \geq 1$.

11.10   REFERENCES AND SELECTED READINGS

The book *The Art of Computer Programming: Fundamental Algorithms*, Volume 1, Third Edition, by D. Knuth, Addison-Wesley, Reading, MA, 1997, is a good reference for material on binary trees. The problem of placing boosters is studied in the following papers: "Deleting Vertices in Dags to Bound Path Lengths" by D. Paik,, S. Reddy, and S. Sahni, *IEEE Transactions on Computers*, 43, 9, 1994, 1091–1096, and "Heuristics for the Placement of Flip-Flops in Partial Scan Designs and for the Placement of Signal Boosters in Lossy Circuits" by D. Paik, S. Reddy, and S. Sahni, *Sixth International Conference on VLSI Design*, 1993, 45–50.

A complete analysis of the tree representations for the inline equivalence problem appears in the paper "Worst Case Analysis of Set Union Algorithms" by R. Tarjan and J. Leeuwen, *Journal of the ACM*, 31, 2, 1984, 245–281.

The Web site for this book develops some tree varieties not covered in the text—pairing heaps, interval heaps, tree structures for double-ended priority queues, tries, and suffix trees. You should look at these only after you have read Chapters 12 through 15.

CHAPTER 12

PRIORITY QUEUES

BIRD'S-EYE VIEW

Unlike the queues of Chapter 9, which are FIFO structures, the order of deletion from a priority queue is determined by the element priority. Elements are removed/deleted either in increasing or decreasing order of priority rather than in the order in which they arrived in the queue.

A priority queue is efficiently implemented with the heap data structure, which is a complete binary tree that is most efficiently stored by using the array representation described in Section 11.4.1. Linked data structures suitable for the implementation of a priority queue include height- and weight-biased leftist trees. This chapter covers both heaps and leftist trees. An additional priority queue data structure—pairing heaps—is developed in the Web site. The Web site also includes data structures for double-ended priority queues that allow you to delete both in increasing and in decreasing order of priority. The C++ STL class `priority_queue` implements a priority queue as a heap.

In the applications section at the end of the chapter, we use heaps to develop an $O(n \log n)$ sorting method called heap sort. The sort methods of Chapter 2 take $O(n^2)$ to sort n elements. Even though the bin sort and radix sort methods of Chapter 6 run in $O(n)$ time, they are limited to elements with keys in an appropriate range. So heap sort is the first general-purpose sort we are seeing that has a complexity better than $O(n^2)$. Chapter 18 discusses other sort methods with this complexity. From the asymptotic-complexity point of view, heap sort is an optimal sorting method because we can show that every general-purpose sorting method that relies on comparing pairs of elements has a complexity that is $\Omega(n \log n)$ (Section 18.4.2).

The other applications considered in this chapter are machine scheduling and the generation of Huffman codes. The machine-scheduling application allows us to introduce the NP-hard class of problems. This class includes problems for which no polynomial-time algorithms are known. As noted in Chapter 3, for large instances only polynomial-time algorithms are practical. As a result, NP-hard problems are often solved by approximation algorithms or heuristics that complete in a reasonable amount of computer time, but do not guarantee to find the best answer. For the machine-scheduling application, we use the heap data structure to obtain an efficient implementation of a much-studied machine-scheduling approximation algorithm.

12.1   DEFINITION AND APPLICATIONS

A **priority queue** is a collection of zero or more elements. Each element has a priority or value. The operations performed on a priority queue are (1) find an element, (2) insert a new element, and (3) remove (or delete) an element. The functions that correspond to the find, insert, and remove operations of a priority queue are, respectively, named *top*, *push* and *pop*. In a **min priority queue**, the find operation finds the element with minimum priority, and the remove operation removes this element. In a **max priority queue**, the find operation finds the element with maximum priority, and the remove operation removes this element. The elements in a priority queue need not have distinct priorities. The find and remove operations may break ties in any manner.

Example 12.1 Suppose that we are selling the services of a machine over a fixed period of time (say, a day or a month). Although each user pays a fixed amount per use, the time needed by each user is different. To maximize the earning from this machine (under the assumption that the machine is not to be kept idle unless no user is available), we maintain a min priority queue of all users waiting for the machine. The priority of a user is the amount of time he/she needs. When a new user requests the machine, his/her request is put into the priority queue. Whenever the machine becomes available, the user with the smallest time requirement (i.e., priority) is selected.

If each user needs the same amount of time on the machine but users are willing to pay different amounts for the service, then we can use a priority queue in which the element priorities are the amount of payment. Whenever the machine becomes available, the user paying the most is selected. This selection requires a max priority queue. ∎

Example 12.2 [Event List] The machine shop simulation problem was introduced in Section 9.5.4. The operations performed on the event queue are (1) find the machine with minimum finish time and (2) change the finish time of this machine. Suppose we set up a min priority queue in which each element represents a machine, and an element's priority is the finish time of the machine it represents. The *top* operation of a min priority queue gives us the machine with the smallest finish time. To change a machine's finish time, we may first do a *top* and a *pop*, and then *push* the removed element/machine with its priority changed to the new finish time. Actually, for event list applications it is desirable for priority queues to include an additional operation to change the priority of the top element. Such an operation would collapse the three step process to change a machine's finish time (*top* followed by *pop* followed by *push*) into one.

Max priority queues may also be used in the machine shop simulation problem. In the simulation programs of Section 9.5.4, each machine served its set of waiting jobs in a first-come-first-served manner. Therefore, we used a FIFO queue at each machine. If the service discipline is changed to "when a machine is ready for a new job, it selects the waiting job with maximum priority," we need a max priority queue at each machine. The operations that are to be performed at each machine are (1) when a new job arrives at the machine, it is inserted into the max priority queue for that machine, and (2) when a machine is ready to work on a new job, a job with maximum priority is removed from its queue and made active.

When the service discipline at each machine is changed as above, the simulation problem of Section 9.5.4 requires a min priority queue for the event list and a max priority queue at each machine.   ∎

In this chapter we develop efficient representations for priority queues. Since the implementations for min and max priority queues are very similar, we explicitly develop only those for max priority queues.

12.2   THE ABSTRACT DATA TYPE

The abstract data type specification for a max priority queue is given in ADT 12.1. The specification for a min priority queue is the same except that *top* and *pop*, respectively, find and remove the element with minimum priority.

AbstractDataType *maxPriorityQueue*
{
    instances
        finite collection of elements, each has a priority

    operations
    empty() : return **true** iff the queue is empty

      size() : return number of elements in the queue

       top() : return element with maximum priority

      pop() : remove the element with largest priority from the queue;

    push(x) : insert the element x into the queue
}

ADT 12.1 Abstract data type specification of a max priority queue

Program 12.1 gives the C++ abstract class that corresponds to the ADT *maxPriorityQueue*. We make the assumption that when two elements of type T are compared using relational operators such as < and <= the element priorities are compared.

```
template<class T>
class maxPriorityQueue
{
    public:
        virtual ~maxPriorityQueue() {}
        virtual bool empty() const = 0;
                    // return true iff queue is empty
        virtual int size() const = 0;
                    // return number of elements in queue
        virtual const T& top() = 0;
                    // return reference to the max element
        virtual void pop() = 0;
                    // remove the top element
        virtual void push(const T& theElement) = 0;
                    // add theElement to the queue
};
```

Program 12.1 The abstract class `maxPriorityQueue`

12.3   LINEAR LISTS

The simplest way to represent a max priority queue is as an unordered linear list. Suppose that we have a priority queue with n elements. If Equation 5.1 is used, new elements are most easily inserted at the right end of this list. Hence the insert or *push* time is $\Theta(1)$. A *pop* operation requires a search for the element with largest priority followed by the removal of this element. Since it takes $\Theta(n)$ time to find the largest element in an n-element unordered list, the removal time is $\Theta(n)$. If a chain is used, *push*s can be performed at the front of the chain in $\Theta(1)$ time. Each *pop* takes $\Theta(n)$ time.

An alternative is to use an ordered linear list. The elements are in nondecreasing order when we use Equation 5.1 and in nonincreasing order when we use an ordered chain. The *pop* time for each representation is $\Theta(1)$, and the *push* time is $O(n)$.

EXERCISES

1. Develop a C++ class for the ADT *maxPriorityQueue*, using an array linear list (see Section 5.3). The *push* time should be $\Theta(1)$, and the *top* and *pop* times should be $O(n)$, where n is the number of elements in the priority queue.

2. Do Exercise 1 using a chain (i.e., use the class **chain** of Section 6.1).

3. Do Exercise 1 using a sorted array linear list. This time the *push* time should be $O(n)$, and the *top* and *pop* times should be $\Theta(1)$.

4. Do Exercise 1 using a sorted chain. The *push* time should be $O(n)$, and the *top* and *pop* times should be $\Theta(1)$.

5. Suppose that the priorities are integers in the range 1 through maxPriority where maxPriority is a small constant such as 3 or 4. Write a C++ class that implements a max priority queue using an array priority[] of FIFO queues; the queue priority[i] holds all elements whose priority is i. Assume that the priority of an element may be determined by typecasting the element to int. The class constructor should require that the value of maxPriority be specified, and the complexity of each ADT operation should be $\Theta(1)$ (exclusive of the time spent resizing arrays). Test your code.

12.4 HEAPS

12.4.1 Definitions

Definition 12.1 *A* **max tree** *(**min tree***) is a tree in which the value in each node is greater (less) than or equal to those in its children (if any).* ∎

Some max trees appear in Figure 12.1, and some min trees appear in Figure 12.2. Although these examples are all binary trees, it is not necessary for a max tree to be binary. Nodes of a max or min tree may have an arbitrary number of children.

(a)   (b)   (c)

Figure 12.1 Max trees

Definition 12.2 *A* **max heap** *(**min heap***) is a max (min) tree that is also a complete binary tree.* ∎

The max tree of Figure 12.1(b) is not a max heap because it is not a complete binary tree. The other two max trees of Figure 12.1 are complete binary trees, so they are max heaps. The min tree of Figure 12.2(b) is not a min heap because it is not a complete binary tree. The other two min trees of Figure 12.2 are complete binary trees; therefore, these two min trees are min heaps.

Figure 12.2 Min trees

Since a heap is a complete binary tree, a heap can be efficiently represented in a one-dimensional array by using the array scheme described in Section 11.4.1. We can use Property 11.4 to move from a node in the heap to its parent or to one of its children. Our subsequent discussion of heaps will refer to nodes in a heap by their position in the array representation. The position of the root is 1, that of its left child is 2, the root's right child is at 3, and so on. Also, note that since a heap is a complete binary tree, a heap with n elements has height $\lceil \log_2(n+1) \rceil$. Consequently, if we can do the *pop* and *push* operations in time $O(height)$, then these operations will have complexity $O(\log n)$.

12.4.2   Insertion into a Max Heap

Figure 12.3(a) shows a max heap with five elements. When an element is added to this heap, the resulting six-element heap must have the structure shown in Figure 12.3(b) because a heap is a complete binary tree. The insertion can be completed by placing the new element into the new node and then bubbling the new element up the tree (along the path from the new node to the root) until the new element has a parent whose priority is $\geq$ that of the new element.

If the element to be inserted has value 1, it may be inserted as the left child of 2. If instead the value of the new element is 5, the element cannot be inserted as the left child of 2 (as otherwise, we will violate the max tree property). Therefore, the 2 is moved down to its left child (Figure 12.3(c)) (equivalently, 5 is bubbled up one node), and we determine whether placing the 5 at the old position of 2 results in a max heap. Since the parent element 20 is at least as large as the element 5 being inserted, we can insert the new element at the position shown in Figure 12.3(c). Next suppose that the new element has value 21, rather than 5. In this case the 2 moves down to its left child as in Figure 12.3(c). The 21 cannot be inserted into the old position occupied by the 2, as the parent 20 of this position is smaller than 21. Hence the 20 is moved down to its right child, and the 21 is inserted in the root of the heap (Figure 12.3(d)).

The insertion strategy just outlined makes a single bubbling pass from a leaf

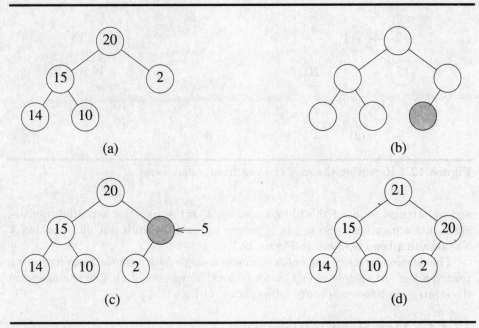

Figure 12.3 Insertion into a max heap

toward the root. At each level we do $\Theta(1)$ work, so we should be able to implement the strategy to have complexity $O(height) = O(\log n)$.

12.4.3   Deletion from a Max Heap

When an element is to be removed from a max heap, it is taken from the root of the heap. For instance, a removal from the max heap of Figure 12.3(d) results in the deletion of the element 21. Since the resulting max heap has only five elements, the binary tree of Figure 12.3(d) needs to be *reheapified* (i.e., restructured to correspond to a complete binary tree, which is a min tree with five elements). To do this reheapification, we remove the element in position 6, that is, the element 2. Now we have the right structure (Figure 12.4(a)), but the root is vacant, and the element 2 is not in the heap. If the 2 is put into the root, the resulting binary tree is not a max tree. The larger of the two children of the root (i.e., the element 20) is moved into the root, thereby creating a vacancy in position 3. Since this position has no children, the 2 may be put here. Figure 12.3(a) shows the resulting max heap.

Now suppose we wish to remove 20. Following this removal the heap has the binary tree structure shown in Figure 12.4(b). To get this structure, the 10 is removed from position 5. If we put the 10 into the root, the result is not a max heap. The larger of the two children of the root (15 and 2) is moved to the root,

(a)   (b)   (c)

Figure 12.4 Removing the max element from a max heap

and we attempt to insert the 10 into position 2. If the 10 is put here, the result is, again, not a max heap. So the 14 is moved up, and the 10 is put into position 4. The resulting heap is shown in Figure 12.4(c).

The deletion strategy just outlined makes a single pass from the heap root down toward a leaf. At each level $\Theta(1)$ work is done, so we should be able to implement the strategy to have complexity $O(height) = O(\log n)$.

12.4.4   Max Heap Initialization

In several max heap applications, including the event list of the machine shop scheduling problem of Example 12.2, we begin with a heap that contains $n > 0$ elements. We can construct this initial nonempty heap by performing n inserts into an initially empty heap. The total time taken by these n inserts is $O(n \log n)$. We may initialize the heap in $\Theta(n)$ time by using a different strategy.

Suppose we begin with an array a of n elements. Assume that $n = 10$ and the priority of the elements in a[1:10] is [20, 12, 35, 15, 10, 80, 30, 17, 2, 1]. This array may be interpreted as representing a complete binary tree as shown in Figure 12.5(a). This complete binary tree is not a max heap.

To *heapify* (i.e., make into a max heap) the complete binary tree of Figure 12.5(a), we begin with the last element that has a child (i.e., 10). This element is at position $i = \lfloor n/2 \rfloor$ of the array. If the subtree that is rooted at this position is a max heap, then no work is done here. If this subtree is not a max heap, then we adjust the subtree so that it is a heap. Following this adjustment, we examine the subtree whose root is at $i - 1$, then $i - 2$, and so on until we have examined the root of the entire binary tree, which is at position 1.

Let us try this process on the binary tree of Figure 12.5(a). Initially, $i = 5$. The subtree with root at i is a max heap, as $10 > 1$. Next we examine the subtree rooted at position 4. This subtree is not a max heap, as $15 < 17$. To convert this subtree into a max heap, the 15 and 17 are interchanged to get the tree of Figure 12.5(b). The next subtree examined has its root at position 3. To make this subtree into a max heap, we interchange the 80 and 35. Next we examine the subtree with its

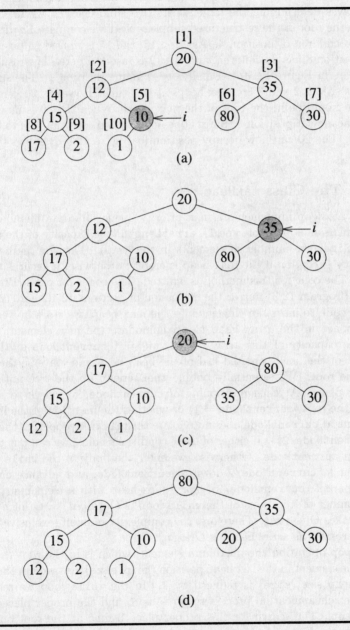

Figure 12.5 Initializing a max heap

root at position 2. From the way the restructuring progresses, the subtrees of this element are guaranteed to be max heaps. So restructuring this subtree into a max heap involves determining the larger of its two children, 17. As $12 < 17$, the 17 should be the root of the restructured subtree. Next we compare 12 with the larger of the two children of position 4. As $12 < 15$, the 15 is moved to position 4. The vacant position 8 has no children, and the 12 is inserted here. The resulting binary tree appears in Figure 12.5(c). Finally, we examine position 1. The subtrees with roots at positions 2 and 3 are max heaps at this time. However, $20 < \max\{17, 80\}$. So the 80 should be in the root of the max heap. When the 80 is moved there, it leaves a vacancy at position 3. Since $20 < \max\{35, 30\}$, position 3 is to be occupied by the 35. The 20 can now occupy position 6. Figure 12.5(d) shows the resulting max heap.

12.4.5   The Class maxHeap

The class maxHeap implements a max priority queue. Its data members are heap (a one-dimensional array of type T), arrayLength (the capacity of the array heap) and heapSize (the number of elements in the heap). The top method throws a queueEmpty exception if the max heap is empty; otherwise, it returns the element heap[1]. The code for this method is omitted. The codes for push (Program 12.2) and pop (Program 12.3) mirror the discussion of Sections 12.4.2 and 12.4.3.

In the code to insert an element into the max heap, we start by verifying that we have space in the array heap to accommodate the new element. If not, we double the capacity of this array. Next, we start currentNode at the position, heapSize, of the newly created leaf of the heap heap and traverse the path from here to the root. We essentially bubble theElement up the tree until it reaches its proper place. At each positioning of currentNode, we check to see whether we are at the root (currentNode $=1$) or whether the insertion of the new element theElement at currentNode does not violate the max tree property (theElement $\leq$ heap[currentNode/2]). If either of these conditions holds, we can put theElement at position currentNode. Otherwise, we enter the body of the while loop, move the element at currentNode/2 down to currentNode, and advance currentNode up to its parent (currentNode/2). For a max heap with n elements (i.e., size $= n$), the number of iterations of the while loop is $O(height) = O(\log n)$, and each iteration takes $\Theta(1)$ time. Therefore, the complexity of push (exclusive of the time needed to resize the array heap) is $O(\log n)$.

For a pop operation the maximum element, which is in the root (heap[1]), is deleted; the element in the last heap position (heap[size]) is saved in lastElement; and the heap size (size) is reduced by 1. In the while loop we reheapify the array. The reheapification process requires us to find the proper place to reinsert lastElement. The search for this proper place begins at the root and proceeds down the heap. For an n-element heap, the number of iterations of the while loop is $O(\log n)$, and each iteration takes $\Theta(1)$ time. Therefore, the overall complexity of pop is $O(\log n)$. Notice that the code works correctly even when the size of the

```
template<class T>
void maxHeap<T>::push(const T& theElement)
{// Add theElement to heap.

   // increase array length if necessary
   if (heapSize == arrayLength - 1)
   {// double array length
      changeLength1D(heap, arrayLength, 2 * arrayLength);
      arrayLength *= 2;
   }

   // find place for theElement
   // currentNode starts at new leaf and moves up tree
   int currentNode = ++heapSize;
   while (currentNode != 1 && heap[currentNode / 2] < theElement)
   {
      // cannot put theElement in heap[currentNode]
      heap[currentNode] = heap[currentNode / 2]; // move element down
      currentNode /= 2;                          // move to parent
   }

   heap[currentNode] = theElement;
}
```

Program 12.2 Inserting an element into a max heap

heap following the deletion is 0. In this case the `while` loop is not entered, and a redundant assignment to position 1 of the heap is made.

The method `initialize` (Program 12.4) heapifies the array `theHeap` by first assigning `theHeap` to `heap`. `theSize` is the number of elements in `theHeap`. In the `for` loop of Program 12.4, we begin at the last node in the binary tree interpretation of the array `heap` (now equivalent to the array `theHeap`) that has a child and work our way to the root. At each positioning of the variable `root`, the embedded `while` loop ensures that the subtree rooted at `root` is a max heap. Notice the similarity between the body of the `for` loop and the code for `pop` (Program 12.3).

Complexity of `initialize`

If the number of elements is n (i.e., `theSize` $= n$), each iteration of the `for` loop of `initialize` (Program 12.4) takes $O(\log n)$ time and the number of iterations is $n/2$. So the complexity of `initialize` is $O(n \log n)$. Recall that the big oh notation provides only an upper bound on the complexity of an algorithm. Consequently,

```
template<class T>
void maxHeap<T>::pop()
{// Remove max element.
   // if heap is empty return null
   if (heapSize == 0)    // heap empty
      throw queueEmpty();

   // Delete max element
   heap[1].~T();

   // Remove last element and reheapify
   T lastElement = heap[heapSize--];

   // find place for lastElement starting at root
   int currentNode = 1,
       child = 2;        // child of currentNode
   while (child <= heapSize)
   {
      // heap[child] should be larger child of currentNode
      if (child < heapSize && heap[child] < heap[child + 1])
         child++;

      // can we put lastElement in heap[currentNode]?
      if (lastElement >= heap[child])
         break;   // yes

      // no
      heap[currentNode] = heap[child]; // move child up
      currentNode = child;             // move down a level
      child *= 2;
   }
   heap[currentNode] = lastElement;
}
```

Program 12.3 Removing the max element from a max heap

the complexity of initialize could be better than suggested by this upper bound. A more careful analysis allows us to conclude that the complexity is actually $\Theta(n)$.

Each iteration of the while loop of initialize takes $O(h_i)$ time where h_i is the height of the subtree with root i. The complete binary tree heap$[1:n]$ has height $h = \lceil \log_2(n+1) \rceil$. It has at most 2^{j-1} nodes at level j. Hence at most 2^{j-1} of the

```
template<class T>
void maxHeap<T>::initialize(T *theHeap, int theSize)
{// Initialize max heap to element array theHeap[1:theSize].
   delete [] heap;
   heap = theHeap;
   heapSize = theSize;

   // heapify
   for (int root = heapSize / 2; root >= 1; root--)
   {
      T rootElement = heap[root];

      // find place to put rootElement
      int child = 2 * root; // parent of child is target
                            // location for rootElement
      while (child <= heapSize)
      {
         // heap[child] should be larger sibling
         if (child < heapSize && heap[child] < heap[child + 1])
            child++;

         // can we put rootElement in heap[child/2]?
         if (rootElement >= heap[child])
            break;   // yes

         // no
         heap[child / 2] = heap[child]; // move child up
         child *= 2;                    // move down a level
      }
      heap[child / 2] = rootElement;
   }
}
```

Program 12.4 Initialize a nonempty max heap

is have $h_i = h - j + 1$. The time to initialize the max heap is therefore:

$$O(\sum_{j=1}^{h-1} 2^{j-1}(h - j + 1)) = O(\sum_{k=2}^{h} k2^{h-k}) = O(2^h \sum_{k=2}^{h} (k/2^k)) = O(2^h) = O(n)$$

This derivation uses the identity (Exercise 10)

$$\sum_{k=1}^{m} \frac{k}{2^k} = 2 - \frac{m+2}{2^m} \qquad (12.1)$$

Since the for loop goes through $n/2$ iterations, the complexity is also $\Omega(n)$. Combining these two bounds, we get $\Theta(n)$ as the complexity of initialize.

12.4.6   Heaps and the STL

The STL class priority_queue employs a vector-based heap to implement a max priority queue. However, since the STL class permits the user to specify the function used to compare priorities, the class may also be used for min priority queues.

EXERCISES

6. Consider the array theHeap = [-, 3, 5, 6, 7, 20, 8, 2, 9, 12, 15, 30, 17].

   (a) Draw the corresponding complete binary tree.
   (b) Heapify the tree by using the method of Program 12.4. Show the result in both tree and array format.
   (c) Now insert the elements 15, 20, and 45 (in this order) using the bubbling up process of Program 12.2. Show the max heap following each insert.
   (d) Perform four remove max operations on the max heap of part (c). Use the remove method of Program 12.3. Show the max heap following each remove.

7. Do Exercise 6 beginning with the array [-, 10, 2, 7, 6, 5, 9, 12, 35, 22, 15, 1, 3, 4].

8. Do Exercise 6 beginning with the array [-, 1, 2, 3, 4, 5, 6, 7, 8, 9, 10, 12, 15, 22, 35].

9. Do Exercise 6 under the assumption that you are to have a min heap. The initial array is [-, 30, 17, 20, 15, 10, 12, 5, 7, 8, 5, 2, 9]. For part (b) insert 1, 10, 6, and 4. For part (d) perform three remove min operations.

10. Use induction on m to prove Equation 12.1.

11. Write a copy constructor for maxHeap. Test the correctness of your code.

12. Extend the class maxHeap by adding a public member changeMax(newElement) that replaces the current maximum element with newElement. newElement may have a value that is either smaller or larger than the current priority of the element in heap[1]. Your code should follow a downward path from the root, as is done in the pop method. The complexity of your code should be $O(\log n)$ where n is the number of elements in the max heap. Show that this is the case. Test the correctness of your code.

13. Extend the class `maxHeap` by adding a public member `remove(i)` that removes and returns the element in `heap[i]`. The complexity of your code should be $O(\log n)$ where n is the number of elements in the max heap. Show that this is the case. Test the correctness of your code.

14. Develop an iterator for the class `maxHeap`. You may enumerate the elements in any order. The time taken to enumerate the elements of an n-element max heap should be $O(n)$. Show that this is the case. Test the correctness of your code.

15. Since the element `lastElement` that is reinserted into the max heap during a `pop` (see Program 12.3) was removed from the bottom of the heap, we expect to reinsert it near the bottom. Write a new version of `pop` in which the vacancy in the root is first moved down to a leaf, and then the place for `lastElement` is determined making an upward pass from this leaf. Experiment with the new code to see whether it works faster than the old one.

16. Rewrite the methods of `maxHeap` under the following assumptions:

    (a) When a heap is created, the creator provides two elements `maxElement` and `minElement`; no element in the heap is larger than `maxElement` or smaller than `minElement`.

    (b) A heap with n elements requires an array `heap[0:2n+1]`.

    (c) The n elements are stored in `heap[1:n]` as described in this section.

    (d) `maxElement` is stored in `heap[0]`.

    (e) `minElement` is stored in `heap[n+1:2n+1]`.

    These assumptions should simplify the codes for `push` and `pop`. Conduct experiments to compare the implementation of this section with the one of this exercise.

17. A d-heap is a complete tree whose degree is d. Develop the concrete class `maxDHeap` which extends the abstract class `maxPriorityQueue` using a d-heap. Compare the performance of your implementation with that of `maxHeap` for d = 2, 3, and 4.

18. Do Exercise 12 for the class `maxDHeap` (see Exercise 17).

12.5   LEFTIST TREES

12.5.1   Height- and Weight-Biased Min and Max Leftist Trees

The heap structure of Section 12.4 is an example of an **implicit data structure**. The complete binary tree representing the heap is stored implicitly (i.e., there are no explicit pointers or other explicit data from which the structure may be deduced) in an array. Since no explicit structural information is stored, the representation is very space efficient; in fact, there is no space overhead. Despite the heap structure being both space and time efficient, it is not suitable for all applications of priority queues. In particular, applications in which we wish to meld (i.e., combine or blend) pairs of priority queues, as well as those in which we have multiple queues of varying size, require a different data structure. Leftist tree structures are suitable for these applications.

Consider a binary tree in which a special node called an **external node** replaces each empty subtree. The remaining nodes are called **internal nodes**. A binary tree with external nodes added is called an **extended binary tree**. Figure 12.6(a) shows a binary tree. Its corresponding extended binary tree is shown in Figure 12.6(b). The external nodes appear as shaded boxes. These nodes have been labeled a through f for convenience.

(a) A binary tree   (b) Extended binary tree

(c) s values   (d) w values

Figure 12.6 s and w values

Let $s(x)$ be the length of a shortest path from node x to an external node in its subtree. From the definition of $s(x)$, it follows that if x is an external node, its s value is 0. Furthermore, if x is an internal node, its s value is

$$\min\{s(L), s(R)\} + 1$$

where L and R are, respectively, the left and right children of x. The s values for the nodes of the extended binary tree of Figure 12.6(b) appear in Figure 12.6(c).

Definition 12.3 *A binary tree is a* **height-biased leftist tree (HBLT)** *iff at every internal node, the s value of the left child is greater than or equal to the s value of the right child.* ∎

The binary tree of Figure 12.6(a) is not an HBLT. To see this, consider the parent of the external node a. The s value of its left child is 0, while that of its right is 1. All other internal nodes satisfy the requirements of the HBLT definition. By swapping the left and right subtrees of the parent of a, the binary tree of Figure 12.6(a) becomes an HBLT.

Theorem 12.1 *Let x be any internal node of an HBLT.*

(a) The number of nodes in the subtree with root x is at least $2^{s(x)} - 1$.

(b) If the subtree with root x has m nodes, $s(x)$ is at most $\log_2(m + 1)$.

(c) The length of the right-most path from x to an external node (i.e., the path obtained by beginning at x and making a sequence of right-child moves) is $s(x)$.

Proof From the definition of $s(x)$, it follows that there are no external nodes on the $s(x) - 1$ levels immediately below node x (as otherwise the s value of x would be less). The subtree with root x has exactly one node on the level at which x is, two on the next level, four on the next, $\cdots$, and $2^{s(x)-1}$ nodes $s(x) - 1$ levels below x. The subtree may have additional nodes at levels more than $s(x) - 1$ below x. Hence the number of nodes in the subtree x is at least $\sum_{i=0}^{s(x)-1} 2^i = 2^{s(x)} - 1$. Part (b) follows from (a). Part (c) follows from the definition of s and the fact that, in an HBLT, the s value of the left child of a node is always greater than or equal to that of the right child. ∎

Definition 12.4 *A* **max HBLT** *is an HBLT that is also a max tree. A* **min HBLT** *is an HBLT that is also a min tree.* ∎

The max trees of Figure 12.1 as well as the min trees of Figure 12.2 are also HBLTs; therefore, the trees of Figure 12.1 are max HBLTs, and those of Figure 12.2 are min HBLTs. A max priority queue may be represented as a max HBLT, and a min priority queue may be represented as a min HBLT.

We arrive at another variety of leftist tree by considering the number of nodes in a subtree, rather than the length of a shortest root to external node path. Define the weight $w(x)$ of node x to be the number of internal nodes in the subtree with root x. Notice that if x is an external node, its weight is 0. If x is an internal node, its weight is 1 more than the sum of the weights of its children. The weights of the nodes of the binary tree of Figure 12.6(a) appear in Figure 12.6(d)

Definition 12.5 *A binary tree is a* **weight-biased leftist tree (WBLT)** *iff at every internal node the w value of the left child is greater than or equal to the w value of the right child. A max (min) WBLT is a max (min) tree that is also a WBLT.* ■

As was the case for HBLTs, the length of the right-most path in a WBLT that has m nodes is at most $\log_2(m+1)$. Using either WBLTs or HBLTs, we can perform the priority queue operations find, insert, and delete in the same asymptotic time as heaps take. Like heaps, WBLTs and HBLTs may be initialized in linear time. Two priority queues represented as WBLTs or HBLTs can be melded into one in logarithmic time. When priority queues are represented as heaps, they cannot be melded in logarithmic time.

The way in which finds, inserts, deletes, melds, and initializations are done in WBLTs and HBLTs is similar. Consequently, we describe these operations for HBLTs only and leave the adaptation of these methods to WBLTs as an exercise (Exercise 24).

12.5.2   Insertion into a Max HBLT

The insertion operation for max HBLTs may be performed by using the max HBLT meld operation. Suppose we are to insert an element x into the max HBLT H. If we create a max HBLT with the single element x and then meld this max HBLT and H, the resulting max HBLT will include all elements in H as well as the element x. Hence an insertion may be performed by creating a new max HBLT with just the element that is to be inserted and then melding this max HBLT and the original.

12.5.3   Deletion from a Max HBLT

The max element is in the root. If the root is deleted, two max HBLTs, the left and right subtrees of the root, remain. By melding together these two max HBLTs, we obtain a max HBLT that contains all elements in the original max HBLT other than the deleted max element. So the delete max operation may be performed by deleting the root and then melding its two subtrees.

12.5.4   Melding Two Max HBLTs

Since the length of the right-most path of an HBLT with n elements is $O(\log n)$, a meld algorithm that traverses only the right-most paths of the HBLTs being melded, spending $O(1)$ time at each node on these two paths, will have complexity logarithmic in the number of elements in the resulting HBLT. With this observation in mind, we develop a meld algorithm that begins at the roots of the two HBLTs and makes right-child moves only.

The meld strategy is best described using recursion. Let A and B be the two max HBLTs that are to be melded. If one is empty, then we may use the other as the result. So assume that neither is empty. To perform the meld, we compare the elements in the two roots. The root with the larger element becomes the root of the melded HBLT. Ties may be broken arbitrarily. Suppose that A has the larger root and that its left subtree is L. Let C be the max HBLT that results from melding the right subtree of A and the max HBLT B. The result of melding A and B is the max HBLT that has A as its root and L and C as its subtrees. If the s value of L is smaller than that of C, then C is the left subtree. Otherwise, L is.

Example 12.3 Consider the two max HBLTs of Figure 12.7(a). The s value of a node is shown outside the node, while the element value is shown inside. When drawing two max HBLTs that are to be melded, we will always draw the one with larger root value on the left. Ties are broken arbitrarily. Because of this convention, the root of the left HBLT always becomes the root of the final HBLT. Also, we will shade the nodes of the HBLT on the right.

Since the right subtree of 9 is empty, the result of melding this subtree of 9 and the tree with root 7 is just the tree with root 7. We make the tree with root 7 the right subtree of 9 temporarily to get the max tree of Figure 12.7(b). Since the s value of the left subtree of 9 is 0 while that of its right subtree is 1, the left and right subtrees are swapped to get the max HBLT of Figure 12.7(c).

Next consider melding the two max HBLTs of Figure 12.7(d). The root of the left subtree becomes the root of the result. When the right subtree of 10 is melded with the HBLT with root 7, the result is just this latter HBLT. If this HBLT is made the right subtree of 10, we get the max tree of Figure 12.7(e). Comparing the s values of the left and right children of 10, we see that a swap is not necessary.

Now consider melding the two max HBLTs of Figure 12.7(f). The root of the left subtree is the root of the result. We proceed to meld the right subtree of 18 and the max HBLT with root 10. The two max HBLTs being melded are the same as those melded in Figure 12.7(d). The resultant max HBLT (Figure 12.7(e)) becomes the right subtree of 18, and the max tree of Figure 12.7(g) results. Comparing the s values of the left and right subtrees of 18, we see that these subtrees must be swapped. Swapping results in the max HBLT of Figure 12.7(h).

As a final example, consider melding the two max HBLTs of Figure 12.7(i). The root of the left max HBLT becomes the root of the result. We proceed to meld the right subtree of 40 and the max HBLT with root 18. These max HBLTs were melded in Figure 12.7(f). The resultant max HBLT (Figure 12.7(g)) becomes the right subtree of 40. Since the left subtree of 40 has a smaller s value than the right has, the two subtrees are swapped to get the max HBLT of Figure 12.7(k). Notice that when melding the max HBLTs of Figure 12.7(i), we first move to the right

Figure 12.7 Melding max HBLTs

child of 40, then to the right child of 18, and finally to the right child of 10. All moves follow the right-most paths of the initial max HBLTs.   ∎

12.5.5 Initialization

It takes $O(n \log n)$ time to initialize a max HBLT with n elements by inserting these elements into an initially empty max HBLT one at a time. To get a linear time initialization algorithm, we begin by creating n max HBLTs with each containing one of the n elements. These n max HBLTs are placed on a FIFO queue. Then max HBLTs are deleted from this queue in pairs, melded, and added to the end of the queue until only one max HBLT remains.

Example 12.4 We wish to create a max HBLT with the five elements 7, 1, 9, 11, and 2. Five single-element max HBLTs are created and placed in a FIFO queue. The first two, 7 and 1, are deleted from the queue and melded. The result (Figure 12.8(a)) is added to the queue. Next the max HBLTs 9 and 11 are deleted from the queue and melded. The result appears in Figure 12.8(b). This max HBLT is added to the queue. Now the max HBLT 2 and that of Figure 12.8(a) are deleted from the queue and melded. The resulting max HBLT (Figure 12.8(c)) is added to the queue. The next pair to be deleted from the queue consists of the max HBLTs of Figures Figure 12.8 (b) and (c). These HBLTs are melded to get the max HBLT of Figure 12.8(d). This max HBLT is added to the queue. The queue now has just one max HBLT, and we are done with the initialization.   ∎

        (a)   (b)   (c)   (d)

Figure 12.8 Initializing a max HBLT

12.5.6 The Class maxHblt

The data type of each node of a max HBLT is `binaryTreeNode<pair<int,T> >`, where `binaryTreeNode` is as in Program 11.1; the first component of the pair is the s value of the node; and the second component is the priority queue element. Our class maxHblt, which implements a max HBLT, extends the class linkedBinaryTree (Program 11.9). The code for the elementary methods empty, size, and top is similar to that for the corresponding methods of maxHeap.

Since the push, pop, and initialize methods of maxHblt use the meld operation, let us examine the meld operation first. The public method meld(maxHblt<T>& theMaxHblt) melds the two max HBLTs *this and theMaxHblt. Upon completion, *this is the resulting melded max HBLT. This method accomplishes its task by invoking a private method meld(x, y) (Program 12.5) that recursively melds the max HBLTs whose roots are x and y. Upon termination, x is the root of the resulting max HBLT.

The private meld method given in Program 12.5 begins by handling the special case when at least one of the trees being melded is empty. When neither tree is empty, we make sure that node x has the larger element (i.e., the tree with larger root is on the left). If the element in x is not larger than that in y, x and y are swapped. Next the right subtree of x and the max HBLT with root y are melded recursively. Following this meld, x is the root of a max tree whose left and right subtrees may need to be swapped so as to ensure that the entire tree is, in fact, a max HBLT. This swapping is done, if necessary, and the s value of x is computed.

To insert theElement into a max HBLT, the code of Program 12.6 creates a max HBLT with the single element theElement and then uses the private method meld to meld this tree and the original one.

The code for pop (Program 12.6) throws a queueEmpty exception in case the max HBLT is empty. When the max HBLT is not empty, the root is deleted and the left and right subtrees of the root are melded to get the desired max HBLT.

The max HBLT initialization code is given in Program 12.7. An array FIFO queue holds the intermediate max HBLTs created by the initialization algorithm. In the first for loop, size single-element max HBLTs are created and added to an initially empty queue. In the next for loop, pairs of max HBLTs are popped from the queue, melded, and the result added to the queue. When this for loop terminates, the queue contains a single max HBLT (provided size > 0), which includes all size elements.

Complexity Analysis

The complexity of the top method is $\Theta(1)$. The complexity of push, pop, and the public method meld is the same as that of the private method meld. Since this private method moves only to right subtrees of the trees with roots x and y that are being melded, the complexity of this private method is $O(s(x) + s(y))$. $s(x)$ and $s(y)$ are at most $\log_2(m+1)$ and $\log_2(n+1)$ where m and n are, respectively, the number of elements in the max HBLTs with roots x and y. As a result, the complexity of the private method meld is $O(\log m + \log n) = O(\log(mn))$.

For the complexity analysis of initialize, assume, for simplicity, that $n =$ size is a power of 2. The first $n/2$ melds involve max HBLTs with one element each, the next $n/4$ melds involve max HBLTs with two elements each; the next $n/8$

```
template<class T>
void maxHblt<T>::meld(binaryTreeNode<pair<int, T> >* &x,
                      binaryTreeNode<pair<int, T> >* &y)
{// Meld leftist trees with roots *x and *y.
 // Return pointer to new root in x.
   if (y == NULL)    // y is empty
      return;
   if (x == NULL)    // x is empty
      {x = y; return;}

   // neither is empty, swap x and y if necessary
   if (x->element.second < y->element.second)
      swap(x, y);

   // now x->element.second >= y->element.second

   meld(x->rightChild,y);

   // swap subtrees of x if necessary and set x->element.first
   if (x->leftChild == NULL)
   {// left subtree empty, swap the subtrees
        x->leftChild = x->rightChild;
        x->rightChild = NULL;
        x->element.first = 1;
   }
   else
   {// swap only if left subtree has smaller s value
      if (x->leftChild->element.first < x->rightChild->element.first)
         swap(x->leftChild, x->rightChild);
      // update s value of x
      x->element.first = x->rightChild->element.first + 1;
   }
}
```

Program 12.5 Melding two leftist trees

melds are with trees that have four elements each; and so on. The time needed to meld two trees with 2^i elements each is $O(i+1)$, and so the total time taken by `initialize` is

$$O(n/2 + 2*(n/4) + 3*(n/8) + \cdots) = O(n \sum \frac{i}{2^i}) = O(n)$$

```
template<class T>
void maxHblt<T>::meld(maxHblt<T>& theHblt)
{// meld *this and theHblt
   meld(root, theHblt.root);
   treeSize += theHblt.treeSize;
   theHblt.root = NULL;
   theHblt.treeSize = 0;
}

template<class T>
void maxHblt<T>::push(const T& theElement)
{// Insert theElement into the leftist tree.
 // Create tree with one node.
   binaryTreeNode<pair<int,T> > *q =
      new binaryTreeNode<pair<int,T> > (pair<int,T>(1, theElement));

   // meld q and original tree
   meld(root,q);
   treeSize++;
}

template<class T>
void maxHblt<T>::pop()
{// Delete max element.
   if (root == NULL)
      throw queueEmpty();

   // tree not empty
   binaryTreeNode<pair<int,T> > *left = root->leftChild,
                                *right = root->rightChild;
   delete root;
   root = left;
   meld(root, right);
   treeSize--;
}
```

Program 12.6 The public methods meld, push, and pop

```
template<class T>
void maxHblt<T>::initialize(T* theElements, int theSize)
{// Initialize hblt with theElements[1:theSize].
   arrayQueue<binaryTreeNode<pair<int,T> >*> q(theSize);
   erase();   // make *this empty

   // initialize queue of trees
   for (int i = 1; i <= theSize; i++)
      // create trees with one node each
      q.push(new binaryTreeNode<pair<int,T> >
                (pair<int,T>(1, theElements[i])));

   // repeatedly meld from queue
   for (i = 1; i <= theSize - 1; i++)
   {// pop and meld two trees from queue
      binaryTreeNode<pair<int,T> > *b = q.front();
      q.pop();
      binaryTreeNode<pair<int,T> > *c = q.front();
      q.pop();
      meld(b,c);
      // put melded tree on queue
      q.push(b);
   }

   if (theSize > 0)
      root = q.front();
   treeSize = theSize;
}
```

Program 12.7 Initializing a max HBLT

EXERCISES

19. Consider the array theElements = [-, 3, 5, 6, 7, 20, 8, 2, 9, 12, 15, 30, 17].

   (a) Draw the max leftist tree created by Program 12.7.

   (b) Now insert the elements 10, 18, 11, and 4 (in this order) using the insert method of Program 12.6. Show the max leftist tree following each insert.

   (c) Perform three remove max operations on the max leftist tree of part (c). Use the remove method of Program 12.6. Show the max leftist tree following each remove.

20. Do Exercise 19 beginning with the element array [-, 10, 2, 7, 6, 5, 9, 12, 35, 22, 15, 1, 3, 4].

21. Write the code for the class minHblt. This class differs from the class maxHblt only in that class members are now min HBLTs rather than max HBLTs.

22. Develop an iterator for the class maxHblt. You may enumerate the elements in any order. The complexity of each of your iterator methods should be $O(1)$. Show that this is the case. Test the correctness of your code.

23. Develop the class maxHbltWithRemoveNode that includes all methods of maxHblt as well as the public methods pushAndReturnNode and removeElementIn-Node. The method pushAndReturnNode(theElement) puts theElement into the leftist tree and returns the node into which the element was put; the method removeElementInNode(theNode) removes and returns the element in theNode; the node theNode is also removed from the tree. *Hint:* add a parent field to each node. The complexity of the methods that are common to maxHblt should be the same as that of the corresponding methods of maxHblt, and the complexity of the new methods should be $O(\log n)$ where n is the number of elements in the leftist tree. Show that this is the case. Test the correctness of your code.

24. [Max WBLTs]

    (a) Which (if any) of the binary trees of Figure 12.1 are WBLTs?

    (b) Let x be a node in a WBLT. Use induction on $w(x)$ to show that the length of the right-most path from x to an external node is at most $\log_2(w(x) + 1)$.

    (c) Develop the class maxWblt as one whose objects are max WBLTs. Your class should include all the methods of maxHblt. Your code for these methods should have the same asymptotic complexity as the corresponding codes for maxHblt. Write the code for the private method meld without using recursion. Note that since the w value of a node can be computed on the way down, the bottom-to-top pass made when recursion unfolds as in Program 12.5 is unnecessary when WBLTs are used but necessary when HBLTs are used.

    (d) Compare the advantages/disadvantages of max WBLTs, max HBLTs, and max heaps as a data structure for max priority queues.

25. Replace the use of the null pointer in the representation of a max HBLT by a pointer to a node that has its element field set to minElement (see Exercise 16). Modify the max HBLT codes to take advantage of this change. Does the new code run faster than the original code?

12.6 APPLICATIONS

12.6.1 Heap Sort

You might have already noticed that a heap can be used to sort n elements in $O(n \log n)$ time. We begin by initializing a max heap with the n elements to be sorted. Then we extract (i.e., delete) elements from the heap one at a time. The elements appear in nonincreasing order. The initialization takes $O(n)$ time, and each deletion takes $O(\log n)$ time. So the total time is $O(n \log n)$. This time is better than the $O(n^2)$ time taken by the sort methods of Chapter 2 .

The sort method that results from the preceding strategy is called **heap sort**. Its implementation, which appears in Program 12.8, employs the max heap method `deactivateArray` that sets `maxHeap<T>::heap` to NULL. This is necessary because `maxHeap<T>::initialize` sets `maxHeap<T>::heap` to the element array a and when we exit the heap sort function, the max heap destructor deletes `maxHeap<T>::heap`. So to prevent the deletion of the element array a, it is necessary to invoke `deactivateArray`.

```
template <class T>
void heapSort(T a[], int n)
{// Sort a[1:n] using the heap sort method.
   // create a max heap of the elements
   maxHeap<T> heap(1);
   heap.initialize(a, n);

   // extract one by one from the max heap
   for (int i = n - 1; i >= 1; i--)
   {
      T x = heap.top();
      heap.pop();
      a[i+1] = x;
   }

   // save array a from heap destructor
   heap.deactivateArray();
}
```

Program 12.8 Sort a[1:n] using heap sort

Figure 12.9 shows the progress of the `for` loop of Program 12.8 for the first few values of i. This loop begins with the max heap of Figure 12.5(d). Circles denote array positions that are part of the max heap, and squares denote array positions that have their sorted values.

Figure 12.9 Heap sort

12.6.2   Machine Scheduling

Consider a machine shop that has m identical machines. We have n jobs that need to be processed. The processing time required by job i is t_i. This time includes the time needed to set up and remove the job on/from a machine. A **schedule** is an assignment of jobs to time intervals on machines such that

- No machine processes more than one job at any time.

- No job is processed by more than one machine at any time.

- Each job i is assigned for a total of t_i units of processing.

Each machine is assumed to be available at time 0. The **finish time** or **length** of a schedule is the time at which all jobs have completed. In a nonpreemptive schedule, each job i is processed by a single machine from some start time s_i to its completion time $s_i + t_i$. We will concern ourselves only with nonpreemptive schedules.

Figure 12.10 shows a three-machine schedule for seven jobs with processing requirements (2, 14, 4, 16, 6, 5, 3). The machines are labeled M1, M2, and M3. Each shaded area represents the duration for which a job is scheduled. The number inside the area is the job index. Job 4 is scheduled on machine 1 (M1) from time 0 to time 16. In these 16 units of time, machine 1 completes the processing of job 4. The schedule for machine 2 is do job 2 from time 0 to time 14 and then do job 7 from time 14 to 17. On machine 3 job 5 is done from 0 to 6, job 6 from 6 to 11, job 3 from 11 to 15, and job 1 from 15 to 17. Notice that each job i is processed on a single machine from a start time s_i to a finish time $s_i + t_i$ and that no machine works on more than one job at any time. The time at which all jobs have completed is 17. So the schedule finish time or length is 17.

Figure 12.10 A three-machine schedule

The schedule of Figure 12.10 is a minimum-finish-time schedule for the given processing requirements. To see this, note the sum of the processing times is 50. Therefore, every three-machine schedule will take at least $\lceil 50/3 \rceil = 17$ time units to complete the jobs.

Our task is to write a program that constructs a minimum-finish-time m-machine schedule for a given set of n jobs. Constructing such a schedule is very hard. In fact, no one has ever developed a polynomial time algorithm (i.e., an algorithm whose complexity is $O(n^k m^l)$ for any constants k and l) to construct a minimum-finish-time schedule.

The scheduling problem we have just defined is a member of the infamous class of NP-hard (NP stands for **nondeterministic polynomial**) problems. The NP-hard and NP-complete problem classes contain problems for which no one has developed a polynomial-time algorithm. The problems in the class NP-complete are decision problems. That is, for each problem instance the answer is either yes or no. Our machine-scheduling problem is not a decision problem, as the answer for each instance is an assignment of jobs to machines such that the finish time is minimum. We may formulate a related machine-scheduling problem in which, in addition to the tasks and machines, we are given a time $TMin$ and are asked to determine whether or not there is a schedule with finish time $TMin$ or less. For this related problem, the answer to each instance is either yes or no. This related problem is a decision problem that is NP-complete. NP-hard problems may or may not be decision problems.

Thousands of problems of practical interest are NP-hard or NP-complete. If anyone discovers a polynomial-time algorithm for an NP-hard or NP-complete problem, then he/she would have simultaneously discovered a way to solve all NP-complete problems in polynomial time. Although we are unable to prove that NP-complete problems cannot be solved in polynomial time, common wisdom very strongly suggests that this is the case. As a result, optimization problems that are NP-hard are often solved by **approximation algorithms**. Although approximation algorithms do not guarantee to obtain optimal solutions, they guarantee solutions "close" to optimal.

In the case of our scheduling problem, we can generate schedules whose lengths are at most $4/3 - 1/(3m)$ of optimal by employing a simple scheduling strategy called **longest processing time** (LPT). In LPT, jobs are assigned to machines in descending order of their processing time requirements t_i. When a job is being assigned to a machine, it is assigned to the machine that becomes idle first. Ties are broken arbitrarily.

For the job set example in Figure 12.10, we may construct an LPT schedule by first sorting the jobs into descending order of processing times. The job order is $(4, 2, 5, 6, 3, 7, 1)$. First, job 4 is assigned to a machine. Since all three machines become available at time 0, job 4 may be assigned to any machine. Suppose we assign it to machine 1. Now machine 1 is unavailable until time 16. Job 2 is next assigned; we can assign it to either machine 2 or 3, as both become available at the same time (i.e., time 0). Assume that we assign job 2 to machine 2. Now machine 2 is unavailable until time 14. Next we assign job 5 to machine 3 from time 0 to time 6. Job 6 is to be assigned next. The first available machine is machine 3. It becomes available at time 6. Following the assignment of job 6 from time 6 to time

11 on this machine, the availability time of machine 3 becomes 11. Job 3 is next considered for scheduling. The first machine to become available is machine 3 at time 11; we assign job 3 to this machine. Continuing in this way, we obtain the schedule of Figure 12.10.

Theorem 12.2 [Graham] *Let $F^*(I)$ be the finish time of an optimal m-machine schedule for a job set I and let $F(I)$ be the finish time of the LPT schedule for this job set. Then*

$$\frac{F(I)}{F^*(I)} \leq \frac{4}{3} - \frac{1}{3m}$$

In practice, LPT schedules are often much closer to optimal than suggested by the bound of Theorem 12.2. In fact, as noted above, the LPT schedule of Figure 12.10 is optimal.

LPT schedules can be constructed in $O(n \log n)$ time by using heaps. First we notice that when $n \leq m$, we need merely assign job i to machine i from time 0 to t_i. When $n > m$, we begin by sorting the jobs into ascending order of processing times using **heapSort** (Program 12.8). To construct the LPT schedule, the jobs are assigned in reverse order. To determine which machine a job is to be assigned to, we need to determine which machine becomes available first. To make this determination, we maintain a min heap of the m machines. Each element on this min heap is of type **machineNode**, which has the data members **avail** (the time at which the machine becomes available) and **id** (the machine identifier). The data type **machineNode** defines a type conversion to **int** as below

```
operator int() const {return avail;}
```

This type conversion enables the comparison of **machineNode** objects via their **avail** fields.

A **pop** is used to extract the machine that becomes available first. The machine's availability time is increased, and the machine is inserted back into the min heap. The min heap of machines is initialized by inserting a node for each machine. Since all machines are initially available at time 0, the **avail** value for each of these machines is 0.

The jobs are represented using the class **jobNode**, which has the data members **id** (the job's unique identifier) and **time** (the processing requirements of the job). Since we will be sorting jobs using **heapSort** and since **heapSort** uses a max heap, **jobNode** defines a type conversion to **int** that simply returns the **time** field.

Program 12.9 gives the code to sort n jobs by their processing times **a[1:n]** and then schedule these jobs on m machines using the LPT method.

```
void makeSchedule(jobNode a[], int n, int m)
{// Output an m machine LPT schedule for the jobs a[1:n].
   if (n <= m)
   {
      cout << "Schedule each job on a different machine." << endl;
      return;
   }

   heapSort(a, n); // in ascending order

   // initialize m machines and the min heap
   minHeap<machineNode> machineHeap(m);
   for (int i = 1; i <= m; i++)
      machineHeap.push(machineNode(i, 0));

   // construct schedule
   for (int i = n; i >= 1; i--)
   {// schedule job i on first free machine
      machineNode x =  machineHeap.top();
      machineHeap.pop();
      cout << "Schedule job " << a[i].id
           << " on machine " << x.id << " from " << x.avail
           << " to " << (x.avail + a[i].time) << endl;
      x.avail += a[i].time;   // new available time for this machine
      machineHeap.push(x);
   }
}
```

Program 12.9 Output an m machine LPT schedule for a[1:n]

Complexity Analysis of makeSchedule

When $n \leq m$, makeSchedule takes $\Theta(1)$ time. When $n > m$, the heap sort takes $O(n \log n)$ time. The heap initialization takes $O(m)$ time, even though we are doing m inserts, because all elements have the same value; therefore, each insert actually takes only $\Theta(1)$ time. In the second for loop, n top, n pop and n push operations are performed. Each top operation takes $O(1)$ time and each pop and push takes $O(\log m)$ time. So the second for loop takes $O(n \log m)$ time. The total time is therefore $O(n \log n + n \log m) = O(n \log n)$ (as $n > m$).

12.6.3   Huffman Codes

In Section 10.6 we developed a text compressor based on the LZW method. This method relies on the recurrence of substrings in a text. Another approach to text compression, **Huffman codes**, relies on the relative frequency with which different symbols appear in a piece of text. Suppose our text is a string that comprises the characters a, u, x, and z. If the length of this string is 1000, then storing it as 1000 one-byte characters will take 1000 bytes (or 8000 bits) of space. If we encode the symbols in the string using 2 bits per symbol ($00 = a$, $01 = x$, $10 = u$, $11 = z$), then the 1000 symbols can be represented with 2000 bits of space. We also need space for the code table, which may be stored in following format:

number of table entries, code 1, symbol 1, code 2, symbol 2, $\cdots$

Eight bits are adequate for the number of entries and for each of the symbols. Each code is of size $\lceil \log_2 (\text{number of table entries}) \rceil$ bits. For our example the code table may be saved in $5 * 8 + 4 * 2 = 48$ bits. The compression ratio is $8000/2048 = 3.9$.

Using the above 2 bits per symbol encoding, the string $aaxuaxz$ is encoded as 00000110000111. The code for each symbol has the same number of bits (i.e., 2). By picking off pairs of bits from the coded string from left to right and using the code table, we can obtain the original string.

In the string $aaxuaxz$, the symbol a occurs three times. The number of occurrences of a symbol is called its **frequency**. The frequencies of the symbols a, x, u, and z in the sample string are 3, 2, 1, and 1, respectively. When there is significant variation in the frequencies of different symbols, we can reduce the size of the coded string by using variable-length codes. If we use the codes ($0 = a$, $10 = x$, $110 = u$, $111 = z$), the encoded version of $aaxuaxz$ is 0010110010111. The length of this encoded version is 13 bits compared to 14 bits using the 2 bits per symbol code! The difference is more dramatic when the spread in frequencies is greater. If the frequencies of the four symbols are (996, 2, 1, 1), then the 2 bits per symbol code results in an encoding that is 2000 bits long, whereas the variable-length code results in an encoding that is 1006 bits.

But how do we decode the encoded string? When each code is 2 bits long, decoding is easy—just pick off every pair of bits and use the code table to determine what these 2 bits stand for. With variable-length codes, we do not know how many bits to pick off. The string $aaxuaxz$ was coded as 0010110010111. When decoding this code from left to right, we need to know whether the code for the first symbol is 0, 00, or 001. Since we have no codes that begin with 00, the first code must be 0. This code is decoded using the code table to get a. The next code is 0, 01, or 010. Again, because no codes begin with 01, the code must be 0. Continuing in this way, we are able to decode the encoded bit string.

What makes this decoding method work? If we examine the four codes in use (0, 10, 110, 111), we observe that no code is a prefix of another. Consequently, when examining the coded bit string from left to right, we can get a match with exactly one code.

We may use extended binary trees (see Section 12.5.1 for a definition) to derive a special class of variable-length codes that satisfy this prefix property. This class of codes is called **Huffman codes**.

The root to external node paths in an extended binary tree may be coded by using 0 to represent a move to a left subtree and 1 to represent a move to a right subtree. In Figure 12.6(b) the path from the root to the external node b gets the code 010. The codes for the paths to the nodes (a, b, c, d, e, f) are $(00, 010, 011, 100, 101, 11)$. Notice that since no root-to-external-node path is a prefix of another such path, no path code is a prefix of another path code. Therefore, these codes may be used to encode the symbols $a, b, \cdots, f$, respectively. Let S be a string made up of these symbols and let $F(x)$ be the frequency of the symbol $x \in \{a, b, c, d, e, f\}$. If S is encoded using these codes, the encoded string has a length

$$2 * F(a) + 3 * F(b) + 3 * F(c) + 3 * F(d) + 3 * F(e) + 2 * F(f)$$

For an extended binary tree with external nodes labeled $1, \cdots, n$, the length of the encoded string is

$$WEP = \sum_{i=1}^{n} L(i) * F(i)$$

where $L(i)$ is the length of the path (i.e., number of edges on the path) from the root to the external node labeled i. WEP is called the **weighted external path length** of the binary tree. To minimize the length of the coded string, we must use codes from a binary tree whose external nodes correspond to the symbols in the string being encoded and whose WEP is minimum. A binary tree with minimum WEP for a given set of frequencies (weights) is called a **Huffman tree**.

To encode a string (or piece of text) using Huffman codes, we need to

1. Determine the different symbols in the string and their frequencies.

2. Construct a binary tree with minimum WEP (i.e., a Huffman tree). The external nodes of this tree are labeled by the symbols in the string, and the weight of each external node is the frequency of the symbol that is its label.

3. Traverse the root-to-external-node paths and obtain the codes.

4. Replace the symbols in the string by their codes.

To facilitate decoding, we need to save a table that contains the symbol to code mapping or a table that contains the frequency of each symbol. In the latter case the Huffman codes can be reconstructed using the method for (2). We will elaborate on step (2) only.

A Huffman tree can be constructed by beginning with a collection of binary trees, each having just an external node. Each external node represents a different string symbol and has a **weight** equal to the frequency of this symbol. Then we repeatedly select two binary trees of lowest weight (ties are broken arbitrarily) from the collection and combine them into one by making them subtrees of a new root node. The weight of the newly formed tree is the sum of the weights of the constituent subtrees. The process terminates when only one tree remains.

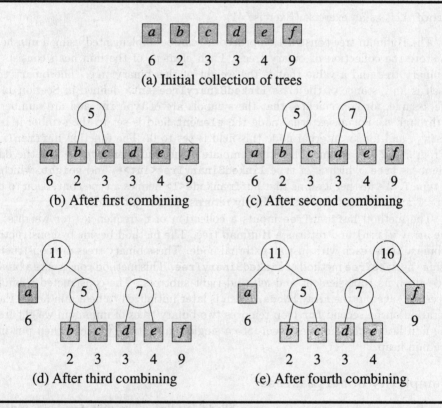

Figure 12.11 Constructing a Huffman tree

Let us try this construction method on a six-symbol (a, b, c, d, e, f) example with frequencies $(6, 2, 3, 3, 4, 9)$. The initial binary trees are shown in Figure 12.11(a). The numbers outside the boxes are the tree weights. The tree with the lowest weight is b. We have a tie for the tree with the second-lowest weight. Suppose that we select tree c. Combining trees b and c yields the configuration of Figure 12.11(b). The root node is labeled with the weight 5. From the five trees of Figure 12.11(b), we select two of lowest weight. Trees d and e are selected and combined to get a tree of weight 7 (Figure 12.11(c)). From the four trees of Figure 12.11(c), we select two of lowest weight to combine. Tree a and the one with weight 5 are selected. Combining these trees results in a tree of weight 11. From the remaining three trees (Figure 12.11(d)), the tree with weight 7 and the tree f are selected for combining. When these two trees are combined, the two trees of Figure 12.11(e) remain. These trees are next combined to get the single tree of Figure 12.6(b), whose weight is 27.

Theorem 12.3 *The procedure outlined above constructs binary trees with minimum WEP.*

Proof Left as an exercise (Exercise 41).   ∎

The Huffman tree construction procedure can be implemented using a min heap to store the collection of binary trees. Each element of the min heap consists of a binary tree and a value that is the weight of this binary tree. The binary tree itself is an instance of the class `linkedBinaryTree<int>` defined in Section 11.8. We assume, for convenience, that the symbols are of type `int` and are numbered 1 through n. For an external node the `element` field is set to the symbol it represents, and for an internal node this field is set to 0. The function `huffmanTree` (Program 12.10) assumes that the template struct `huffmanNode<T>` has the data members `tree`, which is of type `linkedBinaryTree<int>*`, and `weight`, which is of type T. We further assume that `huffmanNode<T>` defines a type conversion to the type T and that this conversion simply returns the `weight` field.

The method `huffmanTree` inputs a collection of n frequencies (or weights) in the array `w[1:n]` and returns a Huffman tree. The method begins by constructing n binary trees, each with just an external node. These binary trees are constructed using the `makeTree` method of `linkedBinaryTree`. This method constructs a binary tree given its root element and left and right subtrees. The constructed n binary trees are saved in the array `hNode`, which is later initialized to be a min heap. Each iteration of the second `for` loop removes two binary trees of minimum weight from the min heap and combines them into a single binary tree, which is then put into the min heap.

Complexity of `huffmanTree`

The time needed to create the array `hNode` is $O(n)$. The first `for` loop and the heap initialization also take $O(n)$ time. In the second `for` loop, a total of $2(n-1)$ `top`, $2(n-1)$ `pop`, and $n-1$ `push` operations are performed, taking $O(n \log n)$ time. The remainder of `huffmanTree` takes $\Theta(n)$ time. So the overall time complexity is $O(n \log n)$.

EXERCISES

26. Show how the array [-, 5, 7, 2, 9, 3, 8, 6, 1] is sorted using heap sort. First draw the corresponding complete binary tree, then draw the heapified tree,

```
template <class T>
linkedBinaryTree<int>* huffmanTree(T weight[], int n)
{// Generate Huffman tree with weights weight[1:n], n >= 1.
   // create an array of single node trees
   huffmanNode<T> *hNode = new huffmanNode<T> [n + 1];
   linkedBinaryTree<int> emptyTree;
   for (int i = 1; i <= n; i++)
   {
      hNode[i].weight = weight[i];
      hNode[i].tree = new linkedBinaryTree<int>;
      hNode[i].tree->makeTree(i, emptyTree, emptyTree);
   }

   // make node array into a min heap
   minHeap<huffmanNode<T> > heap(1);
   heap.initialize(hNode, n);

   // repeatedly combine trees from min heap
   // until only one tree remains
   huffmanNode<T> w, x, y;
   linkedBinaryTree<int> *z;
   for (i = 1; i < n; i++)
   {
      // remove two lightest trees from the min heap
      x = heap.top(); heap.pop();
      y = heap.top(); heap.pop();

      // combine into a single tree
      z = new linkedBinaryTree<int>;
      z->makeTree(0, *x.tree, *y.tree);
      w.weight = x.weight + y.weight;
      w.tree = z;
      heap.push(w);
      delete x.tree;
      delete y.tree;
   }

   return heap.top().tree;
}
```

Program 12.10 Construct a Huffman tree

and then draw figures similar to those in Figure 12.9 to show the state of the tree following each removal from the max heap.

27. Do Exercise 26 using the array [-, 11, 10, 9, 8, 7, 6, 5, 4, 3, 2, 1].

28. Write a heap sort method that uses d-heaps (see Exercise 17). Compare the worst-case run times of heap sort using d-heaps for different d values. What value of d gives best performance?

29. Use the ideas of Exercises 15 and 16 to arrive at an implementation of heap sort that is faster than Program 12.8. Experiment with random data and compare the run times of the two implementations.

30. A sort method is said to be **stable** if the relative order of records with equal keys is the same after the sort as it was before the sort. Suppose that records 3 and 10 have the same key. In a stable sort record 3 will precede record 10 following the sort. Is heap sort a stable sort? How about insertion sort?

31. Draw the three-machine LPT schedule for the processing times [6, 5, 3, 2, 9, 7, 1, 4, 8]. What is the finish time for your schedule. Can you find a schedule with a smaller finish time or is your schedule optimal?

32. Do Exercise 31 using the processing times [20, 15, 10, 8, 8, 8].

33. Each iteration of the second **for** loop of Program 12.9 performs one **pop** and one **push**. The two operations together essentially increase the value of the minimum key by an amount equal to the processing time of the job just scheduled. We can speed up Program 12.9 by a constant factor by using an extended min priority queue. The extension includes the methods normally supported by a min priority queue plus the method **changeMin(x)** that changes the minimum element to **x**. This method moves down the heap (as in a remove min operation), moving elements up the heap until it finds an appropriate place for the changed element.

   (a) Develop a new class **extendedMinHeap** that provides all the methods provided by the class **minHeap** plus the method **changeMin**. The class **extendedMinHeap** should be derived from the class **minHeap** that is available from the Web site for this book.

   (b) Rewrite Program 12.9 using the method **changeMin**.

   (c) Conduct experiments to determine the improvement in run time of your new code versus that of Program 12.9.

34. Construct a machine-scheduling instance for which the two-machine LPT schedule achieves the upper bound given in Theorem 12.2.

35. Do Exercise 34 for a three-machine LPT schedule.

36. n items are to be packed into containers. Item i uses s_i units of space, and each container has a capacity c. The packing is to be done using the **worst-fit** rule in which the items are assigned to containers one at a time. When an item is being assigned, we look for a nonempty container with maximum available capacity. If the item fits in this container, the assignment is made; otherwise, this item starts a new container.

   (a) Develop a program to input n, the s_is, and c and to output the assignment of items to containers. Use a max heap to keep track of the available space in the containers.

   (b) What is the time complexity of your program (as a function of n and the number m of containers used)?

37. Draw the Huffman tree for the weights (frequencies) [3, 7, 9, 12, 15, 20, 25].

38. Do Exercise 37 using the weights (frequencies) [2, 4, 5, 7, 9, 10, 14, 17, 18, 50].

39. A **run** is a sorted sequence of elements. Assume that two runs can be merged into a single run in time $O(r+s)$ where r and s are, respectively, the lengths of the two runs being merged. n runs of different lengths are to be merged into a single run by repeatedly merging pairs of runs until only one run remains. Explain how to use Huffman trees to determine a minimum-cost way to merge the n runs.

40. Suppose you are to code text that uses n symbols. A simple way to assign codes that satisfy the prefix property is to start with a right-skewed extended binary tree that has n external nodes, sort the n symbols in decreasing order of frequency $F()$, and assign symbols to external nodes so that an inorder listing of external nodes gives the symbols in decreasing order of their frequency. The sort step takes $O(n \log n)$ time, and the remaining steps take $O(n)$ time. So this method has the same asymptotic complexity as the optimal method described in Section 12.6.3.

   (a) Draw the Huffman tree and the right-skewed tree for the case when you have $n = 5$ symbols a–e with frequencies [4, 6, 7, 9, 10]. Label each external node with the symbol it represents, list the code for each symbol, and give the WEP of each tree.

   (b) Suppose that the n symbols have the same frequency. What is the ratio of the WEPs of the Huffman tree and the right-skewed tree? Assume that n is a power of 2.

   (c) Write a method to construct the right-skewed extended binary tree as described above.

   (d) Compare the actual run time of your method of part (c) and that of Program 12.10.

    (e) Generate random instances and measure the difference in the WEPs of the trees generated by the two methods.

    (f) Based on your results for parts (b), (d), and (e), can you recommend the use of the method of this exercise over the method of Program 12.10? Why?

41. Prove Theorem 12.3 by using induction on the number of external nodes. The induction step should establish the existence of a binary tree with minimum WEP that has a subtree with one internal node and two external nodes corresponding to the two lowest frequencies.

42. Write a method to take a Huffman tree as created by `huffmanTree` (Program 12.10) and to output the code table. What is the time complexity of your method?

43. Develop a complete compression-decompression package based on Huffman codes. Test your code.

44. A collection of n integers in the range 0 through 511 is to be stored. Develop a compression-decompression package for this application. Use Huffman codes.

12.7   REFERENCES AND SELECTED READINGS

A more detailed study of data structures for priority queues and priority-queue variants can be found in the text *Fundamentals of Data Structures in C++* by E. Horowitz, S. Sahni, and D. Mehta, W. H. Freeman, New York, NY, 1994.

    Height-biased leftist trees are described in the monograph *Data Structures and Network Algorithms* by R. Tarjan, SIAM, Philadelphia, PA, 1983, while weight-biased leftist trees are developed in the paper "Weight Biased Leftist Trees and Modified Skip Lists" by S. Cho and S. Sahni, *ACM Jr. on Experimental Algorithmics*, Article 2, 1998.

    You can find out more about NP-hard problems from the books *Computers and Intractability: A Guide to the Theory of NP-Completeness* by M. Garey and D. Johnson, W. H. Freeman, New York, NY, 1979, and *Computer Algorithms* by E. Horowitz, S. Sahni, and S. Rajasekeran, Computer Science Press, New York, NY, 1998. Chapter 12 of *Computer Algorithms* proves Theorem 12.2.

CHAPTER 13

TOURNAMENT TREES

BIRD'S-EYE VIEW

We have reached the halfway point in our journey through the forest of trees. The new tree variety we encounter in this chapter is the tournament tree. Like the heap of Section 12.4, a tournament tree is a complete binary tree that is most efficiently stored by using the array binary tree representation of Section 11.4.1. The basic operation that a tournament tree supports is replacing the maximum (or minimum) element. If we have n elements, this operation takes $\Theta(\log n)$ time. Although this operation can be done with the same asymptotic complexity—in fact, $O(\log n)$—using either a heap or a leftist tree, neither of these structures can implement a predictable tie breaker easily. The tournament tree becomes the data structure of choice when we need to break ties in a prescribed manner, such as to select the element that was inserted first or to select the element on the left (all elements are assumed to have a left-to-right ordering).

We study two varieties of tournament trees: winner and loser trees. Although winner trees are more intuitive and model real-world tournament trees, loser trees can be implemented more efficiently. The applications section at the end of the chapter considers another NP-hard problem, bin packing. Tournament trees are used to obtain efficient implementations of two approximation algorithms for the bin-packing problem. You will find it instructive to see whether you can implement these algorithms in the same time bounds with any of the other data structures developed so far in this text.

13.1   WINNER TREES AND APPLICATIONS

Suppose that n players enter a tennis tournament. The tournament is to be played in the *sudden-death* mode in which a player is eliminated upon losing a match. Pairs of players play matches until only one player remains undefeated. This surviving player is declared the tournament winner. Figure 13.1(a) shows a possible tennis tournament involving eight players a through h. The tournament is described by a binary tree in which each external node represents a player and each internal node represents a match played between players designated by the children of the node. Each level of internal nodes defines a *round* of matches that can be played in parallel. In the first round players a and b, c and d, e and f, and g and h play. The winner of each match is recorded at the internal node that represents the match. In the case of Figure 13.1(a), the four winners are b, d, e, and h. The remaining four players (i.e., the losers) are eliminated. In the next round of matches, b and d play against each other as do e and h. The winners are b and e, who play the final match. The overall winner is e. Figure 13.1(b) shows a possible tournament that involves five players a through e. The winner in this case is c.

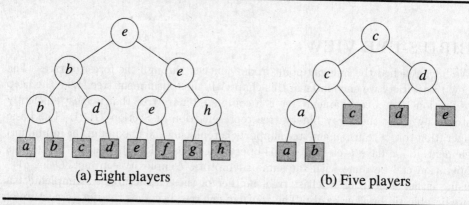

(a) Eight players   (b) Five players

Figure 13.1 Tournament trees

Although both trees of Figure 13.1 are complete binary trees (actually, tree (a) is also a full binary tree), trees that correspond to real-world tournaments do not have to be complete binary trees. However, using complete binary trees minimizes the number of rounds of matches that have to be played. For an n-player tournament, this number is $\lceil \log_2 n \rceil$. The tournament tree depicted in Figure 13.1 is called a **winner tree** because at each internal node, we record the winner of the match played at that node. Section 13.4 considers another variety, called a **loser tree**, in which we record the loser at each internal node. Tournament trees are also known as **selection trees**.

Winner trees may be adapted for computer use. In this adaptation we restrict ourselves to complete binary trees.

Definition 13.1 *A **winner tree** for n players is a complete binary tree with n external and n − 1 internal nodes. Each internal node records the winner of the match played there.* ∎

To determine the winner of a match, we assume that each player has a *value* and that there is a rule to determine the winner based on a comparison of the two players' values. In a **min winner tree**, the player with the smaller value wins, while in a **max winner tree**, the player with the larger value wins. In case of a tie, the player represented by the left child of the node wins. Figure 13.2(a) shows an eight-player min winner tree, while Figure 13.2(b) shows a five-player max winner tree. The number below each external node is the player's value.

(a) Min winner tree   (b) Max winner tree

Figure 13.2 Winner trees

One of the nice things about a winner tree is that we can easily modify the tree to accommodate a change in one of the players. For example, if the value of player *d* changes from 9 to 1, then we need only replay matches on the path from *d* to the root. The change in this value does not affect the outcome of the remaining matches. In some situations we can avoid replaying some of the matches on the path to the root. For example, if in the min winner tree of Figure 13.2(a), the value of player *b* changes from 6 to 5, we play at its parent and *b* loses. There is no need to replay the matches at the grandparent and great-grandparent of *b*, as these matches will have the same outcome as they had before.

Since the number of matches needed to restructure an *n*-player winner tree following a change in one value ranges from a low of 1 to a high of $\lceil \log_2 n \rceil$, the time needed for restructuring is $O(\log n)$. Also, an *n*-player winner tree can be initialized in $\Theta(n)$ time by playing the $n - 1$ matches at the internal nodes by beginning with the matches at the lowest level and working up to the root. Alternatively, the tree can be initialized by performing a postorder traversal. During the visit step, a match is played.

Example 13.1 [Sorting] We may use a min winner tree to sort n elements in $\Theta(n \log n)$ time. First, the winner tree is initialized with the n elements as the players. The sort key is used to decide the outcome of each match. The overall winner is the element with the smallest key. This player's key is now changed to a very large number (say ∞) so that it cannot win against any of the remaining players. We restructure the tree to reflect the change in this player's key. The new overall winner is the element that comes next in sorted order. Its key is changed to ∞, and the tree is restructured. Now the overall winner is the element that is third in sorted order. Continuing in this way, we can sort the n elements. It takes $\Theta(n)$ time to initialize the winner tree. Each key change and restructure operation takes $\Theta(\log n)$ time because when the key of the tournament winner changes, we need to replay all matches on the path to the root. The restructuring needs to be done $n-1$ times, so the overall restructuring time is $\Theta(n \log n)$. Adding in the time needed to initialize the winner tree, the complexity of the sort method becomes $\Theta(n + n \log n)$ $= \Theta(n \log n)$. ∎

Example 13.2 [Run Generation] The sorting methods (insertion sort, heap sort, etc.) we have discussed so far are all **internal sorting methods**. These methods require that the elements to be sorted fit in the memory of our computer. When the element collection does not fit in memory, internal sort methods do not work well because they require too many accesses to the external storage media (say a disk) on which all or part of the collection resides. In this case sorting is accomplished with an **external sorting method**. A popular approach to external sorting involves (1) generating sorted sequences called **runs** and (2) merging these runs together to create a single run.

Suppose we wish to sort a collection of 16,000 records and we are able to sort up to 1000 records at a time using an internal sort. Then in step 1, we do the following 16 times to create 16 runs:

> Input 1000 records.
> Sort these records using an internal sort.
> Output the sorted sequence (or run).

Following this run-generation step, we initiate the run-merging step, step 2. In this step we make several merge passes over the runs. In each merge pass we merge up to k runs, creating a single sorted run. So each merge pass reduces the number of runs by a factor of $1/k$. Merge passes are continued until the number of runs becomes 1.

In our example of 16 runs, we could perform two passes of four-way merges, as in Figure 13.3. The initial 16 runs are labeled R1 $\cdots$ R16. First, runs R1 $\cdots$ R4 merge to obtain the run $S1$, which is 4000 records long. Then R5 $\cdots$ R8 merge, and so on. At the second merge pass, S1 $\cdots$ S4 are merged to create the single run T1, which is the desired output from the external sort.

Figure 13.3 Four-way merging of 16 runs

A simple way to merge k runs is to repeatedly remove the element with smallest key from the front of these k runs. This element is moved to the output run being generated. The process is complete when all elements have been moved from the input k runs to the output run. Notice that to determine the next element in the output run all we need in memory is the key of the front element of each input run. We can merge k runs of arbitrary length as long as we have enough memory to hold k keys. In practice, we will want to input and output many elements at a time so as to reduce the input/output time.

In our 16,000-record example, each run is 1000 records long, and our memory capacity is also 1000 records. To merge the first four runs, we could partition memory into five buffers, each large enough to hold 200 records. Four of these buffers are designated input buffers, and the fifth is an output buffer. Two hundred records from each of the first four runs are input into the four input buffers. The output buffer is used to collect the merged records. Records are merged from the input buffers into the output buffer until one of the following conditions occurs:

- The output buffer becomes full.

- An input buffer becomes empty.

When the first condition occurs, we write the output buffer to disk and resume merging when this write has completed. When the second condition occurs, we read in the next buffer load (if any) for the run that corresponds to the empty input buffer and resume merging when this input has completed. The merge of the four runs is complete when all 4000 records from these runs have been written out as the single run S1. (A more sophisticated run-merging scheme is described in *Fundamentals of Data Structures in C++* by E. Horowitz, S. Sahni, and D. Mehta, Computer Science Press, New York, NY, 1995.)

One of the factors that determines the amount of time spent in the run-merging step is the number of runs generated in step 1. By using a winner tree, we can often reduce the number of runs generated. We begin with a winner tree for p players where each player is an element of the input collection. Each player has an associated key and run number. The first p elements are assigned run number 1. When a match is played between two players, the element with the smaller run number wins. In case of a tie, the keys are compared, and the element with the smaller key wins. If a tie remains, it may be broken arbitrarily. To generate runs, we repeatedly move the overall winner W into the run corresponding to its run-number field and replace the moved element by the next input element N. If the key of N is $\geq$ the key of W, then element N can be output as part of the same run. It is assigned a run number equal to that of W. If the key of N is less than that of W, outputting N after W in the same run violates the sorting constraint on a run. N is assigned a run number that is 1 more than that of W.

When using this method to generate runs, the average run length is $\approx 2p$. When $2p$ is larger than the memory capacity, we expect to get fewer runs than we do by using the simple scheme proposed earlier. In fact, if our input collection is already sorted (or nearly sorted), only one run is generated and we can skip the run-merging step, step 2. ∎

Example 13.3 [k-Way Merging] In a k-way merge (see Example 13.2), k runs are merged to generate a single sorted run. The simple scheme, described in Example 13.2, to perform a k-way merge requires $O(k)$ time per element merged to the output run because in each iteration we need to find the smallest of k keys. The total time to generate a run of size n is, therefore, $O(kn)$. We can reduce this time to $\Theta(k+n\log k)$ using a winner tree. First we spend $\Theta(k)$ time to initialize a winner tree for k players. The k players are the first elements of the k runs to be merged. Then the winner is moved to the output run and replaced by the next element from the corresponding input run. If there is no next element in this run, it is replaced by an element with very large key (say ∞). We remove and replace the winner a total of n times at a cost of $\Theta(\log k)$ each time. The total time needed to perform the k-way merge is $\Theta(k + n \log k)$. ∎

EXERCISES

1. Draw the max and min winner trees for players [3, 5, 6, 7, 20, 8, 2, 9]. Now draw the trees that result when 20 is changed to 1. Obtain the new trees by replaying only the matches on the path from 1 to the root.

2. Draw the max and min winner trees for players [20, 10, 12, 18, 30, 16, 35, 33, 45, 7, 15, 19, 33, 11, 17, 25]. Now draw the trees that result when 17 is changed to 42. Obtain the new trees by replaying only the matches on the path from 42 to the root.

3. Draw the max and min winner trees for players [3, 5, 6, 7, 20, 8, 2, 9, 12, 15, 30, 17]. Now draw the trees that result when 2 is changed to 11. Obtain the new trees by replaying only the matches on the path from 11 to the root.

4. Draw the max and min winner trees for players [10, 2, 7, 6, 5, 9, 12, 35, 22, 15, 1, 3, 4]. Now draw the trees that result when 9 is changed to 0. Obtain the new trees by replaying only the matches on the path from 0 to the root.

5. (a) Describe how a min heap can be used in place of a min winner tree to generate runs (see Example 13.2). How much time does it take to generate each element of a run?

   (b) What are the advantages/disadvantages of using a min winner tree rather than a heap in this application?

6. (a) Describe how a min heap can be used in place of a min winner tree when performing a k-way merge (see Example 13.3).

   (b) What are the advantages/disadvantages of using a min winner tree rather than a heap in this application?

13.2   THE ADT *WinnerTree*

In specifying the abstract data type *WinnerTree*, we make the assumption that the number of players is static. That is, after the tree is initialized for some number n of players, we do not increase or decrease the number of players. The players themselves are not part of the winner tree. So only the internal nodes of Figure 13.1 make up the winner tree. As a result, the operations that a winner tree needs to support are initialize a winner tree for n players, return the winner, and replay the matches on the path from player i to the root. The specification of these operations is provided in ADT 13.1.

Program 13.1 gives the abstract class **winnerTree**. Although the abstract class doesn't specify a mechanism to determine the winner of a match, we assume that this may be done using the <= operator. That is, x <= y iff player x wins the match between players x and y. By suitably overloading the operator <=, we can construct min winner trees, max winner trees, and so forth.

13.3   WINNER TREE IMPLEMENTATION

13.3.1   Representation

We shall represent a winner tree using the array representation of a complete binary tree. A winner tree for n players requires n-1 internal nodes tree[1:n-1]. The players (or external nodes) are represented as an array player[1:n], so tree[i] is an index into the array player and hence is of type int. tree[i] gives the winner of the match played at node i of the winner tree. Figure 13.4 gives the

---

AbstractDataType *WinnerTree*
{
    instances
        complete binary trees with each node pointing to the winner of the match
        played there; the external nodes represent the players

    operations
        initialize(*a*) : initialize a winner tree for the players in the array *a*

        winner() : return the tournament winner

        rePlay(*i*) : replay matches following a change in player *i*
}

ADT 13.1 Abstract data type specification of a winner tree

```
template<class T>
class winnerTree
{
   public:
      virtual ~winnerTree() {}
      virtual void initialize(T *thePlayer,
                              int theNumberOfPlayers) = 0;
         // create winner tree with thePlayer[1:numberOfPlayers]
      virtual int winner() const = 0;
         // return index of winner
      virtual void rePlay(int thePLayer) = 0;
         // replay matches following a change in thePLayer
};
```

Program 13.1 The abstract class winnerTree

---

correspondence between the nodes of a winner tree and the arrays tree and player
for the case of a five-player tree.

    To implement the interface methods, we must be able to determine the parent
tree[p] of an external node player[i]. When the number of external nodes is n,
the number of internal nodes is $n - 1$. The left-most internal node at the lowest
level is numbered s where $s = 2^{\lfloor \log_2(n-1) \rfloor}$. Therefore, the number of internal nodes
at the lowest level is $n - s$, and the number *lowExt* of external nodes at the lowest
level is twice this number. For example, in the tree of Figure 13.4, $n = 5$ and $s = 4$.
The left-most internal node at the lowest level is tree[4], and the total number of

$$t[] = tree[] \text{ and } p[] = player[]$$

Figure 13.4 Tree-to-array correspondence

internal nodes at this level is $n - 4 = 1$. The number of lowest-level external nodes is 2. The left-most external node at the second-lowest level is numbered $lowExt + 1$. Let $offset = 2 * s - 1$. Then we see that for any external node player[i], its parent tree[p] is given by

$$p = \begin{cases} (i + offset)/2 & i \leq lowExt \\ (i - lowExt + n - 1)/2 & i > lowExt \end{cases} \tag{13.1}$$

13.3.2   Initializing a Winner Tree

To initialize a winner tree, we play matches beginning at players that are right children and going up the tree whenever a match is played at a right child. For this purpose right-child players are considered from left to right. So in the tree of Figure 13.4, we first play matches beginning at player 2, then we begin at player 3, and finally, we begin at player 5. When we start at player 2, we play the match at tree[4]. The match at the next level, that is, at tree[2], is not played because tree[4] is a left child. We now start playing at player[3]. The match at tree[2] is played, but the one at tree[1] is not (because tree[2] is a left child). Finally, we start at player[5] and play the matches at tree[3] and tree[1]. Notice that when a match is played at tree[i], the players for this match have already been determined and recorded in the children of tree[i].

13.3.3 Replaying Matches

When the value of player `thePlayer` is changed, it is necessary to replay some or all of the matches on the path from external node `player[thePlayer]` to the root `tree[1]`. For simplicity we replay all matches on this path. Actually, in the applications of Examples 13.1, 13.2, and 13.3, only the value of the winner is changed. Changing the value of the winner requires a replay of all matches on the path from the winner's external node to the root.

13.3.4 The Class `completeWinnerTree`

The winner tree data structure is implemented as the class `completeWinnerTree` (the code is available from the Web site for this book). The complexity of `winner` is $O(1)$, that of `initialize` is $O(n)$, and that of `rePlay` is $O(\log n)$ where n is the number of players. The class constructor creates a winner tree given an array of players. Its complexity is $O(n)$.

Exercises 11, 12, and 13 consider ways to simplify the implementation of a winner tree by using a larger array `tree` than is used in the class `completeWinnerTree`.

EXERCISES

7. Modify the method `completeWinnerTree<T>::rePlay` to play only those matches that are necessary. In particular, we can stop playing when the winner of a match is the same as the previous winner of that match provided this previous winner is not the changed player `thePlayer`.

8. Write a sort function that uses a winner tree to repeatedly extract elements in sorted order (see Example 13.1).

9. Write and test a recursive method to initialize a winner tree. What is the complexity of your method? Is your code any simpler than that of `completeWinnerTree<T>::initialize`?

10. Write and test a simplified version of `completeWinnerTree` for the case when the number of players is a power of 2.

11. Let n be the number of players and let m be the smallest integer that is a power of 2 and is $\geq n$. For example, if $n = 14$, then $m = 16$. We can simplify the implementation of `WinnerTree` by setting up a winner tree for m rather than n players. The parent of the external node `player[thePlayer]` is `tree[m+thePlayer-1]/2`. Note that `player[n+1:m]` is undefined.

   (a) What is the maximum additional space this scheme takes over that taken by the scheme of the text?

   (b) Implement a winner tree class using this scheme.

(c) Test the correctness of your code.

(d) Do you expect any significant difference in the run time between your new implementation and that of the text?

12. The winner tree code of the text is complex because the way we find the players for matches at the leaves of the tree **tree** is different from the way we find these players for the remaining matches. We can eliminate this difference (and hence simplify the code) by increasing the size of **tree** by n and placing the additional nodes between the external/player nodes and the nodes at which matches are played. Now the parent of **player[i]** is **tree[i + offset]** when i $\leq$ lowExt and is **tree[i - lowExt + n - 1]** when i > lowExt. The parent of **player[i]** is initialized with the index i. With this modification, the match at **tree[i]** is always played between **player[tree[2*i]]** and **player[tree[2*i+1]]**, $1 \leq i < n$.

(a) Implement a winner tree class using this scheme.

(b) Test the correctness of your code.

(c) Do you expect any significant difference in the run time between your new implementation and that of the text?

13. In the implementation of **completeWinnerTree**, the special case when n is odd can be eliminated by setting up a tree for **m = n** players when n is even and for **m = n+1** players when n is odd. This method requires us to use $O(1)$ additional space compared to the text's implementation of **completeWinnerTree**. When n is odd, **player[m]** is undefined.

(a) Implement a winner tree class using this scheme.

(b) Test the correctness of your code.

(c) Compare the relative advantages/disadvantages of the winner tree implementations of the text, Exercise 11, and this exercise.

13.4 LOSER TREES

Let us examine the **rePlay** operation on a winner tree. In many applications (see Examples 13.1, 13.2, and 13.3) this operation is performed only after a new player replaces the previous winner. In these applications all matches on the path from the external node that represents the winner up to the root have to be replayed. Consider the min winner tree of Figure 13.2(a). When a player (f') with key 5 replaces the winner f, the first match is played between e and f'. e is the player who lost the match previously played at this node against f. The winner, f', plays the next match at internal node **tree[3]** with g. Notice that g is the player who lost the match previously played at **tree[3]** between g and f. The winner at **tree[3]** is g. Next g plays at the root against a. Again a is the player who lost the match previously played at the root.

We can reduce the work needed to determine the players of each match on the path from the changed winner player[i] to the root if we record in each internal node the loser of the match played at that node, rather than the winner. The overall winner may be recorded in tree[0]. Figure 13.5(a) shows the loser tree for the eight players of Figure 13.2(a). Now when the winner f is changed to have key 5, we move to its parent tree[6]. The match is to be played between player[tree[6]] and player[6]. To determine the opponent for $f' = $ player[6], we simply look at tree[6]. In a winner tree we would need to determine the other child of tree[6]. After playing the match at tree[6], the loser e is recorded here, and f' advances to play at tree[3] with the previous loser of this match. This loser, g, is available from tree[3]. f' loses, and this fact is recorded in tree[3]. The winner g plays with the previous loser of the match at tree[1]. This loser, a, is available from tree[1]. The new loser tree appears in Figure 13.5(b).

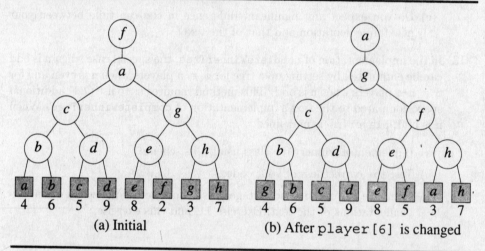

(a) Initial   (b) After player[6] is changed

Figure 13.5 Eight-player min loser trees

Although a loser tree simplifies the replaying of matches following a change in the previous winner, it does not result in a similar simplification when a change is made in other players. For example, suppose that the key of player d is changed from 9 to 3. Matches are to be replayed at tree[5], tree[2], and tree[1]. At tree[5] d has to play c, but c is not the previous loser of this match. At tree[2] d has to play a, but a did not lose the match previously played here. At tree[1] d has to play f, not the player who previously lost at tree[1]. To replay these matches easily, a winner tree is needed. Therefore, we expect a loser tree to give better performance than a winner tree only when the rePlay(i) method is restricted to the case when `player[i]` is the previous tournament winner.

EXERCISES

14. Draw the max and min loser trees for players [3, 5, 6, 7, 20, 8, 2, 9]. Now draw the trees that result when 20 is changed to 10 in the max loser tree and 2 is changed to 4 in the min loser tree. Obtain the new trees by replaying only the matches on the path from the changed element to the root.

15. Draw the max and min loser trees for players [20, 10, 12, 18, 30, 16, 35, 33, 45, 7, 15, 19, 33, 11, 17, 25]. Now draw the trees that result when 45 is changed to 34 in the max loser tree and 7 is changed to 12 in the min loser tree. Obtain the new trees by replaying only the matches on the path from the changed element to the root.

16. Draw the max and min loser trees for players [20, 10, 12, 14, 9, 11, 30, 33, 25, 7, 15]. Now draw the trees that result when 33 is changed to 5 in the max loser tree and 7 is changed to 16 in the min loser tree. Obtain the new trees by replaying only the matches on the path from the changed element to the root.

17. Draw the max and min loser trees for players [3, 5, 6, 7, 20, 8, 2, 9, 12, 15, 30, 17]. Now draw the trees that result when 30 is changed to 19 in the max loser tree and 2 is changed to 14 in the min loser tree. Obtain the new trees by replaying only the matches on the path from the changed element to the root.

18. Draw the max and min loser trees for players [10, 2, 7, 6, 5, 9, 12, 35, 22, 15, 1, 3, 4]. Now draw the trees that result when 35 is changed to 8 in the max loser tree and 1 is changed to 11 in the min loser tree. Obtain the new trees by replaying only the matches on the path from the changed element to the root.

19. (a) Develop a C++ class `completeLoserTree` using a representation similar to that used for winner trees (Section 13.3). The tournament winner should be recorded in `tree[0]`. In place of the public method `rePlay(i)`, define the public method `rePlay()` to replay matches beginning at the winner of the previous tournament.

    (b) A simple way to initialize a loser tree is to first construct a winner tree and then make a level-order traversal, replacing the entry at each internal node with the loser. The traversal is done from top to bottom. When at `tree[i]`, its children tell us who played at `tree[i]`. and from this information we can determine who lost. Write code for `initialize` using this strategy. Show that your code takes $O(n)$ time to initialize a loser tree with n players.

(c) Write a recursive version of `initialize`. The complexity of your code should be $O(n)$.

(d) Write a version of `initialize` that uses the following strategy. Start playing matches at the left-most match node both of whose children are player nodes. Play matches from here to the root as far as you can, recording losers. When a match cannot be played (because one of the players is unknown), record the single player determined for that match. Repeat this process starting at a suitable match node. Continue until all matches have been played. Show that your code takes $O(n)$ time to initialize a loser tree with n players.

20. Develop the C++ class `fullLoserTree` that implements a loser tree as a full binary tree as described in Exercise 11. See Exercise 19 for initialization strategies. Test the correctness of your code.

21. Develop the C++ class `completeLoserTree2` that implements a loser tree using the strategy described in Exercise 12. See Exercise 19 for initialization strategies. Test the correctness of your code.

22. Write a sort program that uses a loser tree to repeatedly extract elements in sorted order. What is the complexity of your program?

13.5   APPLICATIONS

13.5.1   Bin Packing Using First Fit

Problem Description

In the bin-packing problem, we have an unlimited supply of bins that have a capacity `binCapacity` each and n objects that need to be packed into these bins. Object i requires `objectSize[i]`, $0 < $ `objectSize[i]` $\leq$ `binCapacity`, units of capacity. A **feasible** packing is an assignment of objects to bins so that no bin's capacity is exceeded. A feasible packing that uses the fewest number of bins is an **optimal packing**.

Example 13.4 [Truck Loading] A freight company needs to pack parcels into trucks. Each parcel has a weight, and each truck has a load limit (assumed to be the same for all trucks). In the truck-loading problem, we are to pack the parcels into trucks using the fewest number of trucks. This problem may be modeled as a bin-packing problem with each truck being a bin and each parcel an object that needs to be packed. ∎

Example 13.5 [Chip Placement] A collection of electronic chips is to be placed in rows on a circuit board of a given width. The chips have the same height but different widths. The height, and hence area, of the circuit board is minimized by minimizing the number of rows used. The chip-placement problem may also be modeled as a bin-packing problem with each row being a bin and each chip an object that needs to be packed. The board's width is the bin capacity, and the chip's length, the capacity needed by the corresponding object.   ■

Approximation Algorithms

The bin-packing problem, like the machine-scheduling problem of Section 12.6.2, is an NP-hard problem. As a result, it is often solved using an approximation algorithm. In the case of bin packing, such an algorithm generates solutions that use a number of bins that is close to minimum. Four popular approximation algorithms for this problem are

1. *First Fit (FF)*
   Objects are considered for packing in the order 1, 2, $\cdots$, n. We assume a large number of bins arranged from left to right. Object i is packed into the left-most bin into which it fits.

2. *Best Fit (BF)*
   Let bin[j].unusedCapacity denote the capacity available in bin j. Initially, the unused capacity is binCapacity for all bins. Object i is packed into the bin with the least unusedCapacity that is at least objectSize[i].

3. *First Fit Decreasing (FFD)*
   This method is the same as FF except that the objects are first reordered so that objectSize[i] $\geq$ objectSize[i+1], $1 \leq i < n$.

4. *Best Fit Decreasing (BFD)*
   This method is the same as BF except that the objects are reordered as for FFD.

   You should be able to show that none of these methods guarantee optimal packings. All four are intuitively appealing and can be expected to perform well in practice. A worst-fit packing strategy was considered in Exercise 36 of Chapter 12. We may also consider last fit, last-fit decreasing, and worst-fit decreasing strategies.

Theorem 13.1 *Let I be any instance of the bin-packing problem. Let b(I) be the number of bins used by an optimal packing. The number of bins used by FF and BF never exceeds $(17/10)b(I) + 2$, while that used by FFD and BFD does not exceed $(11/9)b(I) + 4$.*

Example 13.6 Four objects with objectSize[1:4] = [3, 5, 2, 4] are to be packed in bins of size 7. When FF is used, object 1 goes into bin 1 and object 2 into bin 2.

Object 3 fits into the first bin and is placed there. Object 4 does not fit into either of the two bins used so far, and a new bin is used. The solution produced utilizes three bins and has objects 1 and 3 in bin 1, object 2 in bin 2, and object 4 in bin 3.

When BF is used, objects 1 and 2 get into bins 1 and 2, respectively. Object 3 gets into bin 2, as this bin provides a better fit than does bin 1. Object 4 now fits into bin 1. The packing obtained uses only two bins and has objects 1 and 4 in bin 1 and objects 2 and 3 in bin 2.

For FFD and BFD the objects are packed in the order 2, 4, 1, 3. In both cases a two-bin packing is obtained. Objects 2 and 3 are in bin 1, and objects 1 and 4 are in bin 2. ∎

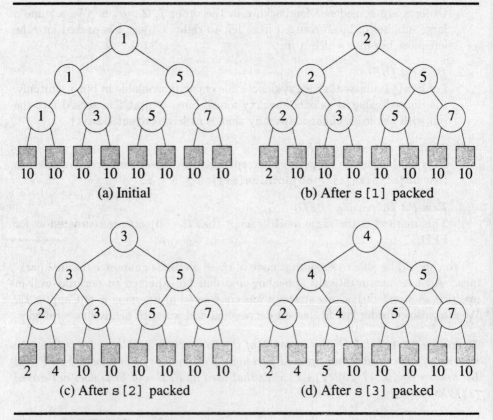

Figure 13.6 First-fit max winner trees

First Fit and Winner Trees

The FF and FFD methods can be implemented so as to run in $O(n \log n)$ time using a winner tree. Since the maximum number of bins ever needed is n, we can begin with n empty bins. Initially, `bin[j].unusedCapacity = binCapacity` for all n bins. Next a max winner tree with the `bin[j]`'s as players is created. Figure 13.6(a) shows the max winner tree for the case n = 8 and `binCapacity = 10`. The external nodes represent bins 1 through 8 from left to right. The number below an external node is the space available in that bin. Suppose that `objectSize[1]` = 8. To find the left-most bin for this object, we begin at the root `tree[1]`. By definition, `bin[tree[1]].unusedCapacity ≥ objectSize[1]`. This relationship simply means that there is at least one bin into which the object fits. To find the left-most bin, we determine whether there is enough space in one of the bins 1 through 4. One of these bins has enough space iff `bin[tree[2]].unusedCapacity ≥ objectSize[1]`. In our example this relationship holds, and so we can continue the search for a bin in the subtree with root 2. Now we determine whether there is adequate space in any bin covered by the left subtree of 2 (i.e., the subtree with root 4). If so, we are not interested in bins in the right subtree. In our example we move into the left subtree as `bin[tree[4]].unusedCapacity ≥ objectSize[1]`. Since the left subtree of 4 is an external node, we know that `objectSize[1]` is to be placed in one of node 4's two children. It goes in the left child provided this child has enough space. When object 1 is placed in bin 1, `bin[1].unused-Capacity` reduces to 2 and we must replay matches beginning at `bin[2]`. The new winner tree appears in Figure 13.6(b). Now suppose that `objectSize[2]` = 6. Since `bin[tree[2]].unusedCapacity ≥ 6`, we know that there is a bin with adequate space in the left subtree. So we move here. Then we move into the left subtree `tree[4]` and place object 2 in bin 2. The new configuration appears in Figure 13.6(c). When `objectSize[3]` = 5, the search for a bin leads us into the subtree with root 2. For its left subtree, `bin[tree[4]].unusedCapacity < objectSize[3]`, so no bin in the subtree with root 4 has enough space. As a result, we move into the right subtree 5 and place the object in bin 3. This placement results in the configuration of Figure 13.6(d). Next, suppose `objectSize[4]` = 3. Our search gets us to the subtree with root 4, as `bin[tree[4]].unusedCapacity ≥ objectSize[3]`, and we add object 3 to bin 2.

C++ Implementation of First Fit

First we add the following public method to the class `completeWinnerTree`.

```
int winner(int i) const
   {return (i < numberOfPlayers) ? tree[i] : 0;}
```

This method returns the winner of the match played at internal node i.

The function `firstFitPack` (Program 13.2) implements the first-fit strategy. This function assumes that the number of objects is at least 2 and that the size of each object is ≤ `binCapacity`. These assumptions are enforced by the `main` function (not shown), which inputs the bin capacity and object sizes and then invokes `firstFitPack`.

The function `firstFitPack` employs the data type `binType` that has the lone instance data member `unusedCapacity`. The data type `binType` overloads the operator `<=` so that `x <= y` returns `true` iff `x.unusedCapacity` ≥ `y.unusedCapacity`.

The function `firstFitPack` begins by initializing a max winner tree for n players, where n is the number of bins. Player i represents the current available capacity of bin i. This capacity is initially `binCapacity` for all bins. The method assumes that when a match is played, the left player is the winner unless the right one is larger.

In the second `for` loop, objects are assigned to bins one by one. When object i is being assigned, we follow a path beginning at the root and leading to the left-most bin with adequate space to accommodate the object. From our current position we see whether the left subtree (the root of this subtree is `child`) has a bin with enough capacity. If not, the right subtree (whose root is `child+1`) is guaranteed to have such a bin. A bin in the left subtree is preferred over one in the right. The `while` loop is exited when the left subtree of the current node is an external node (i.e., `child` ≥ n). Notice that our code does not explicitly record the current position. However, we can always compute the current position by dividing `child` by 2 upon exiting the `while` loop. When n is odd, the current position can be an external node. At this time `child` equals n. In all other cases `child` is an internal node. When `child` is at an external node, the bin represented by this node is the winner of the match played at its parent. That is, it is bin `tree[child/2]`. When `child` is at an internal node, we are assured that bin `tree[child]` has enough capacity. However, if this bin is not the left child of its parent, it may not be the left-most such bin. So we check with the bin on its left. Once the bin (`binToUse`) to assign object i to has been determined, the unused capacity of this bin is reduced by `objectSize[i]` and the winner tree is restructured by replaying the matches on the path from this bin to the root.

Each iteration of the second `for` loop of Program 13.2 takes $\Theta(\log n)$ time, where n is the number of objects to be packed. Therefore, the total time spent in the second `for` loop is $O(n \log n)$ time (note that we may not get as far as the second `for` loop for lack of memory to create the bin array and bin objects). The remainder of the method takes $O(n)$ time, and the total time needed to assign the objects to bins is $O(n \log n)$.

Commentary

The method `firstFitPack` uses intimate details of the implementation of a winner tree. For example, it uses the fact that a winner tree is a complete binary tree represented as an array. As a result, the method is able to move down the tree by multiplying by 2 and possibly by adding 1. Moving down the tree in this way

```
void firstFitPack(int *objectSize, int numberOfObjects,
                                    int binCapacity)
{// output first fit packing into bins of size binCapacity
 // objectSize[1:numberOfObjects] are the object sizes

   int n = numberOfObjects;                 // number of objects

   // initialize n bins and winner tree
   binType *bin = new binType [n + 1];  // bins
   for (int i = 1; i <= n; i++)
      bin[i].unusedCapacity = binCapacity;
   completeWinnerTree<binType> winTree(bin, n);

   // pack objects into bins
   for (int i = 1; i <= n; i++)
   {// put object i into a bin
      // find first bin with enough capacity
      int child = 2;  // start search at left child of root
      while (child < n)
      {
          int winner = winTree.winner(child);
          if (bin[winner].unusedCapacity < objectSize[i])
             child++ ;  // first bin is in right subtree
          child *= 2;   // move to left child
      }

      int binToUse;              // will be set to bin to use
      child /= 2;                // undo last left-child move
      if (child < n)
      {// at a tree node
         binToUse = winTree.winner(child);
         // if binToUse is right child, need to check
         // bin binToUse-1.  No harm done by checking
         // bin binToUse-1 even if binToUse is left child.
         if (binToUse > 1 &&
             bin[binToUse - 1].unusedCapacity >= objectSize[i])
            binToUse--;
      }
      else  // arises when n is odd
         binToUse = winTree.winner(child / 2);
```

Program 13.2 The function firstFitPack (continues)

```
        cout << "Pack object " << i << " in bin "
            << binToUse << endl;
        bin[binToUse].unusedCapacity -= objectSize[i];
        winTree.rePlay(binToUse);
    }
}
```

Program 13.2 The function `firstFitPack` (concluded)

defeats one of the objectives of using a class—information hiding. We wish to keep the implementation details of the class away from the user. When the user and class are so separated, we can change the implementation while keeping the public aspects of the class unchanged. Such changes do not affect the correctness of the applications. In the interests of information hiding, we may add methods to the class `completeWinnerTree` to enable the user to move to the left and right children of an internal node, and then we can use these methods in `firstFitPack`.

13.5.2   Bin Packing Using Next Fit

What Is Next Fit?

Next fit is a bin-packing strategy in which objects are packed into bins one at a time. We begin by packing object 1 in bin 1. For the remaining objects, we determine the next nonempty bin that can accommodate the object by polling the bins in a round-robin fashion, beginning at the bin next to the one last used. In such a polling process, if bins 1 through b are in use, then these bins are viewed as arranged in a circle. The bin next to (or after) bin i is i+1 except when i = b; in this case the next bin is bin 1. If the last object placed went into bin j, then the search for a bin for the current object begins at the bin next to bin j. We examine successive bins until we either encounter a bin with enough space or return to bin j. If no bin with sufficient capacity is found, a new bin is started and the object placed into it.

Example 13.7 Six objects with `objectSize[1:6]` = [3, 5, 3, 4, 2, 1] are to be packed in bins of size 7. When next fit is used, object 1 goes into bin 1. Object 2 doesn't fit into a nonempty bin. So a new bin, bin 2, is started with this object in it. For object 3, we begin by examining the nonempty bin next to the last bin used. The last bin used was bin 2, and the bin next to it is bin 1. Bin 1 has enough space, and object 3 goes in it. For object 4, the search begins at bin 2, as bin 1 was the last one used. This bin doesn't have enough space. The bin next to bin 2 (i.e., bin 1) doesn't have enough space either. So a new bin, bin 3, is started with object 4 in it. The search for a bin for object 5 begins at the bin next to bin 3. This bin is bin 1. From here the search moves to bin 2 where the object is actually packed.

For the last object we begin by examining bin 3. Since this bin has enough space, the object is placed here.   ■

The next-fit strategy described above is modeled after a dynamic memory allocation strategy that has the same name. In the context of bin packing, there is another next-fit strategy in which objects are packed one at a time. If an object does not fit into the current bin, then the current bin is closed and a new bin is started. We do not consider this variant of the next-fit strategy in this section.

Next Fit and Winner Trees

A max winner tree may be used to obtain an efficient implementation of the next-fit strategy. As in the case of first fit, the external nodes represent the bins, and matches are played by comparing the available space in the bins. For an n-object problem, we begin with n bins/external nodes. Consider the max winner tree of Figure 13.7, in which six of eight bins are in use. The labeling convention is the same as that used in Figure 13.6. Although the situation shown in Figure 13.7 cannot arise when n = 8, it illustrates how to determine the bin in which to pack the next object. If the last object was placed in bin lastBinUsed and b bins are currently in use, the search for the next bin to use can be broken into two searches as follows:

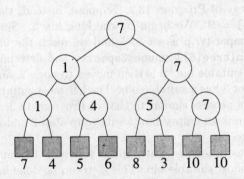

Figure 13.7 A next-fit max winner tree

Step 1: Find the first bin j, j > lastBinUsed into which the object fits. Such a j always exists as the number of bins is n. If this bin is not empty (i.e., j ≤ b), this bin is the bin to use.

Step 2: If step 1 does not find a nonempty bin, find the left-most bin into which the object fits. This bin is now the bin to use.

Consider the situation depicted in Figure 13.7 and suppose that the next object to be placed needs seven units of space. If `lastBinUsed = 3`, then in step 1 we determine that bin 5 has adequate space. Since bin 5 is not an empty bin, the object is placed into it. On the other hand, if `lastBinUsed = 5`, then in step 1 bin 7 is identified as the bin with enough space. Since bin 7 is empty, we move to step 1 and look for the left-most bin with enough capacity. This left-most bin is bin 1, and the object is placed into it.

To implement step 1, we begin at bin $j = $ `lastBinUsed+1`. Notice that if `lastBinUsed = n`, then all n objects must have been packed, as the only way to utilize n bins when the number of objects is n is to pack one object in each bin. So j $\leq$ n. The pseudocode of Figure 13.8 describes the search process adopted from bin j. Basically, we traverse the path from bin j to the root, examining right subtrees until we find the first one that contains a bin with sufficient available capacity. When we find such a subtree, the bin we seek is the left-most bin in this subtree that has sufficient available capacity.

Consider the winner tree of Figure 13.7. Suppose that `lastBinUsed = 1` and `objectSize[i] = 7`. We begin with $j = 2$. First we determine that bin 2 does not have enough capacity. Next we check bin $j+1 = 3$. It doesn't have enough capacity either. So we move to bin j's parent and set p equal to 4. Since p $\neq$ n-1, we reach the `while` loop and determine that the subtree with root 5 does not have a suitable bin. Next we move to node 2 and determine that the subtree with root 3 has a suitable bin. The required bin is the left-most bin in this subtree that has seven or more units of space available. This bin, bin 5, can be found following the strategy of Program 13.2. Suppose, instead, that `lastBinUsed = 3` and `objectSize[i] = 9`. We begin by checking bin 4. Since neither bin 4 nor bin 5 has enough capacity, p is set to 5 and we reach the `while` loop. The first iteration checks `bin[tree[6]].unusedCapacity` and determines that the subtree with root 6 has no suitable bin. p is then moved to node 2, and we determine that the subtree with root 3 has a suitable bin. The left-most suitable bin in this subtree is identified, using a process similar to that of Program 13.2. This left-most bin is bin 7. Since this bin is an empty bin, we move to step 2 and determine that bin 7 is, in fact, the bin to use.

Step 1 requires us to follow a path up the tree and then make a downward pass to identify the left-most suitable bin. This step can be done in $O(\log n)$ time. Step 2 may be done in $O(\log n)$ by following the strategy of Program 13.2, so the overall complexity of the proposed next-fit implementation is $O(n \log n)$.

EXERCISES

23. Suppose that $binCapacity = 10$, $n = 5$, and $objectSize[0 : 4] = [6, 1, 4, 4, 5]$.

    (a) Determine an optimal packing for these objects.

    (b) Give the assignment of objects to bins obtained by using each of these methods: FF, BF, FFD, and BFD.

```
// Find nearest bin to right of lastBinUsed into which object i fits.
j = lastBinUsed + 1;
if (bin[j].unusedCapacity >= objectSize[i])
   return j;
if (bin[j+1].unusedCapacity >= objectSize[i])
   return j + 1;

p = parent of bin[j];
if (p == n - 1)
{// special case
   let q be the external node to the right of tree[p];
   if (bin[q].unusedCapacity >= objectSize[i])
      return q;
}


// Move toward root looking for first right subtree that has a
// bin with enough capacity. Subtree to right of p is p+1.

p /= 2; // move to parent
while (bin[tree[p+1]].unusedCapacity < objectSize[i])
   p /= 2;


return first bin in subtree p+1 into which object i fits;
```

Figure 13.8 Pseudocode for step 1

(c) For the packings of part (b), determine the ratio (number of bins used) / (minimum number of bins needed).

24. Do Exercise 23 for the case when $binCapacity = 11$, $n = 30$, $objectSize[0:9] = 2$, $objectSize[10:19] = 3$, and $objectSize[20:29] = 6$.

25. The function firstFitPack (Program 13.2) takes $\Theta(\log n)$ time to assign an object to a bin, even when the number of bins used so far is much less than n. We can reduce this time by beginning the search for a bin at the root of the smallest subtree that includes both bin 1 and bin b where b is the right-most bin currently in use; that is, we begin at the nearest ancestor of external nodes 1 and b. So when b is 3, we begin at internal node 2. If none of the bins 1 through b has enough space, b is increased by 1. Also, during a replay, matches are played only as far as the nearest common ancestor of 1

and b. Rewrite Program 13.2 using these suggestions and then compare the run times of the two versions using randomly generated instances with n = 1000; 5000; 50,000; and 100,000.

26. (a) Add the public methods root(), leftChild(i), and rightChild(i) to the class completeWinnerTree. These methods, respectively, return the root of the winner tree (i.e., 1) and the left and right children of the internal node i. The last two methods should return 0 in case the respective child is an external node.

   (b) Now rewrite firstFitPack (Program 13.2) so as to conform to the principles of information hiding described in the commentary of Section 13.5.1.

27. Although it is quite difficult to prove that the number of bins used by first fit and best fit never exceeds $\lceil (17/10)b(I) \rceil$, where $b(I)$ is the minimum number of bins needed by instance I, you should be able to prove that the number of bins never exceeds $2b(I)$ with modest effort. Prove this weaker bound.

28. Compare the number of bins required using worst fit (see Exercise 36 of Chapter 12), first fit, first-fit decreasing, and next fit. Do this comparison by generating random instances with $n = 500$, 1000, 2000, and 5000.

29. (a) Write a C++ program for the next-fit strategy to pack bins. Use the two-step approach outlined in Section 13.5.2 and base the implementation of step 1 on the pseudocode of Figure 13.8.

   (b) Compare the number of bins used by next fit and first fit on randomly generated bin-packing instances.

30. Write a C++ program to implement the last-fit bin-packing strategy that puts each object into the right-most bin into which it fits. If an object fits in no bin, a new bin is started. Test your code. What is its time complexity?

13.6   REFERENCES AND SELECTED READINGS

You can learn more about tournament trees from the book *The Art of Computer Programming: Sorting and Searching*, Volume 3, Second Edition, by D. Knuth, Addison-Wesley, Reading, MA, 1998.

The proof of Theorem 13.1 is rather laborious and can be found in the papers "Resource Constrained Scheduling as Generalized Bin-Packing" by M. Garey, R. Graham, D. Johnson, and A. Yao, *Journal of Combinatorial Theory*, Series A, 1976, 257–298 and "Worst-Case Performance Bounds for Simple One-Dimensional Packing Algorithms" by D. Johnson, A. Demers, J. Ullman, M. Garey, and R. Graham, *SIAM Journal on Computing*, 1974, 299–325.

CHAPTER 14

BINARY SEARCH TREES

BIRD'S-EYE VIEW

This chapter and the next develop tree structures suitable for the representation of a dictionary. Although we have already seen data structures such as skip lists and hash tables that can be used to represent a dictionary, the binary search tree data structures developed in this chapter and the balanced search tree structures developed in Chapter 15 provide additional flexibility and/or better worst-case performance guarantees.

This chapter examines binary search trees and indexed binary search trees. Binary search trees provide an asymptotic performance that is comparable to that of skip lists—the expected complexity of a search (or find), insert, or delete (or erase) operation is $\Theta(\log n)$, while the worst-case complexity is $\Theta(n)$; and elements may be output in ascending order in $\Theta(n)$ time. Although the worst-case complexities of the search, insert, and delete operations are the same for binary search trees and hash tables, hash tables have a superior expected complexity—$\Theta(1)$—for these operations. Binary search trees, however, allow you to search efficiently for keys that are close to a specified key. For example, you can find the key nearest to the key k (i.e., either largest key $\leq k$ or smallest key $\geq k$) in expected time $\Theta(n)$. The expected time for this operation is $\Theta(n + D)$ for hash tables, where D is the hash table divisor, and $\Theta(\log n)$ for skip lists.

Indexed binary search trees allow you to perform dictionary operations both by

529

key value and by rank—get the element with the 10th smallest key and remove the element with the 100th smallest key. The expected time for by-rank operations is the same as for by-key operations. Indexed binary search trees may be used to represent linear lists (defined in Chapter 5); the elements have a rank (i.e., index) but no key. The result is a linear list representation in which the expected complexity of the *get*, *erase*, and *insert* operations is $O(\log n)$. Recall that the array and linked representations of linear lists developed in Chapters 5 and 6 perform these operations with expected complexity $\Theta(n)$. The *get* operation for array representations is an exception; it takes $\Theta(1)$ time. Hash tables cannot be extended to support by-rank operations efficiently. Skip lists may be extended to permit by-rank operations with expected time complexity $\Theta(\log n)$.

Although the asymptotic complexity (both expected and worst case) for all tasks stated above is the same for binary search trees and skip lists, we can impose a balancing constraint on binary search trees so that the worst-case complexity for each of the stated tasks is $\Theta(\log n)$. Balanced search trees are the subject of Chapter 15.

Three applications of binary search trees are developed in the applications section. The first is the computation of a histogram. The second application is the implementation of the best-fit approximation method for the NP-hard bin-packing problem of Section 13.5.1. The final application is the crossing-distribution problem that arises when we route wires in a routing channel. We can improve the expected performance of the histogram application by using hashing in place of the search tree. In the best-fit application, the searches are not done by an exact match (i.e., we do a nearest key search), and so hashing cannot be used. In the crossing-distribution problem, the operations are done by rank, and so hashing cannot be used here either. The worst-case performance of each of these applications can be improved by using any of the balanced binary search tree structures developed in Chapter 15 in place of the unbalanced binary search tree developed in this chapter.

14.1   DEFINITIONS

14.1.1   Binary Search Trees

The abstract data type *dictionary* was introduced in Section 10.1, and in Section 10.5 we saw that when a hash table represents a dictionary, the dictionary operations (find, insert, and erase) take $\Theta(1)$ expected time. However, the worst-case time for these operations is linear in the number n of dictionary entries. A hash table no longer provides good expected performance when we extend the ADT *dictionary* to include operations such as

1. Output in ascending order of keys.

2. Get the kth element in ascending order.

3. Delete the kth element.

To perform operation (1), we need to gather the elements from the table, sort them, and then output them. If a divisor D chained table is used, the elements can be gathered in $O(D+n)$ time, sorted in $O(n \log n)$ time, and output in $O(n)$ time. The total time for operation (1) is therefore $O(D + n \log n)$. If linear open addressing is used for the hash table, the gathering step takes $O(b)$ time where b is the number of buckets. The total time for operation (1) is then $O(b + n \log n)$. Operations (2) and (3) can be done in $O(D+n)$ time when a chained table is used and in $O(b)$ time when linear open addressing is used. To achieve these complexities for operations (2) and (3), we must use a linear-time algorithm to determine the kth element of a collection of n elements (explained in Section 18.2.4).

The basic dictionary operations (find, insert, erase) can be performed in $O(\log n)$ time when a balanced search tree is used. Operation (1) can then be performed in $\Theta(n)$ time. By using an indexed balanced search tree, we can also perform operations (2) and (3) in $O(\log n)$ time. Section 14.6 examines other applications where a balanced tree results in an efficient solution, while a hash table does not.

Rather than jump straight into the study of balanced trees, we first develop a simpler structure called a binary search tree.

Definition 14.1 *A **binary search tree** is a binary tree that may be empty. A nonempty binary search tree satisfies the following properties:*

1. *Every element has a key (or value), and no two elements have the same key; therefore, all keys are distinct.*

2. *The keys (if any) in the left subtree of the root are smaller than the key in the root.*

3. *The keys (if any) in the right subtree of the root are larger than the key in the root.*

4. *The left and right subtrees of the root are also binary search trees.*   ∎

There is some redundancy in this definition. Properties 2, 3, and 4 together imply that the keys must be distinct. Therefore, property 1 can be replaced by the following property: The root has a key. The preceding definition is, however, clearer than the nonredundant version.

Some binary trees in which the elements have distinct keys appear in Figure 14.1. The number inside a node is the element key. The tree of Figure 14.1(a) is not a binary search tree despite the fact that it satisfies properties 1, 2, and 3. The right subtree fails to satisfy property 4. This subtree is not a binary search tree, as its right subtree has a key value (22) that is smaller than the key value in the right subtrees' root (25). The binary trees of Figures 14.1(b) and (c) are binary search trees.

Figure 14.1 Binary trees

We can remove the requirement that all elements in a binary search tree need distinct keys. Now we replace smaller in property 2 by smaller or equal and larger in property 3 by larger or equal; the resulting tree is called a **binary search tree with duplicates**.

14.1.2   Indexed Binary Search Trees

An **indexed binary search tree** is derived from an ordinary binary search tree by adding the field leftSize to each tree node. This field gives the number of elements in the node's left subtree. Figure 14.2 shows two indexed binary search trees. The number inside a node is the element key, while that outside is the value of leftSize. Notice that leftSize also gives the index of an element with respect to the elements in its subtree (this condition is a consequence of the fact that all elements in the left subtree of x precede x). For example, in the tree of Figure 14.2 (a), the elements (in sorted order) in the subtree with root 20 are 12, 15, 18, 20, 25, and 30. Viewed as a linear list $(e_0, e_1, \cdots, e_4)$, the index of the root is 3, which equals its leftSize value. In the subtree with root 25, the elements (in sorted order) are 25 and 30, so the index of the root element 25 is 0 and its leftSize value is also 0.

Figure 14.2 Indexed binary search trees

EXERCISES

1. Start with a complete binary tree that has 10 nodes. Place the keys [1, 2, 3, 4, 5, 6, 7, 8, 9, 10], one key per node, so that the result is a binary search tree. Label each node with its leftSize value.

2. Start with a complete binary tree that has 13 nodes. Place the keys [1, 2, 3, 4, 5, 6, 7, 8, 9, 10, 11, 12, 13], one key per node, so that the result is a binary search tree. Label each node with its leftSize value.

14.2   ABSTRACT DATA TYPES

ADT 14.1 gives the abstract data type specification for a binary search tree. An indexed binary search tree supports all the binary search tree operations. In addition, it supports search and deletion by rank. Its abstract data type specification is given in ADT 14.2. The abstract data types *dBSTree* (binary search trees with duplicates) and *dIndexedBSTree* may be specified in a similar way.

Programs 14.1 and 14.2 give C++ abstract classes for the ADTs *bsTree* and *indexedBSTree*, respectively.

EXERCISES

3. How much (expected) time does it take to do the *bsTree* operations of ADT 14.1 using skip lists?

4. Provide a specification for the abstract data type *dBSTree* (binary search tree with duplicates). Define a C++ abstract class that corresponds to this ADT.

AbstractDataType *bsTree*
{

    instances

        binary trees, each node has a pair whose first component is a key and whose second component is the value associated with the key; all keys are distinct; keys in the left subtree of any node are smaller than the key in the node; those in the right subtree are larger

    operations

        $find(k)$: return the pair with key k

        $insert(p)$: insert the pair p into the search tree

        $erase(k)$: delete the pair with key k

        $ascend()$: output all pairs in ascending order of key

}

ADT 14.1 Abstract data type specification of a binary search tree

---

AbstractDataType *IndexedBSTree*
{

    instances

        same as for `bsTree` except that each node also has a `leftSize` field

    operations

        $find(k)$: return the pair with key k

        $get(index)$: return the *index*th pair

        $insert(p)$: insert pair p into the search tree

        $erase(k)$: delete the pair with key k

        $delete(index)$: delete the *index*th pair

        $ascend()$: output all pairs in ascending order of key

}

ADT 14.2 Abstract data type specification of an indexed binary search tree

```
template<class K, class E>
class bsTree : public dictionary<K,E>
{
    public:
        virtual void ascend() = 0;
                        // output in ascending order of key
};
```

Program 14.1 The C++ abstract class `bsTree`

```
template<class K, class E>
class indexedBSTree : public bsTree<K,E>
{
    public:
        virtual pair<const K, E>* get(int) const = 0;
                        // return pointer to pair with given index
        virtual void delete(int) = 0;
                        // delete pair with given index
};
```

Program 14.2 The C++ abstract class `indexedBSTree`

5. Provide a specification for the abstract data type *dIndexedBSTree* (indexed binary search tree with duplicates). Define a C++ abstract class that corresponds to this ADT.

14.3 BINARY SEARCH TREE OPERATIONS AND IMPLEMENTATION

14.3.1 The Class binarySearchTree

Since the number of elements in a binary search tree as well as its shape change as operations are performed, a binary search tree is represented by using the linked representation of Section 11.4.2. We can greatly simplify the task of developing the class `binarySearchTree` if we derive this class from `linkedBinaryTree` (Section 11.8). Each element in the linked binary tree is a pair of type `pair<const K, E>`, where K is the data type of the key and E is the data type of the item associated with the key.

Since `binarySearchTree` is derived from `linkedBinaryTree`, the method `ascend` of the abstract class `bsTree` can be implemented as a call to the `linkedBinaryTree` method inOrderOutput as is done below.

```
void ascend() {inOrderOutput();}
```

The method inOrderOutput first outputs the elements in the left subtree (i.e., smaller elements), then the root element, and finally those in the right subtree (i.e., larger elements). The time complexity is $O(n)$ for an n-element tree.

```
void ascend() {inOrderOutput();}
```

Program 14.3 The method binarySearchTree<K,E>::ascend

14.3.2   Searching

Suppose we wish to search for a pair with key theKey. We begin at the root. If the root is NULL, the search tree contains no pairs and the search is unsuccessful. Otherwise, we compare theKey with the key in the root. If theKey is less than the key in the root, then no pair in the right subtree can have key value theKey and only the left subtree is to be searched. If theKey is larger than the key in the root, only the right subtree needs to be searched. If theKey equals the key in the root, then the search terminates successfully. The subtrees may be searched similarly. Program 14.4 gives the code. The time complexity is $O(h)$ where h is the height of the tree being searched.

14.3.3   Inserting an Element

To insert a new pair thePair into a binary search tree, we must first determine whether its key thePair.first is different from those of existing pairs by performing a search for thePair.first. If the search is successful, we must replace the old value associated with thePair.first with the value thePair.second. If the search is unsuccessful, then the new pair is inserted as a child of the last node examined during the search. For instance, to put a pair with key 80 into the tree of Figure 14.1(b), we first search for 80. This search terminates unsuccessfully, and the last node examined is the one with key 40. The new pair is inserted as the right child of this node. The resulting search tree appears in Figure 14.3(a). Figure 14.3(b) shows the result of inserting a pair with key 35 into the search tree of Figure 14.3(a). Program 14.5 implements this strategy to insert a pair into a binary search tree.

14.3.4   Deleting an Element

For deletion we consider the three possibilities for the node p that contains the pair that is to be removed: (1) p is a leaf, (2) p has exactly one nonempty subtree, and (3) p has exactly two nonempty subtrees.

```
template<class K, class E>
pair<const K, E>* binarySearchTree<K,E>::find(const K& theKey) const
{// Return pointer to matching pair.
 // Return NULL if no matching pair.
   // p starts at the root and moves through
   // the tree looking for an element with key theKey
   binaryTreeNode<pair<const K, E> > *p = root;
   while (p != NULL)
      // examine p->element
      if (theKey < p->element.first)
         p = p->leftChild;
      else
         if (theKey > p->element.first)
            p = p->rightChild;
         else // found matching pair
            return &p->element;

   // no matching pair
   return NULL;
}
```

Program 14.4 Search a binary search tree

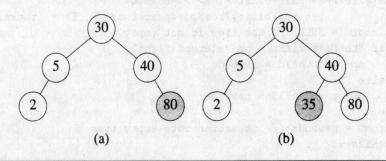

(a)   (b)

Figure 14.3 Inserting elements into a binary search tree

Case (1) is handled by discarding the leaf node, and if the discarded leaf was also the tree root, the root is set to NULL. To delete 35 from the tree of Figure 14.3(b), the left-child field of its parent is set to NULL, and the node discarded. The resulting tree appears in Figure 14.3(a). To delete the 80 from this tree, the right-child field of 40 is set to NULL, obtaining the tree of Figure 14.1(b), and the node containing

```
template<class K, class E>
void binarySearchTree<K,E>::insert(const pair<const K, E>& thePair)
{// Insert thePair into the tree. Overwrite existing
 // pair, if any, with same key.
    // find place to insert
    binaryTreeNode<pair<const K, E> > *p = root,
                                      *pp = NULL;
    while (p != NULL)
    {// examine p->element
        pp = p;
        // move p to a child
        if (thePair.first < p->element.first)
            p = p->leftChild;
        else
            if (thePair.first > p->element.first)
                p = p->rightChild;
            else
            {// replace old value
                p->element.second = thePair.second;
                return;
            }
    }

    // get a node for thePair and attach to pp
    binaryTreeNode<pair<const K, E> > *newNode
                = new binaryTreeNode<pair<const K, E> > (thePair);
    if (root != NULL) // the tree is not empty
        if (thePair.first < pp->element.first)
            pp->leftChild = newNode;
        else
            pp->rightChild = newNode;
    else
        root = newNode; // insertion into empty tree
    treeSize++;
}
```

Program 14.5 Insert an element into a binary search tree

80 is discarded.

Next consider the case when the pair to be removed is in a node p that has only one nonempty subtree. If p has no parent (i.e., it is the root), the root of its single subtree becomes the new search tree root. If **p** has a parent **pp**, then we change the pointer from **pp** so that it points to p's only child. For instance, if we wish to delete the pair with key 5 from the tree of Figure 14.3(b), we change the left-child field of its parent (i.e., the node containing 30) to point to the node containing the 2.

Finally, to remove a pair in a node that has two nonempty subtrees, we replace this pair with either the largest pair in its left subtree or the smallest pair in its right subtree. Following this replacement, the replacing pair is removed from its original node. Suppose we wish to remove the pair with key 40 from the tree of Figure 14.4(a). Either the largest pair (35) from its left subtree or the smallest (60) from its right subtree can replace this pair. If we opt for the smallest pair in the right subtree, we move the pair with key 60 to the node from which the 40 was removed; in addition, the leaf from which the 60 is moved is removed. The resulting tree appears in Figure 14.4(b).

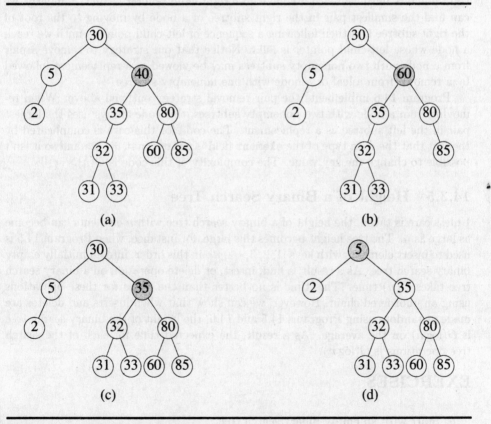

(a)   (b)

(c)   (d)

Figure 14.4 Deletion from a binary search tree

Suppose, instead, that when removing 40 from the search tree of Figure 14.4(a), we had opted for the largest pair in the left subtree of 40. This pair has key 35 and is in a node of degree 1. We move the pair into the node that currently contains 40, and the left-child pointer of this node changes to point to the lone child of the node from which the 35 was moved. The result is shown in Figure 14.4(c).

As another example, consider the removal of 30 from the tree of Figure 14.4(c). We may replace this pair with either the 5 or the 31. If we opt for the 5, then since 5 is currently in a node with degree 1, we change the left-child pointer of the parent node to point to the lone child. The result is the tree of Figure 14.4(d). If we had opted to replace 30 with 31, then since 31 is in a leaf, we need merely remove this leaf.

Notice that the pair with smallest key in the right subtree (as well as that with largest key in the right subtree) is guaranteed to be in a node with either zero or one nonempty subtree. Note also that we can find the largest pair in the left subtree of a node by moving to the root of that subtree and then following a sequence of right-child pointers until we reach a node whose right-child pointer is NULL. Similarly, we can find the smallest pair in the right subtree of a node by moving to the root of the right subtree and then following a sequence of left-child pointers until we reach a node whose left-child pointer is NULL. Notice that our strategy to remove a pair from a node with two nonempty subtrees may be viewed as a replacement followed by a removal from a leaf or a node with one nonempty subtree.

Program 14.6 implements the pair removal strategy outlined above. When removing from a node with two nonempty subtrees, this code always uses the largest pair in the left subtree as a replacement. The code for this case is complicated by the fact that the data type of the **element** field is **pair<const K, E>** and so it isn't possible to change the key value. The complexity of this code is $O(h)$.

14.3.5   Height of a Binary Search Tree

Unless care is taken, the height of a binary search tree with n elements can become as large as n. The tree height becomes this large, for instance, when Program 14.5 is used to insert elements with keys $[1, 2, 3, \cdots, n]$, in this order, into an initially empty binary search tree. As a result, a find, insert, or delete operation on a binary search tree takes $O(n)$ time. This time is no better than the times for these operations using an unordered chain. However, we can show that when inserts and deletes are made at random using Programs 14.5 and 14.6, the height of the binary search tree is $O(\log n)$ on the average. As a result, the expected time for each of the search tree operations is $O(\log n)$.

EXERCISES

6. Start with an empty binary search tree.

   (a) Insert the keys 4, 12, 8, 16, 6, 18, 24, 2, 14, 3 in this order. Draw the tree following each insert. Use the insert method described in this section.

```
template<class K, class E>
void binarySearchTree<K,E>::erase(const K& theKey)
{// Delete the pair, if any, whose key equals theKey.

   // search for node with key theKey
   binaryTreeNode<pair<const K, E> > *p = root,
                                     *pp = NULL;
   while (p != NULL && p->element.first != theKey)
   {// move to a child of p
      pp = p;
      if (theKey < p->element.first)
         p = p->leftChild;
      else
         p = p->rightChild;
   }
   if (p == NULL)
      return; // no pair with key theKey

   // restructure tree
   // handle case when p has two children
   if (p->leftChild != NULL && p->rightChild != NULL)
   {// two children
      // convert to zero or one child case
      // find largest element in left subtree of p
      binaryTreeNode<pair<const K, E> > *s = p->leftChild,
                                        *ps = p;  // parent of s
      while (s->rightChild != NULL)
      {// move to larger element
         ps = s;
         s = s->rightChild;
      }
```

Program 14.6 Deleting a pair from a binary search tree (continues)

   (b) From the tree of (a) delete the keys 6, 14, 16, and 4 in this order. Draw
       the search tree following each deletion. Use the deletion method of this
       section.

7. Do Exercise 6 using the key sequence 10, 5, 20, 14, 30, 8, 6, 35, 25, 3, 12, 17
   for part (a). For part (b) delete 35, 30, 20, and 10 in this order.

8. Extend the class **binarySearchTree** by adding a public method **outputIn-**

```
   // move largest from s to p, can't do a simple move
   // p->element = s->element as key is const
   binaryTreeNode<pair<const K, E> > *q =
      new binaryTreeNode<pair<const K, E> >
         (s->element, p->leftChild, p->rightChild);
   if (pp == NULL)
      root = q;
   else if (p == pp->leftChild)
         pp->leftChild = q;
      else
         pp->rightChild = q;
   if (ps == p) pp = q;
   else pp = ps;
   delete p;
   p = s;
}

// p has at most one child
// save child pointer in c
binaryTreeNode<pair<const K, E> > *c;
if (p->leftChild != NULL)
   c = p->leftChild;
else
   c = p->rightChild;

// delete p
if (p == root)
   root = c;
else
{// is p left or right child of pp?
   if (p == pp->leftChild)
      pp->leftChild = c;
   else pp->rightChild = c;
}
treeSize--;
delete p;
}
```

Program 14.6 Deleting a pair from a binary search tree (concluded)

Range(theLow, theHigh) that outputs, in ascending order of key, all elements in a binary search tree whose key lies between theLow and theHigh.
Use recursion and avoid entering subtrees that cannot possibly contain any
elements with keys in the desired range. Test the correctness of your code.

9. Develop a modified version of Program 14.4 in which the first comparison in
the while loop is theKey == p->element.first. Measure the time it takes
to search for all elements in a binary search tree using Program 14.4 as well
as the modified version just described. What conclusion can you draw?

10. A binary search tree can be used to sort n elements. Write a sort procedure
that inserts the n elements a[0:n-1] into an initially empty binary search tree
and then performs an inorder traversal putting the elements into a in sorted
order. For simplicity, assume that the keys of the elements in a are distinct.
Compare the average run time of the resulting sort procedure with that for
insertion sort and heap sort.

11. In Section 12.5 we saw how to initialize an n-element leftist tree in linear
time and also how to meld/combine two leftist trees into one in logarithmic
time. This exercise establishes that the asymptotic time complexity of the
initialize and combine operations for binary search trees is larger than that
for the corresponding operations for leftist trees. To establish this result, we
will use the known lower bound on the asymptotic complexity of sorting. In
Section 18.4.2 we will see that every algorithm that sorts n elements has a
complexity that is at least $O(n \log n)$.

  (a) Use this result to prove that it is not possible to initialize/create an
  n-pair binary search tree in less than $O(n \log n)$ time.

  (b) Use the above lower bound on the complexity of sorting to show that it
  is not possible to combine two binary search trees into a single binary
  search tree in less than $O(n + m)$ time, where n and m are, respectively,
  the number of pairs in the two trees that are to be combined.

12. Extend the class binarySearchTree by adding a method split(theKey,
lessThan, greaterThan) that splits the binary search tree *this into two
binary search trees—lessThan contains all elements of *this whose keys are
less than theKey, and greaterThan contains all elements of *this whose keys
are greater than theKey. If the binary search tree *this has a pair whose
key equals theKey, a pointer to this pair is returned as by the split method;
otherwise, NULL is returned. Following the operation, *this is an empty binary search tree. The complexity of your method should be $O(h)$, where h is
the height of the tree being split. Test the correctness of your code.

13. Generate a random permutation of the integers 1 through n. Put the keys
1 through n into an initially empty binary search tree. Perform the put

operations in the order specified by the random permutation. Measure the height of the resulting search tree. Repeat this experiment for several random permutations and compute the average of the measured heights. Compare this figure with $2\lceil\log_2(n+1)\rceil$. For n use the values 100; 500; 1000; 10,000; 20,000; and 50,000.

14. Extend the class `binarySearchTree` by including an iterator that allows you to examine the pairs in ascending order of the key. The time taken to enumerate all pairs of an n-element binary tree should be $O(n)$, the complexity of no method should exceed $O(h)$ where h is the tree height, and the space requirements should be $O(h)$. Show that this is the case. Test your code.

15. Write a method to delete the pair with largest key from a binary search tree. Your method must have time complexity $O(h)$ where h is the height of the binary search tree. Show that your code has this complexity.

    (a) Use suitable test data to test the correctness of your delete max method.

    (b) Create a random list of n pairs and a random sequence of insert and delete max operations of length m. Create the latter sequence so that the probability of an insert operation is approximately 0.5 (therefore, the probability of a delete max operation is also 0.5). Initialize a max heap and a binary search tree with duplicates to contain the n pairs in the first random list. Now measure the time to perform the m operations, using the max heap as well as the binary search tree. Divide this time by m to get the average time per operation. Do this experiment for n = 100, 500, 1000, 2000, $\cdots$, and 5000. Let m be 5000. Tabulate your computing times.

    (c) Based on your experiments, what can you say about the relative merits of the two priority queue schemes?

14.4   BINARY SEARCH TREES WITH DUPLICATES

The class for the case when the binary search tree is permitted to contain two or more pairs that have the same key is called dBinarySearchTree. We can implement this class by changing the `while` loop of binarySearchTree<K,E>::insert (Program 14.5) to that shown in Program 14.7 and by changing the second occurrence of the line

```
if (thePair.first < pp->element.first)
```

to

```
if (thePair.first <= pp->element.first)
```

```
while (p != NULL)
{// examine p->element
   pp = p;
   // move p to a child
   if (thePair.first <= p->element.first)
       p = p->leftChild;
   else
       p = p->rightChild;
}
```

Program 14.7 New while loop for Program 14.5 to permit duplicates

If we insert n pairs, all of which have the same key, into an an initially empty binary search tree, the result is a left-skewed tree whose height is n. An alternative approach that uses random numbers and results in trees with better height properties is considered in Exercise 17.

EXERCISES

16. Start with an empty binary search tree with duplicates and insert the keys 2, 2, 2, and 2 using the `insert` method described in this section. Draw your tree following each insert. What is the tree height following the insertion of n 2s?

17. Develop a new implementation of the C++ class `dBinarySearchTree`. During an insert, instead of consistently moving to the left subtree of a node that contains a key equal to `thePair.first` (see Program 14.7), use a random number generator to move to the left or right subtree with equal probability. Test the correctness of your implementation.

14.5   INDEXED BINARY SEARCH TREES

The class `indexedBinarySearchTree` may also be defined as a derived class of `linkedBinaryTree` (see Exercise 19). For the class `indexedBinarySearchTree`, the `element` field of a node is a triple `leftSize`, `key`, and `value`.

We can perform an indexed search in a manner similar to that used to search for a pair (a pair is now defined by the fields `key` and `value`). Consider the tree of Figure 14.2(a). Suppose we are looking for the pair whose index is 2. The `leftSize` field (and hence index) of the root is 3. So the pair we desire is in the left subtree. Furthermore, the pair we desire has index 2 in the left subtree. The root, 15, of the left subtree has leftSize = 1. So the pair we desire is in the right subtree of 15. However, the index, in the right subtree of 15, of the pair we desire is no longer 2 because all pairs in the right subtree of 15 follow the pairs in the left subtree of 15 as well as the pair 15. To determine the index of the desired pair in the right subtree, we subtract leftSize + 1. Since the leftSize value of 15 is 1, the index of the desired pair in its right subtree is $2 - (1+1) = 0$. Since leftSize $= 0$ (which equals the index of the pair we seek) for the root of the right subtree of 15, we have found the desired pair 18.

When inserting a pair into an indexed binary search tree, we use a procedure similar to Program 14.5. This time, though, we also need to update leftSize fields on the path from the root to the newly inserted node.

A delete by index is done by first performing an indexed search to locate the pair to be deleted. Next we delete the pair as outlined in Section 14.3.4 and update leftSize fields on the path from the root to the physically deleted node as necessary.

The time required to find, insert, and delete is $O(h)$ time where h is the height of the indexed search tree.

EXERCISES

18. Start with an empty indexed binary search tree.

    (a) Insert the keys 4, 12, 8, 16, 6, 18, 24, 2, 14, 3 in this order. Draw the tree following each insert. Show leftSize values. Use the insert method described in this section.

    (b) Use the method of this section to find the keys with index 3, 6, and 8. Describe the search process used in each case.

    (c) Start with the tree of (a) and remove the keys whose index is 7, 5, and 0 in this order. Draw the search tree following each deletion. Use the deletion method of this section.

19. Develop the C++ class indexedBinarySearchTree. You should derive from the abstract class indexedBSTree. Test the correctness of your code. Express the time complexity of each method in terms of the number of elements and/or the height of the tree.

20. Do Exercise 19 for the class dIndexedBinarySearchTree, which represents an indexed binary search tree with duplicates.

21. You are to represent a linear list as an indexed binary tree which is like an indexed binary search tree except that no node has a key value. Each node of the indexed binary tree contains exactly one element of the linear list. When an indexed binary tree is traversed in inorder, we visit the elements in linear list order from left to right.

(a) Start with a complete binary tree that has 11 nodes. Label each node with its leftSize value. Place the elements of the linear list $A = $ [a, b, c, d, e, f, g, h, i, j, k] into this indexed binary tree. Note that when you traverse the binary tree in inorder, you must visit the elements in linear list order.

(b) Perform the following linear list insert operations on the tree of part (a): insert(4, m), insert(9, n), insert(0, p), and insert(14, q). Do these in the given order using a method similar to that used to insert into a binary search tree. Search for the proper place to add the new node using leftSize values.

(c) Perform the following linear list delete operations on the tree of part (b): erase(0), erase(3), erase(8), and erase(7). Do these in the given order using a method similar to that used to delete from an indexed binary search tree.

22. Develop a class linearListAsBinaryTree that represents a linear list as an indexed binary tree (see Exercise 21). Your implementation should support all the linear list operations defined in Program 5.1.

A simple way to implement the insert(index, theElement) operation is to first find the index − 1th node p, make the new element the right child of p, and finally make the original right subtree of the p the right subtree of the newly inserted element. However, since this insertion method never makes an element a left child of another, the trees that are constructed are right skewed (i.e., all left-child fields are 0) and have height equal to the number of elements in the tree.

To construct binary trees with expected height logarithmic in the number of elements, we must create both left and right subtrees. When the index − 1th node p is found, we can (1) make the new element the right child of p and make the former right subtree of p the right subtree of the new element or (2) make the new element the left or right child of the parent of p (depending on which child p is of its parent), make p the left child of the new element, and make the original right subtree of p the right subtree of the new element or (3) insert the new element as the left-most node in the right subtree of p. By making this decision randomly, we can obtain better balanced trees. Your insert code should select from the available options randomly.

Other than the method indexOf, all methods should run in logarithmic or less expected time. Show that this is the case. You may assume that the expected height of the binary tree constructed is logarithmic in the number of elements.

14.6   APPLICATIONS

14.6.1   Histogramming

What Is Histogramming?

In the histogramming problem we start with a collection of n keys and must output a list of the distinct keys and the number of times (i.e., frequency) each occurs in the collection. Figure 14.5 gives an example with 10 keys. The problem input appears in Figure 14.5(a), and the histogram is presented in Figure 14.5(b) as a table and as a bar chart in Figure 14.5(c). Histogramming is commonly performed to determine the distribution of data. For example, we may histogram the scores on a test, the grayscale values in an image, the cars registered in Gainesville (the key being the manufacturer), and the highest degree earned by persons living in Los Angeles.

$$n = 10;\ keys = [2, 4, 2, 2, 3, 4, 2, 6, 4, 2]$$
(a) Input

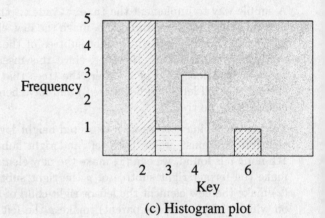

Key	Frequency
2	5
3	1
4	3
6	1

(b) Output histogram table

(c) Histogram plot

Figure 14.5 Histogramming example

Simple Histogramming Program

When the key values are integers in the range 0 through r and r is reasonably small, the histogram can be computed in linear time by a rather simple procedure (Program 14.8) that uses the array element $h[i]$ to determine the frequency of the key i. Other integral key types may be mapped into this range to use Program 14.8. For example, if the keys are lowercase letters, we may use the mapping [a, b, $\cdots$, z] = [0, 1, $\cdots$, 25].

```
void main(void)
{// Histogram of nonnegative integer values.
   int n,  // number of elements
       r;  // values between 0 and r
   cout << "Enter number of elements and range"
        << endl;
   cin >> n >> r;

   // create histogram array h
   int *h = new int[r+1];

   // initialize array h to zero
   for (int i = 0; i <= r; i++)
      h[i] = 0;

   // input data and compute histogram
   for (i = 1; i <= n; i++)
   {// assume input values are between 0 and r
      int key;  // input value
      cout << "Enter element " << i << endl;
      cin >> key;
      h[key]++;
   }

   // output histogram
   cout << "Distinct elements and frequencies are"
        << endl;
   for (i = 0; i <= r; i++)
      if (h[i] != 0)
         cout << i << "    "  << h[i] << endl;
}
```

Program 14.8 Simple histogramming program

Histogramming with a Binary Search Tree

Program 14.8 becomes infeasible when the key range is very large as well as when the key type is not integral (for example, when the keys are real numbers). Suppose we are determining the frequency with which different words occur in a text. The number of possible different words is very large compared to the number that might actually appear in the text. In such a situation we can use hashing to arrive at a solution whose expected complexity is $O(n)$ (Exercise 24). Alternatively, we may sort the keys and then use a simple left-to-right scan to determine the number of keys for each distinct key value. The sort can be accomplished in $O(n \log n)$ time (using heapSort (Program 12.8), for example), and the ensuing left-to-right scan takes $\Theta(n)$ time; the overall complexity is $O(n \log n)$.

The histogramming-by-sorting solution can be improved when the number m of distinct keys is small compared to n. By using balanced search trees such as AVL and red-black trees (see Chapter 15), we can solve the histogramming problem in $O(n \log m)$ time. Furthermore, the balanced search tree solution requires only the distinct keys to be stored in memory. Therefore, this solution is appropriate even in situations when n is so large that we do not have enough memory to accommodate all keys (provided, of course, there is enough memory for the distinct keys).

The solution we describe in this section uses a binary search tree that may not be balanced. Therefore, this solution has expected complexity $O(n \log m)$.

The Class binarySearchTreeWithVisit

For our binary search tree solution, we first define the class binarySearchTree-WithVisit that extends the class binarySearchTree by adding the public method

```
void insert(const pair<const K, E>& thePair, void(*visit)(E&))
```

This method inserts thePair into the search tree provided no pair with key equal to thePair.first exists. If the tree already contains a pair p that has the key thePair.first, the method visit(p.second) is invoked.

Back to Histogramming with a Binary Search Tree

Program 14.9 gives the code to histogram using a binary search tree. This method inputs the data, enters it into an object of type binarySearchTreeWithVisit, and finally outputs the histogram by invoking the ascend method. The first component of each pair stored in the binary search tree is its key and the second if the frequency of the key. During a visit of a pair, the frequency count of the key is incremented by 1.

14.6.2   Best-Fit Bin Packing

Using a Binary Search Tree with Duplicates

The best-fit method to pack n objects into bins of capacity c was described in Section 13.5.1. By using a binary search tree with duplicates, we can implement the method to run in $O(n \log n)$ expected time. The worst-case complexity becomes $\Theta(n \log n)$ when a balanced search tree is used.

In our implementation of the best-fit method, the binary search tree (with duplicates) will contain one element for each bin that is currently in use and has nonzero unused capacity. Suppose that when object i is to be packed, there are nine bins (a

```
int main(void)
{// Histogram using a search tree.
   int n;   // number of elements
   cout << "Enter number of elements" << endl;
   cin >> n;

   // input elements and enter into tree
   binarySearchTreeWithVisit<int, int> theTree;
   for (int i = 1; i <= n; i++)
   {
      pair<int, int> thePair;  // input element
      cout << "Enter element " << i << endl;
      cin >> thePair.first;    // key
      thePair.second = 1;      // frequency
      // insert thePair in tree unless match already there
      // in latter case increase count by 1
      theTree.insert(thePair, add1);
   }

   // output distinct elements and their counts
   cout << "Distinct elements and frequencies are"
        << endl;
   theTree.ascend();
}
```

Program 14.9 Histogramming with a search tree

through i) in use that still have some space left. Let the unused capacity of these bins be 1, 3, 12, 6, 8, 1, 20, 6, and 5, respectively. Notice that it is possible for two or more bins to have the same unused capacity. The nine bins may be stored in a binary search tree with duplicates (i.e., an instance of **dBinarySearchTree**) using as key the unused capacity of a bin.

Figure 14.6 shows a possible binary search tree for the nine bins. For each bin the unused capacity is shown inside a node, and the bin name is shown outside. If the object i that is to be packed requires **objectSize[i]** $= 4$ units, we can find the bin that provides the best fit by starting at the root of the tree of Figure 14.6. The root tells us bin h has an unused capacity of 6. Since object i fits into this bin, bin h becomes the candidate for the best bin. Also, since the capacity of all bins in the right subtree is at least 6, we need not look at the bins in this subtree in our quest for the best bin. The search proceeds to the left subtree. The capacity of bin b isn't adequate to accommodate our object, so the search for the best bin moves into the right subtree of bin b. The bin, bin i, at the root of this subtree has enough capacity, and it becomes the new candidate for the best bin. From here the search moves into the left subtree of bin i. Since this subtree is empty, there are no better candidate bins and bin i is selected.

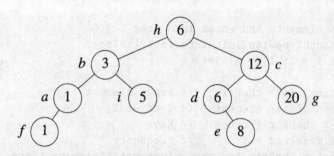

Figure 14.6 Binary search tree with duplicates

As another example of the search for the best bin, suppose objectSize[i] = 7. The search again starts at the root. The root bin, bin h, does not have enough capacity for this object, so our quest for a bin moves into the right subtree. Bin c has enough capacity and becomes the new candidate bin. From here we move into c's left subtree and examine bin d. It does not have enough capacity to accommodate the object, so we continue with the right subtree of d. Bin e has enough capacity and becomes the new candidate bin. We then move into its left subtree, which is empty. The search terminates.

When we find the best bin, we can delete it from the search tree, reduce its capacity by objectSize[i], and reinsert it (unless its remaining capacity is 0). If we do not find a bin with enough capacity, we can start a new bin.

C++ Implementation

To implement this scheme, we can use the class dBinarySearchTree to obtain $O(n \log n)$ expected performance or the class davlTree (Section 15.1) for $O(n \log n)$ performance in all instances. In either case we must first extend the class to include the public method findGE(theKey) that returns the smallest bin capacity that is $\geq$ theKey. This method takes the form given in Program 14.10. Its complexity is $O(height)$. The code for the method is unchanged if the class davlTree is extended instead of dBinarySearchTree.

The function bestFitPack (Program 14.11), which implements the best-fit packing strategy, uses pairs whose second component is a bin identifier (bin number) and whose first component is the unused capacity of the bin.

```
template<class K, class E>
pair<const K, E>* dBinarySearchTreeWithGE<K,E>::
                         findGE(const K& theKey) const
{// Return pointer to pair with smallest key >= theKey.
 // Return NULL if no element has key >= theKey.
  binaryTreeNode<pair<const K, E> > *currentNode = root;
    pair<const K, E> *bestElement = NULL; // element with smallest key
                                          // >= theKey found so far

    // search the tree
    while (currentNode != NULL)
       // is currentNode->element a candidate?
       if (currentNode->element.first >= theKey)
       {// yes, currentNode->element is
        // a better candidate than bestElement
          bestElement = &currentNode->element;
          // smaller keys in left subtree only
          currentNode = currentNode->leftChild;
       }
       else
          // no, currentNode->element.first is too small
          // try right subtree
          currentNode = currentNode->rightChild;

    return bestElement;
}
```

Program 14.10 Finding the smallest key $\geq$ theKey

14.6.3   Crossing Distribution

Channel Routing and Crossings

In the crossing-distribution problem, we start with a routing channel with n pins on both the top and bottom of the channel. Figure 14.7 shows an instance with $n = 10$. The routing region is the shaded rectangular region. The pins are numbered 1 through n, left to right, on both the top and bottom of the channel. In addition, we have a permutation C of the numbers $[1, 2, 3, \cdots, n]$. We must use a wire to connect pin i on the top side of the channel to pin C_i on the bottom side. The example in Figure 14.7 is for the case $C = [8, 7, 4, 2, 5, 1, 9, 3, 10, 6]$. The n wires needed to make these connections are numbered 1 through n. Wire i connects top pin i to bottom pin C_i. Wire i is to the left of wire j iff $i < j$.

No matter how we route wires 9 and 10 in the given routing region, these wires

```
void bestFitPack(int *objectSize, int numberOfObjects, int binCapacity)
{// Output best-fit packing into bins of size binCapacity.
 // objectSize[1:numberOfObjects] are the object sizes.
   int n = numberOfObjects;
   int binsUsed = 0;
   dBinarySearchTreeWithGE<int,int> theTree;  // tree of bin capacities
   pair<int, int> theBin;

   // pack objects one by one
   for (int i = 1; i <= n; i++)
   {// pack object i
      // find best bin
      pair<const int, int> *bestBin = theTree.findGE(objectSize[i]);
      if (bestBin == NULL)
      {// no bin large enough, start a new bin
         theBin.first = binCapacity;
         theBin.second = ++binsUsed;
      }
      else
      {// remove best bin from theTree
         theBin = *bestBin;
         theTree.erase(bestBin->first);
      }

      cout << "Pack object " << i << " in bin "
           << theBin.second << endl;

      // insert bin in tree unless bin is full
      theBin.first -= objectSize[i];
      if (theBin.first > 0)
         theTree.insert(theBin);
   }
}
```

Program 14.11 Bin packing using best fit

must cross at some point. Crossings are undesirable as special care must be taken at the crossing point to avoid a short circuit. This special care, for instance, might involve placing an insulator at the point of crossing or routing one wire onto another layer at this point and then bringing it back after the crossover point. Therefore, we seek to minimize the number of crossings. You may verify that the minimum number of crossings is made when the wires are run as straight lines as in Figure 14.7.

Each crossing is given by a pair (i, j) where i and j are the two wires that cross.

$$C = [8, 7, 4, 2, 5, 1, 9, 3, 10, 6]$$

Figure 14.7 A wiring instance

To avoid listing the same pair of crossing wires twice, we require $i < j$ (note that the crossings $(9, 10)$ and $(10, 9)$ are the same). Note that wires i and j, $i < j$, cross iff $C_i > C_j$. Let k_i be the number of pairs (i, j), $i < j$, such that wires i and j cross. For the example of Figure 14.7, $k_9 = 1$ and $k_{10} = 0$. In Figure 14.8 we list all crossings and k_i values for the example of Figure 14.7. Row i of this table first gives the value of k_i and then the values of j, $i < j$, such that wires i and j cross. The total number of crossings K may be determined by adding together all k_is. For our example $K = 22$. Since k_i counts the crossings of wire i only with wires to its right (i.e., $i < j$), k_i gives the number of right-side crossings of wire i.

Distributing the Crossings

To balance the routing complexity in the top and lower halves of the channel, we require that each half have approximately the same number of crossings. (The top half should have $\lfloor K/2 \rfloor$ crossings, and the bottom should have $\lceil K/2 \rceil$ crossings.) Figure 14.9 shows a routing of Figure 14.7 in which we have exactly 11 crossings in each half of the channel.

The connections in the top half are given by the permutation $A = [1, 4, 6, 3, 7, 2, 9, 5, 10, 8]$. That is, top pin i is connected to center pin A_i. The connections in the bottom half are given by the permutation $B = [8, 1, 2, 7, 3, 4, 5, 6, 9, 10]$. That is, center pin i is connected to bottom pin B_i. Observe that $C_i = B_{A_i}$, $1 \leq i \leq n$. This equality is essential if we are to accomplish the connections given by C.

In this section we develop algorithms to compute the permutations A and B so that the top half of the channel has $\lfloor K/2 \rfloor$ crossings where K is the total number of crossings.

i	k_i	Crossings
1	7	2 3 4 5 6 8 10
2	6	3 4 5 6 8 10
3	3	4 6 8
4	1	6
5	2	6 7
6	0	
7	2	8 10
8	0	
9	1	10
10	0	

Figure 14.8 Crossing table

Figure 14.9 Splitting the crossings

Crossing Distribution Using a Linear List

The crossing numbers k_i and the total number of crossings K can be computed in $\Theta(n^2)$ time by examining each wire pair (i, j). The partitioning of C into A and B can then be computed by using an **arrayList** as in Program 14.12.

In the **while** loop, we scan the wires from right to left, determining their relative order at the center of the routing channel. The objective is to have a routing order at the center that requires exactly **crossingsNeeded = theK/2** crossings in the top half of the routing channel.

The linear list **theList** keeps track of the current ordering, at the center, of the

```
void main(void)
{
   // define the instance to be solved
   // connections at bottom of channel, theC[1:10]
   int theC[] = {0, 8, 7, 4, 2, 5, 1, 9, 3, 10, 6};
   // crossing numbers, k[1:10]
   int k[] = {0, 7, 6, 3, 1, 2, 0, 2, 0, 1, 0};
   int n = 10;        // number of pins on either side of channel
   int theK = 22;     // total number of crossings

   // create data structures
   arrayList<int> theList(n);
   int *theA = new int[n + 1],   // top-half permutation
       *theB = new int[n + 1],   // bottom-half permutation
       *theX = new int[n + 1];   // center connections

   int crossingsNeeded = theK / 2;  // remaining number of crossings
                                    // needed in top half

   // scan wires right to left
   int currentWire = n;
   while (crossingsNeeded > 0)
   {// need more crossings in top half
      if (k[currentWire] < crossingsNeeded)
      {// use all crossings from currentWire
         theList.insert(k[currentWire], currentWire);
         crossingsNeeded -= k[currentWire];
      }
      else
      {// use only crossingsNeeded crossings from currentWire
         theList.insert(crossingsNeeded, currentWire);
         crossingsNeeded = 0;
      }
      currentWire--;
   }

   // determine wire permutation at center
   // first currentWire wires have same ordering
   for (int i = 1; i <= currentWire; i++)
      theX[i] = i;
```

Program 14.12 Crossing distribution using a linear list (continues)

```
    // ordering of remaining wires is from list
    for (int i = currentWire + 1; i <= n; i++)
        theX[i] = theList.get(i - currentWire - 1);

    // compute top-half permutation
    for (int i = 1; i <= n; i++)
        theA[theX[i]] = i;

    // compute bottom-half permutation
    for (int i = 1; i <= n; i++)
        theB[i] = theC[theX[i]];

    cout << "A is ";
    for (int i = 1; i <= n; i++)
        cout << theA[i] << " ";
    cout << endl;

    cout << "B is ";
    for (int i = 1; i <= n; i++)
        cout << theB[i] << " ";
    cout << endl;
}
```

Program 14.12 Crossing distribution using a linear list (concluded)

wires so far considered. When wire currentWire is considered, we can allocate up to k[currentWire] of its crossings with right-side wires to the upper half. The first crossing is with the zeroth wire in list, the second with the next wire in theList, and so on. If c of the k[currentWire] right-side crossings of wire currentWire are allocated to the upper half, then this wire must cross the first c wires in theList. In addition, the ordering of wires currentWire through n is obtained by inserting currentWire after the cth wire in theList. Notice that when wire currentWire is considered in the while loop of Program 14.12, wires currentWire+1 through n have already been considered and so are in theList. Further, since k[currentWire] cannot exceed the number of wires to the right of currentWire, theList has at least k[w] wires in it when currentWire is considered.

When currentWire is considered in the while loop of Program 14.12, all of its right-side crossings are allocated to the top half unless the remaining number crossingsNeeded of crossings needed in the top half is less than k[currentWire]. Then crossingsNeeded of the possible k[currentWire] right-side crossings are allocated to the upper half.

When the `while` loop terminates, the wire ordering `theX` at the center of the routing channel may be constructed by noting that wires 1 through `w` have no crossings in the upper half and so do not change their relative order in this half. Therefore, `theX[1:currentWire]` $= [1, 2, \cdots, \texttt{currentWire}]$. The ordering of the remaining wires is given by the list `theList`. The first two `for` loops of Program 14.12 construct `theX`.

An Example

Let us go through the construction of `theX` using our example of Figure 14.7. We begin by inserting wire 10 into `theList` to get `theList` $= (10)$. No crossings are generated. Next we insert wire 9 to get `theList` $= (10, 9)$. The insertion of this wire generates one upper-half crossing. Then we insert wire 8 after the k_8th element to get `theList` $= (8, 10, 9)$. The total number of right-side crossings in the upper half remains 1. Next we insert wire 7 after the second element of `theList`, generating two upper-half crossings. `theList` becomes $(8, 10, 7, 9)$, and the additional crossings needed `r` drops to 8. When wire 6 is inserted, we get `theList` $= (6, 8, 10, 7, 9)$; `r` $= 8$. The insertion of wire 5 generates two crossings and results in `theList` $= (6, 8, 5, 10, 7, 9)$; `r` $= 6$. When wire 4 is inserted after the first element of `theList`, one crossing is generated and we get `theList` $= (6, 4, 8, 5, 10, 7, 9)$; `r` $= 5$. Next we add wire 3 to get `theList` $= (6, 4, 8, 3, 5, 10, 7, 9)$; `r` $= 2$. Finally, when wire 2 is considered, we see that although it is capable of generating $k_2 = 6$ crossings, only two of these crossings can be assigned to the top half of the channel. So it is inserted after the second element of the list to get `theList` $= (6, 4, 2, 8, 3, 5, 10, 7, 9)$. The remaining wires retain their current relative order.

Now we compute the wire permutation following the routing of the top half by appending `theList` to the ordering $(1, 2, \cdots, \texttt{w})$ to obtain `theX` $= [1, 6, 4, 2, 8, 3, 5, 10, 7, 9]$.

The permutation `theA` $= A$ is closely related to `theX`. `theA[j]` tells us which center pin wire j should go to, while `theX[i]` tells us which wire comes to center pin j. The third `for` loop of Program 14.12 uses this information to compute `theA`. From `theX` and `theC`, `theB` $= B$ may be computed, as in the fourth `for` loop.

Complexity Analysis

Since the time needed to insert an element into a linear list of size s is $O(s)$, the `while` loop of Program 14.12 takes $O(n^2)$ time. The remainder of the code takes $O(n)$ time, so the overall complexity of Program 14.12 is $O(n^2)$. Combining the time requirements of Program 14.12 with the time needed to compute `theK` and the `k[i]`s, we see that the overall time needed to solve the crossing-distribution problem is $O(n^2)$ when a linear list is used.

We can reduce the complexity of our solution to $O(n \log n)$ by using a balanced search tree rather than a linear list. To obtain a solution with expected complexity

$O(n \log n)$, we may use an indexed binary search tree rather than an indexed balanced search tree. The technique is the same in both cases. We will use an indexed binary search tree to illustrate this technique.

Using an Indexed Binary Search Tree

First let us see how to compute the crossing numbers k_i, $1 \leq i \leq n$. Suppose we examine the wires in the order n, $n-1$, $\cdots$, 1 and put C_i into an indexed search tree when wire i is examined. For the example of Figure 14.7, we start with an empty tree. We examine wire 10 and insert $C_{10} = 6$ into an empty tree to get the tree of Figure 14.10(a). The number outside the node is its leftSize value, and that inside the node is its key (or C value). Note that k_n is always 0, so we set $k_n = 0$. Next we examine wire 9 and insert $C_9 = 10$ into the tree to get the tree of Figure 14.10(b). To make the insertion, we pass over the root that has leftSize $= 1$. From this leftSize value, we know that wire 9's bottom endpoint is to the right of exactly one of the wires seen so far, so $k_9 = 1$. We examine wire 8 and insert $C_8 = 3$ to get the tree of Figure 14.10(c). Since C_8 is the smallest entry in the tree, no wires are crossed and $k_8 = 0$. For wire 7, $C_7 = 9$ is inserted to obtain tree (d). C_7 becomes the third-smallest entry in the tree. We can determine that C_7 is the third-smallest entry by keeping a running sum of the leftSize values of the nodes whose right subtree we enter. When C_7 is inserted, this sum is 2. So the new element is currently the third smallest. From this information we conclude that its bottom endpoint is to the right of two others in the tree. As a result, $k_7 = 2$. Proceeding in this way, the trees of Figures 14.10(e) through 14.10(i) are generated when we examine wires 6 through 2. Finally, when we examine wire 1, we insert $C_1 = 8$ as the right child of the node with key 7. The sum of the leftSize values of the nodes whose right subtrees we enter is $6 + 1 = 7$. Wire 1 has a bottom endpoint that is to the right of seven of the wires in the tree, and so $k_1 = 7$.

The time needed to examine wire i and compute k_i is $O(h)$ where h is the current height of the indexed search tree. So all k_is can be computed in expected time $O(n \log n)$ by using an indexed binary search tree or in time $O(n \log n)$ by using an indexed balanced search tree.

To compute A, we can implement the code of Program 14.12, using an indexed binary tree representation of a linear list. To list the elements in order of rank, we can do an inorder traversal. The expected time needed by this implementation of Program 14.12 is $O(n \log n)$ when the linear list implementation of Exercise 22 is used; the worst-case time is $O(n \log n)$ when an indexed balanced tree implementation (see Exercise 20 in Chapter 15) is used.

Another way to obtain the permutation A is to first compute $r = \sum_{i=1}^{n} k_i / 2$ and $s =$ smallest i such that $\sum_{l=i}^{n} k_l \leq r$. For our example, $r = 11$ and $s = 3$. We see that Program 14.12 does all crossings (i.e., with wires whose top point is to the right) for wires n, $n-1$, $\cdots$, s and $r - \sum_{l=s}^{n} k_l$ of the crossings for wire $s - 1$ in the top half. The remaining crossings are done in the bottom half. To get these top-half crossings, we examine the tree following the insertion of C_s. For our

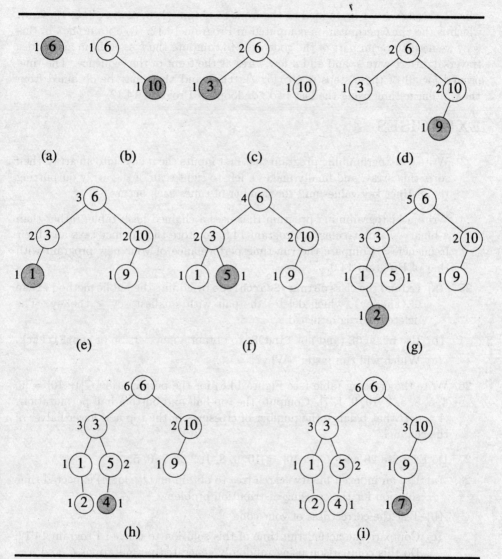

Figure 14.10 Computing the number of crossings

example we examine tree (h) of Figure 14.10. An inorder traversal of tree (h) yields the sequence (1, 2, 3, 4, 5, 6, 9, 10). Replacing these bottom endpoints with the corresponding wire numbers, we get the sequence (6, 4, 8, 3, 5, 10, 7, 9), which gives the wire permutation following the nine crossings represented in Figure 14.10(h). For the additional two crossings, we insert wire $s = 2$ after the second wire in the sequence to get the new wire sequence (6, 4, 2, 8, 3, 5, 10, 7, 9). The remaining wires 1 through $s-1$ are added at the front to obtain $(1, 6, 4, 2, 8, 3, 5, 10, 7, 9)$, which is the theX permutation computed in Program 14.12. To obtain theX in this way, we need to rerun part of the code used to compute the k_is, perform an inorder traversal, insert wire s, and add a few wires at the front of the sequence. The time needed for all of these steps is $O(n \log n)$. theA and theB may be obtained from theX in linear time using the last two for loops of Program 14.12.

EXERCISES

23. Write a histogramming program that first inputs the n keys into an array, then sorts this array, and finally makes a left-to-right scan of the array outputting the distinct key values and the number of times each occurs.

24. Write a histogramming program that uses a chained hash table, rather than a binary search tree as in Program 14.9, to store the distinct keys and their frequencies. Compare the run-time performance of your new program with that of Program 14.9.

25. (a) Extend the class dBinarySearchTree by adding the public method erase-GE(theKey), which deletes the pair with smallest key $\geq$ theKey. The deleted pair is returned.

    (b) Use eraseGE (and not findGE) to obtain a new version of bestFitPack.

    (c) Which will run faster? Why?

26. Write the crossing table (see Figure 14.8) for the permutation $C[1:10] = [6, 4, 5, 8, 3, 2, 10, 9, 1, 7]$. Compute the top-half and bottom-half permutations A and B that balance the number of crossings in the top and lower halves of the channel.

27. Do Exercise 26 with $C[1:10] = [10, 9, 8, 1, 2, 3, 7, 6, 5, 4]$.

28. (a) Use an indexed binary search tree to obtain an $O(n \log n)$ expected time solution for the crossing-distribution problem.

    (b) Test the correctness of your code.

    (c) Compare the actual run time of this solution to that of Program 14.12. Do this comparison using randomly generated permutations C and $n = 1000$; 10,000; and 50,000.

29. Write a program to create a concordance for a piece of text (see Exercise 48 in Chapter 10). Use a binary search tree to construct the concordance entries and then perform an inorder traversal of this AVL tree to output the concordance entries in sorted order. Comment on the merits of using a binary search tree versus a hash table. In particular, what can you say about the expected performance of the two approaches when the input text has n words and only $m \leq n$ of these are distinct?

CHAPTER 15

BALANCED SEARCH TREES

BIRD'S-EYE VIEW

This last chapter on trees develops balanced tree structures—tree structures whose height is $O(\log n)$. We develop two balanced binary tree structures, AVL and red black, and one tree structure, B-tree, whose degree is more than 2. AVL and red-black trees are suitable for internal memory applications, and the B-tree is suitable for external memory (e.g., a large dictionary that resides on disk) applications. These balanced structures allow you to perform dictionary operations as well as by-rank operations in $O(\log n)$ time in the worst case. When a linear list is represented as an indexed balanced tree, the *get*, *insert*, and *erase* operations take $O(\log n)$ time.

The splay tree is another data structure that is developed in this chapter. Although the height of a splay tree is $O(n)$ and an individual dictionary operation performed on a splay tree takes $O(n)$ time, every sequence of u operations performed on a splay tree takes $O(u \log u)$ time. The asymptotic complexity of a sequence of u operations is the same regardless of whether you use splay trees, AVL trees, or red-black trees.

The following table summarizes the asymptotic performance of the various dictionary structures considered in this text. All complexities are theta of the given function.

563

Method	Worst Case			Expected		
	Search	Insert	Delete	Search	Insert	Delete
sorted array	$\log n$	n	n	$\log n$	n	n
sorted chain	n	n	n	n	n	n
skip lists	n	n	n	$\log n$	$\log n$	$\log n$
hash tables	n	n	n	1	1	1
binary search tree	n	n	n	$\log n$	$\cdot \log n$	$\log n$
AVL tree	$\log n$	$\log n$	$\log n$	$\log n$	$\log n$	$\log n$
red-black tree	$\log n$	$\log n$	$\log n$	$\log n$	$\log n$	$\log n$
splay tree	n	n	n	$\log n$	$\log n$	$\log n$
B-trees	$\log n$	$\log n$	$\log n$	$\log n$	$\log n$	$\log n$

The STL classes `map` and `multimap` use red-black trees to guarantee logarithmic performance for the search, insert, and delete operations.

In practice, we expect hashing to outperform balanced search trees when the desired operations are search, insert, and delete (all by key value); therefore, hashing is the preferred method in these applications. When the dictionary operations are done solely by key value, balanced search trees are recommended only in time-critical applications in which we must guarantee that no dictionary operation ever takes more than a specified amount of time. Balanced search trees are also recommended when the search and delete operations are done by rank and for applications in which the dictionary operations are not done by exact key match. An example of the latter would be finding the smallest element with a key larger than k.

The actual run-time performance of both AVL and red-black trees is similar; in comparison, splay trees take less time to perform a sequence of u operations. In addition, splay trees are easier to implement.

Both AVL and red-black trees use "rotations" to maintain balance. AVL trees perform at most one rotation following an insert and $O(\log n)$ rotations following a delete. However, red-black trees perform a single rotation following either an insert or delete. This difference is not important in most applications where a rotation takes $\Theta(1)$ time. It does, however, become important in advanced applications where a rotation cannot be performed in constant time. One such application is the implementation of the balanced priority search trees of McCreight. These priority search trees are used to represent elements with two-dimensional keys. In this case each key is a pair (x, y). A priority search tree is a tree that is simultaneously a min (or max) tree on y and a search tree on x. When rotations are performed in these trees, each has a cost of $O(\log n)$. Since red-black trees perform a single rotation following an insert or delete, the overall insert or delete time remains $O(\log n)$ if we use a red-black tree to represent a priority search tree. When we use an AVL tree, the time for the delete operation becomes $O(\log^2 n)$.

Although AVL trees, red-black trees, and splay trees provide good performance when the dictionary being represented is sufficiently small to fit in our computer's memory, they are quite inadequate for larger dictionaries. When the dictionary resides on disk, we need to use search trees with a much higher degree and hence a much smaller height. An example of such a search tree, the B-tree, is also considered in this chapter.

Although C++ codes are not given for any of the data structures developed in this chapter, several codes are available on the Web site as solutions to exercises. The Web site also has material on other search structures such as tries and suffix trees.

This chapter does not have an applications section because the applications of balanced search trees are the same as those of binary search trees (Chapter 14). By using a balanced search tree in these applications, we obtain code whose worst-case asymptotic complexity is the same as the expected complexity when unbalanced binary search trees are used.

15.1   AVL TREES

15.1.1   Definition

We can guarantee $O(\log n)$ performance for the search, insert and delete operations of a search tree by ensuring that the search tree height is always $O(\log n)$. Trees with a worst-case height of $O(\log n)$ are called **balanced trees**. One of the more popular balanced trees, known as an **AVL tree**, was introduced in 1962 by Adelson-Velskii and Landis.

Definition 15.1 *An empty binary tree is an AVL tree. If T is a nonempty binary tree with T_L and T_R as its left and right subtrees, then T is an AVL tree iff (1) T_L and T_R are AVL trees and (2) $|h_L - h_R| \leq 1$ where h_L and h_R are the heights of T_L and T_R, respectively.* ∎

An **AVL search tree** is a binary search tree that is also an AVL tree. Trees (a) and (b) of Figure 14.1 are AVL trees, while tree (c) is not. Tree (a) is not an AVL search tree, as it is not a binary search tree. Tree (b) is an AVL search tree. The trees of Figure 14.3 are AVL search trees.

An **indexed AVL search tree** is an indexed binary search tree that is also an AVL tree. Both the search trees of Figure 14.2 are indexed AVL search trees. In the remainder of this section, we will not consider indexed AVL search trees explicitly. However, the techniques we develop carry over in a rather straightforward manner to such trees. We will use the terms *insert* and *put* as well as the terms *remove* and *delete* interchangeably.

If we are to use AVL search trees to represent a dictionary and perform each dictionary operation in logarithmic time, then we must establish the following properties:

1. The height of an AVL tree with n elements/nodes is $O(\log n)$.

2. For every value of n, $n \geq 0$, there exists an AVL tree. (Otherwise, some insertions cannot leave behind an AVL tree, as no such tree exists for the current number of elements.)

3. An n-element AVL search tree can be searched in $O(height) = O(\log n)$ time.

4. A new element can be inserted into an n-element AVL search tree so that the result is an $n + 1$ element AVL tree and such an insertion can be done in $O(\log n)$ time.

5. An element can be deleted from an n-element AVL search tree, $n > 0$, so that the result is an $n - 1$ element AVL tree and such a deletion can be done in $O(\log n)$ time.

Property 2 follows from property 4, so we will not show property 2 explicitly. Properties 1, 3, 4, and 5 are established in the following subsections.

15.1.2   Height of an AVL Tree

We will obtain a bound on the height of an AVL tree that has n nodes in it. Let N_h be the minimum number of nodes in an AVL tree of height h. In the worst case the height of one of the subtrees is $h-1$, and the height of the other is $h-2$. Both these subtrees are also AVL trees. Hence

$$N_h = N_{h-1} + N_{h-2} + 1, \quad N_0 = 0, \quad \text{and} \quad N_1 = 1$$

Notice the similarity between this definition for N_h and the definition of the Fibonacci numbers

$$F_n = F_{n-1} + F_{n-2}, \quad F_0 = 0, \quad \text{and} \quad F_1 = 1$$

It can be shown (see Exercise 9) that $N_h = F_{h+2} - 1$ for $h \geq 0$. From Fibonacci number theory we know that $F_h \approx \phi^h/\sqrt{5}$ where $\phi = (1 + \sqrt{5})/2$. Hence $N_h \approx \phi^{h+2}/\sqrt{5}-1$. If there are n nodes in the tree, then its height h is at most $\log_\phi(\sqrt{5}(n+1)) - 2 \approx 1.44 \log_2(n+2) = O(\log n)$.

15.1.3   Representation of an AVL Tree

AVL trees are normally represented by using the linked representation scheme for binary trees. However, to facilitate insertion and deletion, a balance factor bf is associated with each node. The balance factor $bf(x)$ of a node x is defined as

height of left subtree of x $-$ height of right subtree of x

From the definition of an AVL tree, it follows that the permissible balance factors are -1, 0, and 1. Figure 15.1 shows two AVL search trees and the balance factors for each node.

15.1.4   Searching an AVL Search Tree

To search an AVL search tree, we may use the code of Program 14.4 without change. Since the height of an AVL tree with n elements is $O(\log n)$, the search time is $O(\log n)$.

15.1.5   Inserting into an AVL Search Tree

If we use the strategy of Program 14.5 to insert an element into an AVL search tree, the tree following the insertion may no longer be AVL. For instance, when an element with key 32 is inserted into the AVL tree of Figure 15.1(a), the new search tree is the one shown in Figure 15.2(a). Since this tree contains nodes with balance

The number outside each node is its balance factor

Figure 15.1 AVL search trees

factors other than −1, 0, and 1, it is not an AVL tree. When an insertion into an AVL tree using the strategy of Program 14.5 results in a search tree that has one or more nodes with balance factors other than −1, 0, and 1, the resulting search tree is **unbalanced**. We can restore balance (i.e., make all balance factors −1, 0, and 1) by shifting some of the subtrees of the unbalanced tree as in Figure 15.2(b).

(a) Immediately after insertion   (b) Following rebalancing

Figure 15.2 Sample insertion into an AVL search tree

Before examining the subtree movement needed to restore balance, let us make some observations about the unbalanced tree that results from an insertion. I1 denotes insertion observation 1.

I1: In the unbalanced tree the balance factors are limited to −2, −1, 0, 1, and 2.

I2: A node with balance factor 2 had a balance factor 1 before the insertion.

Similarly, a node with balance factor -2 had a balance factor -1 before the insertion.

I3: The balance factors of only those nodes on the path from the root to the newly inserted node can change as a result of the insertion.

I4: Let A denote the nearest ancestor of the newly inserted node whose balance factor is either -2 or 2. (In the case of Figure 15.2(a), the A node is the node with key 40.) The balance factor of all nodes on the path from A to the newly inserted node was 0 prior to the insertion.

Node A (see I4) may be identified while we are moving down from the root searching for the place to insert the new element. From I2 it follows that $bf(A)$ was either -1 or 1 prior to the insertion. Let X denote the last node encountered that has such a balance factor. When inserting 32 into the AVL tree of Figure 15.1(a), X is the node with key 40; when inserting 22, 28, or 50 into the AVL tree of Figure 15.1(b), X is the node with key 25; and when inserting 10, 14, 16, or 19 into the AVL tree of Figure 15.1(b), there is no node X.

When node X does not exist, all nodes on the path from the root to the newly inserted node have balance factor 0 prior to the insertion. The tree cannot be unbalanced following the insertion because an insertion changes balance factors by -1, 0, or 1, and only balance factors on the path from the root may change. Therefore, if the tree is unbalanced following the insertion, X exists. If $bf(X) = 0$ after the insertion, then the height of the subtree with root X is the same before and after the insertion. For example, if this height was h before the insertion and if $bf(X)$ was 1, the height of its left subtree X_L was $h-1$ and that of its right subtree X_R was $h - 2$ before the insertion (see Figure 15.3(a)). For the balance factor to become 0, the insertion must be made in X_R resulting in an X'_R of height $h - 1$ (see Figure 15.3(b)). The height of X'_R must increase to $h-1$ as all balance factors on the path from X to the newly inserted node were 0 prior to the insertion. The height of X remains h, and the balance factors of the ancestors of X are the same before and after the insertion, so the tree is balanced.

The only way the tree can become unbalanced is if the insertion causes $bf(X)$ to change from -1 to -2 or from 1 to 2. For the latter case to occur, the insertion must be made in the left subtree X_L of X (see Figure 15.3(c)). Now the height of X'_L must become h (as all balance factors on the path from X to the newly inserted node were 0 prior to the insertion). Therefore, the A node referred to in observation I4 is X.

When the A node has been identified, the imbalance at A can be classified as either an L (the newly inserted node is in the left subtree of A) or R type imbalance. This imbalance classification may be refined by determining which grandchild of A is on the path to the newly inserted node. Notice that such a grandchild exists, as the height of the subtree of A that contains the new node must be at least 2 for the balance factor of A to be -2 or 2. With this refinement of the imbalance classification, the imbalance at A is of one of the types LL (new node is in the left

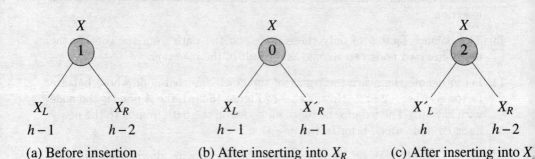

(a) Before insertion   (b) After inserting into X_R (c) After inserting into X

Balance factor of X is inside the node
Subtree heights are below subtree names

Figure 15.3 Inserting into an AVL search tree

subtree of the left subtree of A), LR (new node is in the right subtree of the left subtree of A), RR, and RL.

A generic LL type imbalance appears in Figure 15.4. Figure 15.4(a) shows the conditions before the insertion, and Figure 15.4(b) shows the situation following the insertion of an element into the left subtree B_L of B. The subtree movement needed to restore balance at A appears in Figure 15.4(c). B becomes the root of the subtree that A was previously root of, B'_L remains the left subtree of B, A becomes the root of B's right subtree, B_R becomes the left subtree of A, and the right subtree of A is unchanged. The balance factors of nodes in B'_L that are on the path from B to the newly inserted node change as does the balance factor of A. The remaining balance factors are the same as before the rotation. Since the heights of the subtrees of Figures 15.4(a) and (c) are the same, the balance factors of the ancestors (if any) of this subtree are the same as before the insertion. So no nodes with a balance factor other than -1, 0, or 1 remain. A single LL rotation has rebalanced the entire tree! You may verify that the rebalanced tree is indeed a binary search tree.

Figure 15.5 shows a generic LR type imbalance. Since the insertion took place in the right subtree of B, this subtree cannot be empty following the insertion; therefore, node C exists. However, its subtrees C_L and C_R may be empty. The rearrangement of subtrees needed to rebalance appears in Figure 15.5(c). The values of $bf(B)$ and $bf(A)$ following the rearrangement depend on the value, b, of $bf(C)$ just after the insertion but before the rearrangement. The figure gives these values as a function of b. The rearranged subtree is seen to be a binary search tree. Also, since the heights of the subtrees of Figures 15.5(a) and (c) are the same, the balance factors of their ancestors (if any) are the same before and after the insertion. So a single LR rotation at A rebalances the entire tree.

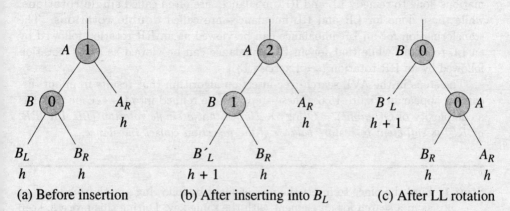

(a) Before insertion   (b) After inserting into B_L (c) After LL rotation

Balance factors are inside nodes
Subtree heights are below subtree names

Figure 15.4 An LL rotation

(a) Before insertion (b) After inserting into B_R (c) After LR rotation

$$b = 0 \Rightarrow bf(B) = bf(A) = 0 \text{ after rotation}$$
$$b = 1 \Rightarrow bf(B) = 0 \text{ and } bf(A) = -1 \text{ after rotation}$$
$$b = -1 \Rightarrow bf(B) = 1 \text{ and } bf(A) = 0 \text{ after rotation}$$

Figure 15.5 An LR rotation

The cases RR and RL are symmetric to the ones we have just seen. The transformations done to remedy LL and RR imbalances are often called **single rotations**, while those done for LR and RL imbalances are called **double rotations**. The transformation for an LR imbalance can be viewed as an RR rotation followed by an LL rotation, while that for an RL imbalance can be viewed as an LL rotation followed by an RR rotation (see Exercise 13).

The steps in the AVL search-tree-insertion algorithm that results from our discussion appear in Figure 15.6. These steps can be refined into C++ code that has a complexity of $O(height) = O(\log n)$. *Notice that a single rotation (LL, LR, RR, or RL) is sufficient to restore balance if the insertion causes imbalance.*

Step 1: Find the place to insert the new element by following a path from the root as in a search for an element with the same key. During this process, keep track of the most recently seen node with balance factor -1 or 1. Let this node be A. If an element with the same key is found, the insert fails and the remaining steps are not performed.

Step 2: If there is no node A, then make another pass from the root, updating balance factors. Terminate following this pass.

Step 3: If $bf(A) = 1$ and the new node was inserted in the right subtree of A or if $bf(A) = -1$ and the insertion took place in the left subtree, then the new balance factor of A is 0. In this case update balance factors on the path from A to the new node and terminate.

Step 4: Classify the imbalance at A and perform the appropriate rotation. Change balance factors as required by the rotation as well as those of nodes on the path from the new subtree root to the newly inserted node.

Figure 15.6 Steps for AVL search tree insertion

15.1.6 Deletion from an AVL Search Tree

To delete an element from an AVL search tree, we proceed as in Program 14.6. Let q be the parent of the node that was physically deleted. For example, if the element with key 25 is deleted from the tree of Figure 15.1(b), the node containing this element is deleted and the right-child pointer from the root diverted to the only child of the deleted node. The parent of the deleted node is the root, so q is the root. If instead, the element with key 15 is deleted, its spot is used by the element with key 12 and the node previously containing this element is deleted. Now q is the node that originally contained 15 (i.e., the left child of the root). Since the balance factors of some (or all) of the nodes on the path from the root to q have changed as a result of the deletion, we retrace this path backward from q toward the root.

If the deletion took place from the left subtree of q, $bf(q)$ decreases by 1, and if it took place from the right subtree, $bf(q)$ increases by 1. We may make the following observations (D1 denotes deletion observation 1):

D1: If the new balance factor of q is 0, its height has decreased by 1; we need to change the balance factor of its parent (if any) and possibly those of its other ancestors.

D2: If the new balance factor of q is either -1 or 1, its height is the same as before the deletion and the balance factors of its ancestors are unchanged.

D3: If the new balance factor of q is either -2 or 2, the tree is unbalanced at q.

Since balance factor changes may propagate up the tree along the path from q to the root (see observation D1), it is possible for the balance factor of a node on this path to become -2 or 2. Let A be the first such node on this path. To restore balance at node A, we classify the type of imbalance. The imbalance is of type L if the deletion took place from A's left subtree. Otherwise, it is of type R. If $bf(A) = 2$ after the deletion, it must have been 1 before. So A has a left subtree with root B. A type R imbalance is subclassified into the types R0, R1, and R-1, depending on $bf(B)$. The type R-1, for instance, refers to the case when the deletion took place from the right subtree of A and $bf(B) = -1$. Similarly, type L imbalances are subclassified into the types L0, L1, and L-1.

An R0 imbalance at A is rectified by performing the rotation shown in Figure 15.7. Notice that the height of the shown subtree was $h+2$ before the deletion and is $h+2$ after. So the balance factors of the remaining nodes on the path to the root are unchanged. As a result, the entire tree has been rebalanced.

(a) Before deletion   (b) After deleting from A_R (c) After R0 rotation

Figure 15.7 An R0 rotation (single rotation)

Figure 15.8 shows how to handle an R1 imbalance. While the pointer changes are the same as for an R0 imbalance, the new balance factors for A and B are different and the height of the subtree following the rotation is now $h + 1$, which is 1 less than before the deletion. So if A is not the root, the balance factors of some of its ancestors will change and further rotations may be necessary. Following an R1 rotation, we must continue to examine nodes on the path to the root. *Unlike the case of an insertion, one rotation may not suffice to restore balance following a deletion. The number of rotations needed is* $O(\log n)$.

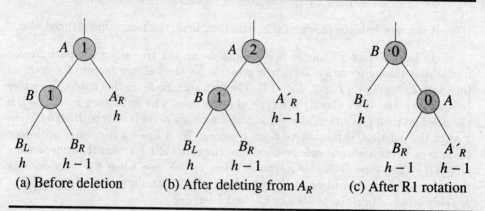

(a) Before deletion   (b) After deleting from A_R (c) After R1 rotation

Figure 15.8 An R1 rotation (single rotation)

The transformation needed when the imbalance is of type R−1 appears in Figure 15.9. The balance factors of A and B following the rotation depend on the balance factor b of the right child of B. This rotation leaves behind a subtree of height $h + 1$, while the subtree height prior to the deletion was $h + 2$. So we need to continue on the path to the root.

LL and R1 rotations are identical; LL and R0 rotations differ only in the final balance factors of A and B; and LR and R−1 rotations are identical.

EXERCISES

1. Start with an empty AVL search tree and insert the following keys in the given order: 15, 14, 13, 12, 11, 10, 9, 8, 7, 6, 5, 4, 3, 2, 1. Draw figures similar to Figures 15.2 and 15.3 depicting your tree immediately after each insertion and following the rebalancing rotation (if any). Label all nodes with their balance factors and identify the rotation type (if any) that is done.

2. Do Exercise 1 using the insert key sequence: 1, 2, 3, 4, 5, 6, 7, 8, 9, 10, 11, 12, 13, 14, 15.

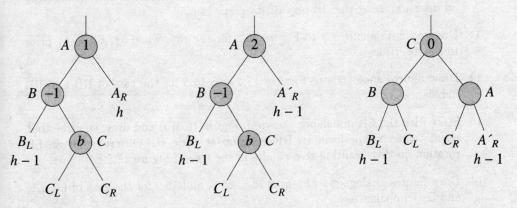

(a) Before deletion   (b) After deleting from A_R (c) After R−1 rotation

$$b = 0 \Rightarrow bf(A) = bf(B) = 0 \text{ after rotation}$$
$$b = 1 \Rightarrow bf(A) = -1 \text{ and } bf(B) = 0 \text{ after rotation}$$
$$b = -1 \Rightarrow bf(A) = 0 \text{ and } bf(B) = 1 \text{ after rotation}$$

Figure 15.9 An R−1 rotation (double rotation)

3. Do Exercise 1 using the insert key sequence: 20, 10, 5, 30, 40, 3, 4, 25, 23, 27, 50.

4. Do Exercise 1 using the insert key sequence: 40, 50, 70, 30, 20, 45, 25, 10, 5, 22, 1, 35.

5. Start with an AVL search tree that is a 15-node full binary tree; the keys are 1–15. Remove the keys in the order 15, 14, 13, $\cdots$, 1. Draw your tree immediately following each deletion and immediately after each rotation that is performed. Label all nodes with their balance factors and identify the rotation type (if any) that is done.

6. Do Exercise 5 but this time remove the keys in the order 1, 2, 3, $\cdots$, 15.

7. Do Exercise 5 but this time remove keys in the order 6, 7, 5, 10, 9, 11, 15, 12, 13, 1, 2, and 3.

8. Do Exercise 5 but this time remove keys in the order 11, 14, 13, 15, 9, 2, 3, 1, 6, 5, and 7.

9. Prove by induction that the minimum number of nodes in an AVL tree of height h is $N_h = F_{h+2} - 1$, $h \geq 0$.

10. Prove observations I1 through I4 regarding an unbalanced tree resulting from an insertion using the strategy of Program 14.5.

11. Draw a figure analogous to Figure 15.3 for the case when $bf(X) = -1$ prior to the insertion.

12. Draw figures analogous to Figures 15.4 and 15.5 for the case of RR and RL imbalances.

13. Start with the LR imbalance shown in Figure 15.5(b) and draw the tree that results when we perform an RR rotation at node B. Observe that an LL rotation on this resulting tree results in the tree of Figure 15.5(b).

14. Draw figures analogous to Figures 15.7, 15.8, and 15.9 for the case of L0, L1, and L−1 imbalances.

15. Develop the concrete class `avlTree` that derives from the abstract class `indexed-BSTree` (Program 14.2). Fully code all your methods and test their correctness. Your implementations for `find`, `get`, `insert`, `erase` and `delete` must have complexity $O(\log n)$, and that for `ascend` should be $O(n)$. Show that this is the case.

16. Do Exercise 15 for the case when the search tree may contain several elements with the same key. Call the new class `davlTree`.

· 17. Develop a C++ class `indexedAVLtree` that includes the indexed binary search tree methods `find(theKey)`, `insert`, `delete(theKey)`, `get(theIndex)`, `erase(theIndex)`, and `ascend`. Fully code all your methods and test their correctness. Your implementations for the first five operations must have complexity $O(\log n)$ and that for the last operation should be $O(n)$. Show that this is the case.

18. Do Exercise 17 for the case when the search tree may contain several elements with the same key. Call the new class `dIndexedAVLtree`.

19. Explain how you could use an AVL tree to reduce the asymptotic complexity of our solution to the railroad car rearrangement problem of Section 8.5.3 to $O(n \log k)$.

20. Develop the class `linearListAsIndexedAVLtree` that derives from the abstract class `linearList` (Program 5.1). See Exercise 21 in Chapter 14 for some clues. Other than the operation `indexOf`, all operations should run in logarithmic or less time.

21. Replace the use of a binary search tree in Program 14.11 with an AVL search tree with duplicates. Measure the performance of the two versions of the best-fit bin-packing codes.

22. (a) Use an indexed AVL search tree to obtain an $O(n \log n)$ solution for the crossing-distribution problem (Section 14.6.3).

    (b) Test the correctness of your code.

    (c) Compare the actual run time of this solution to that of the $\Theta(n^2)$ solution described in Section 14.6.3 (see Program 14.12). Do this comparison using randomly generated permutations C and $n = 1000$; 10,000; and 50,000.

15.2   RED–BLACK TREES

15.2.1   Definition

A **red-black tree** is a binary search tree in which every node is colored either red or black. The remaining properties satisfied by a red-black tree are best stated in terms of the corresponding extended binary tree. Recall, from Section 12.5.1, that we obtain an extended binary tree from a regular binary tree by replacing every null pointer with an external node. The additional properties are

RB1. The root and all external nodes are colored black.

RB2. No root-to-external-node path has two consecutive red nodes.

RB3. All root-to-external-node paths have the same number of black nodes.

An equivalent definition arises from assigning colors to the pointers between a node and its children. The pointer from a parent to a black child is black and to a red child is red. Additionally,

RB1′. Pointers from an internal node to an external node are black.

RB2′. No root-to-external-node path has two consecutive red pointers.

RB3′. All root-to-external-node paths have the same number of black pointers.

Notice that if we know the pointer colors, we can deduce the node colors and vice versa. In the red-black tree of Figure 15.10, the external nodes are shaded squares, black nodes are shaded circles, red nodes are unshaded circles, black pointers are thick lines, and red pointers are thin lines. Notice that every path from the root to an external node has exactly two black pointers and three black nodes (including the root and the external node); no such path has two consecutive red nodes or pointers.

Let the **rank** of a node in a red-black tree be the number of black pointers (equivalently the number of black nodes minus 1) on any path from the node to any external node in its subtree. So the rank of an external node is 0. The rank of the root of Figure 15.10 is 2, that of its left child is 2, and of its right child is 1.

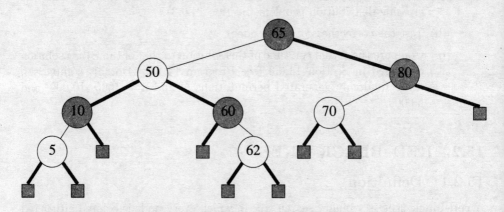

Figure 15.10 A red-black tree

Lemma 15.1 *Let the length of a root-to-external-node path be the number of pointers on the path. If P and Q are two root-to-external-node paths in a red-black tree, then* $length(P) \leq 2length(Q)$.

Proof Consider any red-black tree. Suppose that the rank of the root is r. From RB1′ the last pointer on each root-to-external-node path is black. From RB2′ no such path has two consecutive red pointers. So each red pointer is followed by a black pointer. As a result, each root-to-external-node path has between r and $2r$ pointers, so $length(P) \leq 2length(Q)$. To see that the upper bound is possible, consider the red-black tree of Figure 15.10. The path from the root to the left child of 5 has length 4, while that to the right child of 80 has length 2. ∎

Lemma 15.2 *Let h be the height of a red-black tree (excluding the external nodes), let n be the number of internal nodes in the tree, and let r be the rank of the root.*

(a) $h \leq 2r$

(b) $n \geq 2^r - 1$

(c) $h \leq 2\log_2(n+1)$

Proof From the proof of Lemma 15.1, we know that no root-to-external-node path has length $> 2r$, so $h \leq 2r$. (The height of the red-black tree of Figure 15.10 with external nodes removed is $2r = 4$.)

Since the rank of the root is r, there are no external nodes at levels 1 through r, so there are $2^r - 1$ internal nodes at these levels. Consequently, the total number of internal nodes is at least this much. (In the red-black tree of Figure 15.10, levels 1 and 2 have $3 = 2^2 - 1$ internal nodes. There are additional internal nodes at levels 3 and 4.)

From (b) it follows that $r \leq \log_2(n+1)$. This inequality together with (a) yields (c). ∎

Since the height of a red-black tree is at most $2\log_2(n+1)$, search, insert, and delete algorithms that work in $O(h)$ time have complexity $O(\log n)$.

Notice that the worst-case height of a red-black tree is more than the worst-case height (approximately $1.44\log_2(n+2)$) of an AVL tree with the same number of (internal) nodes.

15.2.2   Representation of a Red-Black Tree

Although it is convenient to include external nodes when defining red-black trees, in an implementation null pointers, rather than physical nodes, represent external nodes. Further, since pointer and node colors are closely related, with each node we need to store only its color or the color of the two pointers to its children. Node colors require just one additional bit per node, while pointer colors require two. Since both schemes require almost the same amount of space, we may choose between them on the basis of actual run times of the resulting red-black tree algorithms.

In our discussion of the insert and delete operations, we will explicitly state the needed color changes only for the nodes. The corresponding pointer color changes may be inferred.

15.2.3   Searching a Red-Black Tree

We can search a red-black tree with the code we used to search an ordinary binary search tree (Program 14.4). This code has complexity $O(h)$, which is $O(\log n)$ for a red-black tree. Since we use the same code to search ordinary binary search trees, AVL trees, and red-black trees and since the worst-case height of an AVL tree is least, we expect AVL trees to show the best worst-case performance in applications where search is the dominant operation.

15.2.4   Inserting into a Red-Black Tree

Elements may be inserted using the strategy used for ordinary binary trees (Program 14.5). When the new node is attached to the red-black tree, we need to assign the node a color. If the tree was empty before the insertion, then the new node is the root and must be colored black (see property RB1). Suppose the tree was not empty prior to the insertion. If the new node is given the color black, then we will have an extra black node on paths from the root to the external nodes that are children of the new node. On the other hand, if the new node is assigned the color red, then we might have two consecutive red nodes. Making the new node black is guaranteed to cause a violation of property RB3, while making the new node red may or may not violate property RB2. We will make the new node red.

If making the new node red causes a violation of property RB2, we will say that the tree has become imbalanced. The nature of the imbalance is classified by examining the new node u, its parent pu, and the grandparent gu of u. Observe that since property RB2 has been violated, we have two consecutive red nodes. One of these red nodes is u, and the other must be its parent; therefore, pu exists. Since pu is red, it cannot be the root (as the root is black by property RB1); u must have a grandparent gu, which must be black (property RB2). When pu is the left child of gu, u is the left child of pu and the other child of gu is black (this case includes the case when the other child of gu is an external node); the imbalance is of type LLb. The other imbalance types are LLr (pu is the left child of gu, u is the left child of pu, the other child of gu is red), LRb (pu is the left child of gu, u is the right child of pu, the other child of gu is black), LRr, RRb, RRr, RLb, and RLr.

Imbalances of the type XYr (X and Y may be L or R) are handled by changing colors, while those of type XYb require a rotation. When we change a color, the RB2 violation may propagate two levels up the tree. In this case we will need to reclassify at the new level, with the new u being the former gu, and apply the transformations again. When a rotation is done, the RB2 violation is taken care of and no further work is needed.

Figure 15.11 shows the color changes performed for LLr and LRr imbalances; these color changes are identical. Black nodes are shaded, while red ones are not. In Figure 15.11(a), for example, gu is black, while pu and u are red; the pointers from gu to its left and right children are red; gu_R is the right subtree of gu; and pu_R is the right subtree of pu. Both LLr and LRr color changes require us to change the color of pu and of the right child of gu from red to black. Additionally, we change the color of gu from black to red provided gu is not the root. Since this color change is not done when gu is the root, the number of black nodes on all root-to-external-node paths increases by 1 when gu is the root of the red-black tree.

If changing the color of gu to red causes an imbalance, gu becomes the new u node, its parent becomes the new pu, its grandparent becomes the new gu, and we continue to rebalance. If gu is the root or if the color change does not cause an RB2 violation at gu, we are done.

Figure 15.12 shows the rotations performed to handle LLb and LRb imbalances. In Figures 15.12(a) and (b), u is the root of pu_L. Notice the similarity between these rotations and the LL (refer to Figure 15.4) and LR (refer to Figure 15.5) rotations used to handle an imbalance following an insertion in an AVL tree. The pointer changes are the same. In the case of an LLb rotation, for example, in addition to pointer changes we need to change the color of gu from black to red and of pu from red to black.

In examining the node (or pointer) colors after the rotations of Figure 15.12, we see that the number of black nodes (or pointers) on all root-to-external-node paths is unchanged. Further, the root of the involved subtree (gu before the rotation and pu after) is black following the rotation; therefore, two consecutive red nodes cannot exist on the path from the tree root to the new pu. Consequently, no additional

(a) LLr imbalance

(b) After LLr color change

(c) LRr imbalance

(d) After LRr color change

Figure 15.11 LLr and LRr color changes

rebalancing work is to be done. *A single rotation (preceded possibly by $O(\log n)$ color changes) suffices to restore balance following an insertion!*

Example 15.1 Consider the red-black tree of Figure 15.13(a). External nodes are shown for convenience. In an actual implementation, the shown black pointers to external nodes are simply null pointers and external nodes are not represented. Notice that all root-to-external-node paths have three black nodes (including the external node) and two black pointers.

To insert 70 into this red-black tree, we use the algorithm of Program 14.5. The new node is added as the left child of 80. Since the insertion is done into a nonempty tree, the new node is assigned the color red. So the pointer to it from its parent (80) is also red. This insertion does not result in a violation of property RB2, and no remedial action is necessary. Notice that the number of black pointers on all root-to-external-node paths is the same as before the insertion.

Next insert 60 into the tree of Figure 15.13(b). The algorithm of Program 14.5

(a) LLb imbalance

(b) After LLb rotation

(c) LRb imbalance

(d) After LRb rotation

Figure 15.12 LLb and LRb rotations for red-black insertion

attaches a new node as the left child of 70, as is shown in Figure 15.13(c). The new node is red, and the pointer to it is also red. The new node is the u node, its parent (70) is pu, and its grandparent (80) is gu. Since pu and u are red, we have an imbalance. This imbalance is classified as an LLr imbalance (as pu is the left child of gu, u is the left child of pu, and the other child of gu is red). When the LLr color change of Figure 15.11(a) and (b) is performed, we get the tree of Figure 15.13(d). Now u, pu, and gu are each moved two levels up the tree. The node with 80 is the new u node, the root becomes pu, and gu is null. Since there is no gu node, we cannot have an RB2 imbalance at this location and we are done. All root-to-external-node paths have exactly two black pointers.

Now insert 65 into the tree of Figure 15.13(d). The result appears in Figure 15.13(e). The new node is the u node. Its parent and grandparent are, respectively, the pu and gu nodes. We have an LRb imbalance that requires us to perform the rotation of Figure 15.12(c) and (d). The result is the tree of Figure 15.13(f).

Finally, insert 62 to obtain the tree of Figure 15.13(g). We have an LRr imbalance that requires a color change. The resulting tree and the new u, pu, and gu nodes appear in Figure 15.13(h). The color change just performed has caused an

(a) Initial

(b) Insert 70

(c) Insert 60

(d) LLr color change

(e) Insert 65

(f) LRb rotation

Figure 15.13 Insertion into a red-black tree (continues)

(g) Insert 62   (h) LRr color change

(i) RLb rotation

Figure 15.13 Insertion into a red-black tree (concluded)

RLb imbalance two levels up, so we now need to perform an RLb rotation. The rotation results in the tree of Figure 15.13(i). Following a rotation, no further work is needed, and we are done.   ■

15.2.5   Deletion from a Red-Black Tree

Deletions are performed by first using the deletion algorithm for ordinary binary search trees (Program 14.6) and then performing remedial color changes and a single rotation if necessary. Consider the red-black tree of Figure 15.14(a). If Program 14.6 is used to delete 70, the node containing 70 is physically removed (deleted) from the tree and we get the tree of Figure 15.14(b). (If pointer colors are represented, we will also need to change the color of 90's left pointer to get this tree.) When 90 is deleted from tree (a), the node that contains 90 is physically removed from the tree, the right-child pointer from its parent is changed to point to the left subtree of the physically removed node, and tree (c) results. The deletion of 65 from tree (a) is done by moving 62 into the root and then physically removing the node that originally contained 62; the result is tree (d). Let y denote the node that takes the place of the node that is physically removed (or deleted). The y nodes for the deletion examples appear in Figure 15.14. In the case of Figure 15.14(b), for example, the left child of 90 was deleted. Its new left child is the external node y.

(a) A red-black tree

(b) Delete 70

(c) Delete 90

(d) Delete 65

Figure 15.14 Red-black deletion examples

In the case of tree (b), the deleted node (i.e., the one that contained 70 in tree (a)) was red. Its deletion does not affect the number of black nodes on root-to-external-node paths, and no remedial work is necessary. In tree (c) the deleted node (i.e., the one with 90 in tree (a)) was black, and the number of black nodes (and hence pointers) on paths from the root-to-external-nodes in y is 1 less than before. Since y is not the new root, an RB3 violation occurs. In tree (d) the deleted node was red, and no RB3 violation occurs. *An RB3 violation occurs only when the deleted node was black and y is not the root of the resulting tree.* No other red-black property violations are possible following a deletion using Program 14.6.

When an RB3 violation occurs, the subtree rooted at y is one black node (or equivalently, one black pointer) deficient; therefore, the number of black nodes (and hence pointers) on paths from the root to external nodes in the subtree y is 1 less than on paths to other external nodes. We will say that the tree has become **imbalanced**. We classify the nature of the imbalance by identifying the parent py and sibling v of y. When y is the right child of py, the imbalance is of type R. Otherwise, it is of type L. Observe that since y is one black node deficient, v cannot be an external node. If v is a black node, the imbalance is of type Lb or Rb. When v is red, the imbalance is of type Lr or Rr.

First consider an Rb imbalance. Imbalances of type Lb are handled in a similar way. Rb imbalances may be divided into three subcases on the basis of the number of v's red children. The three subcases are Rb0, Rb1, and Rb2.

When the imbalance type is Rb0, a color change is performed (Figure 15.15). Figure 15.15 shows the two possibilities for the color of py. If py was black prior to the color change, then the color change causes the subtree rooted at py to be one black node deficient. Also, in Figure 15.15(b) the number of black nodes on paths to external nodes in v is 1 less than before the color change. Therefore, regardless of whether the path goes to an external node in v or y, following the color change, it is one black node deficient. If py is the root of the whole red-black tree, nothing more is to be done. If it is not, then py becomes the new y; the imbalance at y is reclassified, and appropriate remedial action occurs at this new y.

(a) Rb0 imbalance   (b) Rb0 color change

Figure 15.15 Rb0 color change for red-black deletion

When py was red before the color change, the number of black nodes on paths to external nodes in y increases by 1 but is unchanged for those in v. The entire tree becomes balanced, and we are done.

Rotations are performed when the imbalance type is Rb1 or Rb2. These rotations appear in Figure 15.16. A thatched node denotes a node that may be either red or black. The color of such a node is not changed as a result of the rotation. Therefore, in Figure 15.16(b) the root of the shown subtree has the same color before and after the rotation—the color of v in (b) is the same as that of py in (a). You should verify that following the rotation the number of black nodes (and hence black pointers) on paths from the root-to-external-nodes in y is increased by 1 and unchanged on paths from the root to the remaining external nodes. As a result, a rotation rebalances the tree, and no further work is to be done.

(a) Rb1(i) imbalance

(b) After Rb1(i) rotation

(c) Rb1(ii) imbalance

(d) After Rb1(ii) rotation

(e) Rb2 imbalance

(f) After Rb2 rotation

Figure 15.16 Rb1 and Rb2 rotations for red-black deletion

Next consider imbalances of type Rr. The case of Lr imbalances is symmetric. Since y is one black node deficient and v is red, both v_L and v_R have at least one black node that is not an external node; therefore, both children of v are internal nodes. Rr imbalances may be subdivided into three cases according to the number of red children (0, 1, or 2) that v's right child has. All three cases of an Rr imbalance are handled by a rotation. The rotations appear in Figures 15.17 and 15.18. Once again, you can verify that the shown rotation restores balance to the entire tree.

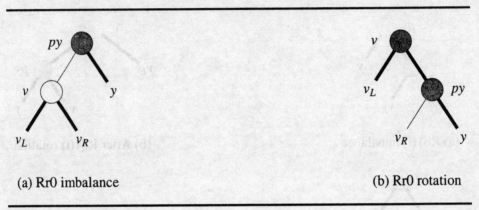

(a) Rr0 imbalance   (b) Rr0 rotation

Figure 15.17 Rr0 rotation for red-black deletion

Example 15.2 If we delete 90 from the red-black tree of Figure 15.13(i), we get the tree of Figure 15.19(a). Since the deleted node was not the root and was black, we have an imbalance. The imbalance is of type Rb0, and a color change is performed to get the tree of Figure 15.19(b). Since py was originally a red node, this color change rebalances the tree and we are done.

If we now delete 80 from tree (b), tree (c) results. A red node was deleted, so the tree remains balanced. When 70 is deleted from tree (c), we get tree (d). This time a nonroot black node was deleted, and the tree is unbalanced. The imbalance type is Rr1(ii) (the right child w of v has one red pointer, which is itself the right-child pointer of w). Following an Rr1(ii) rotation, tree (e) is obtained. This tree is balanced.   ■

15.2.6   Implementation Considerations and Complexity

The remedial action taken to rebalance a red-black tree following an insertion or deletion requires us to move back on the path taken from the root to the point of insertion or deletion. This backward movement is easy to do if each node has a parent field in addition to data, left child, right child, and color fields. An alternative to adding a parent field to each node is to save, on a stack, pointers to nodes encountered on the downward path from the root to the point of insertion/deletion.

(a) Rr1(i) imbalance

(b) After Rr1(i) rotation

(c) Rr1(ii) imbalance

(d) After Rr1(ii) rotation

(e) Rr2 imbalance

(f) After Rr2 rotation

Figure 15.18 Rr1 and Rr2 rotations for red-black deletion

(a) 90 deleted

(b) After Rb0 color change

(c) 80 deleted

(d) 70 deleted

(e) After Rr1(ii) rotation

Figure 15.19 Deletion from a red-black tree

Now we may move back toward the root by performing deletes from the stack of saved pointers. For an n-element red-black tree, the addition of parent fields increases the space requirements by $\Theta(n)$, while the use of a stack increases the space requirements by $\Theta(\log n)$. Although the stack scheme is more efficient on space requirements, the parent-pointer scheme runs slightly faster.

Since the color changes performed following an insert or delete may propagate back toward the root, $O(\log n)$ of these color changes may be performed. Rotations, on the other hand, guarantee to rebalance the tree. As a result, at most one rotation may be performed following each insert/delete. The time needed for each color change or rotation operation is $\Theta(1)$; the total time needed to insert/delete is $O(\log n)$.

As a final note, red-black trees are used in the C++ STL implementation of dictionaries (`map`) and dictionaries with duplicates (`multimap`).

EXERCISES

23. Start with an empty red-black tree and insert the following keys in the given order: 15, 14, 13, 12, 11, 10, 9, 8, 7, 6, 5, 4, 3, 2, 1. Draw figures similar to Figure 15.13 depicting your tree immediately after each insertion and following the rebalancing rotation or color change (if any). Label all nodes with their color and identify the rotation type (if any) that is done.

24. Do Exercise 23 using the insert key sequence: 1, 2, 3, 4, 5, 6, 7, 8, 9, 10, 11, 12, 13, 14, 15.

25. Do Exercise 23 using the insert key sequence: 20, 10, 5, 30, 40, 57, 3, 2, 4, 35, 25, 18, 22, 21.

26. Do Exercise 23 using the insert key sequence: 40, 50, 70, 30, 42, 15, 20, 25, 27, 26, 60, 55.

27. Start with a red-black tree that is a 15-node full binary tree; the keys are 1–15. All nodes are black. Remove the keys in the order 15, 14, 13, $\cdots$, 1. Draw your tree immediately following each deletion and immediately after each rotation or color change that is performed. Label all nodes with their colors and identify the rotation type (if any) that is done.

28. Do Exercise 27 but this time remove the keys in the order 1, 2, 3, $\cdots$, 15.

29. Do Exercise 27 but this time remove keys in the order 6, 7, 5, 10, 9, 11, 15, 12, 13, and 2.

30. Do Exercise 27 but this time remove keys in the order 11, 14, 13, 15, 9, 12, 2, 3, and 1.

31. Draw the RRr and RLr color changes that correspond to the LLr and LRr changes of Figure 15.11.

32. Draw the RRb and RLb rotations that correspond to the LLb and LRb changes of Figure 15.12.

33. Draw the Lb0 color change that corresponds to the Rb0 change of Figure 15.15.

34. Draw the Lb1 and Lb2 rotations that correspond to the Rb1 and Rb2 rotations of Figure 15.16.

35. Draw the Lr0, Lr1, and Lr2 rotations that correspond to the Rr0, Rr1, and Rr2 rotations of Figures 15.17 and 15.18.

36. Develop the concrete C++ class `redBlackTree` that derives from the abstract class `bsTree` (Program 14.1). Fully code all your methods and test their correctness. Your implementations for `find`, `insert`, and `delete` must have complexity $O(\log n)$, and that for the `ascend` should be $O(n)$. Show that this is the case. The implementations of `insert` and `delete` should follow the development in the text.

37. Develop the concrete C++ class `dRedBlackTree` that derives from `dBSTree` (see Exercise 4). Fully code all your methods and test their correctness. Your implementations for `find`, `insert`, and `delete` must have complexity $O(\log n)$, and that for the `ascend` should be $O(n)$. Show that this is the case.

38. Develop the C++ concrete class `indexedRedBlackTree` that derives from the abstract class `indexedBSTree` (Program 14.2). Fully code all your methods and test their correctness. Your implementations for `find`, `get`, `insert`, `erase`, and `delete` must have complexity $O(\log n)$, and that for the `ascend` should be $O(n)$. Show that this is the case.

39. Develop the C++ concrete class `dIndexedRedBlackTree` that implements the interface `dIndexedBSTree` (see Exercise 5). Fully code all your methods and test their correctness. Your implementations for `find`, `get`, `insert`, `delete`, and `erase` must have complexity $O(\log n)$, and that for the `ascend` should be $O(n)$. Show that this is the case.

40. Develop the C++ concrete class `linearListAsRedBlackTree` that derives from the abstract class `linearList`. Fully code all your methods and test their correctness.

15.3   SPLAY TREES

15.3.1   Introduction

When either AVL trees or red-black trees are used to implement a dictionary, the worst-case complexity of each dictionary operation is logarithmic in the dictionary size. No known data structures provide a better worst-case time complexity for these operations. However, in many applications of a dictionary, we are less interested in the time taken by an individual operation than we are in the time taken by a sequence of operations. This is the case, for example, for the applications considered at the end of Chapter 14. The complexity of each of these applications depends on the time taken to perform a sequence of dictionary operations, not on the time taken for any one of them.

Splay trees are binary search trees in which the complexity of an individual dictionary operation is $O(n)$. However, every sequence of f find, i insert, and d delete operations is done in $O((f+i+d)\log i)$ time, the same asymptotic complexity as when AVL trees or red-black trees are used. Experimental studies indicate that for random sequences of dictionary operations, splay trees are actually faster than AVL trees and red-black trees are. Moreover, splay trees are easier to code.

15.3.2   The Splay Operation

In a splay tree the dictionary operations are performed exactly as they are by the methods of the class `binarySearchTree` (Section 14.3). However, the operations *get*, *put*, and *remove* are followed by a splay operation that starts at a splay node. At the end of the splay operation, the splay node is the root of the binary search tree. The **splay node** is selected to be the highest level (i.e, deepest) node, in the resulting tree, that was examined (i.e., a comparison was done with the key in this node, the node was newly created, the node was removed, or we moved to the left or right child of the node) during the dictionary operation.

Example 15.3 Consider the binary search tree of Figure 14.4(a). When performing the operation $find(80)$, the deepest node examined is the node with key 80; this node is the splay node. When the operation $find(31)$ is performed, the deepest node examined is the node with key 31; this node becomes the splay node. The operation $find(55)$ follows the path from 30 to 60; the deepest node examined is the one with key 60. So this node becomes the splay node.

An *insert* operation might create a new node or overwrite the element in an existing node. When a new node is created, this new node is the deepest node examined. Therefore, this new node becomes the splay node. When an existing element is overwritten, the node containing this overwritten element is the deepest node examined. Therefore, this node becomes the splay node. In the tree of Figure 14.4(a), the splay node for $insert(5, e)$ is the left child of the root. The splay node for $insert(65, e)$ is the newly created node, which becomes the right child of 60.

When the binary search tree has an element with key k, the deepest node examined by $delete(k)$ is the node that is removed from the tree. This node does not become the splay node because it is not a node in the resulting tree. The parent of the removed node becomes the splay node because it is the deepest of the examined nodes that remain. In the tree of Figure 14.4(a), the splay node for $delete(33)$ is the node with key 32, for $delete(35)$ the splay node is the node with key 40, for $delete(40)$ the splay node is the node with key 32, and for $delete(30)$ the splay node is the node with key 5. ∎

The **splay operation** comprises a sequence of **splay steps**. When the splay node is the root of the binary search tree, this sequence of steps is empty. When the splay node is not the root node, each splay step moves the splay node either one level or two levels up the tree. A one-level move is made only when the splay node is at level 2 of the binary search tree.

There are two types of one-level splay steps. One is done when the splay node q is the left child of its parent p; the other is done when the splay node q is the right child of its parent. The first type is called a type L splay step, and the second is a type R step. Figure 15.20 shows a type L splay step. Notice that following the splay step the splay node becomes the root of the binary search tree. A type R splay step is similar.

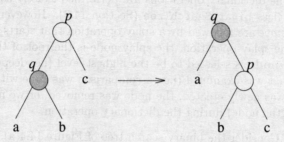

a, b, and c are subtrees
Shaded node is the splay node

Figure 15.20 Type L splay step

Two-level splay steps are done whenever the level of the splay node is > 2. Therefore, when a two-level splay step is done, the splay node q has a parent p and a grandparent gp. There are four types of two-level splay steps: LL, LR, RR, and RL. In an LR splay step, for example, p is the left child of gp, and q is the right child of p. Figure 15.21 shows a type LL and a type LR splay step. In each the splay node is moved two levels up the tree. Splay steps of type RR and LR are similar. Notice the similarity between splay steps and AVL tree rotations (Figures 15.4 and 15.5).

Example 15.4 Consider the binary search tree of Figure 15.22(a). Suppose that a $find(2)$ operation is performed. The shaded node becomes the splay node and a splay operation is initiated. This splay operation will first move the splay node from level 6 to level 4 by using an LL splay step (Figure 15.22(b)); next a type LR splay step moves the splay node to level 2 (Figure 15.22(c)); finally, a type L splay step moves the splay node to level 1.   ∎

Although we can move the splay node from any level of the binary search tree to level 1 by performing one-level splay steps alone (i.e., types L and R), limiting

(a) Type LL

(b) Type LR

a, b, c, and d are subtrees
Shaded node is the splay node

Figure 15.21 Types LL and LR splay steps

a splay operation to one-level splay steps does not ensure that every sequence of f *find*, i *insert*, and d *delete* operations is done in $O((f + i + d) \log i)$ time. To establish this time bound, it is necessary to use a sequence of two-level splay steps terminated by at most 1 one-level splay step.

15.3.3   Amortized Complexity

Unlike the actual and worst-case complexities of an operation, which are closely related to the step count for that operation, the **amortized complexity** of an operation is an accounting artifact that often bears no direct relationship to the actual complexity of that operation. The amortized complexity of an operation could be

(a) Initial search tree

(b) After type LL splay step

(c) After type LR splay step

(d) After type L splay step

a–g are subtrees
Shaded node is the splay node

Figure 15.22 Sample splay operation

anything. *The only requirement is that the sum of the amortized complexities of all operations in the sequence be greater than or equal to the sum of their actual complexities.* That is

$$\sum_{i=1}^{n} amortized(i) \geq \sum_{i=1}^{n} actual(i) \qquad (15.1)$$

where $amortized(i)$ and $actual(i)$, respectively, denote the amortized and actual complexities of the ith operation in a sequence of n operations. Because of this requirement on the sum of the amortized complexities of the operations in any sequence of operations, we may use the sum of the amortized complexities as an upper bound on the complexity of any sequence of operations.

You may view the amortized cost of an operation as being the amount you charge the operation rather than the amount the operation costs. You can charge an operation any amount you wish so long as the amount charged to all operations in the sequence is at least equal to the actual cost of the operation sequence.

Theorem 15.1 *The amortized complexity of a* find, insert, *or* delete *operation performed on a splay tree with n elements is $O(\log n)$.*

From Theorem 15.1 and Equation 15.1, it follows that the actual complexity of any sequence of f *find*, i *insert*, and d *delete* operations is $O((f + i + d) \log i)$ time.

EXERCISES

41. Start with a splay tree that is a 15-node full binary tree; the keys are 1–15. Search for the keys in the order 15, 14, 13, $\cdots$, 1. Draw your tree after each rotation that is performed and label the rotation type.

42. Do Exercise 41 but this time search for the keys in the order 1, 15, 8, 7, 12, 10, 6, 2, 14.

43. Start with an empty splay tree and insert the following keys in the given order: 20, 10, 5, 30, 40, 25, 8, 35, 7, 23. Draw figures similar to Figures 15.20 through 15.22, depicting your tree immediately after each insertion and following each rotation (if any). Label each rotation with the rotation type.

44. Do Exercise 43 using the insert key sequence: 40, 50, 70, 30, 35, 75, 25, 10, 15, 22, 16, 23.

45. Start with a splay tree that is a 15-node full binary tree; the keys are 1–15. Remove the keys in the order 15, 14, 13, $\cdots$, 1. Draw your tree immediately following each deletion and immediately after each rotation that is performed. Label each rotation with the rotation type.

46. Do Exercise 45 but this time remove the keys in the order 1, 2, 3, $\cdots$, 15.

47. Do Exercise 45 but this time remove keys in the order 6, 7, 5, 10, 9, 11, 15, 12, 13, and 14.

48. Do Exercise 45 but this time remove keys in the order 11, 14, 13, 15, 9, 12, 2, 3, and 1.

49. (a) Draw figures similar to Figures 15.20 and 15.21 for type R, RR, and RL splay steps.

    (b) Draw a figure similar to Figure 15.22 that begins with a binary search tree and performs type RR, RL, and R splay steps on the splay node while moving the splay node from its initial level to level 1.

50. Give an example of an n-node splay tree that has height n. From this conclude that the time of complexity of the *find*, *insert*, and *delete* operations for splay trees is $O(n)$.

51. Explain how a splay operation can be used to implement the `split` method of Exercise 12.

52. Develop the concrete class `splayTree` that uses a splay tree to implement all methods of the abstract class `bsTree`. Test the correctness of all methods.

53. Develop the class `dSplayTree` that uses a splay tree to implement all methods of the abstract class `dBSTree` (see Exercise 4). Test the correctness of all methods.

54. Develop the class `indexedSplayTree` that uses a splay tree to implement all methods of the abstract class `indexedBSTree`. Test the correctness of all methods.

55. Develop the class `dIndexedSplayTree` that uses a splay tree to implement all methods of the abstract class `dIndexedBSTree` (see Exercise 5). Test the correctness of all methods.

56. Develop the class `linearListAsSplayTree` that uses a splay tree to implement all methods of the abstract class `linearList`. Test the correctness of all methods.

15.4   B-TREES

15.4.1   Indexed Sequential Access Method (ISAM)

AVL and red-black trees guarantee good performance when the dictionary is small enough to reside in internal memory. For larger dictionaries (called **external dictionaries** or **files**) that must reside on a disk, we can get improved performance using search trees of higher degree. Before we jump into the study of these high-degree search trees, let us take a look at the popular **indexed sequential access method** (ISAM) for external dictionaries. This method provides good sequential and random access.

In the ISAM method the available disk space is divided into blocks, a block being the smallest unit of disk space that will be input or output. Typically, a block is one track long and can be input or output with a single seek and latency delay. The dictionary elements are packed into the blocks in ascending order, and the blocks are used in an order that minimizes the delay in going from one block to the next.

For sequential access the blocks are input in order, and the elements in each block are retrieved in ascending order. If each block contains m elements, the number of disk accesses per element retrieved is $1/m$.

To support random access, an index is maintained. This index contains the largest key in each block. Since the index contains only as many keys as there are blocks and since a block generally houses many elements (i.e., m is usually large), the index is generally small enough to reside in internal memory. To perform a random access of an element with key k, the index is searched for the single block that can contain the corresponding element; this block is retrieved from the disk and searched internally for the desired element. As a result, a single disk access is sufficient to perform a random access.

This technique may be extended to larger dictionaries that span several disks. Now the elements are assigned to disks in ascending order and then to blocks within a disk also in ascending order. Each disk maintains a block index that retains the largest key in each block. Additionally, an overall disk index maintains the largest key in each disk. This index generally resides in memory.

To perform a random access, the disk index is searched to determine the single disk that the desired record might reside on. Next the block index for this disk is retrieved from the appropriate disk and searched for the block that is to be fetched from the disk. The block is then fetched and searched internally. In the extended scheme a random access requires two disk accesses (one to fetch a block index and another to fetch a block).

Since the ISAM method is essentially an array representation scheme, it runs into difficulty when inserts and deletes are performed. We can partially alleviate this difficulty by leaving space in each block so that a few inserts can be performed without moving elements across block boundaries. Similarly, we can leave empty space in the block after deletes, rather than perform an expensive shift of the elements across block boundaries to use the new free space.

We can overcome these difficulties with the ISAM method at the expense of making sequential access more expensive. Elements are stored in any arbitrary order, and an index with an entry for each key is maintained. All elements are accessed via this index. The B-tree is a data structure that is suitable for indexes that reside on disk.

15.4.2 m-Way Search Trees

Definition 15.2 *An* **m-way search tree** *may be empty. If it is not empty, it is a tree that satisfies the following properties:*

1. *In the corresponding extended search tree (obtained by replacing null pointers*

with external nodes), each internal node has up to m children and between 1 and m − 1 elements. (External nodes contain no elements and have no children.)

2. *Every node with p elements has exactly p + 1 children.*

3. *Consider any node with p elements. Let k_1, ···, k_p be the keys of these elements. The elements are ordered so that $k_1 < k_2 < ··· < k_p$. Let c_0, c_1, ···, c_p be the p + 1 children of the node. The elements in the subtree with root c_0 have keys smaller than k_1, those in the subtree with root c_p have keys larger than k_p, and those in the subtree with root c_i have keys larger than k_i but smaller than k_{i+1}, $1 \le i < p$.*   ∎

Although it is useful to include external nodes when defining an m-way search tree, external nodes are not physically represented in actual implementations. Rather, a null pointer appears wherever there would otherwise be an external node.

Figure 15.23 shows a seven-way search tree. External nodes are shown as solid squares. All other nodes are internal nodes. The root has two elements (with keys 10 and 80) and three children. The middle child of the root has six elements and seven children; six of these children are external nodes.

Figure 15.23 A seven-way search tree

Searching an m-Way Search Tree

To search the seven-way search tree in Figure 15.23 for an element with key 31, we begin at the root. Since 31 lies between 10 and 80, we follow the middle pointer. (By definition, all elements in the first subtree have key < 10, and all in the third have key > 80.) The root of the middle subtree is searched. Since $k_2 < 31 < k_3$, we move to the third subtree of this node. Now we determine that $31 < k_1$ and move into the first subtree. This move causes us to fall off the tree; that is, we reach an external node. We conclude that the search tree contains no element with key 31.

Inserting into an m-Way Search Tree

If we wish to insert an element with key 31, we search for 31 as above and fall off the tree at the node [32,36]. Since this node can hold up to six elements (each node of a seven-way search tree can have up to six elements), the new element may be inserted as the first element in the node.

To insert an element with key 65, we search for 65 and fall off the tree by moving to the sixth subtree of the node [20,30,40,50,60,70]. This node cannot accommodate additional elements, and a new node is obtained. The new element is put into this node, and the new node becomes the sixth child of [20,30,40,50,60,70].

Deleting from an m-Way Search Tree

To delete the element with key 20 from the search tree of Figure 15.23, we first perform a search. The element is the first element in the middle child of the root. Since $k_1 = 20$ and $c_0 = c_1 = 0$, we may simply delete the element from the node. The new middle child of the root is [30,40,50,60,70]. Similarly, to delete the element with key 84, we first locate the element. It is the second element in the third child of the root. Since $c_1 = c_2 = 0$, the element may be deleted from this node and the new node configuration is [82,86,88].

When deleting the element with key 5, we have to do more work. Since the element to be deleted is the first one in its node and since at least one of its neighboring children (these children are c_0 and c_1) is nonnull, we need to replace the deleted element with an element from a nonempty neighboring subtree. From the left neighboring subtree (c_0), we may move up the element with largest key (i.e., the element with key 4).

To delete the element with key 10 from the root of Figure 15.23, we may replace this element with either the largest element in c_0 or the smallest element in c_1. If we opt to replace it with the largest in c_0, then the element with key 5 moves up and we need to find a replacement for this element in its original node. The element with key 4 is moved up.

Height of an m-Way Search Tree

An m-way search tree of height h (excluding external nodes) may have as few as h elements (one node per level and one element per node) and as many as $m^h - 1$. The upper bound is achieved by an m-way search tree of height h in which each node at levels 1 through $h - 1$ has exactly m children and nodes at level h have no children. Such a tree has $\sum_{i=0}^{h-1} m^i = (m^h - 1)/(m - 1)$ nodes. Since each of these nodes has $m - 1$ elements, the number of elements is $m^h - 1$.

As the number of elements in an m-way search tree of height h ranges from a low of h to a high of $m^h - 1$, the height of an m-way search tree with n elements ranges from a low of $\log_m(n + 1)$ to a high of n.

A 200-way search tree of height 5, for example, can hold $32 * 10^{10} - 1$ elements but might hold as few as 5. Equivalently, a 200-way search tree with $32 * 10^{10} - 1$

elements has a height between 5 and $32 * 10^{10} - 1$. When the search tree resides on a disk, the search, insert, and delete times are dominated by the number of disk accesses made (under the assumption that each node is no larger than a disk block). Since the number of disk accesses needed for the search, insert, and delete operations are $O(h)$ where h is the tree height, we need to ensure that the height is close to $\log_m(n+1)$. This assurance is provided by balanced m-way search trees.

15.4.3   B-Trees of Order m

Definition 15.3 *A* **B-tree of order** m *is an m-way search tree. If the B-tree is not empty, the corresponding extended tree satisfies the following properties:*

1. *The root has at least two children.*

2. *All internal nodes other than the root have at least $\lceil m/2 \rceil$ children.*

3. *All external nodes are at the same level.*   ∎

The seven-way search tree of Figure 15.23 is not a B-tree of order 7, as it contains external nodes at more than one level (levels 3 and 4). Even if all its external nodes were at the same level, it would fail to be a B-tree of order 7 because it contains nonroot internal nodes with two (node [5]) and three (node [32,36]) children. Nonroot internal nodes in a B-tree of order 7 must have at least $\lceil 7/2 \rceil = 4$ children. A B-tree of order 7 appears in Figure 15.24. All external nodes are at level 3, the root has three children, and all remaining internal nodes have at least four children. Additionally, it is a seven-way search tree.

Figure 15.24 A B-tree of order 7

In a B-tree of order 2, no internal node has more than two children. Since an internal node must have at least two children, all internal nodes of a B-tree of order 2 have exactly two children. This observation, coupled with the requirement that all external nodes be on the same level, implies that B-trees of order 2 are full binary trees. As such, these trees exist only when the number of elements is $2^h - 1$ for some integer h.

In a B-tree of order 3, internal nodes have either two or three children. So a B-tree of order 3 is also known as a 2-3 tree. Since internal nodes in B-trees of order 4 must have two, three, or four children, these B-trees are also referred to as 2-3-4 (or simply 2,4) trees. A 2-3 tree appears in Figure 15.25. Even though this tree has no internal node with four children, it is also an example of a 2-3-4 tree. To build a 2-3-4 tree in which at least one internal node has four children, simply add elements with keys 14 and 16 into the left child of 20.

Figure 15.25 A 2-3 tree or B-tree of order 3

15.4.4   Height of a B-Tree

Lemma 15.3 *Let T be a B-tree of order m and height h. Let $d = \lceil m/2 \rceil$ and let n be the number of elements in T.*

(a) $2d^{h-1} - 1 \leq n \leq m^h - 1$

(b) $\log_m(n+1) \leq h \leq \log_d(\frac{n+1}{2}) + 1$

Proof The upper bound on n follows from the fact that T is an m-way search tree. For the lower bound, note that the external nodes of the corresponding extended B-tree are at level $h + 1$. The minimum number of nodes on levels 1, 2, 3, 4, $\cdots$, $h + 1$ is 1, 2, 2d, $2d^2$, $\cdots$, $2d^{h-1}$, so the minimum number of external nodes in the B-tree is $2d^{h-1}$. Since the number of external nodes is 1 more than the number of elements

$$n \geq 2d^{h-1} - 1$$

Part (b) follows directly from (a).   ∎

From Lemma 15.3 it follows that a B-tree of order 200 and height 3 has at least 19,999 elements, and one of the same order and height 5 has at least $2 * 10^8 - 1$ elements. Consequently, if a B-tree of order 200 or more is used, the tree height is quite small even when the number of elements is rather large. In practice, the

B-tree order is determined by the disk block size and the size of individual elements. There is no advantage to using a node size smaller than the disk block size, as each disk access reads or writes one block. Using a larger node size involves multiple disk accesses, each accompanied by a seek and latency delay, so there is no advantage to making the node size larger than one block.

Although in actual applications the B-tree order is large, our examples use a small m because a two-level B-tree of order m has at least $2d - 1$ elements. When m is 200, d is 100 and a two-level B-tree of order 200 has at least 199 elements. Manipulating trees with this many elements is quite cumbersome. Our examples involve 2-3 trees and B-trees of order 7.

15.4.5   Searching a B-Tree

A B-tree is searched using the same algorithm as is used for an m-way search tree. Since all internal nodes on some root-to-external-node path may be retrieved during the search, the number of disk accesses is at most h (h is the height of the B-tree).

15.4.6   Inserting into a B-Tree

To insert an element into a B-tree, we first search for the presence of an element with the same key. If such an element is found, the insert fails because duplicates are not permitted. When the search is unsuccessful, we attempt to insert the new element into the last internal node encountered on the search path. For example, when inserting an element with key 3 into the B-tree of Figure 15.24, we examine the root and its left child. We fall off the tree at the second external node of the left child. Since the left child currently has three elements and can hold up to six, the new element may be inserted into this node. The result is the B-tree of Figure 15.26(a). Two disk accesses are made to read in the root and its left child. An additional access is necessary to write out the modified left child.

Next let us try to insert an element with key 25 into the B-tree of Figure 15.26(a). This element is to go into the node [20,30,40,50,60,70]. However, this node is full. *When the new element needs to go into a full node, the full node is split.* Let P be the full node. Insert the new element e together with a null pointer into P to get an overfull node with m elements and $m + 1$ children. Denote this overfull node as

$$m, \ c_0, \ (e_1, c_1), \ \cdots, \ (e_m, c_m)$$

where the e_is are the elements and the c_is are the children pointers. The node is split around element e_d where $d = \lceil m/2 \rceil$. Elements to the left remain in P, and those to the right move into a new node Q. The pair (e_d, Q) is inserted into the parent of P. The format of the new P and Q is

$$P: \ d - 1, \ c_0, \ (e_1, c_1), \ \cdots, \ (e_{d-1}, c_{d-1})$$

$$Q: \ m - d, \ c_d, \ (e_{d+1}, c_{d+1}), \ \cdots (e_m, c_m)$$

(a) Insert 3 into Figure 15.24

(b) Insert 25 into (a)

(c) Insert 44 into Figure 15.25

Figure 15.26 Inserting into a B-tree

Notice that the number of children of both P and Q is at least d.

In our example, the overfull node is

$$7, 0\ (20,0), (25,0), (30,0), (40,0), (50,0), (60,0), (70,0)$$

and $d = 4$. Splitting around e_4 yields the two nodes

$$P : 3, 0, (20,0), (25,0), (30,0)$$
$$Q : 3, 0, (50,0), (60,0), (70,0)$$

When the pair $(40, Q)$ is inserted into the parent of P, we get the B-tree of Figure 15.26(b).

To insert 25 into Figure 15.26(a), we need to get the root and its middle child from the disk. Then we write to disk the two split nodes and the modified root. The total number of disk accesses is 5.

As a final example, consider inserting an element with key 44 into the 2-3 tree of Figure 15.25. This element goes into the node [35,40]. Since the node is full, we get the overfull node

$$3, 0, (35,0), (40,0), (44,0)$$

Splitting around $e_d = e_2$ yields the two nodes

$$P : 1, 0, (35,0)$$
$$Q : 1, 0, (44,0)$$

When we attempt to insert the pair $(40,Q)$ into the parent A of P, we see that this node is full. Following the insertion, we get the overfull node

$$A : 3, P, (40,Q), (50,C), (60,D)$$

where C and D are pointers to the nodes [55] and [70]. The overfull node A is split to create a new node B. The new A and B are

$$A : 1, P, (40,Q)\ B : 1, C, (60,D)$$

Now we need to insert the pair $(50,B)$ into the root. Prior to this insertion, the root has the format

$$R: 2, S, (30,A), (80,T)$$

where S and T are, respectively, pointers to the first and third subtrees of the root. Following the insertion of the pair $(50,B)$, we get the overfull node

$$R: 3, \; S, \; (30,A), \; (50,B), \; (80,T)$$

This node is split around the element with key 50 to create a new R and a new node U as below:

$$R: 1, \; S, \; (30,A)$$
$$U: 1, \; B, \; (80,T)$$

The pair $(50,U)$ would normally be inserted into the parent of R. However, since R has no parent, we create a new root with the format

$$1, \; R, \; (50,U)$$

The resulting 2-3 tree appears in Figure 15.26(c).

Three disk accesses are made to read in nodes [30,80], [50,60], and [35,40]. For each node that splits, two accesses are made to write the modified node and the newly created node. In our case three nodes are split, so six write accesses are made. Finally, a new root is created and written out. This write takes an additional disk access. The total number of disk accesses is 10.

When an insertion causes s nodes to split, the number of disk accesses is h (to read in the nodes on the search path) $+ \; 2s$ (to write out the two split parts of each node that is split) $+ \; 1$ (to write the new root or the node into which an insertion that does not result in a split is made). Therefore, the number of disk accesses needed for an insertion is $h + 2s + 1$, which is at most $3h + 1$.

15.4.7   Deletion from a B-Tree

Deletion is first divided into two cases: (1) the element to be deleted is in a node whose children are external nodes (i.e., the element is in a leaf), and (2) the element is to be deleted from a nonleaf. Case (2) is transformed into case (1) by replacing the deleted element with either the largest element in its left-neighboring subtree or the smallest element in its right-neighboring subtree. The replacing element is guaranteed to be in a leaf.

Consider deleting the element with key 80 from the B-tree of Figure 15.26(a). Since the element is not in a leaf, we find a suitable replacement. The possibilities are the element with key 70 (i.e., the largest element in the left-neighboring subtree) and 82 (i.e., the smallest element in the right-neighboring subtree). When we use the 70, the problem of deleting this element from the leaf [20,30,40,50,60,70] remains.

If we are to delete the element with key 80 from the 2-3 tree of Figure 15.26(c), we replace it with either the element with key 70 or that with key 82. If we select the 82, the problem of deleting 82 from the leaf [82,85] remains.

Since case (2) may be transformed into case (1) quite easily, we concern ourselves with case (1) only. To delete an element from a leaf that contains more than the minimum number of elements (1 if the leaf is also the root and $\lceil m/2 \rceil - 1$ if it is not) requires us to simply write out the modified node. (In case this node is the root, the B-tree becomes empty.) To delete 50 from the B-tree of Figure 15.26(a), we write out the modified node [20,30,40,60,70], and to delete 85 from the 2-3 tree of Figure 15.26(c), we write out the node [82]. Both cases require h disk accesses to follow the search path down to the leaf and an additional access to write out the modified version of the leaf that contained the deleted element.

When the element is being deleted from a nonroot node that has exactly the minimum number of elements, we try to replace the deleted element with an element from its nearest-left or -right sibling. Notice that every node other than the root has either a nearest-left sibling or a nearest-right sibling or both. For example, suppose we wish to delete 25 from the B-tree of Figure 15.26(b). This deletion leaves behind the node [20,30], which has just two elements. However, since this node is a nonroot node of a B-tree of order 7, it must contain at least three elements. Its nearest-left sibling, [2,3,4,6], has an extra element. The largest element from here is moved to the parent node, and the intervening element (i.e., with key 10) is moved down to create the B-tree of Figure 15.27(a). The number of disk accesses is 2 (to go from the root to the leaf that contains 25) + 1 (to read in the nearest-left sibling of this leaf) + 3 (to write out the changed leaf, its sibling, and its parent) = 6.

Suppose that instead of checking the nearest-left sibling of [20,30], we had checked its nearest-right sibling, [50,60,70]. Since this node has only three elements, we cannot delete an element. (If the node had four elements or more, we would have moved its smallest element to the parent and moved the element in the parent that lies between these two siblings into the leaf that is one element short.) Now we can check the nearest-left sibling of [20,30]. Performing this check requires an additional disk access, and we are not certain that this nearest sibling will have an extra element. *In the interest of keeping the worst-case disk-access count low, we will check only one of the nearest siblings of a node that is one element short.*

When the nearest sibling that is checked has no extra elements, we merge the two siblings with the element between them in the parent into a single node. Since the siblings have $d - 2$ and $d - 1$ elements, respectively, the merged node has $2d - 2$ elements. As $2d - 2$ equals $m - 1$ when m is odd and $m - 2$ when m is even, there is enough space in a node to hold this many elements.

In our example the siblings [20,30] and [50,60,70] and the element with key 40 are merged into the single node [20,30,40,50,60,70]. The resulting B-tree is that of Figure 15.26(a). This deletion requires two disk accesses to get to the node [20,25,30], another access to read in its nearest-right sibling, and then two more accesses to write out the two nodes that are modified. The total number of disk accesses is 5.

Notice that since merging reduces the number of elements in the parent node, the parent may end up being one element short. If the parent becomes one element short, we will need to check the parent's nearest sibling and either get an element from there or merge with it. If we get an element from the nearest-right (-left) sibling, then the left-most (right-most) subtree of this sibling is also taken. If we

(a) Delete 25 from Figure 15.26(b)

(b) After merging at leaf node

(c) Delete 10 from Figure 15.25

Figure 15.27 Deleting from a B-tree

merge, the grandparent may become one element short and the process will need to be applied at the grandparent. At worst the shortage will propagate back to the root. When the root is one element short, it is empty. The empty root is discarded, and the tree height decreases by 1.

Suppose we wish to delete 10 from the 2-3 tree of Figure 15.25. This deletion leaves behind a leaf with zero elements. Its nearest-right sibling [25] does not have an extra element. Therefore, the two sibling leaves and the in-between element in the parent (10) are merged into a single node. The new tree structure appears in Figure 15.27(b). We now have a node at level 2 that is an element short. Its nearest-right sibling has an extra element. The left-most element (i.e., the one with key 50) moves to the parent, and the element with key 30 moves down. The resulting 2-3 tree appears in Figure 15.27(c). Notice that the left subtree of the former [50,60] has moved also. This deletion took three read accesses to get to the leaf that contained the element that was to be deleted; two read accesses to get the nearest-right siblings of the level 3 and 2 nodes; and four write accesses to write out the four nodes at levels 1, 2, and 3 that were modified. The total number of disk accesses is 9.

As a final example, consider the deletion of 44 from the 2-3 tree of Figure 15.26(c). When the 44 is removed from the leaf it is in, this leaf becomes short one element. Its nearest-left sibling does not have an extra element, and so the two siblings to-

(a) After merging at leaf level

(b) After merging at level 3

Figure 15.28 Deleting 44 from the 2-3 tree of Figure 15.26(c) (continues)

(c) After merging at level 2

(d) After deletion of root

Figure 15.28 Deleting 44 from the 2-3 tree of Figure 15.26(c) (concluded)

gether with the in-between element in the parent are merged to get the tree of Figure 15.28(a). We now have a node at level 3 that is one element short. Its nearest-left sibling is examined and found to have no extra elements, so the two siblings and the in-between element in their parent are merged. The tree of Figure 15.28(b) is obtained. Now we have a level 2 node that is one element short. Its nearest-right sibling has no extra elements, and we perform another merge to get the tree of Figure 15.28(c). Now the root is an element short. Since the root becomes an element short only when it is empty, the root is discarded. The final 2-3 tree is shown in Figure 15.28(d). Notice that when the root is discarded, the tree height reduces by 1.

We need four disk accesses to find the leaf that contains the element to be deleted, three nearest-sibling accesses, and three write accesses. The total number is 10.

The worst case for a deletion from a B-tree of height h is when merges take place at levels h, $h-1$, $\cdots$, and 3 and we get an element from a nearest sibling at level 2. The worst-case disk access count is $3h$; (h reads to find the leaf with the element to be deleted) + ($h-1$ reads to get nearest siblings at levels 2 through h) + ($h-2$ writes of merged nodes at levels 3 through h) + (3 writes for the modified root and 2 level 2 nodes).

15.4.8   Node Structure

Our discussion has assumed a node structure of the form

$$s, c_0, (e_1, c_1), (e_2, c_2), \cdots, (e_s, c_s)$$

where s is the number of elements in the node, the e_is are the elements in ascending order of key, and the c_is are children pointers. When the element size is large relative to the size of a key, we may use the node structure

$$s, c_0, (k_1, c_1, p_1), (k_2, c_2, p_2), \cdots, (k_s, c_s, p_s)$$

where the k_is are the element keys and the p_is are the disk locations of the corresponding elements. By using this structure, we can use a B-tree of a higher order. An even higher-order B-tree, called a B'-tree, becomes possible if nonleaf nodes contain no p_i pointers and if, in the leaves, we replace the null children pointers with p_i pointers.

Another possibility is to use a balanced binary search tree to represent the contents of each node. Using a balanced binary search tree in this way reduces the permissible order of the B-tree, as with each element we need a left- and right-child pointer as well as a balance factor or color field. However, the CPU time spent inserting/deleting an element into/from a node decreases. Whether this approach results in improved overall performance depends on the application. In some cases a smaller m might increase the B-tree height, resulting in more disk accesses for each search/insert/delete operation.

EXERCISES

57. Start with an empty 2-3 tree and insert the keys 20, 40, 30, 10, 25, 28, 27, 32, 36, 34, 35, 8, 6, 2, and 3 in this order. Draw the 2-3 tree following each insert.

58. Start with an empty 2-3 tree and insert the keys 2, 1, 5, 6, 7, 4, 3, 8, 9, 10, and 11 in this order. Draw the 2-3 tree following each insert.

59. From the 2-3 tree of Figure 15.25, remove the keys 55, 40, 70, 35, 60, 95, 90, 82, 80 in this order. Draw a figure similar to Figure 15.28 showing the different steps in each remove.

60. (a) Remove 10 from the 2-3 tree of Figure 15.26(c). Draw a figure similar to Figure 15.28 showing the different steps in the delete.

    (b) Do part (a) but this time remove 70 from Figure 15.26(c).

    (c) Do part (a) but this time remove 95 and 85 (in this order) from Figure 15.26(c).

61. What is the maximum number of disk accesses made during a search of a B-tree of order $2m$ if each node is two disk blocks and requires two disk accesses to retrieve? Compare this number with the corresponding number for a B-tree of order m that uses nodes that are one disk block in size. Based on this analysis, what can you say about the merits of using a node size larger than one block?

62. What is the maximum number of disk accesses needed to delete an element that is in a nonleaf node of a B-tree of order m?

63. Suppose we modify the way an element is deleted from a B-tree as follows: If a node has both a nearest-left and nearest-right sibling, then both are checked before a merge is done. What is the maximum number of disk accesses that can be made when deleting from a B-tree of height h?

64. A 2-3-4 tree may be represented as a binary tree in which each node is colored black or red. A 2-3-4 tree node that has just one element is represented as a black node; a node with two elements is represented as a black node with a red child (the red child may be either the left or right child of the black node); a node with three elements is represented as a black node with two red children.

    (a) Draw a 2-3-4 tree that contains at least one node with two elements and one with three. Now draw it as a binary tree with colored nodes using the method just described.

    (b) Verify that the binary tree is a red-black tree.

    (c) Prove that when any 2-3-4 tree is represented as a colored binary tree as described here, the result is a red-black tree.

    (d) Prove that every red-black tree can be represented as a 2-3-4 tree using the inverse mapping.

    (e) Verify that the color changes and rotations given in Section 15.2.4 for an insertion into a red-black tree are obtainable from the B-tree insertion method using the mapping in (d).

    (f) Do part (e) for the case of deletion from a red-black tree.

65. Develop the concrete class `twoThree` that derives from the abstract class `dictionary` (Program 10.1) using a 2-3 tree. Test the correctness of your code.

66. Develop the concrete class `twoThreeFour` that derives from the abstract class `dictionary` (Program 10.1) using a 2-3-4 tree. Test the correctness of your code.

15.5 REFERENCES AND SELECTED READINGS

AVL trees were invented by G. Adelson-Velskii and E. Landis in 1962. More material on these and other search trees developed in this chapter can be found in the book *The Art of Computer Programming: Sorting and Searching*, Volume 3, Second Edition, by D. Knuth, Addison-Wesley, Reading, MA, 1998.

Red-black trees were invented by R. Bayer in 1972. However, Bayer called these trees "symmetric balanced B-trees." The red-black terminology is from Guibas and Sedgewick who studied these trees in greater detail in 1978. The pioneering papers are "Symmetric Binary B-Trees: Data Structures and Maintenance Algorithms" by R. Bayer, *Acta Informatica*, 1, 1972, 290–306, and "A Dichromatic Framework for Balanced Trees" by L. Guibas and R. Sedgewick, *Proceedings of the 10th IEEE Symposium on Foundations of Computer Science*, 1978, 8–21.

The application of red-black trees to the implementation of priority search trees is described in the paper "Priority Search Trees" by E. McCreight, *SIAM Journal on Computing*, 14, 2, 1985, 257–276.

Various balanced search-tree structures that have the same asymptotic complexity as do AVL and red-black trees are described in the text *Fundamentals of Data Structures in C++* by E. Horowitz, S. Sahni, and D. Mehta, W. H. Freeman, New York, NY, 1994. This text also has the complexity analysis for splay trees and describes B'-trees and B*-trees, which are variants of B-trees.

You can find a detailed development of amortized complexity in the Web site for this book. And don't forget, you can learn about other search structures, such as tries and suffix trees, by visiting the Web site.

CHAPTER 16

GRAPHS

BIRD'S-EYE VIEW

Congratulations! You have successfully journeyed through the forest of trees. Awaiting you now is the study of the graph data structure. Surprisingly, graphs are used to model literally thousands of real-world problems. Not so surprisingly, we will see only a very small fraction of these problems in the remainder of this book. This chapter covers the following topics:

- Graph terminology including these terms: *vertex, edge, adjacent, incident, degree, cycle, path, connected component,* and *spanning tree.*

- Different types of graphs: undirected, directed, and weighted.

- Common graph representations: adjacency matrix, array adjacency lists, and linked adjacency lists.

- Standard graph search methods: breadth-first and depth-first search.

- Algorithms to find a path in a graph, to find the connected components of an undirected graph, and to find a spanning tree of a connected undirected graph.

Additional graph algorithms—topological sorting, bipartite covers, shortest paths. minimum-cost spanning trees, max clique, and traveling salesperson—are developed in the remaining chapters of this book.

615

16.1   DEFINITIONS

Informally, a graph is a collection of vertices or nodes, pairs of which are joined by lines or edges. More formally, a **graph** $G = (V,E)$ is an ordered pair of finite sets V and E. The elements of V are called **vertices** (vertices are also called **nodes** and **points**). The elements of E are called **edges** (edges are also called **arcs** and **lines**). Each edge in E joins two different vertices of V and is denoted by the tuple (i,j), where i and j are the two vertices joined by E.

A graph is generally displayed as a figure in which the vertices are represented by circles and the edges by lines. Examples of graphs appear in Figure 16.1. Some of the edges in this figure are oriented (i.e., they have arrow heads), while others are not. An edge with an orientation is a **directed** edge, while an edge with no orientation is an **undirected** edge. The undirected edges (i,j) and (j,i) are the same; the directed edge (i,j) is different from the directed edge (j,i), the former being oriented from i to j and the latter from j to i.[1]

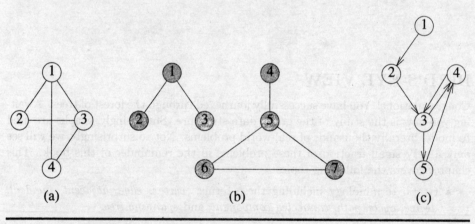

(a)   (b)   (c)

Figure 16.1 Graphs

Vertices i and j are **adjacent** vertices iff (i,j) is an edge in the graph. The edge (i,j) is **incident** on the vertices i and j. Vertices 1 and 2 of Figure 16.1(a) are adjacent, as are vertices 1 and 3; 1 and 4; 2 and 3; and 3 and 4. This graph has no other pairs of adjacent vertices. The edge (1,2) is incident on the vertices 1 and 2 and the edge (2,3) is incident on the vertices 2 and 3.

It is sometimes useful to have a slightly refined notion of adjacency and incidence for directed graphs. The directed edge (i,j) is **incident to** vertex j and **incident from** vertex i. Vertex i is **adjacent to** vertex j, and vertex j is **adjacent from**

---

[1]Some books use the notation i,j for an undirected edge and (i,j) for a directed one. Others use (i,j) for an undirected edge and $< i,j >$ for a directed one. This book uses the same notation, (i,j), for both kinds of edges. Whether an edge is directed or not will be clear from the context.

vertex i. In the graph of Figure 16.1(c), vertex 2 is adjacent from 1, while 1 is adjacent to 2. Edge (1,2) is incident from 1 and incident to 2. Vertex 4 is both incident to and from 3. Edge (3,4) is incident from 3 and incident to 4. For an undirected edge, the refinements "to" and "from" are synonymous.

Using set notation, the graphs of Figure 16.1 may be specified as $G_1 = (V_1, E_1)$; $G_2 = (V_2, E_2)$; and $G_3 = (V_3, E_3)$ where

$$
\begin{aligned}
V_1 &= \{1,2,3,4\}; & E_1 &= \{(1,2),\ (1,3),\ (2,3),\ (1,4),\ (3,4)\} \\
V_2 &= \{1,2,3,4,5,6,7\}; & E_2 &= \{(1,2),\ (1,3),\ (4,5),\ (5,6),\ (5,7),\ (6,7)\} \\
V_3 &= \{1,2,3,4,5\}; & E_3 &= \{(1,2),\ (2,3),\ (3,4),\ (4,3),\ (3,5),\ (5,4)\}
\end{aligned}
$$

If all the edges in a graph are undirected, then the graph is an **undirected** graph. The graphs of Figures 16.1(a) and (b) are undirected graphs. If all the edges are directed, then the graph is a **directed** graph. The graph of Figure 16.1(c) is a directed graph.

By definition, a graph does not contain multiple copies of the same edge. Therefore, an undirected graph can have at most one edge between any pair of vertices, and a directed graph can have at most one edge from vertex i to vertex j and one from j to i. Also, a graph cannot contain any **self-edges**; that is, edges of the form (i, i) are not permitted. A self-edge is also called a **loop**.

A directed graph is also called a **digraph**. In some applications of graphs, we will assign a weight or cost to each edge. When weights have been assigned to edges, we use the terms **weighted undirected graph** and **weighted digraph** to refer to the resulting data object. The term **network** is often used to refer to a weighted undirected graph or digraph. Actually, all the graph variants defined here may be regarded as special cases of networks—an undirected (directed) graph may be viewed as an undirected (directed) network in which all edges have the same weight.

16.2   APPLICATIONS AND MORE DEFINITIONS

Graphs are used in the analysis of electrical networks; the study of the molecular structure of chemical compounds (particularly hydrocarbons); the representation of airline routes and communication networks; in planning projects, genetic studies, statistical mechanics, and social sciences; and in many other situations. In this section we formulate some real-world problems as problems on graphs.

Example 16.1 [Path Problems] In a city with many streets, we can say that each intersection is a vertex in a digraph. Each segment of a street that is between two adjacent intersections is represented by either one or two directed edges. Two directed edges, one in either direction, are used if the street segment is two way, and a single directed edge is used if it is a one-way segment. Figure 16.2 shows a hypothetical street map and the corresponding digraph. In this figure there are three streets—1St, 2St, and 3St—and two avenues—1Ave and 2Ave The intersections are labeled 1 through 6. The vertices of the corresponding digraph (Figure 16.2(b)) have the same labels as given to the intersection in Figure 16.2(a).

(a) Street map

(b) Digraph

Figure 16.2 Street map and corresponding digraph

A sequence of vertices $P = i_1, i_2, \cdots, i_k$ is an i_1 to i_k **path** in the graph $G = (V, E)$ iff the edge (i_j, i_{j+1}) is in E for every j, $1 \leq j < k$. There is a path from intersection i to intersection j iff there is a path from vertex i to vertex j in the corresponding digraph. In the digraph of Figure 16.2(b), 5, 2, 1 is a path from 5 to 1. There is no path from 5 to 4 in this digraph.

A **simple path** is a path in which all vertices, except possibly the first and last, are different. The path 5, 2, 1 is a simple path, whereas the path 2, 5, 2, 1 is not.

Each edge in a graph may have an associated **length**. The length of a path is the sum of the lengths of the edges on the path. The shortest way to get from intersection i to intersection j is obtained by finding a shortest path from vertex i to vertex j in the corresponding network (i.e., weighted digraph). ∎

Example 16.2 [Spanning Trees] Let $G = (V, E)$ be an undirected graph. G is **connected** iff there is a path between every pair of vertices in G. The undirected graph of Figure 16.1(a) is connected, while that of Figure 16.1(b) is not. Suppose that G represents a possible communication network with V being the set of cities and E the set of communication links. It is possible to communicate between every pair of cities in V iff G is connected. In the communication network of Figure 16.1(a), cities 2 and 4 can communicate by using the communication path 2,3,4, while in the network of Figure 16.1(b), cities 2 and 4 cannot communicate.

Suppose that G is connected. Some of the edges of G may be unnecessary in that G remains connected even if these edges are removed. In the graph of Figure 16.1(a), for example, the graph remains connected even if we remove the edges (2,3) and (1,4).

A graph H is a **subgraph** of another graph G iff its vertex and edge sets are subsets of those of G. A **cycle** is a simple path with the same start and end vertex. For example, 1, 2, 3, 1 is a cycle in the graph of Figure 16.1(a). A connected undirected graph that contains no cycles is a **tree**. A subgraph of G that contains all the vertices of G and is a tree is a **spanning tree** of G. Figure 16.3 gives some of the spanning trees of Figure 16.1(a).

(a)   (b)   (c)

(d)   (e)   (f)

Figure 16.3 Some spanning trees of Figure 16.1(a)

A connected undirected graph with n vertices must have at least $n-1$ edges. Hence when each link of a communication network has the same construction cost, the construction of all links on any one spanning tree minimizes network construction cost and ensures that a communication path exists between every pair of cities. Further, if the links have different (but nonnegative) costs, then the links on a minimum-cost spanning tree (the cost of a spanning tree is the sum of the costs of the edges on it) are to be constructed. Figure 16.4 shows a graph and two of its spanning trees. ∎

(a) Graph

(b) Spanning tree
Cost = 110

(c) Spanning tree
Cost = 129

Figure 16.4 Connected graph and two of its spanning trees

Example 16.3 [Interpreters] Suppose that you are planning an international convention. All the speakers at this convention know English only. The remaining participants know one of the languages L1, L2, L3, $\cdots$, Ln. You have available a set of interpreters who can translate between English and some of the other languages. Your task is to select the fewest number of interpreters to do the job.

We can formulate the problem as a graph problem in which the graph has two sets of vertices. One set corresponds to interpreters and the other to languages (Figure 16.5). An edge exists between interpreter i and language Lj iff interpreter i can translate between English and this language. Interpreter i **covers** language Li iff an edge connects the interpreter and the language. We want to find the smallest subset of the interpreter vertices that cover the language vertices.

The graph of Figure 16.5 has an interesting property: We can partition the vertex set into two subsets, A (the interpreter vertices) and B (the language vertices), so that every edge has one endpoint in A and the other in B. Graphs with this property are **bipartite graphs**.　■

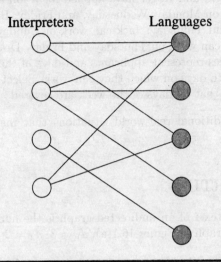

Figure 16.5 Interpreters and languages

EXERCISES

1. Consider the graph of Figure 16.4(b). Which of the following are simple paths? Why?

    (a) 6, 1, 2, 7, 4

    (b) 1, 2, 3, 4

    (c) 7, 2, 3, 2, 1, 6

    (d) 4, 5, 7, 2

2. (a) List all simple paths between vertices 1 and 4 in Figure 16.1(a).

    (b) List all simple paths between vertices 1 and 7 in Figure 16.4(a).

    (c) List all simple paths between vertices 3 and 6 in Figure 16.4(a).

    (d) List all simple paths from vertex 4 to vertex 1 in Figure 16.1(c).

    (e) List all simple paths from vertex 4 to vertex 1 in Figure 16.2(b).

3. Draw all subgraphs of Figure 16.1(a).

4. List all cycles of the graph of Figure 16.4(a).

5. List all cycles of the graph of Figure 16.2(b).

6. Draw two more spanning trees of the graph of Figure 16.4(a). Give the cost of each spanning tree.

7. Anita, Beth, Jack, and Roger have applied for a job at the local bookstore. Anita can work on Monday, Wednesday, and Friday; Beth can work on Monday, Tuesday, and Thursday; Jack can work on Sunday, Monday, and Saturday; and Roger can work on Thursday and Friday. Draw a bipartite graph in which the vertices represent applicants and days of the week, and edges connect applicants to days on which they can work. Select the minimum number of applicants so that all days of the week are covered.

8. Identify two additional real-world situations that may be modeled with a bipartite graph.

16.3   PROPERTIES

The **degree** d_i of vertex i of an undirected graph is the number of edges incident on vertex i. For the graph of Figure 16.1(a), $d_1 = 3$; $d_2 = 2$; $d_3 = 3$; and $d_4 = 2$.

Property 16.1 *Let $G = (V, E)$ be an undirected graph. Let $n = |V|$ and $e = |E|$.*

(a) $\sum_{i=1}^{n} d_i = 2e$

(b) $0 \le e \le n(n-1)/2$

Proof To prove (a), note that each edge in an undirected graph is incident on exactly two vertices. Hence the sum of the degrees of the vertices equals two times the number of edges. For (b), observe that the degree of a vertex lies between 0 .and $n - 1$, so the sum of the degrees lies between 0 and $n(n-1)$. From (a), it now follows that e lies between 0 and $n(n-1)/2$.   ∎

An n-vertex undirected graph with $n(n-1)/2$ edges is a **complete** graph. Figure 16.6 gives the complete undirected graphs for $n = 1, 2, 3,$ and 4. The complete undirected graph on n vertices is denoted K_n.

(a) K_1 (b) K_2 (c) K_3 (d) K_4

Figure 16.6 Complete undirected graphs

Let G be a digraph. The **in-degree** d_i^{in} of vertex i is the number of edges incident to i (i.e., the number of edges coming into this vertex). The **out-degree** d_i^{out} of vertex i is the number of edges incident from this vertex (i.e., the number of edges leaving vertex i). For the digraph of Figure 16.1(c), $d_1^{in} = 0$; $d_1^{out} = 1$; $d_2^{in} = 1$; $d_2^{out} = 1$; $d_3^{in} = 2$; and $d_3^{out} = 2$.

Property 16.2 *Let $G = (V, E)$ be a directed graph. Let $n = |V|$ and $e = |E|$.*

(a) $0 \le e \le n(n-1)$

(b) $\sum_{i=1}^{n} d_i^{in} = \sum_{i=1}^{n} d_i^{out} = e$

Proof Exercise 10 asks you to prove this property.   ∎

A **complete** digraph (also denoted K_n) on n vertices contains exactly $n(n-1)$ directed edges. Figure 16.7 gives the complete digraphs for $n = 1, 2, 3,$ and 4.

(a) K_1 (b) K_2 (c) K_3 (d) K_4

Figure 16.7 Complete digraphs

In the context of undirected graphs, the terms *in-degree* and *out-degree* may be used as synonyms for the term *degree*. The definitions provided in this section extend to networks in a rather straightforward way.

EXERCISES

9. For each graph in Figure 16.8, determine the following:

  (a) The in-degree of each vertex.
  (b) The out-degree of each vertex.
  (c) The set of vertices adjacent from vertex 2.
  (d) The set of vertices adjacent to vertex 1.
  (e) The set of edges incident from vertex 3.
  (f) The set of edges incident to vertex 4.
  (g) All directed cycles and their lengths.

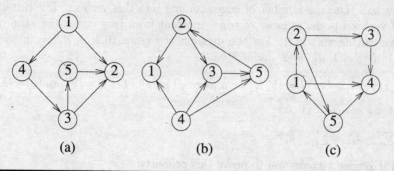

Figure 16.8 Digraphs

10. Prove Property 16.2.

11. Let G be any undirected graph. Show that the number of vertices with odd degrees is even.

12. Let $G = (V, E)$ be a connected graph with $|V| > 1$. Show that G contains either a vertex of degree 1 or a cycle (or both).

13. Let $G = (V, E)$ be a connected undirected graph that contains at least one cycle. Let $(i, j) \in E$ be an edge that is on at least one cycle of G. Show that the graph $H = (V, E - \{(i, j)\})$ is also connected.

14. Prove the following:

    (a) For every n there exists a connected undirected graph containing exactly $n - 1$ edges, $n \geq 1$.

    (b) Every n-vertex connected undirected graph contains at least $n - 1$ edges. You may use the results of the previous two exercises.

15. A digraph is **strongly connected** iff it contains a directed path from i to j and from j to i for every pair of distinct vertices i and j.

    (a) Show that for every n, $n \geq 2$, there exists a strongly connected digraph that contains exactly n edges.

    (b) Show that every n vertex strongly connected digraph contains at least n edges, $n \geq 2$.

16.4   THE ADT *graph*

The abstract data type *graph* refers to all varieties of graphs, whether directed, undirected, weighted, or unweighted. The abstract data type specification of ADT theChapter.1 lists only a few of the many operations commonly performed on a graph. As we progress through this text, we will add operations.

AbstractDataType *graph*
{

    instances
        a set V of vertices and a set E of edges

    operations
numberOfVertices() : return the number of vertices in the graph

  numberOfEdges() : return the number of edges in the graph

    existsEdge(i, j) : return **true** if edge (i, j) exists; **false** otherwise

insertEdge(*theEdge*) : insert the edge *theEdge* into the graph

    eraseEdge(i, j) : delete the edge (i, j)

      degree(i) : return the degree of vertex i, defined only for undirected
          · graphs

    inDegree(i) : return the in-degree of vertex i

  outDegree(i) : return the out-degree of vertex i

}

ADT 16.1 Abstract data type specification of a graph

Unlike the abstract classes for the data structures seen so far, the abstract class corresponding to the ADT *graph* will contain pure virtual methods as well as methods for which an implementation is provided in the abstract class. These latter methods, to be introduced later in this chapter and in succeeding chapters, will employ an iterator that will sequence through the vertices adjacent from a given vertex. Some of these methods also will need to tell whether the graph being worked on is directed and/or weighted. So we augment the ADT specification of *graph* (ADT 16.1) with methods to support these tasks. Program 16.1 is the resulting C++ abstract class. For weighted graphs, T is the data type of the edge weights; and for unweighted graphs, T is bool.

The template class **edge**, which gives the data type of the input to the **insertEdge** method is an abstract class that has the methods **vertex1**, **vertex2**, and **weight**

```
template<class T>
class graph
{
    public:
        virtual ~graph() {}

        // ADT methods
        virtual int numberOfVertices() const = 0;
        virtual int numberOfEdges() const = 0;
        virtual bool existsEdge(int, int) const = 0;
        virtual void insertEdge(edge<T>*) = 0;
        virtual void eraseEdge(int, int) = 0;
        virtual int degree(int) const = 0;
        virtual int inDegree(int) const = 0;
        virtual int outDegree(int) const = 0;

        // Additional methods
        virtual bool directed() const = 0;
                // return true iff the graph is directed
        virtual bool weighted() const = 0;
                // return true iff the graph is weighted
        virtual vertexIterator<T>* iterator(int) = 0;
                // access adjacent vertices of specified vertex
};
```

Program 16.1 The abstract class graph

that, respectively, return the first vertex, second vertex, and weight (if any) of an edge. The template class vertexIterator used in Program 16.1 is an abstract class that contains only a virtual destructor and the pure virtual methods

```
virtual int next() = 0;
virtual int next(T&) = 0;
```

Let g be a pointer to a graph. We may create an iterator for vertex 5 of g as below:

```
vertexIterator<T> *vertex5Iterator = iterator(5);
```

Successive invocations of vertex5Iterator->next() will return vertices j such that $(5, j)$ is an edge of the graph. The method returns 0 if there is no remaining adjacent vertex to return. The invocation vertex5Iterator->next(w), in addition to returning the next adjacent vertex j, sets w to be the weight of the edge $(5, j)$ when g is a weighted graph and to = true when g is an unweighted graph.

16.5   REPRESENTATION OF UNWEIGHTED GRAPHS

The most frequently used representation schemes for unweighted graphs are adjacency based: adjacency matrices, linked adjacency lists, and array adjacency lists.

16.5.1   Adjacency Matrix

The **adjacency matrix** of an n-vertex graph $G = (V, E)$ is an $n \times n$ matrix A. Each element of A is either 0 or 1. We will assume that $V = \{1, 2, \cdots, n\}$. If G is an undirected graph, then the elements of A are defined as follows:

$$A(i,j) = \begin{cases} 1 & \text{if } (i,j) \in E \text{ or } (j,i) \in E \\ 0 & \text{otherwise} \end{cases} \tag{16.1}$$

If G is a digraph, then the elements of A are defined as follows:

$$A(i,j) = \begin{cases} 1 & \text{if } (i,j) \in E \\ 0 & \text{otherwise} \end{cases} \tag{16.2}$$

The adjacency matrices for the graphs of Figure 16.1 appear in Figure 16.9.

Figure 16.9 Adjacency matrices for the graphs of Figure 16.1

The validity of the following statements is an immediate consequence of Equations 16.1 and 16.2:

1. $A(i,i) = 0$, $1 \le i \le n$ for all n-vertex graphs.

2. The adjacency matrix of an undirected graph is symmetric. That is, $A(i,j) = A(j,i)$, $1 \le i \le n$, $1 \le j \le n$.

3. For an n-vertex undirected graph, $\sum_{j=1}^{n} A(i,j) = \sum_{j=1}^{n} A(j,i) = d_i$. (Recall that d_i is the degree of vertex i.)

4. For an n-vertex digraph, $\sum_{j=1}^{n} A(i,j) = d_i^{out}$ and $\sum_{j=1}^{n} A(j,i) = d_i^{in}$, $1 \leq i \leq n$.

Mapping the Adjacency Matrix into an Array

The $n \times n$ adjacency matrix A may be mapped into an $(n+1) \times (n+1)$ array a of type **bool** by using the mapping $A(i,j)$ equals 1 iff a$[i][j]$ is **true**, $1 \leq i \leq n$, $1 \leq j \leq n$. This representation requires $(n+1)^2 = n^2 + 2n + 1$ bytes. Alternatively, we may use an $n \times n$ array—a$[n][n]$—and the mapping $A(i,j)$ equals 1 iff a$[i-1][j-1]$ is **true**, $1 \leq i \leq n$, $1 \leq j \leq n$. Since this alternative requires n^2 bytes, the storage requirement is reduced by $2n+1$ bytes.

A further reduction by n bytes results if we use the fact that all diagonal entries are 0 and so need not be stored. When the diagonal is eliminated, an upper- and a lower-triangular matrix remain (see Section 7.3.4). These triangular matrices may be compacted into an $(n-1) \times n$ matrix as in Figure 16.10. The shaded entries represent the lower triangle of the original adjacency matrix.

Figure 16.10 Adjacency matrices of Figure 16.9 with diagonals eliminated

The preceding methods to reduce the storage requirements yield a very small reduction and come at the cost of causing a mismatch between the vertex indexes used in the external and internal representation of a graph. This mismatch has the potential of causing errors in our codes. Further, the reduced storage methods require more time to access an edge. Therefore, we will use the $(n+1) \times (n+1)$ array mapping.

For undirected graphs the adjacency matrix is symmetric (see Section 7.3.5), so only the elements above (or below) the diagonal need to be stored explicitly. Hence we need only $(n^2 - n)/2$ bytes. By using the method of Section 7.3.5, we reduce the space requirement by about 50 percent. This reduction is significant for large graphs.

When adjacency matrices are used, we need $\Theta(n)$ time to determine the set of vertices adjacent to or from any given vertex. However, we can add or delete an edge in $\Theta(1)$ time.

16.5.2   Linked Adjacency Lists

The **adjacency list** for vertex i is a linear list that includes all vertices adjacent from i. In an **adjacency-list representation** of a graph, we maintain an adjacency list for each vertex of the graph. When these adjacency lists are represented as chains, we get the linked-adjacency-list representation.

We may use an array `aList` of type `chain` to represent all the adjacency lists. `aList[i].firstNode` points to the first node in the adjacency list for vertex `i`. If `x` points to a node in the chain `aList[i]`. then `(i, x->element)`, where the data type of `element` is `int`, is an edge of the graph. Figure 16.11 gives some linked-adjacency-list representations.

Since each pointer and integer is 4 bytes long, the space needed by the linked-adjacency-list representation of an n-vertex graph is $8(n+1)$ (for the $n+1$ `firstNode` pointers and `listSize` fields of the chains of `aList`) $+ 4*2*m$ (m chain nodes, 4 bytes for each of the two fields (`next` and `element`) of a chain node) $= 8(n+m+1)$ bytes where $m = 2e$ for an undirected graph, $m = e$ for a digraph, and e is the number of edges.

When e is much less than n^2, the linked-adjacency-list representation takes less space than does the adjacency-matrix representation. For example, a digraph with $e = n$ edges requires $16n + 8$ bytes of space when linked adjacency lists are used; the same digraph requires n^2 bytes when a compacted adjacency matrix is used. So when $e = n \geq 17$, the linked-list representation takes less space.

When linked adjacency lists are used, we can determine the vertices adjacent from vertex i in time Θ(number of vertices adjacent from vertex i). The time needed to add or delete the edge (i, j) is $O(d_i + d_j)$ or $O(d_i^{out})$, depending on whether the graph is undirected or directed.

16.5.3   Array Adjacency Lists

In the **array-adjacency-list** representation of a graph, each adjacency list is represented by using an array linear list representation rather than a chain. So, for example, the data type of the array `aList` of the linked-adjacency-list representation may now be `arrayList` (Program 5.3). Alternatively, we may use a two-dimensional irregular array (Section 7.1.6) `aList[][]` with `aList[i]` having a capacity equal to the size of the adjacency list for vertex `i`. Figure 16.12 gives some array-adjacency-list representations. You may interpret each `aList[i]` as a one-dimensional array or as an instance of `arrayList`.

Figure 16.11 Linked adjacency lists for the graphs of Figure 16.1

The array-adjacency-list representation requires $4m$ bytes of space less than that required by linked adjacency lists, because, in the array-adjacency-list representation, we do not have the m **next** pointer fields that are present in the linked-adjacency-list representation. Most of the operations commonly performed on a graph can be done in the same asymptotic complexity by using either linked or array adjacency lists. Based on the experimental results of Sections 6.1.6 and 8.4.3, we expect array adjacency lists to outperform linked adjacency lists for most graph

Figure 16.12 Array adjacency lists for graphs of Figure 16.1

applications.

A word of caution–the space analyses we have done for adjacency matrices and lists are approximate analyses. Actual implementations may take slightly more space because in an actual implementation we may store additional data such as the number of vertices and edges in a graph. It is expected, however, that the space unaccounted for in our analyses will not affect the relative comparisons made by us.

EXERCISES

16. Draw the following representations for the digraph of Figure 16.2(b).

   (a) Adjacency matrix.
   (b) Linked adjacency lists.
   (c) Array adjacency lists.

17. Do Exercise 16 for the graph of Figure 16.4(a).

18. Do Exercise 16 for the graph of Figure 16.5.

19. Do Exercise 16 for the digraph of Figure 16.8(a).

20. Do Exercise 16 for the digraph of Figure 16.8(b).

21. Suppose that the adjacency matrix of a graph is represented using a Boolean array as in Figure 16.10. Note that in this representation, the diagonal of the adjacency matrix is not stored (see Figure 16.10). Write methods **set** and **get** to, respectively, store and retrieve the value of $A(i, j)$. The complexity of each method should be $\Theta(1)$.

22. Do Exercise 21 for the case of an undirected graph for which only the lower triangle is explicitly stored in a one-dimensional **bool** array **a**.

23. Assume that a directed $n \times n$ adjacency matrix is represented in an $n \times n$ **bool** array **a**. Write a method to determine the number of edges in the graph. The complexity of your method should be $O(n^2)$. Show that this is the case.

24. Suppose that an undirected graph is represented with the array-adjacency-list representation (see Figure 16.12).

    (a) Write a method to delete the edge (i, j). What is the time complexity of your code?

    (b) Write a method to insert an edge into the array-adjacency-list representation. What is the time complexity of your code?

25. Do Exercise 23 for the case when linked adjacency lists (see Figure 16.11) are used.

26. Do Exercise 24 for the case when linked adjacency lists are used.

27. Do Exercise 24 for the case of a directed graph.

28. Let G be an n-vertex e-edge undirected graph. What is the least value of e for which the adjacency-matrix representation of G uses less space than the array-adjacency-list representation uses?

29. Do Exercise 28 for the case of a directed graph G.

16.6   REPRESENTATION OF WEIGHTED GRAPHS

Weighted graphs are generally represented with schemes that are simple extensions of those used for unweighted graphs. The **cost-adjacency-matrix** representation uses a matrix C just like the adjacency-matrix representation does. If $C(i, j)$ is the cost (or weight) of the edge (i, j). In this representation, we need to assign a cost-value for edges that are not present in the graph. Typically, one assigns absent edges a very high cost. In our implementations, we shall require the user to specify a cost **noEdge** that is to be assigned to absent edges. Figure 16.13 gives possible cost-adjacency matrices for the graphs of Figure 16.1. Absent edges are denoted by dashes.

	1	2	3	4
1	-	4	7	8
2	4	-	2	-
3	7	2	-	6
4	8	-	6	-

(a)

	1	2	3	4	5	6	7
1	-	9	5	-	-	-	-
2	9	-	-	-	-	-	-
3	5	-	-	-	-	-	-
4	-	-	-	-	3	-	-
5	-	-	-	3	-	6	4
6	-	-	-	-	6	-	1
7	-	-	-	-	4	1	-

(b)

	1	2	3	4	5
1	-	8	-	-	-
2	-	-	3	-	-
3	-	-	-	2	7
4	-	-	6	-	-
5	-	-	-	5	-

(c)

The small dash (-) denotes the value noEdge

Figure 16.13 Possible cost-adjacency matrices for the graphs of Figure 16.1

We can obtain the linked-adjacency-list representation of a weighted graph from that of the corresponding graph by using chains whose elements have the two fields `vertex` and `weight`. Figure 16.14 shows the representation for the weighted graph that corresponds to the cost-adjacency matrix of Figure 16.13(a). The first component of each node in this figure is `vertex`, and the second is `weight`.

N denotes a null link

Figure 16.14 Linked adjacency lists for weighted graph of Figure 16.13(a)

We can obtain the array-adjacency-list representation of a weighted graph from that of the corresponding unweighted graph by replacing each entry with a (vertex, weight) pair. The representation differs from that shown in Figure 16.14 only in that there are no next pointers. Notice that when using adjacency lists, we do not assign costs to absent edges.

EXERCISES

30. Draw the array-adjacency-list representations of the weighted graphs that correspond to the cost-adjacency matrices of Figures 16.13(a) and (b).

31. Draw the linked-adjacency-list representations of the weighted graphs that correspond to the cost-adjacency matrices of Figures 16.13(b) and (c).

16.7   CLASS IMPLEMENTATIONS

16.7.1   The Different Classes

For each of the four graph types—unweighted undirected graphs, weighted undirected graphs, unweighted digraphs, and weighted digraphs—we considered three possible representations (matrix, linked, and array) in Sections 16.5 and 16.6. With one C++ class for each graph type and representation combination, we will have 12 classes. Only eight of these classes are explicitly considered in this text. We develop the four that correspond to the array-adjacency-list representation in Exercises 37 through 40.

The eight classes we will develop are adjacencyGraph (unweighted undirected graphs using the matrix representation), adjacencyWGraph, adjacencyDigraph, adjacencyWDigraph, linkedGraph, linkedWGraph, linkedDigraph, and linked-WDigraph.

Several pairs of our four graph types have an "IsA" relationship between them. For example, an undirected graph may be viewed as a directed graph in which edge (i, j) is present whenever edge (j, i) is present; as a weighted undirected graph in which all edge weights are 1; or as a weighted digraph in which all edge weights are 1 and edge (j, i) is present whenever edge (i, j) is present. Similarly, a digraph may be viewed as a weighted digraph in which all edge weights are 1.

The presence of these relationships makes it easier to develop the eight classes because we can derive one class from another. Although many IsA relationships exist, we will employ just a few. Figure 16.15 shows the derivation hierarchy we use. The class adjacencyGraph, for example, is derived from the class adjacencyWGraph, which is derived from adjacencyWDigraph. The abstract class graph is a common superclass for all our graph classes. We will use this class in later sections to house methods that are implementation independent. These implementation-independent methods are inherited by all of our graph classes.

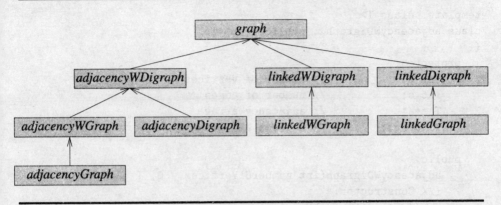

Figure 16.15 Class derivation hierarchy

16.7.2   Adjacency-Matrix Classes

The adjacency-matrix classes for weighted edges are similar to those for unweighted edges. The primary difference is that the weighted-edge classes use a two-dimensional array of type T, where T is the type of the edge weights; whereas the classes for unweighted graphs use a two-dimensional array of type bool. We describe only the weighted-graph classes adjacencyWDigraph and adjacencyWGraph here. Although only partial code for the class adjacencyWDigraph is given in the book, you can obtain complete codes for all adjacency-matrix classes from the Web site.

The Class adjacencyWDigraph

Program 16.2 gives the code for adjacencyWDigraph.

The constructor creates the cost-adjacency matrix a for a weighted directed graph with n = numberOfVertices vertices and zero edges. All positions of the two-dimensional array a are initialized to noEdge and e is set to 0. Therefore, the complexity of the constructor is $O(n^2)$.

The method insertEdge first verifies that the endpoints of the input edge theEdge are in the range [1, n] and that the endpoints are different; that is, the endpoints correspond to vertices of the weighted digraph and the edge is not a self-edge. If the edge theEdge that is to be added to the weighted digraph fails this test, an exception of type illegalParameterValue is thrown. If the edge passes the test, we must verify whether theEdge already exists in the graph. When theEdge exists in the graph, we must update the weight of the edge, but not increase the edge count. When theEdge is a new edge, we must set the edge weight in a and increase the edge count.

eraseEdge first verifies that the edge to be removed exists. If the edge exists, the corresponding entry in a is set to noEdge and the edge count reduced by 1.

```
template <class T>
class adjacencyWDigraph : public graph<T>
{
   protected:
      int n;              // number of vertices
      int e;              // number of edges
      T **a;              // adjacency array
      T noEdge;           // denotes absent edge

   public:
      adjacencyWDigraph(int numberOfVertices = 0, T theNoEdge = 0)
      {// Constructor.
         // validate number of vertices
         if (numberOfVertices < 0)
         throw illegalParameterValue("number of vertices must be >= 0")
         n = numberOfVertices;
         e = 0;
         noEdge = theNoEdge;
         make2dArray(a, n + 1, n + 1);
         for (int i = 1; i <= n; i++)
            // initialize adjacency matrix
            fill(a[i], a[i] + n + 1, noEdge);
      }

      ~adjacencyWDigraph() {delete2dArray(a, n + 1);}

      int numberOfVertices() const {return n;}

      int numberOfEdges() const {return e;}

      bool directed() const {return true;}

      bool weighted() const {return true;}

      bool existsEdge(int i, int j) const
      {// Return true iff (i,j) is an edge of the graph.
         if (i < 1 || j < 1 || i > n || j > n || a[i][j] == noEdge)
            return false;
         else
            return true;
      }
```

Program 16.2 Cost-adjacency matrix for weighted directed graphs (continues)

```
void insertEdge(edge<T> *theEdge)
{// Insert edge theEdge into the digraph; if the edge is already
 // there, update its weight to theEdge.weight().
   int v1 = theEdge->vertex1();
   int v2 = theEdge->vertex2();
   if (v1 < 1 || v2 < 1 || v1 > n || v2 > n || v1 == v2)
   {
      ostringstream s;
      s << "(" << v1 << "," << v2
        << ") is not a permissible edge";
      throw illegalParameterValue(s.str());
   }

   if (a[v1][v2] == noEdge)  // new edge
      e++;
   a[v1][v2] = theEdge->weight();
}

void eraseEdge(int i, int j)
{// Delete the edge (i,j).
   if (i >= 1 && j >= 1 && i <= n && j <= n && a[i][j] != noEdge)
   {
      a[i][j] = noEdge;
      e--;
   }
}

void checkVertex(int theVertex) const
{// Verify that theVertex is a valid vertex.
   if (theVertex < 1 || theVertex > n)
   {
      ostringstream s;
      s << "no vertex " << theVertex;
      throw illegalParameterValue(s.str());
   }
}

int degree(int theVertex) const
   {throw undefinedMethod("degree() undefined");}
```

Program 16.2 Cost-adjacency matrix for weighted directed graphs (continues)

```
int outDegree(int theVertex) const
{// Return out-degree of vertex theVertex.
   checkVertex(theVertex);

   // count out edges from vertex theVertex
   int sum = 0;
   for (int j = 1; j <= n; j++)
      if (a[theVertex][j] != noEdge)
         sum++;

   return sum;
}

int inDegree(int theVertex) const
{// Return in-degree of vertex theVertex.
   checkVertex(theVertex);

   // count in edges at vertex theVertex
   int sum = 0;
   for (int j = 1; j <= n; j++)
      if (a[j][theVertex] != noEdge)
         sum++;

   return sum;
}

class myIterator : public vertexIterator<T>
{
   public:
      myIterator(T* theRow, T theNoEdge, int numberOfVertices)
      {
         row = theRow;
         noEdge = theNoEdge;
         n = numberOfVertices;
         currentVertex = 1;
      }

      ~myIterator() {}
```

Program 16.2 Cost-adjacency matrix for weighted directed graphs (continues)

```
            int next(T& theWeight)
            {// Return next vertex if any. Return 0 if no next vertex.
             // Set theWeight = edge weight.
               // find next adjacent vertex
               for (int j = currentVertex; j <= n; j++)
                  if (row[j] != noEdge)
                  {
                     currentVertex = j + 1;
                     theWeight = row[j];
                     return j;
                  }
               // no next adjacent vertex
               currentVertex = n + 1;
               return 0;
            }

            // code for next() is similar to above

      protected:
         T* row;                // row of adjacency matrix
         T noEdge;              // theRow[i] == noEdge iff no edge to i
         int n; .               // number of vertices
         int currentVertex;
      };

      myIterator* iterator(int theVertex)
      {// Return iterator for vertex theVertex.
         checkVertex(theVertex);
         return new myIterator(a[theVertex], noEdge, n);
      }
};
```

Program 16.2 Cost-adjacency matrix for weighted directed graphs (concluded)

The method **degree** simply throws an exception of type **undefinedMethod** because **degree** is defined only for undirected graphs (whether weighted or unweighted). The out-degree of vertex **theVertex** is computed by determining the number of entries **a[theVertex][*]** that are not equal to **noEdge**, and the in-degree of vertex **theVertex** is the number of entries **a[*][theVertex]** that are not equal to **noEdge**.

For the iterator, we define the class **myIterator**, which is a member class of **adjacencyWDigraph**. Recall from our discussion of the abstract class **graph** (Section 16.4) that the iterator is to return, one by one, the vertices that are adjacent from the vertex that is being iterated. The code for **next** scans the adjacency matrix row of the vertex being iterated beginning at the current position **currentVertex** searching for the first entry that is not equal to **noEdge**. When such an entry is found, it returns a pointer to a pair which includes the column index (i.e., next adjacent vertex) and the edge weight. If such an entry is not found, the method returns 0.

The complexity of **existsEdge**, **numberOfVertices**, **numberOfEdges**, **directed**, **weighted**, **insertEdge**, **eraseEdge**, **degree**, and **iterator** is $\Theta(1)$. The complexity of **outDegree** and **inDegree**, and **next** is $O(n)$. The complexity of **outDegree** and **inDegree** may be reduced to $\Theta(1)$ by keeping an array of out-degree values and an array of in-degree values.

The Class adjacencyWGraph

Since this class is derived from **adjacencyWDigraph**, it inherits all the data members and methods of the superclass. We need to override those methods that are to work differently. The method **insertEdge** must set both **a[v1][v2]** and **a[v2][v1]** to the weight of **theEdge**; **eraseEdge** must set both **a[i][j]** and **a[j][i]** to **noEdge**; **degree** should be defined to return the number of entries **a[theVertex][*]** that are not equal to **noEdge**, and **directed** should return the value **false**. The code for the overriding methods is quite similar to code we have already seen for the methods of **adjacencyWDigraph**. We do not include this code in the book, but you can get the code from the Web site.

16.7.3   An Extension to the Class chain

In the linked-list representations of a graph, we employ an array of chains. For our application here, we need to extend the class **chain** (Section 6.1) by adding in the method **eraseElement(theVertex)**. This method searches the chain for an element whose vertex equals **theVertex**. If a matching element is found, it is deleted from the chain and a pointer to the deleted element is returned. The extension of **chain** that includes the new method is called **graphChain**.

16.7.4   Linked-List Classes

Program 16.3 gives the data members and some of the methods of the class **linked-Digraph**. The complexity of constructor is $O(n)$ ($n = $ **numberOfVertices**) and that of **existsEdge(i,j)** is $O(d_i^{out})$.

To insert an edge (**v1**, **v2**) into a digraph, we first verify that the edge is not already in the digraph, and then we insert **v2** at the front of the chain **aList[v1]**. To erase the edge (**i**, **j**) we use **graphChain::eraseElement** to erase j from the chain **aList[i]**. The complexity of **insertEdge** is $O(d_{v1}^{out})$, and that of **eraseEdge** is $O(d_i^{out})$.

```
class linkedDigraph : public graph<bool>
{
   protected:
      int n;                           // number of vertices
      int e;                           // number of edges
      graphChain<int> *aList;          // adjacency lists

   public:
      linkedDigraph(int numberOfVertices = 0)
      {// Constructor.
         if (numberOfVertices < 0)
            throw illegalParameterValue
                  ("number of vertices must be >= 0");
         n = numberOfVertices;
         e = 0;
         aList = new graphChain<int> [n + 1];
      }

      ~linkedDigraph() {delete [] aList;}

      // code for numberOfVertices, numberOfEdges, directed
      // and weighted is same as for adjacencyWDigraph

      bool existsEdge(int i, int j) const
      {// Return true iff (i,j) is an edge.
         if (i < 1 || j < 1 || i > n || j > n
             || aList[i].indexOf(j) == -1)
            return false;
         else
            return true;
      }

      void insertEdge(edge<bool> *theEdge)
      {// Insert an edge.
         // code to set and validate v1 and v2 is same as
         // for adjacencyWDigraph

         if (aList[v1].indexOf(v2) == -1)
         {// new edge
            aList[v1].insert(0, v2);
            e++;
         }
      }
```

Program 16.3 The class linkedDigraph (continues)

```
void eraseEdge(int i, int j)
{
   if (i >= 1 && j >= 1 && i <= n && j <= n)
   {
      int *v = aList[i].eraseElement(j);
      if (v != NULL)  // edge (i,j) did exist
         e--;
   }
}

void checkVertex(int theVertex) const
{// Verify that theVertex is a valid vertex.
   // code is same as for adjacencyWDigraph
}

int degree(int theVertex) const
   {throw undefinedMethod("degree() undefined");}

int outDegree(int theVertex) const
{// Return out-degree of vertex theVertex.
   checkVertex(theVertex);
   return aList[theVertex].size();
}

int inDegree(int theVertex) const
{
   checkVertex(theVertex);

   // count in-edges at vertex theVertex
   int sum = 0;
   for (int j = 1; j <= n; j++)
      if (aList[j].indexOf(theVertex) != -1)
         sum++;

   return sum;
}

   // code for iterator omitted
};
```

Program 16.3 The class linkedDigraph (concluded)

The method `degree` is undefined for a directed graph. The out-degree of vertex `theVertex` is just `aList[theVertex].listSize()`. Since the complexity of `chain::listSize()` is $\Theta(1)$, the out-degree of a vertex is determined in $\Theta(1)$ time. Computing the in-degree of a vertex is far more expensive. To compute the in-degree of vertex `theVertex`, we must search all the adjacency lists, keeping a count of the number of lists that contain `theVertex` (Program 16.3). The complexity of `inDegree` is $O(n + e)$, where n and e are, respectively, the number of vertices and the number of edges in the digraph; this complexity may be reduced to $\Theta(1)$ by keeping an array of in-degree values.

Other Linked Classes

The codes for the remaining linked classes may be obtained with modest effort and can be found at the Web site.

EXERCISES

32. Write the method `adjacencyWDigraph::input`, which inputs a weighted directed graph. Assume that the input consists of the number of vertices and edges in the graph together with a list of edges. Each edge is given as a pair of vertices plus the edge weight. Note that your input method is inherited by the remaining adjacency-matrix classes. Does your input method work correctly for these remaining adjacency-matrix classes? If not, override the input method by writing new ones as needed.

33. Write and test a copy constructor for `adjacencyWDigraph`.

34. Write the method `linkedDigraph::input`, which inputs a digraph. The complexity of your method should be linear in the number of vertices and edges in the input graph. Show that this is the case.

35. Write the method `linkedWDigraph::input`, which inputs a weighted digraph. The complexity of your method should be linear in the number of vertices and edges in the input graph. Show that this is the case.

36. We can speed `linkedWGraph` and `linkedWDigraph` if we include a new version of the `indexOf` method in `graphChain`. The new version updates the element in case it is already in the chain. Develop such an `indexOf` method and modify the `insertEdge` methods of the linked adjacency list classes to utilize this new method.

37. Develop the C++ class `arrayDigraph` in which digraphs are represented with array adjacency lists.

38. Develop the C++ class `arrayGraph` in which undirected graphs are represented with array adjacency lists.

39. Develop the C++ class `arrayWDigraph` in which weighted digraphs are represented with array adjacency lists.

40. Develop the C++ class `arrayWGraph` in which weighted undirected graphs are represented with array adjacency lists.

16.8   GRAPH SEARCH METHODS

The operations that are performed on graphs are too numerous to list here. We saw some of these operations (e.g., find a path, find a spanning tree, determine whether the undirected graph is connected) in Section 16.2, and we will see some others later in this book. Many operations require us to visit all vertices that can be reached from a given start vertex. (A vertex u is reachable from vertex v iff there is a (directed) path from v to u.) The two standard ways to search for these vertices are **breadth-first search** (BFS) and **depth-first search** (DFS). Although both search methods are popular, the depth-first method is used more frequently to obtain efficient graph algorithms.

16.8.1   Breadth-First Search

Consider the directed graph of Figure 16.16(a). One way to determine all the vertices reachable from vertex 1 is to first determine the set of vertices adjacent from 1. This set is {2,3,4}. Next we determine the set of new vertices (i.e., vertices not yet reached) that are adjacent from vertices in {2,3,4}. This set is {5,6,7}. The set of new vertices adjacent from vertices in {5,6,7} is {8,9}. No new vertices are adjacent from a vertex in {8,9}; therefore, {1,2,3,4,5,6,7,8,9} is the set of vertices reachable from vertex 1.

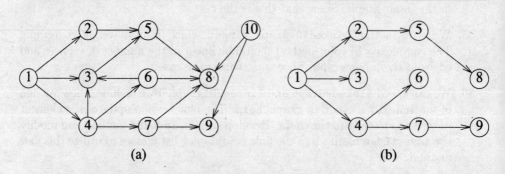

(a)   (b)

Figure 16.16 Breadth-first search

    This method of starting at a vertex and identifying all vertices reachable from it is called breadth-first search (BFS). Such a search may be implemented using a queue. A pseudocode version of a possible implementation appears in Figure 16.17. Notice the similarity between BFS and level-order traversal of a binary tree.

```
breadthFirstSearch(v)
{
    Label vertex v as reached.
    Initialize Q to be a queue with only v in it.
    while (Q is not empty)
    {
        Delete a vertex w from the queue.
        Let u be a vertex (if any) adjacent from w.
        while (u != NULL)
        {
            if (u has not been labeled)
            {
                Add u to the queue.
                Label u as reached.
            }
            u = next vertex that is adjacent from w.
        }
    }
}
```

Figure 16.17 Pseudocode for BFS

If we use the pseudocode of Figure 16.17 on the graph of Figure 16.16(a) with $v = 1$, then vertices 2, 3, and 4 will get added to the queue (assume that they get added in this order) during the first iteration of the outer **while** loop. In the next iteration of this loop, 2 is removed from the queue, and vertex 5 added to it. Next 3 is deleted from the queue, and no new vertices are added. Then 4 is deleted and 6 and 7 added; 5 is deleted and 8 added; 6 is deleted and nothing added; and 7 is deleted and 9 added. Finally, 8 and 9 are deleted, and the queue becomes empty. The procedure terminates, and vertices 1 through 9 have been marked as reached. Figure 16.16(b) shows the subgraph formed by the edges used to reach the nodes that get visited.

Theorem 16.1 *Let G be an arbitrary graph and let v be any vertex of G. The pseudocode of Figure 16.17 labels all vertices that are reachable from v (including vertex v).*

Proof Exercise 43(a) asks you to prove this theorem. ∎

16.8.2   Implementation of Breadth-First Search

As indicated by the pseudocode of Figure 16.17, at a suitably high level the manner in which a BFS is performed is independent of whether we are dealing with an undirected graph, digraph, weighted undirected graph, or weighted digraph and is also independent of the particular representation used. However, to implement statements such as

u = next vertex that is adjacent from w

we need to know the implementation in use. We can avoid writing separate code to perform a BFS for each of our implementations by making our BFS method a member of the class graph, which is a superclass of all of the implementation classes, and using graph iterators to go from one adjacent vertex to the next.

The implementation-independent code for BFS (see Program 16.4) closely follows the pseudocode of Figure 16.17. Program 16.4 assumes that reach[i] = 0 initially for all vertices and that label ≠ 0. All reachable vertices have reach[i] set to label upon termination.

16.8.3   Complexity Analysis of graph::bfs

Each vertex that is reachable from the start vertex v is labeled, added to the queue exactly once, deleted from the queue exactly once, and its row in the adjacency matrix or its linked adjacency list traversed exactly once. If s vertices are labeled, then the time for all of these operations is $O(sn)$ when an adjacency matrix is used and $O(\sum_i d_i^{out})$ when a linked adjacency list is used. In the latter case the sum is done over all i where i is a labeled vertex. For an undirected graph the out-degree of a vertex is considered equal to its degree.

At this point we may wonder what the unified BFS code costs compared to codes customized for each representation. We need three customized codes—one is a member of adjacencyWDigraph, another is a member of linkedWDigraph, and the third is a member of linkedDigraph. The remaining methods inherit the customized code from their superclass. Programs 16.5 and 16.6 give the customized codes for adjacencyWDigraph and linkedDigraph, respectively.

On our 1.7 GHz Pentium 4 PC, graph::bfs took 0.18 milliseconds (ms) to do a BFS on a 100-vertex, unweighted complete undirected graph represented by its adjacency matrix. The corresponding time for adjacencyWDigraph::bfs was 0.06 ms. So we pay a 3-fold performance penalty to use the implementation-independent method graph::bfs. For the linked representation the implementation-independent code took 1.0 ms, while the customized code took 0.9 ms. The performance penalty for this case is 11%

We see that there is a performance penalty associated with using the implementation-independent BFS code rather than the customized versions. This penalty, which is rather significant in the case of the adjacency matrix representation, is due largely to the use of iterators. However, we should keep in mind that several merits are associated with the implementation-independent code. For example, this single code

```
virtual void bfs(int v, int reach[], int label)
{// Breadth-first search. reach[i] is set to label for
 // all vertices reachable from vertex v.
   arrayQueue<int> q(10);
   reach[v] = label;
   q.push(v);
   while (!q.empty())
   {
      // remove a labeled vertex from the queue
      int w = q.front();
      q.pop();

      // mark all unreached vertices adjacent from w
      vertexIterator<T> *iw = iterator(w);
      int u;
      while ((u = iw->next()) != 0)
         // visit an adjacent vertex of w
         if (reach[u] == 0)
         {// u is an unreached vertex
            q.push(u);
            reach[u] = label; // mark reached
         }
      delete iw;
   }
}
```

Program 16.4 Implementation-independent BFS code

works with all representations, whereas the customized route requires several codes. Consequently, if we introduce new representations (for example array adjacency lists), we can use the implementation-independent code with no change. When developing code for a new graph application, we can first develop the implementation-independent code. This approach enables all graph implementations to make use of this application. Then as time and resources permit, we can develop the more efficient customized codes for individual representations.

16.8.4   Depth-First Search

Depth-first search (DFS) is an alternative to BFS. The DFS strategy has already been used in the rat-in-a-maze problem (Section 8.5.6) and is quite similar to preorder traversal of a binary tree.

Figure 16.18 gives the pseudocode for DFS. Starting at a vertex v, a DFS pro-

```
void bfs(int v, int reach[], int label)
{// Breadth-first search. reach[i] is set to label for
 // all vertices reachable from vertex v.
   arrayQueue<int> q(10);
   reach[v] = label;
   q.push(v);
   while (!q.empty())
   {
      // remove a labeled vertex from the queue
      int w = q.front();
      q.pop();

      // mark all unreached vertices adjacent from w
      for (int u = 1; u <= n; u++)
         // visit an adjacent vertex of w
         if (a[w][u] != noEdge && reach[u] == 0)
         {// u is an unreached vertex
            q.push(u);
            reach[u] = label; // mark reached
         }
   }
}
```

Program 16.5 Direct BFS implementation for `adjacencyWDigraph`

ceeds as follows: First the vertex v is marked as reached, and then an unreached
vertex u adjacent from v is selected. If such a vertex does not exist, the search
terminates. Assume that a u as described exists. A DFS from u is now initiated.
When this search is completed, we select another unreached vertex adjacent from v.
If such a vertex does not exist, then the search terminates. If such a vertex exists,
a DFS is initiated from this vertex, and so on.

```
depthFirstSearch(v)
{
    Label vertex v as reached.
    for (each unreached vertex u adjacent from v)
        depthFirstSearch(u);
}
```

Figure 16.18 Pseudocode for DFS

```
void bfs(int v, int reach[], int label)
{// Breadth-first search. reach[i] is set to label for
 // all vertices reachable from vertex v.
   arrayQueue<int> q(10);
   reach[v] = label;
   q.push(v);
   while (!q.empty())
   {
      // remove a labeled vertex from the queue
      int w = q.front();
      q.pop();

      // mark all unreached vertices adjacent from w
      for (chainNode<int>* u = aList[w].firstNode;
                           u != NULL; u = u->next)
         // visit an adjacent vertex of w
         if (reach[u->element] == 0)
         {// u->element is an unreached vertex
            q.push(u->element);
            reach[u->element] = label; // mark reached
         }
   }
}
```

Program 16.6 Direct BFS implementation for linkedDigraph

Let us try out depthFirstSearch on the digraph of Figure 16.16(a). If v = 1, then vertices 2, 3, and 4 are the candidates for the first choice of u. Suppose that the first value assigned to u is 2. A DFS from 2 is now initiated. Vertex 2 is marked as reached. The only candidate for u this time is vertex 5, and a DFS from 5 is initiated. Vertex 5 is marked as reached, and then a DFS from 8 is initiated. Next vertex 8 is marked. From 8 there are no unreached adjacent vertices, so the algorithm backs up to vertex 5. There are no new candidates for u here, so we back up to 2 and then to 1.

At this point we have two candidates: vertices 3 and 4 for u. Assume that 4 is selected. A DFS from 4 is initiated, and vertex 4 is marked as reached. Vertices 3, 6, and 7 are now the candidates for u. Assume that vertex 6 is selected. When v = 6, vertex 3 is the only candidate for u. A DFS from 3 is initiated, and vertex 3 gets labeled as reached. No new vertices are adjacent from 3, and we back up to vertex 6. No new vertices are adjacent from here, so we back up to 4. From 4 we initiate a DFS with u = 7. Next we reach vertex 9 from which there are no new adjacent vertices. This time we back up all the way to 1. As there are no new vertices adjacent from 1, the algorithm terminates.

For depthFirstSearch we can prove a theorem analogous to Theorem 16.1; depthFirstSearch labels vertex v and all vertices reachable from v (Exercise 43(b)).

Theorem 16.2 *Let G be an arbitrary graph and let v be any vertex of G. Procedure* depthFirstSearch *labels all vertices that are reachable from v (including vertex v).*

Proof Exercise 43(b) asks you to prove this theorem.   ∎

16.8.5   Implementation of Depth-First Search

Program 16.7 gives the public method graph::dfs as well as the protected method graph::rDfs. The code of Program 16.7 assumes that graph<T>::reach and graph<T>::label are static data members of graph. In the implementation of DFS, it is easier to let u run through all vertices adjacent from v, rather than just through the unreached vertices adjacent from v.

```
void dfs(int v, int reach [], int label)
{// Depth-first search. reach[i] is set to label for all
 // vertices reachable from vertex v
   graph<T>::reach = reach;
   graph<T>::label = label;
   rDfs(v);
}


void rDfs(int v)
{// Recursive dfs method.
   reach[v] = label;
   vertexIterator<T> *iv = iterator(v);
   int u;
   while ((u = iv->next()) != 0)
      // visit an adjacent vertex of v
      if (reach[u] == 0)
         rDfs(u);  // u is an unreached vertex
   delete iv;
}
```

Program 16.7 Depth-first search

16.8.6 Complexity Analysis of graph::dfs

You can verify that the methods dfs and bfs have the same time and space complexities. However, the instances for which dfs takes maximum space (i.e., stack space for the recursion) are those on which bfs takes minimum space (i.e., queue space); and the instances for which bfs takes maximum space are those on which dfs takes minimum space. Figure 16.19 gives the best-case and worst-case instances for dfs and bfs.

(a) Worst case for dfs(1) ; best case for bfs(1)

(b) Best case for dfs(1) ; worst case for bfs(1)

Figure 16.19 Worst-case and best-case space complexity graphs

EXERCISES

41. Consider the graph of Figure 16.4(a).

    (a) Draw an adjacency-list representation (either linked or array) for this graph.

    (b) Label the vertices in the order in which they are visited in a BFS that starts at vertex 4. Use your representation of part (a) and the code of Program 16.4.

    (c) Show the subgraph formed by the edges used to reach new vertices during your search of part (b).

    (d) Redo parts (b) and (c), but this time do a DFS using the code of Program 16.7.

42. Do Exercise 41 using vertex 7 as the start vertex for the search.

43. (a) Prove Theorem 16.1.

    (b) Prove Theorem 16.2.

44. Develop customized DFS codes for `adjacencyWDigraph` and `linkedDigraph`.

(a) Test the correctness of your codes.

(b) Determine the speedup obtained by the customized codes over the implementation-independent code of Program 16.7 on a complete digraph with 100 vertices.

16.9   APPLICATIONS REVISITED

16.9.1   Finding a Path

We can find a path (see Example 16.1) from a source vertex `theSource` to a destination vertex `theDestination` by starting a search (either breadth first or depth first) at `theSource` and terminating the search as soon as we reach `theDestination`. To actually construct the path, we need to remember the edges used to move from one vertex to the next. For the path problem, the needed set of edges is implicitly stored in the depth-first recursion, so it is easier to develop a path-finding code by using the depth-first strategy. As the recursion unfolds following the labeling of `theDestination`, the path is constructed backward from `theDestination` to `theSource`. The code for `graph::findPath` appears in Program 16.8. Program 16.9 gives the code for `rFindPath`.

If there is no path from `theSource` to `theDestination`, `findPath` returns NULL; otherwise , it returns an array `path` such that `path[0]` is the number of edges on the path that is found; `path[1]` = `theSource` ⋯ `path[path[0] + 1]` = `theDestination` gives the actual path.

`findPath` first initializes the following static data members of `graph`: `destination`, `path`, `length`, and `reach`. The DFS for the path is actually performed by the protected method `graph::rFindPath`, which returns `false` iff no path to the destination is found. The method `graph::rFindPath` is a modified DFS. There are essentially two modifications that have been made to a standard DFS: (1) `rFindPath` discontinues the search for reachable vertices as soon as the destination vertex `destination` is reached, and (2) `rFindPath` records the vertices on the path from `theSource` to the current vertex u in the array `path`. Notice that `rFindPath` is invoked only when `theSource` ≠ `theDestination`. Also, notice that `rFindPath` does not necessarily find a shortest path (i.e., a path with the fewest number of edges) to the destination. When a BFS is used in place of a DFS, a shortest path is found (Exercise 45).

`findPath` and `dfs` have the same complexity.

16.9.2   Connected Graphs and Components

We can determine whether an undirected graph G is connected (see Example 16.2) by performing either a DFS or BFS from any vertex and then verifying that all

```
int* findPath(int theSource, int theDestination)
{// Find a path from theSource to theDestination. Return the
 // path in an array using positions 1 on up. path[0] is
 // path length. Return NULL if there is no path.
   // initialize for recursive path finder
   int n = numberOfVertices();
   path = new int [n + 1];
   path[1] = theSource;        // first vertex is always s
   length = 1;                 // current path length + 1
   destination = theDestination;
   reach = new int [n + 1];
   for (int i = 1; i <= n; i++)
      reach[i] = 0;

   // search for path
   if (theSource == theDestination || rFindPath(theSource))
      // a path was found
      path[0] = length - 1;
   else
   {
      delete [] path;
      path = NULL;
   }

   delete [] reach;
   return path;
}
```

Program 16.8 Preprocessor to find a path in a graph

vertices have been labeled as reached. Although this strategy directly verifies only that there is a path from the start vertex of the DFS or BFS to every other graph vertex, this verification is sufficient to conclude that a path exists between every pair of vertices. To see the validity of this claim, suppose that i is the start vertex of the search and that the search reaches all vertices of the graph. We may construct a path between any two vertices u and v by using the path from i to u in the reverse direction and then the path from i to v. Method connected (Program 16.10) returns false if the graph is not connected and true if it is. Since the notion of connectedness is defined only for undirected graphs, we test that the graph *this is undirected by invoking the method directed, which returns the value true iff *this is a directed graph.

```
bool rFindPath(int s)
{// Real path finder, performs a depth-first search from s.
 // s should not equal the destination.
 // Return true iff a path to destination is found.
    reach[s] = 1;
    vertexIterator<T>* is = iterator(s);
    int u;
    while ((u = is->next()) != 0)
    {// visit an adjacent vertex of s
        if (reach[u] == 0)    // u is an unreached vertex
        {// move to vertex u
            path[++length] = u; // add u to path
            if (u == destination || rFindPath(u))
                return true;
            // no path from u to destination
            length--;    // remove u from path
        }
    }
    delete is;
    return false;
}
```

Program 16.9 Recursive method to find a path in a graph

In an undirected graph the set C of vertices that are reachable from a vertex i, together with the edges that connect pairs of vertices in C, is a **connected component**. The undirected graph of Figure 16.1(b) has two connected components. One consists of the vertices $\{1,2,3\}$ and the edges $\{(1,2), (1,3)\}$, and the other consists of the remaining vertices and edges. In the **component-labeling problem**, we are to label the vertices of an undirected graph so that two vertices are assigned the same label iff they belong to the same component. In the example of Figure 16.1(b), vertices 1, 2, and 3 can be labeled 1, and the remaining vertices labeled 2.

We can label components by making repeated invocations of either a DFS or BFS. We start each invocation at an as-yet-unlabeled vertex and perform a search. For each search a new label is used to mark the vertices that are reached. So vertices that are in different components have different labels. The method graph::labelComponents (Program 16.11) solves the component-labeling problem. It returns the number of components in the undirected graph. The component labels are returned in the array c[1:n] where n is the number of vertices in the graph. We may use dfs in place of bfs in Program 16.11 and obtain the same results. The complexity of Program 16.11 is $O(n^2)$ when the graph is represented as an adjacency

```
bool connected()
{// Return true iff graph is connected.
   // make sure this is an undirected graph
   if (directed())
      throw undefinedMethod
      ("graph::connected() not defined for directed graphs");

   int n = numberOfVertices();

   reach = new int [n + 1];  // by default reach[i] = 0

   // mark vertices reachable from vertex 1
   dfs(1, reach, 1);

   // check if all vertices marked
   for (int i = 1; i <= n; i++)
      if (reach[i] == 0)
         return false;
   return true;
}
```

Program 16.10 Determine whether an undirected graph is connected

matrix and $O(n+e)$ when we use the linked-adjacency-list representation.

16.9.3   Spanning Trees

If a BFS is carried out starting from any vertex in a connected undirected graph
or network with n vertices, then from Theorem 16.1 we know that all vertices will
get labeled. Exactly n-1 of these vertices are reached in the inner while loop of
graph::bfs (Program 16.4). When a new vertex u is reached in this loop, the edge
used to reach u is (w,u). The set of edges used in the inner while loop to reach
previously unreached vertices is of size n-1. Since this set of edges contains a path
from v to every other vertex in the graph, it defines a connected subgraph, which
is a spanning tree of G.

Consider the graph of Figure 16.20(a). If a BFS is started at vertex 1, then
the edges {(1,2), (1,3), (1,4), (2,5), (4,6), (4,7), (5,8)} are used to reach previously unreached vertices. This set of edges corresponds to the spanning tree of
Figure 16.20(b).

A **breadth-first spanning tree** is any spanning tree obtained in the manner
just described from a BFS. We can verify that the spanning trees of Figures 16.20
(b), (c), and (d) are all breadth-first spanning trees of the graph of Figure 16.20

```
int labelComponents(int c[])
{// Label the components of an undirected graph.
 // Return the number of components.
 // Set c[i] to be the component number of vertex i.
    // make sure this is an undirected graph
    if (directed())
        throw undefinedMethod
        ("graph::labelComponents() not defined for directed graphs");

    int n = numberOfVertices();

    // assign all vertices to no component
    for (int i = 1; i <= n; i++)
        c[i] = 0;

    label = 0;  // ID of last component
    // identify components
    for (int i = 1; i <= n; i++)
        if (c[i] == 0)  // vertex i is unreached
        {// vertex i is in a new component
            label++;
            bfs(i, c, label); // mark new component
        }

    return label;
}
```

Program 16.11 Component labeling

(a); the start vertex for each BFS is the shaded node.

When a DFS is performed in a connected undirected graph or network, exactly $n-1$ edges are used to reach new vertices. The subgraph formed by these edges is also a spanning tree. Spanning trees obtained in this manner from a DFS are called **depth-first spanning trees**. Figure 16.21 shows some of the depth-first spanning trees of Figure 16.20(a). In each case the start vertex is vertex 1.

EXERCISES

45. Write a version of Program 16.8 that uses a BFS rather than a DFS. Show that this version finds a shortest path from theSource to theDestination.

46. For the graph of Figure 16.20(a), do the following:

Figure 16.20 A graph and some of its breadth-first spanning trees

(a) Draw a breadth-first spanning tree starting at vertex 3.

(b) Draw a breadth-first spanning tree starting at vertex 7.

(c) Draw a depth-first spanning tree starting at vertex 3.

(d) Draw a depth-first spanning tree starting at vertex 7.

47. Do Exercise 46 using the graph of Figure 16.4(a).

48. Write code for the method **graph::bfSpanningTree(theVertex)**, which finds a breadth-first spanning tree of a connected undirected graph by initiating a BFS at **theVertex**. Your code should return NULL if it fails because there is no spanning tree (i.e., the graph is not connected). When a spanning tree is found, your method should return an array of edges that make up the spanning tree. The data type of the edge array that is returned is **pair<int, int>**.

49. Do Exercise 48 for the case of **graph::dfSpanningTree(theVertex)**, which finds a depth-first spanning tree beginning at **theVertex**.

(a)   (b)

(c)   (d)

Figure 16.21 Some depth-first spanning trees of Figure 16.20(a)

50. Write code for the public method `graph::cycle()`, which determines whether an undirected graph has a cycle. Base your code on either a DFS or a BFS.

    (a) Prove the correctness of your code.

    (b) Determine the time and space complexities of your code.

51. Let G be an undirected graph. Write code for the method `graph::bipartite()`, which returns NULL if G is not a bipartite graph (see Example 16.3) and an integer array `label` if it is. When G is bipartite, the array `label` is a labeling of the vertices such that `label[i]` = 1 for vertices in one subset and `label[i]` = 2 for vertices in the other subset. The complexity of your code should be $O(n^2)$ if G has n vertices and is represented as a matrix and $O(n+e)$ if a linked list representation is used. Show that this is the case. (*Hint:* Perform several BFSs, each time beginning at an as-yet-unreached vertex. Assign this unreached vertex to set 1; vertices adjacent from this vertex are assigned to set 2, those adjacent to these set 2 vertices are assigned to set 1,

and so on. Also check for conflicting assignments, i.e., the set assignment of a vertex is changed.)

52. Let G be an undirected graph. Its **transitive closure** is a 0/1 valued array tc such that tc[i][j] $= 1$ iff G has a path with one or more edges from vertex i to vertex j. Write a method graph::undirectedTC() to compute and return the transitive closure of G. The time complexity of your method should be $O(n^2)$ where n is the number of vertices in G. (*Hint:* Use component labeling.)

53. Do Exercise 52 for graph::directedTC(), which is to be used when G is directed. What is the complexity of your algorithm?

CHAPTER 17

THE GREEDY METHOD

BIRD'S-EYE VIEW

Exit the world of data structures. Enter the world of algorithm-design methods. In the remainder of this book, we study methods for the design of good algorithms. Although the design of a good algorithm for any given problem is more an art than a science, some design methods are effective in solving many problems. You can apply these methods to computer problems and see how the resulting algorithm works. Generally, you must fine-tune the resulting algorithm to achieve acceptable performance. In some cases, however, fine-tuning is not possible, and you will have to think of some other way to solve the problem.

Chapters 17 through 21 present five basic algorithm-design methods: the greedy method, divide and conquer, dynamic programming, backtracking, and branch and bound. This list excludes several more advanced methods, such as linear programming, integer programming, neural networks, genetic algorithms, and simulated annealing, that are also widely used. These methods are typically covered in courses and texts dedicated to them.

This chapter begins by introducing the notion of an optimization problem. Next the greedy method, which is a very intuitive method, is described. Although it is usually quite easy to formulate a greedy algorithm for a problem, the formulated algorithm may not always produce an optimal answer. Therefore, *it is essential that we prove that our greedy algorithms actually work.* Even when greedy algorithms do not guarantee optimal answers, they remain useful, as they often get us answers that are close to optimal. We use the greedy method to obtain algorithms for the container-loading, knapsack, topological-ordering, bipartite-cover, shortest-path, and minimum-cost spanning-tree problems.

17.1   OPTIMIZATION PROBLEMS

Many of the examples used in this chapter and in the remaining chapters are **optimization problems**. In an optimization problem we are given a set of **constraints** and an **optimization function**. Solutions that satisfy the constraints are called **feasible solutions**. A feasible solution for which the optimization function has the best possible value is called an **optimal solution**.

Example 17.1 [Thirsty Baby] A very thirsty, and intelligent, baby wants to quench her thirst. She has access to a glass of water, a carton of milk, cans of various juices, and bottles and cans of various sodas. In all the baby has access to n different liquids. From past experience with these n liquids, the baby knows that some are more satisfying than others. In fact, the baby has assigned satisfaction values to each liquid. s_i units of satisfaction are obtained by drinking 1 ounce of the ith liquid.

Ordinarily, the baby would just drink enough of the liquid that gives her greatest satisfaction per ounce and thereby quench her thirst in the most satisfying way. Unfortunately, there isn't enough of this most satisfying liquid available. Let a_i be the amount in ounces of liquid i that is available. The baby needs to drink a total of t ounces to quench her thirst. How much of each available liquid should she drink?

We may assume that satisfaction is additive. Let x_i denote the amount of liquid i that the baby should drink. The solution to her problem is obtained by finding real numbers x_i, $1 \le i \le n$ that maximize $\sum_{i=1}^{n} s_i x_i$ subject to the constraints $\sum_{i=1}^{n} x_i = t$ and $0 \le x_i \le a_i$, $1 \le i \le n$.

Note that if $\sum_{i=1}^{n} a_i < t$, then there is no solution to the baby's problem. Even if she drinks all the liquids available, she will be unable to quench her thirst.

This precise mathematical formulation of the problem provides an unambiguous specification of what the program is to do. Having obtained this formulation, we can provide the input/output specification, which takes the form:

[Input] n, t, s_i, a_i, $1 \le i \le n$. n is an integer, and the remaining numbers are positive reals.

[Output] Real numbers x_i, $1 \le i \le n$, such that $\sum_{i=1}^{n} s_i x_i$ is maximum, $\sum_{i=1}^{n} x_i = t$, and $0 \le x_i \le a_i$, $1 \le i \le n$. Output a suitable message if $\sum_{i=1}^{n} a_i < t$.

The constraints are $\sum_{i=1}^{n} x_i = t$ and $0 \le x_i \le a_i$, and the optimization function is $\sum_{i=1}^{n} s_i x_i$. Every set of x_is that satisfies the constraints is a feasible solution. Every feasible solution that maximizes $\sum_{i=1}^{n} s_i x_i$ is an optimal solution.   ∎

Example 17.2 [Loading Problem] A large snip is to be loaded with cargo. The cargo is containerized, and all containers are the same size. Different containers may have different weights. Let w_i be the weight of the ith container, $1 \leq i \leq n$. The cargo capacity of the ship is c. We wish to load the ship with the maximum number of containers.

This problem can be formulated as an optimization problem in the following way: Let x_i be a variable whose value can be either 0 or 1. If we set x_i to 0, then container i is not to be loaded. If x_i is 1, then the container is to be loaded. We wish to assign values to the x_is that satisfy the constraints $\sum_{i=1}^{n} w_i x_i \leq c$ and $x_i \in \{0, 1\}$, $1 \leq i \leq n$. The optimization function is $\sum_{i=1}^{n} x_i$.

Every set of x_is that satisfies the constraints is a feasible solution. Every feasible solution that maximizes $\sum_{i=1}^{n} x_i$ is an optimal solution.   ∎

Example 17.3 [Minimum-Cost Communication Network] We introduced this problem in Example 16.2. The set of cities and possible communication links can be represented as an undirected graph. Each edge has a cost (or weight) assigned to it. This cost is the cost of constructing the link represented by the edge. Every connected subgraph that includes all the vertices represents a feasible solution. Under the assumption that all weights are nonnegative, the set of feasible solutions can be narrowed to the set of spanning trees of the graph. An optimal solution is a spanning tree with minimum cost.

In this problem we need to select a subset of the edges. This subset must satisfy the following constraint: *The set of selected edges forms a spanning tree.* The optimization function is the sum of the weights of the selected edges.   ∎

17.2   THE GREEDY METHOD

In the **greedy method** we attempt to construct an optimal solution in stages. At each stage we make a decision that appears to be the best (under some criterion) at the time. A decision made in one stage is not changed in a later stage, so each decision should assure feasibility. The criterion used to make the greedy decision at each stage is called the **greedy criterion**.

Example 17.4 [Change Making] A child buys candy valued at less than $1 and gives a $1 bill to the cashier. The cashier wishes to return change using the fewest number of coins. Assume that an unlimited supply of quarters, dimes, nickels, and pennies is available. The cashier constructs the change in stages. In each stage a coin is added to the change. This coin is selected using the greedy criterion: *At each stage increase the total amount of change constructed by as much as possible.* To assure feasibility (i.e., the change given exactly equals the desired amount) of the solution, the selected coin should not cause the total amount of change given so far to exceed the final desired amount.

Suppose that 67 cents in change is due the child. The first two coins selected are quarters. A quarter cannot be selected for the third coin because such a selection results in an infeasible selection of coins (change exceeds 67 cents). The third coin selected is a dime, then a nickel is selected, and finally two pennies are added to the change.

The greedy method has intuitive appeal in that we construct the change by using a strategy that our intuition tells us should result in the fewest (or at least close to the fewest) number of coins being given out. We can actually prove that the greedy algorithm just described does indeed generate change with the fewest number of coins (see Exercise 1).   ∎

Example 17.5 [Machine Scheduling] You are given n tasks and an infinite supply of machines on which these tasks can be performed. Each task has a start time s_i and a finish time f_i, $s_i < f_i$. $[s_i, f_i]$ is the processing interval for task i. Two tasks i and j overlap iff their processing intervals overlap at a point other than the interval start or end. For example, the interval $[1, 4]$ overlaps with $[2, 4]$, but not with $[4, 7]$. A **feasible** task-to-machine assignment is an assignment in which no machine is assigned two overlapping tasks. Therefore, in a feasible assignment each machine works on at most one task at any time. An **optimal assignment** is a feasible assignment that utilizes the fewest number of machines.

Suppose we have $n = 7$ tasks labeled a through g and that their start and finish times are as shown in Figure 17.1(a). The following task-to-machine assignment is a feasible assignment that utilizes seven machines: Assign task a to machine $M1$, task b to machine $M2$, $\cdots$, task g to machine $M7$. This assignment is not an optimal assignment because other assignments use fewer machines. For example, we can assign tasks a, b, and d to the same machine, reducing the number of utilized machines to five.

A greedy way to obtain an optimal task assignment is to assign the tasks in stages, one task per stage and in nondecreasing order of task start times. Call a machine **old** if at least one task has been assigned to it. If a machine is not old, it is **new**. For machine selection, use the greedy criterion: *If an old machine becomes available by the start time of the task to be assigned, assign the task to this machine; if not, assign it to a new machine.*

For the data of Figure 17.1(a), the tasks in nondecreasing order of task start time are a, f, b, c, g, e, d. The greedy algorithm assigns tasks to machines in this order. The algorithm has $n = 7$ stages, and in each stage one task is assigned to a machine. Stage 1 has no old machines, so a is assigned to a new machine (say, $M1$). This machine is now busy from time 0 to time 2 (see Figure 17.1(b)). In stage 2 task f is considered. Since the only old machine is busy when task f is to start, it is assigned to a new machine (say, $M2$). When task b is considered in stage 3, we find that the old machine $M1$ is free at time $s_b = 3$, so b is assigned to $M1$. The availability time for $M1$ becomes $f_b = 7$, and that for M_2 is $f_f = 5$. In stage 4 task c is considered. Since neither of the old machines is available at time $s_c = 4$, task c is assigned to a new machine (say, $M3$). The availability time of this machine becomes $f_c = 7$. Task g is considered in stage 5 and assigned to machine $M2$, which is the first to become available. Task e is assigned in stage 6 to machine

task	a	b	c	d	e	f	g
start	0	3	4	9	7	1	6
finish	2	7	7	11	10	5	8

(a) Seven tasks

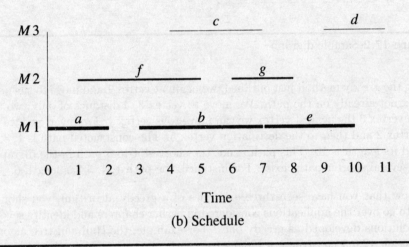

(b) Schedule

Figure 17.1 Tasks and a three-machine schedule

$M1$ or $M3$ (assume it is assigned to $M1$), and finally, in stage 7, task d is assigned to machine $M2$ or $M3$ (Figure 17.1(b) assumes task d is assigned to $M3$).

The proof that the described greedy algorithm generates optimal assignments is left as an exercise (Exercise 7). The algorithm may be implemented to have complexity $O(n \log n)$ by sorting the tasks in nondecreasing order of s_i, using an $O(n \log n)$ sort (such as heap sort) and then using a min heap of availability times for the old machines. ∎

Example 17.6 [Shortest Path] You are given a directed network as in Figure 17.2. The length of a path is defined to be the sum of the costs of the edges on the path. You are to find a shortest path from a start vertex s to a destination vertex d.

A greedy way to construct such a path is to do so in stages. In each stage a vertex is added to the path. Suppose that the path built so far ends at vertex q and q is not the destination vertex d. The vertex to add in the next stage is obtained using the greedy criterion: *Select a nearest vertex adjacent from q that is not already on the path.*

This greedy method does not necessarily obtain a shortest path. For example, suppose we wish to construct a shortest path from vertex 1 to vertex 5 in Figure 17.2.

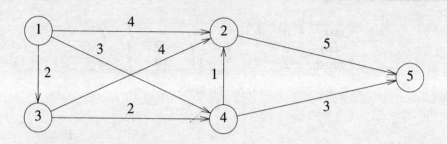

Figure 17.2 Sample digraph

Using the greedy method just outlined, we begin at vertex 1 and move to the nearest vertex not already on the path. We move to vertex 3, a distance of only two units. From vertex 3 the nearest vertex we can move to is vertex 4. From vertex 4 we move to vertex 2 and then to the destination vertex 5. The constructed path is 1, 3, 4, 2, 5, and its length is 10. This path is not the shortest 1-to-5 path in the digraph. In fact, several shorter paths exist. For instance, the path 1, 4, 5 has length 6.   ■

Now that you have seen three examples of a greedy algorithm, you should be able to go over the applications considered in earlier chapters and identify several of the solutions developed as greedy ones. For example, the Huffman tree algorithm of Section 12.6.3 constructs a binary tree with minimum weighted external path length in $n - 1$ stages. In each stage two binary trees are combined to create a new binary tree. This algorithm uses the greedy criterion: Of the available binary trees, combine two with the least weight.

The LPT-scheduling (longest processing time first) rule of Section 12.6.2 is a greedy one. It schedules the n jobs in n stages. First the jobs are ordered by length. Then in each stage a machine is selected for the next job. The machine is selected using the greedy criterion: *Minimize the length of the schedule constructed so far.* This criterion translates into scheduling the job on the machine on which it finishes first. This machine is also the machine that becomes idle first.

Notice that in the case of the machine-scheduling problem of Section 12.6.2, the greedy algorithm does not guarantee optimal solutions. However, it is intuitively appealing and generally produces solutions that are very close in value to the optimal. It uses a rule of thumb that we might expect a human machine scheduler to use in a real scheduling environment. Algorithms that do not guarantee optimal solutions but generally produce solutions that are close to optimal are called **heuristics**. So the LPT method is a heuristic for machine scheduling. Theorem 9.2 states a bound between the finish time of LPT schedules and optimal schedules, so the LPT heuristic has **bounded performance**. A heuristic with bounded performance is an **approximation algorithm**.

Section 13.5.1 stated several bounded performance heuristics (i.e., approximation algorithms) for the bin-packing problem. Each of these heuristics is a greedy heuristic. The LPT method of Section 12.6.2 is also a greedy heuristic. All these heuristics have intuitive appeal and, in practice, yield solutions much closer to optimal than suggested by the bounds given in that section.

The rest of this chapter presents several applications of the greedy method. In some applications the result is an algorithm that always obtains an optimal solution. In others the algorithm is just a heuristic that may or may not be an approximation algorithm.

EXERCISES

1. Show that the greedy algorithm for the change-making problem (Example 17.4) generates change with the fewest number of coins when the cashier has an unlimited supply of quarters, dimes, nickels, and pennies.

2. Consider the change-making problem of Example 17.4. Suppose that the cashier has only a limited number of quarters, dimes, nickels, and pennies. Formulate a greedy solution to the change-making problem. Does your algorithm always use the fewest number of coins? Prove your result.

3. Extend the algorithm of Example 17.4 to the case when the cashier has $100, $50, $20, $10, $5, and $1 bills in addition to coins and a customer gives u dollars and v cents as payment toward a purchase of x dollars and y cents. Does your algorithm always generate change with the fewest total number of bills and coins? Prove this.

4. Write a C++ program implementing the change-making solution of Example 17.4. Assume that the cashier has bills in the denominations $100, $50, $20, $10, $5, and $1 in addition to coins. Your program should include a method to input the purchase amount and the amount given by the customer as well as a method to output the amount of change and a breakdown by denomination.

5. Suppose that some country has coins in the denominations 14, 12, 5, and 1 cents. Will the greedy method of Example 17.4 always generate change with the fewest number of coins? Prove your answer.

6. (a) Show that the greedy algorithm of Example 17.5 always finds an optimal task assignment.

   (b) Program your algorithm so that its complexity is $O(n \log n)$; n is the number of tasks.

7. Consider the machine-scheduling problem of Example 17.5. Assume that only one machine is available and that we are to select the largest number of tasks that can be scheduled on this machine. For the example, the largest task

selection is $\{a, b, e\}$. A greedy algorithm for this task-selection problem would select the tasks in stages. In each stage one task is selected using the following criterion: *From the remaining tasks, select the one that has the least finish time and does not overlap with any of the already selected tasks.*

(a) Show that this greedy algorithm obtains optimal selections.

(b) Develop an $O(n \log n)$ implementation of this algorithm. (*Hint:* Use a min heap of finish times.)

17.3   APPLICATIONS

17.3.1   Container Loading

A Greedy Solution

The terminology is from Example 17.2. The ship may be loaded in stages; one container per stage. At each stage we need to decide which container to load. For this decision we may use the greedy criterion: *From the remaining containers, select the one with least weight.* This order of selection will keep the total weight of the selected containers minimum and hence leave maximum capacity for loading more containers. Using the greedy algorithm just outlined, we first select the container that has least weight, then the one with the next smallest weight, and so on until either all containers have been loaded or there isn't enough capacity for the next one.

Example 17.7 Suppose that $n = 8$, $[w_1, \cdots, w_8] = [100, 200, 50, 90, 150, 50, 20, 80]$, and $c = 400$. When the greedy algorithm is used, the containers are considered for loading in the order 7, 3, 6, 8, 4, 1, 5, 2. Containers 7, 3, 6, 8, 4, and 1 together weigh 390 units and are loaded. The available capacity is now 10 units, which is inadequate for any of the remaining containers. In the greedy solution we have $[x_1, \cdots, x_8] = [1, 0, 1, 1, 0, 1, 1, 1]$ and $\sum x_i = 6$.   ∎

Correctness of Greedy Algorithm

Theorem 17.1 *The greedy algorithm generates optimal loadings.*

Proof Let $x = [x_1, \cdots, x_n]$ be the solution produced by the greedy algorithm and let $y = [y_1, \cdots, y_n]$ be any feasible solution. We will show that $\sum_{i=1}^{n} x_i \geq \sum_{i=1}^{n} y_i$. Without loss of generality we may assume that the containers have been ordered so that $w_i \leq w_{i+1}$, $1 \leq i < n$. From the way the greedy algorithm works, we know that there is a k, $0 \leq k \leq n$ such that $x_i = 1$, $i \leq k$, and $x_i = 0$, $i > k$.

We use induction on the number p of positions i such that $x_i \neq y_i$. For the induction base, we see that when $p = 0$, x and y are the same. So $\sum_{i=1}^{n} x_i \geq$

$\sum_{i=1}^{n} y_i$. For the induction hypothesis, let m be an arbitrary natural number and assume that $\sum_{i=1}^{n} x_i \geq \sum_{i=1}^{n} y_i$ whenever $p \leq m$.

In the induction step, we show that $\sum_{i=1}^{n} x_i \geq \sum_{i=1}^{n} y_i$ when $p = m + 1$. Find the least integer j, $1 \leq j \leq n$, such that $x_j \neq y_j$. Since $p \neq 0$, such a j exists. Also, $j \leq k$, as otherwise y is not a feasible solution. Since $x_j \neq y_j$ and $x_j = 1$, $y_j = 0$. Set y_j to 1.

If the resulting y is a feasible solution, let z denote the·resulting y. If the resulting y denotes an infeasible solution, there must be an l in the range $[k+1, n]$ for which $y_l = 1$. Set y_l to 0. Let z denote the resulting y. As $w_j \leq w_l$, z is a feasible loading.

In either case, $\sum_{i=1}^{n} z_i \geq \sum_{i=1}^{n} y_i$, and z differs from x in at most $p - 1 = m$ positions. From the induction hypothesis, it follows that $\sum_{i=1}^{n} x_i \geq \sum_{i=1}^{n} z_i, \geq \sum_{i=1}^{n} y_i$. ■

C++ Implementation

Program 17.1 gives the C++ code for the greedy container-loading algorithm since the greedy method loads containers in increasing order of their weight. The data type `container`, which has the integer data members `id` (an identifier in the range 1 through number of containers) and `weight` (container weight), defines a type conversion to `int` that simply returns the `weight` field. Because of this type conversion, when objects of type `container` are compared, this comparison is done by container weight.

Program 17.1 begins by sorting the containers by weights using the heap sort method (Program 12.8). Following the sort, containers are loaded in increasing order of weight. The sort takes $O(n \log n)$ time, where n is the number of containers. Since the remainder of the algorithm takes $O(n)$ time, the overall time complexity of Program 17.1 is $O(n \log n)$.

17.3.2   0/1 Knapsack Problem

Problem Description

In the 0/1 knapsack problem, we wish to pack a knapsack (bag or sack) with a capacity of c. From a list of n items, we must select the items that are to be packed into the knapsack. Each object i has a weight w_i and a profit p_i. In a feasible knapsack packing, the sum of the weights of the packed objects does not exceed the knapsack capacity. An optimal packing is a feasible one with maximum profit. The problem formulation is

$$\text{maximize} \sum_{i=1}^{n} p_i x_i$$

```
void containerLoading(container* c, int capacity,
                      int numberOfContainers, int x)
{// Greedy algorithm for container loading.
 // Set x[i] = 1 iff container i, i >= 1 is loaded.
   // sort into increasing order of weight
   heapSort(c, numberOfContainers);

   int n = numberOfContainers;

   // initialize x
   for (int i = 1; i <= n; i++)
      x[i] = 0;

   // select containers in order of weight
   for (int i = 1; i <= n && c[i].weight <= capacity; i++)
   {// enough capacity for container c[i].id
      x[c[i].id] = 1;
      capacity -= c[i].weight;   // remaining capacity
   }
}
```

Program 17.1 Loading containers

subject to the constraints

$$\sum_{i=1}^{n} w_i x_i \leq c \text{ and } x_i \in \{0,1\}, \ 1 \leq i \leq n$$

In this formulation we are to find the values of x_i. $x_i = 1$ means that object i is packed into the knapsack, and $x_i = 0$ means that object i is not packed. The 0/1 knapsack problem is really a generalization of the container-loading problem to the case where the profit earned from each container is different. In the context of the knapsack problem, the ship is the *knapsack*, and the containers are *objects* that may be packed into the knapsack.

Example 17.8 You are the first-prize winner in a grocery-store contest, and the prize is a free cart load of groceries. There are n different items available in the store, and the contest rules stipulate that you can pick at most one of each. The cart has a capacity of c, and item i takes up w_i amount of cart space. The cost of item i is p_i. Your objective is to fill the cart with groceries that have the maximum value. Of course, you cannot exceed the cart capacity, and you cannot take two of any item. The problem may be modeled by using the 0/1 knapsack formulation.

The cart corresponds to the knapsack, and the available grocery items correspond to the objects. ∎

Possible Greedy Strategies

Several greedy strategies for the 0/1 knapsack problem are possible. In each of these strategies, the knapsack is packed in several stages. In each stage one object is selected for inclusion into the knapsack using a greedy criterion. One possibility for this greedy criterion is as follows: *From the remaining objects, select the object with maximum profit that fits into the knapsack.* Using this criterion, the object with the largest profit is packed first (provided enough capacity is available), then the one with next largest profit, and so on. This strategy does not guarantee an optimal solution. For instance, consider the case $n = 3$, $w = [100, 10, 10]$, $p = [20, 15, 15]$, and $c = 105$. When we are greedy on profit, we obtain the solution $x = [1, 0, 0]$. The total profit from this solution is 20. The optimal solution is $[0, 1, 1]$. This solution has profit 30.

An alternative is to be greedy on weight. This time we use the following selection criterion: *From the remaining objects, select the one that has minimum weight and also fits into the knapsack.* Although the use of this criterion yields an optimal solution for the preceding instance, it does not do so in general. Consider the instance $n = 2$, $w = [10, 20]$, $p = [5, 100]$, and $c = 25$. When we are greedy on weight, we obtain the solution $x = [1, 0]$, which is inferior to the solution $[0, 1]$.

Yet another possibility is to be greedy on the profit density p_i/w_i. The new selection criterion is as follows: *From the remaining objects, select the one with maximum p_i/w_i that fits into the knapsack.* This strategy does not guarantee optimal solutions either. For example, try this strategy on the instance $n = 3$, $w = [20, 15, 15]$, $p = [40, 25, 25]$, and $c = 30$.

Greedy Heuristics

We should not be too disheartened that none of the considered greedy algorithms can guarantee optimal solutions. The 0/1 knapsack problem is an NP-hard problem (see Section 12.6.2 for a discussion of NP-hard problems), and we probably cannot find a polynomial-time algorithm that solves it. Although packing a knapsack in nonincreasing order of the ratio p_i/w_i does not guarantee an optimal packing, this approach is intuitively appealing. We expect it to be a good heuristic and produce solutions that are very close to optimal most of the time. In an experiment that involved 600 randomly generated knapsack instances, this greedy heuristic generated optimal solutions for 239. For 583 instances the generated solution had a value within 10 percent of optimal, and all 600 solutions were within 25 percent of optimal. Quite an impressive performance by an algorithm that runs in $O(n \log n)$ time.

We may ask whether the greedy heuristic guarantees solutions that have a value that is within x percent of the optimal value for some x, $x < 100$. The answer is no. To see this, consider the instance $n = 2$, $w = [1, y]$, $p = [10, 9y]$, and $c = y$. The greedy solution is $x = [1, 0]$. This solution has value 10. For $y \geq 10/9$, the optimal solution has value $9y$. Therefore, the value of the greedy solution is $(9y - 10)/(9y) * 100$ percent away from the optimal value. For large y this value approaches 100 percent.

We can modify the greedy heuristic to provide solutions within x percent of optimal for $x < 100$. First we place a subset of at most k objects into the knapsack. If this subset has weight greater than c, we discard it. Otherwise, the remaining capacity is filled by considering the remaining objects in decreasing order of p_i/w_i. The best solution obtained considering all possible subsets with at most k objects is the solution generated by the heuristic.

Example 17.9 Consider the knapsack instance $n = 4$, $w = [2, 4, 6, 7]$, $p = [6, 10, 12, 13]$, and $c = 11$. When $k = 0$, the knapsack is filled in nonincreasing order of profit density. First we place object 1 into the knapsack, then object 2. The capacity that remains at this time is five units. None of the remaining objects fits, and the solution $x = [1, 1, 0, 0]$ is produced. The profit earned from this solution is 16.

Let us now try the greedy heuristic with $k = 1$. The subsets to begin with are $\{1\}$, $\{2\}$, $\{3\}$, and $\{4\}$. The subsets $\{1\}$ and $\{2\}$ yield the same solution as obtained with $k = 0$. When the subset $\{3\}$ is considered, x_3 is set to 1. Five units of capacity remain, and we attempt to use this capacity by considering the remaining objects in nonincreasing order of profit density. Object 1 is considered first. It fits, and x_1 is set to 1. At this time only three units of capacity remain, and none of the remaining objects can be added to the knapsack. The solution obtained when we begin with the subset $\{3\}$ in the knapsack is $x = [1, 0, 1, 0]$. The profit earned from this solution is 18. When we begin with the subset 4, we produce the solution $x = [1, 0, 0, 1]$ that has a profit value of 19. The best solution obtained considering subsets of size 0 and 1 is $[1, 0, 0, 1]$. This solution is produced by the greedy heuristic when $k = 1$.

If $k = 2$, then in addition to the subsets considered for $k < 2$, we need to consider the subsets $\{1, 2\}$, $\{1, 3\}$, $\{1, 4\}$, $\{2, 3\}$, $\{2, 4\}$, and $\{3, 4\}$. The last of these subsets represents an infeasible starting point and is discarded. For the remaining, the solutions obtained are $[1, 1, 0, 0]$, $[1, 0, 1, 0]$, $[1, 0, 0, 1]$, $[0, 1, 1, 0]$, and $[0, 1, 0, 1]$. The last of these solutions has the profit value 23, which is higher than that obtained from the subsets of size 0 and 1. This solution is therefore the solution produced by the heuristic. ∎

The solution produced by the modified greedy heuristic is $k - optimal$. That is, if we remove up to k objects from the solution and put back up to k, the new solution is no better than the original. Further, the value of a solution obtained in this manner comes within $100/(k + 1)$ percent of optimal. Therefore, we refer to this heuristic as a *bounded performance* heuristic. When $k = 1$, the solutions are guaranteed to have value within 50 percent of optimal; when $k = 2$, they are guaranteed to have value within 33.33 percent of optimal; and so on. The run time of the bounded performance heuristic increases with k. The number of subsets to be tried is $O(n^k)$, and $O(n)$ time is spent on each. Also, $O(n \log n)$ time is needed to order the objects by p_i/w_i. So the total time taken is $O(n^{k+1})$ when $k > 0$.

The observed performance is far better than suggested by the worst-case bounds. Figure 17.3 summarizes the results of 600 random tests.

k	0	Percent Deviation			
	0	1%	5%	10%	25%
0	239	390	528	583	600
1	360	527	598	600	
2	483	581	600		

Figure 17.3 Number of solutions within x percent out of 600

17.3.3   Topological Sorting

Problem Description

Often a complex project may be decomposed into a collection of simpler tasks with the property that the completion of all these tasks implies that the project has been completed. For example, the automobile-assembly project may be decomposed into these tasks: place chassis on assembly line, mount axles, mount wheels onto axles, fit seats onto chassis, paint, install brakes, install doors, and so on. A precedence relation exists between certain pairs of tasks. For example, the chassis must be placed on the assembly line before we can mount the axles. The set of tasks together with the precedences may be represented as a digraph—called an **activity on vertex** (AOV) network. The vertices of this digraph represent the tasks, and the directed edge (i, j) denotes the following precedence: Task i must complete before task j can start. A six-task project appears in Figure 17.4. The edge (1,4) implies that task 1 is to be done before task 4. Similarly, the edge (4,6) implies that task 4 is to be done before task 6. The edges (1,4) and (4,6) together imply that task 1 is to be done before task 6. So the precedence relation is transitive. As a result of this observation, we see that the edge (1,4) is redundant, as the edges (1,3) and (3,4) imply (1,4).

In many situations we must perform the tasks consecutively, for example, to solve the automobile-assembly problem or to put together a consumer product (bicycle, child's swing set, lawn mower, etc.) labeled "some assembly required." We perform the assembly tasks in a sequence dictated by the accompanying instructions. This sequence has the property that for every edge (i, j) in the task digraph for the assembly project, task i comes before task j in the assembly sequence. Sequences that satisfy this property are **topological orders** or **topological sequences**, and

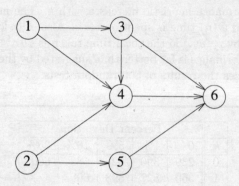

Figure 17.4 A task digraph

the process of constructing a topological order from a task digraph is **topological sorting**.

The task digraph of Figure 17.4 has several topological orders. Three of these orders are 123456, 132456, and 215346. The sequence 142356 is not a topological order, as (for example) task 4 precedes task 3 in this sequence, whereas the task digraph contains the edge (3,4). This sequence violates the precedence dictated by this edge (and others).

A Greedy Solution

We may formulate a greedy algorithm to construct a topological order or sequence. This algorithm constructs the sequence from left to right in stages. In each stage we add a vertex to the sequence. We select the new vertex using the greedy criterion: *From the remaining vertices, select a vertex w that has no incoming edge (v, w) with the property that v hasn't already been placed into the sequence.* Notice that if we add a vertex w that violates this criterion (i.e., the digraph has an edge (v, w) and vertex v is not part of the constructed sequence), then we cannot complete the sequence in a topological order, as vertex v will necessarily come after vertex w. A high-level statement of the greedy algorithm appears in Figure 17.5. Each iteration of the **while** loop represents a stage of the greedy algorithm.

Let us try out this algorithm on the digraph of Figure 17.4. We start with an empty sequence *theOrder*. In the first stage we select the first vertex for *theOrder*. The digraph has two candidate vertices, 1 and 2, for the first position in the sequence. If we select vertex 2, the sequence becomes *theOrder* = 2 and stage 1 is complete. In stage 2 we select the second vertex for *theOrder*. Applying the greedy criterion with *theOrder* = 2, we see that the candidate vertices are 1 and 5. If we select vertex 5, then *theOrder* = 25. For the next stage vertex 1 is the only candidate for w. Following stage 3 *theOrder* = 251. In stage 4 vertex 3 is the only

Let n be the number of vertices in the digraph.
Let *theOrder* be an empty sequence.
```
while (true)
{
```
   Let w be any vertex that has no incoming edge (v, w) such that v is not in
   theOrder.
   if there is no such w, **break**.
   Add w to the end of *theOrder*.
```
}
```
if (*theOrder* has fewer than n vertices)
   the algorithm fails.
else
   theOrder is a topological sequence.

Figure 17.5 Topological sorting

candidate for w. Thus we add vertex 3 to *theOrder* to get *theOrder* $= 2513$. In
the next two stages, we add vertices 4 and 6 to get *theOrder* $= 251346$.

Correctness of the Greedy Algorithm

To establish the correctness of the greedy algorithm, we need to show (1) that when
the algorithm fails, the digraph has no topological sequence and (2) that when the
algorithm doesn't fail, *theOrder* is, in fact, a topological sequence. Item (2) is a
direct consequence of the greedy criterion used to select the next vertex. For (1) we
show in Lemma 17.1 that when the algorithm fails, the digraph has a cycle. When
the digraph has a cycle, $q_j q_j + 1 \cdots q_k q_j$, there can be no topological order, as the
sequence of precedences defined by the cycle implies that q_j must finish before q_j
can start.

Lemma 17.1 *If the algorithm of Figure 17.5 fails, the digraph has a cycle.*

Proof Note that upon failure $|theOrder| < n$ and there are no candidates for
inclusion in *theOrder*. So there is at least one vertex, q_1, that is not in *theOrder*.
The digraph must contain an edge (q_2, q_1) where q_2 is not in *theOrder*; otherwise,
q_1 is a candidate for inclusion in *theOrder*. Similarly, there must be an edge (q_3, q_2)
such that q_3 is not in *theOrder*. If $q_3 = q_1$, then $q_1 q_2 q_3$ is a cycle in the digraph. If
$q_3 \neq q_1$, there must be a q_4 such that (q_4, q_3) is an edge and q_4 is not in *theOrder*;
otherwise, q_3 is a candidate for inclusion in *theOrder*. If q_4 is one of q_1, q_2, or
q_3, then again the digraph has a cycle. Since the digraph has a finite number n of
vertices, continued application of this argument will eventually detect a cycle. ∎

Selection of Data Structur

To refine the algorithm of Figure 17.5 into C++ code, we must decide on a representation for the sequence *theOrder*, as well as how to detect candidates for inclusion into *theOrder*. An efficient implementation results if we represent *theOrder* as a one-dimensional array; use a stack to keep track of all vertices that are candidates for inclusion into *theOrder*; and use a one-dimensional array inDegree such that inDegree[j] is the number of vertices i for which (i, j) is an edge of the digraph and i is not a member of *theOrder*. A vertex j becomes a candidate for inclusion in *theOrder* when inDegree[j] becomes 0. *theOrder* is initially the empty sequence, and inDegree[j] is simply the in-degree of vertex j. Each time we add a vertex to x, inDegree[j] decreases by 1 for all j that are adjacent from the added vertex.

For the digraph of Figure 17.4, inDegree[1:6] $= [0, 0, 1, 3, 1, 3]$ in the beginning. Vertices 1 and 2 are candidates for inclusion in *theOrder*, as their inDegree value is 0. Therefore, we start with 1 and 2 on the stack. In each stage we remove a vertex from the stack and add that vertex to *theOrder*. We also reduce the inDegree values of the vertices that are adjacent from the vertex just added to *theOrder*. If vertex 2 is removed from the stack and added to *theOrder* in stage 1, we get theOrder[0] $= 2$ and inDegree[1:6] $= [0, 0, 1, 2, 0, 3]$. Since inDegree[5] has just become 0, it is added to the stack.

C++ Implementation

Program 17.2 gives the resulting C++ code. This code is defined as a method of the abstract class graph (Program 16.1). Consequently, it can be used for digraphs with and without edge weights. The method topologicalOrder returns true if a topological order is found and false if the input digraph does not have a topological order. When a topological order is found, the order is returned in theOrder[0:n-1], where n is the number of vertices in the digraph.

Complexity Analysis

The total time spent in the first for loop is $O(n^2)$ if we use an adjacency-matrix representation and $O(n+e)$ if we use a linked-adjacency-list representation. Here n is the number of vertices and e is the number of edges. The second for loop takes $O(n)$ time. Of the two nested while loops, the outer one is iterated at most n times. Each iteration adds a vertex nextVertex to theOrder and initiates the inner while loop. When adjacency matrices are used, this inner while loop takes $O(n)$ time for each nextVertex. When we use linked adjacency lists, this loop takes $d_{nextVertex}^{out}$ time. Therefore, the time spent on the inner while loop is either $O(n^2)$ or $O(n+e)$. Hence the complexity of Program 17.2 is $O(n^2)$ when we use adjacency matrices and $O(n+e)$ when we use linked adjacency lists.

```
bool topologicalOrder(int *theOrder)
{// Return false iff the digraph has no topological order.
 // theOrder[0:n-1] is set to a topological order when
 // such an order exists.

   // code to verify that *this is a digraph comes here

   int n = numberOfVertices();
   // compute in-degrees
   int *inDegree = new int [n + 1];
   fill(inDegree + 1, inDegree + n + 1, 0);
   for (int i = 1; i <= n; i++)
   {// edges out of vertex i
      vertexIterator<T> *ii = iterator(i);
      int u;
      while ((u = ii->next()) != 0)
         // visit an adjacent vertex of i
         inDegree[u]++;
   }
   // stack vertices with zero in-degree
   arrayStack<int> stack;
   for (int i = 1; i <= n; i++)
      if (inDegree[i] == 0)
         stack.push(i);
   // generate topological order
   int j = 0;  // cursor for array theOrder
   while (!stack.empty())
   {// select from stack
      int nextVertex = stack.top();
      stack.pop();
      theOrder[j++] = nextVertex;
      // update in-degrees
      vertexIterator<T> *iNextVertex = iterator(nextVertex);
      int u;
      while ((u = iNextVertex->next()) != 0)
      {// visit an adjacent vertex of nextVertex
         inDegree[u]--;
         if (inDegree[u] == 0)
            stack.push(u);
      }
   }
   return (j == n);
}
```

Program 17.2 Topological sorting

17.3.4   Bipartite Cover

Problem Description

A bipartite graph (see Example 16.3) is an undirected graph in which the n vertices may be partitioned into two sets A and B so that no edge in the graph connects two vertices that are in the same set (i.e., every edge in the graph has one endpoint in A and the other in B). A subset A' of the set A is said to **cover** the set B (or simply, A' is a cover) iff every vertex in B is connected to at least one vertex of A'. The size of the cover A' is the number of vertices in A'. A' is a minimum cover iff A has no subset of smaller size that covers B.

Example 17.10 Consider the 17-vertex bipartite graph of Figure 17.6. $A = \{1, 2, 3, 16, 17\}$, and $B = \{4, 5, 6, 7, 8, 9, 10, 11, 12, 13, 14, 15\}$. The subset $A' = \{1, 2, 3, 17\}$ covers the set B. Its size is 4. The subset $A' = \{1, 16, 17\}$ also covers B and is of size 3. A has no subset of size less than 3 that covers B. Therefore, $A' = \{1, 16, 17\}$ is a minimum cover of B. ∎

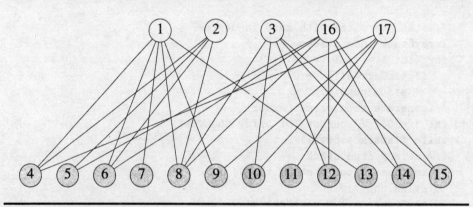

Figure 17.6 Figure for Example 17.10

We will refer to the problem of finding a minimum cover in a bipartite graph as the **bipartite-cover** problem. In the context of Example 16.3, a minimum cover is useful because it identifies the fewest number of interpreters who can handle the translations at the convention. The bipartite-cover problem is identical to the **set-cover** problem. In this latter problem we are given a collection $S = \{S_1, S_2, \cdots, S_k\}$ of k sets. The members of each set S_i are from the universe U. A subset S' of S covers U iff $\cup_{i \in S'} S_i = U$. The number of sets in S' is the size of the cover, and S' is a minimum cover iff there is no cover of U of smaller size. We can transform the set-cover problem into the bipartite-cover problem (and vice versa) by using the vertices in A to represent the sets $S_1, \cdots, S_k$ and the vertices in B to represent the elements of the universe U. An edge exists between a vertex in A and one in B iff the corresponding element of U is in the corresponding set of S.

Example 17.11 Let $S = \{S_1, \cdots, S_5\}$, $U = \{4, 5, \cdots, 15\}$, $S_1 = \{4, 6, 7, 8, 9, 13\}$, $S_2 = \{4, 5, 6, 8\}$, $S_3 = \{8, 10, 12, 14, 15\}$, $S_4 = \{5, 6, 8, 12, 14, 15\}$, and $S_5 = \{4, 9, 10, 11\}$. $S' = \{S_1, S_4, S_5\}$ is a cover of size 3. No smaller cover exists, so it is a minimum cover. The set-cover instance may be mapped into the bipartite graph of Figure 17.6 using vertices 1, 2, 3, 16, and 17 to represent sets S_1, S_2, S_3, S_4, and S_5, respectively. Vertex j represents universe element j, $4 \leq j \leq 15$. ∎

A Greedy Heuristic

The set-cover problem is known to be NP-hard. Since the set-cover and bipartite-cover problems are identical, the bipartite-cover problem is also NP-hard. As a result we probably will not be able to develop a fast algorithm to solve it. We can, however, use the greedy method to develop a fast heuristic. One possiblity is to construct the cover A' in stages. In each stage we select a vertex of A for inclusion into the cover. This vertex is selected by using the greedy criterion: *Select a vertex of A that covers the largest number of uncovered vertices of B.*

Example 17.12 Consider the bipartite graph of Figure 17.6. Initially $A' = \phi$, and no vertex of B is covered. Vertices 1 and 16 each covers six uncovered vertices of B; vertex 3 covers five; and vertices 2 and 17 each covers four. Therefore, in the first stage, we add either vertex 1 or vertex 16 to A'. If we add vertex 16, it covers the vertices $\{5, 6, 8, 12, 14, 15\}$. The uncovered vertices are $\{4, 7, 9, 10, 11, 13\}$. Vertex 1 of A covers four of these uncovered vertices ($\{4, 7, 9, 13\}$), vertex 2 covers one ($\{4\}$), vertex 3 covers one ($\{10\}$), vertex 16 covers zero, and vertex 17 covers four. In the next stage, either 1 or 17 is selected for inclusion into A'. If we choose vertex 1, vertices $\{10, 11\}$ remain uncovered. Vertices 1, 2, and 16 cover none of these uncovered vertices; vertex 3 covers one; and vertex 17 covers two. Therefore, we select vertex 17. Now no uncovered vertices remain, and we are done. $A' = \{1, 16, 17\}$. ∎

A high-level statement of the greedy covering heuristic appears in Figure 17.7. You should be able to show (1) that the algorithm fails to find a cover iff the initial bipartite graph does not have a cover, and (2) that bipartite graphs exist on which the heuristic will fail to find a minimum cover.

Selection of Data Structur   and Complexity

To implement the algorithm of Figure 17.7, we need to select a representation for A' and to decide how to keep track of the number of uncovered vertices of B that each vertex of A covers. Since only additions are made to the set A', we can represent A' as a one-dimensional integer array theCover and use coverSize

---

$A' = \phi$
while (more vertices can be covered)
    Add the vertex that covers the largest number of uncovered vertices to A'.
if (some vertices are uncovered) fail.
else a cover has been found.

Figure 17.7 High-level statement of greedy covering heuristic

to keep track of the number of elements in A'. We store the members of A' in
theCover[0:coverSize-1].

For a vertex i of A, let new_i be the number of uncovered vertices of B that i
covers. In each stage we need to select the vertex with maximum new_i and then
update the new_is, as some previously uncovered vertices are now covered. For this
update we examine the vertices of B that are newly covered by v. Let j be one
such vertex. The new_i value of all vertices of A that cover j is to be reduced by 1.

Example 17.13 Consider the graph of Figure 17.6. Initially $(new_1, new_2, new_3,$
$new_{16}, new_{17}) = (6, 4, 5, 6, 4)$. Suppose we select vertex 16 in stage 1, as in
Example 17.12. To update the new_is, we examine all the newly covered vertices of
B. These vertices are 5, 6, 8, 12, 14, and 15. When we examine vertex 5, we reduce
the new_i values of vertices 2 and 16 by 1 because vertex 5 is no longer an uncovered
vertex being covered by either 2 or 16. When we examine vertex 6, the counts for
vertices 1, 2, and 16 are reduced by 1. Similarly, when we examine vertex 8, the
counts of 1, 2, 3, and 16 are reduced by 1. After we examine all the newly covered
vertices, the new_i values are $(4, 1, 1, 0, 4)$. In the next stage we select vertex 1.
The newly covered vertices are 4, 7, 9, and 13. When we examine vertex 4, new_1,
new_2, and new_{17} are reduced by 1; and when we examine vertex 7, only new_1 is
reduced by 1 because vertex 1 is the only vertex that covers 7.   ∎

To implement the vertex-selection process, we need to know the new_i values and
also which vertices have already been covered. We can use 2 one-dimensional arrays
for this purpose. newVerticesCovered is an integer array such that newVertices-
Covered[i] equals new_i, and covered is a boolean array such that covered[i]
equals **false** if vertex i is not covered and **true** if it is. We can now refine the
high-level statement of Figure 17.7 to obtain the version in Figure 17.8.

The time spent updating newVerticesCovered is $O(e)$ where e is the number
of edges in the bipartite graph. It takes $\Theta(n^2)$ time to find the edges of a graph
represented by an adjacency matrix and $\Theta(n + e)$ time when we use a linked-
adjacency list. The actual update time is either $O(n^2)$ or $O(n + e)$ depending on
the graph representation.

The selection of vertex v at the start of each stage takes $\Theta(SizeOfA)$ time where
$SizeOfA = |A|$. Since all vertices of A may need to be selected, the number of

```
coverSize = 0; // current size of cover
newVerticesCovered[i] = degree[i] for all i in A.
covered[i] = false for all i in B.
while (newVerticesCovered[i] > 0 for some i in A)
{
    Let v be a vertex with largest newVerticesCovered[i].
    theCover[coverSize++] = v;
    for (all vertices j adjacent from v)
    {
        if (!covered[j])
        {
            covered[j] = true;
            Reduce newVerticesCovered[k] by 1 for all vertices
                adjacent from j.
        }
    }
}
if (some vertices are uncovered)
    fail
else
    a cover has been found
```

Figure 17.8 Refined version of Figure 17.7

stages is $O(SizeOfA)$ and the overall complexity of the cover algorithm is either $O(SizeOfA^2 + n^2) = O(n^2)$ or $O(SizeOfA^2 + n + e)$.

Reducing the Complexity

We can reduce the complexity of selecting vertex v at the start of each stage to $\Theta(1)$ time by using a sorted array of new_i values, a max heap, or a max selection tree. With the sorted-array approach, the new_i values need to be sorted at the end of each stage. This sort takes $\Theta(SizeOfB)$ time ($SizeOfB = |B|$) when we use the bin sort (see bin sort in Section 6.5.1) method. As $SizeOfB$ is generally much larger than $SizeOfA$, the sorted-array approach does not yield an overall improvement.

If we use a max heap, then following each stage we need to restructure the heap to account for the change in newVerticesCovered values. We can do this restructuring each time a newVerticesCovered value is reduced by 1. Such a reduction can cause the reduced newVerticesCovered value to move at most one level down the heap; therefore, this restructuring costs $\Theta(1)$ per newVerticesCovered reduction of 1. The total number of reductions is $O(e)$. Hence over all stages of the algorithm, only

$O(e)$ time is spent maintaining the max heap. Therefore, when we use a max heap, the overall complexity of the cover algorithm is either $O(n^2)$ or $O(n+e)$.

When we use a max winner tree, restructuring the winner tree following the update of each newVerticesCovered takes $\Theta(\log SizeOfA)$ time. The best time to do this restructuring is at the end of each stage, rather than after each reduction of a newVerticesCovered value by 1. The number of restructurings needed is $O(e)$, so the total restructuring time is $O(e \log SizeOfA)$. This time is larger than the restructuring time for a max heap.

However, we can obtain the same time bound as we do when we use a heap by maintaining bins of vertices with the same newVerticesCovered value. Since newVerticesCovered values may range from zero to $SizeOfB$, $SizeOfB + 1$ bins are needed. Each bin i is a doubly linked list of vertices that have newVertices-Covered value i. At the end of a stage, if newVerticesCovered[6], for example, has changed from 12 to 4, then we need to move it from bin 12 to bin 4. We can make this move in $\Theta(1)$ time using simulated pointers and an array node of nodes such that node[i] represents vertex i and node[i].left and node[i].right are the doubly linked list pointers. To move vertex 6 from bin 12 to bin 4, we delete node[6] from bin 12 and insert it into bin 4. With this bin scheme the complexity of the covering heuristic is $O(n^2)$ or $O(n+e)$, depending on whether the adjacency matrix or list representation of a graph is used.

The refinement of Figure 17.8 into C++ code that uses bins that are doubly linked lists with simulated pointers is available from the Web as the method graph::bipartiteCover.

17.3.5   Single-Source Shortest Paths

Problem Description

In this problem we are given a weighted graph G with the property that each edge (i, j) has a nonnegative cost (or length) a[i][j]. The length of a path is the sum of the costs of the edges on the path. Figure 17.9(a) shows a five-vertex weighted digraph. The number on each edge is its cost. The length of the path 1, 2, 5 from vertex 1 to vertex 5 is $4 + 5 = 9$; the length of the path 1, 5 is 8; and the length of the path 1, 3, 4, 5 is 6.

In the **single-source, all-destinations, shortest-path** problem, we must find a shortest path from a given source vertex to each of the vertices (called destinations) in the graph to which there is a path. Figure 17.9(b) lists the shortest paths from vertex 1 of the digraph of Figure 17.9(a); these paths are listed in increasing order of length. The number preceding each path is its length.

A Greedy Solution

We can solve the shortest-path problem using a greedy algorithm, developed by E. Dijkstra, that generates the shortest paths in stages. In each stage a shortest

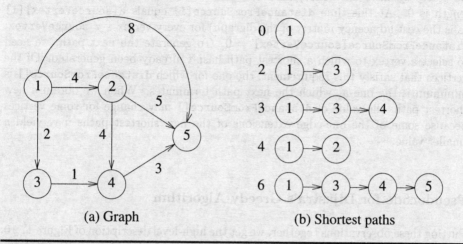

(a) Graph   (b) Shortest paths

Figure 17.9 Shortest-paths example

path to a new destination vertex is generated. The destination vertex for the next shortest path is selected using the greedy criterion: *From the vertices to which a shortest path has not been generated, select one that results in the least path length.* In other words, Dijkstra's method generates the shortest paths in increasing order of length.

We begin with the trivial path from the source vertex to itself. This path has no edges and has a length of 0. In each stage of the greedy algorithm, the next shortest path is generated. This next shortest path is the shortest possible one-edge extension of an already generated shortest path (Exercise 31). For the example of Figure 17.9, the second path of (b) is a one-edge extension of the first; the third is a one-edge extension of the second; the fourth is a one-edge extension of the first; and the fifth is a one-edge extension of the third.

This observation results in a convenient way to store the shortest paths. We can use an array predecessor such that predecessor[i] gives the vertex that immediately precedes vertex i on the shortest sourceVertex to i path. For our example predecessor[1:5] = [0, 1, 1, 3, 4]. The path from sourceVertex to any vertex i may be constructed backward from i and following the sequence predecessor[i], predecessor[predecessor[i]], predecessor[predecessor[predecessor[i]]], $\cdots$ until we reach sourceVertex. If we begin our example with i = 5, we get the vertex sequence predecessor[i] = 4, predecessor[4] = 3, predecessor[3] = 1 = sourceVertex. Therefore, the path is 1, 3, 4, 5.

To facilitate the generation of shortest paths in increasing order of length, we define distanceFromSource[i] to be the length of the shortest one-edge extension of a path already generated so that the extended path ends at vertex i. When we start, we have only the path from sourceVertex to sourceVertex and its length is 0. At this time distanceFromSource[i] equals a[sourceVertex][i] (a is the cost-adjacency matrix of the digraph) for every vertex i ≠ sourceVertex; distanceFromSource[sourceVertex] = 0. To generate the next path, we need to select a vertex to which a shortest path hasn't already been generated. Of the vertices that satisfy this requirement, the one for which distanceFromSource[] is minimum is the one at which the next path terminates. When we obtain a new shortest path, the value of distanceFromSource[] may change for some vertices because some of the one-edge extensions of the new shortest paths may yield a smaller value.

Pseudocode for Dijkstra's Greedy Algorithm

Putting these observations together, we get the high-level description of Figure 17.10. Step 1 initializes predecessor to sourceVertex for all vertices adjacent from sourceVertex. This initialization records the best information currently available. That is, the shortest path from sourceVertex to i is a one-edge extension of the shortest path from sourceVertex to sourceVertex. As shorter paths are discovered, predecessor[i] will be updated. When the next shortest path is generated, we need to update distanceFromSource by looking at the one-edge extensions of this path (step 4). The list newReachableVertices contains all vertices that have been determined to be reachable from sourceVertex and to which the shortest path is yet to be generated.

Selection of Data Structure and Complexity

We need to choose a data structure for the list newReachableVertices. From this list, we need to extract a vertex with least distanceFromSource (step 3). This extraction can be done in logarithmic time if newReachableVertices is maintained as a min heap (see Section 12.4). Since step 3 is executed $O(n)$ times, the total time spent in step 3 is $O(n \log n)$. However, in step 4 we need to possibly change some distanceFromSource values, as some one-edge extensions of the newly generated shortest path may yield a smaller value of distanceFromSource for some of the unreached vertices. Although key reduction is not a standard min heap operation, it can be done in logarithmic time. Since the total number of key reductions is O(number of edges in the digraph) $= O(n^2)$, the key reduction time is $O(n^2 \log n)$.

The time spent in steps 3 and 4 is $O(n^2)$ if newReachableVertices is maintained as an unordered chain. Now each execution of step 3 takes $O(|$newReachableVertices$|) = O(n)$ time, and each key reduction takes $\Theta(1)$ time. (distanceFromSource[j] needs to be reduced, and no change is to be made in the chain.)

```
void shortestPaths(int sourceVertex,
                   T* distanceFromSource, int* predecessor)
{// Find shortest paths from sourceVertex.
 // Return shortest distances in distanceFromSource.
 // Return predecessor information in predecessor.
   if (sourceVertex < 1 || sourceVertex > n)
      throw illegalParameterValue("Invalid source vertex");

   // code to verify that *this is weighted comes here

   graphChain<int> newReachableVertices;

   // initialize
   for (int i = 1; i <= n; i++)
   {
      distanceFromSource[i] = a[sourceVertex][i];
      if (distanceFromSource[i] == noEdge)
      predecessor[i] = -1;
      else
      {
         predecessor[i] = sourceVertex;
         newReachableVertices.insert(0, i);
      }
   }
   distanceFromSource[sourceVertex] = 0;
   predecessor[sourceVertex] = 0;  // source vertex has no predecessor

   // update distanceFromSource and predecessor
   while (!newReachableVertices.empty())
   {// more paths exist
      // find unreached vertex v with least distanceFromSource
      chain<int>::iterator iNewReachableVertices
                           = newReachableVertices.begin();
      chain<int>::iterator theEnd = newReachableVertices.end();
      int v = *iNewReachableVertices;
      iNewReachableVertices++;
      while (iNewReachableVertices != theEnd)
      {
         int w = *iNewReachableVertices;
         iNewReachableVertices++;
         if (distanceFromSource[w] < distanceFromSource[v])
            v = w;
      }
```

Program 17.3 Shortest-path program (continues)

Step 1: Initialize `distanceFromSource[i] = a[sourceVertex][i], 1 ≤ i ≤ n`.
Set `predecessor[i] = sourceVertex` for all `i` adjacent from `sourceVertex`.
Set `predecessor[sourceVertex] = 0` and `predecessor[i] = −1` for all other vertices.
Create a list `newReachableVertices` of all vertices for which `predecessor[i] > 0` (i.e., `newReachableVertices` now contains all vertices that are adjacent from `sourceVertex`).

Step 2: If `newReachableVertices` is empty, terminate. Otherwise, go to step 3.

Step 3: Delete from `newReachableVertices` the vertex `i` with least value of `distanceFromSource` (ties are broken arbitrarily).

Step 4: Update `distanceFromSource[j]` to `min{distanceFromSource[j], distanceFromSource[i]+a[i][j]}` for all vertices `j` adjacent from `i`. If `distanceFromSource[j]` changes, set `predecessor[j] = i` and add `j` to `newReachableVertices` in case it isn't already there. Go to step 2.

Figure 17.10 High-level description of Dijkstra's shortest-path algorithm

C++ Implementation

The refinement of Figure 17.10 into the C++ method `adjacencyWDigraph::shortestPaths` appears in Program 17.3. This code uses the class `graphChain` (Section 16.7.3).

Comments on Complexity

The complexity of Program 17.3 is $O(n^2)$. Any shortest-path algorithm must examine each edge in the graph at least once, since any of the edges could be in a shortest path. Hence the minimum possible time for such an algorithm would be $O(e)$. Since cost-adjacency matrices were used to represent the graph, it takes $O(n^2)$ time just to determine which edges are in the digraph. Therefore, any shortest-path algorithm that uses this representation must take $O(n^2)$. For this representation, then, Program 17.3 is optimal to within a constant factor. Even if a change to adjacency lists is made, only the overall time for the last `for` loop can be brought down to $O(e)$ (because `distanceFromSource` can change only for vertices adjacent from `i`). The total time spent selecting and deleting the minimum-distance vertex from `newReachableVertices` remains $O(n^2)$.

```
    // next shortest path is to vertex v, delete v from
    // newReachableVertices and update distanceFromSource
    newReachableVertices.eraseElement(v);
    for (int j = 1; j <= n; j++)
    {
        if (a[v][j] != noEdge && (predecessor[j] == -1 ||
      distanceFromSource[j] > distanceFromSource[v] + a[v][j]))
        {
            // distanceFromSource[j] decreases
            distanceFromSource[j] = distanceFromSource[v] + a[v][j];
            // add j to newReachableVertices
            if (predecessor[j] == -1)
                // not reached before
                newReachableVertices.insert(0, j);
            predecessor[j] = v;
        }
    }
  }
}
```

Program 17.3 Shortest-path program (concluded)

17.3.6   Minimum-Cost Spanning Trees

This problem was considered in Examples 16.2 and 17.3. Since every spanning tree
of an n-vertex undirected network G has exactly $n - 1$ edges, the problem is to
select $n - 1$ edges in such a way that the selected edges form a least-cost spanning
tree of G. We can formulate at least three different greedy strategies to select these
$n - 1$ edges. These strategies result in three greedy algorithms for the minimum-
cost spanning-tree problem: Kruskal's algorithm, Prim's algorithm, and Sollin's
algorithm.

Kruskal's Algorithm

The Method

Kruskal's algorithm selects the $n - 1$ edges one at a time using the greedy criterion:
From the remaining edges, select a least-cost edge that does not result in a cycle
when added to the set of already selected edges. Note that a collection of edges that
contains a cycle cannot be completed into a spanning tree. Kruskal's algorithm
has up to e stages where e is the number of edges in the network. The e edges
are considered in order of increasing cost, one edge per stage. When an edge is
considered, it is rejected if it forms a cycle when added to the set of already selected

edges. Otherwise, it is accepted.

Consider the network of Figure 17.11(a). We begin with no edges selected. Figure 17.11(b) shows the current state of affairs. Edge (1,6) is the first edge picked. It is included into the spanning tree that is being built, and the graph of Figure 17.11(c) obtained. Next the edge (3,4) is selected and included into the tree (Figure 17.11(d)). The next edge to be considered is (2,7). Its inclusion into the tree being built does not create a cycle, so we get the graph of Figure 17.11(e). Edge (2,3) is considered next and included into the tree (Figure 17.11(f)). Of the edges not yet considered, (7,4) has the least cost. It is considered next. Its inclusion into the tree results in a cycle, so this edge is rejected. Edge (5,4) is the next edge to be added to the tree being built. The new configuration appears in Figure 17.11(g). The next edge to be considered is the edge (7,5). It is rejected, as its inclusion creates a cycle. Finally, edge (6,5) is considered and included into the tree being built. The inclusion of this edge completes the spanning tree (Figure 17.11(h)). The resulting tree has cost 99.

Figure 17.11 Constructing a minimum-cost spanning tree (continues)

Figure 17.12 gives a high-level statement of Kruskal's algorithm.

Correctness Proof

We need to establish the following: (1) Kruskal's method results in a spanning tree whenever a spanning tree exists, and (2) the spanning tree generated is of minimum cost.

Figure 17.11 Constructing a minimum-cost spanning tree (concluded)

Let G be any weighted undirected graph (i.e., G is an undirected network). From Section 16.9.3 we know that an undirected graph G has a spanning tree iff it is connected. Further, the only edges that get rejected (or discarded) in Kruskal's method are those that are currently on a cycle. The deletion of a single edge that

---

// Find a minimum-cost spanning tree in an n-vertex network.
    Let T be the set of selected edges. Initialize $T = \phi$.
    Let E be the set of network edges.
    `while` $(E \neq \phi)$ `&&` $(|T| \neq n - 1)$
    {
        Let (u, v) be a least-cost edge in E.
        $E = E - \{(u,v)\}$. // delete edge from E
        `if` $((u,v)$ does not create a cycle in $T)$
            Add edge (u, v) to T.
    }
    `if` $(|T| == n - 1)$
        T is a minimum-cost spanning tree.
    `else`
        The network is not connected and has no spanning tree.

Figure 17.12 High-level statement of Kruskal's algorithm

is on a cycle of a connected graph results in a graph that is also connected. Hence if G is initially connected, the set of edges in T and E always forms a connected graph. Consequently, if G is initially connected, the algorithm cannot terminate with $E = \phi$ and $|T| < n - 1$.

Now let us prove that the constructed spanning tree T is of minimum cost. Since G has a finite number of spanning trees, it has at least one of minimum cost. Let $minTrees$ be the set of minimum-cost spanning trees of G. For any $W \in minTrees$, let d_W be the number of edges in T that are also in W. Let k, $k < n$, be $\max\{d_W | W \in minTrees\}$. If $k = n - 1$, $T \in minTrees$. So assume $k < n - 1$. The proof is by contradiction.

Let $U \in minTrees$ be a minimum-cost spanning tree for which $d_U = k$. We add to U one edge, e, from T and remove one edge, f, from U. The edges e and f are selected in the following way:

1. Let e be the least-cost edge in T that is not in U. Such an edge must exist because $k < n - 1$.

2. When e is added to U, a unique cycle is created. Let f be any edge on this cycle that is not in T. Note that at least one of the edges on this cycle is not in T, because T contains no cycles.

From the way e and f are selected, it follows that $V = U + \{e\} - \{f\}$ is a spanning tree and that T has exactly $k + 1$ edges that are also in V. Now if we can show that V is a minimum-cost spanning tree, then we would have a contradiction with the assumption that $k = \max\{d_W | W \in minTrees\}$, and the proof would be complete.

Clearly, the cost of V is the cost of U plus the cost of edge e minus the cost of edge f. If the cost of e is less than the cost of f, then the spanning tree V has a smaller cost than the tree U, which is impossible (U is a minimum-cost spanning tree).

If e has a higher cost than f, then f is considered before e by Kruskal's algorithm. Since f is not in T, Kruskal's algorithm must have discarded f when f was considered for inclusion in T. Hence f together with edges in T having a cost less than or equal to the cost of f must form a cycle. Since e is a least-cost edge of T that is not in U, all edges of T whose cost is less than that of e (and hence all edges of T whose cost is $\leq$ that of f) are also in U. Hence U must also contain a cycle, but it does not because it is a spanning tree. The assumption that e is of higher cost than f therefore is invalid.

The only possibility left is that e and f have the same cost. Hence V has the same cost as U, and so V is a minimum-cost spanning tree.

Choice of Data Structures and Complexity

To select edges in nondecreasing order of cost, we can set up a min heap and extract edges one by one as needed. When there are e edges in the graph, it takes $O(e)$ time to initialize the heap and $O(\log e)$ time to extract each edge.

The edge set T together with the vertices of G define a graph that has up to n connected components. Let us represent each component by the set of vertices in it. These vertex sets are disjoint. To determine whether the edge (u, v) creates a cycle, we need merely check whether u and v are in the same vertex set (i.e., in the same component). If so, then a cycle is created. If not, then no cycle is created. Hence two finds on the vertex sets suffice. When an edge is included in T, two components are combined into one and a unite is to be performed on the two sets. The set operations find and unite can be carried out efficiently using the tree scheme (together with the weighting rule and path compaction) of Section 11.9.2. The number of finds is at most $2e$, and the number of unites at most $n-1$ (exactly $n - 1$ if the weighted undirected graph is connected). Including the initialization time for the trees, this part of the algorithm has a complexity that is just slightly more than $O(n + e)$.

The only operation performed on the set T is that of adding a new edge to it. T may be implemented as an array spanningTreeEdges with additions being performed at one end. We can add at most $n - 1$ edges to T. So the total time for operations on T is $O(n)$.

Summing up the various components of the computing time, we get $O(n+e \log e)$ as the asymptotic complexity of Figure 17.12.

C++ Implementation

Using the data structures just described, Figure 17.12 may be refined into C++ code. Program 17.4 gives the resulting code. The method of Program 17.4 is a

```
bool kruskal(weightedEdge<T> *spanningTreeEdges)
{// Find a min cost spanning tree using Kruskal's method.
 // Return false iff the weighted undirected graph is not connected.
 // spanningTreeEdges[0:n-2] has the min-cost-tree edges when done.

    // code to verify that *this is undirected and weighted comes here

    int n = numberOfVertices();
    int e = numberOfEdges();
    // set up array of graph edges
    weightedEdge<T> *edge = new weightedEdge<T> [e + 1];
    int k = 0;                // cursor for edge[]
    for (int i = 1; i <= n; i++)
    {// get all edges incident to i
        vertexIterator<T> *ii = iterator(i);
        int j;
        T w;
        while ((j = ii->next(w)) != 0)
            if (i < j)  // add to edge array
                edge[++k] = weightedEdge<int> (i, j, w);
    }
    // put edges in min heap
    minHeap<weightedEdge<T> > heap(1);
    heap.initialize(edge, e);

    fastUnionFind uf(n); // union/find structure

    // extract edges in cost order and select/reject
    k = 0;  // use as cursor for t now
    while (e > 0 && k < n - 1)
    {// spanning tree not complete & edges remain
        weightedEdge<T> x =  heap.top();
        heap.pop();
        e--;
        int a = uf.find(x.vertex1());
        int b = uf.find(x.vertex2());
        if (a != b)
        {// select edge x
            spanningTreeEdges[k++] = x;
            uf.unite(a,b);
        }
    }
    return (k == n - 1);
}
```

Program 17.4 C++ code for Kruskal's algorithm

member of **graph** and has been written so as to work with all representations of a
weighted undirected graph The class **weightedEdge<T>** defines a type conversion to
the data type **T**. This type conversion returns the weight of the edge. Consequently,
when edges are extracted from the min heap of Program 17.4 these edges are in
ascending order of weight.

The code of Program 17.4 returns **false** if there is no spanning tree and **true**
otherwise. Note that when the code returns **true**, a minimum-cost spanning tree
is returned in the array **spanningTreeEdges**.

Prim's Algorithm

Prim's algorithm, like Kruskal's, constructs the minimum-cost spanning tree by
selecting edges one at a time. The greedy criterion used to determine the next edge
to select is *From the remaining edges, select a least-cost edge whose addition to the
set of selected edges forms a tree.* Consequently, at each stage the set of selected
edges forms a tree. By contrast, the set of selected edges in Kruskal's algorithm
forms a forest at each stage.

Prim's algorithm begins with a tree T that contains a single vertex. This vertex
can be any of the vertices in the original graph. Then we add a least-cost edge (u, v)
to T such that $T \cup \{(u, v)\}$ is also a tree. This edge-addition step is repeated until
T contains $n - 1$ edges. Notice that edge (u, v) is always such that exactly one of u
and v is in T. A high-level description of Prim's algorithm appears in Figure 17.13.
This description also provides for the possibility that the input graph may not be
connected. In this case there is no spanning tree. Figure 17.14 shows the progress
of Prim's algorithm on the graph of Figure 17.11(a). The refinement of Figure 17.13
into a C++ program and its correctness proof are left as Exercise 37.

Prim's algorithm can be implemented to have a time complexity $O(n^2)$ if we
associate with each vertex v not in TV a vertex $near(v)$ such that $near(v) \in TV$
and $cost(v, near(v))$ is minimum over all such choices for $near(v)$. The next edge
to add to T is such that $cost(v, near(v))$ is minimum and $v \notin TV$.

Sollin's Algorithm

Sollin's algorithm selects several edges at each stage. At the start of a stage, the
selected edges together with the n vertices of the graph form a spanning forest.
During a stage we select one edge for each tree in this forest. This edge is a
minimum-cost edge that has exactly one vertex in the tree. The selected edges are
added to the spanning tree being constructed. Note that two trees in the forest can
select the same edge, so we must eliminate duplicates. When several edges have the
same cost, two trees can select different edges that connect them. In this case also,
we must discard one of the selected edges. At the start of the first stage, the set of
selected edges is empty. The algorithm terminates when only one tree remains at
the end of a stage or when no edges remain to be selected.

```
// Assume that the network has at least one vertex.
    Let T be the set of selected edges. Initialize T = φ.
    Let TV be the set of vertices already in the tree. Set TV = {1}.
    Let E be the set of network edges.
    while (E ≠ φ) && (|T| ≠ n − 1)
    {
        Let (u, v) be a least-cost edge such that u ∈ TV and v ∉ TV.
        if (there is no such edge)
            break.
        E = E − {(u, v)}. // delete edge from E
        Add edge (u, v) to T.
        Add vertex v to TV.
    }
    if (|T| == n − 1)
        T is a minimum-cost spanning tree.
    else
        The network is not connected and has no spanning tree.
```

Figure 17.13 Prim's minimum-spanning-tree algorithm

Figure 17.15 shows the stages in Sollin's algorithm when it begins with the graph of Figure 17.11(a). The initial configuration of zero selected edges is the same as that shown in Figure 17.11(b). Each tree in this spanning forest is a single vertex. The edges selected by vertices $1, 2, \cdots, 7$ are, respectively, $(1, 6), (2, 7), (3, 4), (4, 3),$ $(5, 4), (6, 1), (7, 2)$. The distinct edges in this selection are $(1, 6), (2, 7), (3, 4),$ and $(5, 4)$. Adding these edges to the set of selected edges results in the configuration of Figure 17.15(a). In the next stage the tree with vertex set $1, 6$ selects edge $(6, 5)$, and the remaining two trees select the edge $(2, 3)$. Following the addition of these two edges to the set of selected edges the spanning-tree construction is complete. The constructed spanning tree appears in Figure 17.15(b). The development of Sollin's algorithm into a C++ program and its correctness proof are left as Exercise 38.

Which Algorithm Should You Use?

We have seen three greedy algorithms for the minimum-cost spanning-tree problem. Since all three always construct a minimum-cost spanning tree, you should select one based on performance criteria. Because the space requirements of all three are approximately the same, the decision is made based on their relative time complexities. The asymptotic complexity of Kruskal's method is $O(n + e \log e)$ and that of Prim's method is $O(n^2)$ (though an $O(e + n \log n)$ implementation is also possible; see the solution to Exercise 37 on the Web site); Sollin's method was not analyzed in this text. Experimental results indicate that Prim's method is generally the fastest. Therefore, this method should be used.

Figure 17.14 Stages in Prim's algorithm

EXERCISES

8. Extend the greedy solution for the loading problem to the case when there are two ships. Does the algorithm always generate optimal solutions?

9. We are given n tasks to perform in sequence. Suppose that task i needs t_i units of time. If the tasks are done in the order $1, 2, \cdots, n$, then task i completes at time $c_i = \sum_{j=1}^{i} t_j$. The average completion time (ACT) is $\frac{1}{n} \sum_{i=1}^{n} c_i$.

   (a) Consider the case of four tasks with task times (4, 2, 8, 1). What is the ACT when the task order is 1, 2, 3, 4?

   (b) What is the ACT when the task order is 2, 1, 4, 3?

Figure 17.15 Stages in Sollin's algorithm

(c) The following method constructs a task order that tries to minimize the ACT: *Construct the order in n stages; in each stage select from the remaining tasks one with least task time.* For the example of part (a), this strategy results in the task order 4, 2, 1, 3. What is the ACT for this greedy order?

(d) Write a C++ program that implements the greedy strategy of (c). The complexity of your program should be $O(n \log n)$. Show that this is so.

(e) Show that the greedy strategy of (c) results in task orders that have minimum ACT.

10. If two people perform the n tasks of Exercise 9, we need an assignment of tasks to each and an order in which each person is to perform his/her assigned tasks. The task completion times and ACT are defined as in Exercise 9. A possible greedy method that aims to minimize the ACT is as follows: *The two workers select tasks alternately and one at a time; from the remaining tasks, one with least task time is selected; each person does his/her tasks in the order selected.* For the example of Exercise 9(a), if person 1 begins the selection process, he/she selects task 4, person 2 selects task 2, person 1 selects task 1, and finally person 2 selects task 3.

(a) Write a C++ program to implement this strategy. What is its time complexity?

(b) Does the outlined greedy strategy always minimize the ACT? Prove your answer.

11. (a) Extend the greedy algorithm of Exercise 10 to the case when m persons are available to do the tasks.

(b) Does your algorithm guarantee optimal solutions? Prove your answer.

(c) Write C++ code for your algorithm. What is its complexity?

12. Consider the stack-folding problem of Example 7.5.

   (a) Develop a greedy algorithm to fold the carton stack into the fewest number of substacks such that no substack is of height more than *height*.

   (b) Does your algorithm guarantee to fold into the fewest number of substacks always? Prove your answer.

   (c) Write C++ code for your algorithm of (a).

   (d) What is the time complexity of your code of (c)?

13. Write a C++ program for the 0/1 knapsack problem using this heuristic: Pack the knapsack in nonincreasing order of profit density.

14. Write a C++ program for the 0/1 knapsack problem using the bounded-performance heuristic with $k = 1$.

15. Prove the error bound on the bounded-performance heuristic for the 0/1 knapsack problem for the case $k = 1$.

16. Write a C++ program for the 0/1 knapsack problem using the bounded-performance heuristic with $k = 2$.

17. Consider the **continuous-knapsack problem** in which we require $0 \le x_i \le 1$, rather than $x_i \in 0, 1$. A possible greedy algorithm is *Consider objects in nonincreasing order of profit density; if there is enough remaining capacity to accommodate the object, put it in; if not, put in a fraction to fill the knapsack.*

   (a) What is the packing obtained for the instance $n = 3$, $w = [100, 10, 10]$, $p = [20, 15, 15]$, and $c = 105$?

   (b) Prove that this greedy algorithm always generates an optimal solution.

   (c) Write a C++ program that implements this algorithm.

18. The thirsty-baby problem of Example 17.1 is a generalization of the continuous-knapsack problem of Exercise 17. Extend the greedy method of Exercise 17 to this problem. Does the algorithm guarantee optimal solutions? Prove your answer.

19. [AOE Networks] The task digraph of Figure 17.4 is called an activity on vertex (AOV) network because the vertices of the digraph represent tasks or activities. The activity on edge (AOE) network is a related network in which the edges represent activities (or tasks) and the vertices represent events. One of the vertices of the AOE network represents the start event s, and another vertex represents the finish event f. The in-degree of the start event and the

out-degree of the finish event are 0. An event i, other than the start event, occurs when all activities coming into the event (i.e., all activities denoted by edges of the form (j, i)) complete; and activity (i, k) can start only after event i has occurred. In an AOE network several activities can be done in parallel.

Figure 17.16 shows an eight-event, 12-activity AOE network. The number on an edge is the time it takes to complete that activity. So activity (1,4) takes five time units. Vertex 1 is the start event, and vertex 8 is the finish event.

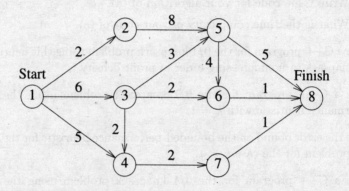

Figure 17.16 An AOE network

By definition, the start event occurs at time 0.

(a) List the events of Figure 17.16 in topological order.

(b) Let $earliestEventTime(i)$, be the earliest time at which event i can occur. Prove that, for i not the start event,

$$earliestEventTime(i) = \max_{(j,i)\in E} \{earliestEventTime(j) + length(j, i)\}$$

(17.1)

where E is the set of edges of the AOE network and $length(j, i)$ is the time required by activity (j, i). Keep in mind that you can do as many activities as you wish concurrently.

(c) Use Equation 17.1 and the topological order of part (a) to compute the earliest event times for the events of Figure 17.16.

(d) The earliest event time of the finish event is called the **project length**. What is the project length for the project represented by the AOE network of Figure 17.16?

(e) The latest event time $latestEventTime(i)$ of event i is the latest time by which event i must occur; if event i does not occur by this time, then the project cannot complete in time equal to the project length. Clearly, the latest event time for the finish event is the same as its earliest event time. Prove that, for i not the finish event,

$$latestEventTime(i) = \min_{(i,j)\in E} \{latestEventTime(j) - length(i,j)\}$$

$$(17.2)$$

(f) Use Equation 17.2 and the reverse of the topological order of part (a) to compute the latest event times for the events of Figure 17.16.

(g) From the definition of an AOE network, it follows that the earliest time, $earliestActivityTime(i,j)$, at which activity (i,j) can commence is $earliestEventTime(i)$; if the activity starts later than

$$latestActivityTime(i,j) = latestEventTime(j) - length(i,j)$$

then the project cannot finish in time equal to the project length. Compute the earliest and latest activity times for the activities of Figure 17.16.

(h) The **slack time**, $slack(i,j)$, of activity (i,j) is

$$latestActivityTime(i,j) - earliestActivityTime(i.j)$$

Compute the slack times for all activities.

(i) A **critical activity** is an activity whose slack is 0. Identify the critical activities of Figure 17.16.

20. Write a program to input an AOE network (see Exercise 19) and output the project length, earliest and latest event and activity times, slack times, and critical activities. The complexity of your program should be $O(n+e)$ where n is the number of events and e is the number of activities. Test your code.

21. (a) Show that the algorithm of Figure 17.7 fails to find a cover iff the input bipartite graph does not have a cover.

(b) Give a bipartite graph that has a cover and on which the algorithm of Figure 17.7 fails to find a minimum cover.

22. Trace the working of Figure 17.8 on the graph of Figure 17.6.

23. Devise another greedy heuristic for the bipartite-cover problem. This time use the following greedy criterion: *If there is a vertex of B that can be covered by only a single vertex of A, select this vertex; otherwise, select a vertex of A that covers the largest number of uncovered vertices.*

    (a) Write a high-level statement of the greedy heuristic.

    (b) Refine this greedy heuristic into a C++ method that is a member of the class **graph**.

    (c) What is the time complexity of your method?

    (d) Test the correctness of your code.

24. Let G be an undirected graph. A subset S of the vertices of G is a **clique** iff there is an edge between every pair of vertices in S. The size of the clique is the number of vertices in S. A **maximum clique** is a clique of largest size. The problem of finding a maximum clique (i.e., the max-clique problem) in a graph is NP-hard.

    (a) Provide a high-level statement of a possible greedy heuristic for the max-clique problem.

    (b) Give an example of a graph on which your heuristic actually produces a maximum clique and also an example on which it does not.

    (c) Refine the heuristic of (a) into the public method **graph::maxClique(int *cliqueVertices)** that returns the size of the largest clique found and puts the vertices of this largest clique into the array **cliqueVertices**.

    (d) What is the time complexity of your code?

25. Let G be an undirected graph. A subset S of the vertices of G is an **independent set** iff no two vertices of S are connected by an edge. A maximum independent set is an independent set with the maximum number of vertices. Finding the maximum independent set of a graph is NP-hard. Do Exercise 24 for the maximum-independent-set problem.

26. A **coloring** of an undirected graph G is an assignment of the labels $\{1, 2, \cdots\}$ to the vertices of G such that no two vertices connected by an edge have the same label. In the graph-coloring problem, we are to color G using the fewest number of distinct colors (labels). The graph-coloring problem is NP-hard. Do Exercise 24 for the graph-coloring problem.

27. List all simple paths from vertex 1 to vertex 3 in the weighted digraph of Figure 17.17. What is the length of each path? Which is the shortest path?

28. List the shortest paths from vertex 1 to each vertex of Figure 17.17 in ascending order of length. Observe that each path, other than the first, is a one-edge extension of a previous path.

Figure 17.17 A weighted digraph

29. (a) For the graph of Figure 17.17, show the initial `distanceFromSource` and `predecessor` arrays for Dijkstra's method (Figure 17.10). Use vertex 1 as the source vertex.

    (b) Now show these two arrays following each iteration of the loop of steps 2, 3, and 4.

    (c) Use the final `predecessor` array to determine the shortest paths from vertex 1.

30. Do Exercise 29 using vertex 5 as the source vertex.

31. Show that when shortest paths are generated in order of length, the next shortest path to be generated is always a one-edge extension of an already generated shortest path.

32. Show that the greedy algorithm of Figure 17.10 may not correctly compute the lengths of the shortest paths in a digraph that has one or more edges with negative cost.

33. Write a method `path(predecessor, sourceVertex, destinationVertex)` that uses the `predecessor` values computed by the method `shortestPaths` and outputs a shortest path from vertex `sourceVertex` to vertex `destination-Vertex`. What is the time complexity of your method?

34. Write a version of Program 17.3 for the case when the weighted digraph is a member of the class `linkedWDigraph`. Your method should be defined as a member of this class. What is the time complexity of your method?

35. Write a version of Program 17.3 for the case when the weighted digraph is a member of the class `linkedWDigraph` and has only $O(n)$ edges. This time implement `newReachableVertices` as a min heap. Use a vertex's `distanceFromSource` value as the priority. What is the time complexity of your method?

36. Write a version of Program 17.3 that works for weighted undirected and directed graphs and is independent of the representation that is used. Your method will be a member of `graph`.

37. (a) Provide a correctness proof for Prim's method (Figure 17.13).

   (b) Refine Figure 17.13 into a C++ method `graph::prim` with complexity $O(n^2)$. (*Hint:* Use a strategy similar to that used in the shortest paths code of Program 17.3.)

   (c) Show that the complexity of your method is indeed $O(n^2)$.

38. (a) Prove that Sollin's algorithm finds a minimum-cost spanning tree for every connected undirected graph.

   (b) What is the maximum number of stages in Sollin's algorithm? Give this as a function of the number of vertices n in the graph.

   (c) Write a C++ method, `graph::sollin`, that finds a minimum-cost spanning tree using Sollin's algorithm.

   (d) What is the complexity of your method?

39. Let T be a tree (not necessarily binary) in which a length is associated with each edge. Let S be a subset of the vertices of T and let T/S denote the forest that results when the vertices of S are deleted from T. We wish to find a minimum-cardinality subset S such that no forest in T/S has a root-to-leaf path whose length exceeds d.

   (a) Develop a greedy algorithm to find a minimum-cardinality S. (*Hint:* Start at the leaves and move toward the root.)

   (b) Prove the correctness of your algorithm.

   (c) What is the complexity of your algorithm? In case it is not linear in the number of vertices in T, redesign your algorithm so that its complexity is linear.

40. Do Exercise 39 for the case when T/S denotes the forest that results from making two copies of each vertex in S. The pointer from the parent goes to one copy, and pointers to the children go from the other copy.

41. A convex polygon (Section 6.5.3) with $n > 2$ vertices is to be triangulated (i.e., partitioned or cut into triangles; each corner of a triangle is a vertex of the polygon). A cut starts at a polygon vertex u and ends at a nonadjacent vertex v. The cost of the cut (u, v) is $c(u, v)$. A total of $n - 2$ cuts are required to triangulate the polygon.

   (a) Formulate a greedy strategy to find a triangulation with minimum cost.

   (b) Does your strategy always find a minimum-cost triangulation? Prove your answer.

(c) Write a program that implements your strategy. Test your code.

(d) What is the complexity of your code?

17.4 REFERENCES AND SELECTED READINGS

Greedy approximation algorithms for several problems appear in the paper "A Survey of Approximately Optimal Solutions to Some Covering and Packing Problems" by V. Paschos, *ACM Computing Surveys*, 29, 2, 1997, 171–209. An experimental evaluation of greedy algorithms for the minimum-cost spanning-tree problem appears in the paper "An Empirical Assessment of Algorithms for Constructing a Minimum Spanning Tree" by B. Moret and H. Shapiro, *DIMACS Series in Discrete Mathematics*, 15, 1994, 99–117.

Section 17.4 References and Selected Readings 703

(c) Write a program that implements your strategy. Test your code.

CHAPTER 18

DIVIDE AND CONQUER

BIRD'S-EYE VIEW

The divide-and-conquer strategy so successfully used by monarchs and colonizers may also be applied to the development of efficient computer algorithms. We begin this chapter by showing how to adapt this ancient strategy to the algorithm-development arena. Then we use the strategy to obtain good algorithms for the minmax problem; matrix multiplication; a problem from recreational mathematics—the defective-chessboard problem; sorting; selection; and a computational geometry problem—find the closest pair of points in two-dimensional space.

Since divide-and-conquer algorithms decompose a problem instance into several smaller independent instances, divide-and-conquer algorithms may be effectively run on a parallel computer; the independent smaller instances can be worked on by different processors of the parallel computer.

This chapter develops the mathematics needed to analyze the complexity of frequently occurring divide-and-conquer algorithms and proves that the divide-and-conquer algorithms for the minmax and sorting problems are optimal by deriving lower bounds on the complexity of these problems. The derived lower bounds agree with the complexity of the divide-and-conquer algorithms for these problems.

704

18.1   THE METHOD

The divide-and-conquer methodology is very similar to the modularization approach to software design. Small instances of a problem are solved using some direct approach. To solve a large instance, we (1) divide it into two or more smaller instances, (2) solve each of these smaller problems, and (3) combine the solutions of these smaller problems to obtain the solution to the original instance. The smaller instances are often instances of the original problem and may be solved by using the divide-and-conquer strategy recursively.

Example 18.1 [Detecting a Counterfeit Coin] You are given a bag with 16 coins and told that one of these coins may be counterfeit. Further, you are told that counterfeit coins are lighter than genuine ones. Your task is to determine whether the bag contains a counterfeit coin. To aid you in this task, you have a machine that compares the weights of two sets of coins and tells you which set is lighter or whether both sets have the same weight.

We can compare the weights of coins 1 and 2. If coin 1 is lighter than coin 2, then coin 1 is counterfeit and we are done with our task. If coin 2 is lighter than coin 1, then coin 2 is counterfeit. If both coins have the same weight, we compare coins 3 and 4. Again, if one coin is lighter, a counterfeit coin has been detected and we are done. If not, we compare coins 5 and 6. Proceeding in this way, we can determine whether the bag contains a counterfeit coin by making at most eight weight comparisons. This process also identifies the counterfeit coin.

Another approach is to use the divide-and-conquer methodology. Suppose that our 16-coin instance is considered a large instance. In step 1, we divide the original instance into two or more smaller instances. Let us divide our 16-coin instance into two 8-coin instances by arbitrarily selecting 8 coins for the first instance (say A) and the remaining 8 coins for the second instance B. In step 2, we need to determine whether A or B has a counterfeit coin. For this step we use our machine to compare the weights of the coin sets A and B. If both sets have the same weight, a counterfeit coin is not present in the 16-coin set. If A and B have different weights, a counterfeit coin is present and it is in the lighter set. Finally, in step 3 we take the results from step 2 and generate the answer for the original 16-coin instance. For the counterfeit-coin problem, step 3 is easy. The 16-coin instance has a counterfeit coin iff either A or B has one. So with just one weight comparison, we can complete the task of determining the presence of a counterfeit coin.

Now suppose we need to identify the counterfeit coin. We will define a "small" instance to be one with two or three coins. Note that if there is only one coin, we cannot tell whether it is counterfeit. All other instances are "large" instances. If we have a small instance, we may identify the counterfeit coin by comparing one of the coins with up to two other coins, performing at most two weight comparisons.

The 16-coin instance is a large instance. So it is divided into two 8-coin instances A and B as above. By comparing the weights of these two instances, we determine whether or not a counterfeit coin is present. If not, the algorithm terminates. Otherwise, we continue with the subinstance known to have the counterfeit coin.

Suppose B is the lighter set. It is divided into two sets of four coins each. Call these sets $B1$ and $B2$. The two sets are compared. One set of coins must be lighter. If $B1$ is lighter, the counterfeit coin is in $B1$ and $B1$ is divided into two sets of two coins each. Call these sets $B1a$ and $B1b$. The two sets are compared, and we continue with the lighter set. Since the lighter set has only two coins, it is a small instance. Comparing the weights of the two coins in the lighter set, we can determine which is lighter. The lighter one is the counterfeit coin.   ■

Example 18.2 [Gold Nuggets] Your boss has a bag of gold nuggets. Each month two employees are given one nugget each for exemplary performance. By tradition, the first-ranked employee gets the heaviest nugget in the bag, and the second-ranked employee gets the lightest. This way, unless new nuggets are added to the bag, first-ranked employees get heavier nuggets than second-ranked employees get. Since new nuggets are added periodically, it is necessary to determine the heaviest and lightest nugget each month. You have a machine that can compare the weights of two nuggets and report which is lighter or whether both have the same weight. As this comparison is time-consuming, we wish to determine the heaviest and lightest nuggets, using the fewest number of comparisons.

Suppose the bag has n nuggets. We can use the strategy used in method max (Program 1.37) to find the heaviest nugget by making $n - 1$ comparisons. After we identify the heaviest nugget, we can find the lightest from the remaining $n - 1$ nuggets using a similar strategy and performing an additional $n - 2$ comparisons. The total number of weight comparisons is $2n - 3$. Two alternative strategies appear in Programs 2.24 and 2.25. The first strategy performs $2n - 2$ comparisons, and the second performs at most $2n - 2$ comparisons.

Let us try to formulate a solution that uses the divide-and-conquer method. When n is small, say, $n \leq 2$, one comparison is sufficient to identify the heaviest and lightest nuggets. When n is large (in this case $n > 2$), in step 1 we divide the instance into two or more smaller instances. Suppose we divide the bag of nuggets into two smaller bags A and B, each containing half the nuggets. In step 2 we determine the heaviest and lightest nuggets in A and B. Let these nuggets be H_A (heaviest in A), L_A, H_B, and L_B. Step 3 determines the heaviest overall nugget by comparing H_A and H_B and the lightest by comparing L_A and L_B. We can use the outlined divide-and-conquer scheme recursively to perform step 2.

Suppose $n = 8$. The bag is divided into two bags A and B with four nuggets each (Figure 18.1(a)). To find the heaviest and lightest nuggets in A, the four nuggets in A are divided into two groups $A1$ and $A2$. Each group contains two nuggets. We can identify the heavier nugget H_{A1} and the lighter one L_{A1} in $A1$ with one comparison (Figure 18.1(b)). With another comparison, we can identify H_{A2} and L_{A2}. Now by comparing H_{A1} and H_{A2}, we can identify H_A. A comparison between L_{A1} and L_{A2} identifies L_A. So with four comparisons we have found H_A and L_A. We need another four comparisons to determine H_B and L_B. By comparing H_A and H_B (L_A and L_B), we determine the overall heaviest (lightest) nugget. Therefore, the divide-and-conquer approach requires 10 comparisons when $n = 8$. In contrast,

Program 1.37 requires 13 comparisons, and both Programs 2.24 and 2.25 require up to 14 comparisons.

(a) Dividing into smaller bags   (b) Finding heavy and light nuggets in a bag

Figure 18.1 Finding the heaviest and lightest of eight nuggets

Let $c(n)$ be the number of comparisons used by the divide-and-conquer approach. For simplicity, assume that n is a power of 2. When $n = 2$, $c(n) = 1$. For larger n, $c(n) = 2c(n/2) + 2$. Using the substitution method (see Example 2.20), this recurrence can be solved to obtain $c(n) = 3n/2 - 2$ when n is a power of 2. The divide-and-conquer approach uses almost 25 percent fewer comparisons than the alternative schemes suggested in this example use.   ∎

Example 18.3 [Matrix Multiplication] The product of two $n \times n$ matrices A and B is a third $n \times n$ matrix C where $C(i, j)$ is given by

$$C(i,j) = \sum_{k=1}^{n} A(i,k) * B(k,j), \quad 1 \le i \le n, \quad 1 \le j \le n \qquad (18.1)$$

If each $C(i, j)$ is computed by using this equation, then the computation of each requires n multiplications and $n - 1$ additions. The total operation count for the computation of all terms of C is therefore $n^3 m + n^2(n - 1)a$ where m denotes a multiplication and a an addition or subtraction.

To formulate a divide-and-conquer algorithm to multiply the two matrices, we need to define a "small" instance, specify how small instances are multiplied, determine how a large instance may be subdivided into smaller instances, state how these smaller instances are to be multiplied, and finally describe how the solutions of these smaller instances may be combined to obtain the solution for the larger instance. To keep the discussion simple, let's assume that n is a power of 2 (i.e., n is one of the numbers 1, 2, 4, 8, 16, $\cdots$).

To begin with, let us assume that $n = 1$ is a small instance and that $n > 1$ is a large instance. We will modify this assumption later if we need to. Since a small matrix is a 1×1 matrix, we can multiply two such matrices by multiplying together the single element in each.

Consider a large instance, that is, one with $n > 1$. We can divide such a matrix A into four $n/2 \times n/2$ matrices A_1, A_2, A_3, and A_4 as shown in Figure 18.2(a). When n is greater than 1 and a power of 2, $n/2$ is also a power of 2. So the smaller matrices satisfy our assumption on the matrix size also. The matrices B_i and C_i, $1 \leq i \leq 4$, are defined in a similar way. The matrix product we are to perform may be represented as in Figure 18.2(b). We may use Equation 18.1 to verify that the following equations are valid:

$$C_1 = A_1 B_1 + A_2 B_3 \tag{18.2}$$
$$C_2 = A_1 B_2 + A_2 B_4 \tag{18.3}$$
$$C_3 = A_3 B_1 + A_4 B_3 \tag{18.4}$$
$$C_4 = A_3 B_2 + A_4 B_4 \tag{18.5}$$

These equations allow us to compute the product of A and B by performing eight multiplications and four additions of $n/2 \times n/2$ matrices. We can use these equations to complete our divide-and-conquer algorithm. In step 2 of the algorithm, the eight multiplications involving the smaller matrices are done using the divide-and-conquer algorithm recursively. In step 3 the eight products are combined using a direct matrix addition algorithm (see Program 2.21). The complexity of the resulting algorithm is $\Theta(n^3)$, the same as the complexity of Program 2.22, which uses Equation 18.1 directly. The divide-and-conquer algorithm will actually run slower than Program 2.22 because of the overheads introduced by the instance-dividing and -recombining steps.

(a) Dividing A into four   (b) $A * B = C$

Figure 18.2 Dividing a matrix into smaller matrices

To get a faster algorithm, we need to be more clever about the instance-dividing and -recombining steps. A scheme, known as Strassen's method, involves the computation of seven smaller matrix products (versus eight in the preceding scheme).

The results of these seven smaller products are matrices $D, E, \cdots, J$, which are defined as

$$
\begin{aligned}
D &= A_1(B_2 - B_4) \\
E &= A_4(B_3 - B_1) \\
F &= (A_3 + A_4)B_1 \\
G &= (A_1 + A_2)B_4 \\
H &= (A_3 - A_1)(B_1 + B_2) \\
I &= (A_2 - A_4)(B_3 + B_4) \\
J &= (A_1 + A_4)(B_1 + B_4)
\end{aligned}
$$

The matrices D through J may be computed by performing seven matrix multiplications, six matrix additions, and four matrix subtractions. The components of the answer may be computed by using another six matrix additions and two matrix subtractions as below:

$$
\begin{aligned}
C_1 &= E + I + J - G \\
C_2 &= D + G \\
C_3 &= E + F \\
C_4 &= D + H + J - F
\end{aligned}
$$

Let us try this scheme on a multiplication instance with $n = 2$. Sample A and B matrices together with their product C are given below:

$$
\begin{bmatrix} 1 & 2 \\ 3 & 4 \end{bmatrix} * \begin{bmatrix} 5 & 6 \\ 7 & 8 \end{bmatrix} = \begin{bmatrix} 19 & 22 \\ 43 & 50 \end{bmatrix}
$$

Since $n > 1$, the matrix multiplication instance is divided into four smaller matrices as in Figure 18.2(a); each smaller matrix is a 1×1 matrix and has a single element. The 1×1 multiplication instances are small instances, and they are solved directly. Using the equations for D through J, we obtain the values that follow.

$$
\begin{aligned}
D &= 1(6 - 8) = -2 \\
E &= 4(7 - 5) = 8
\end{aligned}
$$

$$\begin{aligned}
F &= (3+4)5 = 35 \\
G &= (1+2)8 = 24 \\
H &= (3-1)(5+6) = 22 \\
I &= (2-4)(7+8) = -30 \\
J &= (1+4)(5+8) = 65
\end{aligned}$$

From these values the components of the answer are computed as follows:

$$\begin{aligned}
C_1 &= 8 - 30 + 65 - 24 = 19 \\
C_2 &= -2 + 24 = 22 \\
C_3 &= 8 + 35 = 43 \\
C_4 &= -2 + 22 + 65 - 35 = 50
\end{aligned}$$

For our 2×2 instance, the divide-and-conquer algorithm has done seven multiplications and 18 add/subtracts. We could have computed C by performing eight multiplications and four add/subtracts by using Equation 18.1 directly. For the divide-and-conquer scheme to be faster, the time cost of a multiplication must be more than the time cost of 14 add/subtracts.

If Strassen's instance-dividing scheme is used only when $n \geq 8$ and smaller instances are solved using Equation 18.1, then the case $n = 8$ requires seven multiplications of 4×4 matrices and 18 add/subtracts of matrices of this size. The multiplications take $64m + 48a$ operations each, and each matrix addition or subtraction takes $16a$ operations. The total operation count is $7(64m + 48a) + 18(16a) = 448m + 624$. The direct method has an operation count of $512m + 448a$. A minimum requirement for Strassen's method to be faster is that the cost of $512 - 448$ multiplications be more than that of $624 - 448$ add/subtracts. Or one multiplication should cost more than approximately 2.75 add/subtracts.

If we consider a "small" instance to be one with $n < 16$, the Strassen's decomposition scheme is used only for matrices with $n \geq 16$; smaller matrices are multiplied using Equation 18.1. The operation count for the divide-and-conquer algorithm becomes $7(512m + 448a) + 18(64a) = 3584m + 4288a$ when $n = 16$. The direct method has an operation count of $4096m + 3840a$. If the cost of a multiplication is the same as that of an add/subtract, then Strassen's method needs time for 7872 operations plus overhead time to do the problem division. The direct method needs time for 7936 operations plus time for the `for` loops and other overhead items in the program. Even though the operation count is less for Strassen's method, it is not expected to run faster because of its larger overhead.

For larger values of n, the difference between the operation counts of Strassen's method and the direct method becomes larger and larger. So for suitably large n,

Strassen's method will be faster. Let $t(n)$ denote the time required by Strassen's divide-and-conquer method. Since large instances are recursively divided into smaller ones until each instance becomes of size k or less (k is at least eight and may be larger depending on the implementation and computer characteristics), the recurrence for t is

$$t(n) = \begin{cases} d & n \le k \\ 7t(n/2) + cn^2 & n > k \end{cases} \qquad (18.6)$$

where cn^2 represents the time to perform 18 add/subtracts of $n/2 \times n/2$ matrices as well as the time to divide the instance of size n into the smaller instances. Using the substitution method, this recurrence may be solved to obtain $t(n) = \Theta(n^{\log_2 7})$. Since $\log_2 7 \approx 2.81$, the divide-and-conquer matrix multiplication algorithm is asymptotically faster than Program 2.22. $\blacksquare$

Implementation Note

The divide-and-conquer methodology naturally leads to recursive algorithms. In many instances, these recursive algorithms are best implemented as recursive programs. In fact, in many cases all attempts to obtain nonrecursive programs result in the use of a stack to simulate the recursion stack. However, in some instances we can implement the divide-and-conquer algorithm as a nonrecursive program without the use of such a stack and in such a way that the resulting program is faster, by a constant factor, than the natural recursive implementation. The divide-and-conquer algorithms for both the gold nuggets problem (Example 18.2) and the merge sort method (Section 18.2.2) can be implemented without the use of recursion so as to obtain fast programs that do not directly simulate the recursion.

Example 18.4 [Gold Nuggets] The work done by the algorithm of Example 18.2 to find the lightest and heaviest of eight nuggets is described by the binary tree of Figure 18.3. The leaves of this tree denote the eight nuggets (a, b, $\cdots$, h). Each shaded node represents an instance containing all the leaves in its subtree. Therefore, root A represents the problem of finding the lightest and heaviest of all eight nuggets, while node B represents the problem of finding the lightest and heaviest of the nuggets a, b, c, and d. The algorithm begins at the root. The eight-nugget instance represented by the root is divided into 2 four-nugget instances represented by the nodes B and C. At B the four-nugget instance is divided into the two-nugget instances D and E. We solve the two-nugget instance at node D by comparing the nuggets a and b to determine which is heavier. After we solve the problems at D and E, we solve the problem at B by comparing the lighter nuggets from D and E, as well as the heavier nuggets at D and E. We repeat this process at F, G, and C and then at A.

We can classify the work of the recursive divide-and-conquer algorithm as follows:

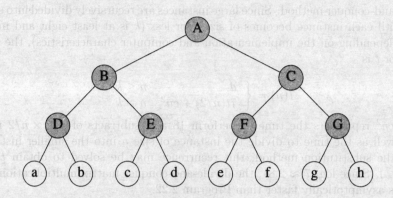

Figure 18.3 Finding the lightest and heaviest of eight nuggets

1. Divide a large instance into many smaller ones, each of size 1 or 2, during a downward root-to-leaf pass of the binary tree of Figure 18.3.

2. Compare the nuggets in each smaller size 2 instance to determine which nugget is heavier and which is lighter. This comparison is done at nodes D, E, F, and G. For size 1 instances the single nugget is both the smaller and lighter nugget.

3. Compare the lighter nuggets to determine which is lightest. Compare the heavier nuggets to determine which is heaviest. These comparisons are done at nodes A through C.

This classification of the work leads to the nonrecursive code of Program 18.1 to find the locations of the minimum and maximum of the n weights a[0:n-1]. These locations are returned in the variables indexOfMin and indexOfMax.

The cases n < 1 and n = 1 are handled first. If n > 1 and odd, the first weight a[0] becomes the candidate for minimum and maximum, and we are left with an even number of weights a[1:n-1] to account for in the for loop. When n is even, the first two weights are compared outside the for loop and indexOfMin and indexOfMax are set to the location of the smaller and larger weight, respectively. Again, we are left with an even number of weights a[2:n-1] to account for in the for loop.

In the for loop the outer if finds the larger and smaller of the pair (a[i],a[i+1]) being compared. This work corresponds to the category 2 work in our classification of the work of our divide-and-conquer algorithm. The embedded ifs find the smallest of the smaller weights and the largest of the larger weights. This work is the category 3 work.

The for loop compares the smaller of each pair to the current minimum weight

```
template<class T>
bool minmax(T a[], int n, int& indexOfMin, int& indexOfMax)
{// Locate min and max elements in a[0:n-1].
   if (n < 1) return false;
   if (n == 1)
   {
      indexOfMin = indexOfMax = 0;
      return true;
   }
   // n > 1
   int s = 1;                    // start point for loop
   if (n % 2 == 1)  // n is odd
      indexOfMin = indexOfMax = 0;
   else
   {// n is even, compare first pair
      if (a[0] > a[1])
         {indexOfMin = 1; indexOfMax = 0;}
      else
         {indexOfMin = 0; indexOfMax = 1;}
      s = 2;
   }

   // compare remaining pairs
   for (int i = s; i < n; i += 2)
   {
      // find larger of a[i] and a[i + 1], then compare larger one
      // with a[p.second] and smaller one with a[p.first]
      if (a[i] > a[i + 1])
      {
         if (a[i] > a[indexOfMax])
            indexOfMax = i;
         if (a[i + 1] < a[indexOfMin])
            indexOfMin = i + 1;
      }
      else
      {
         if (a[i + 1] > a[indexOfMax])
            indexOfMax = i + 1;
         if (a[i] < a[indexOfMin])
            indexOfMin = i;
      }
   }
   return true;
}
```

Program 18.1 Nonrecursive code to locate the min and max in a[0:n-1] a[indexOfMin] and compares the larger to the current maximum weight a[index-OfMax]; indexOfMin and indexOfMax are updated if necessary.

For the complexity analysis, we see that when n is even, one comparison is made outside the for loop and 3(n/2-1) inside. The total number of comparisons is 3n/2-2. When n is odd, no comparisons are made outside the for loop. However, 3(n-1)/2 comparisons are made inside. Therefore, regardless of whether n is odd or even, a total of $\lceil 3n/2 \rceil - 2$ comparisons are made, n > 0. In Section 18.4.1 we show that this is the minimum number of comparisons that every algorithm that finds the minimum and the maximum of n weights must make.   ∎

EXERCISES

1. Extend the divide-and-conquer method of Example 18.1 to the case of $n > 1$ coins. How many weight comparisons are done?

2. Consider the counterfeit-coin problem of Example 18.1. Suppose that the information "counterfeit coins are lighter than genuine ones" is changed to "counterfeit coins and genuine coins do not have the same weight." Also assume that the coin bag contains n coins.

    (a) Formulate a divide-and-conquer algorithm that either outputs the message "there is no counterfeit coin" or identifies the counterfeit coin. Your algorithm should recursively divide large problem instances into two smaller ones. How many weight comparisons are needed to identify the counterfeit coin (in case such a coin exists)?

    (b) Repeat part (a) with the requirement that large instances are divided into three smaller ones.

3. (a) Write C++ programs that implement both schemes of Example 18.2 to find the maximum and minimum of n elements. Use recursion to implement the divide-and-conquer scheme.

    (b) Programs 2.24 and 2.25 are two other codes to find the maximum and minimum of n elements. What are the minimum and maximum number of comparisons made by each?

    (c) Compare the run times of the codes of (a) and (b) as well as the code of Program 18.1 for $n = 100$; 1000; and 10,000. For the code of Program 2.25 use both the average- and worst-case times. The two codes of (a) and that of Program 2.24 should have the same average- and worst-case times.

    (d) Note that unless the comparison cost is very high, the divide-and-conquer algorithm will not outperform the others on worst-case data. Why? Will it ever outperform Program 2.25 on the average-time measure? Why?

4. Show that the divide-and-conquer matrix-multiplication algorithm that results from the direct application of Equations 18.2 through 18.5 has complexity $\Theta(n^3)$. From this analysis conclude that the resulting program will be slower than Program 2.22.

5. Use the substitution method to show that the solution to the recurrence Equation 18.6 is $\Theta(n^{\log_2 7})$.

6. Program Strassen's matrix-multiplication algorithm and experiment with different values of k (see Equation 18.6) to determine which value results in best performance. Now compare the run times of your program with those for Program 2.22. It is sufficient to do this comparison for the case when n is a power of 2.

7. When n is not a power of 2, we may add rows and columns to the matrices to obtain larger matrices whose size is a power of 2. Suppose that the smallest number of rows and columns are added so that the resulting matrix size m is a power of 2.

   (a) How large can the ratio m/n be?

   (b) What matrix entries should you use for the new rows and columns so that when the new matrices A' and B' are multiplied, the product of the original matrices A and B appears in the top-left corner of C'?

   (c) The run time of Strassen's method to multiply A' and B' is $\Theta(m^{2.81})$. What is the run time as a function of n?

18.2 APPLICATIONS

18.2.1 Defective Chessboard

Problem Description

A **defective chessboard** is a $2^k \times 2^k$ board of squares with exactly one defective square. Figure 18.4 shows some of the possible defective chessboards for $k \leq 2$. The defective square is shaded. Note that when $k = 0$, there is only one possible defective chessboard (Figure 18.4(a)). In fact, for any k there are exactly 2^{2k} different defective chessboards.

In the defective-chessboard problem, we are required to tile a defective chessboard using triominoes (Figure 18.5). In this tiling two triominoes may not overlap, triominoes should not cover the defective square, and triominoes must cover all other squares. With these constraints the number of triominoes to be used becomes $(2^{2k} - 1)/3$. We can verify that $(2^{2k} - 1)/3$ is an integer. A defective chessboard with $k = 0$ is easily tiled, as it has no nondefective squares. The number of triominoes used in the tiling is zero. When $k = 1$, there are exactly three nondefective

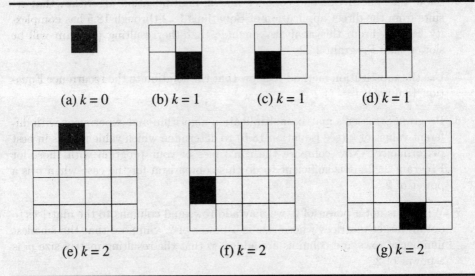

Figure 18.4 Defective chessboards

squares and these squares are covered using a triomino in one of the orientations of Figure 18.5.

Figure 18.5 Triominoes with different orientations

Solution Strategy

The divide-and-conquer method leads to an elegant solution to the defective-chessboard problem. The method suggests reducing the problem of tiling a $2^k \times 2^k$ defective chessboard to that of tiling smaller defective chessboards. A natural partitioning of a $2^k \times 2^k$ chessboard would be into four $2^{k-1} \times 2^{k-1}$ chessboards as in Figure 18.6(a). Notice that when such a partitioning is done, only one of the four smaller boards has a defect (as the original $2^k \times 2^k$ board had exactly one defective square). Tiling one of the four smaller boards corresponds to tiling a defective

$2^{k-1} \times 2^{k-1}$ chessboard. To convert the remaining three boards to defective boards, we place a triomino at the corner formed by these three. Figure 18.6(b) shows this placement for the case when the defect in the original $2^k \times 2^k$ chessboard falls into the upper left $2^{k-1} \times 2^{k-1}$ board. We can use this partitioning technique recursively to tile the entire $2^k \times 2^k$ defective chessboard. The recursion terminates when the chessboard size has been reduced to 1×1. The chessboard's only square now has a defect, and no triominoes are to be placed.

| (a) Partitioning | (b) Triomino placed |

Figure 18.6 Partitioning a $2^k \times 2^k$ board

C++ Implementation

We can code this divide-and-conquer algorithm as the recursive C++ function `tileBoard` (Program 18.2). This function employs two global variables `board` and `tile`. `board` is a two-dimensional integer array that represents the chessboard, and `board[0][0]` represents the top-left corner square of the chessboard; `tile`, an integer variable with initial value 1, gives the index of the next tile to use.

The initial invocation is `tileBoard(0,0,dRow,dCol,size)` where `size` = 2^k, and `dRow` and `dCol` give the row and column index of the defect. The number of tiles needed to tile the defective chessboard is $(\text{size}^2 - 1)/3$. Function `tileBoard` represents these tiles by the integers 1 through $(\text{size}^2 - 1)/3$ and labels each nondefective square of the chessboard with the number of the tile that covers it.

Complexity Analysis

Let $t(k)$ denote the time taken by `tileBoard` to tile a $2^k \times 2^k$ defective chessboard. When $k = 0$, `size` equals 1 and a constant d amount of time is spent. When $k > 0$,

```
// global variables
int **board;        // the chessboard
int tile;           // current tile to use

void tileBoard(int topRow, int topColumn,
               int defectRow, int defectColumn, int size)
{// topRow is row number of top-left corner of board.
 // topColumn is column number of top-left corner of board.
 // defectRow is row number of defective square.
 // defectColumn is column number of defective square.
 // size is length of one side of chess board.
   if (size == 1) return;
   int tileToUse = tile++,
       quadrantSize = size / 2;

   // tile top-left quadrant
   if (defectRow < topRow + quadrantSize &&
       defectColumn < topColumn + quadrantSize)
      // defect is in this quadrant
      tileBoard(topRow, topColumn, defectRow, defectColumn,
                quadrantSize);
   else
   {// no defect in this quadrant
      // place a tile in bottom-right corner
      board[topRow + quadrantSize - 1][topColumn + quadrantSize - 1]
           = tileToUse;
      // tile the rest
      tileBoard(topRow, topColumn, topRow + quadrantSize - 1,
                topColumn + quadrantSize - 1, quadrantSize);
   }

   // code for remaining three quadrants is similar
}
```

Program 18.2 Tiling a defective chessboard

four recursive calls are made. These calls take $4t(k-1)$ time. In addition to this time, time is spent testing the if conditionals and tiling three nondefective squares. Let this time be denoted by the constant c. We obtain the following recurrence for t:

$$t(k) = \begin{cases} d & k = 0 \\ 4t(k-1) + c & k > 0 \end{cases} \tag{18.7}$$

We may solve this recurrence using the substitution method (see Example 2.20) to obtain $t(k) = \Theta(4^k) = \Theta(\text{number of tiles needed})$. Since we must spend at least $\Theta(1)$ time placing each tile, we cannot obtain an asymptotically faster algorithm than divide and conquer.

18.2.2   Merge Sort

The Sort Method

We can apply the divide-and-conquer method to the sorting problem. In this problem we must sort n elements into nondecreasing order. The divide-and-conquer method suggests sorting algorithms with the following general structure: If n is 1, terminate; otherwise, partition the collection of elements into two or more subcollections; sort each; combine the sorted subcollections into a single sorted collection.

Suppose we limit ourselves to partitioning the n elements into two subcollections. Now we need to decide how to perform this partitioning. One possibility is to put the first $n-1$ elements into the first subcollection (say, A) and the last element into the second subcollection (say, B). A is sorted using this partitioning scheme recursively. Since B has only one element, it is already sorted. Following the sort of A, we need to combine A and B, using the method insert of Program 2.10. Comparing the resulting sort algorithm with insertionSort (Program 2.15), we see that we have really discovered the recursive version of insertion sort. The complexity of this sort algorithm is $O(n^2)$.

Another possibility for the two-way partitioning of n elements is to put the element with largest key in B and the remaining elements in A. Then A is sorted recursively. To combine the sorted A and B, we need merely append B to the sorted A. If we find the element with largest key using the function Max of Program 1.37, the resulting sort algorithm is a recursive formulation of selectionSort (Program 2.7). If we use a bubbling process (Program 2.8) to locate and move the element with largest key to the right-most position, the resulting algorithm is a recursive version of bubbleSort (Program 2.9). In either case the sort algorithm has complexity $\Theta(n^2)$. This complexity can be made $O(n^2)$ by terminating the recursive partitioning of A as soon as A is known to be in sorted order (see Examples 2.16 and 2.17).

The partitioning schemes used to arrive at the three preceding sort algorithms partitioned the n elements into two very unbalanced collections A and B. A has $n-1$ elements, while B has only 1 element. Let us see what happens when this partitioning is done in a more balanced way, that is, when A gets a fraction n/k of the elements and B gets the rest. Now both A and B are to be sorted by recursive application of the divide-and-conquer scheme. To combine the sorted A and B, we use a process called *merge*, which combines two sorted sequences into one.

Example 18.5 Consider the eight elements with keys [10, 4, 6, 3, 8, 2, 5, 7]. If we pick $k = 2$, then [10, 4, 6, 3] and [8, 2, 5, 7] are to be sorted independently. The result is [3, 4, 6, 10] and [2, 5, 7, 8]. To merge these two sorted sequences, we begin at the front of each. The smaller element, 2, is moved to the result sequence. Next 3 and 5 are compared, and 3 is moved to the result sequence. Then 4 and 5 are compared, and 4 is placed in the result sequence. Next 6 and 5 are compared, and so on.

If we pick $k = 4$, then the sequences [10, 4] and [6, 3, 8, 2, 5, 7] are to be sorted. The result of sorting these sequences independently is [4, 10] and [2, 3, 5, 6, 7, 8]. When these sorted sequences are merged, we obtain the desired eight-element sorted sequence.   ∎

Figure 18.7 is a high-level statement of the divide-and-conquer sort algorithm that results when the number of smaller instances created is 2 and the partitioning is such that A gets n/k elements.

```
void sort(E, n)
{// Sort the n elements in E.  k is global.
   if (n >= k)
   {
      i = n / k;
      j = n - i;
      Let A consist of the first i elements in E.
      Let B consist of the remaining j elements in E.
      sort(A, i);
      sort(B, j);
      merge(A, B, E, i, j); // merge from A and B into E
   }
   else
      sort E using insertion sort.
}
```

Figure 18.7 Pseudocode for divide-and-conquer sort

From our brief description of merge, it is evident that n elements can be merged in $O(n)$ time. Let $t(n)$ be the worst-case time of the divide-and-conquer sort algorithm (Figure 18.7). We obtain the following recurrence for t

$$t(n) = \begin{cases} d & n < k \\ t(n/k) + t(n - n/k) + cn & n \geq k \end{cases} \tag{18.8}$$

where c and d are constants. From Equation 18.8 it follows that $t(n)$ is minimum when $t(n/k) + t(n - n/k)$ is minimum.

Theorem 18.1 *Let* $f(x)$ *satisfy*

$$f(y + d) - f(y) \geq f(z + d) - f(z) \qquad (18.9)$$

for all $y \geq z$ *and all positive* d. *For every real number* w, $f(w/k) + f(w - w/k)$ *is minimum when* $k = 2$.

Proof Substituting $z = y - d$ into Equation 18.9, we get

$$f(y + d) - f(y) \geq f(y) - f(y - d)$$

or

$$2f(y) \leq f(y + d) + f(y - d) \qquad (18.10)$$

Substituting $d = w/2 - w/k$ when $k \geq 2$, $d = w/k - w/2$ when $k < 2$, and $y = w/2$ into Equation 18.10, we get

$$2f(w/2) \leq f(w/k) + f(w - w/k) \qquad \blacksquare$$

Every sort algorithm has complexity $\Omega(n \log n)$ (see Section 18.4.2). Therefore, $f(n) = t(n)$ satisfies Equation 18.9, and the complexity of Figure 18.7 is minimum when $k = 2$, that is, when the two smaller instances are of approximately the same size. (Actually, a complexity of $\Omega(n)$ is sufficient to satisfy Equation 18.9.) *Divide-and-conquer algorithms usually have optimal performance when the smaller instances created are of approximately the same size.*

Setting $k = 2$ in the recurrence for $t(n)$, we get the following recurrence:

$$t(n) = \begin{cases} d & n \leq 1 \\ t(\lfloor n/2 \rfloor) + t(\lceil n/2 \rceil) + cn & n > 1 \end{cases}$$

The presence of the floor and ceiling operators makes this recurrence difficult to solve. We can overcome this difficulty by solving the recurrence only for values of n that are a power of 2. In this case the recurrence takes the simpler form

$$t(n) = \begin{cases} d & n \leq 1 \\ 2t(n/2) + cn & n > 1 \end{cases}$$

We can solve this recurrence using the substitution method, and the result is $t(n) = \Theta(n \log n)$. Although the recurrence that was solved is valid only when n is a power of 2, the asymptotic bound obtained is valid for all n because $t(n)$ is a nondecreasing function of n. Since $t(n) = \Theta(n \log n)$, this time represents the best- and worst-case complexity of merge sort. Further, since the best- and worst-case complexities are the same, the average complexity of merge sort is also given by $\Theta(n \log n)$.

C++ Implementation

Figure 18.7 with $k = 2$ is the sorting method known as **merge sort** (or more precisely **two-way merge sort**). Let us now proceed to refine Figure 18.7 with $k = 2$ (i.e., merge sort) into a C++ function to sort n elements. The easiest way to do this refinement is to represent the elements as a chain (i.e., as a member of the class **chain** (Section 6.1)). In this case we divide E into two roughly equal lists by moving down to the $(n/2)$th node and breaking the chain. The merge procedure should be capable of merging together two sorted chains. We will not complete the refinement using chains, as we wish to compare the performance of the resulting C++ code with those of heap sort and insertion sort. Neither of these latter sorting methods was coded using a linked representation for the collection of elements.

To be compatible with our earlier sort methods, the merge sort method must begin with the element collection E in an array a and return the sorted sequence in the same array. With this requirement the refinement of Figure 18.7 takes the following course. When E is divided in two, we can avoid copying both halves into A and B and simply keep track of the left and right ends of each half. We can then perform the merge with the sequences to be merged in a initially. We can merge the sequences into a new array b and then copy them back into a. The refined version of Figure 18.7 appears in Figure 18.8.

```
void mergeSort(T *a, int left, int right)
{// sort a[left:right]
   if (left < right)
   {// at least 2 elements
      int midddle = (left + right) / 2;
      mergeSort(a, left, middle);
      mergeSort(a, middle + 1, right);
      merge(a, b, left, middle, right); // merge from a to b
      copy(b, a, left, right);          // copy result back to a
   }
}
```

Figure 18.8 Divide-and-conquer sort refinement

We can improve the performance of Figure 18.8 in many ways. For example, we can easily eliminate the recursion. If we examine this program carefully, we see that the recursion simply divides the element list repeatedly until we are left with segments of size 1. The merging that takes place after this division into segments of size 1 is best described for the case when n is a power of 2. The segments of size 1 are merged to get sorted segments of size 2. These segments of size 2 are then merged to get sorted segments of size 4. The merge process is repeated until a single sorted sequence of size n remains. Figure 18.9 shows the merging (and copying) that takes place when $n = 8$. The square brackets denote the start and end of sorted segments.

initial segments	[8]	[4]	[5]	[6]	[2]	[1]	[7]	[3]
merge to b	[4	8]	[5	6]	[1	2]	[3	7]
copy to a	[4	8]	[5	6]	[1	2]	[3	7]
merge to b	[4	5	6	8]	[1	2	3	7]
copy to a	[4	5	6	8]	[1	2	3	7]
merge to b	[1	2	3	4	5	6	7	8]
copy to a	[1	2	3	4	5	6	7	8]

Figure 18.9 Merge sort example

An iterative version of merge sort begins by merging pairs of adjacent segments of size 1, then it merges pairs of adjacent segments of size 2, and so on. We can eliminate virtually all the copying from b to a by merging alternately from a to b and from b to a. The iterative merge sort algorithm appears in Program 18.3.

To complete our sorting code, we need to specify the method `mergePass`. In our C++ development, the method `mergePass` (Program 18.4) simply determines the left and right ends of the segments to be merged. The actual merging of a pair of segments is done by the function `merge` (Program 18.5).

Natural Merge Sort

The merge sort method of Program 18.3 is also known as `straight merge sort`. In a **natural merge sort**, we start by identifying the existing sorted segments within the input sequence. For example, the element list [4, 8, 3, 7, 1, 5, 6, 2] contains the sorted segments [4, 8], [3, 7], [1, 5, 6], and [2]. These segments may be identified by making a left-to-right scan of the element list, looking for positions i such that element i is larger than element $i + 1$. Once the initial segments have been identified, we repeatedly make merge passes over the segments until only one segment remains.

As noted above, the element list [4, 8, 3, 7, 1, 5, 6, 2] has four segments. Segments 1 and 2 are merged to get [3, 4, 7, 8], and segments 3 and 4 are merged to get [1, 2,

```
template <class T>
void mergeSort(T a[], int n)
{// Sort a[0 : n - 1] using the merge sort method.
   T *b = new T [n];
   int segmentSize = 1;
   while (segmentSize < n)
   {
      mergePass(a, b, n, segmentSize); // merge from a to b
      segmentSize += segmentSize;
      mergePass(b, a, n, segmentSize); // merge from b to a
      segmentSize += segmentSize;
   }
}
```

Program 18.3 Sort a[0:n-1] using merge sort

```
template <class T>
void mergePass(T x[], T y[], int n, int segmentSize)
{// Merge adjacent segments from x to y.
   int i = 0;   // start of the next segment
   while (i <= n - 2 * segmentSize)
   {// merge two adjacent segments from x to y
      merge(x, y, i, i + segmentSize - 1, i + 2 * segmentSize - 1);
      i = i + 2 * segmentSize;
   }

   // fewer than 2 full segments remain
   if (i + segmentSize < n)
      // 2 segments remain
      merge(x, y, i, i + segmentSize - 1, n - 1);
   else
      // 1 segment remains, copy to y
      for (int j = i; j < n; j++)
         y[j] = x[j];
}
```

Program 18.4 Merge pairs of adjacent segments from x to y

5, 6]. Finally, these two segments are merged to get the single sorted segment [1, 2, 3, 4, 5, 6, 7, 8]. Thus only two merge passes are made over the data. Program 18.3

```
template <class T>
void merge(T c[], T d[], int startOfFirst, int endOfFirst,
                         int endOfSecond)
{// Merge two adjacent segments from c to d.
   int first = startOfFirst,        // cursor for first segment
       second = endOfFirst + 1,     // cursor for second
       result = startOfFirst;       // cursor for result

   // merge until one segment is done
   while ((first <= endOfFirst) && (second <= endOfSecond))
      if (c[first] <= c[second])
         d[result++] = c[first++];
      else
         d[result++] = c[second++];

   // take care of leftovers
   if (first > endOfFirst)
      for (int q = second; q <= endOfSecond; q++)
         d[result++] = c[q];
   else
      for (int q = first; q <= endOfFirst; q++)
         d[result++] = c[q];
}
```

Program 18.5 Merge two adjacent segments from c to d

would begin with segments of size 1 and make three merge passes.

The best case for natural merge sort is when the input element list is already sorted. Natural merge sort would identify exactly one sorted segment and make no merge passes, while Program 18.3 would make $\lceil \log_2 n \rceil$ merge passes. So natural merge sort would complete in $\Theta(n)$ time, while Program 18.3 would take $\Theta(n \log n)$ time.

The worst case for natural merge sort is when the input elements are in decreasing order of their keys. With this input, n initial segments are identified; both merge sort and natural merge sort make the same number of passes, but natural merge sort has a higher overhead in keeping track of segment boundaries. The worst-case performance of natural merge sort is worse than that of straight merge sort.

On average, we expect a list of n elements to have $n/2$ segments because, on average, the ith key is larger than the $i + 1$st key with probability 0.5. Starting with half as many segments, natural merge sort is expected to make one fewer merge pass than is made by straight merge sort. However, the time saved is offset by the cost of the initial sorted segment-finding pass and the added cost of keeping track of segment boundaries. Because of these observations, natural merge sort is recommended only in situations where we expect the input data to have few segments.

18.2.3   Quick Sort

The Sort Method

We can also use the divide-and-conquer approach to arrive at another totally different sort method called **quick sort**. In this method the n elements to be sorted are partitioned into three segments (or groups)—a left segment *left*, a middle segment *middle*, and a right segment *right*. The middle segment contains exactly one element; no element in *left* has a key larger than the key of the element in *middle*; and no element in *right* has a key that is smaller than that of the middle element. As a result, the elements in *left* and *right* can be sorted independently, and no merge is required following the sorting of *left* and *right*. The element in *middle* is called the **pivot** or **partitioning element**. The sort method is described more precisely by the code of Figure 18.10.

```
// Sort a[0:n-1] using quick sort.
```
Select an element from a[0:n-1] for *middle*. This element is the pivot.
Partition the remaining elements into the segments *left* and *right* so that
    no element in *left* has a key larger than that of the pivot and
    no element in *right* has a key smaller than that of the pivot.
Sort *left* using quick sort recursively.
Sort *right* using quick sort recursively.
The answer is *left* followed by *middle* followed by *right*.

Figure 18.10 High-level statement of quick sort

Consider the element list [4, 8, 3, 7, 1, 5, 6, 2]. Suppose we pick the element with key 6 as the pivot. Then 6 is in *middle*; 4, 3, 1, 5, and 2 are in *left*; and 8 and 7 are in *right*. When *left* has been sorted, the keys are in the order 1, 2, 3, 4, 5. When *right* has been sorted, its keys are in the order 7, 8. Putting the elements in *right* after the element in *middle* and those in *left* before the one in *middle*, we get the sorted sequence [1, 2, 3, 4, 5, 6, 7, 8]. The left segment [4, 3, 1, 5, 2], for example, is sorted recursively. We start by selecting a pivot; then the segment is partitioned into the three subsegments *left*, *middle*, and *right*; and the *left* and *right* subsegments are sorted recursively. If 3 is selected as the pivot, *left* contains 1 and 2, *middle* is 3, and *right* contains 4 and 5. When the sorted left segment, the middle segment, and the sorted right segment are concatenated, we get the sorted segment [1, 2, 3, 4, 5].

C++ Implementation

The `quickSort` function of Program 18.6 moves the largest element of the element array `a` to the right-most position of the array; and invokes the recursive function `quickSort` of Program 18.7, which does the actual sorting. We move the largest element to the right-most position because our element partitioning scheme (Program 18.7) requires that each segment either has its largest element on the right or is followed by an element that is $\geq$ all elements in the segment; in case this condition is not satisfied, the first **do** loop of Program 18.7 results in a left cursor value larger than `n - 1` when the pivot is the largest element, for example.

```
template <class T>
void quickSort(T a[], int n)
{// Sort a[0 : n - 1] using the quick sort method.
   if (n <= 1) return;
   // move largest element to right end
   int max = indexOfMax(a,n);
   swap(a[n - 1], a[max]);
   quickSort(a, 0, n - 2);
}
```

Program 18.6 Driver for recursive quick sort function

The partitioning of the element list into *left, middle,* and *right* is done in place (Program 18.7). In this implementation the pivot is always the element at the left end of the segment that is to be sorted. Other choices that result in improved performance are possible. One such choice is discussed later in this section.

Program 18.7 remains correct when we change the $<$ and $>$ in the conditionals of the **do-while** statements to $<=$ and $>=$, respectively (provided the right-most element of a segment is larger than the pivot). Experiments suggest that the average performance of quick sort is better when it is coded as in Program 18.6. All attempts to eliminate the recursion from this procedure result in the introduction of a stack. The last recursive call, however, can be eliminated without the introduction of a stack. We leave the elimination of this recursive call as Exercise 21.

Complexity Analysis

Program 18.6 requires $O(n)$ recursion stack space. The space requirements can be reduced to $O(\log n)$ by simulating the recursion using a stack. In this simulation the smaller of the two segments *left* and *right* is sorted first. The boundaries of the other segment are put on the stack.

The worst-case computing time for quick sort is $\Theta(n^2)$, and it is achieved, for instance, when *left* is always empty. However, if we are lucky and *left* and *right*

```
template <class T>
void quickSort(T a[], int leftEnd, int rightEnd)
{// Sort a[leftEnd:rightEnd], a[rightEnd+1] >= a[leftEnd:rightEnd].
   if (leftEnd >= rightEnd) return;

   int leftCursor = leftEnd,           // left-to-right cursor
       rightCursor = rightEnd + 1;  // right-to-left cursor
   T pivot = a[leftEnd];

   // swap elements >= pivot on left side
   // with elements <= pivot on right side
   while (true)
   {
      do
      {// find >= element on left side
         leftCursor++;
      } while (a[leftCursor] < pivot);

      do
      {// find <= element on right side
         rightCursor--;
      } while (a[rightCursor] > pivot);

      if (leftCursor >= rightCursor) break;  // swap pair not found
      swap(a[leftCursor], a[rightCursor]);
   }

   // place pivot
   a[leftEnd] = a[rightCursor];
   a[rightCursor] = pivot;

   quickSort(a, leftEnd, rightCursor - 1);   // sort left segment
   quickSort(a, rightCursor + 1, rightEnd);  // sort right segment
}
```

Program 18.7 Recursive quick sort function

are always of about the same size, then the complexity is $\Theta(n \log n)$. Therefore, the best-case complexity of quick sort is $\Theta(n \log n)$ (Exercise 24). Surprisingly, the average complexity of quick sort is also $\Theta(n \log n)$.

Theorem 18.2 *The average complexity of* quickSort *is* $\Theta(n \log n)$ *where* n *is the* *number of elements to be sorted.*

Proof Let $t(n)$ denote the average time needed to sort an n-element array. When $n \leq 1$, $t(n) \leq d$ for some constant d. Suppose that $n > 1$. Let s be the size of the left segment following the partitioning of the elements. Because the pivot element is in the middle segment, the size of the right segment is $n - s - 1$. The average times to sort the left and right segments are $t(s)$ and $t(n - s - 1)$, respectively. The time needed to partition the elements is bounded by cn where c is a constant. Since s can have any of the n values 0 through $n - 1$ with equal probability, we obtain the following recurrence:

$$t(n) \leq cn + \frac{1}{n} \sum_{s=0}^{n-1} [t(s) + t(n - s - 1)]$$

We can simplify this recurrence as follows:

$$t(n) \leq cn + \frac{2}{n} \sum_{s=0}^{n-1} t(s) \leq cn + \frac{4d}{n} + \frac{2}{n} \sum_{s=2}^{n-1} t(s) \tag{18.11}$$

Now using induction on n we show that $t(n) \leq kn \log_e n$ for $n > 1$ and $k = 2(c + d)$. Here $e \approx 2.718$ is the base of natural logarithms. The induction base covers the case $n = 2$. From Equation 18.11 we obtain $t(2) \leq 2c + 2d \leq kn \log_e 2$. For the induction hypothesis we assume $t(n) \leq kn \log_e n$ for $2 \leq n < m$ where m is an arbitrary integer that is greater than 2. In the induction step we need to prove $t(m) \leq km \log_e m$. From Equation 18.11 and the induction hypothesis, we obtain

$$t(m) \leq cm + \frac{4d}{m} + \frac{2}{m} \sum_{s=2}^{m-1} t(s) \leq cm + \frac{4d}{m} + \frac{2k}{m} \sum_{s=2}^{m-1} s \log_e s \tag{18.12}$$

To proceed further we use the following facts:

- $s \log_e s$ is an increasing function of s.
- $\int_2^m s \log_e s \, ds < \frac{m^2 \log_e m}{2} - \frac{m^2}{4}$.

Using these facts and Equation 18.12, we obtain

$$
\begin{aligned}
t(m) \ &< \ cm + \frac{4d}{m} + \frac{2k}{m} \int_2^m s \log_e s \, ds \\
&< \ cm + \frac{4d}{m} + \frac{2k}{m} \left[\frac{m^2 \log_e m}{2} - \frac{m^2}{4} \right] \\
&= \ cm + \frac{4d}{m} + km \log_e m - \frac{km}{2} \\
&< \ km \log_e m
\end{aligned}
$$

So the average complexity of `quickSort` is $O(n \log n)$. In Section 18.4.2 we show that the complexity of every comparison sort method (including `quickSort`) is $\Omega(n \log n)$. Therefore, the average complexity of `quickSort` is $\Theta(n \log n)$.   ■

The table of Figure 18.11 compares the average and worst-case complexities of the sort methods developed in this book.

Method	Worst	Average
bubble sort	n^2	n^2
count sort	n^2	n^2
insertion sort	n^2	n^2
selection sort	n^2	n^2
heap sort	$n \log n$	$n \log n$
merge sort	$n \log n$	$n \log n$
quick sort	n^2	$n \log n$

Figure 18.11 Comparison of sort methods

Median-of-Three Quick Sort

Our implementation of quick sort exhibits its worst-case performance when presented with a sorted list. It is distressing to have a sort program that takes more time on a sorted list than on an unsorted one. We can remedy this problem and, at the same time, improve the average performance of quick sort by selecting the pivot element using the **median-of-three rule**.

In a median-of-three quick sort, the pivot is chosen to be the median of the three elements {a[leftEnd], a[(leftEnd+rightEnd)/2], a[rightEnd]}. For example, if these elements have keys {5, 9, 7}, then a[rightEnd] is used as the value of pivot. To implement the median-of-three rule, it is easiest to swap the element in the median position with that at a[leftEnd] and then proceed as in Program 18.6. If a[rightEnd] is the median element, then we swap a[leftEnd] and a[rightEnd] just before pivot is set to a[leftEnd] in Program 18.7 and proceed as in the remainder of the code.

When the median-of-three rule is used, quick sort takes $O(n \log n)$ time when the input list is in sorted order. Moreover, the case when one of the two partitions is empty is eliminated (except when we have duplicates). In other words, the median-of-three rule ensures a better balance between the two partitions. Is this improvement in balance enough to pay for the added cost of computing the pivot? Only an experiment can answer this question.

Performance Measurement

The observed average times for quickSort appear in Figure 18.12. These times are
for Program 18.6 with the pivot being the first element of the segment. This figure
includes the average times for merge, heap, and insertion sort. For each n at least
100 randomly generated integer instances were run. These random instances were
constructed by making repeated calls to the C++ function rand. If the time taken
to sort these instances was less than 1 second (see Section 4.4), then additional
random instances were sorted until the total time taken was at least this much.
The times reported in Figure 18.12 include the time taken to set up the random
data. For each n the time taken to set up the data and the time for the remaining
overheads included in the reported numbers is the same for all sort methods. As
a result, the data of Figure 18.12 is useful for comparative purposes. The data of
this figure is plotted in Figure 18.13.

n	Insert	Heap	Merge	Quick
0	0.000	0.000	0.000	0.000
50	0.004	0.009	0.008	0.006
100	0.011	0.019	0.017	0.013
200	0.033	0.042	0.037	0.029
300	0.067	0.066	0.059	0.045
400	0.117	0.090	0.079	0.061
500	0.179	0.116	0.100	0.079
1000	0.662	0.245	0.213	0.169
2000	2.439	0.519	0.459	0.358
3000	5.390	0.809	0.721	0.560
4000	9.530	1.105	0.972	0.761
5000	15.935	1.410	1.271	0.970

Times are in milliseconds

Figure 18.12 Average times for sort methods

As Figure 18.13 shows, quick sort outperforms the other sort methods for suitably large n. We see that the break-even point between insertion and quick sort is
a between 50 and 100. The exact break-even point can be found experimentally by
obtaining run-time data for n between 50 and 100. Let the exact break-even point
be nBreak. For average performance, insertion sort is the best sort method (of those
tested) to use when n ≤ nBreak, and quick sort is the best when n > nBreak. We
can improve on the performance of quick sort for n > nBreak by combining insertion
and quick sort into a single sort function by replacing the following statement in
Program 18.6

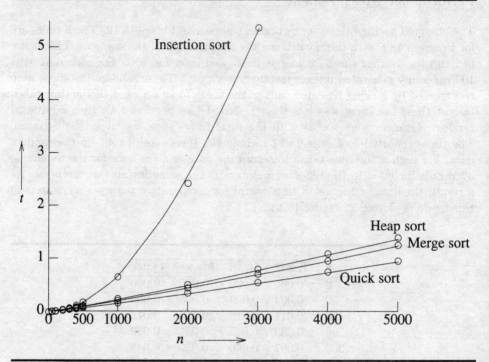

Figure 18.13 Plot of average times (milliseconds)

```
if (leftEnd >= rightEnd) return;
```

with the code

```
if (rightEnd - leftEnd < nBreak)
{
    insertionSort(a, leftEnd, rightEnd);
    return;
}
```

Here `insertionSort(a, leftEnd, rightEnd)` is a function that sorts `a[leftEnd:rightEnd]`, using the insertion sort method. The performance measurement of the modified quick sort code is left as Exercise 28. Further improvement in performance may be possible by replacing `nBreak` with a smaller value (see Exercise 28).

For worst-case behavior most implementations will show merge sort to be best for n > c where c is some constant. For n ≤ c insertion sort has the best worst-case behavior. The performance of merge sort can be improved by combining insertion sort and merge sort (see Exercise 29).

The run-time results for the sort methods point out some of the limitations of asymptotic complexity analysis. Asymptotic analysis is not a good predictor of performance for small instances—insertion sort with its $O(n^2)$ complexity is better than all of the $O(n \log n)$ methods for small instances. Programs that have the same asymptotic complexity often have different actual run times.

C++'s Sort Methods

If you had to develop the STL sort function `sort`, what would you do? The results of Figures 18.12 and 18.13 leave you in a quandary. Should you pick a method that optimizes worst-case performance, or should you pick one that optimizes average performance? Should you limit your choice to a sort method that is stable (i.e., a method that does not alter the relative order of equal elements)?

The developers of C++'s sort function opted to optimize average performance and use a modified quick sort that reverts to a heap sort when the number of subdivisions exceeds some constant times $\log_n$ and to an insertion sort when the segment size becomes small. The STL function `stable_sort` is a merge sort that reverts to an insertion sort when the segment size becomes small.

18.2.4   Selection

Problem Description

In this problem we are given an array $a[0 : n-1]$ of n elements and are to determine the kth smallest element. This element is the element in position `a[k-1]` following a sort of the array. Consider the case $n = 8$; each element has the two fields, `key` and `id`, where `key` is an integer and `id` is a character. Let the eight elements be $[(12, a), (4, b), (5, c), (4, d), (5, e), (10, f), (2, g), (20, h)]$. Then suppose that following a sort we have the array $[(2, g), (4, d), (4, b), (5, c), (5, e), (10, f), (12, a), (20, h)]$. If $k = 1$, we return the element with id g; if $k = 8$, we return the element with id h; if $k = 6$, we return the element with id f; and if $k = 2$, we return the element with id d. Actually, in this last case we have some flexibility, as the sort could have placed either of the elements with ids d and b into `a[1]`, because both have the same `key`. Therefore, either may be returned. However, if one element is returned when $k = 2$, the other should be returned when $k = 3$.

One application of the selection problem is finding the median element. In this case $k = \lceil n/2 \rceil$. Medians are useful statistical quantities that are reported often in the media, for example, median salary, median age, and median height. Other values of k are also useful. For example, we can divide a population into quartiles by finding the $n/4$, $n/2$, and $3n/4$ elements.

Solution Strategy and Implementation

We can solve the selection problem in $O(n \log n)$ time by first sorting the n elements (for example, using heap sort or merge sort) and then picking off the element in position a[k-1]. We can obtain better average performance by using quick sort (see Figure 18.12), even though this method has an inferior asymptotic complexity of $O(n^2)$.

We can adapt the code of Program 18.6 to the selection problem so as to obtain an even faster solution. If the pivot a[leftEnd] is to be placed in a[j] following the execution of the two while loops, then a[leftEnd] is known to be the j-leftEnd+1th element of a[leftEnd:rightEnd]. If we are looking for the kth element in a[leftEnd:rightEnd] and j-leftEnd+1 equals k, then the answer is a[leftEnd]; if j-leftEnd+1 < k, then the element we are looking for is the k-j+leftEnd-1th element of *right*; otherwise, it is the kth element of *left*. Therefore, we need to make either zero or one recursive call. The code for the new selection program appears in Programs 18.8 and 18.9. A for or while loop can replace the recursive calls made by select (see Exercise 35).

```
template <class T>
T select(T a[], int n, int k)
{// Return k'th smallest element in a[0 : n - 1].
   if (k < 1 || k > n)
      throw illegalParameterValue("k must be between 1 and n");

   // move largest element to right end
   int max = indexOfMax(a, n);
   swap(a[n-1], a[max]);
   return select(a, 0, n - 1, k);
}
```

Program 18.8 Preprocessor to find the *k*th element

Complexity Analysis

The worst-case complexity of Program 18.8 is $\Theta(n^2)$. This worst case is achieved, for example, when *left* is always empty and the kth element is in *right*. However, if *left* and *right* are always of the same size or differ in size by at most 1, then we get the following recurrence for the time needed by Program 18.8:

$$t(n) \leq \begin{cases} d & n \leq 1 \\ t(\lfloor n/2 \rfloor) + cn & n > 1 \end{cases} \tag{18.13}$$

If we assume that n is a power of 2, the floor operator may be dropped and the recurrence solved, using the substitution method, to obtain $t(n) = \Theta(n)$. By selecting the partitioning element more carefully, the worst-case time also becomes $\Theta(n)$. The more careful way to select the partitioning element is to use the **median-of-medians** rule in which the n elements of a are divided into $\lfloor n/r \rfloor$ groups for some

```
template <class T>
T select(T a[], int leftEnd, int rightEnd, int k)
{// Return k'th element in a[leftEnd:rightEnd].
   if (leftEnd >= rightEnd)
      return a[leftEnd];
   int leftCursor = leftEnd,         // left-to-right cursor
       rightCursor = rightEnd + 1;   // right-to-left cursor
   T pivot = a[leftEnd];

   // swap elements >= pivot on left side
   // with elements <= pivot on right side
   while (true)
   {
      do
      {// find >= element on left side
         leftCursor++;
      } while (a[leftCursor] < pivot);

      do
      {// find <= element on right side
         rightCursor--;
      } while (a[rightCursor] > pivot);

      if (leftCursor >= rightCursor) break;  // swap pair not found
      swap(a[leftCursor], a[rightCursor]);
   }

   if (rightCursor - leftEnd + 1 == k)
      return pivot;

   // place pivot
   a[leftEnd] = a[rightCursor];
   a[rightCursor] = pivot;

   // recursive call on one segment
   if (rightCursor - leftEnd + 1 < k)
      return select(a, rightCursor + 1, rightEnd,
                       k - rightCursor + leftEnd - 1);
   else return select(a, leftEnd, rightCursor - 1, k);
}
```

Program 18.9 Recursive method to find the kth element

integer constant r. Each of these groups contains exactly r elements. The remaining $n \bmod r$ elements are not used in the selection of the pivot. Next we find the median of each group by sorting the r elements in each group and then selecting the one in the middle position (i.e., in position $\lceil r/2 \rceil$). The median of these $\lfloor n/r \rfloor$ medians is computed, using the selection algorithm recursively, and is used as the partitioning element.

Example 18.6 [Median of Medians] Consider the case $r = 5$, $n = 27$, and $a = [2, 6, 8, 1, 4, 9, 20, 6, 22, 11, 9, 8, 4, 3, 7, 8, 16, 11, 10, 8, 2, 14, 15, 1, 12, 5, 4]$. These 27 elements may be divided into the five groups $[2, 6, 8, 1, 4]$, $[9, 20, 6, 22, 11]$, $[9, 8, 4, 3, 7]$, $[8, 16, 11, 10, 8]$, and $[2, 14, 15, 1, 12]$. The remaining elements, 5 and 4, are not used when selecting the pivot. The medians of these five groups are 4, 11, 7, 10, and 12, respectively. The median of the elements $[4, 11, 7, 10, 12]$ is 10. This median is used as the partitioning element. With this choice of the pivot, we get $left = [2, 6, 8, 1, 4, 9, 6, 9, 8, 4, 3, 7, 8, 8, 2, 1, 5, 4]$, $middle = [10]$, and $right = [20, 22, 11, 16, 11, 14, 15, 12]$. If we are to find the kth element for $k < 19$, only $left$ needs to be examined; if $k = 19$, the element is the pivot; and if $k > 19$, the eight elements of $right$ need to be examined. In this last case we need to find the $k - 19$th element of $right$.   ∎

Theorem 18.3 *When the partitioning element is chosen using the median-of-medians rule, the following statements are true:*

(a) *If $r = 9$, then $\max\{|left|, |right|\} \le 7n/8$ for $n \ge 90$.*

(b) *If $r = 5$ and all elements of a are distinct, then $\max\{|left|, |right|\} \le 3n/4$ for $n \ge 24$.*

Proof Exercise 33 asks you to prove this theorem.   ∎

From Theorem 18.3 and Program 18.8, it follows that if the median-of-medians rule with $r = 9$ is used, the time $t(n)$ needed to select the kth element is given by the following recurrence:

$$t(n) = \begin{cases} cn \log n & n < 90 \\ t(\lfloor n/9 \rfloor) + t(\lfloor 7n/8 \rfloor) + cn & n \ge 90 \end{cases} \tag{18.14}$$

where c is a constant. This recurrence assumes that an $n \log n$ method is used when $n < 90$ and that larger instances are solved using divide and conquer with the median-of-medians rule. Using induction, you can show (Exercise 34) that $t(n) \le 72cn$ for $n \ge 1$. When the elements are distinct, we may use $r = 5$ to get linear-time performance.

18.2.5   Closest Pair of Points

Problem Description

In this problem you are given n points (x_i, y_i), $1 \le i \le n$, and are to find two that are closest. The distance between two points i and j is given by the following formula:

$$\sqrt{(x_i - x_j)^2 + (y_i - y_j)^2}$$

Example 18.7 Suppose that n equal-size holes are to be drilled into a sheet of metal. If any two holes are too close, metal failure may occur during the drilling process. By determining the minimum distance between any two holes, we can assess the probability of such a failure. This minimum distance corresponds to the distance between a closest pair of points. ∎

Solution Strategy

We can solve the closest-pair-of-points problem in $O(n^2)$ time by examining all $n(n-1)/2$ pairs of points, computing the distance between the points in each pair, and determining the pair for which this distance is minimum. We will call this method the *direct approach*. The divide-and-conquer method suggests the high-level algorithm of Figure 18.14.

```
if (n is small)
{
    Find the closest pair using the direct approach.
    return;
}

// n is large
Divide the point set into two roughly equal parts A and B.
Determine the closest pairs of points in A and B.
Determine the closest point pair such that one point is in A and the other in B.
From the three closest pairs computed, select the one with least distance.
```

Figure 18.14 Finding a closest pair of points

This algorithm uses the direct approach to solve small instances and solves large instances by dividing them into two smaller instances. One instance (say, A) will be of size $\lceil n/2 \rceil$, and the other (say, B) of size $\lfloor n/2 \rfloor$. The closest pair of points in the original instance falls into one of the three categories: (1) both points are in A (i.e., it is a closest pair of A); (2) both points are in B; and (3) one point is in A, and the other in B. Suppose we determine the closest pair in each of these categories. The pair with the least distance is the overall closest pair. The closest pair in category 1 can be determined by using the closest-pair algorithm recursively on the smaller point set A. The closest pair in B can be similarly determined.

To determine the closest pair in category 3, we need a different method. The method depends on how the points are divided into A and B. A reasonable way to do this division is to cut the plane by a vertical line that goes through the median x_i value. All points to the left of this line are in A; all to the right are in B; and those on the line are distributed between A and B so as to meet the size requirements on A and B.

Example 18.8 Consider the 14 points a through n of Figure 18.15(a). These points are plotted in Figure 18.15(b). The median $x_i = 1$, and the vertical line $x = 1$ is shown as a broken line in Figure 18.15(b). The points to the left of this line (i.e., points b, c, h, and n) are in A, and those to the right of the line (i.e., points a, e, f, j, k, and l) are in B. Of the points d, g, and m that are on the line, two are added to A and one to B so that A and B have seven points each. Suppose that d and m are assigned to A, and g is assigned to B.   ∎

Let δ be the smaller of the distances between the points in the closest pairs of A and B. For a pair in category 3 to be closer than δ, each point of the pair must be less than distance δ from the dividing line. Therefore, we can eliminate from consideration all points that are a distance $\geq \delta$ from this line. The broken line of Figure 18.16 is the dividing line. The shaded box has width 2δ and is centered at the dividing line. Points on or outside the boundary of this box are eliminated. Only the points inside the shaded region need be retained when determining whether there is a category 3 pair with distance less than δ.

Let R_A and R_B, respectively, denote the points of A and B that remain. If there is a point pair (p, q) such that $p \in A$, $q \in B$, and p and q are less than δ apart, then $p \in R_A$ and $q \in R_B$. We can find this point pair by considering the points in R_A one at a time. Suppose that we are considering point p of R_A and that p's y-coordinate is $p.y$. We need to look only at points q in R_B with y-coordinate $q.y$ such that $p.y - \delta < q.y < p.y + \delta$ and see whether any point is less than distance δ from p. The region of R_B that contains these points q appears in Figure 18.17(a). Only the points of R_B within the shaded $\delta \times 2\delta$ box need be paired with p to see whether p is part of a category 3 pair with distance less than δ. This $\delta \times 2\delta$ region is p's **comparing region**.

Example 18.9 Consider the 14 points of Example 18.8. The closest point pair in A (see Example 18.8) is (b, h) with a distance of approximately 0.316. The closest point pair in B is (f, j) with a distance of 0.3. Therefore, $\delta = 0.3$. When determining whether there is a category 3 pair with distance less than δ, all points

label	a	b	c	d	e	f	g
x_i	2	0.5	0.25	1	3	2	1
y_i	2	0.5	1	2	1	0.7	1
label	h	i	j	k	l	m	n
x_i	0.6	0.9	2	4	1.1	1	0.7
y_i	0.8	0.5	1	2	0.5	1.5	2

(a) The 14 points

(b) Plot of points

Figure 18.15 Fourteen-point instance

other than d, g, i, l, and m are eliminated from consideration, as each is $\geq \delta$ distant from the dividing line that has x-coordinate 1. We have $R_A = \{d, i, m\}$ and $R_B = \{g, l\}$. Since there are no points in the comparing regions of d and g, only point i needs to be considered further. The comparing region of i contains only point l. We compute the distance between i and l and find that it is less than δ. (i, l) is therefore the closest pair.   ∎

Since all points on the boundary of or inside the $\delta \times 2\delta$ comparing region are at least δ apart, the number of such points cannot exceed six. Figure 18.17(b) shows the only way to place six points while satisfying the minimum distance δ requirement. So each point of R_A is paired with at most six points of R_B when determining a closer category 3 pair.

Points shown by × are eliminated

Figure 18.16 Eliminating points that are too far from the dividing line

Figure 18.17 Comparing region for p

Choice of Data Structures

To implement the divide-and-conquer algorithm of Figure 18.14, we need to decide what exactly is a "small" instance and also decide how to represent the points. Since the closest pair of a set of fewer than 2 points is not defined, we must ensure that our division process does not create sets of size less than 2. The creation of sets with fewer than two points can be avoided if our divide-and-conquer algorithm considers sets with fewer than four points as small.

Our implementation utilizes four structs for points. The struct `point` has two data members x and y to store the x- and y-coordinates of a point, and both x and y are of type double. The struct point1 derives from point and adds the additional data member id, which is of type int. The struct point1 defines a type conversion to double that returns the value of x. This type conversion allows us to use merge sort (Program 18.3) to sort the points into ascending order of x-coordinate. The third class for points is point2. This class also derives from point, and adds the integer data member p whose significance is described below. The struct point2 defines a type conversion to double that returns the y-coordinate of the point. This type conversion allows us to use merge sort (Program 18.3) to sort the points into ascending order of y-coordinate. The fourth and last point struct is pointPair. This struct has the data members a (first point in the pair), b (second point in the pair), and dist (distance between the points a and b). a and b are of type point1, and dist is of type double.

The input points may be represented in an array x of type point1. Suppose that the points in x have been sorted by their x-coordinate. If at any stage of the division process the points under consideration are x$[l : r]$, then we may obtain A and B by first computing $m = (l + r)/2$. The points X$[l : m]$ are in A, and the remaining points are in B.

After we compute the closest pairs in A and B, we need to compute R_A and R_B and then determine whether there is a closer pair with one point in R_A and the other in R_B. The test of Figure 18.17 may be implemented in a simple way if the points are sorted by their y-coordinate. A list of the points sorted by y-coordinate is maintained in another array using the struct point2. Notice that for this struct, the type conversion to double has been implemented so as to facilitate sorting by y-coordinate. The field p is used to index back to the same point in the array x.

C++ Implementation

With the necessary data structures determined, let us examine the resulting code. First we define a function dist (Program 18.10) that computes the distance between two points a and b. Notice that Program 18.10 may also be used to compute the distance between points of type point1 and point2 because the class point is the base class of point1 and point2.

```
double dist(const point& u, const point& v)
{// return distance between points u and v.
    double dx = u.x - v.x;
    double dy = u.y - v.y;
    return sqrt(dx * dx + dy * dy);
}
```

Program 18.10 Computing the distance between two points

The function closestPair of Program 18.11 throws an exception if the number of points is fewer than 2. When the number of points exceeds 1, the function

returns the closest pair of points. Function `closestPair` begins by verifying that
we have at least two points. Then the points in x are sorted by x-coordinate, using
`mergeSort` (Program 18.3). Next the points are copied into an array y and sorted
by y-coordinate. Following this sort, $y[i].y \leq y[i+1].y$, and for each i, $y[i].p$ gives
point i's location in the array x. After this preprocessing, we invoke the function
`closestPair` of Program 18.12, which does the actual determination of the closest
pair.

```
pointPair closestPair(point1 x[], int numberOfPoints)
{// Return closest pair of points in x[0:numberOfPoints-1].
 // Throw an exception if fewer than two points.
   int n = numberOfPoints;
   if (n < 2)
      throw illegalParameterValue("Number of points must be > 1");

   // sort on x-coordinate
   mergeSort(x, n);

   // create a point array sorted on y-coordinate
   point2 *y = new point2 [n];
   for (int i = 0; i < n; i++)
      // copy point i from x to y and index it
      y[i] = point2(x[i].x, x[i].y, i);
   mergeSort(y, n);  // sort on y-coordinate

   // create a temporary array
   point2 *z = new point2 [n];

   // find closest pair
   return closestPair(x, y, z, 0, n - 1);
}
```

Program 18.11 Driver for recursive `closestPair` function

The recursive `closestPair` function (Program 18.12) determines the closest
pair from among the points x[1:r]. These points are assumed to be sorted by their
x-coordinate. y[1:r] is the same points sorted by their y-coordinate. z[1:r] is
available as space for temporary results. Upon completion the closest pair of points
is returned as an instance of `pointPair`, and the array y is restored to its input
status. The function does not modify the array x.

We begin by taking care of small instances; that is, instances with fewer than
four points. Since no instance of size less than two is created by the division process,

```
pointPair closestPair(point1 x[], point2 y[], point2 z[], int l, int r)
{// x[l:r] points sorted by x-coordinate, r > l.
 // y[l:r] points sorted by y-coordinate.
 // z[l:r] is used for work space.
 // Return closest pair of points in x[l:r].
   if (r - l == 1)  // only two points
      return pointPair(x[l], x[r], dist(x[l], x[r]));

   if (r - l == 2)
   {// three points
      // compute distance between all pairs
      double d1 = dist(x[l], x[l + 1]);
      double d2 = dist(x[l + 1], x[r]);
      double d3 = dist(x[l], x[r]);
      // find closest pair
      if (d1 <= d2 && d1 <= d3)
         return pointPair(x[l], x[l + 1], d1);
      if (d2 <= d3)
         return pointPair(x[l + 1], x[r], d2);
      else
         return pointPair(x[l], x[r], d3);
   }

   // more than three points, divide into two
   int m = (l + r) / 2;     // x[l:m] in A, rest in B

   // create sorted-by-y lists in z[l:m] & z[m+1:r]
   int f = l,        // cursor for z[l:m]
       g = m + 1;    // cursor for z[m+1:r]
   for (int i = l; i <= r; i++)
      if (y[i].p > m) z[g++] = y[i];
      else z[f++] = y[i];

   // solve the two parts
   pointPair best = closestPair(x, z, y, l, m);
   pointPair right = closestPair(x, z, y, m + 1, r);

   // make best closer pair of the two
   if (right.dist < best.dist)
      best = right;
```

Program 18.12 Determination of closest pair of points (continues)

```
    merge(z, y, l, m, r);    // reconstruct y

    // put points within best.d of midpoint in z
    int k = 1;                          // cursor for z
    for (int i = 1; i <= r; i++)
        if (fabs(x[m].x - y[i].x) < best.dist)
            z[k++] = y[i];

    // search for closer category 3 pair
    // by checking all pairs from z[1:k-1]
    for (int i = 1; i < k; i++)
    {
        for (int j = i + 1; j < k && z[j].y - z[i].y < best.dist; j++)
        {
            double dp = dist(z[i], z[j]);
            if (dp < best.dist) // closer pair found
                best = pointPair(x[z[i].p], x[z[j].p], dp);
        }
    }
    return best;
}
```

Program 18.12 Determination of closest pair of points (concluded)

we need to handle the cases of two and three points. These cases are handled by trying out all possibilities. When the number of points exceeds 3, the instance is divided into two smaller instances A and B by computing $m = (1+r)/2$. The points $x[1:m]$ are in A, and the points $x[m+1:r]$ are in B. The corresponding sorted-by-y lists are created in $z[1:m]$ and $z[m+1:r]$ from the sorted-by-y list $y[1:r]$ by scanning the list y from left to right and determining which points are in A and which in B. The roles of the arrays y and z are interchanged, and two recursive calls are made to obtain the closest pairs in A and B. Upon return from these recursive calls, array z is guaranteed to be unaltered, but array y is not. However, only $y[1:r]$ may have changed. $y[1:r]$ is reconstructed from $z[1:r]$ by merging (Program 18.5) the sublists corresponding to A and B.

To implement the test of Figure 18.17, we first scan the array segment $y[1:r]$ that contains the points under consideration sorted by y and accumulate points that are $< \delta$ from the dividing line (see Figure 18.16) in sorted order of y-coordinate in another array $z[1:k-1]$. The pairing of each point p of R_A with all points in its comparing region of R_B is divided into two parts: (1) pairing with points in the comparing region of R_B that have y-coordinate $\geq$ p.y and (2) pairing with points that have y-coordinate $\leq$ p.y. These two parts may be implemented by pairing each point z[i], $1 \leq$ i $<$ k (regardless of whether it is in R_A or R_B) with a point z[j], i $<$ j, for which z[j].y-z[i].y $< \delta$. For each z[i] the points that get examined lie inside the $2\delta \times \delta$ region shown in Figure 18.18. Since the points in each $\delta \times \delta$ subregion are at least δ apart, the number in each subregion cannot exceed four. So the number of points z[j] that each z[i] is paired with is at most seven.

(a)   (b)

Figure 18.18 Region of points paired with z[i]

Complexity Analysis

Let $t(n)$ denote the time taken by the recursive function closestPair on a set of n points. When $n < 4$, $t(n)$ equals some constant d. When $n \geq 4$, it takes $\Theta(n)$ time to divide the instance into two parts, reconstruct y after the two recursive calls, eliminate points that are too far from the dividing line, and search for a better category 3 pair. The recursive calls take $t(\lceil n/2 \rceil)$ and $t(\lfloor n/2 \rfloor)$ time, respectively. Therefore, we obtain the recurrence

$$t(n) = \begin{cases} d & n < 4 \\ t(\lfloor n/2 \rfloor) + t(\lceil n/2 \rceil) + cn & n \geq 4 \end{cases}$$

which is the same as the recurrence for merge sort. Its solution is $t(n) = \Theta(n \log n)$. The additional work done by the driver function closestPair of Program 18.11 consists of sorting x, creating y and z, and sorting y. The total time for this additional work is also $\Theta(n \log n)$. The overall time complexity of the divide-and-conquer closest-pair code is $\Theta(n \log n)$ under the assumption that no exception is thrown.

EXERCISES

8. Write a complete program for the defective-chessboard problem. Include modules to welcome the user to the program; input the chessboard size and location

of the defect; and output the tiled chessboard. The output is to be provided on a color monitor using colored tiles. No two tiles that share a common boundary should be colored the same. Since the chessboard is a planar figure, it is possible to color the tiles in this way using at most four colors. However, for this exercise, it is sufficient to devise a greedy coloring heuristic that attempts to use as few colors as possible.

9. Solve the recurrence of Equation 18.7 using the substitution method.

10. Does $f(x) = \sqrt{x}$ satisfy Equation 18.9?

11. Show that $f(x) = x^a \log^b x$ satisfies Equation 18.9 for all $a \geq 1$, all integer $b \geq 0$, and all $x \geq 1$.

12. Start with the array [11, 2, 8, 3, 6, 15, 12, 0, 7, 4, 1, 13, 5, 9, 14, 10] and draw a figure similar to Figure 18.9 that shows the steps involved in a merge sort.

13. Do Exercise 12 using the array [11, 3, 8, 7, 5, 10, 0, 9, 4, 2, 6, 1].

14. Write a merge sort code that works on chains of elements. The output should be a sorted chain. Make your sort method a member of the class **chain** or of a class that extends **chain** (Section 6.1).

15. Start with the array [2, 3, 6, 8, 11, 15, 0, 7, 12, 1, 4, 13, 5, 9, 10, 14] and draw a figure similar to Figure 18.9 that shows the steps involved in a natural merge sort.

16. Do Exercise 15 using the array [11, 3, 8, 5, 7, 10, 0, 9, 2, 4, 6, 1].

17. Write the function **naturalMergeSort** that implements a natural merge sort. The input and output configurations are the same as for Program 18.3.

18. Write a natural merge sort code that sorts a chain of elements. Your function should be a member of the class **chain** or of a class that extends **chain** (Section 6.1).

19. Start with the segment [5, 3, 8, 4, 7, 1, 0, 9, 2, 10, 6, 11] and draw a figure to show the status of this segment following each swap that is done in the **while** loop of Program 18.7. Also show the segment after the pivot is properly placed. Use 5 as the pivot.

20. Do Exercise 19 using the array [7, 3, 6, 8, 11, 14, 0, 2, 12, 1, 4, 13, 5, 9, 10, 15]. Use 7 as the pivot.

21. Replace the last recursive call to **quickSort** in Program 18.7 with a **while** loop. Compare the average run time of the resulting sort method with that of Program 18.7.

22. Rewrite the quick sort code (Programs 18.6 and 18.7) using a stack to simulate the recursion. The new code should stack the boundaries of only the larger of the segments *left* and *right*.

    (a) Show that the stack space needed is $O(\log n)$.

    (b) Compare the average run time of your nonrecursive code with that of the recursive code given in the text.

23. Show that the worst-case time complexity of `quickSort` is $\Theta(n^2)$.

24. Suppose that the partitioning into *left*, *middle*, and *right* is always such that *left* and *right* have the same size when n (n is the number of elements in the segment being sorted) is odd and *left* has one element more than *right* when n is even. Show that under this assumption, the time complexity of Program 18.6 is $O(n \log n)$.

25. Show that $\int s \log_e s \, ds = \frac{s^2 \log_e s}{2} - \frac{s^2}{4}$. Use this result to show that $\int_2^m s \log_e s \, ds < \frac{m^2 \log_e m}{2} - \frac{m^2}{4}$.

26. Compare the worst-case and average times of Program 18.7 when the median-of-three rule is used to the times when it is not used. Do this comparison experimentally; use suitable test data and $n = 10, 20, \cdots, 100, 200, 300, 400, 500, 1000$.

27. Do Exercise 26 using a random number generator rather than the median-of-three rule to select the pivot element.

28. At the end of the quick sort section, we suggested combining two sort methods: quick sort and insertion sort. The combined algorithm is essentially a quick sort that reverts to an insertion sort when the size of a segment is less than or equal to `changeOver = nBreak`. Can we obtain a faster algorithm by using a different value for `changeOver`? Why? Modify Program 18.7 to use the median-of-three rule; experiment with different values of `changeOver` and see what happens. Determine the best value of `changeOver` for the case of average performance. After you have optimized your quick sort code, compare the average performance of your code and that of the C++ STL function `sort`.

29. In this exercise we will develop a sort procedure with best worst-case performance.

    (a) Compare the worst-case run times of insertion, bubble, selection, heap, merge, and quick sort. The worst-case input data for insertion, bubble, selection, and quick sort are easy to generate. For merge sort, write a program to generate the worst-case data. This program will essentially unmerge a sorted sequence of n elements. For heap sort, estimate the worst-case time using random permutations.

(b) Use the results of part (a) to obtain a composite sort function that has the best worst-case performance. More likely than not, your composite procedure will include only merge and insertion sort.

(c) Run an experiment to determine the worst-case run time of your composite function. Compare the performance with that of the original sort functions and of the STL function stable_sort.

(d) Plot the worst-case times of the eight sort methods on a single graph sheet.

30. Start with the array $[4, 3, 8, 5, 7, 10, 0, 9, 2, 11, 6, 1]$ and draw a figure to show the progress of Programs 18.8 and 18.9 when started with $k = 7$. You should show the segment to be searched following each partitioning pass and also give the new k value.

31. Do Exercise 30 using the array $[7, 3, 6, 8, 11, 15, 0, 2, 12, 1, 4, 13, 5, 9, 10, 14]$ and $k = 5$.

32. Use the substitution method to solve Equation 18.13 for the case when n is a power of 2.

33. Prove Theorem 18.3.

34. Use induction to show that Equation 18.14 implies $t(n) \leq 72cn$ for $n \geq 1$.

35. Programs 18.8 and 18.9 need $O(n)$, where n is the number of elements, space for the recursion stack. This space can be entirely eliminated by replacing the recursive calls with a while or for loop. Rewrite the code in this way. Compare the run time of the two versions of the selection code.

36. (a) Recode Program 18.9 using a random number generator to select the partitioning element. Conduct experiments to compare the average performance of the two codes.

(b) Recode Program 18.9 using the median-of-medians rule with $r = 9$.

37. In an attempt to speed Program 18.12, we might eliminate the square root operator from the computation of the distance between two points and instead work with the square of the distance. Finding the closest pair is the same as finding a pair with minimum squared distance. What changes need to be made to Program 18.12? Experiment with the two versions and measure the performance improvement you can achieve.

38. Devise a faster algorithm to find the closest pair of points when all points are known to lie on a straight line. For example, suppose the points are on a horizontal line. If the points are sorted by x-coordinate, then the nearest pair contains two adjacent points. Although this strategy results in an $O(n \log n)$ algorithm if we use mergeSort (Program 18.3), the algorithm has considerably less overhead than Program 18.11 has and so runs faster.

39. Consider the closest-pair-of-points problem. Suppose that instead of sorting the points by x-coordinate initially, we use function `select` (Program 18.8) to find the median x_i and divide the points into A and B.

   (a) Write a high-level description of the resulting algorithm for the closest-pair problem.

   (b) What is the complexity of your algorithm?

   (c) Comment on whether or not you expect the new algorithm to be faster than Program 18.12.

18.3   SOLVING RECURRENCE EQUATIONS

Several techniques—substitution, induction, characteristic roots, and generating function—are available to solve recurrence equations. You can find a detailed development of these methods in the Web site for this book. In this section, we describe a table look-up method that can be used to solve many recurrences associated with divide-and-conquer algorithms.

The complexity of many divide-and-conquer algorithms is given by a recurrence of the form

$$t(n) = \begin{cases} t(1) & n = 1 \\ a * t(n/b) + g(n) & n > 1 \end{cases} \qquad (18.15)$$

where a and b are known constants. We will assume that $t(1)$ is known and that n is a power of b (i.e., $n = b^k$). Using the substitution method (see the Web site), we can show that

$$t(n) = n^{\log_b a}[t(1) + f(n)] \qquad (18.16)$$

where $f(n) = \sum_{j=1}^{k} h(b^j)$ and $h(n) = g(n)/n^{\log_b a}$.

Figure 18.19 tabulates the asymptotic value of $f(n)$ for various values of $h(n)$. This table allows us to easily obtain the asymptotic value of $t(n)$ for many of the recurrences we encounter when analyzing divide-and-conquer algorithms.

Let us solve a few recurrences using this table. The recurrence for binary search when n is a power of 2 is

$$t(n) = \begin{cases} t(1) & n = 1 \\ t(n/2) + c & n > 1 \end{cases}$$

Comparing this recurrence with Equation 18.14, we see that $a = 1$, $b = 2$, and $g(n) = c$. Therefore, $\log_b(a) = 0$, and $h(n) = g(n)/n^{\log_b a} = c = c(\log n)^0 = \Theta((\log n)^0)$. From Figure 18.19, we obtain $f(n) = \Theta(\log n)$. Therefore, $t(n) = n^{\log_b a}(c + \Theta(\log n)) = \Theta(\log n)$.

$h(n)$	$f(n)$
$O(n^r)$, $r < 0$	$O(1)$
$\Theta((\log n)^i)$, $i \geq 0$	$\Theta(((\log n)^{i+1})/(i+1))$
$\Omega(n^r)$, $r > 0$	$\Theta(h(n))$

Figure 18.19 $f(n)$ values for various $h(n)$ values

For the merge sort recurrence, we obtain $a = 2$, $b = 2$, and $g(n) = cn$. So $\log_b a = 1$, and $h(n) = g(n)/n = c = \Theta((\log n)^0)$. Hence $f(n) = \Theta(\log n)$ and $t(n) = n(t(1) + \Theta(\log n)) = \Theta(n \log n)$.

As another example, consider the recurrence

$$t(n) = 7t(n/2) + 18n^2, \ n \geq 2 \text{ and a power of 2}$$

that corresponds to the recurrence for Strassen's matrix-multiplication method (Equation 18.6) with $k = 1$ and $c = 18$. We obtain $a = 7$, $b = 2$, and $g(n) = 18n^2$. Therefore, $\log_b a = \log_2 7 \approx 2.81$, and $h(n) = 18n^2/n^{\log_2 7} = 18n^{2 - \log_2 7} = O(n^r)$ where $r = 2 - \log_2 7 < 0$. Therefore, $f(n) = O(1)$. The expression for $t(n)$ is

$$t(n) = n^{\log_2 7}(t(1) + O(1)) = \Theta(n^{\log_2 7})$$

as $t(1)$ is assumed to be a constant.

As a final example, consider the following recurrence:

$$t(n) = 9t(n/3) + 4n^6, \ n \geq 3 \text{ and a power of 3}$$

Comparing this recurrence with Equation 18.14, we obtain $a = 9$, $b = 3$, and $g(n) = 4n^6$. Therefore, $\log_b a = 2$ and $h(n) = 4n^6/n^2 = 4n^4 = \Omega(n^4)$. From Figure 18.13 we see that $f(n) = \Theta(h(n)) = \Theta(n^4)$. Therefore,

$$t(n) = n^2(t(1) + \Theta(n^4)) = \Theta(n^6)$$

as $t(1)$ may be assumed constant.

EXERCISES

40. Use the substitution method to show that Equation 18.16 is the solution to the recurrence 18.15.

41. Use the table of Figure 18.19 to solve the following recurrences. In each case assume $t(1) = 1$.

   (a) $t(n) = 10t(n/3) + 11n$, $n \geq 3$ and a power of 3.

   (b) $t(n) = 10t(n/3) + 11n^5$, $n \geq 3$ and a power of 3.

   (c) $t(n) = 27t(n/3) + 11n^3$, $n \geq 3$ and a power of 3.

   (d) $t(n) = 64t(n/4) + 10n^3 \log^2 n$, $n \geq 4$ and a power of 4.

   (e) $t(n) = 9t(n/2) + n^2 2^n$, $n \geq 2$ and a power of 2.

   (f) $t(n) = 3t(n/8) + n^2 2^n \log n$, $n \geq 8$ and a power of 8.

   (g) $t(n) = 128t(n/2) + 6n$, $n \geq 2$ and a power of 2.

   (h) $t(n) = 128t(n/2) + 6n^8$, $n \geq 2$ and a power of 2.

   (i) $t(n) = 128t(n/2) + 2^n/n$, $n \geq 2$ and a power of 2.

   (j) $t(n) = 128t(n/2) + \log^3 n$, $n \geq 2$ and a power of 2.

18.4   LOWER BOUNDS ON COMPLEXITY

$f(n)$ is an **upper bound** on the complexity of a problem iff at least one algorithm solves this problem in $O(f(n))$ time. One way to establish an upper bound of $f(n)$ on the complexity of a problem is to develop an algorithm whose complexity is $O(f(n))$. Each algorithm developed in this book established an upper bound on the complexity of the problem it solved. For example, until the discovery of Strassen's matrix-multiplication algorithm (Example 18.3), the upper bound on the complexity of matrix multiplication was n^3, as the algorithm of Program 2.22 was already known and this algorithm runs in $\Theta(n^3)$ time. The discovery of Strassen's algorithm reduced the upper bound on the complexity of matrix multiplication to $n^{2.81}$.

  $f(n)$ is a **lower bound** on the complexity of a problem iff every algorithm for this problem has complexity $\Omega(f(n))$. To establish a lower bound of $g(n)$ on the complexity of a problem, we must show that *every* algorithm for this problem has complexity $\Omega(g(n))$. Making such a statement is usually quite difficult as we are making a claim about all possible ways to solve a problem, rather than about a single way to solve it.

  For many problems we can establish a trivial lower bound based on the number of inputs and/or outputs. For example, every algorithm that sorts n elements must have complexity $\Omega(n)$, as every sorting algorithm must examine each element at least once or run the risk that the unexamined elements are in the wrong place. Similarly, every algorithm to multiply two $n \times n$ matrices must have complexity $\Omega(n^2)$, as the result contains n^2 elements and it takes $\Omega(1)$ time to produce each of these elements, and so on. Nontrivial lower bounds are known for a very limited number of problems.

In this section we establish nontrivial lower bounds on two of the divide-and-conquer problems studied in this chapter—finding the minimum and maximum of n elements and sorting. For both of these problems, we limit ourselves to **comparison algorithms**. These algorithms perform their task by making comparisons between pairs of elements and possibly moving elements around; they do not perform other operations on elements. The minmax algorithms of Chapter 2, as well as those proposed in this chapter, satisfy this property, as do all the sort methods studied in this book except for bin sort and radix sort (Sections 6.5.1 and 6.5.2).

18.4.1   Lower Bound for the Minmax Problem

Program 18.1 gave a divide-and-conquer function to find the minimum and maximum of n elements. This function makes $\lceil 3n/2 \rceil - 2$ comparisons between pairs of elements. We will show that every comparison algorithm for the minmax problem must make at least $\lceil 3n/2 \rceil - 2$ comparisons between the elements. For purposes of the proof, we assume that the n elements are distinct. This assumption does not affect the generality of the proof, as distinct element inputs form a subset of the input space. In addition, every minmax algorithm must work correctly on these inputs as well as on those that have duplicates.

The proof uses the **state space method**. In this method we describe the start, intermediate, and finish states of every algorithm for the problem as well as how a comparison algorithm can go from one state to another. Then we determine the minimum number of transitions needed to go from the start state to the finish state. This minimum number of transitions is a lower bound on the complexity of the problem. The start, intermediate, and finish states of an algorithm are abstract entities, and there is no requirement that an algorithm keep track of its state explicitly.

For the minmax problem the algorithm state can be described by a tuple (a, b, c, d) where a is the number of elements that the minmax algorithm still considers candidates for the maximum and minimum elements; b is the number of elements that are no longer candidates for the minimum, but are still candidates for the maximum; c is the number of elements that are no longer candidates for the maximum, but are still candidates for the minimum; and d is the number of elements that the minmax algorithm has determined to be neither the minimum nor the maximum. Let A, B, C, and D denote the elements in each of the preceding categories.

When the minmax algorithm starts, all n elements are candidates for the min and max. So the start state is $(n,0,0,0)$. When the algorithm finishes, there are no elements in A, one in B, one in C, and $n-2$ in D. Therefore, the finish state is $(0, 1, 1, n-2)$. Transitions from one state to another are made on the basis of comparisons between pairs of elements. When two elements from A are compared, the smaller element can be placed in C and the larger in B. (Recall that all elements are distinct, so we cannot get an equal compare.) The following state transition is possible:

$$(a, b, c, d) \rightarrow (a - 2, b + 1, c + 1, d)$$

Other possible transitions follow.

- When comparisons between elements of B are made, the possible transition is

$$(a, b, c, d) \rightarrow (a, b - 1, c, d + 1)$$

- When comparisons between elements of C are made, the possible transition is

$$(a, b, c, d) \rightarrow (a, b, c - 1, d + 1)$$

- When an element of A is compared with an element of B, the possible transitions are

$(a, b, c, d) \rightarrow (a - 1, b, c, d + 1)$ (the A element is greater than the B element)
$(a, b, c, d) \rightarrow (a - 1, b, c + 1, d)$ (the A element is smaller than the B element)

- When an element of A is compared with an element of C, the possible transitions are

$(a, b, c, d) \rightarrow (a - 1, b, c, d + 1)$ (the A element is smaller than the C element)
$(a, b, c, d) \rightarrow (a - 1, b + 1, c, d)$ (the A element is greater than the C element)

Although other comparisons are possible, none of these comparisons can guarantee a state change. Examining the possible state changes, we see that when n is even, the quickest way to go from the start state $(n,0,0,0)$ to the finish state $(0, 1, 1, n - 2)$ is to do $n/2$ comparisons between elements in A, $n/2 - 1$ between those in B, and $n/2 - 1$ between those in C. The total number of comparisons is $3n/2 - 2$. When n is odd, the fastest way to go from the start state to the finish state is to make $\lfloor n/2 \rfloor$ comparisons between elements in A, $\lfloor n/2 \rfloor - 1$ comparisons between elements in B, $\lfloor n/2 \rfloor - 1$ comparisons between elements in C, and up to two more comparisons involving the remaining element of A. The total count is $\lceil 3n/2 \rceil - 2$.

Since no comparison algorithm for the minmax problem can go from the start state to the finish state making fewer than $\lceil 3n/2 \rceil - 2$ comparisons between pairs of elements, this number is a lower bound on the number of comparisons every minmax comparison algorithm must make. Hence Program 18.1 is an optimal comparison algorithm for the minmax problem.

18.4.2   Lower Bound for Sorting

A lower bound of $n \log n$ on the worst-case complexity of every comparison algorithm that sorts n elements can be established by using the state space method. This time the algorithm state is given by the number of permutations of the n elements that are still candidates for the output permutation. When the sort algorithm starts, all $n!$ permutations of the n elements are candidates for the sorted output and when the algorithm terminates, only one candidate permutation remains. (As for the minmax problem, we assume the n elements to be sorted are distinct.)

When two elements a_i and a_j are compared, the current set of candidate permutations is divided into two groups—one group retains permutations that are consistent with the outcome $a_i < a_j$, and the other set retains those that are consistent with the outcome $a_i > a_j$. Since we have assumed that the elements are distinct, the outcome $a_i = a_j$ is not possible. For example, suppose that $n = 3$ and that the first comparison is between a_1 and a_3. Prior to this comparison, as far as the algorithm is concerned, all six permutations of the elements are candidates for the sorted permutation. If $a_1 < a_3$, then the best the algorithm can do is eliminate the permutations (a_3, a_1, a_2), (a_3, a_2, a_1), and (a_2, a_3, a_1). The remaining three permutations must be retained as candidates for the output.

If the current candidate set has m permutations, then a comparison produces two groups, one of which must have at least $\lceil m/2 \rceil$ permutations. A worst-case execution of the sort algorithm begins with a candidate set of size $n!$, reduces this set to one of size at least $n!/2$, then reduces the candidate set further to one of size at least $n!/4$, and so on until the size of the candidate set becomes 1. The number of reduction steps (and hence comparisons needed) is at least $\lceil \log n! \rceil$.

Since $n! \geq \lceil n/2 \rceil^{\lceil n/2 \rceil - 1}$, $\log n! \geq (n/2 - 1) \log(n/2) = \Omega(n \log n)$. Hence every sort algorithm that is a comparison algorithm must make $\Omega(n \log n)$ comparisons in the worst case.

We can arrive at this same lower bound from a **decision-tree** proof. In such a proof we model the progress of an algorithm by using a tree. At each internal node of this tree, the algorithm makes a comparison and moves to one of the children based on the outcome of this comparison. External nodes are nodes at which the algorithm terminates. Figure 18.20 shows the decision tree for `insertionSort` (Program 2.15) while sorting the three-element sequence `a[0:2]`. Each internal node has a label of the type i:j. This label denotes a comparison between a[i] and a[j]. If a[i] < a[j], the algorithm moves to the left child. A right child move occurs when a[i] > a[j]. Since the elements are distinct, the case a[i] = a[j] is not possible. The external nodes are labeled with the sorted permutation that is generated. The left-most path in the decision tree of Figure 18.20 is followed when a[1] < a[0], a[2] < a[0], and a[2] < a[1]; the permutation at the left-most external node is (a[2],a[1],a[0]).

Notice that each leaf of a decision tree for a comparison sort algorithm defines a unique output permutation. Since every correct sorting algorithm must be able to produce all $n!$ permutations of n inputs, the decision tree for every correct comparison sort algorithm must have at least $n!$ external nodes. Because a tree whose height is h has at most 2^h external nodes, the decision tree for a correct comparison sort algorithm must have a height that is at least $\lceil \log_2 n! \rceil = \Omega(n \log n)$. Therefore, every comparison sort algorithm must perform $\Omega(n \log n)$ comparisons in the worst case. Further, since the average height of every binary tree that has $n!$ external nodes is also $\Omega(n \log n)$ (Exercise 47), the average complexity of every comparison sort algorithm is also $\Omega(n \log n)$.

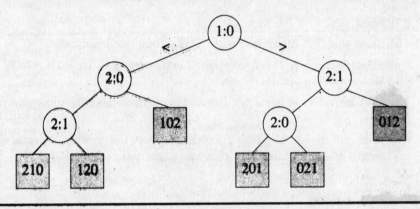

Figure 18.20 Decision tree for insertionSort when n = 3

The preceding lower-bound proof shows that heap sort and merge sort are optimal worst-case sort methods (as far as asymptotic complexity is concerned) and that heap sort, merge sort, and quick sort are optimal average-case methods.

EXERCISES

42. Use the state space method to show that every comparison algorithm that finds the maximum of n elements makes at least $n - 1$ comparisons between pairs of elements.

43. Show that $n! \geq \lceil n/2 \rceil^{\lceil n/2 \rceil - 1}$.

44. Draw the decision tree for `insertionSort` when $n = 4$.

45. Draw the decision tree for `mergeSort` (Program 18.3) when $n = 4$.

46. Let $a_1, \cdots, a_n$ be a sequence of n elements. Elements a_i and a_j, $i < j$, are **inverted** iff $a_i > a_j$. The number of pairs (i, j) such that a_i and a_j are inverted is the **inversion number** of the element sequence.

    (a) What is the inversion number of the sequence 6, 2, 3, 1?

    (b) What is the maximum inversion number possible for a sequence of n elements?

    (c) Suppose that a sort function compares only pairs of adjacent elements and then possibly swaps them (this is essentially what bubble, selection, and insertion sorts do). Show that sort methods of this type must perform $\Omega(n^2)$ comparisons in the worst case.

47. Let T be an extended binary tree with n internal nodes; let I, the internal path length of T, be the sum of the lengths of the paths from the root to each of the internal nodes; let E, the external path length of T, be the sum of the lengths of the paths from the root to each of the external nodes.

    (a) Show that $E = I + 2n$.

    (b) Show that I is minimized when T is a complete binary tree.

    (c) Show that when T is a complete binary tree, $I = (n + 1)p - 2^{p+1} + 2$ where $p = \lfloor \log_2(n + 1) \rfloor$.

    (d) Use the results of parts (a), (b), and (c) to determine the minimum value of E.

    (e) From the result of part (d), conclude that the average external path length of every binary tree that has n internal nodes is $\Omega(\log n)$.

CHAPTER 19

DYNAMIC PROGRAMMING

BIRD'S-EYE VIEW

Dynamic programming is arguably the most difficult of the five design methods we are studying. It has its foundations in the principle of optimality. We can use this method to obtain elegant and efficient solutions to many problems that cannot be so solved with either the greedy or divide-and-conquer methods. After describing the method, we consider its application to the solution of the knapsack, matrix multiplication chains, shortest-path, and noncrossing subset of nets problems. Additional applications (e.g., image compression and component folding) are developed on the Web site. You should study these as well as the exercise solutions to gain mastery of dynamic programming.

19.1   THE METHOD

In dynamic programming, as in the greedy method, we view the solution to a problem as the result of a sequence of decisions. In the greedy method we make irrevocable decisions one at a time, using a greedy criterion. However, in dynamic programming we examine the decision sequence to see whether an optimal decision sequence contains optimal decision subsequences. Some examples that illustrate this point are given below.

Example 19.1 [Shortest Path] Consider the digraph of Figure 17.2. We wish to find a shortest path from the source vertex $s = 1$ to the destination vertex $d = 5$. We need to make decisions on the intermediate vertices. The choices for the first decision are 2, 3, and 4. That is, from vertex 1 we may move to any one of these vertices. Suppose we decide to move to vertex 3. Now we need to decide on how to get from 3 to 5. If we go from 3 to 5 in a suboptimal way, then the 1-to-5 path constructed cannot be optimal, even under the restriction that from vertex 1 we must go to vertex 3. For example, if we use the suboptimal path 3, 2, 5 with length 9, the constructed 1-to-5 path 1, 3, 2, 5 has length 11. Replacing the suboptimal path 3, 2, 5 with an optimal one 3, 4, 5 results in the path 1, 3, 4, 5 of length 9.

For this shortest-path problem, suppose that our first decision gets us to some vertex v. Although we do not know how to make this first decision we do know that the remaining decisions must be optimal for the problem of going from v to d. ∎

Example 19.2 [0/1 Knapsack Problem] Consider the 0/1 knapsack problem of Section 17.3.2. We need to make decisions on the values of $x_1, \cdots, x_n$. Suppose we are deciding the values of the x_is in the order $i = 1, 2, \cdots, n$. If we set $x_1 = 0$, then the available knapsack capacity for the remaining objects (i.e., objects 2, 3, $\cdots$, n) is c. If we set $x_1 = 1$, the available knapsack capacity is $c - w_1$. Let $r \in \{c, c - w_1\}$ denote the remaining knapsack capacity.

Following the first decision, we are left with the problem of filling a knapsack with capacity r. The available objects (i.e., 2 through n) and the available capacity r define the *problem state* following the first decision. Regardless of whether x_1 is 0 or 1, $[x_2, \cdots, x_n]$ must be an optimal solution for the problem state following the first decision. If not, there is a solution $[y_2, \cdots, y_n]$ that provides greater profit for the problem state following the first decision. So $[x_1, y_2, \cdots, y_n]$ is a better solution for the initial problem.

Suppose that $n = 3$, $w = [100, 14, 10]$, $p = [20, 18, 15]$, and $c = 116$. If we set $x_1 = 1$, then following this decision, the available knapsack capacity is 16. $[x_2, x_3] = [0, 1]$ is a feasible solution to the two-object problem that remains. It returns a profit of 15. However, it is not an optimal solution to the remaining two-object problem, as $[x_2, x_3] = [1, 0]$ is feasible and returns a greater profit of 18. So $x = [1, 0, 1]$ can be improved to $[1, 1, 0]$. If we set $x_1 = 0$, the available capacity for the two-object instance that remains is 116. If the subsequence $[x_2, x_3]$ is not an optimal solution for this remaining instance, then $[x_1, x_2, x_3]$ cannot be optimal for the initial instance.   ∎

Example 19.3 [Airfares] A certain airline has the following airfare structure: From Atlanta to New York or Chicago, or from Los Angeles to Atlanta, the fare is \$100; from Chicago to New York, it is \$20; and for passengers connecting through Atlanta, the Atlanta to Chicago segment is only \$20. A routing from Los Angeles to New York involves decisions on the intermediate airports. If problem states are encoded as (origin, destination) pairs, then following a decision to go from Los Angeles to Atlanta, the problem state is *We are at Atlanta and need to get to New York.* The cheapest way to go from Atlanta to New York is a direct flight with cost \$100. Using this direct flight results in a total Los Angeles–to–New York cost of \$200. However, the cheapest routing is Los Angeles–Atlanta–Chicago–New York with a cost of \$140, which involves using a suboptimal decision subsequence for the Atlanta–to–New York problem (Atlanta–Chicago–New York).

If instead we encode the problem state as a triple *(tag, origin, destination)* where *tag* is 0 for connecting flights and 1 for all others, then once we reach Atlanta, the state becomes (0, Atlanta, New York) for which the optimal routing is through Chicago.   ∎

When optimal decision sequences contain optimal decision subsequences, we can establish recurrence equations, called **dynamic-programming recurrence equations**, that enable us to solve the problem in an efficient way.

Example 19.4 [0/1 Knapsack] In Example 19.2 we saw that for the 0/1 knapsack problem, optimal decision sequences were composed of optimal subsequences. Let $f(i, y)$ denote the value of an optimal solution to the knapsack instance with remaining capacity y and remaining objects $i, i+1, \cdots, n$. From Example 19.2 it follows that

$$f(n, y) = \begin{cases} p_n & y \geq w_n \\ 0 & 0 \leq y < w_n \end{cases} \qquad (19.1)$$

and

$$f(i, y) = \begin{cases} \max\{f(i+1, y), f(i+1, y - w_i) + p_i\} & y \geq w_i \\ f(i+1, y) & 0 \leq y < w_i \end{cases} \qquad (19.2)$$

By making use of the observation that optimal decision sequences are made up of optimal subsequences, we have obtained a recurrence for f. $f(1, c)$ is the value of the optimal solution to the knapsack problem we started with. Equation 19.2 may be used to determine $f(1, c)$ either recursively or iteratively. In the iterative approach, we start with $f(n, *)$, as given by Equation 19.1, and then obtain $f(i, *)$.

in the order $i = n-1,\ n-2,\ \cdots,\ 2$, using Equation 19.2. Finally, $f(1,c)$ is computed by using Equation 19.2.

For the instance of Example 19.2, we see that $f(3,y) = 0$ if $0 \leq y' < 10$, and 15 if $y \geq 10$. Using Equation 19.2, we obtain $f(2,y) = 0$ if $0 \leq y < 10$, 15 if $10 \leq y < 14$, 18 if $14 \leq y < 24$, and 33 if $y \geq 24$. The optimal solution has value $f(1,116) = \max\{f(2,116),\ f(2,\ 116\ -w_1) + p_1\} = \max\ \{f(2,116),\ f(2,16) + 20\} = \max\{33,\ 38\} = 38$.

To obtain the values of the x_is, we proceed as follows: If $f(1,c) = f(2,c)$, then we may set $x_1 = 0$ because we can utilize the c units of capacity getting a return of $f(1,c)$ from objects $2,\ \cdots,\ n$. In case $f(1,c) \neq f(2,c)$, then we must set $x_1 = 1$. Next we need to find an optimal solution that uses the remaining capacity $c - w_1$. This solution has value $f(2, c - w_1)$. Proceeding in this way, we may determine the value of all the x_is.

For our sample instance we see that $f(2,116) = 33 \neq f(1,116)$. Therefore, $x_1 = 1$, and we need to find x_2 and x_3 so as to obtain a return of $38 - p_1 = 18$ and use a capacity of at most $116 - w_1 = 16$. Note that $f(2,16) = 18$. Since $f(3,16) = 15 \neq f(2,16)$, $x_2 = 1$; the remaining capacity is $16 - w_2 = 2$. Since $f(3,2) = 0$, we set $x_3 = 0$. ∎

The **principle of optimality** states that no matter what the first decision, the remaining decisions must be optimal with respect to the state that results from this first decision. This principle implies that an optimal decision sequence is comprised of optimal decision subsequences. Since the principle of optimality may not hold for some formulations of some problems, it is necessary to verify that it does hold for the problem being solved. *Dynamic programming cannot be applied when this principle does not hold.*

The steps in a dynamic-programming solution are

- Verify that the principle of optimality holds.

- Set up the dynamic-programming recurrence equations.

- Solve the dynamic-programming recurrence equations for the value of the optimal solution.

- Perform a **traceback** step in which the solution itself is constructed.

It is very tempting to write a simple recursive program to solve the dynamic-programming recurrence. *However, as we will see in subsequent sections, unless care is taken to avoid recomputing previously computed values, the recursive program will have prohibitive complexity.* When the recursive program is designed to avoid this recomputation, the complexity is drastically reduced. The dynamic-programming recurrence may also be solved by iterative code that naturally avoids recomputation of already computed values. Although this iterative code has the same time complexity as the "careful" recursive code, the former has the advantage of not requiring additional space for the recursion stack. As a result, the iterative code generally runs faster than the careful recursive code.

19.2   APPLICATIONS

19.2.1   0/1 Knapsack Problem

Recursive Solution

The dynamic-programming recurrence equations for the 0/1 knapsack problem were developed in Example 19.4. A natural way to solve a recurrence such as Equation 19.2 for the value $f(1, c)$ of an optimal knapsack packing is by a recursive program such as Program 19.1, which employs the global variables profit, weight and numberOfObjects. The profits and weights of the objects are profit[1:number-OfObjects] and weight[1:numberOfObjects].

```
int f(int i, int theCapacity)
{// Return f(i,theCapacity).
   if (i == numberOfObjects)
      return (theCapacity < weight[numberOfObjects])
             ? 0 : profit[numberOfObjects];
   if (theCapacity < weight[i])
      return f(i + 1, theCapacity);
   return max(f(i + 1, theCapacity),
              f(i + 1, theCapacity - weight[i]) + profit[i]);
}
```

Program 19.1 Recursive function for knapsack problem

Let $t(n)$ be the time this code takes to solve an instance with n objects. We see that $t(1) = a$ and $t(n) \leq 2t(n-1) + b$ for $n > 1$. Here a and b are constants. This recurrence solves to $t(n) = O(2^n)$.

Example 19.5 Consider the case $n = 5$, $p = [6, 3, 5, 4, 6]$, $w = [2, 2, 6, 5, 4]$, and $c = 10$. To determine $f(1, 10)$, function f is invoked as f(1,10). The recursive calls made are shown by the tree of Figure 19.1. Each node has been labeled by the value of y. Nodes on level j have $i = j$. So the root denotes the invocation f(1,10). Its left and right children, respectively, denote the invocations f(2,10) and f(2,8). In all, 27 invocations are made. Notice that several invocations redo the work of previous invocations. For example, $f(3, 8)$ is computed twice, as are $f(4, 8)$, $f(4, 2)$, $f(5, 8)$, $f(5, 3)$, and $f(5, 2)$. If we save the results of previous invocations, we can reduce the number of invocations to 21 because we eliminate the shaded nodes of Figure 19.1.　■

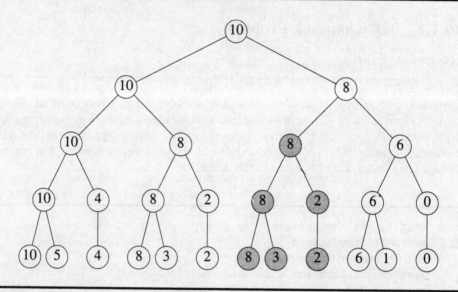

Figure 19.1 Tree of recursive calls

Recursive Solution without Recomputations

As observed in Example 19.5, Program 19.1 is doing more work than necessary. To avoid recomputing the same $f(i, y)$ value, we may keep a list of $f(i, y)$s that have already been computed. The elements of this list are triples of the form $(i, y, f(i, y))$. Before making an invocation f(i,y), we see whether the list contains a triple of the form $(i, y, *)$ where $*$ denotes a wildcard. If so, $f(i, y)$ is retrieved from the list. If not, the invocation is made and then the triple $(i, y, f(i, y))$ added to the list. The list of triples may be implemented as a hash table (see Section 10.5) or as a binary search tree (see Chapter 15).

When the weights are integer, we may use an integer array fArray[i][y] such that f[i][y] equals -1 iff $f(i, y)$ has not been computed before. Program 19.2 gives the recursive code that avoids recomputation of previously computed f values. This code assumes that fArray is an $(n + 1) \times (c + 1)$ global integer array that has been initialized to -1.

To determine the time complexity of Program 19.2, we will use an accounting scheme in which we charge different components of the total time to different $f(i, y)$s and then add up the amounts charged to each $f(i, y)$. When computing an $f(i, y)$, the cost of an invocation f(i+1,z) is charged to $f(i + 1, z)$ if $f(i + 1, z)$ has not been computed and to $f(i, z)$ otherwise. (This $f(i + 1, z)$ in turn offloads the cost of computing new $f(*, *)$s to the individual $f(*, *)$s that are computed.) The cost of the remainder of Program 19.2 is charged to $f(i, y)$. This remaining cost is $\Theta(1)$.

```
int f(int i, int theCapacity)
{// Return f(i,theCapacity). Do not recpute an f value.
   // check if already computed
   if (fArray[i][theCapacity] >= 0)
      return fArray[i][theCapacity];

   // not yet computed
   if (i == numberOfObjects)
   {// use Equation 19.1
      // compute and save f(i,theCapacity)
      fArray[i][theCapacity] = (theCapacity < weight[numberOfObjects])
                               ? 0 : profit[numberOfObjects];
      return fArray[i][theCapacity];
   }
   // use Equation 19.2
   if (theCapacity < weight[i])
      // object i does not fit
      fArray[i][theCapacity] = f(i + 1, theCapacity);
   else
      // object i fits, try both possibilities
      fArray[i][theCapacity] = max(f(i + 1, theCapacity),
                  f(i + 1, theCapacity - weight[i]) + profit[i]);

   return fArray[i][theCapacity];
}
```

Program 19.2 Recursive function for knapsack problem with no recomputations

The total amount charged to each $f(i, y)$ is constant, and the number of $f(i, y)$s is $(c + 1)(n + 1)$. Therefore, the total time is $O(cn)$ (recall that c denotes the knapsack capacity and n is the number of objects). By avoiding the recomputation of previously computed $f(i, y)$s, we have cut the running time of the recursive code from an impractical $O(2^n)$ to a very practical $O(cn)$!

Iterative Solution with Integer Weights

We can devise a fairly simple iterative code (Program 19.3) to solve for $f(1, c)$ when the weights are integer. This code, based on the strategy outlined in Example 19.4, computes each $f(i, y)$ exactly once. Program 19.3 uses a two-dimensional array f[][] to store the values of the function f. Program 19.4 gives the code for the traceback needed to determine the x_i values that result in the optimal filling.

```
void knapsack(int *profit, int *weight, int numberOfObjects,
              int knapsackCapacity, int **f)
{// Iterative method to solve dynamic programming recurrence.
 // Computes f[1][knapsackCapacity] and f[i][y],
 // 2 <= i <= numberOfObjects, 0 <= y <= knapsackCapacity.
 // profit[1:numberOfObjects] gives object profits.
 // weight[1:numberOfObjects] gives object weights.

   // initialize f[numberOfObjects][]
   int yMax = min(weight[numberOfObjects] - 1, knapsackCapacity);
   for (int y = 0; y <= yMax; y++)
      f[numberOfObjects][y] = 0;
   for (int y = weight[numberOfObjects]; y <= knapsackCapacity; y++)
      f[numberOfObjects][y] = profit[numberOfObjects];

   // compute f[i][y], 1 < i < numberOfObjects
   for (int i = numberOfObjects - 1; i > 1; i--)
   {
      yMax = min(weight[i] - 1, knapsackCapacity);
      for (int y = 0; y <= yMax; y++)
         f[i][y] = f[i + 1][y];
      for (int y = weight[i]; y <= knapsackCapacity; y++)
         f[i][y] = max(f[i + 1][y], f[i + 1][y - weight[i]] + profit[i]
   }

   // compute f[1][knapsackCapacity]
   f[1][knapsackCapacity] = f[2][knapsackCapacity];
   if (knapsackCapacity >= weight[1])
      f[1][knapsackCapacity] = max(f[1][knapsackCapacity],
                    f[2][knapsackCapacity-weight[1]] + profit[1]);
}
```

Program 19.3 Iterative computation of f

Example 19.6 Figure 19.2 shows the f array computed by Program 19.3 using the data of Example 19.5. The data are computed by rows from top to bottom and within a row from left to right. The value f[1][10] = 15 is not shown.

To determine the x_i values, we begin with x_1. Since $f(1, 10) \neq f(2, 10)$, $f(1, 10)$ must equal $f(2, 10-w_1)+p_1 = f(2, 8)+6$. Therefore, $x_1 = 1$. Since $f(2, 8) \neq f(3, 8)$, $f(2, 8)$ must equal $f(3, 8 - w_2) + p_2 = f(3, 6) + 3$ and $x_2 = 1$. $x_3 = x_4 = 0$ because $f(3, 6) = f(4, 6) = f(5, 6)$. Finally, since $f(5, 4) \neq 0$, $x_5 = 1$. ∎

```
void traceback(int **f, int *weight, int numberOfObjects,
                int knapsackCapacity, int *x)
{// Compute solution vector x.
   for (int i = 1; i < numberOfObjects; i++)
      if (f[i][knapsackCapacity] == f[i+1][knapsackCapacity])
         // do not include object i
         x[i] = 0;
      else
      {// include object i
         x[i] = 1;
         knapsackCapacity -= weight[i];
      }
   x[numberOfObjects] = (f[numberOfObjects][knapsackCapacity] > 0)
                        ? 1 : 0;
}
```

Program 19.4 Iterative computation of x

i	0	1	2	3	4	5	6	7	8	9	10
						y					
5	0	0	0	0	6	6	6	6	6	6	6
4	0	0	0	0	6	6	6	6	6	10	10
3	0	0	0	0	6	6	6	6	6	10	11
2	0	0	3	3	6	6	9	9	9	10	11

Figure 19.2 f function/array for Example 19.6

The complexity of the iterative knapsack code is $\Theta(nc)$ and that of traceback is $\Theta(n)$.

Tuple Method *(Optional)*

The code of Program 19.3 has two drawbacks. First, it requires that the weights be integer. Second, it is slower than Program 19.1 when the knapsack capacity is large. In particular, if $c > 2^n$, its complexity is $\Omega(n2^n)$. We can overcome both of these shortcomings by using a tuple approach in which for each i, $f(i, y)$ is stored as an ordered list $P(i)$ of pairs $(y, f(i, y))$ that correspond to the y values at which the function f changes. The pairs in each $P(i)$ are in increasing order of y. In addition, since $f(i, y)$ is a nondecreasing function of y, the pairs are also in increasing order of $f(i, y)$.

Example 19.7 Consider the f function of Figure 19.2. When $i = 5$, the function f is completely specified by the pairs $P(5) = [(0, 0), (4, 6)]$. The pairs $P(i)$ for $i = 4, 3,$ and 2 are $[(0, 0), (4, 6), (9, 10)]$, $[(0, 0), (4, 6), (9, 10), (10, 11)]$, and $[(0, 0), (2, 3), (4, 6), (6, 9), (9, 10), (10, 11)]$.

To compute $f(1, 10)$, we use Equation 19.2, which yields $f(1, 10) = \max\{f(2, 10), f(2, 8) + p_1\}$. From $P(2)$ we get $f(2, 10) = 11$, and $f(2, 8) = 9$ ($f(2, 8) = 9$ comes from the pair $(6, 9)$). Therefore, $f(1, 10) = \max\{11, 15\} = 15$.

To determine the x_i values, we begin with x_1. Since $f(1, 10) = f(2, 6) + p_1$, $x_1 = 1$. Since $f(2, 6) = f(3, 6 - w_2) + p_2 = f(3, 4) + p_2$, $x_2 = 1$. $x_3 = x_4 = 0$ because $f(3, 4) = f(4, 4) = f(5, 4)$. Finally, since $f(5, 4) \neq 0$, $x_5 = 1$.   ■

If we examine the pairs in each $P(i)$, we see that each pair $(y, f(i, y))$ corresponds to a different combination of 0/1 assignments to the variables $x_i, \cdots, x_n$. Let (a, b) and (c, d) be pairs that correspond to two different 0/1 assignments to $x_i, \cdots, x_n$. If $a \geq c$ and $b < d$, then (a, b) is dominated by (b, c). Dominated assignments do not contribute pairs to $P(i)$. If two or more assignments result in the same pair, only one is in $P(i)$.

Under the assumption that $w_n \leq c$, $P(n) = [(0, 0), (w_n, p_n)]$. These two pairs correspond to x_n equal to 0 and 1, respectively. For each i, $P(i)$ may be obtained from $P(i + 1)$. First, compute the ordered set of pairs Q such that (s, t) is a pair of Q iff $w_i \leq s \leq c$ and $(s - w_i, t - p_i)$ is a pair of $P(i + 1)$. Now Q has the pairs with $x_i = 1$, and $P(i + 1)$ has those with $x_i = 0$. Second, merge Q and $P(i + 1)$ eliminating dominated as well as duplicate pairs to get $P(i)$.

Example 19.8 Consider the data of Example 19.7. $P(5) = [(0, 0), (4, 6)]$, so $Q = [(5, 4), (9, 10)]$. When merging $P(5)$ and Q to create $P(4)$, the pair $(5, 4)$ is eliminated because it is dominated by the pair $(4, 6)$. As a result, $P(4) = [(0, 0), (4, 6), (9, 10)]$. To compute $P(3)$, we first obtain $Q = [(6, 5), (10, 11)]$ from $P(4)$. Next merging with $P(4)$ yields $P(3) = [(0, 0), (4, 6), (9, 10), (10, 11)]$. Finally, to get $P(2)$, $Q = [(2, 3), (6, 9)]$ is computed from $P(3)$. Merging $P(3)$ and Q yields $P(2) = [(0, 0), (2, 3), (4, 6), (6, 9), (9, 10), (10, 11)]$.   ■

Since the pairs in each $P(i)$ represent different 0/1 assignments to $x_i, \cdots, x_n$, no $P(i)$ has more than 2^{n-i+1} pairs. When computing $P(i)$, Q may be computed in $\Theta(|P(i+1)|)$ time. The time needed to merge $P(i + 1)$ and Q is also $\Theta(|P(i+1)|)$. So all the $P(i)$s may be computed in $\Theta(\sum_{i=2}^{n} |P(i + 1)|) = O(2^n)$ time. When the weights are integer, $|P(i)| \leq c + 1$. In this case the complexity becomes $O(\min\{nc, 2^n\})$.

19.2.2   Matrix Multiplication Chains

Problem Description

An $m \times n$ matrix A and an $n \times p$ matrix B can be multiplied in $\Theta(mnp)$ time (see Exercise 2.24). We will use mnp as a measure of the time needed to multiply the two matrices. Suppose we are to multiply three matrices A, B, and C. There are two ways in which we can accomplish this task. In the first, we multiply A and B to get the product matrix D and then multply D and C to get the desired result. This multiplication order can be written as $(A * B) * C$. The second way is $A * (B * C)$. Although both multiplication orders obtain the same result, one may take a lot more computing time than the other.

Example 19.9 Suppose that A is a 100×1 matrix, B is a 1×100 matrix, and C is a 100×1 matrix. Then the time needed to compute $A * B$ is 10,000. Since the result is a 100×100 matrix, the time needed to perform the multiplication with C is 1,000,000. The overall time needed to compute $(A * B) * C$ is therefore 1,010,000. $B * C$ can be computed in 10,000 units of time. Since the result is a 1×1 matrix, the time needed for the multiplication with A is 100. The total time needed to compute $A * (B * C)$ is therefore 10,100! Furthermore, when computing $(A*B)*C$, we need 10,000 units of space to store $A * B$; however, when $A * (B * C)$ is computed, only one unit of space is needed for $B * C$.

As an example of a real problem that can benefit from computing the matrix product $A*B*C$ in the proper order, consider the registration of 2 three-dimensional images. In the registration problem, we are to determine the amount by which one image needs to be rotated, translated, and shrunk (or expanded) so that it approximates the second. One way to perform this registration involves doing about 100 iterations of computation. Each iteration computes the following 12×1 vector T:

$$T = \sum A(x,y,z) * B(x,y,z) * C(x,y,z)$$

Here A, B, and C are, respectively, 12×3, 3×3, and 3×1 matrices. (x,y,z) gives the coordinates of a voxel, and the sum is done over all voxels. Let t be the number of computations needed to compute $A(x,y,z) * B(x,y,z) * C(x,y,z)$ for a single voxel. Assume that the image is of size $256 \times 256 \times 256$ voxels. In this case the total number of computations needed for the 100 iterations is approximately $100 * 256^3 * t \approx 1.7 * 10^9 t$. When the three matrices are multiplied from left to right, $t = 12 * 3 * 3 + 12 * 3 * 1 = 144$. When we multiply from right to left, $t = 3 * 3 * 1 + 12 * 3 * 1 = 45$. The left-to-right computation requires approximately $2.4 * 10^{11}$ operations, while the right-to-left computation requires about $7.5 * 10^{10}$ operations. On a computer that can do 100 million operations per second, the first scheme would take 40 minutes and the second would take 12.5 minutes. ∎

When we are to compute the matrix product $A * B * C$, only two multiplication orders are possible (left to right and right to left). We can determine the number of operations each order requires and go with the cheaper one. In a more general situation, we are to compute the matrix product $M_1 \times M_2 \times \cdots \times M_q$ where M_i is an $r_i \times r_{i+1}$ matrix, $1 \leq i \leq q$. Consider the case $q = 4$. The matrix product $A * B * C * D$ may be computed in any of the following five ways:

$$A * ((B * C) * D) \qquad A * (B * (C * D))$$
$$(A * B) * (C * D) \qquad ((A * B) * C) * D \qquad (A * (B * C)) * D$$

The number of different ways in which the product of q matrices may be computed increases exponentially with q. As a result, for large q it is not practical to evaluate each multiplication scheme and select the cheapest.

Dynamic-Programming Formulation

We can use dynamic programming to determine an optimal sequence of pairwise matrix multiplications to use. The resulting algorithm runs in $O(q^3)$ time. Let M_{ij} denote the result of the product chain $M_i \times \cdots \times M_j$, $i \leq j$, and let $c(i, j)$ be the cost of the optimal way to compute M_{ij}. Let $kay(i, j)$ be such that the optimal computation of M_{ij} computes $M_{ik} \times M_{k+1,j}$. An optimal computation of M_{ij} therefore comprises the product $M_{ik} \times M_{k+1,j}$ preceded by optimal computations of M_{ik} and $M_{k+1,j}$. The principle of optimality holds, and we obtain the dynamic-programming recurrence that follows.

$$
\begin{aligned}
c(i, i) &= 0, 1 \leq i \leq q \\
c(i, i+1) &= r_i r_{i+1} r_{i+2} \text{ and } kay(i, i+1) = i, \ 1 \leq i < q \\
c(i, i+s) &= \min_{i \leq k < i+s} \{ c(i, k) + c(k+1, i+s) + r_i r_{k+1} r_{i+s+1} \}, \\
& \qquad\qquad 1 \leq i \leq q-s, \ 1 < s < q \\
kay(i, i+s) &= \text{value of } k \text{ that obtains the above minimum}
\end{aligned}
$$

The above recurrence for c may be solved recursively or iteratively. $c(1, q)$ is the cost of the optimal way to compute the matrix product chain, and $kay(1, q)$ defines the last product to be done. The remaining products can be determined by using the kay values.

Recursive Solution

As in the case of the 0/1 knapsack problem, any recursive solution must be implemented so as to avoid computing the same $c(i, j)$ and $kay(i, j)$ values more than once otherwise, the complexity of the algorithm is too high.

Example 19.10 Consider the case $q = 5$ and $r = (10, 5, 1, 10, 2, 10)$. The dynamic-programming recurrence yields

$$
\begin{aligned}
c(1, 5) = \min\{ &c(1, 1) + c(2, 5) + 500, c(1, 2) + c(3, 5) + 100, \qquad (19.3) \\
&c(1, 3) + c(4, 5) + 1000, c(1, 4) + c(5, 5) + 200 \}
\end{aligned}
$$

Four of the needed cs have $s = 0$ or 1. Their values are immediately computable from the dynamic-programming equations. We get $c(1,1) = c(5,5) = 0$; $c(1,2) = 50$; $c(4,5) = 200$. For $c(2,5)$, we get

$$c(2,5) = \min\{c(2,2) + c(3,5) + 50, c(2,3) + c(4,5) + 500, \qquad (19.4)$$
$$c(2,4) + c(5,5) + 100\}$$

$c(2,2) = c(5,5) = 0$; $c(2,3) = 50$; and $c(4,5) = 200$. For $c(3,5)$ and $c(2,4)$ we need to use the recurrences

$$
\begin{aligned}
c(3,5) &= \min\{c(3,3) + c(4,5) + 100, c(3,4) + c(5,5) + 20\} \\
&= \min\{0 + 200 + 100, 20 + 0 + 20\} \\
&= 40
\end{aligned}
$$

and

$$
\begin{aligned}
c(2,4) &= \min\{c(2,2) + c(3,4) + 10, c(2,3) + c(4,4) + 100\} \\
&= \min\{0 + 20 + 10, 50 + 0 + 20\} \\
&= 30
\end{aligned}
$$

These computations also yield $kay(3,5) = 4$ and $kay(2,4) = 2$. Now we know all the values needed to compute $c(2,5)$. Substituting these values in Equation 19.4, we get

$$c(2,5) = \min\{0 + 40 + 50, 50 + 200 + 500, 30 + 0 + 100\} = 90$$

and so $kay(2,5) = 2$. To use Equation 19.3 to compute $c(1,5)$, we still need values for $c(3,5)$, $c(1,3)$, and $c(1,4)$. Proceeding as above, we obtain the values 40, 150, and 90. The corresponding kay values are 4, 2, and 2. Substituting into Equation 19.3, we get

$$
\begin{aligned}
c(1,5) &= \min\{0 + 90 + 500, 50 + 40 + 100, 150 + 200 + 1000, \\
&\qquad 90 + 0 + 200\} = 190
\end{aligned}
$$

and $kay(1,5) = 2$.

The optimal multiplication sequence has cost 190. The sequence can be determined by examining $kay(1,5)$, which equals 2. So the last multiplication to perform is $M_{12} \times M_{35}$. Since both M_{12} and M_{35} are to be computed optimally, the kay values may be used to figure out how. $kay(1,2) = 1$, so M_{12} is computed as $M_{11} \times M_{22}$. Also, since $kay(3,5) = 4$, M_{35} is optimally computed as $M_{34} \times M_{55}$. M_{34} in turn is computed as $M_{33} \times M_{44}$, so the optimal multiplication sequence is

Multiply M_{11} and M_{22} to get M_{12}

Multiply M_{33} and M_{44} to get M_{34}

Multiply M_{34} and M_{55} to get M_{35}

Multiply M_{12} and M_{35} to get M_{15}

■

The recursive code to determine $c(i,j)$ and $kay(i,j)$ appears in Program 19.5. This code assumes that the one-dimensional integer array r and the two-dimensional integer array kay are global. The code computes the value of $c(i,j)$ and also sets kay[a][b] = $kay(a,b)$ for all a and b for which $c(a,b)$ is computed during the computation of $c(i,j)$. The function traceback uses the kay values computed by the function c to determine the optimal multiplication sequence.

Let $t(q)$ be the complexity of function c when $j - i + 1 = q$ (i.e., when M_{ij} is composed of q matrices). We see that when q is 1 or 2, $t(q) = d$ where d is a constant. When $q > 2$, $t(q) = 2 \sum_{k=1}^{q-1} t(k) + eq$ where e is a constant. For $q > 2$, $t(q) > 2t(q-1) + e$. So $t(q) = \Omega(2^q)$. The complexity of function traceback is $O(q)$.

Recursive Solution without Recomputations

By avoiding the recomputation of c (and hence kay) values previously computed, the complexity can be reduced to $O(q^3)$. To avoid the recomputation, we need to save the values of the $c(i,j)$s in a global two-dimensional array theC[][] whose initial values are 0. Program 19.6 gives the new recursive code for function c.

To analyze the complexity of the new function c (Program 19.6), we will again use the cost amortization method. Observe that the invocation c(1,q) causes each $c(i,j)$, $1 \le i \le j \le q$ to be computed exactly once. For $s = j - i > 1$, the computation of each requires s amount of work in addition to the work done computing the needed $c(a,b)$s that haven't as yet been computed. This additional work is charged to the $c(a,b)$s that are being computed for the first time. These $c(a,b)$s, in turn, offload some of this charge to the first-time cs that need to be computed during the computation of $c(a,b)$. As a result, each $c(i,j)$ is charged s amount of work. For each s, $q - s + 1$ $c(i,j)$s are computed. The total cost is therefore $\sum_{s=1}^{q-1} s(q - s + 1) = O(q^3)$.

Iterative Solution

The dynamic-programming recurrence for c may be solved iteratively, computing each c and kay exactly once, by computing the $c(i, i+s)$s in the order $s = 2, 3, \cdots, q - 1$.

```
int c(int i, int j)
{// Return c(i,j) and compute kay[i][j] = kay(i,j).
   if (i == j)
      return 0;   // one matrix
   if (i == j - 1)
   {// two matrices
      kay[i][i + 1] = i;
      return r[i] * r[i + 1] * r[i + 2];
   }

   // more than two matrices
   // set u to min term for k = i
   int u = c(i,i) + c(i + 1, j) + r[i] * r[i + 1] * r[j + 1];
   kay[i][j] = i;

   // compute remaining min terms and update u
   for (int k = i + 1; k < j; k++)
   {
      int t = c(i, k) + c(k + 1, j) + r[i] * r[k + 1] * r[j + 1];
      if (t < u)
      {// smaller min term found, update u and kay[i][j]
         u = t;
         kay[i][j] = k;
      }
   }

   return u;
}

void traceback(int i, int j)
{// Output best way to compute Mij.
   if (i == j)  // only one matrix
      return;
   traceback(i, kay[i][j]);
   traceback(kay[i][j] + 1, j);
   cout << "Multiply M " << i << ", " << kay[i][j] <<
           " and M " << (kay[i][j] + 1) << ", " << j << endl;
}
```

Program 19.5 Recursive computation of $c(i,j)$ and $kay(i,j)$

```
int c(int i, int j)
{// Return c(i,j) and compute kay[i][j] = kay(i,j).
   // check if already computed
   if (theC[i][j] > 0)  // c(i,j) was computed earlier
      return theC[i][j];

   // c(i,j) not computed before, compute it now
   if (i == j)
      return 0;   // one matrix
   if (i == j - 1)
   {// two matrices
      kay[i][i + 1] = i;
      theC[i][j] = r[i] * r[i + 1] * r[i + 2];
      return theC[i][j];
   }

   // more than two matrices
   // set u to min term for k = i
   int u = c(i,i) + c(i + 1, j) + r[i] * r[i + 1] * r[j + 1];
   kay[i][j] = i;

   // compute remaining min terms and update u
   for (int k = i + 1; k < j; k++)
   {
      int t = c(i, k) + c(k + 1, j) + r[i] * r[k + 1] * r[j + 1];
      if (t < u)
      {// smaller min term found, update u and kay[i][j]
         u = t;
         kay[i][j] = k;
      }
   }

   theC[i][j] = u;
   return theC[i][j];
}
```

Program 19.6 Computing $c(i,j)$ without recomputations

Example 19.11 Consider the five-matrix instance of Example 19.10. We begin by initializing $c(i,i)$ to 0, $1 \leq i \leq 5$. Next we compute $c(i, i+1)$ for $i = 1, \cdots, 4$. $c(1,2)$ $= r_1 r_2 r_3 = 50$, $c(2,3) = 50$, $c(3,4) = 20$, and $c(4,5) = 200$. The corresponding *kay* values are 1, 2, 3, and 4.

When $s = 2$, we get

$$
\begin{aligned}
c(1,3) &= \min\{c(1,1) + c(2,3) + r_1 r_2 r_4, c(1,2) + c(3,3) + r_1 r_3 r_4\} \\
&= \min\{0 + 50 + 500, 50 + 0 + 100\} = 150
\end{aligned}
$$

and $kay(1,3) = 2$. $c(2,4)$ and $c(3,5)$ are computed in a similar way. Their values are 30 and 40. The corresponding kay values are 2 and 3.

When $s = 3$, we compute $c(1,4)$ and $c(2,5)$. All the values needed to compute $c(2,5)$ (see Equation 19.4) are known. Substituting these values, we get $c(2,5) = 90$ and $kay(2,5) = 2$. $c(1,4)$ is computed from a similar equation. Finally, when $s = 4$, only $c(1,5)$ is to be computed. The equation is 19.3. All quantities on the right side are known. ∎

The iterative code to compute the c and kay values is function `matrixChain` (Program 19.7). Its complexity is $O(q^3)$. We can use a traceback to determine the optimal multiplication sequence following the computation of `kay`.

19.2.3 All-Pairs Shortest Paths

Problem Description

In the **all-pairs shortest-path problem**, we are to find a shortest path between every pair of vertices in a directed graph G. That is, for every pair of vertices (i, j), we are to find a shortest path from i to j as well as one from j to i. These two paths are the same when G is undirected.

When no edge has a negative length, the all-pairs shortest-path problem may be solved by using Dijkstra's greedy single-source algorithm (Section 17.3.5) n times, once with each of the n vertices as the source vertex. This process results in an $O(n^3)$ solution to the all-pairs problem. The dynamic-programming solution we develop in this section, called Floyd's algorithm, runs in $\Theta(n^3)$ time. Floyd's algorithm works even when the graph has negative-length edges (provided there are no negative-length cycles). Also, the constant factor associated with Floyd's algorithm is smaller than that associated with Dijkstra's algorithm. Therefore, Floyd's algorithm takes less time than the worst-case time for n applications of Dijkstra's algorithm.

Dynamic-Programming Formulation

We permit negative-length edges but require that G not contain any negative-length cycles. Under this assumption, every pair of vertices (i, j) always has a shortest path that contains no cycle. When the graph has a cycle whose length is less than 0, some shortest paths have length $-\infty$, as they involve going around the negative-length cycle indefinitely.

```
void matrixChain(int q)
{// Compute costs and kay for all Mij's iteratively.
 // r[] is array of dimensions; q is number of matrices;
 // c is cost matrix; kay is recurrence selector.

   // initialize c[i][i], c[i][i+1], and kay[i][i+1]
   for (int i = 1; i < q; i++)
   {
      c[i][i] = 0;
      c[i][i + 1] = r[i] * r[i + 1] * r[i + 2];
      kay[i][i + 1] = i;
   }
   c[q][q] = 0;

   // compute remaining c's and kay's
   for (int s = 2; s < q; s++)
      for (int i = 1; i <= q - s; i++)
      {// min term for k = i
         c[i][i+s] = c[i][i] + c[i + 1][i + s]
                   + r[i] * r[i + 1] * r[i + s + 1];
         kay[i][i + s] = i;

         // remaining min terms
         for (int k = i + 1; k < i + s; k++)
         {
            int t = c[i][k] + c[k + 1][i + s]
                  + r[i] * r[k + 1] * r[i + s + 1];
            if (t < c[i][i + s])
            {// smaller min term, update c and kay
               c[i][i + s] = t;
               kay[i][i + s] = k;
            }
         }
      }
}
```

Program 19.7 Iterative computation of c and kay

Let the n vertices of G be numbered 1 through n. Let $c(i,j,k)$ denote the length of a shortest path from i to j that has no intermediate vertex larger than k. Hence $c(i,j,0)$ is the length of the edge (i,j) in case this edge is in G. It is 0 if $i = j$ and

∞ otherwise. $c(i, j, n)$ is the length of a shortest path from i to j.

Example 19.12 For the digraph of Figure 17.17, $c(1, 3, k) = \infty$ for $k = 0, 1, 2, 3$; $c(1, 3, 4) = 28$; $c(1, 3, k) = 10$ for $k = 5, 6, 7$; and $c(1, 3, k) = 9$ for $k = 8, 9, 10$. Hence the shortest 1-to-3 path has length 9. ∎

How can we determine $c(i, j, k)$ for any k, $k > 0$? There are two possibilities for a shortest i-to-j path that has no intermediate vertex larger than k. This path may or may not have k as an intermediate vertex. If it does not, then its length is $c(i, j, k-1)$. If it does, then its length is $c(i, k, k-1) + c(k, j, k-1)$. $c(i, j, k)$ is the smaller of these two quantities. So we obtain the recurrence

$$c(i, j, k) = \min\{c(i, j, k-1), c(i, k, k-1) + c(k, j, k-1)\}, \quad k > 0$$

The above recurrence formulates the solution for one k in terms of the solutions for $k - 1$. Obtaining solutions for $k - 1$ should be easier than obtaining those for k directly.

Recursive Solution

If the above recurrence is solved recursively, the complexity of the resulting procedure is excessive. Let $t(k)$ be the time needed to solve the recurrence recursively for any i, j, k combination. From the recurrence, we see that $t(k) = 3t(k-1) + c$. Using the substitution method, we obtain $t(n) = \Theta(3^n)$. So the time needed to obtain all the $c(i, j, n)$ values is $\Theta(n^2 3^n)$.

Iterative Solution

The values $c(i, j, n)$ may be obtained far more efficiently by noticing that some $c(i, j, k-1)$ values get used several times. By avoiding the recomputation of $c(i, j, k)$s that were computed earlier, all c values may be determined in $\Theta(n^3)$ time. This strategy may be implemented recursively as we did for the matrix chain problem (see Program 19.6) or iteratively. We will develop only the iterative code. Our first attempt at developing this iterative code results in the pseudocode of Figure 19.3.

Observe that $c(i, k, k) = c(i, k, k-1)$ and that $c(k, i, k) = c(k, i, k-1)$ for all i. As a result, if $c(i, j)$ replaces $c(i, j, *)$ throughout Figure 19.3, the final value of $c(i, j)$ will be the same as $c(i, j, n)$.

C++ Implementation

With this observation Figure 19.3 may be refined into the C++ code of Program 19.8. This refinement uses the class `adjacencyWDigraph` defined in Program 16.2. Method `allPairs` returns, in `c`, the lengths of the shortest paths. In case there is no path from i to j, `c[i][j]` is set to `noEdge`, which is the weight used to designate an edge that is absent from the digraph. This method also computes

```
// Find the lengths of the shortest paths.
  // initialize c(i,j,0)
  for (int i = 1; i <= n; i++)
     for (int j = 1; j <= n; j++)
```
$c(i,j,0) = a(i,j);$ // a is the cost adjacency matrix

```
  // compute c(i,j,k) for 0 < k <= n
  for (int k = 1; k <= n; k++)
     for (int i = 1; i <= n; i++)
        for (int j = 1; j <= n; j++)
```
            if $(c(i,k,k-1) + c(k,j,k-1) < c(i,j,k-1))$
                $c(i,j,k) = c(i,k,k-1) + c(k,j,k-1);$
```
           else
```
                $c(i,j,k) = c(i,j,k-1);$

Figure 19.3 Initial shortest-paths algorithm

kay[i][j] such that kay[i][j] is the largest k that is on a shortest i-to-j path. The kay values may be used to construct a shortest path from one vertex to another (see method outputPath of Program 19.9).

The time complexity of Program 19.8 is readily seen to be $\Theta(n^3)$. Program 19.9 takes $O(n)$ time to output a shortest path.

Example 19.13 A sample cost array a appears in Figure 19.4(a). Figure 19.4(b) gives the c array computed by Program 19.8, and Figure 19.4(c) gives the kay values. From these kay values we see that the shortest path from 1 to 5 is the shortest path from 1 to kay[1][5] = 4 followed by the shortest path from 4 to 5. The shortest path from 4 to 5 has no intermediate vertex on it, as kay[4][5] = 0. The shortest path from 1 to 4 goes through kay[1][4] = 3. Repeating this process, we determine that the shortest 1-to-5 path is 1, 2, 3, 4, 5.   ∎

19.2.4   Single-Source Shortest Paths with Negative Costs

Introduction

Do graphs with negative edge costs actually arise in practice? They must; otherwise, we would not study such graphs. Consider a graph in which vertices represent cities, and an edge cost gives the cost of renting a car in one city and dropping it off in another. Most edge costs are positive. However, if there is a net migration into Florida, then Florida will have a surplus of cars and cities that are losing population will have no cars. To fix this imbalance in rental cars, the rental company will

```
template <class T>
void allPairs(T **c, int **kay)
{// Dynamic programming all pairs shortest paths algorithm.
 // Compute c[i][j] and kay[i][j] for all i and j.

   // code to verify *this is weighted comes here

   // initialize c[i][j] = c(i,j,0)
   for (int i = 1; i <= n; i++)
      for (int j = 1; j <= n; j++)
      {
         c[i][j] = a[i][j];
         kay[i][j] = 0;
      }
   for (int i = 1; i <= n; i++)
      c[i][i] = 0;

   // compute c[i][j] = c(i,j,k)
   for (int k = 1; k <= n; k++)
      for (int i = 1; i <= n; i++)
         for (int j = 1; j <= n; j++)
            if (c[i][k] != noEdge && c[k][j] != noEdge &&
               (c[i][j] == noEdge || c[i][j] > c[i][k] + c[k][j]))
            {// smaller value for c[i][j] found
                c[i][j] = c[i][k] + c[k][j];
                kay[i][j] = k;
            }
}
```

Program 19.8 Computation of c and kay

0	1	4	4	8		0	1	2	3	4		0	0	2	3	4
3	0	1	5	9		3	0	1	2	3		0	0	0	3	4
2	2	0	1	8		2	2	0	1	2		0	0	0	0	4
8	8	9	0	1		5	5	3	0	1		5	5	5	0	0
8	8	2	9	0		4	4	2	3	0		3	3	0	3	0
	(a)						(b)						(c)			

Figure 19.4 Shortest-paths example

```
template <class T>
void outputPath(T **c, int **kay, T noEdge, int i, int j)
{// Output shortest path from i to j.
   if (c[i][j] == noEdge)
      cout << "There is no path from " << i << " to " << j << endl;
   else
   {
      cout << "The path is " << i << " ";
      outputPath(kay, i, j);
      cout << endl;
   }
}

void outputPath(int **kay, int i, int j)
{// Actual code to output i to j path.
   if (i == j)
      return;
   if (kay[i][j] == 0)  // no intermediate vertices on path
      cout << j << " ";
   else
   {// kay[i][j] is an intermediate vertex on the path
      outputPath(kay, i, kay[i][j]);
      outputPath(kay, kay[i][j], j);
   }
}
```

Program 19.9 Output a shortest path

actually pay you to drive a car from a select Florida city to one that is short of cars. So some edges have a negative cost. The Web site shows how to solve a scheduling problem and a system of difference equations by finding shortest paths in a graph that has negative edge costs.

The single-source, all-destinations, greedy algorithm developed in Section 17.3.5 cannot be used to obtain the shortest paths when the digraph has one or more edges whose cost is less than 0 (see the solution to Exercise 32). However, the dynamic-programming all-pairs shortest-path algorithm of Section 19.2.3 works as long as the graph/digraph has no cycle whose length/cost is less than 0. As pointed out in Section 19.2.3, the shortest-path problem is not well-defined when we have cycles whose length/cost is negative, because now some shortest paths have an infinite number of edges on them. Therefore, it is reasonable to assume that the graph/digraph we are dealing with has no cycle whose length/cost is negative.

Since the dynamic-programming algorithm of Section 19.2.3 finds shortest paths in a graph/digraph that has edges whose cost is less than 0 (but no cycle whose cost is less than 0) in $\Theta(n^3)$ time, the single-source all-destinations algorithm that we develop should run in less time to be a useful algorithm. The complexity of the algorithm we will develop here is $O(n^3)$ when the adjacency-matrix representation is used and is $O(ne)$ when the adjacency-list representation is used (e is the number of edges). Therefore, the new algorithm has a run-time advantage over the algorithm of Section 19.2.3 when we are interested in finding the shortest paths from a single source vertex. The new algorithm is due to Bellman and Ford and is known as the Bellman-Ford algorithm.

Dynamic-Programming Formulation

Since the graph/digraph has no negative length/cost cycles, we can assume that all shortest paths have at most $n - 1$ edges. Note that a path with n or more edges must contain a cycle; this cycle has length/cost ≥ 0, and so the path that remains following the deletion of this cycle is no longer than the original path. Therefore, between any two connected vertices there is always a shortest path that has no cycle and hence has at most $n - 1$ edges.

As in Sections 17.3.5 and 19.2.3, we first assume that we are interested only in the lengths of the shortest paths. Let $d(v, k)$ be the length of a shortest path from the source vertex to vertex v under the constraint that the path has at most k edges. We see that $d(v, n - 1)$ is the length of a shortest path from the source vertex to vertex v under no constraint and is the answer we seek. Further, $d(v, 0)$ is the length of a shortest path from the source vertex to vertex v using at most zero edges. Therefore, $d(v, 0)$ is 0 when $v = s$ and is infinity otherwise. For $k > 0$, the shortest path has between 0 and k edges. When the number of edges on this shortest path is at least 1,

$$d(v, k) = \min\{d(u, k - 1) + cost(u, v) | (u, v) \text{ is an edge of the graph}\}$$

where u denotes the vertex just before vertex v on this shortest path. We, therefore, obtain the following dynamic-programming recurrence

$$d(v, k) = \min\{d(v, 0), \min\{d(u, k - 1) + cost(u, v) | (u, v) \text{ is an edge of the graph}\}\}$$

This recurrence can be used to compute $d(*, n - 1)$ by computing the ds in the order $d(*, 1), d(*, 2), \cdots, d(*, n - 1)$.

Iterative Solution

Although we can solve the dynamic-programming recurrence for d recursively or recursively without recomputations, an iterative solution results in the least run time. Figure 19.5 gives the pseudocode for the iterative algorithm.

```
initialize d(*, 0);

// compute remaining d(*, k)s
for (int k = 1; k < n; k++)
{
    d(v, k) = d(v, 0) for all v;
    for (each edge (u, v))
        d(v, k) = min{d(v, k), d(u, k − 1) + cost(u, v)};
}
```

Figure 19.5 Pseudocode for Bellman-Ford algorithm

Figure 19.6 gives a refinement of Figure 19.5 in which the computation is done in place, that is, using a d that has only one subscript.

```
initialize d(*) = d(*, 0);

// compute d(*) = d(*, n − 1)s
for (int k = 1; k < n; k++)
    for (each edge (u, v))
        d(v) = min{d(v), d(u) + cost(u, v)};
```

Figure 19.6 Refined pseudocode for Bellman-Ford algorithm

Notice that while the in-place computation does not have $d(*) = d(*, k)$ at the end of each iteration of the outer loop, the value of $d(*)$ on termination is $d(*, n−1)$. Basically, the original code computes the min function $n−1$ times at each vertex and ensures that in the end there is no vertex whose $d(v)$ can be reduced by performing the min function again at this vertex. The modified in-place code does this also. The assurance that no further reduction in d is possible follows from the fact that the graph/digraph has no cycle with negative cost. In fact, on termination we can check each $d(v)$ to see whether it can be reduced by applying the min operation of the pseudocode. If any d can be reduced, the original graph has a cycle of negative length/cost.

Two other observations that can be used to reduce the computation time are (1) if for some k, $d(v)$ does not change for any v, then we can abort the outer **for** loop, and (2) the inner **for** loop need be done only for those edges (u, v) for which $d(u)$ changed on the previous iteration of the outer loop. Figure 19.7 gives the pseudocode for the Bellman-Ford algorithm with these observations incorporated.

```
initialize d(*) = d(*, 0);
put the vertices that are adjacent from the source vertex onto a list list1;

// compute d(*) = d(*, n − 1)
put the source vertex into list1;
for (int k = 1; k < n; k++)
{
    // see if there are vertices whose d value has changed
    if (list1 is empty) break;   // no such vertex
    while (list1 is not empty)
    {
        delete a vertex u from list1;
        for (each edge (u, v))
        {
            d(v) = min{d(v), d(u) + cost(u, v)};
            if (d(v) has changed and v is not on list2) add v to list2;
        }
        list1 = list2;
        make list2 empty;
    }
}
```

Figure 19.7 Final pseudocode for Bellman-Ford algorithm

C++ Implementation

When implementing the pseudocode of Figure 19.7, it is useful to maintain an array inList2 such that inList2[v] is true iff vertex v is in list2. This array needs to be reset to **false** at the end of each iteration of the outer **for** loop. This resetting is done efficiently by going through the vertices that are in list2 and resetting only the corresponding array values.

Although any list structure that permits constant time insertion and deletion may be used (for example, a stack or a queue), we will use arrayList because we have defined an enumerator for this class and because this class has better best-case performance than any of the other linear list classes we have developed. Using the enumerator, we can reset the array inList2 easily at the end of each iteration of the outer **for** loop.

Program 19.10 gives our implementation of the Bellman-Ford algorithm. This code includes the predecessor array p as used in shortest-path code of Program 17.3. Using the terminal p values, we can construct the shortest paths as described in the solution to Exercise 33.

```
void bellmanFord(int s, T *d, int *p)
{// Bellman and Ford algorithm to find the shortest paths from vertex s.
 // Graph may have edges with negative cost but should not have a
 // cycle with negative cost.
 // Shortest distances from s are returned in d.
 // Predecessor info in returned p.
   if (!weighted())
      throw undefinedMethod
      ("graph::bellmanFord() not defined for unweighted graphs");

   int n = numberOfVertices();
   if (s < 1 || s > n)
      throw illegalParameterValue("illegal source vertex");

   // define two lists for vertices whose d has changed
   arrayList<int> *list1 = new arrayList<int>;
   arrayList<int> *list2 = new arrayList<int>;

   // define an array to record vertices that are in list2
   bool *inList2 = new bool [n+1];

   // initialize p[1:n] = 0 and inList2[1:n] = false
   fill(p + 1, p + n + 1, 0);
   fill(inList2 + 1, inList2 + n + 1, false);

   // set d[s] = d^0(s) = 0
   d[s] = 0;
   p[s] = s;  // p[i] != 0 means vertex i has been reached
              // will later reset p[s] = 0

   // initialize list1
   list1->insert(0, s);

   // do n - 1 rounds of updating d
   for (int k = 1; k < n; k++)
   {
      if (list1->empty())
         break;  // no more changes possible
```

Program 19.10 Bellman-Ford algorithm (continues)

```
    // process vertices on list1
    for (arrayList<int>::iterator iList1 = list1->begin();
         iList1 != list1->end(); ++iList1)
    {// update d for the neighbors v of vertex u =. *iList1
        int u = *iList1;
        vertexIterator<T> *iu = iterator(u);
        int v;
        T w;
        while ((v = iu->next(w)) != 0)
        {
            if (p[v] == 0 || d[u] + w < d[v])
            {
                // this is either the first path to v
                // or is a shorter path than earlier ones
                d[v] = d[u] + w;
                p[v] = u;
                // put v into list2 unless it is already there
                if (!inList2[v])
                {// put at end of list
                    list2->insert(list2->size(), v);
                    inList2[v] = true;
                }
            }
        }
    }

    // set list1 and list2 for next update round
    list1 = list2;
    list2 = new arrayList<int>;

    // reset inList2[1:n] to false
    for (arrayList<int>::iterator iList1 = list1->begin();
         iList1 != list1->end(); ++iList1)
        inList2[*iList1] = false;
    }
    p[s] = 0;  // s has no predecessor
}
```

Program 19.10 Bellman-Ford algorithm (concluded)

Complexity Analysis

At the start of each iteration of the for (int k ...) loop, there are $O(n)$ vertices in list1. Therefore, the innermost while loop iterates $O(e)$ (e is the number of edges) times for each value of k. So each iteration of the for (int k ...) loop takes $O(n^2)$ time when the adjacency-matrix representation is used and $O(e)$ time when the adjacency-list representation is used. Therefore, the overall complexity is $O(n^3)$ when the adjacency-matrix representation is used and $O(ne)$ when the adjacency-list representation is used.

19.2.5 Noncrossing Subset of Nets

Problem Description

In the crossing-distribution problem of Section 14.6.3, we are given a routing channel with n pins on either side and a permutation C. Pin i on the top side of the channel is to be connected to pin C_i on the bottom side, $1 \leq i \leq n$. The pair (i, C_i) is called a **net**. In all we have n nets that are to be connected or routed. Suppose that we have two or more routing layers of which one is a *preferred layer*. For example, in the preferred layer it may be possible to use much thinner wires, or the resistance in the preferred layer may be considerably less than in other layers. Our task is to route as many nets as possible in the preferred layer. The remaining nets will be routed, at least partially, in the other layers. Since two nets can be routed in the same layer iff they do not cross, our task is equivalent to finding a maximum noncrossing subset (MNS) of the nets. Such a subset has the property that no two nets of the subset cross. Since net (i, C_i) is completely specified by i, we may refer to this net as net i.

Example 19.14 Consider the example of Figure 14.7 that has been redrawn as Figure 19.8. The nets (1,8) and (2,7) (or equivalently, the nets 1 and 2) cross and so cannot be routed in the same layer. The nets (1,8), (7,9), and (9,10) do not cross and so can be routed in the same layer. These three nets do not constitute an MNS, as a larger subset of noncrossing nets exists. The set of four nets (4,2), (5,5), (7,9), (9,10) is an MNS of the routing instance given in Figure 19.8.   ∎

Dynamic-Programming Formulation

Let $MNS(i, j)$ denote an MNS under the constraint that all pairs (u, C_u) in the MNS have $u \leq i$ and $C_u \leq j$. Let $size(i, j)$ be the size (i.e., number of nets) of $MNS(i, j)$. Note that $MNS(n, n)$ is an MNS for the input instance and that $size(n, n)$ is its size.

Example 19.15 For the example of Figure 19.8, $MNS(10, 10)$ is the answer we seek. As pointed out in Example 19.14, $size(10, 10) = 4$. Nets (1,8), (2,7), (7,9), (8,3), (9,10), and (10,6) cannot be members of $MNS(7, 6)$ because either their top

$$C = [8, 7, 4, 2, 5, 1, 9, 3, 10, 6]$$

Figure 19.8 A wiring instance

pin number is greater than 7 or their bottom pin number is greater than 6. So we are left with four nets that are eligible for membership in $MNS(7, 6)$. These nets appear in Figure 19.9. The subset $(3,4)$, $(5,5)$ is a noncrossing subset of size 2. There is no noncrossing subset of size 3. So $size(7,6) = 2$. ∎

Figure 19.9 Nets of Figure 19.8 that may be in $MNS(7,6)$

When $i = 1$, the net $(1, C_1)$ is the only candidate for membership in $MNS(1, j)$. This net can be a member only when $j \geq C_1$. So we obtain

$$size(1,j) = \begin{cases} 0 & \text{if } j < C_1 \\ 1 & j \geq C_1 \end{cases} \qquad (19.5)$$

Next consider the case $i > 1$. If $j < C_i$, then the net (i, C_i) cannot be part of $MNS(i, j)$. In this case all nets (u, C_u) in $MNS(i, j)$ have $u < i$ and $C_u < j$. Therefore

$$size(i, j) = size(i - 1, j), \quad j < \dot{C}_i \tag{19.6}$$

If $j \geq C_i$, then the net (i, C_i) may or may not be in $MNS(i, j)$. If it is, then no nets (u, C_u) such that $u < i$ and $C_u > C_i$ can be members of $MNS(i, j)$, as nets of this form cross (i, C_i). All other nets in $MNS(i, j)$ must have $u < i$ and $C_u < C_i$. The number of such nets in $MNS(i, j)$ must be M_{i-1, C_i-1}; otherwise, $MNS(i, j)$ doesn't have the maximum number of nets possible. If (i, C_i) is not in $MNS(i, j)$, then all nets in $MNS(i, j)$ have $u < i$; therefore, $size(i, j) = size(i-1, j)$. Although we do not know whether the net (i, C_i) is in $MNS(i, j)$, of the two possibilities, the one that gives the larger MNS must hold. Therefore

$$size(i, j) = \max\{size(i - 1, j), size(i - 1, C_i - 1) + 1\}, \quad j \geq C_i \tag{19.7}$$

Iterative Solution

Although Equations 19.5 through 19.7 may be solved recursively, our earlier examples have shown that the recursive solution of dynamic-programming recurrences is inefficient even when we avoid recomputation of previously computed values. So we consider only an iterative solution. For this iterative solution, we use Equation 19.5 to first compute $size(1, j)$. Next we compute $size(i, j)$ for $i = 2, 3, \cdots, n$ in this order of i using Equations 19.6 and 19.7. Finally, we use a traceback to determine the nets in $MNS(n, n)$.

Example 19.16 Figure 19.10 shows the $size(i, j)$ values obtained for the example of Figure 19.8. Since $size(10, 10) = 4$, we know that the MNS for this instance has four nets. To find these four nets, we begin at $size(10, 10)$. $size(10, 10)$ was computed using Equation 19.7. Since $size(10, 10) = size(9, 10)$, it follows from the reasoning used to obtain Equation 19.7 that there is an MNS of size 4 that does not include net 10. We must now find $MNS(9, 10)$. Since $size(9, 10) \neq size(8, 10)$, $MNS(9, 10)$ must include net 9. The remainder of the nets in $MNS(9, 10)$ also constitute $MNS(8, C_9 - 1) = MNS(8, 9)$. Since $size(8, 9) = size(7, 9)$, net 8 may be excluded from the MNS. So we proceed to determine $MNS(7, 9)$, which must include net 7 as $size(7, 9) \neq size(6, 9)$. The remainder of the MNS is $MNS(6, C_7 - 1)$ $= MNS(6, 8)$. Net 6 is excluded as $size(6, 8) = size(5, 8)$. Net 5 is added to the MNS, and we proceed to determine $MNS(4, C_5 - 1) = MNS(4, 4)$. Net 4 is excluded, and then net 3 is added to the MNS. No other nets are added. The traceback yields the size 4 MNS $\{3, 5, 7, 9\}$.

Notice that the traceback does not require $size(10, j)$ for values of j other than 10. We need not compute the values that are not required.   ∎

i	j									
	1	2	3	4	5	6	7	8	9	10
1	0	0	0	0	0	0	0	1	1	1
2	0	0	0	0	0	0	1	1	1	1
3	0	0	0	1	1	1	1	1	1	1
4	0	1	1	1	1	1	1	1	1	1
5	0	1	1	1	2	2	2	2	2	2
6	1	1	1	1	2	2	2	2	2	2
7	1	1	1	1	2	2	2	2	3	3
8	1	1	2	2	2	2	2	2	3	3
9	1	1	2	2	2	2	2	2	3	4
10	1	1	2	2	2	3	3	3	3	4

Figure 19.10 $size(i, j)$s for the instance of Figure 19.8

C++ Implementation

Program 19.11 gives the iterative codes to compute the $size(i, j)$s and then the MNS. Function mns computes the $size(i, j)$ values in a two-dimensional array size. The mapping is $size(i, j) =$ size[i][j]. size[i][j] $= size(i, j)$ is computed for $1 \leq i < n$, $0 \leq j \leq n$ as well as for $i = j = n$. The time taken by this computation is $\Theta(n^2)$. Function traceback (Program 19.12) returns, in net[0:sizeOfMNS], the nets that form an MNS. This function takes $\Theta(n)$ time, so the total time taken by the dynamic-programming algorithm for the MNS problem is $\Theta(n^2)$.

EXERCISES

1. Let $n = 5$, $p = [7, 3, 5, 2, 4]$, $w = [3, 1, 2, 1, 2]$, and $c = 6$. Draw a figure similar to Figure 19.1 that shows the recursive class made by Program 19.1. Label each node by the y value and shade nodes that represent the recomputation of a previously computed value.

2. Use the data of Exercise 1 and arrive at a table similar to that of Figure 19.2. Use the iterative function of Program 19.3. Now trace back from $f(1, c)$ and determine the x_i values.

```
void mns(int *c, int numberOfNets, int **size)
{// Compute size[i][j] for all i and j.
   // initialize size[1][*]
   for (int j = 0; j < c[1]; j++)
      size[1][j] = 0;
   for (int j = c[1]; j <= numberOfNets; j++)
      size[1][j] = 1;

   // compute size[i][*], 1 < i < numberOfNets
   for (int i = 2; i < numberOfNets; i++)
   {
      for (int j = 0; j < c[i]; j++)
         size[i][j] = size[i - 1][j];
      for (int j = c[i]; j <= numberOfNets; j++)
         size[i][j] = max(size[i - 1][j], size[i - 1][c[i] - 1] + 1);
   }

   size[numberOfNets][numberOfNets] =
         max(size[numberOfNets - 1][numberOfNets],
            size[numberOfNets - 1][c[numberOfNets] - 1] + 1);
}
```

Program 19.11 Compute $size(i, j)$ for all i and j

3. Modify Program 19.1 so that it also computes the values of the x_is that result in an optimal packing.

4. Write C++ code implementing the tuple method. You code should determine the x_i values that define an optimal packing.

5. [0/1/2 Knapsack] Define the 0/1/2 knapsack problem to be

$$\text{maximize} \sum_{i=1}^{n} p_i x_i$$

subject to the constraints

$$\sum_{i=1}^{n} w_i x_i \leq c \text{ and } x_i \in \{0, 1, 2\}, \ 1 \leq i \leq n$$

Let f be as defined for the 0/1 knapsack problem.

```
int traceback(int *c, int numberOfNets, int **size, int *net)
{// Put max noncrossing subset in net[0:sizeOfMNS-1].
 // Return size of MNS.
   int maxAllowed = numberOfNets;    // max bottom pin number allowed
   int sizeOfMNS = 0;
   for (int i = numberOfNets; i > 1; i--)
      // is net i in MNS?
      if (size[i][maxAllowed] != size[i - 1][maxAllowed])
      {// yes, net i is in the MNS
         net[sizeOfMNS++] = i;
         maxAllowed = c[i] - 1;
      }

   // is net 1 in MNS?
   if (maxAllowed >= c[1])
      net[sizeOfMNS++] = 1;  // yes

   return sizeOfMNS;
}
```

Program 19.12 Find a maximum noncrossing subset of nets

(a) Determine equations similar to Equations 19.1 and 19.2 for the 0/1/2 knapsack problem.

(b) Assume that the ws are integer. Write a function similar to Program 19.3 to compute f as a two-dimensional array and then to determine an optimal assignment of values for x.

(c) What is the complexity of your function?

6. [Two-dimensional Knapsack] The two-dimensional 0/1 knapsack problem is defined as

$$\text{maximize } \sum_{i=1}^{n} p_i x_i$$

subject to the constraints

$$\sum_{i=1}^{n} v_i x_i \le c, \ \sum_{i=1}^{n} w_i x_i \le d, \text{ and } x_i \in \{0,1\}, \ 1 \le i \le n$$

Let $f(i,y,z)$ denote the value of an optimal solution to the two-dimensional knapsack problem with objects i through n, $c = y$, and $d = z$.

(a) Determine equations similar to Equations 19.1 and 19.2 for $f(n, y, z)$ and $f(i, y, z)$.

(b) Assume that the vs and ws are integer. Write a function similar to Program 19.3 to compute f as a three-dimensional array and then to determine an optimal assignment of values for x.

(c) What is the complexity of your function?

7. Use the dynamic-programming recurrence for the matrix chains problem to compute $c(i, j)$ and $kay(i, j)$, $1 \le i \le j \le q$ for $q = 5$ and $r = (100, 10, 100, 2, 50, 4)$. What is the cost of the best way to multiply the q matrices? Use the kay values to determine that best way to multiply the q matrices.

8. Do Exercise 7 using $q = 6$ and $r = (2, 100, 4, 100, 2, 200, 3)$.

9. Show that $\sum_{s=1}^{q-1} s(q - s + 1) = O(q^3)$.

10. Only the upper triangle of the arrays c and kay are used when solving the matrix multiplication recurrence. Rewrite the code of Program 19.7, defining c and kay to be members of the class upperTriangularMatrix (see Section 7.3.4). Comment on the merits of using two-dimensional arrays versus upper-triangular matrices for this program.

11. Use the dynamic-programming recurrence equations for the all-pairs shortest-path problem to determine all $c(i, j, k)$ values for the graph of Figure 17.9. Present your results as a sequence of matrices $c(*, *, k)$, one matrix for each k. Also, give the final kay array computed by Floyd's algorithm.

12. Do Exercise 11 using the undirected graph that corresponds to the digraph of Figure 17.9 (this graph is obtained by replacing each directed edge with an undirected edge).

13. Write a version of Program 19.8 that will work on members of the class linkedWDigraph. The asymptotic complexity of your code should be the same as that of Program 19.8.

14. Let G be a weighted directed acyclic graph with n vertices. Assume that the vertices in G have been labeled 1 through n such that if (i, j) is an edge of G, then $i < j$. Let $l(i, j)$ be the length of the edge (i, j).

(a) Use dynamic programming to obtain a method that determines the length of a longest path in G. Your method should work in $O(n + e)$ time where e is the number of edges in G.

(b) Write a method that uses the results of your method for part (a) and constructs the longest possible path. The complexity of your new method should be $O(p)$ where p is the number of vertices on the longest path.

15. [Reflexive Transitive Closure] Modify Program 19.8 so that it starts with an adjacency matrix of a directed graph and computes its reflexive transitive closure matrix rtc. rtc[i][j] = 1 if there is a directed path from vertex i to vertex j that uses zero or more edges. rtc[i][j] = 0 otherwise. The complexity of your code should be $O(n^3)$ where n is the number of vertices in the graph.

16. Use Equations 19.5 through 19.7 to compute the *size* values for the case when $C = [4, 2, 6, 8, 9, 3, 1, 10, 7, 5]$. Present your results as is shown in Figure 19.10. Use these results to determine an MNS.

17. In Section 17.3.3 we saw that a project may be decomposed into several tasks and that these tasks may be performed in topological order. Let the tasks be numbered 1 through n so that task 1 is done first, then task 2 is done, and so on. Suppose that we have two ways to perform each task. Let $C_{i,1}$ be the cost of doing task i the first way, and let $C_{i,2}$ be the cost of doing it the second way. Let $T_{i,1}$ be the time it takes to do task i the first way, and let $T_{i,2}$ be the time when the task is done the second way. Assume that the Ts are integers. Develop a dynamic-programming algorithm to determine the least-cost way to complete the entire project in no more than t time. Assume that the cost of the project is the sum of the task costs and the total time is the sum of the task times. (*Hint:* Let $c(i, j)$ be the least cost with which tasks i through n can be completed in time j.) What is the complexity of your algorithm?

18. A machine has n components. For each component, there are three suppliers. The weight of component i from supplier j is $W_{i,j}$, and its cost is $C_{i,j}$, $1 \le j \le 3$. The cost of the machine is the sum of the component costs, and its weight is the sum of the component weights. Assume that all costs are positive integers. Write a dynamic-programming algorithm to determine from which supplier to buy each component so as to have the lightest machine with cost no more than c. Assume that the costs are integer. (*Hint:* Let $w(i, j)$ be the weight of the lightest machine composed of components i through n that costs no more than j.) What is the complexity of your algorithm?

19. Do Exercise 18 but this time define $w(i, j)$ to be the weight of the lightest machine, with components 1 through i, that costs no more than j.

20. [Longest Common Subsequence] String s is a subsequence of string a if s can be obtained from a by deleting some of the characters in a. The string "onion" is a subsequence of "recognition." s is a common subsequence of a and b iff it is a subsequence of both a and b. The length of s is its number of characters. Develop a dynamic-programming algorithm to find a longest common subsequence of the strings a and b. (*Hint:* Let $a = a_1 a_2 \cdots a_n$ and $b = b_1 b_2 \cdots b_m$. Define $l(i, j)$ to be the length of a longest common subsequence of the strings $a_i \cdots a_n$ and $b_j \cdots b_m$.) What is the complexity of your algorithm?

21. Do Exercise 20 but this time define $l(i,j)$ to be the length of a longest common subsequence of the strings $a_1 \cdots a_i$ and $b_1 \cdots b_j$.

22. [Longest Sorted Subsequence] Write an algorithm to find a longest sorted subsequence (see Exercise 20) of a sequence of integers. What is the complexity of your algorithm?

23. Let x_1, x_2, $\cdots$, be a sequence of integers. Let $sum(i,j) = \sum_i^j x_k$, $i \leq j$. Write an algorithm to find i and j for which $sum(i,j)$ is maximum. What is the complexity of your algorithm?

24. [String Editing] In the **string-editing problem**, you are given two strings $a = a_1 a_2 \cdots a_n$ and $b = b_1 b_2 \cdots b_m$ and three cost functions C, D, and I. $C(i,j)$ is the cost of changing a_i to b_j, $D(i)$ is the cost of deleting a_i from a, and $I(i)$ is the cost of inserting b_i into a. String a may be changed to string b by performing a sequence of change, delete, and insert operations. Such a sequence is called an **edit sequence**. For example, we could delete all the a_is and then insert the b_is, or when $n \geq m$, we could change a_i to b_i, $1 \leq i \leq n$, and then delete the remaining a_is. The cost of a sequence of operations is the sum of the individual operation costs. Write a dynamic-programming algorithm to determine a least-cost edit sequence. (*Hint:* Define $c(i,j)$ to be the cost of a least-cost edit sequence that transforms $a_1 \cdots a_i$ into $b_1 \cdots b_j$.) What is the complexity of your algorithm?

25. Do Exercise 41 in Chapter 17 using dynamic programming.

19.3   REFERENCES AND SELECTED READINGS

An $O(n \log n)$ algorithm for the matrix multiplication chains problem may be found in the papers "Computation of Matrix Chain Products" parts I & II by T. Hu and M. Shing, *SIAM Journal on Computing*, 11, 1982, 362–372 and 13, 1984, 228–251.

   The dynamic-programming algorithm for the noncrossing subset of nets problem is based on the work reported in the paper "Finding a Maximum Planar Subset of a Set of Nets in a Channel" by K. Supowit, *IEEE Transactions on Computer-Aided Design of Integrated Circuits and Systems*, 6, 1, 1987, 93–94.

Chapters 20 and 21 are available from the Web site for this book. The URL for this site is

```
http://www.cise.ufl.edu/~sahni/dsaac
```

INDEX